Contrasts and Solutions
in the Middle East

Contrasts and Solutions in the Middle East

Edited by Ole Høiris
and Sefa Martin Yürükel

AARHUS UNIVERSITY PRESS

AARHUS UNIVERSITY PRESS
University of Aarhus
DK-8000 Aarhus C
Fax (+ 45) 8619 8433

73 Lime Walk
Headington, Oxford OX3 7AD
Fax (+ 44) 1865 750 079

Box 511
Oakville, Conn. 06779
Fax (+ 1) 860 945 9468

ANSI/NISO
Z39.48-1992

Published with the support of the University of Aarhus and the Danish Institute of International Affairs. Attention is drawn to the fact that the opinions expressed in this book are those of individual authors; therefore the aforementioned Institutions do not assume responsibility for the said opinions.

Contents

Iran — Syria — Iraq

Turkey

The Kurdish Question

Preface

In April 1995, an international conference was held at the University of Aarhus, Denmark, under the title *Contradictions in the Middle East — A Token of National or Religious Identifications in a Local-Global Perspective*. (See Appendix, p. 553). This was the second in a series of conferences organized under the heading *Aarhus Debates: The Focal Issues of the World*.

As an extension of the conference on the Middle East it was decided to publish this book containing contributions made at the conference itself and supplemented with commentaries by experts and politicians with knowledge of and influence in the four main regions: Palestine, Israel, the Kurdish regions and Turkey. The intention was to make available the many conflicting and informative viewpoints, not only to a public audience, but also to the various parties involved in the conflict itself. In this sense we hope that the book will be of some practical application in an educational context within a range of subjects dealing with the conditions in the region.

We would also like to thank the many people who have helped to make this project possible; some have given their time and effort and others have contributed financially. In connection with the conference as much as with the publication of this book we would like to give a special thanks to Henning Lehmann, Vice-Chancellor of the University of Aarhus; André Wang Hansen, Dean of the Faculty of Arts, the University of Aarhus; and Prof. Torben Vestergaard and Prof. Jens Pinholt, Heads of the Department of Ethnography and Social Anthropology, the University of Aarhus, for their encouragement and support through the entire project.

In connection with the staging of the conference itself we would like to send a warm thanks to Mette Fenger and Dorthe Laustrup Nielsen (both reading for masters in Anthropology); Senior Lecturer, Prof. Mikael Gravers, of the Department of Ethnography and Social Anthropology, the University of Aarhus, for his considerable and voluntary contribution to the preparations for the conference. In addition, we would like to thank the following for their financial and other contributions: the University of Aarhus: the Faculty of Arts, the Faculty of Social Sciences, the Faculty of Theology, the Department of Ethnography and Social Anthropology, the Department of Information and Media Studies, the Department of the History of Ideas, the Centre for Cultural

Research, Director M.C. Holst's Endowment Fund to the University of Aarhus, and Miss Charlotte Trap de Thygesons Endowment Fund for teachers at the University of Aarhus. A number of institutions outside the University also deserve thanks; these include The Security and Disarmament Committee, The International Forum of The Workers Movement and Jacob's Pita.

In relation to those involved in the publication of the book we would like to thank masters student Dorthe Laustrup Nielsen for her great help with the editing work. Thanks must also go to Prof. Torben Vestergaard and Research Prof. Elisabeth Vestergaard, the University of Aarhus, for their tremendous assistance and undying patience in the matter of converting the innumerable word processing systems into one we could use, and Jamal Mahjoub for his work in translating and correcting the papers we received. Finally, we would like to thank the following for their financial support, without which the editing and publishing of the book would not have been possible: the University of Aarhus; the Department of Ethnography and Social Anthropology, University of Aarhus; the Faculty of Arts, University of Aarhus; the Faculty of Social Sciences, University of Aarhus; the Faculty of Theology, University of Aarhus; the Aarhus University Research Foundation; and the Danish Institute of International Affairs (DUPI).

Finally a great debt is owed to all the people who have contributed their knowledge, opinions and ideas in the articles which make up this book.

Sefa Martin Yürükel and Ole Høiris

Introduction and General Survey

National or Religious Identification seen in a Local and Global Perspective

Peder Mortensen

National and religious identification are key-words. As we all know, the Middle East with its mountains, fertile hills and valleys, deserts, oases and rivers offers a richly varied geographical stage for the development of human life. Nomads, farmers and people living in towns and cities are all one way or another involved in ethnic conflicts, religious intolerance, linguistic divergences, cultural, social or political antagonisms, problems with national identification, fights over oil and water, etc. In the Middle East such problems are defined by two characteristics: their *variety* and their complex mutual *integration* throughout history. Trying to isolate and solve one conflict often leads to the uncovering of underlying problems of a slightly different character. Being an archaeologist, I am tempted to describe the Middle Eastern scenario of conflicts as a very complex stratification of interrelated problems. Many of these can be traced very far back in time. They appear almost immediately in the first written sources more than 5,000 years ago. I shall briefly mention four examples chosen from this temporal stratification: problems concerning the role of water, the relationship between settled people and nomads, the suppression of ethnic and religious minorities, and national versus ethnic identification.

It is said that land goes with water, meaning that land is not enough for those who want to cultivate, — it needs water. This is why water — together with security — has been a key issue in Israel's negotiations with Jordan, PLO and Syria. And since three major sources of the river Jordan originate in the Lebanon and the Golan heights, it clearly shows why Israel and Syria have both been interested in controlling these areas. However, disputes and wars in order to control the flow of water were known already more than 4,000 years ago in Sumeria where some of the larger city states like Ur, Uruk, and Nippur were quarrelling and sometimes fighting to get enough water for canal irrigation from the river Tigris and the Euphrates. The real loosers at that time were the farmers living in small towns and villages east of the Tigris: during years with little water in the main river, the far eastern end of the canals would dry out, so that irrigation was impossible. As the population of the large cities near the river increased, more water was needed here, which forced those farmers who could not get any water for their fields, either to move to the cities or to lead a half-nomadic life in the Zagros mountains. In the Middle East this problem of controlling the water from rivers and wells has been known ever since, and it has been the main reason for a great number of conflicts in countries with arable land or with nomads wanting access to water for their herds of goats, sheep, and camels.

From the earliest times conflicts, and a mutual lack of understanding of one another, have characterized the relationship between settled peoples and nomads, often of different ethnic origin. The hostilities range from small local incidents — like when the Kassite governor of Bahrain in the 14th century BC complains that the Ahlamu nomads have stolen all his dates, to tribally organized invaders appearing in Palestine, Syria and Mesopotamia. They came from the Zagros mountains and from Arabia in the 3rd, 2nd and 1st millennium BC: Akkadians, Amorites, Kassites, Aramaeans, Caldaeans, and Suti, and finally in the centuries before and after Muhammed: Arabs. Some of these invaders, the Akkadians, for example, came with a new language, others like the Arabs brought a new religion. They added new layers of potential problems, one on top of the other, to the cultural stratification forming the surface we are looking at today.

Kingdoms and states come and go. But the first Middle Eastern empire was founded by the Assyrians who, at a certain time ruled over most countries from the Mediterranean to western Iran and from the Gulf in the South to the Tauros mountains in the North. I only mention this empire, because we have all the elements of later conflicts assembled and testified in connection with one dynasty of rulers: a cruel oriental despoty, elimination of religious and ethnic minorities, whole populations forcibly moved from one end of the empire to another, economic enervation and cultural suppression combined with efficiency, monumental art, and a tendency to be proud of having created waste lands and killed the people who resisted domination. All this commemorated in long, victorious, boasting inscriptions. An example from a 9th century BC stela:

Chemosh said to me: go and take Nebo from Israel. So I went by night, and fought against it from break of dawn till noon. And I took it and slew all in it: seven thousand men and women, both natives and aliens, and female slaves, — for I had devoted it to Ashtar-Chemosh. I took from thence the vessels of Yahweh and dragged them before Chemosh (King of Moab).

A cruel way of ruling by suppression, immitated by Egyptians, Hittites, and many others. Unfortunately, it is an oriental heritage, deeply rooted, but not entirely buried in the cultural stratigraphy of the Middle East.

After the First World War, most of the Middle East became heavily dominated by British and French interests. Persia and the old Ottoman Empire, now under the names of Iran and Turkey, were ruled by new regimes who wanted reforms in accordance with western standards. In Iran, Reza Shah sought control over the enormous tribal areas bordering the central part of the country by breaking up the tribal structures, killing the leaders and forcing the nomads to settle in villages, and to behave and look civilized, i.e. to adopt the European style of dress, to cut their hair etc. In Turkey, Mustafa Kemal Atatürk went even further in his westernization of the country, by changing the alphabet, rejecting religious institutions, establishing Turkish as the only written language from Edirne to Kars in Eastern Anatolia, and by an effective control of political and religious opponents. There was of course no tradition for democracy in the Middle East, and in both cases the suppression of religious, ethnic, social and political minorities has caused a serious reaction within the last ten years. In a provocative statement the modern Turkish author Orhan Pamuk writes about his people: '... they are possessed by the question of their identity. This happens when modernization — as in Turkey — cuts off a people from its past. Culture in this way is discontinued.' In this context I might add a remark by a Danish political observer. He says that it is this attitude that created a blindness towards the Kurdish wish to be recognized as an ethnic minority.

Similar problems of identity also appeared in most of the nation states created by France and Britain, when they gave up their mandates and protectorates. Asking a man at the Meidan al-Husein in Cairo about his identity might perhaps, after some confusion, lead him to identify himself as a Muslim and an Arab, but he would not necessarily reveal his national identity — not because he wanted to hide it, but because it would seem inferior to him compared to his ethnic and religious status. In this perspective the themes of today 'national or religious identification' may appear rather opaque, but we can easily agree that such problems are not solved by ignoring their existence. An awareness of the historical stratification and integration of conflicts is absolutely essential in creating a future, not only based on historical claims, but on a positive self-identification on which a mutual understanding, respect for, and interaction with other ethnic, religious or political groups can be built.

Quite recently I heard a Palestinian openly discussing with an Israeli the problems of Jericho in relation to Israel: the economic depression on the

Palestinian side and increased security problems for Israel. 'Yes', one of them said '... but after all *shouting* is better than *shooting*, isn't it?'

If people with an historical consciousness and respect for other ethnic groups, religions or nations might succeed in solving some of the problems facing us today, the Middle East could again develop its cultural complexity into a rich and powerful stimulation, much needed right now in our western civilization.

Universal Human Rights, Particular Cultural Rights and Peaceful Co-existence. Models for Conflicts and their Solution in the Middle East

Ole Høiris

Background

Throughout the 1950s and 60s, liberation movements in the colonized world fought for their national freedom and to establish free and democratic states upon the ruins of the European-dominated, global power system which World War II had finally undermined. The colonies became independent states and were accepted into the international community as such. Their ruling systems, however, were, in by far the majority of cases, neither the liberal nor socialist democracies which the liberation movements fought to achieve. Internal colonization, ethnic, political and religious oppression, and despotism in the name of modernization was often the result. Since the direct intervention of international organizations in the internal affairs of these countries was out of the question, this situation was accepted. Many analyses suggested that the situation was the result of colonialism and neo-colonialism. Under the given circumstances, one could not expect that either liberal or socialist democracies could develop so quickly after their liberation from a despotic, colonial situation. The development which had taken several hundred years in Europe would take time in these new states. Implicit in this was the consideration of the new states from an evolutionist theory angle: that they were backward or pre-modern and would have to progress along the long road to modern democracy. Various conditions, such as a dual-economy structure with a large, traditional and smaller modern sector, over-development of the state apparatus and underdevelopment in a global capitalist central-peripheral structure, or dependent development along with the distorted class system resulting from colonialism, etc, were described as being part of the problem. In the case of all the models, it was vital that the specific conditions pertaining in the individual regions, be seen in a universal perspective. In terms of its future outlook this would envisage a uniform, modern condition as the goal of development. This was either delayed or stagnated in the global — and especially the economic — world order. Cultural differences were considered as being phenomena of lesser importance, or variations in the context of the global system. Foreign aid, which was expanded at this time, was regarded as one of the means by which to establish this universal order. Among other things, this would be achieved by helping to develop a middle-class which would bring these states to the point of 'take-off', from which point their development would be self-perpetuating. At more optimistic moments, the project seemed as though it would succeed because of the rise in the global economy, which was the case in the first two decades of the independence of these states.

In addition to this, the third world was a central part of the cold war throughout this period. As long as these states delivered the raw materials which the industrialized world had need of, and did not change sides in the cold war, the ruling powers and abuse of human rights remained internal matters. Apart from there being, particularly among the European public, a reluctance to be seen as any kind of extension of the former colonialist involvement, the despots in the new countries were often regarded as guarantees of political and economic stability in the polarized world. It was only the states which continued to maintain a type of colonialistic status, or else were subject to direct colonization, which found themselves on the agenda of world opinion, such as the Portuguese colonies in Africa, Southern Rhodesia, South Africa, Vietnam and Afghanistan — as well as in the longest lasting case — Palestine, after the establishment and subsequent expansion of the Israeli state. Although, in relation to this last conflict, signs of solidarity were less unequivocal. This was partly due to the fact that the state of Israel was the result of a United Nations decision in the wake of the atrocities of the Second World War, and partly due to the globalization of the Palestinian resistance movement and the Orientalization of the world press. In addition, there were of course the Latin American countries which were subject to direct military attack by the USA. Typical of world opinion, the reaction focussed on the assault by the invaders and was aimed at forcing them to withdraw. When it was all over, interest declined and there was no continued criticism of the political systems which were left in place. There was even less interest in internal aggression within the 'free' states, since any involvement in such situations could be regarded as a form of neo-colonialism.

But strong conflicts developed in the new states on a broader level too. The two most significant factors were the extension of the cold war into the Third World and later, the spread of the global economic crisis.

The cold war created many bloody conflicts in the Third World. Shortly after the establishment of the colonies as independent states, internal contrasts became apparent in these countries. Freedom, which was the intended goal of the war of liberation against the European colonial powers, in an extension of what could be called internal colonization as a consequence of the national rebuilding of the new states, excluded a series of different population groups. This often occurred in such a way that participation or exclusion from state power was decided along ethnic lines. It was on these contrasts that global polarization was to play a part.

Frequently, the different groups in political or economically strategic regions were supported financially, or with arms, each with its own great power. This contributed to a sharpening of these conflicts which made them even harder to resolve. In many cases, the root of the problem lay in deciding which representative of the great powers was to rule the country. Compromise at the local level was therefore rarely a feasible option. But despite the chaos and poverty which this created, there was also an inbuilt mechanism controlling the escalation of the conflict. These wars were not allowed to develop beyond a certain limit; they were not allowed to pose a threat to 'world peace'. They were sealed in by the overriding interests which the superpowers had in keeping the wars well away from their centres in the industrialized north.

In many places, the global economic crisis heralded the definitive undermining of the building up of these new states: Modernistic values and national myths, which were a central part of the ideological construction of citizenship in these states, lost their value in the eyes of the population. The modernistic development was at heart, an - often forcible - universal acceptance of Western conditions and thereby a total break with regional and local cultures.

Following the economic collapse, this development was the aim of this reaction, which in turn allied resistance to the West with an assertion of regional, cultural or religious values. When modernism proved incapable of delivering prosperity, cultural/ethnic or religious fundamentalism was seen as a suitable alternative; references to a mythological, romanticized past had a strong mobilizing effect. Similarly, this particularity united strong local opponents in places where it crystallized into several different groups' struggle over power.

The Ethnification of Contrasts

The gap between the struggle against the powers in the former colonies and the struggle for the establishment of the new states is not a wide one. This was a logical consequence of the conflicts being along ethnic lines. The new national states were divided territorially according to the old borders between the colonial powers and the divisions which they managed to reach during the 19th century. This meant that the borders between the new states divided, in many cases, people who, as a consequence of the conflict's ethnic mix were to feel as one people. To some extent a number of states made demands on the territories of neighbouring states on the basis that the people who lived there actually belonged to the population of another nation. Furthermore, larger ethnic groups which did not gain a role in the running of the state, but instead lived under the oppression of the ethnic group in power, demanded and struggled for their freedom as a people within their own state. The popular mobilization on ethnic grounds founded revolt against the national states and was not based on the German romantic folk and cultural idea of 'one people, one state', as it was later claimed, but on the ethnic element in their oppression. The common oppression founded ethnically created ethnic group identities which were the basis for the mobilization of the resistance. Where the ethnic groups were placed within the borders of several states, the situation became even more complex as it became part of the conflicts between the states. Support for groups revolting in neighbouring states could contribute to the weakening and destablising of these areas.

These groups primarily emerged from the resistance to internal colonization. During the 1980s they managed to emerge as ethnic groups/people in the Western European tradition. In order to understand how this happened we have to briefly turn our attention to a smaller less violent development in that period. During the 1970s and 1980s, the autochthonous populations of the industrialized liberal countries demanded greater territorial autonomy with regard to the respect of their cultural particularity and traditions. This was in line with the idea that modernization on the terms of the conditions of modern capitalism, and in the name of equality, contained the threat of the eradication of their characteristic traits, thereby making them the same as the dominant population. Along with the rising influence of universal modernity and economic stagnation in the Western world, some of these populations were trapped both culturally and economically. With the educational explosion, members of these groups were educated to the point where they could formulate their demands for relative independence. Via alliances with, and appeals to, international organizations along with the use of modern mass media, these demands became a national, and later an international, affair. The most obvious examples of this are the Native Americans in North America, the Saami in Scandinavia and the Inuit in the Arctic. Some of these achieved success by referring to history, cultural autonomy and democracy, that is to say their own particular culture, their original right to a region and the relevant states' democratic tradition to gain extensive self autonomy. This is a process which is still ongoing. The aim was to achieve respect for their character and administrative powers within a territorial frame with various links to the states within which they lay. The central crux in this struggle was not the demand for independent state formation, but simply the expansion of autonomous administrative authority within a given territory.

The new tone in world opinion was clearly heard in the Western world, because it challenged democratic traditions, on a very serious political and argumentative level. This in turn could form the framework for the new independent states in providing a forum for the ethnic groups in which their struggle against the assault of the new states could be conducted. It became quite legitimate to demand relative autonomy on grounds of culture, origin and democracy. Modernism, with its emphasis on the universal and the common was replaced by post-modernism and the weight shifted to the specific and the varied, prompted by the global economic crisis in particular. The contrasts between the evolutionary lenience towards despotic political regimes and the demand for the right of all people to have their specific culture respected thus became obvious. At the same time, the colonial age was so far off that references to this in excusing despotic political regimes, along with the worry about neo-colonial interference, were no longer valid in Western opinion.

But first and foremost, the collapse of the polarized world order and the subsequent founding of new states provided much needed space. This made it possible to ensure that the debate, which up until this point had only really affected a few relatively small, groups at the democratic end of the world now became, not only valid, but of consqeuence in the Third World. A double process took place: The superpower conflict vanished from the local level, 'ethnic' conflicts and the separate sides in the conflict no longer had an economic pillar upon which to support themselves and to propagate the conflict. Secondly, the new states entered into a process whereby, as was the case in the states which emerged from the collapse of the Soviet Union, they demanded autonomy or independent state formation. This was an extension of the process of dissolution in which the minority populations raised their demands for more lasting solutions within a forseeable future. In itself, the issue of human rights for example, became relevant in the debate on internal conditions in the Third World at the popular level of debate and opinion. This was accentuated by the establishment of a kind of Kurdish national state in what was formerly Northern Iraq, and an autonomous Palestinian territory, which will, within a forseeable space of time become a self governing state. In all of this one can begin to glimpse the outline of a process whereby the international community — at least in strategically and economically valuable regions — and with a view towards increasing stability, will demand some fundamental cultural and human rights within the states themselves. This part of the Third World, which has a world economic interest has become a part of the international society in the sense that we now expect that universal, fundamental human rights which are internationally recognized, are also observed here. Let it not be said that those states which are engaged in the establishment of these rights are not doing it for their own political or economic interests; such as, for example, is shown by the oil interests in the Middle East and Central Asia. The central point, however, is that these interests are no longer implemented by the state-ruling political power groups, since economic integration in the world market today is based on an infrastructure which demands peace and stability. This peace and stability can be established in two ways, partly by creating a popular acceptance in the relevant regions as a positive element, and partly, as has occurred in the Kurdish regions of Turkey, by carrying out brutal, forcible relocations of the civilian population from the sensitive areas. The latter, however, cannot take place today without there being a strong reaction in world opinion. In part this is due to the global communication resources which have given all sides in the various conflicts a voice in the world. And partly it is because such a displacement of people nowadays has consequences of a global nature — in the form of great numbers of refugees streaming out into the world.

Popular, Historic and Cultural Identity

One of the sure signs that an area has become part of the modern world is that the basic identity references of the modern state become the identity of the people. In an extension of the bourgeois revolution and the romantic wave upon which it was built in Europe, language and history became raised to the status of central identity markers. These were the essential worldly markers in the nation forming process in relation to the former role of religion and reference to the regent. Language, religion and history were turned into culture and were considered inherent to man, despite the fact that they were in practice taught and developed with each generation. Language itself was a part of the family's socialization in fields where the local and the national language were the same. History on the other hand, had to be created and taught, and the same applied to language in those places where the national language was different from the local. This required an 'Enlightenment' project carried out by schools, the literary sources and the electronic forms such as radio and television. The fight for a national culture and the right to function in a society under prevailing local cultural conditions became a central factor in the struggle for international approval of self autonomy. This was made clear not only in traditional matters such as language in the schools and in the administration, but also in the importance of using ones own language in the written and electronic media. Equally, history became a battlefield where the common history became a necessary fundament of national identity. Separate individual histories, on the other hand, with their inherently ethnic based assault and suffering, became the fundaments of the separatist groups. New histories were created which made the population, which until then had not had language or history as central identity markers, into cultural descendents in an almost biological sense, descended from parents who had no idea that they actually belonged to the culture in question. The European 'Enlightenment' project did not exist in an age and a region where it was the clan, the religion or the ruler, who was the most important focus of identity, as it was, for example, in the case of the Ottoman Empire.

When the goal is a legal, internationally recognized demand on territorial autonomy, there are a series of different and often quite incompatible legal factors. The goal is often the same: one people with one culture, religion and language in a state with sovereign territorial power. The most important legalizing references are the justification of history — 'we were here first' — that we are one people, which is often linked to culture and language and in some cases race — a people on the strength of a common origin, culture and language — along with religion in some cases; if distinct from that of the group from which one is seeking separation. The historical construction is linked to internationally recognized treaties or to former international recognition.

This legalizing construction creates a lot of problems. It is modernist in the sense that it refers to a scientific documentation of rights in the form of cultural and historical academics. But it becomes sectarian because the reference is in an unlimited space with no clearly defined limitations. History is endless and manifold. If it is connected to a particular, well defined territory, it is often the case that history cannot prove that a particular people have occupied a particular region since time immemorial. In by far the most regions, and not least in the Middle East, it can be shown that a people with a given culture, language and religion which today are a majority of some kind, are not indigenous to the region. The problem is that 'Year Zero' can only be fixed arbitrarily, and usually relative to various power interests. To be the first inhabitants really has little bearing in a world where, if such a condition were applied, large parts of the world should be returned to indigenous peoples. One only has to consider what the consequences would be in, say America, Turkey, or Australia — where the period of occupation is relatively short compared to the case of the Middle East. Historical arguments are good as an instrument of mobilization in the modern world. They cannot, however, clear up the problems because none of the people in question have always been exclusively dominant in the relevant regions in terms of culture, race and religion etc.

The historical argument is further complicated by the fact that the focus is on a modern group, whose culture, language and religion are presented as being constant over time. The historical argument can only be applied in terms of a cultural concept, which can most closely be likened to an almost biological essence of the population. That 'we' are not just those living at present, but in fact comprise several previous generations. This, however, requires that 'we' have something in common, and quite everlasting, in relation to the attempts at legalizing the formation of a state on the basis of the historical argument. This gives rise to two problem areas: Partly it is in identifying that which is common, and connecting it to something which is relevant in terms of separatism. In other words, something distinctive in relation to other groups. The other problem is in proving that this distinctive element is very old in order to justify the historical argument. The great problem is that the element which is quite central to the way of life, which has a background stretching back in time (such as a trade) is neither distinct, nor cultural, but rather a symbol of poverty — the life of the poor peasants for example, or of the nomads.

In addition to this, the internal differences, such as economic, occupational, educational aspects and so on, are often greater than the differences betweeen the individual groups and the respective groups elsewhere in the world. The modern, middle class lives of the ethnic groups are often not that different from that of middle class groups in other parts of the world. Just as there is no great variation in the condition of the poor in various regions of the world. The distinctive must therefore refer to some ideological element, to that which can broadly be described as being identity. These people have, since the dawn of time, felt themselves to be one people. But this too is not valid. Nowadays, modern national identity is often described as an imagined community, and this imagined community is not something very old, but is intrinsically tied to and built up along with the nation state over the last 150 years. A real community, based on marriage or kinship has been in existence for a long time, as has the idea of a religious community. Neither of these, however, is connected to the national state. The idea of a national community was established when the state authority could not only reach the individual but could also become a central part of the formation and maintenance of the individual's identity; something which requires a steady influence. This came about through the socializing influence of schools and competence building in the form of widespread proficiency in reading in particular. This socializing and competence building was in turn maintained by a daily press, centralized 'union formation' such as the trade unions for example and the political parties, and the added influence resulting from involvement in the political process. Modern national identity, where people, culture and language are bound to a state and a territory are relatively new, as such, in Europe where it actually emerged, and even newer in the rest of the world. That a region previously took part in a bloody war is in itself not proof of the existence at the time of a national feeling.

The connection of history, people and identity can then only legalize the formation of a state if behind these mobilizing elements, there is a considerably large and real force capabale of creating recognition of territorial demands made on other national states, and/or in the state which one wishes to separate oneself from. Or, looked at in another way, the legalizing of relevant changes must have a pertinent reference. Where the idea of a thousand year-old common culture can be left flapping in the wind; the peoples right to self autonomy, as it would be expressed in a democratic process in the actual situation, or as a military *fait accompli*, would be a weapon of quite another magnitude.

Culture and identity are often alienated and cited as a reason for mobilization. This is done on the basis of language and history, and at times also of that which, with a suggestion of biology or race, is referred to as a people. Furthermore, it is also declared natural, as an objective condition which on the one hand cites the right to an independent state, making any objective compromise impossible, and on the other hand turning whole population groups into actors in the conflicts. If one did not actively support ones people, then one was automatically against them; it was not possible to change from one people to another, or remain neutral. This contributed to making the civilian cost of these conflicts very bloody; people which one group did not execute or incarcerate had to be enemies of the others. The wars therefore filled every individual with terror and the consequences were the large flows of refugees.

What made it possible then, and still does now, for such a mobilization to take place, despite illiteracy and other aspects of education that are lacking?

Answer — the electronic media, because this makes it possible to reach large numbers without educational conditions being necessary, and it is the surrounding powerful authority. The term ethnic group introduces a biological element to the matter of culture. This makes it possible to force large population groups into fighting for a project that is presented as an extension of their ancestral project. The national mobilization plan can therefore be undertaken without the democratic foundation which an informative, written form of publicity would demand. The project of the national state can thus be contained within despotic structures.

Models for Conflict and Solution

While relative comparisons of language, history, people, culture and ethnicity can perhaps explain certain elements of the conflict mobilization and development, taking into account the fact they are a central part of such conflicts in the 1990s, they cannot, therefore, be simply ignored as being 'imagined', or dismissed as being 'irrelevant'. Ethnicity — the sense of a cultural particularity, which is worth going to war over, has become a reality which must be incorporated into any proposed solution. That this was created by history — perhaps even within the last few years — does not change with the awareness that many people now regard themselves within, and subsequently act in accordance with, such categories. The solution to ethnic co-existence under such circumstances is unavoidable - their relatedness can only be a part of the process.

The second part of this process is that a dialogue between the conflict representatives and strategists is established. This requires some agreement - not necessarily in their view of the situation, but in the ground - rules of analysis - in the theoretical understanding of the background. This is due to the fact that the possible solutions to the problem are to be found within the theoretical view of the situation. This matter will be taken up in the last section, since, as is made clear in this book, there are a wide variety of differing viewpoints.

Opinions of the reasons for the conflicts can be arranged in a list of straight opposites, which, individually or combined, can be identified as the individual conflict identifications, and which contain their own possible solutions:

1) Imperialism versus national autonomy: The region in question is a part of the global economy and supplier of raw materials — particularly oil — which is of global significance. Both assurances of access to local oil and of the route into the oil-rich parts of the former Soviet Union mean that the area is not only

subject to a struggle between the imperialist states and the local populations, but also in a struggle between the imperial states themselves - particularly the USA, Germany, Japan, France, and the European Union - for dominance in the region. In an extention of this, local powers such as Turkey and Israel in particular, can be described as dependent, sub-imperialist powers. The solution to the conflict in this perspective is a common anti-imperialist struggle. That is to say a detachment from the global, capitalist economy. Ethnic and religious contrasts are seen in this perspective as an instrument for the imperialist powers and as something that will cease when the influence of these powers is eliminated. One problem with this model is that it is difficult to imagine economic welfare without integration in the world market.

2) Contrasts between the states: In an extension of the imperialist conflicts, the states are also mutually at odds over the central economic position in the supply of raw materials. This being considered as a condition for economic development as much as for regional political power. In addition to this there are contrasts on the national scale due to critical local resources - water in particular, which on the one hand demands a common authority if it is to be utilised to the benefit of everyone's interests, but which on the other hand provides an important development resource for the individual states in the form of hydro-electric power and the expansion of industrial production as well as food production. Water crosses borders which makes some states entirely dependent on the consumption of other states. One cannot expect international guarantees to apply because this would be an intervention in the internal affairs of another state. Here too, the cultural and religious contrasts can be regarded as secondary effects of the internal power stuggles between the individual states. This implies that a solution can only be achieved when the power struggles are replaced by cooperation.

Both of these models lay down the causes of the local despotic conditions as a dialectic between the foreign powers assurance of the actual power situation and the local groups' establishment of their own power. Analyses of the background would therefore be evolutionist and/or historical. The position of the despotic, patriarchal, ethnic power elite is due to a persitent adherence to the ways of the past. This is not only in contrast to modernity but is also a hindrance to economic development which can be taken as a prerequisite for democratization. This archaic aspect is often analysed in reference to, either European feudalism, which is artificially maintained by interests in power in contrast to the necessity of global development, or to the conflicts that existed in Europe when modernism emerged. In particular, the establishment of an informed, literate public is seen as a pre-condition for the creation of an 'imagined community', which is the fundament of the modern national state. Finally, there is a third and possibly more overtly political variant which is compared with European fascism. The transition to modern, democratic conditions would be a historic change. The speed and foundation of such a movement in the various regions is open to debate. It should be noted that the reference to a certain kind of archaism is quite acceptable to the European public. It is seen as being linked to the evolutionary or historical representation of the region here. An impression that is still, for example, presented in tourist advertising for the region. In this respect it is not so much a question of democracy, but of history. This is what legitimizes the lack of human rights, not just to a local society, but also to a Western public opinion, which recognizes exactly the same break with feudalism and religious domination in their own history as marking the birth of democracy. Again, this is a reason why the democratic rights of religious fundamentalist groups do not receive support. They are seen in the light of their religious background and with reference to the European prehistoric forces; something that does not simply fit into Western Orientalism, but is also actively used by local regimes to secure their international support as a bolster against backward looking religious fundamentalism.

3) Contrasts within the States: There are three main regions of conflict in existence at this time: a) Class conflicts, b) Cultural/Religious contrasts, and c) Despotic/Democratic contrasts. These contrasts are also involved in relation to the categories mentioned earlier:

(a) Within the collection of Middle East states, there are large contrasts in welfare. These can be ascribed to the persistence of prehistoric forms within historical or evolutionary perceptions of the world. In such cases it is the perpetuation of feudalism, usually, but also in certain cases of tribalism, in these modern states which is emphasized. Eradicating this apparent archaism is seen as a necessary condition for the establishment of the antagonism operating in the modern state, which, again, is supposed to lead towards socialism. This process can be taken as having been delayed as a consequence of a period of large oil revenues. This put leaders into a position where they were able to buy peace by (bribing) the public. With falling oil prices this system collapsed. The class struggle can also be perceived as a quite modern phenomenon in which capital and workers are brought into direct confrontation. This can be seen in, for example, the analysis of the capital interests running the media. This model also encompasses the fact that peace is a necessary development for the assurance of the national capitalists' capital accumulation. So long as the exploitation continues, this analytical model means that there is no possibility of peace in the form of some kind of class compromise. Cultural and religious differences have no analytical significance in this class struggle. However, class cooperation in the imperialist context is incorporated as the international dimension of an understanding of the core of the conflict.

(b) The ethnic, religious or cultural contrasts can be partly analysed in religious terms as a question of true/false religion; a matter which has not been addressed in this book. Alternatively they can be analysed in a modernist sense with reference to modern human rights; the right of culturally distinct groups in a region to some degree of autonomy, the freedom to practice their own religion, freedom of speech and expression and the freedom to organize gatherings etc. In the analysis of these conflicts, the right to a certain degree of autonomy is legitimized on the basis of historical evidence of an original claim to the region along with oppression by another - state bearing - group. History is quite central to the matter of justifying the right to autonomy and the struggle for the 'true' history becomes central. It can be said that autonomy is demanded, partly in reference to universal human rights: when the right to be different is threatened by suppression by the state, coexistence is replaced by the autonomy. On the other hand, it is demanded by references to historical and cultural rights: claims of indigenous occupation, or at the very least, an unbroken occupation of a particular area (Israel is something of an exception in this case due to the quite unique historical details caused by the Second World War) over a very long period of time can be used to secure the right to autonomy. It therefore appears that arguments for a group's right to relative or absolute state autonomy requires extensive historical evidence with the weight partly on the long unbroken presence — or at least the oldest presence in relation to other groups in the region — and a history of suffering documenting the assaults on them. This results in an argument for the intervention from outside if genocide is to be prevented from become total or if local conflicts are to be prevented from spreading.

(c) Whilst both the class contrast model and the cultural contrast model arise in the form of a struggle about the interpretation of culture and history, the democracy/despot model is represented as the cultural model for universal rights based on universal equality. The conflicts in society are seen as being the result of the assaults of despotic power, or in a milder form, as the state's inability to resolve its central task as redistributor of resources. The solution is seen as being the establishment of democracy and this can happen here and now so long as the archaic element is not taken as a part of the despotic conditions. These are purely modern power relations based on a modern foundation. In this model there is no room for any kind of larger cultural autonomy, in that the uniformity of the citizens overrides the cultural differences. The cultural differentiation can be dealt with within the frame of democracy, in that people are first and foremost people (or citizens) — it is only after this that they are Kurds or Turks or Palestinians. This argument is coupled with the idea that despotism is the cause of the poverty which in turn created the conflicts. Democracy on the other hand is seen as leading to economic development and thereby to the modernization of man. This would then reduce the significance of cultural and religious differences by moving them from the public to the private sphere along the lines of the situation in Europe. The democracy argument can be taken as an argument for the majority in the sense that democracy holds no guarantee of cultural autonomy as far as minority groups are concerned. One argument is therefore that the minority groups will become in effect a majority in the future. Extrapolating their high birth rate is presented as the threat of the minorities to the majority population if democracy is introduced. As several of the articles here point out, the problem is also that the term democracy is lacking in content. Its achievement meanwhile, in the form of definitions of the implications of citizenship - the imagined community - immediately invites the question of both linguistic and cultural problems. The conflicts arise when laying down the rules of how the national identity is to be expressed in the unifying elements of the education system, the administration, and the state information system. In terms of identity, common citizenship cannot be empty of content. The alternative solution to this is subsequently presented as being a federal system. A federal system can retain the original states at the same time as a common, political citizenship. It would also be open to the expression of cultural differences in the public sphere; in administration, media and education. Federalism as such is thus seen as a compromise between the independence of ethno-nations and the united state.

4) Conflict within the groups: The internal conflicts within the individual groups is at the basic level an explanation of the conflicts, or the lack of effectiveness in the struggles for democracy or autonomy. These can be reproduced with reference to a part of the above mentioned models: as class, or religious conflicts within the ethnic groups, as contrasts between the sexes, as contrast between local and displaced members of the culture (country and city contrasts, or the contrast beteen migrants/refugees and those who remained at home). These contrasts can also be attributed to the influence of

other states, such as, for example, the exploitation by the four neighbouring countries of the Kurds and their setting them up against one another.

At the root of all of the various conflict models there is evidence of a contrasting relationship, the dissolution of which — that is to say the model's resolution of the conflicts — consists of equalizing the opposing elements. This equalling-out would naturally vary according to the conflict model in question: the equal right and authority of the states in the international community in 1 and 2 above, the classless society with the total victory of one class or the cooperation of the classes for the common good in 3a, a common citizenship with a reduction of the differences to the private sphere, a federal co-existence or separate free and equal states as in 3b, a popular democracy in 3c, and popular solidarity despite internal opposites in 4.

In general, there seems to be agreement over the fact that the conflicts cannot be resolved militarily. Likewise a lasting peace needs two central requirements, the realization of which is a matter of disagreement: Economic development and democratic institutions. In a number of the contributions here these two requirements have been linked in so much as they are mutually dependent. Democracy is not possible without a certain degree of economic development and welfare, and economic development and prosperity require stability, which in turn requires an informed public and democratic social institutions. These would guarantee human rights in relation to both individuals, for whom these internationally recognized rights are intended as well as for the minority rights of groups on a cultural and/or religious basis. Economic development also needs a solid infrastructure. This, in turn, calls for large state investment which demands that military spending is considerably reduced. For this to happen there has to be popular support since any investment in the infrastructure could not be defended militarily against the local population.The aim must be to create sufficient mutual economic dependency so that military intervention would always incur greater loss than gain. This was the case in the wealthier parts of the world after the Second World War. The great problem is the route to achieving this goal. Depending on which conflict model is chosen, economic prosperity is therefore dependent on either greater integration into world economy, including the EU or else greater independence from this.

Fundamental to all these projections is the idea that while analyses of history and the past are made, future possibilities are considered independently of the limitations imposed by the past. It is the process of moving towards the future condition which is to be seen in a historical perspective. History, or the stories created around the particular models must, in relation to the proposed solutions, be set in parentheses. In actual fact this is already the case, in the sense that the definition of contrasts and solutions in relation to this uses history to legitimize a particular analysis of the actual situation, but which in terms of their form are quite modern. Even though various actual conditions can be understood in relation to European history or development, this is not an argument for the idea that European history should be repeated in order to create the desired solution.

The fact remains that the contrasts are now so deeply entrenched and have in fact become a part of the local cultures involved that they cannot be ignored. This is a part of the nation-building process and not something which is rooted in place. As it appears, this problem can be avoided by expressing a rhetoric of peace submerged within a rhetoric of security. This, however, does not prevent the establishment of a common national mythology as a grounding for an imagined national community since the two rhetorics must, by their very nature, have the same consequences.

Altogether it has to be said that the contributions in this book point towards a federal solution of cultural and religious problems. The length and brutality of the conflicts, for the moment at least, make it impossible to create a common modern identity. Also, taking account of the fact that this can be regarded as being, at one and the same time, a peace and security arrangement. In addition to this, there must be, in one correlation or another, economic development. In part, this has to come from assistance from abroad and partly as a result of a redistribution of state resources and from the democratization process which must be based on a project of education which can give rise to modern, informed and critical citizens.

Bibliography

Amin, S. 1970. *L'accumulation à l'échelle mondiale*. Paris.

Amin, S. 1973. *Le développement inégal*. Paris.

Anderson, B. 1983. *Imagined Communities: Reflections on the Origin and Spread of Nationalism*. London

Appadurai, A. 1990. 'Disjuncture and Difference in the Global Cultural Economy'. M Featherstone (ed.), *Global Culture - Nationalism, Globalization and Modernity*. London.

Balibar, E. & Wallerstein, I. 1991. *Race, Nation, Class - Ambigous Identities*. London.

Cardoso, F.H. 1972. 'Dependency and Development in Latin America'. *New Left Review* No. 74. London.

Eriksen, T.H. 1993. *Ethnicity and Nationalism. Anthropological Perspectives*. London.

Frank, A.G. 1969. *Capitalism and Underdevelopment in Latin America*. New York.

Friedman, J. 1987. 'Beyond Otherness: The Spectacularization of Anthropology'. *Telos*, No. 71.

Friedman, J. 1990. 'Being in the World: Globalization and Localization'. M Featherstone (ed.), *Global Culture - Nationalism, Globalization and Modernity*. London.

Friedman, J. 1995. 'History and the Politics of Identity'. J. Friedman (ed.), *Cultural Identity and Global Process*. London.

Gellner, E. 1983. *Nations and Nationalisms*. Oxford.

Hannerz, U. 1989. 'Culture between Centre and Periphery: Toward a Macroanthropology'. *Ethnos* Vol. 54, No. 3/4. Stockholm.

Hobsbawm, E. 1983. 'The Invention of Tradition — Introduction'. E. Hobsbawm & T. Ranger (eds.), *The Invention of Tradition*. Cambridge.

Hobsbawm, E. 1992. *Nations and Nationalism since 1780*. Cambridge.

Jenkins, R. 1994. 'Rethinking Ethnicity: Identity, Categorization and Power'. *Ethnic and Racial Studies* Vol. 17, No. 2. London.

Laclau, E. 1971. 'Feudalism and Capitalism in Latin America'. *New Left Review* No. 67. London.

Lash, S. & Urry, J. 1994. *Economies of Signs and Space*. London.

Rey, P.P. 1973. *Les alliances de classes*. Paris.

Roosens, E.E. 1989. *Creating Ethnicity: The Process of Ethnogenesis*. London.

Rostow, W.W. 1960. *The Stages of Economic Growth*. Oxford.

Sanders, E. D. 1977. *The Formation of the World Council of Indigenous Peoples*. IWGIA Document 29. Copenhagen.

Smith, A.D. 1994. 'The Problem of National Identity: ancient, medieval and modern' *Ethnic and Racial Studies* Vol. 17, No. 3.

Smith, A.D. 1994. *National Identity*. London.

Tambiah, S.J. 1994. 'The Politics of Ethnicity'. R. Borofsky (ed.), *Assessing Cultural Anthropology*. New York.

Wallerstein, I. 1990. 'Culture as the Ideological Battleground in Modern World System'. M. Featherstone (ed.), *Global Culture — Nationalism, Globalization and Modernity*. London.

The New Map of the Middle East

Faik Bulut

What is the Middle East? The term 'Middle East' was not created by the people of the region. To the Semitic peoples, the present day Middle East was the centre of the world. This concept is also to be found in the Quran, the Muslim holy book. In the *Hadith*, the selected speeches of the prophet Muhammed, this way of thinking is clearly reflected. If we look at the origins of Islam and its expansion during the age of the Ummayads and Abbassids, under whose leadership the Islamic empires were forged, it is clear that they considered themselves to be at the centre of the world; Europe and the Far East were peripheral. To the Semitic peoples and the Persians, the Middle East stretched from the Amuderya river in Central Asia, to the Nile.

It was during the 17th century that the term 'The Middle East' first emerged as a consequence of the colonialist mentality of Eurocentric capitalists. This marked the beginnings of imperialism. Taking the cultural and political aspects into account, the 'white man' divided the world into High and Low civilizations. The Europeans saw it as their mission to civilize the backward people of the region. In this sense, the Middle East is an invention of the Europeans. In German, the term is *Nahosten*; in French, *Proche-Orient*; in English, *Middle East*. With all of these terms, the three imperialist nations applied a geo-strategic and geo-political dimension to the region. The British influence stretched across Egypt, Palestine, Iraq, Saudi Arabia, the Gulf States, Sudan, Yemen, and from there through Iran, Afghanistan, and China, to India, Hong Kong, New Zealand and Australia. The very terms — Middle, Near and Far East were all created to indicate the distance from the centre of the British Empire.

To the Germans and the French, who had relatively speaking much smaller empires, there were only two divisions by the end of the 19th century; *Proche-Orient*, and *Nahosten*. These terms were also based on the distance from their European centre. Social researchers and historians in the colonial period coined the term 'Orientalism' for the study of these regions. All Western Orientalists made the basic division in their theories between 'Western' and 'Eastern' and this in turn prejudiced their view of Arabs, Afghanis, Indians and Turks alike. The same objective approach was applied to the religions of the region;

Judaism, Christianity and Islam. The prejudice of the Orientalists produced the idea that European culture arose from Graeco-Roman civilisation and a Judaeo-Christian synthesis. The Islamicists of today (traditional and fundamentalist) support this prejudice, despite the fact that they use another argument: when they say, 'Muslim is Muslim and Christian is Christian and there is no similarity between them. Graeco-Roman and Judaeo-Christian systems of belief have no connection with Islam', they are in effect evoking a reverse form of Orientalism. This way of thinking is not far from the racist mentality of the English writer Rudyard Kipling, or the term 'Clash of Civilizations' by which the American Samuel Huntington describes the present situation. In actual fact they both betray their ignorance; when Alexander the Great of Macedonia went to war with the Persians and conquered Egypt, he carried elements of ancient Babylonian civilization to the Greeks. In effect, he created a cultural bridge between the Nile, Hellas and Mesopotamia. The truth is that the cultural roots of Judaeo-Christian civilization come from the Middle East and the East. In the monotheistic religions and their Scriptures, the roots of the three religions show the strong influence of Mesopotamian culture, as well as the effects of Zoroastrianism.

In today's world, because of the geo-political interests, the term, 'The Middle East' is defined somewhat differently. In July 1995, at the Technical University of Middle East Studies in Ankara, an international conference was held under the title; 'New borders for the security of the Middle East'. A number of experts, of a variety of nationalities, took part. What emerged was that the New World Order regarded the Middle East as a very elastic term. Discussions of the term Middle East itself produced a variety of responses from the delegates. Out of the heated debate which followed came the statement that, 'The Middle East can be defined in a wide range of ways and is not independent of political interests'.

There are several examples which confirm this. In the USA there are two versions of the Middle East. The first is defined by Washington as the 'illegal Middle East' and includes Libya, Sudan, Iran and Iraq. These countries are regarded as being impossible to convert or form alliances with. The other group is made up of those countries which are taking part in the peace process. These include Israel, Jordan and Palestine and were all present in 1994 at the international summit in Morocco. They are all involved in a trade, economical and industrial cooperation. The USA regards these as being the countries of 'The Middle East Peace Process'. If we look at the first group, those opposed to the *Pax Americana* policy, the USA sees them as being against the goals which they would like to achieve.

At the same time, the USA realizes that the first group exists, but regards them as 'demons' which have to be destroyed. The other group are, in an ideal map of the region, the 'friends of peace'.

If we look at how Israel defines the region, there are also several 'Middle Easts'. In the 'demonic' geography, those countries which possess nuclear weapons, 'Islamic Atom', are a threat to Israel's existence one way or another. Pakistan and Iran fall into this category. To Israel, the build up of arms in these countries is an immediate threat to the state of Israel. Turkey is also in the process of building up its weaponry, but it is a member of NATO and is not a threat in Israel's mind. Israel's geography of the Middle East is circumstantial; it changes with time. When the subject turns to water, the map changes and includes countries with water resources, such as Jordan, Lebanon, Syria, Turkey and Saudi-Arabia. The Tigris and Euphrates rivers and the Seyhan and Ceyhan rivers all flow out of Turkish Kurdistan and are important to Israel's existence. Israel's map of water in the Middle East includes the possibility of 'water wars'. At times, the Israeli geography of the Middle East stretches as far as the Nile in the Sudan and Ethiopia.

In the Middle East, after Israel and Turkey, the third strongest land is Egypt. Egypt wishes to expand its influence to Jordan, Palestine, Syria, Iraq etc. Egypt's definition of the Middle East: the Egyptian map, cannot withstand the intentions of either Israel or the USA.

How Turkey defines the Middle East: To Turkey, the Middle East consists of water, oil and security interests. Turkey borders on Iran, Syria, Iraq and Iraqi Kurdistan all of which support the Kurdish separatist movement. Turkey is thus surrounded by a series of 'unfriendly' neighbours. To the Turkish intelligentsia, the Middle East includes the Caucasus and the Balkan region.

Looking at it from the universal point of view, there is a difference between the European and the American definitions of the region. Their definition is based on political and economic interests. The European map of the Middle East for example, includes much of the Mediterranean axis. Morocco, Tunisia, Palestine, Egypt, Jordan, Syria, Lebanon and Turkey were all represented at the conference of Europe and the Mediterranean lands held in September 1995, in Barcelona. It was important to the French and Spanish that they developed further cooperation with the North African countries. Morocco, Algeria, Tunisia and Libya are defined by France as being 'North Africa'. Following on from its colonial history, these are defined as the 'Francophone' lands and are, at times, included in the French map of the Middle East.

The American and British influence in the Middle East is centred on the Arabian Peninsula and the lands of the Arab oil sheiks. On the global level, it is here that the 'strategic natural resources' are, which they regard as being important. As the Gulf War proved, the USA was prepared to take any steps necessary to protect her economic interests. The Gulf War was also a clear signal to the rest of the world. To Germany, the map of the Middle East includes countries with large agricultural projects: Morocco, Algeria, Libya, Egypt, Palestine, Israel, Syria, Iraq and Turkey, Iran and their interests stretch further into Central Asia.

If we look forward into the 21st century, apart from the existing local conflicts, we can see that the Middle East will be divided into two blocs; the first being those which have access to the Mediterranean coast: Turkey, Syria, Egypt and Palestine and the European community. The other being the petrodollar Gulf lands under the leadership of Saudi-Arabia.But these two blocs will not be totally separate from one another, sometimes they will work together, but their development could be different. These two blocs are similar to the pre- and post- First World War divisions.

For us, the Middle East is a very large geographic area which is defined by three features:

1)   The 21 Arab countries which lie between the Atlas Mountains and the Gulf of Basra. These countries have the Islamic/Arabic culture and a similar political and social character in common.

2)   Historical, cultural and political similarities: In the second half of the 19th century, the Islamic philosopher Jamal ad-Din al Afghani saw the Middle East as an Islamic union which included the countries of the Ottoman Empire: Egypt, Lebanon Iraq, Iran and Aghanistan and also to a degree, those who struggled against the French and British colonialists.

The Lebanese Druse aristocrat and great Islamic Arabic personality, Shakib Arslan, also inspired similar reactions among the people of Morocco and Algeria at the start of the 20th century. Arslan's organisation fought against colonialism in the triangle formed by Egypt, Syria and Lebanon. It is also very important to note that up until 1920, the Islamic intellectuals of Iran and Egypt cooperated in cultural and political actions along the Teheran-Cairo axis. This also gives some idea of how important the above mentioned factors of culture, history and politics are in defining the unity of the Middle East lands.

Also in 1920, in Alexandria, Egypt, Hassan al-Banna established a social Muslim brotherhood which only became politicised by later events. This organisation became the focal point for all political activities in Sudan, Palestine and Syria and later spread over the entire region. The influence of the *Jama'at-i Islami*'s leader in Pakistan, Abu'l Ala Mevdudi, was an important political inspiration in Turkey and all the Arab lands. The Muslim Brotherhood's greatest theoretician, Sayed Kuttub, in the 1960s radical ideas, was an influence on the entire Islamic/Arab world. This is also proof of the close political and cultural bonds which exist in this region.

3)   In the present state of imbalance in the world and the ideological vacuum, the ideology of political Islam is seen as the 'only solution and route to independence'. This aspect produces another map of the Middle East — a much broader one. For instance, in the 1980s, in the Pakistani town of Peshawar, many guerillas of the Islamic *Mujahiddin* were being trained; Today, the *Mujahiddin* play a significant role in Afghanistan, Tajikistan, Bosnia-Herzegovina, Turkey, Iran, Lebanon, Yemen, Bahrain, Sudan, Egypt, Tunisia and Algiers. The fact that arms were taken up almost simultaneously in Kabul, Dushambe, Peshawar, Grozny, Negev, Tehran, Ankara, Beirut, Gaza, Cairo, Khartoum, Algiers and Aden, testifies as to how broad the true scope of the Middle East is and how tightly it is linked together.

Historical Panorama

Taken together, the above mentioned definitions of the Middle East form a pattern which can be analysed. In the 20th century, the European colonialists in Africa conquered Algeria, Morocco, Libya, Sudan and Egypt. This created an anti-colonialist movement which employed Islamic arguments. One example of this was the Kaddiri sect in the 1830s in Algeria led by Emir Abdul Kadir which resisted the French invasion. Another was the Mahdist revolution in the Sudan in the 1880s against the Turko-Egyptian forces. At the same time, the Kurdish Kaddiri leader, Sheik Obeid Ullah and his movement were fighting the British in Iran. In Afghanistan the *Bacay-I-Saka* movement resisted the British invasion. In India, the Islam-Deoband school of learning led the fight against the British. All of these examples can be seen in the same context. At the end of the 19th century, a Pan-Islamist politicization arose in the Islamic world, in the territories of the Ottoman Empire which was to counter Pan-Slavism. This Pan-Islamism was actually a strategy created by the Ottomans in order to create a strong position for themselves at the centre of the Muslim world. Thus an anti-capitalist, anti-colonialist feeling was created and this in turn gave rise to cultural and ideological growth. This was also the intention of the Pan-Islamists. More specifically, their ideas were those of Ottoman intellectuals such as Namik Kemal and Ali Suavi, as well as the Islamic scholar, Jamal ad-Din al Afghani and his Egyptian follower, Muhammed Abdu, and the Lebanese Rashid Rida, who together represented the other aspect of Pan-

Islamism. To this group, the *Salafiya*, Islam had no need of western civilization. Islams religious and political system provided alternative terms and mechanisms to counter western thinking. For example, instead of the term 'Democracy' there is *Shura*; for 'Equality' they use *Adalet*; for 'Fraternity' they use 'Brotherhood' meaning that it is enough that one is a Muslim. For the *Salafiya*, the most important thing in the struggle against Western influence was the principles of the first Islamic society, *Asr-i-Saadet* (The Golden Age) which was established by the Prophet Muhammed. In itself, the Islamic faith is a pure one, but is misinterpreted by authority. To understand Islam and draw strength from it, one has only to look at the basis of the religion the *Koran-al-Karim* and the sayings of the Prophet (*hadith*).

The *Salafiya* were regarded as 'fundamentalists'. Their main adversary was not other religions, but Western development of positivism. The *Salafiya* arose out of the reaction to Western cultural and political expansionism, but they were also influenced by Western positivist thinking. Economic and social development was also a goal to them. At the same time, the *Salafiya* were influenced by such 19th century social institutions as the Mazzini-Karbonari Masonic group, which they used as a model. Unintentionally perhaps, the *Salafiya* therefore played a significant role in implementing colonialist politics to the Middle East. Islamic movements today also draw on *Salafiya* ideas.

The other large movement in Islamic thinking was that of the reformists. They were called the partisans/ followers of the New Order or *Nizam-i Ceditci*. These movements were influenced by Western thought, but more specifically by the French bourgeois revolutionaries, who promoted nationalist ideas. At the start of the 20th century, nationalistic separatism and consciousness grew and anti-colonialist national resistance clashed with ethnic groups who were supported by the West. Turk, Arab, Afghan, Iran and the nationalist movement in Central Asia were all, generally speaking, affected by this trend. The above named three points effectively give us a broad picture of the political, social and cultural geography of the Middle East. What is interesting is that these phenomena became a passive ideology in the 18th century armed struggles. At the same time, the different movements influenced the development of each other. But the question is how and why. The problems of the people of the Middle East and solutions to these were a common motive for all of them. The problems with the colonial presence were the same everywhere: in North Africa and the Damascus region (Lebanon, Syria, Jordan and Palestine), in the Fertile Crescent of Mesopotamia, and the Gulf countries, in the Arabian Peninsula and Central Asia. What they had in common was, primarily, the conflict with imperial colonialist policy and the struggle for freedom by the people of the East. The second conflict was between the feudal classes who collaborated with the colonialists and the millions of oppressed peasants in the same region. At that time, the area held the largest collection of peasants in the world. The system of feudal production was an exploitative one. The farmers were very poor. The modern classes of the bourgeois and the proletariat were yet to evolve.

The Islamic ideology which had been in place for 1,300 years lost its political authority at the end of the First World War. At the same time, at universal level, socialist ideology had developed. Socialist ideology became wedded to nationalist ideology in a mixture that became representative of a growing bourgeoisie who in historical perspective appear as the leaders of the nationalist freedom movement. The population of all the large and small towns, small traders and merchants, all played a major role in providing members of the national and nationalistic movements. This was the case throughout the entire Middle East. In the final analysis, the colonialists of France, Russia, Britain and Germany, tore up the map of the Middle East and created a series of new borders and states, new countries and new provinces. In addition, there was the actual physical invasion in the establishment of the Protectorates. This led to the direct colonization of lands such as Turkey, Lebanon, Palestine, Algeria etc. As a result, there was little faith in the idea of a peaceful resolution for the countries of the Middle East. Strength and physical power dominated events. After 1919 and the Turkish freedom struggle, the Palestinian armed struggle against the Anglo-Zionist invasion of 1917-36, popular uprisings continued: in Iran in 1905, with the Mashruta, Constitutional movement and the outcome of the tobacco strike; in Syria the struggle against the French lasted from 1920-45; in Egypt, there was Said Zaghloul's popular movement in 1919; in Afghanistan and in India, there were armed uprisings and peaceful strikes aimed at the British colonial occupation; the national liberation struggle in Algeria between 1930 and 1962; in Kurdistan (parts of Iran, Iraq and Turkey) national and religious movements emerged to confront the French and English colonialists, especially in the Iraqi-Kurdish regions; the Kaddiri sects and Sheik Mahmud Berzenci from 1919-22 which marked the high point of the fight, etc. All of these events show the similarity of various aspects of the history of the Middle Eastern lands.

The Three Corners of the Middle East, or the Collapse of Nationalism

We have looked at the collapse of the political authority of Islam, and the rise of nationalism at the end of the 19th century. This continued up into the middle of the 1960s. The bourgeoisie's implementation of the national development project (NDP) went through a historical battle against Islamic ideology and experienced three major breaks:

1)   The historical events marking the start of the 1940s: firstly, there was the birth of the state of Pakistan. Following the peaceful, anti-colonialist freedom struggle in India, Pakistan separated from India and formed a state based on religion. In the Islamic world this meant that political Islam had once again become a reality and the Islamic model of a political state could be achieved with the assistance of the British colonialists. This provided the inspiration for the passive Islamic movements to begin legal and illegal opposition to the alliance of nationalism and socialism. The society of the Muslim Brotherhood in Egypt for example, began to organize cells within the military. They formed alliances with officers to create opportunities for themselves. In confronting Israel's invasion of Palestinian territory, Islamicists and the military fought side by side. In 1952, the Movement of Free Officers overthrew King Farouk and for a time remained an invisible part of the ruling authority.

2)   The second break came in 1948 when the state of Israel was founded. At that time, the feudal Arab regime lost their authority and the Islamic movement attempted to increase their opposition to them. To explain their losses, the Arab regimes began to produce demagogic and obscure arguments:

The Zionist colonialists have studied the Torah well, and they have learnt it by heart, therefore they have established the state of Israel, but we have distanced ourselves from our book, the Quran and are far removed from the religion of Allah, and this is why we have now been punished.[1]

In any case, the establishment of Pakistan and the 1948 Arab-Israeli war with the subsequent Arab defeat, created an alternative Islamic 'state model and project'. This gave rise to a new vision. The colonial powers had a strong foothold in the Middle East and so the conflict was to be between them and the Islamic movements. Political Islam did not have an opportunity at that time to make any gains over the nationalist movements. The nationalists of the day mobilized the peasants and small traders against imperialism. They used 'strongly Arab-Islamic motifs'. Time after time, national leaders expressed 'the

---

1. See Hugh Robert's article, 'Radical Islamism and the Impasse of Algerian Nationalism', translated and published in *Dünya ve Islam magazine*, Winter 1990, Istanbul; also quoted from reports of al Azhar Islamic Academy's serial meetings (4th, 5th, 6th), 1967, 1968, in Cairo; also see Yvonne Haddad 'Islamicist and the Israeli Question: Rising of 1967', Middle East Journal, Spring 1992; See Bruno Etienne, *l'Islamisme Radical*, Hachette, 1987, Paris.

glorious, progressive and anti-imperialist nature of Islam'. This was really a strategy aimed at the Islamicists in order to disarm them of the religious argument. They hoped that degrading the idea of political Islam in power would help them.

Later on this tactic was to backfire. For example, the Egyptian leader, Gamal Abdel Nasser, came up with an ideology of Islamic-Arab socialism. In Tunisia, the historical nationalist leader, Habib Bourguiba, saw himself as the greatest defender of the *Jihad* (holy war). His plan for national development was modelled on the Prophet Mohammed. In Algeria, Huwari Boumedien, during the struggle for national liberation, used the mosques as rallying places in order to create a *Jihad*. 'The best order is the order of Islam', Boumedien said, because we are the best interpreters and practitioners of Arab-Islam socialism. In Turkey, the 'Kemalists' who struggled against the Islamicists also used Islamic motifs in an opportunist fashion. In the interests of power, the Islamicist opposition was not averse to entering into alliances with foreign powers. The first model for a modern Islamic state, was that created by Muhammed Iqbal and Muhammed Jinnah, in the creation of Pakistan by breaking away from the Indian liberation struggle and the British colonialists in order to create their own state.

The Afghani Islamic opposition parties who fought against the pro-Soviet forces had close ties with the intelligence services of Pakistan, USA and Britain. The Islamicists in Algeria have been linked with the reactionary, feudal landowners in opposing the national classes in the cities to hinder the national development project. In Egypt, the Islamic Brotherhood which fought against Nasser's administration, had financial advisors from England as well as assistance from the CIA in their efforts to overthrow Nasser. In Jordan and Kuwait, the *Hizb al-Tahrir* was created by the British and their activities were sponsored by ARAMCO (the Arab-American Oil Company).

Therefore, it seems likely that the reason why the Islamicists never enjoyed the same popularity as the Nationalists was because people were aware of these alliances. It was the Nationalists and not the Islamicists who resisted the incursion of the Western powers into the Middle East. In 1956 for example, Egypt nationalized the Suez Canal. France, England and Israel took an aggressive stance. Many Arab countries also raised objections. But because of the aims of Pan-Arabism, millions of people from the Atlas Mountains to the Gulf of Basra stood up to resist the attack of the imperialists and their collaborators. The national freedom movements became political parties in the end and the imperialist collaborators, who were the reactionary feudal authority, which existed in Jordan, Saudi-Arabia and the Gulf kingdoms and principalities, gave themselves up for the sake of the nationalist movement.

They were also worried about the risk of military action in support of the nationalists. Where they lost local support, these feudalists went into alliances with France, Britain and the USA.

The Islamicists were also more interested in their own agenda than in the nationalist plan. Therefore, the nationalist movement worked with the socialist system, against the imperialist, feudal, reactionary and Islamicist alliance. In this way they rapidly gained strength. The Iranian nationalist (*Musaddik*) movement was a product of this time. The *Ba'ath* movement in Syria and Iraq also emerged from this trend. There was no compromise in the conflict between colonialism and the nationalists — as was shown by the Algerian war of liberation beginning in 1954 and the Palestinian resistance movement at the start of 1960 — both were symbolic of this trend. These two events gave new life to the national development project on both political and ideological levels which had been lacking since the setbacks in the 1940s (Pakistan and the founding of the state of Israel) when the movement had lost much of its momentum.

The League of Non-Aligned Nations was founded at the Bandung Conference (1955). This formed a large lobby opposed to colonialism and its collaborators by nationalist movements throughout the Third World. Many reforms were made on the behalf of the population at large. In particular, regarding the National Development Project (NDP), or the national 'Utopia', groups mobilized almost all categories and classes with regard to this reform. At the time, national and class politics were the order of the day. Broadly speaking, the population was unaware that it was up against the colonialists and class exploitation - there was a general lack of political awareness at this time. In the Middle East, the national classes had not radically defined their relationship with the colonialists and the capitalist world system. This meant that the exploitation of the classes was still effectively in operation at the local level. The exploitation continued and this delayed the NDP. The national 'Utopia' plan thus went through a phase of disillusionment. This meant that instead of being united under a banner of national identity, the population formed *Jama'at* or communities. Therefore, the NDP was incapable of solving ethnic and religious problems at the national level. This problem has now resurfaced once again. Foreign aggressors and local warriors were also a reason for the NDP not achieving its aims. Islamicists in the opposition at that time exploited the NDP's failure and created a political platform for itself. They called themselves the 'The voice of society's conscience'. Every mistake made by the so-called socialists in implementing the NDP was thus utilised by the Islamicists to disprove their claims and in turn assert that the other parties were demagogic and that the only real alternative was Islam.

The end of the nationalist movements came in 1967 with the Arab defeat in the Arab-Israeli war. This failure prompted the Islamicists, with support from the Colonialists and the local feudal regimes to claim that the defeat was 'a punishment from God' and that, once again, the only thing to do was to return to Islam. After the defeat, Gamal Abdel Nasser, the Egyptian leader and symbol of the Pan-Arabist movement, set up an investigative Commission, the majority of whose members were religious Ulema (scholars). Their conclusion was that 'we have forgotten Allah and he in turn has forgotten us'. In short, this was a lesson and required an immediate return to the ways of Islam. In actual fact, Nasser's establishment of the Commission was a final declaration of bankruptcy by the nationalist movement — in effect Nasser was bowing to the Islamicists and the colonial powers — the nationalists were waving the white flag. This turn of events did not end with Nasser; the phenomenon was widespread. Nasser's successor, Anwar Sadat, supported the Islamicist movement against nationalist and liberationist movements. This was known as the *Infitah* policy and was a combination of free market economy and the capitalist system. In Tunis, the Bourguiba regime in the 1970s implemented a policy of compromise on an Islamic platform, which developed into an open alliance with French capitalists. In Algeria, Boumedien declared that 'we must be open to the West'. Later, in Chadli Ben Jedid's day, this policy was coated with Islamic terminology and later with liberalism. They began to build mosques and supermarkets; the first with the assistance of imported Egyptian personnel, and the second by inviting French investors.

In Turkey on March 12th, 1970 and September 12th, 1980, there were military coups d'état staged with American support. They used Communism and Kurdish separatism as their excuse. They were so demagogic that the leader of the second coups d'état, Chief-of-Staff General Kenan Evren, announced his theory that: 'Fundamentalism is a socialist ploy and communist plot'. Later the Turkish-Islamic synthesis became the country's official ideology. Turkey today is effectively ruled by the *Diyanet Isleri Baskanligi* (Department of Religious Affairs) whose budget was raised to three times that of the National Education Ministry. While Iran is constantly criticized for exporting the *Sharia* system, in effect Turkey is an even greater exporter of this policy. Since its start in 1975, the religious war in Lebanon continued for fifteen years. Gaafar Nimeiri, former president of the Sudan, introduced a Sharia system to that country. In Syria, the only active organization was the Muslim Brotherhood. In 1982, with help from Turkey, USA, Israel and Lebanese Christians, a large uprising began in the town of Hama. This was harshly subdued by Assad. The Shia population of Iraq, who were the strongest supporters of the Communist party, inspired by the *Havdat-u Medreset-u Necef,* the School of Theology in Najaf, switched their alliance to an Islamic-Economic order and became militant supporters of Islamic alternative systems. In Afghanistan, the Soviet invasion gave rise to an Islamic resistance movement. In the 1970s, the silent policy in Saudi-Arabia protected the country from such nationalist movements. Following the 1973 Arab-Israeli war, Saudi-Arabia gained much greater influence in the region. The American-Saudi alliance built up a strategy known as 'Islam Hilal' which was also known as 'Yesil Kusak'; the Green Belt, which effectively was to surround the Soviet Union.

The examples mentioned show how the initiatives taken at the Bandung conference were turned to the advantage of the imperialist powers and the reactionary regimes in the Middle East.

Three Important Developments and Their Consequences

The first of these three developments was the overthrow of the Shah of Iran in 1979 which led to the establishment of the Islamic Republic under the leadership of Ayatollah Khomeini.

The second was the Soviet military invasion of Afghanistan to install a puppet regime. This created the well known *Mujaheddin* movement.

The third factor was supplied by Mikhail Gorbachov's initiatives in the '80s which were to end the cold war and lead to the collapse of the Soviet Union.

The importance of the first development lies in the internal and external factors which gave rise to the Islamic opposition to the Shah's regime. The Islamic movement was thus in direct confrontation with the nationalists and provided an alternative to the authorities at the time. Inspired by Iran, Islamic movements began to grow in a number of Middle Eastern countries, in the form of demonstrations and uprisings. The protest movement was created in this way. This was the case in Egypt for example, as well as Tunisia, and Algeria. Islamic protest movements gave rise to the 'bread riots' over shortages and prices in these places. In the holy lands, in Mecca, there was the Juhaini uprising and in Bahrain and Kuwait bomb explosions detonated by the Shi'ites. In Beirut, Shi'ite movements in the slums played a major role in the civil war in Lebanon; and in southern Lebanon, Hizbollah mobilized resistance against the Israelis — they too were inspired by the Iranian revolution.

On the second point, Islamic fundamentalists received political, military and ideological training in the Afghanistan-Pakistan axis. The Afghani Mujahed resistance in Peshawar became an attractive place for all the Islamic movements. They played a role similar in importance to that of the Syria-Lebanon axis in the Palestinian movement in the 1960s and 70s. The Islamicists fighting the Soviet 'bear' formed alliances with Uncle Sam and Western friends. The American régime of the day, which today regards the fundamentalists as being the devil, were the same people who trained them, through the CIA and the Pentagon, in Afghanistan and Pakistan. Islam as an ideology took off in Afghanistan and became a realistic contender for power in that country.

The consequences of the third point were very destructive. Until the collapse of the former Soviet Union, the world was ruled by the balance in the system between East and West. Even the USA was shocked by the consequences of this collapse which had a powerful impact on the balance in the Middle East. The Arab lands which were opposed to the State of Israel were supported by the Soviets. They now found themselves in a vacuum. The PLO signed on under the platform of the New World Order, despite the possible consequences for its own people. Turkey and Israel gained more influence in the region. Syria conducted a series of political manoeuvres to stay afloat. Iraq, which did not understand the consequences of the New World Order, invaded Kuwait in 1990, in what was to be a decisive confrontation with the imperialist powers. Iraq paid very dearly for this misunderstanding in the Gulf War.

There are also two subsidiary factors to be taken into account. The first was the Iran-Iraq war between 1980 and 1988 which came about as a consequence of a vacuum within the balance between the superpowers. The USA pushed Iraq against Iran in seeking a regional conflict. Internal conflicts within Iran were put aside until after the war. The national demands of the Kurdish, Belugi and Turcoman peoples were put down by the Iranian regime during the war. The Iranian regime did not, at the time, develop a progressive solution for the population. The internal power struggle and the euphoria over the Islamic revolution led to its export to other countries. They gave the impression to the world of being the centre of Anti-Imperialism. The regime supported all forms of opposition in countries which refused to compromise with Iran.

Israel took advantage of the opportunity presented by the conflict within the Arab world and invaded Lebanon in 1982, surrounding Beirut. As a consequence, the PLO leadership and bases, which had been located in Lebanon since 1960, were now dispersed and forced to move further away from Israel.

These two factors led to the nationalist movements losing what influence they had to the Islamicists. Radical Shi'a movements, organizations of the Hizbollah type, emerged in Lebanon, Iraq and the Gulf states. At the same time, in lands such as Egypt, Palestine, Tunisia, Syria and Algeria, radical fundamentalist Sunni movements, inspired by the Iranian revolution (Hamas, FIS, Jihad, Jami'at al-Islamia, etc.) began to appear.

The New World Order: Questions and Problems

The collapse of the Soviet Union and the Eastern Bloc marked the end of the balance in the world and created a new polarization. We must look at this in a historical context. The Soviet Union was by name socialist but in effect practised capitalist exploitation. An ultra-centralist, state capitalist system; the many rewards from the enormous machinery of state first reached those in power in the 1960s. The USA lost its influence in the world gradually, while at the same time, the Soviet Union took advantage of this opportunity and used the huge state mechanism to create an expansion of its global hegemony over the needs of the people. The conservatism of the central bureaucracy gave rise to an exploitative class and a number of national problems which were not solved by reasonable methods. During the Second World War a lot of mistakes were made. Out of a fear of collaboration with the German Imperialists, many people were deported to various Soviet republics. Ethnic 'islands' were thus created within the republics. Instead of building up a socialist identity, an ethnic one was created. Because of this, the Soviet type of capitalism became stagnant. Finally, due to the state capitalism of the time, a class of liberal economists emerged calling for a free market economy. In this way, Soviet society in the historical context ceased to develop. The spokesman for the new bourgeoisie, Gorbachov opened the road for the liberal class and their expectations. With the collapse of the Soviet Union, one of the world's military superpowers withdrew from the game. They gave up the global race and created an image of themselves as being in need of the West and the USA. The collapse of the Soviet Union gave the USA an opportunity to emerge once again as a political, military and ideological power in the world. Many supported the USA which was suddenly the unchallenged ruler and sole leader of the world. In actual fact the Americans were also caught unawares by these events. Reagan's 'Star Wars' project was created to destroy the Soviet Unions economy. Despite this, the USA never expected such drastic changes. The National Security Advisor to President Jimmy Carter, Zbigniew Brzezinski, was very much mistaken, however, in believing that the Soviet Union could be brought down through external pressure via the so-called 'Green Belt' of Islamic countries on the borders of Soviet Central Asia. In the end it was internal dynamics which brought on the collapse and not external factors.

Today, it appears that there is only one ruler in the world; in actual fact this is not so; the balance between the USA and the Soviet Union was a transition period leading to a polarization of the world. Therefore, the USA's present position is not permanent. In my opinion, by the year 2000, the USA will have lost its superior position. The authority of the USA is based on the system of balance between itself and one enemy. Today, there are numerous enemies. This means that we must begin to think in terms of different blocks and economic competition. In the European Union, France and Germany, while competing with one another are not in conflict. In the collapse of former Yugoslavia, the pro-Serb French-English axis is often at odds with the pro-Croatian politics of the Germans. This type of polarization is very interesting for it is apparent that the political interests of France, Britain and Russia are in opposition to those of the USA, Germany, Holland and Italy. France, for example, would like to see a policy that centres the Middle East around the Mediterranean and also include Iran and Iraq. Germany on the other hand sees the map running from Morocco through Egypt to Iran and Turkey. The USA supports another alternative; as embodied by NAFTA, which is based on Mexico, Canada and the USA in opposition to the new economic bloc in the Pacific consisting of Taiwan, Singapore, South Korea and Japan. China remains a potential threat to the new balance in the world system.

The USA is the only superpower in the world at present: The term 'New World Order' is not a coincidence. In effect, it is a much more barbaric version of the old colonialist order. Not only invading and colonizing other lands but also taking resources from the poorer countries in a very crude manner. The intellectual and political systems of the poor countries, their way of life, natural resources, national markets are being plundered by the New World Order. The ultimate policy of the New World Order is to destroy their psychological and intellectual balance. This can be taken so far as to almost be saying, 'This is the way you shall live, the way you shall think and consume'. The New World Order is also involved in the day to day life of ordinary people. The same mentality divides the world into a rich North and a poor South. This is the end result of the Imperialist-Capitalist system. This is a typical 'White Man' mentality which suggests that history is at an end, or speaks of a 'clash of civilizations'. In this way they hope to create a system without opposition from the rest of the world. At the same time, this results in a North-South and East-West conflict. In other words, it is a conflict between 'the modern high civilizations and the poor, primitive civilizations'. In this way their strategy is aimed at destroying all the so-called 'primitive' or 'low' civilizations.

This can create local conflicts, wars, ethnic-religious conflicts or civil wars. Of course we can certainly see the effect of the policies of the New World Order in the Middle East: the war between Azerbaijan and Armenia, conflicts such as; Georgia-Abkhazian, Kurdish-Turkish, Kurdish-Arab, Iran-Iraq, Sunni-

Shi'a, Secular-Islamic, Egypt-Sudan, Somalia-Somalia, Jew-Muslim — these are all the products of the New World Order in the Middle East. It is important, therefore, that we put the following questions to the New World Order:

a) Could the Western imperialists, and the USA in particular, surround the poorer countries, known as the Third World, or carry out a military invasion of them in order to create their New World Order in these regions?
b) Can these new geo-political strategies create a new world map and give rise to a new world order?
c) Can the strategic importance of the Middle East still give new border divisions for the New World Order?
d) What role will Israel play in this NWO?
e) Are there any alternative resources in the NWO to compete with the oil of the Middle East?
f) Can NATO play a new role in the region and if so, in alliance with whom?
g) Is it possible to reach a settlement between the lands of the Middle East under the New World Order, and how should this be achieved?
h) Is it possible for external forces to intervene in the Middle East?
i) What will be the result of the formation of new blocs in the Middle East and of separate agreements between parties without an overall common agreement?
j) How will the internal conflicts resolve themselves?
k) What is the role of Israel and Turkey in the imperialist strategy?
l) Is there any future for the anti-imperialist political movements and to what degree will the Islamic and nationalist groups resist this?
m) Can the Islamic and nationalist movements continue with their anti-imperialist politics and can they be part of the solution?

There are a lot of other questions which we could ask, but we need to analyse the politics of the New World Order in the Middle East.

The Middle East: A Testing Ground for the New World Order

In August 1990, the invasion of Kuwait and the expulsion of its oil-sheikhs by Saddam Hussein announced the New World Order in the Middle East. In February 1991, the American-Allied military attack on Iraq was greatly assisted by CNN. This was the first test for the New World Order in the Middle East. Many believed that this conflict was simply between Kuwait and Iraq. In fact it was something very different. That is to say, it marked the new divisions of the world, motivated by imperialist conflict and interests and possibly also laid the seeds for the Third World War. This is because prior to the collapse of the Soviet Union and the USA's withdrawal from Cambodia, Vietnam and Laos, the Middle East created an attractive and irresistible opportunity for the West. The oil factor made this area strategically very important. The USA saw Europe and Japan as being their new competitors and therefore needed to gain control of these most valuable assets to increase its power in this competition. Alliances made prior to and after the Gulf War created an internal Arab conflict as well as a pro-American pact. During the War, Syria and Egypt along with six of the Arab Gulf states issued the Damascus Declaration voicing their protest against Iraq. They also provided soldiers for the Allied forces facing Iraq. This showed very clearly the divisions that existed within the Arab world. It also produced a strong dependency on the USA: Syria, for example, in order to avoid being attacked by the Americans, reached a compromise with the West, while Saudi-Arabia and the other Gulf states allowed the Americans to establish military bases on their land. Saddam Hussein, known as a great tactician in the Middle East, made a number of strategic mistakes which allowed his country to be partly occupied and divided into three parts by the West. Following the collapse of the Soviet Union, the PLO lost one of its most important supporters, and so entered into a hopeless alliance with Saddam Hussein against Israel. But when Saddam lost the war, the PLO waved the white flag and bowed towards the New World Order. It is in these dark times that Israel and the Palestinians have signed the Peace Treaty. The fact is that what the Palestinians were signing in Oslo in 1993 was their acceptance of the New World Order.

The consequences of the Gulf War was an extension of NATO influence in the Middle East. Turkey plays a role in Caucasus and the Middle East on the basis of its historical background in the region. The New World Order provided Turkey with the excuse needed to occupy Mosul and Kirkuk in northern Iraq. During the Gulf War, with the consent of former President Özal, plans were laid by Turkish and Allied military experts for the occupation of Mosul.

Consequences of the Gulf War

It is important that we analyse the consequences of the war:

1) The Middle East, Balkans and the Caucasus are areas in which the superpowers are competing for influence:

Russian military documents from the 1994 NATO summit show that NATO's sphere of influence is to be expanded southwards, and is to include all three of the above regions. In particular, the document known as 'Scenario Number Seven' outlines Turkey's role regarding Bosnia-Herzegovina, Kirim, Azerbaijan and Central Asia. At the same time it covers military operations across the borders into Iran, Iraq and Syria. Of course this kind of operation would be explained as being undertaken 'in the interests of Turkey's internal security and unity against Kurdish separatists'. In March 1995, Turkey crossed into Iraqi Kurdistan with 35,000 soldiers. In June 1995, they also went into Iran. Turkey's threat to Syria is also included in this 'Scenario Number Seven'.

2) The Balkan area, the Middle East and the Caucasus, look very similar to the way they did in the days of the First World War. Over the last fifty to sixty years, national boundaries have existed in these areas and today these are collapsing. We know how many states will emerge out of the collapse of former Yugoslavia. In Armenia and Azerbaijan, the conflict region of Nagorno-Karabak has collapsed to the advantage of Armenia. After Iraq's invasion of Kuwait, the northern Iraqi border was changed in favour of the Kurds. At the same time the Palestinians and Israelis entered into the peace process, and this can be taken as evidence of the strategy of the New World Order.

3) In line with these developments, the Kurdish question becomes very pertinent at the international level. The unsolved Kurdish question is added to the problems of the region. This is another key question in the area and one which could have a decisive influence on the future of the region. The West is still divided as to whether or not there should be a Kurdish state. The USA and the Western lands use the Kurdish problem to their advantages while not seeking a solution that will not harm their interests in the region. Despite this, I believe that in the long term it is still possible for a Kurdish state to emerge. The continued significance of the Kurdish problem is an indication of this.

4) At the same time, the USA is working on the project of removing all obstacles from their path. This is done by announcing countries which, for example, actively support terrorism; Countries such as: Libya, Sudan, Syria and Iran, as well as organizations such as PKK and Hizbollah. The USA therefore supports Turkey's attacks on the PKK in Iraqi territory and Israel's attacks on Hizbollah camps on Lebanese soil.

5) The USA surrounds Iran and Iraq. In the short term, the plan is to overthrow the regimes, but in the longer term the USA will extend its interests from the Middle East in order to reach the wealth of natural resources in Central Asia.

6) The American strategy is not simply to control oil in the Middle East, but also, additionally the oil resources in Central Asia in the future. Therefore, there is a conflict with Russia, which in turn explains why the USA supports the Turkish pipeline project which is to run from Baku to Turkey. In support of this project the USA would like to protect the Kurdish areas through which the line would run.

7) The unstable republics in Central Asia have 'radical Islamic' groups. These movements threaten American interests in the region. The American strategy is to strike its own balance in the region and therefore support Turkey over the Iranians. At the same time, they support Pakistan in order to gain influence in Afghanistan. In this way, the Kashmir-Peshtun-Afghanistan-Pakistan chain will surround the China-India-Iran-SNG area. Iran is therefore seeking to enter into an alliance with India, China and Russia to break the American plan.

8) In North Africa: The USA, opposing French influence in Algeria, supports FIS's 'Reformist Islamic' government against the French-supported government. Jacques Chirac's visit to North Africa in July 1995 was a move to counter American ambitions in the region. The Americans are trying to redress the loss of face they suffered in Somalia with their involvement in the conflict between Egypt and the Sudan - in the hope that this will increase their standing in the region.

9) In the Gulf region, the USA would like, under the leadership of the Saudi-Arabians, to create a new bloc. During the war in 1994 between North and South Yemen, the USA supported, along with Saudi-Arabia, South against North Yemen. North Yemen had always been a friend of the Americans, but during the Gulf War North Yemen joined the Iraqi side. This is a classic example. In Bahrain, the crown prince overthrew his father and this was to the advantage of the Saudi - Arabians and the Americans. In an extension of this strategy, the Americans transferred the 5th Fleet to the waters of the Gulf region — allowing the Americans to launch lightning attacks to protect their interests.

10) The American project in actual fact is based on the large roles played by Turkey, Saudi-Arabia and Israel; they are not only the guardians of the region, but at the same time form a bridge to Central Asia and the Caucasus. In Turkish-Kurdistan for example, the largest water dam is the GAP South-Eastern Anatolian Project. Israeli and Western finances are invested in this project which is an indication of how much this alliance is an economic cooperation between these countries. In this sense, Israel has had a long term interest in the Kurdish problem. The investment in the GAP project makes it much easier for them to keep an eye on events in the Kurdish territory.

The War Between Projects

The interests of the Western great powers in the Middle East can be typified by their economic projects. Here are some examples:

1) American Projects: After the peace agreement between the Palestinians and the Israelis a number of water projects emerged. The Turkish rivers which will supply water to the Arabian Peninsula via Syria, Israel, Palestine, Iraq and Kuwait is called the 'Water for Peace' project and is to be carried out by an American firm. The second project is to built a large road connecting Turkey to those countries which lie on the Mediterranean coast: Syria, Lebanon, Israel, Egypt. The third is the Middle East Economic Cooperation project. The fourth is the Middle East Peace and Cooperation project. All these projects are sponsored by the USA. Their intention is to create a regional economic unity with Turkey and Israel playing an active role, with the stipulation that this development and international politics are under the control of American multinationals. One of the proposed ideas is to found a Middle East-African Development Bank. 50 percent of the bank would be owned by 10 capitalist countries such as the USA and various European countries. In contrast, 30 different countries in the Middle East would share the other 50 percent of the shares. This would mean that the financial capital would effectively be controlled by the imperialist colonialists. One of the main conditions for this project is that all the countries involved have a free market economy based on Petro-dollar finances. This would mean that the USA would create an enormous market for itself and at the same time playing the role of the `Guardian of Peace' in the region. It would also secure American arms sales in the region and in this way finance their large projects in the countries of the region. The real intention is to increase American strength in the region and improve its interests in Central Asia ahead of the other competitors.

2) The German Project: A large economic and agricultural conference was held in Morocco in 1994. The outcome of this was a large agricultural project in North Africa and the Middle East; from Morocco to Egypt, Turkey and Iran and including Afghanistan. Germany also uses the Black Sea Economic Cooperation Council to create advantages for Germany to go in via the Caucasus to Central Asia. It is obvious that Germany is using both of these ways to improve its interests in the region. It is very important to look closely at this project. One good example here is Chancellor Helmut Kohl's visit to Jordan, Egypt and Israel, Palestine, Libya, and Syria in 1995 created hope for those who were wary of the Americans. German influence is strong on the Iraqi and Iranian markets. This visit showed that Germany is very busy improving its competitive edge over the Americans.

3) The French Project: The French are mainly interested in those countries which border on the Mediterranean coast. This project is based on mutual economic cooperation and export. This is to take place with Europe at the centre. In September 1995, a large conference was held in Barcelona and French interests were discussed. The French were the secret architects of the Oslo negotiations of the peace agreement between Israel and the Palestinians. They are continuing in their plans to create a confederation between Jordan, Palestine and Israel. Like its neighbour Germany, France is also developing its economic links with Iraq and Iran. France is also interested in using the Georgian-Armenian axis to reach the resources in Central Asia and would also like to be involved in the Kurdish question to increase its interests in the Middle East.

4) The Japanese Project: This obscure involvement is based on an oil pipeline from Baghdad to Gaza. This would be run by Japanese firms.

All of these examples show that the proposed projects of the imperialist countries would provide them with a base in the Middle East from which they could reach Central Asia. The common theme is to build a chain linking Mesopotamia, Kurdistan and the Caucasus. Therefore, the change in the different national boundaries in the region and Turkey's large role in this project, and the question of the establishment a Kurdish state, are all related to the competition between the various powers and the realization of their ambitions. The role of the rivers, Tigris, Euphrates and the Nile, have all been politicized. There is a real possibility of war over water resources in the Middle East. Considering the sources of these rivers, two of them, the Tigris and Euphrates, are in Kurdistan. The geography of Kurdistan places it between the Caucasus and the Gulf of Basra. The great superpowers — Russia, USA and Europe, and the regional powers — Turkey, Iran, Syria, Iraq and Israel, all have a great interest in the Kurdish problem because of its importance. The USA has not completely decided the outcome of the question of a Kurdish state, but the Palestinian-Israeli model would suggest an autonomous, federal state. Slowly, the USA is trying to put this into practice and would incorporate Iranian and Iraqi-Kurds into Turkey to create a large Kurdistan under the protection of Turkey. This formulation is one of the American projects.

I will not go any further into this topic but wish to stress the matter of how much of an advantage such a proposal would be to the countries of the Middle East. I would also like to speak about the other projects. For example, the idea of creating a Middle East African Development Bank, the common market of the Middle East, and an Israeli-led, Jordan, Israeli, Palestinian federation. Both of these to be created using Arab finance and Israeli technology. Although the countries of the Middle East are strong enough, if the international financial sector conquers the Middle Eastern market neither Turkey, Israel, Egypt nor Saudi-Arabia would escape becoming the entrepreneurs of the great powers. They would also be called upon to act as the *gendarmes* of the region. The economic and financial interests have to be protected. At the same time, the national and religious wars and conflicts exist in the Middle East and these will not stop by themselves. Therefore, they will either be broken down or provoked by the prevailing circumstances at the time.

This will be one outcome of Western interest in the region. But we should not forget the Arab-Israeli peace treaty and the end of the Iran-Iraq war have also helped in reducing the possibility of national conflicts to a minimum. This will have consequences in countries such as Syria, Iraq, Israel, Jordan, Iran, and Egypt and may give rise to the demands of a class struggle or social problems which can create a period of internal power struggle. In these countries, the rise of Islamic movements can be seen as a protest on behalf of the poverty stricken populations. This factor will not be the decisive determining one. The newly converted capitalist countries in the Middle East do not have well developed economic structures and will be colonized by multinational firms which will create a large pirate economy; 'Islamic non-interest banks' are also a part of this pirate economy. The unstable economies in the Middle East will create a broad middle class and encourage its growth in these countries. Workers and peasants will move from one class to another. Ideological vacuum creates a large oppression of the population and this creates a desire for equality and freedom. In this way, although people may not be aware of it, they are vulnerable to the slogans of the political Islamicists for whom 'the only solution is Islam'. This has a destabilising effect on society and the class struggle and gives rise to ethnic and religious conflicts in the region: In Iraq the Shi'a Mohalafat (opposition); in Iran the Kurdish and Baluchi questions; in Egypt the conflict between Muslims and Copts; and in Turkey, the Refah party and the problems between Alawi and Sunni; in Lebanon, the Druse — Shi'a-Maronite-Muslim conflict; in Algeria, Islamicists versus the military regime, etc.

All of these are examples. In the Middle East today, former nationalist voices and politics still survive. In fact, today the political Islamicists can be seen as a form of anti-imperialist nationalism in the Middle East. But we cannot predict how this type of Islamic reaction, which has limited social and ideological dimensions, will develop. In the future, however, other forms of social reaction may emerge as a result of the unrest in these societies and we cannot say whether these may lead to patriotic, nationalist or socialist developments in society, or alternatively, a mixture of the three. In any case, for the moment it is not possible to say that lasting peace will develop in the Middle East, firstly, because the West is very concerned about this unstable period which could produce some unseen surprises. These may not be Saddam Hussein's superficial form of socialism, and nor will they be anti-Western movements. In fact the direction in which popular democracy in the Middle East is developing is turning towards the Western imperialist system. This cannot come about without breaking with Islamic fundamentalism and the classic forms of nationalism. But, by doing this they would be able to achieve their utopian project.

Bibliography

Aflaq, Michael. *Arab Baath Socialist Party; The Starting Point.*

Agha, J. Hussein-Khalidi, and S. Ahmad 1995; *Syria and Iran: Rivalry and Cooperation*, London: Pinter Publishers.

Amiranmadi, Hooshang 1994. 'The Islamic Republic and the Question of Palestine', *Middle East Insight*, May-August.

Avrasya Magazine 1996. 'The Kurdish Question', special issue, Ankara.

Barnes, Jack 1991. *Washington's Assault on Iraq: Opening Guns of World War III*, special isue, New International, No. 7.

Bostancioglu, Burcu 1996. 'Soguk Savas Güdülenmesi ve Ortadogu', *Avrasya Magazine*, Summer. Ankara.

Bulut, Faik 1994. *Seriat Gölgesinde Cezayir (Canonical Obligation: Algeria Under The Shadow of Shari'a)*, Istanbul: Cem Yayinlari.

Bulut, Faik 1993. *Islamci Örgütler (Islamic Societes/Organizations)*, third edition, Ankara: Tümzamanlar Yayincilik.

Bulut, Faik. *Türkiye'de Tarikat Sermayesinin Yükselisi ve Islam Ekonomisinin Elestirisi (A Research into Economiy and The Capital of Orders/Sects)*, second edition, Ankara: Doruk Yayinlari.

Etienne, Bruno 1987. *L'Islamisme Radical*, Paris: Hachette.

Fuller, G. Graham and O. Ian Lessler, 1995. *A Sense of Siege: The Geopolitics of Islam and West*, Washington: Westview Press.

Funabashi, Yoichi, 1991. 'The New Order and Japan', *Foreign Affairs*, Vol. 4.

Güldemir, Ufuk 1987. *Cevik Kuvvetin Gölgesinde Türkiye (1980-1984)*, Istanbul: Tekin Yayinlari.

Gunter, Michael 1993. 'de facto Kurdish State in Northern Iraq', *Third World Quarterly*, Vol. 14, No. 2.

Haddad, Yvonne 1992. 'Islamist and the Israeli Question: Rising of 1967', *Middle East Journal*, Spring.

Haikal, M. Hasanain. *The 1973 Arab-Israeli War anda the Middle East*, Cairo.

Halloum, Rubhi (Abu Firas) 1988. *Palestine through documents*, Istanbul: Yazir Matbaacilik.

Hilal, Hasan 1994. 'Are the Arab Ready for Peace with Israel?', *Middle East Quarterly* 1, No. 1.

Hugh, Robert 1990. 'Radical Islamism and the Impasse of Algerian Nationalism', translated and published in *Dünya magazine*, Winter, Istanbul.

Köni, Hasan 1994. 'Misir-Türkiye-Israil Ücgeni' (The triangle of Egypt-Turkey-Israel), *Avrasya magazine*.

Lepoer, Leitch Barbara. 'Pakistan-U.S. Relations', *CRS issue brief 94-041*.

Ma'oz, Moshe 1990. *Assad — The Sphinx of Damascus (A political biography)*.

Migdalovitz, Carol 1994. 'Turkey's Kurdish Imbroglio and U.S. Policy', *CRS Report 94-267*, March 18th.

Mark, Clyde and Kenneth Katzman, 1994. 'Hamas and Palestinian Islamic Jihad; Recent Developments, Sources of Support, and Implications for U.S. Policy', *CRS Report 94-993*, December 12th.

Odeh, B. D. 1985. *Lebanon: Dynamics of Conflict*. Beirut.

O'Neil, Dan and Dan Wagner 1993. *Peace or Armaggedo: Unfolding of the Middle East Peace Accord*, London: Harper and Collins.

Özdag, Muzaffer 1994. 'Türkiye'nin Asya Politikasi', *Avrasya magazine*, Summer, Ankara.

Rode, Reinhard 1994. 'Aus Politik und Zeitgeschishte' (translated into Turkish and published in *Avrasya Magazine*), Winter, Ankara.

Sestanovich, Stephen 1994. *Rethinking Russia's National Interest*. Centre for Strategic and International Studies, Washington.

Shafiq, Munir 1983. *al Islam ve'L Tahaddiyat-ul inhitat-iL Muasir. The Islam and Contemporary Decadence Challange*, London: Dar-ul Tha.

Shukri, Ghali 1992. *Some articles on the Islamism and fundamentalism problem in the Arab World*, published in *Al Watan al Arabi magazine*, August 21st-28th, and September 4th, Cairo.

Rushdie, Fundamentalism and Politics

Lars Erslev Andersen

The Middle East is a region with the specific characteristic that it has the constant attention of the media, generally speaking. The reason for this is that the area is a centre for Ethnic conflicts; conflicts about resources like water and oil and, not least, religious conflicts. Primarily the conflict between Muslims and Christians followed by conflicts between Jews and Muslims and most recently, the religious conflicts between Muslims and Muslims. The latter naturally referring to the phenomenon which is called fundamentalism in Europe as well as in the Middle East. Now fundamentalism, other things being equal, is not a new phenomenon. Saudi Arabia's traditions for a fundamentalistic government whose legislation is based on Sharia or Islamic law go way back. The political, often militaristic, groupings that have grown in countries like Egypt and Algeria are relatively new phenomena and they have caused fear as well as confusion among the Western public. The shooting of Western tourists in Egypt is, automatically, bound to spawn questions like: what is this fundamentalism and what are the fundamentalists basically after? Also, there is a tendency to see fundamentalist violence as a built-in element in the Muslim religion, Islam. Thus, the Gulf war was personified by the good, and Christian, George Bush, in contrast to the evil, and Muslim, Saddam Hussein. A well-known Danish writer, theologian and broadcaster, (now deceased) went so far as to present Islam as the religion of hate — as opposite the religion of love, Christianity. I think it is wrong to focus on the strictly religious to such an extent in an analysis of fundamentalism. To put it simplistically: Islam is one thing; the use of Islam is another.

Islamic fundamentalism is not just a religious revival but also an extremely political revival that has to do with modernity. In the following, I shall argue in favour of the idea that Islamic fundamentalism primarily is to be understood as a special political language and not as a religious movement; that it is a phenomenon of modernity which, in a certain sense, carries the future with it. I plan to do this by resuming the discussion on the Rushdie case which, to me, is a conflict between Western liberal systems inveterated in the novel, and the Middle Eastern full — and semi dictatorships — that is to say, more politics than religion.

The Novel — The Essence of Europe

In his short essay *Is Nothing Sacred?* Salman Rushdie writes that:

literature is the one place in any society where one, within the secrecy of our own heads, can hear voices that speak about all kinds of things in all thinkable ways. The reason for ensuring that that privileged arena is preserved is not that writers want absolute freedom to say and do whatever they please. It is that we, all of us, readers and writers and citizens and generals and godmen need that little, unimportant-looking room. We do not need to call it sacred, we just need to remember that it is necessary.[1]

From the context, it is evident that the literature to which Rushdie is referring is the novel and, on my own account, it can be added that it is not a 'small, insignificant-looking room'. On the contrary the fact is that the novel is, if anything, the phenomenon which incarnates the European civilization. In his salute to the novel, Milan Kundera writes that it constitutes an 'espace imaginaire est né avec l'Europe moderne, il est l'image de l'Europe ou, au moins, notre rêve de l'Europe'.[2]

The fact that the novel was born along with modern Europe, as Kundera expresses it, makes it special among literary genres: All other genres were known before modernity as well as in other cultures; it is only the novel that is dependent on the book and, as such, developed into a genre according to Gutenberg's invention. It is the only genre that has been developed along with the European writing culture, and it is writing in particular, and the propagation of writing that characterizes Europe as being a literary place where everyone can read and where the messages of all political parties are freely distributed. Furthermore, the establishment of a literary public is an irreversable process: if the technology, the market, and the public is realized, then restrictions on the propagation of writing is impossible in practice. In the Middle East, there is no literary public, even though, of course, there are writers, intellectuals, readers and printing houses. However,all writing productivity is subject to censorship. There has not yet been established a free market for literature and this is partly due to the fact that at least half of the population does not know how to read. It is clear that the present Middle Eastern regimes see this situation as being to their advantage. For this makes it easier for them to restrict the political discussion. There can be no doubt that the establishment of a literary public for these regimes would have enormous consequences.

In the formation of the European literary public, the novel, as a genuine

---

1. Salman Rushdie: *Is Nothing Sacred?* in 'Imaginary Homelands', London, 1991: 429.
2. Milan Kundera: *L'art du Roman.* Paris, 1986: 199.

writing genre, took on a belatedly, exceptional position. The experience it provides is individual and the community it creates is formal and abstract. Two million people can read the same novel at the same time but they each do it in private, away from one another and the only thing tying them together is actually fictional. It is hardly incidental that, temporally, the development of this fiction coincides with the development of another modern phenomenon: the national state. As Timothy Brennan writes in his book *Salman Rushdie and the Third World*:

The development of the modern national state in Europe is inseparable from the development of forms and issues in literature. On one side, the political issues which control literature and lead in the direction of romantic ideas as for instance 'the people charactaristic' and 'the national language' were for use in catagorizing the literature within the national literature. On the other side and just as fundamental, literature was a part of the establishment of states through the development of a nationally published media: the newspaper and the novel.[3]

It is through newspapers and novels that a population receives an identity, for instance, through a national language which is characterized as a 'grapholect' that sets a standard for the language which is to be spoken in a given area. To marginalize the dialects is an expression of the fact that it is writing as a formal, national 'grapholect' which decides the speech and not the local language. In other words, the development or the establishment is carried by a special discourse about the national issues found in newspapers and novels.

Somewhat more starkly, it could be said that the novel is the mediator of the metaphysics of our time, the national state ideology having taken over the previously religious discourse about origin, cohesion and target. People of different ethnic nationalities, different languages (dialects), different rank in a social and economical hierachy are brought together as one people with only one language and one origin. The local and specific traces of life are erased in favour of a formal and abstract relation. An example is one of the new national state projects in Europe, namely Turkey. Or rather, one could, in this connection, speak of a purposely planned Europeanization of a Middle Eastern way of life. A process which, according to Søren Mørch was:

systematically carried out in a series of 'revolutions' through which all kinds of outer signs of Oriental affiliations were removed. The written language was changed from Arabic characters to the Latin alphabet, the public were given first and last names according to European customs, their apparel was Europeanized, the Gregorian calender

3. Timothy Brennan: *Salman Rushdie and the Third World*. London, 1989.

was introduced and most important of all — politics were secularized: The state and 'the church' were separated and legislation was altered to eliminate any trace of Sharia. Religion is distinctively a private matter despite 98 percent of the public being Muslim. Turkey is therefore not a Muslim state but a worldly state. There is just one problem: not everyone in Turkey approves of this process. The Kurds have held onto their particular ethnic characteristics and onto their language as well, even though it is prohibited to teach it in class or to use it in print. For many years, the authorities simply denied the existence of the Kurdish language. They claimed that Kurdish was just a variation of the Turkish language and they regarded the Kurds as 'mountain-Turks'. In the meantime, things have improved. During the war in Kuwait, President Özal allowed Kurdish to be spoken and sung. As the government officially denies the existence of serious ethnic contrasts, it is difficult to get reliable information about their extent. The number of Kurds is much discussed and statements vary from 2 to 20 million. A 'guesstimate' of a number in between (8-10 million) would probably be fairly accurate.[4]

Turkey has attempted to undergo a process — which has taken Europe several centuries to implement — over a period of half a century; this of course has caused problems. Nevertheless, the premises are clear: one common language, one common national identity, one common time, a secularization and de-politicization of religion.

In Europe, the novel played, as mentioned, an important role in this development, as did the newspaper. This is not to say that the novel, and the whole industry built around it — the first writers able to earn money from the distribution of their work were novelists — is the prime mover in this development; that would be to assign too big a significance to it in the historical context; it was, however, an extremely important link in the staging of the discourse on nationalism and, in this respect, in the foundation of an 'audience': A highly abstract entity who have nothing else in common besides the fact that they speak the same language, live within the same borders, and all have the ability to read. As Walter J. Ong expresses it: 'The writer's audience is always a fiction'.[5] However, fundamentally and ideally, the audience is something other than a mere anonymous crowd of readers; it is also among them that new thoughts can be passed on, where questions to the current views can be posed and where, as Rushdie puts it, 'one can hear voices talking about all kinds of things in all sorts of ways'. The first literature to find an audience, a market, was the novel and it is still the form of literature making the most money, and thereby the form reaching the most people. In that way, the novel is, like a laboratory of ideas and the dux of market

---

4. Søren Mørch: 'Landeprofil: Tyrkiet' in *Mellemøst-Information* February, 1992.
5. Walter J. Ong: *Orality and Literacy.* London, 1982.

economy beyond good and evil, a strong metaphor for 'print capitalism' - civilization as named by Benedict Anderson.[6] Being a pure product of 'print capitalism', the novel must look like a cancerous tumor, whose distribution can only be destroyed at the stake; to systems and cultures like those in the Middle East which are seeking to maintain a powerful integration of morals, religion and politics. To a person from the Western world who has had free access to novels ever since he reached the age of discretion, the reactions of the Muslim world toward Rushdie's book seem both shocking and out of proportion — as if they are shooting sparrows with cannons. I would claim that the only reason for the reaction being so strong is because *The Satanic Verses* is a novel: A novel that poses embarrassing questions to the religion is, both because of its potential large audience and because it incarnates a whole way of life — that of Western civilization; much more dangerous than many poems or scientific essays. The latter would most probably invoke censorship and anger, but hardly murder, death sentences, and severed diplomatic relations.

Religion and Political Staging

When it has been proven, that an essential condition for the duration of the Rushdie affair is the simple fact that it is centred around a novel, then it does not automatically follow that this is the only reason. Other conditions, such as the content of the book; the conjunction of sociological, political and other circumstances must also be present — and they were:

1) The publishing of the book on September 26th, 1988 coincided at that time with an impending election in India and Rajiv Gandhi's Congress Party needed the Muslim votes. Its condemnation as early as October 5th has to be seen in the light of this and Rushdie himself reacted quickly in a letter to Gandhi in which he wrote regarding the leaders of the opposition, that; 'they really don't care about my novel one way or another. The real issue is, who is to get the Muslim vote'.

2) In Pakistan, the Muslim fundamentalists could not let the opportunity pass without employing the anti-Rushdie movement to shake Benazir Bhutto's new government. And it was also a painful decision for her, as leader of the first democratic government for over a decade, to ban the book.

3) In England, the relationship between the Muslim immigrants and the native

---

6. Benedict Anderson: *Imagined Communities*. London, 1991.

British had been tense for a long time. The unemployment rate among Muslims
was high. They were particularly affected by the readjustments of the system
of taxation. And, in contrast to other minorities such as, for instance, the Jews
and the Catholics, they had no right to their own schools; Feminist criticism
of family patterns in the Third World were only directed at Muslims; and the
blasphemy clause in British law only applies to Christianity. Attempts made
by the Muslims to draw the attention of politicians and other initiatives taken
in order to improve the terms, had not only been unsuccessful, but had
generally also been systematically ignored. The dissatisfaction among the
Muslims was manifested in those areas where many are gathered, such as
Bradford, Yorkshire. In the media, the violent demonstrations were portrayed
as spontaneous acts by dogmatic Muslims. In actual fact, it was a well-planned
course of action whereby pages of the book had been photocopied and passed
around. A demonstration had thereafter been called in which, naturally, it had
been seen to that the media were informed to ensure that they would be there.
But it was probably more out of social indignation than spite, regarding a book
that nobody had read, which came to the surface on that and other occasions
as well. 'In other words, the political arena in Britain is a fascinating and
serious one, but the political relationship of Rushdie's novel to it had more
to do with the social relations beyond the text than with the content of the text
itself'.[7]

4) The Iranians were late in presenting their case. However, it had just as great
an effect when the famous and inadmissible *fatwa* was issued by Khomeini
on the February 14th 1989. In the war-devastated areas of Iran, the Islamic
revolution was taking place on a 'low key' level only, and although the forces
in the country had made attempts to normalize the tense relationship with the
Western world, any kind of process that might have made things normal again
was stopped, at least for a period of time. The fact that the Rushdie case in
Iran was more of a political conflict than a religious one, is also supported by
the fact that the book was actually reviewed in the country without having
given rise to further concern. Added to this is the fact that Rushdie's earlier
novels *Shame* and *Midnights Children*, were not only well-known and translated
into Persian, *Shame* had actually received an award for the best translated
novel, which had been presented by the president at the time and present
religious leader, Ali Khamenei. In other words, a perception of the Rushdie

---

7. Michael M.J. Fischer & Mehdi Abedi: *Debating Muslims. Cultural Dialogues in
   Postmodernity and Tradition.* London, 1990: 396. Moreover, a lot of the material and
   documentation regarding the Rushdie case is collected in Lisa Appignanesi & Sarah
   Maitland: *The Rushdie File.* London, 1989.

affair which puts all its faith in the allegations of religious offence and blasphemy is misjudged. There is a lot more than religion at stake: For the Muslim countries, it is not about prohibiting freedom of speech because of religious reasons, but because of power and political reasons. To the Western countries, it is not a question that we face some Islamic regimes to whom it is crucial that Islam and faith be protected against violations; it is about State centralistic, paramilitary regimes who couch political discourse in religious rhetoric. They can get away with this as long as the common Muslim is kept from having any political influence and this in turn is possible as long as they are successful in keeping writing out of society.

Islam and Modernity

However, changes do take place in the Middle Eastern countries. Modernity phenomena appear here too. Paradoxically, the Rushdie affair would never have materialized had it not been for the modern typographic and electronic media. The same thing can be said about Khomeini's revolution in Iran. In this case, it was not enough for the mosques to present the message, and therefore, audio- and video cassettes were brought into use.

Fundamentalism is, in many ways, proof that something political is happening in the Middle East. On the surface, fundamentalism may well seem like a regressive nostalgic wave rolling through the most westernized countries, such as Algeria and Egypt. In actual fact, I think, in this case, it has to do with a modernity phenomenon, meaning a politically-religious current which has been made possible by the introduction of typographical and electronical medias, urbanity, education, and the development of a form of politcal culture which, in any event, resembles that of the Western World.

In general, the content of the fundamentalistic programmes is just as abstract as it is stereotypical: on one side, a broadside toward the West because it spreads decadent and destructive thoughts and ideas; on the other, an insistence to preserve traditional Islamic values such as sexual segregation and veiling of the woman's body, prohibition, pro-Arab unity and the introduction of Islamic principals regarding economy: for example, no taxes and no interest rates. Except for the part about Arab unity, this was identical to the programme in Iran, and it is the programme for FIS and the different movements in Egypt. In Iran, the Islamic republic still exists but the problems are great everywhere which is demonstrated by the amplitudic movements' attitude toward the Western market. Concerning Algeria and Egypt, the fact is that here we are confronted with countries who suffer serious problems regarding economy, population and administration. For both countries in question, resources are few and demands are great: the need for housing, jobs and foodstuffs has increased along with an incompetent, centralistic, bureaucratic line of politics which is continually growing worse.There are differences between the two countries: because of its strategic location and openness toward the Western World which Sadat introduced, Egypt has had more success in acquiring a couple of billion US dollars compared to Algeria who has tried to make a type of Eastern European régime work for a long time.

Fundamentalism and Modernity

Patternwise, the fundamental rebellions still look alike: they are big-city phenomena, the activists are generally recruited among young people who come from families living in the country, and who have both been able to afford and give their daughter or son the opportunity to study in the city, often in technical-scientific faculties. Their perception of Islam is different from the common 'people's religion'; it is a perception which calls for reflection and a certain form of reading; The messages are passed out through personal contact, but also through printed papers. Those who organize and present the fundamentalistic Islamic message are, at the same time — hypothetically speaking — the ones who basically present a civilization or a social construction; meaning the establishment of a political public. Those who present the message 'Death to the West, death to the USA' in Algeria are, at the same time, the ones who most persistently insist on democratic elections. Islam is, in this respect, also a political rhetoric through which dissatisfaction with unreasonable terms of living and resentment to the fact that an impotent regime is given the power to rule. It is also most probable that the democracy will not be permitted to exist much longer than the next election. The point is not to make the Islamic fundamentalists look like heroic advocates of democracy in this case either — not at all, but to make them see that the battle they are fighting is only possible because of modernity.

It could be that the thesis about implementation of the secularized modern Western society through a Christian fundamentalism as outlined in the book *Die protestantische Ethik und der Geist des Kapitalismus* by the sociologist Max Weber,[8] is repeating itself in this case. The Islamic countries have not experienced feudalism as we know it in Europe and, therefore, it is wrong to consider the Middle East as 'the dark Middle Ages'. Nevertheless, there appear to be characteristics which we recognize from European history: Firstly, there is a paradoxical connection between fundamentalism and modernity and secondly, the conflicts of reading; as a matter of fact, there are Islamic

8. Max Weber: *Gesammelte Aufsätze zur Religionssoziologie, Vol.* 1, Tübingen, 1920.

intellectuals who have expressed their support of Rushdie and pointed out that he is, as a Muslim, part of an Islamic satiric tradition. The conflicts of reading in the Islamic World resemble the battles that were fought in the 18th and 19th century in England regarding the inconvenience that the workers and (in America) slaves were to be taught to read. In any case, it is an expression of Orientalism, that is, a romanticization and demonization of the Middle East; to challenge them on their resentment over Rushdie as well as the fundamentalistic movements' religious rhetoric and ignore the political contents.

As Ümit Necef[9] has proven, this was what many well-meaning Danes did regarding the Rushdie debate in Denmark: Worried about sounding disloyal to the foreigners, 'the others', they chose not to take a stand; using, among others, the excuse that ultimately one must respect other cultures. They cut in on a story or a discourse which immediately identified the Islamic humiliation as a respectable token of another culture, the values of which one cannot do anything about, except allowing oneself to accept. However, this view is quite senseless: first of all, it shows obviously that one does not respect other cultures as it only confirms one's own — in this connection, overreflected culture; secondly, thereby just that freedom of thought is prized — the freedom to write literature which is, according to Rushdie as well as Kundera, not an entirely unimportant scope for Europe — rather on the contrary: 'Express yourself' as Madonna sings.

Bibliography

Anderson, Benedict 1991. *Imagined Communities*, London.

Appignanesi, Lisa and Sarah Maitland, 1989. *The Rushdie File*, London.

Brennan, Timothy 1989. *Salman Rushdie and the Third World*, London.

Fisher, Michael M.J. and Mehdi Abedi, 1990. *Debating Muslims. Cultural Dialogues in Postmodernity and Tradition*, London.

Kundera, Milan 1986. *L'art du Roman*, Paris.

Mørch, Søren, February 1992. 'Landeprofil Tyrkiet' in *Mellemøst-Information*, Odense University.

Necef, Mehmet Ümit 1989. 'Rushdie-debatten, indvandrerforskerne og indvandrerne' in Torben Hansen (ed.), *Islam! En Religion, en historie, en kultur*, Copenhagen.

Ong, Walter J. 1982. *Orality and Literacy*, London.

9. Read the subtle portrayal in the article (in Danish) *Rushdie-debatten, indvandrerforskerne og indvandrerne*. In antologien: *Islam! En religion, en historie, en kultur*. Edited by Torben Hansen, Copenhagen, 1989.

Rushdie, Salman 1991. *Imaginary Homelands*, London.
Weber, Max 1920. *Gesammelte Aufsätze zur Religionssoziologie,* vol. 1, Tübingen.

The Mosque and Fear of Fundamentalism

Anders Jerichow

The West is clearly afraid of it, and Middle Eastern governments are no less worried about the challenge coming from it — the Mosque.

One word, one image, has cast its shadow upon current usage of the word mosque, and that is 'fundamentalism'. Few words as this have managed to set an international agenda. And even fewer images of comparable strength have been interpreted so widely and so differently. In most of the Western press, fundamentalism has become the image of a violent terrorist campaign led by fanatics, for the re-establishment of a medieval society under the banner of Islam.

In the Middle Eastern, the Arab, as well as the Persian press, the mere word 'fundamentalism' — which does not hold any meaning locally — is taken as evidence of Western stereotyping, putting all variety of Muslim activity in the same basket. Yet, Middle Eastern governments share Western fears of any such activity which offers an alternative to traditional government rule.

In the centre of this debate and fear: The mosque. Thus, with minimal clarification of the simple meaning of the word 'fundamentalist', a few simple questions remain, calling for academic research, Muslim consideration and Western soul searching: Who, where, why, how, to what purpose - and so what?

A search for an answer to the first question — who? — does, in itself, invoke the confusion surrounding the image of fundamentalism and the power of the mosque. After all, those perceived to be 'fundamentalists' range from the Sunni Moslem Brotherhood in Egypt to politically active tribal forces in Yemen, semi-military Shia movements in the Lebanon to opposition priests in Saudi Arabia and terrorists, as well as the opposition in Algeria, and to the political, though unarmed, uprising in Tunisia. And this without mentioning Muslim militias in Afghanistan and radical movements in Malaysia and Indonesia - although they too are usually counted within the same category of 'fundamentalists'.

Categorizing them by the word 'Muslim' may be correct, yet both superficial and wrong if meant to distinguish them from their opposites — usually the local governments — who are no less Muslim by faith or origin. What does call for a common description of these groups may be the word 'activist', which would seem to be a rather bleak description of a phenomenon which has attracted so much attention for its dramatic expression. Still, activism rather than religious belief may be what separates these groups from government and national majority.

Leading to the third question of 'why', it will be worth dwelling a moment with the second, 'where', i.e. with the geopolitical arena or the countries involved in the conflict with religious (Muslim, since they are all Muslim communities) activism. It is hardly a coincidence or irrelevant that none of these countries offers a free, let alone democratic, outlet for popular criticism. On the contrary, all of them are characterized by a high degree of political government control; all of them are in a process of social and economic modernization; all of them are struggling to keep population growth down or at least economic growth at a higher rate relative to that of the population. All of them have been ruled by the same families — along the Arab Gulf — or the same political-military bureaucracies — in the centre of the Middle East and in North Africa — for decades, and all of them face the challenge of combining traditional control with the introduction of new information technology.

This, in itself, need not explain why these countries face religiously dominated activism. It does, however, suggest one reason - among other possibilities — for political turbulence, at least if the impact of development and modernization in other parts of the world holds some truth in The Middle East and North Africa.

Although the Arab nations are split between relatively wealthy and relatively poor countries, between oil exporters and labour force exporters, countries in affluence and some in need, they all face the same challenge of solidarity, within and among nations, and the same challenge of sharing limited resources. In the end, of course, this leaves only two options concerning the means: by ruling decree or by national consensus. The first rests on a use of power and control, the latter requires not only room for national consideration, a civil institution most of the Arab nations still have to experience, but also a well established acceptance of the decisions made by civil society, which is only slowly taking over from totalitarian tradition.

On the other hand, the totalitarian tradition leaves another reason for religious activism — or for the use of the mosque in political activity. Quite simply, none of the countries in this case have developed civil institutions that allow the formation of free political movement; a free press, free political organizations, including free labour and women's movements, and very few of them allow political campaigns or meetings to take place - whether in public or in private.

Only one institution has survived centuries of governments: the mosque. Never just a place for prayer, but always a forum for rest, dialogue and social gathering, the mosque in most Muslim countries has provided what governments did otherwise not permit: A place to meet and talk freely, a place to distribute and share ideas - and in quite a few countries, an institution to deal with social affairs, to arrange alternative education for the poor and to offer social services for people in need.

Be it by deed or by lack of popular choice — populations in many Muslim communities have not enjoyed the existence of any alternative social institution other than the state and the mosque. Again, be it by deed, by religious or cultural authority, or by lack of choice — populations in many Muslim communities have seen no candidates for leadership other than the representative of the state or of the mosque. Strong traders or 'bazaries' as they are called in Teheran could have offered their own leadership, but have seldom had reason for conflict with local governmental power (when the Shah of Iran did confront his bazaries, he may have paved the way for his own demise, seeing business people side with the upcoming ayatollahs).

This takes us back to the question of 'who' in religious activism (fundamentalism). While still keeping the same countries in mind, it is no coincidence that practically no Muslim activist movements operate without religious leaders, mullahs, sheiks, either in front or as a source of inspiration.

Though similar in character by education and position, the leading activists (fundamentalist) clearly differ. Not least of all along lines determined by the societies in which they live. In Egypt, leading clerics are split between government consultative bodies and semi-autonomous religious and social institutions, competing for the highest authority. In the Lebanon, religious communities enjoy a relative freedom of the still-fractioned state, to some point still suffering from 15 years of civil war that allowed leaders of religious communities as well as of armed militias to thrive. To a very large extent this has resulted in religious states-within-the-state, each of them accepting wide social, cultural and political responsibilities. In Saudi Arabia, the traditional alliance between the ruling family and the dominating *ulema* only suffers dissent as a result of heavy criticism of the family's call for Western assistance, and due to the assertion by religious leaders of immoral lifestyles behind the royal walls. Contrary to decades of tradition the *ulema* now seem to be split on the need to ally with (apparently) discredited members of the royal family.

No wonder then, in the light of this, that most Middle Eastern governments insist on keeping local preachers — potential leaders — on the national payroll, i.e. under national control. Egypt presently is in the process of reinstituting total government control of the nation's mosques. In practically all other Middle Eastern and North African societies, the state is similarly insisting on government control to the extent of overseeing the kind of preachers, if not by prior censorship then by current 'security check ups' with agents of the security police keeping an eye on mosques and active preachers (fundamentalists) before, during and after the Friday prayers.

Remembering that religion has been a catalyst of change in other cultures, one of them being Christianity, Muslim activism as such can hardly be seen as a crime. According to universally accepted values, priests — of any religion — are given the right to speak, to think, to publish and to organize. According to Muslim tradition they are bestowed with — and must be respected for — traditional wisdom.

What makes Muslim activists feared among governments in Arabia and in the West alike — and partly respected and loved by others in their own communities — is their claim to having the right to oppose the established governmental authority. And, even more challenging, by stirring up fears by refuting traditional religious interpretation, claiming their own right to interpret holy books and accumulated tradition in a new light. Their messages often deal with social, economic, educational, moral issues and contain political critique, but all of them stem from the seeds of religious interpretation and argument. Other cultural values or material logic might lead to the same argument or campaign. However, only religious interpretation is, at the same time, able to maintain religious trust and to thrive within the privileged manoeuvering space provided by the mosque.

The Western public naturally should have no choice but to grant Muslim scholars and preachers certain universally accepted rights, including the right to voicing non-violent dissent against an established power or wisdom. Whether Muslim activist priests and others conform with their own holy books is for the Muslim society to decide.

Back to the first question: Who, in the Muslim world, is to decide who has the right to interpret the holy book and the traditions (*Hadith*) of the Prophet Muhammed? Who decides on the status of preachers; those who pay their salary or those who attend their Friday prayers? Who elects the *ulema*? Who selects the religious leaders?

Leaving the answers to these questions to a Muslim response, it is a current trend that individual 'freelance' religious leaders, with no mandate but the affection of their followers, are popping up all over the Muslim world. They attract crowds where governments would prefer silence. In Egypt, they inspire religious opposition to Western influences, and opposition to peace with

Israel, heavily criticizing the Egyptian president for his economic and social policies. In Saudi Arabia, likewise, they find religious justification for a strong moral critique of immorality in the House of Saud. In the Lebanon, they lend religious justification to a political, and armed, resistance to Israel in the south and to the Christian polity in Lebanon itself. In Algiers, they have legitimized popular uprising — only some of them by the means of violent struggle — against the corrupt and inefficient military-political policies of the past three decades. In Tunisia, Muslim preachers in involuntary exile in Europe call for a peaceful campaign against the local, governing military bureaucracy.

All of them, however different they may be, qualify for the term 'fundamentalist'. All of them challenge the existing order from the mosque, however different the society, the economic situation or the need for political change. All of them can be attributed a traditional religious role in society as well as an untraditional use of their religious platform.

Whereas the term 'fundamentalist' is of hardly any relevance with regard to preachers as a group, the phenomenon of religious activism calls for analysis of the purpose of this religious renaissance in the political arena.

Excluding the demand for the right to interpret Islam and the demands for a say in national or social policies, the religious activists do not conform to any common aim. Some of them call for the overthrow of a government. Some do it peacefully, some — though only a few — do it by violent means; often the brutality of these activists only matches the brutality of the relevant government. Some just call for more proper government, better moral standards and governmental accountability, but not necessarily for a change of government. Some of them accept a social responsibility in local affairs. Some demand all encompassing influence in national affairs.

Even more importantly in the context of future prognosis, they do not agree with one anothers interpretation of Islamic law, when it comes to governmental right, obligation and eventual succession. The Tunisian renaissance movement, *En-Nahda*, officially subscribes to pluralism and free speech. The Saudi preachers criticizing the House of Saud do not accept either. In Egypt, as in Saudi Arabia, Tunisia, and most other Arab states, (with Jordan and Palestine as possible near-future exceptions) the religious activists are not given a simple chance to seek the backing of the population ('voters') by means of open competition, neither in elections nor in any other kind of selective process — be it offers of sermons, or other media. This is due to government control and regulation not only of the mosques, but also of the media and private organizations etc.

Legitimacy? Religious activism? Government control and/or suppression? According to universal values, non-violent activism should enjoy full freedom, including protection from any sort of aggression. Yet even, hitherto, non-violent religious activists are often suppressed and even feared by Muslim and Western governments alike.

So what? Deeming all and every Muslim activist a 'fundamentalist' hardly contributes to the understanding of the source of religious activism in the first place. Academic study of the phenomenon may add to our knowledge, although Muslim consideration of rights and privileges seem imperative too.

A degree of Western soul-searching, looking into the question of whether universal values and rights can or should be attributed to Muslims as well as Christians, might also facilitate some understanding across the cultural barriers.

History as Mythos: On the Question of Religious Language and Historiography in Middle Eastern Politics

Jan Hjärpe

A narrative providing an explanation or interpretation of the conditions of human life is called a *myth*. Myths are patterns of interpretation and perception in the form of stories given significance beyond the content of the narrative, beyond the very events being told. For the believer, the myth is true - in two respects: The story contains a factual element; the events have really happened. But more important is its truth in the way that it explains one's *own* conditions, and gives them a meaning. It also decides the interpretation of the world beyond oneself and its behaviour which one meet daily. The myth functions as a pattern of perception, a filter which influences the choice selected from the huge amount of stimuli reaching one's senses. We see in what happens to us *signs*, signs of those conditions for which the myth has given expression.

The historian of religions is often very eager to point out that the myth belongs to a ritual context. Its content is repeated frequently, ritually, regularly. One experiences in the ritual commemoration a *participation* in the events of the narrative.

For the non-believer the myth is no longer true in the first respect, it is no longer regarded as history, as expressing a historical fact. But this does not necessarily imply that it loses its function as 'true' in the other, symbolic meaning, its existential significance. It still contains a conceptual and interpretational pattern expressing the conditions of existence.

Myths can develop into history, become historicized epics. Myths about gods and heroes, beyond time and space, have sometimes lost their mythical function. But the narratives remain, changed into legend or historiography: The epics of the Persian Kings, the stories of the Pandavas in the Mahabharata, the history of early Rome, all seem to be historicized myths. But we also meet the opposite process, i.e. that history obtains the *function* of the myth. History and historiography function as patterns of perception, explaining the conditions of man, giving the feeling of belonging, of *having a part* in significant events in the past, and become ritualized: Historical events are 'remembered' in ritualized commemorations: One uses the words 'we' and 'us' of events that happened before one was even born. Narratives of what happened in the past function as patterns steering our perception and interpretation of what happens today.

Historiography is never a totally innocent phenomenon. It is always a question of choice; a choice of what in the past we have chosen to regard as significant events. The parts in any conflict choose their significant historical events differently. As a rule all parts in the conflict present events in the past which have really happened, but not the *same* events.

Of special importance is very often what might be called 'the chosen trauma'; a catastrophe in the past, a disaster. The battle of Kosovo is such a 'chosen trauma' for Serbian Nationalism. In the 'ethnic' cleansing which took place in former Yugoslavia, the narratives of the atrocities during the Second World War play a central role as a 'chosen trauma' in the consciousness of the parts — Serbs are called 'cetniks', and Croats 'Ustasja'. Albanians and Bosnians are called 'Turks', with allusion to the conditions of the Ottoman Empire.

In modern Turkish historiography, the 'chosen trauma' — the event regarded as especially significant in national history — is evidently the Treaty of Sevres (1923).

We can see that in Shi'a Islamic historiography the central point, the most significant event in history, is the disaster of Karbala, in 680, where the grandson of the Prophet, Husayn, was killed along with the 72 martyrs; a pattern very much used in interpreting contemporary events — as we know from the Iranian revolution and from the Iran-Iraq war of the 1980s.

In Christian historiography and theology, the main event is the drama of Calvary, which is ritually remembered. ('Were you there when they crucified my Lord?', as it is put in a very popular hymn). In Judaism, the role of the Exodus narrative, ritually and existentially, is well known (as we can see in the ritual function of the Haggadah shel Pesach). For modern Judaism, the most significant historical event is Auschwitz, also ritually remembered, and functioning as a pattern of interpretation.

The narrative of the disaster signifies group belonging and creates a pattern of behaviour, the 'Never again' pattern. History is seen as warnings. To doubt or to deny the historical facticity of 'the chosen trauma', or its significance, is considered the worst of heresies.

We can see that the significant events of a particular historiography are not scattered evenly over the centuries. They occur in clusters, constituting significant eras. In Christian historiography, the most significant era is the life of Jesus and the time of the early church. Without doubt, the most important time in Islamic history is the life of the Prophet and his Companions, regarded as *normative*; and the era of the first four caliphs, including the period of 'the great *fitna*', the disaster of the disintegration of the community.

In contemporary 'European identity', I would say that the remembrance, the commemoration, of the era of the Second World War — its preludes and its course of events, is *the* significant era in the political interpretational pattern of European policy — 'Never again', 'no new München'.

Changes in the political (or for that part: existential) situation, are reflected in a change in the choice of history. This was the case when Anwar Sadat legitimized the Camp David Treaty in 1978 by alluding to the Prophet Muhammed's treaty with the Quraysh tribe at *al-Hudaybiya* (in 628). Yasir Arafat also alluded to the same event in his much discussed speech on the ongoing peace process, in a South African mosque, in May 1994 (in connection with Nelson Mandela's inauguration as president). The same allusion was made in the *fatwa* on the peace process and the new Saudi policy of normalization with Israel made by the Saudi Grand Mufti Abd al Aziz ibn Baz, in December 1994. The Mufti cited the al-*Hudaybiya* treaty as one precedent. The other one that he chose was the so called Madina Constitution, in the year 622. At the time of the Prophet's *hijira* to Madina an agreement was concluded; the point of this treaty was that the old and the new inhabitants should constitute one *umma* ('nation'). The treaty thus included the three Jewish tribes of Madina in the new *umma*. This Saudi Arabian *fatwa* provoked much controversy. The interesting feature is that of change, a change in the choice of historiography. The 'Madina Constitution' has traditionally been seen as having been superseded by later developments, later precedents, which have legitimized the *dhimmi* system, totally different from the idea of *umma* now projected into the story of the Madina Constitution. In modern times it has been alluded to almost only by those who argue for secularism as being an Islamically legitimate idea.

A very good example of change in the choice of history is to be found in connection with the long diplomatic efforts to bring about a cease fire in the Iran-Iraq war (1980-88): The change from a 'Husayni' to a 'Hasani' perspective. In the Iranian mobilizing propaganda during the war, the most important historical event was the tragedy of Karbala (in 680) when the Prophet's grandson Husayn was martyred in his rebellion against the Umayyad calif Yazid. Imam Husayn was then the impeccable example of martyrdom and strife against tyranny: No cease fire was possible so long as 'Yazid' (=Saddam) was still in power in Baghdad. The Battle of Karbala was the most significant event in history, giving the battle its 'meaning'. But in late 1987 and early 1988, readers of Iranian newspapers and pamphlets would have observed that the stories about Imam Husayn became less frequent, while material featuring the life of the second Shi'a Imam, Hasan, became more common. One could then have made the prognosis that the regime in Teheran was preparing to accept a cease fire. In contrast to the fighting martyr, Hasan was the one who had accepted a 'cease fire,' a settlement with the Umayyad calif Mu'awiya; in a situation where rebellion was not profitable or even possible.

In 1988, it became obvious that Teheran had to yield and accept a cease fire. The public was prepared in advance by the articles on Hasan. When the UN Security Council's Resolution 598 was accepted in July, Ayatollah Khomeini made the comment that the treaty was a necessity, although 'it was worse than drinking poison.' According to the Shiite tradition, Hasan was murdered by poison. The historical allusion to the death of Imam Hasan served, in a subtle way, as a legitimation of the change in policy from war to a cease fire.

During the Kuwait crisis of 1990-91 we could see how the conflict, in the European debate, was compared to and interpreted using comparisons to European history and the Second World War (Saddam=Hitler) in particular. In Israel the threat of a gas attack immediately provoked associations with the Holocaust in Europe. In the Muslim world, the centre of the conflict was not over the question of Kuwait but of Mekka: There was real concern over the fact that Mekka and Madina were, in a way, under non-Muslim sovereignty due to the massive American and European military presence. The historical comparison was with the Crusades (as-salibiya). In the Iraqi propaganda this was very much in the focus: George Bush was called 'the Crusader', and Saddam Hussein was given the role of Salah ad-Din al-Ayyubi; the chivalrous victor over both the Crusaders and the Fatimid califate. In the same Iraqi propaganda language, King Fahd of Saudi Arabia was frequently referred to as 'Abu Sufyan' - an allusion to the siege of Madina in the time of Muhammad, the 'battle of the Ditch' (al-Khandaq). All these historical allusions and comparisons became obsolete as a result of the actual development, both during and after the crisis.

During the ongoing peace process there has been an increasing interest in the history of al-Andalus, especially for those periods in the history of Muslim Spain which can be described as periods of coexistence, cooperation and mutual cultural exchange between Muslims-Christians-Jews. Such a historiography has an instrumental value in legitimizing the peace.

The symbolically significant cooperation seen in the provision of humanitarian aid to Bosnia is also — in a way — a part of the process of peace and normalization in the Middle East. At the end of July 1995, a shipment of humanitarian aid was organized in a joint operation between Jordan, Israel and the Palestinian administration. A television programme in Jordan triggered off an immense surge of generosity. But here again we can detect a slight shift in historiography: The atrocities in Bosnia were due to the fact that the people there were Muslims, and 'this is the way in which the Europeans have always treated us'. 'We' in this case means 'us Jews and Muslims'. Again it became relevant to refer to the Crusades, and the atrocities committed against Jews, Muslims, and Eastern Christians. It was no coincidence that the Spanish king, in his speech at the Barcelona Conference in November 1995, mentioned the fact that it was exactly 900 years since the infamous proclamation of the Crusade in Clermont by Pope Urban II, and he underlined the fact that the purpose of today's policy was the opposite: Peaceful cooperation.

The analysis of historical allusions in the use of names (e.g. the appellations chosen by different groups), in the propaganda, in the common discourse, provides us with a useful tool of prognostic value, but also one that can be used actively to legitimize and promote desirable changes in society and politics.

The Muslim Woman — A Battlefield

Connie Carøe Christiansen & Lene Kofoed Rasmussen

When the subject of research is Islam or the Middle East, the scholar has to watch his, or her, step. The traps into which he or she risks falling include apologeticism, Orientalism, reversed Orientalism, Eurocentrism, cultural essentialism, just to mention a few of the most common terms of abuse in current literature on the subject. These dangers are no less imminent when it comes to the study of Islam and women, or — as in our case — to female adherents of political Islam. We would, however, argue that the current danger lies rather in becoming trapped in a polarized political climate, which makes claims of approval or rejection of political Islam hard to avoid. Far from advocating a withdrawal of researchers from the political debate, we will in the following discuss one approach to the study of female Islamists, where politics — global as well as local — is still in focus, but as a stage for contrasts and interactions other than the essentialized polarization between secularists and Islamists.

The discussion of political Islam and Islamist movements has often centred around women, with predictions of the consequences for women in the case of an Islamist group gaining governmental control, and usually taking Iran as a model. This example from real life has allowed only few contradictions, regardless of the specific Iranian circumstances and historical convergences. Such a consensus on the tragedy of the Iranian revolution when it comes to women's rights and general status is now about to dissolve as international attitudes towards Iran are becoming milder. Likewise, recent studies of female Islamists have stressed that for women there is a liberating impetus in joining Islamist groups in Middle Eastern societies.[1] This, to the annoyance of those scholars who vehemently attack Islamism wherever it is to be found, accusing it of trapping women and turning them into the scapegoats of general social problems and of trying to prevent women from taking part in public life (to mention just a couple of several points of critique).[2] We do not intend to argue that neither of those points have any truth in them, but instead would suggest that the premises upon which this polarization is built are wrong. Most writing

1. Búcaille, 1994; Mir-Hosseini, 1996; Hessini, 1994.
2. Mernissi, 1993; Hakiki-Talahite, 1991.

on women's history and social reality in the Middle East reflects an unspecified idea of women's ultimate emancipation as being the goal.[3] This is not to say that there is no mention of relative improvements for women in this type of writing, but it is paired with a lack of recognition of the conditions that have been the starting point for young women attracted to Islamism. Thus, it is both too naive to celebrate Islamic activism as a liberating act for the women concerned, and too narrow to ignore the gains stemming from a female Islamist position. After all, the fact that these gains are relative does not make them any less real.

An Exercise in Freedom of Choice?

In 1986 a scholar warned against any depiction of the current trend of wearing the veil as 'an exercise in freedom of choice',[4] a warning often reflected in subsequent writings on Middle Eastern women.[5] However, with Foucault's analysis of Western civilization as a grid of discourses in which any individual is placed — not without the opportunity to move, to change and create discourses, but always at the same time changed and created by them, the image of an individual choosing his or her own destiny, free of any restrictions, is fading away.[6]

Well aware that female Islamists, according to Foucault, like anybody else, are not exercising an absolute freedom of choice, we have titled our previous published work on young women in political Islam: 'Choosing the veil'.[7] While an overall emancipation is certainly not the effect of the trend of veiling, young women living in Middle Eastern cities, who approve of an Islamization of their society and show their approval by covering their hair, have knowledge — as do other women living in an urban environment — about options for identification other than the Islamist ideal. At the same time these women are situated in a social and political context, where this specific choice seems appealing, and for some groups of women even the most obvious choice. This is probably also the case for women who become feminists or, say, supporters of the ruling party.

---

3. One example here is Göcek & Balaghi, 1994, who in their introduction refer to liberation and discuss strategies of Middle Eastern women in that regard, but do not, however, discuss or question their notion of liberation.
4. Hatem, 1986.
5. Moghadam, 1994; Mernissi, 1993.
6. Foucault, 1978.
7. 'Choosing the Veil'. *At Vælge Sløret. Unge kvinder i politisk Islam*, Christiansen & Rasmussen, 1994.

To proceed in a Foucauldian fashion, we will refer to the current *discourse* on 'the Muslim woman'. This discourse is highly contested, or rather, analogous to a battlefield. Female Islamists themselves do relate to the discourse on the Muslim woman, and we therefore put forward some consequences of that.

Empowerment

While it is not reasonable to expect the total emancipation of women to emanate from Islamism, it would be appropriate to point to other gains of women taking part in shaping the discourse on the Muslim woman. A distinctive feature of the discourse of female Islamists themselves is a narrative of conversion: Female Islamists report (in interviews in Cairo and Istanbul 1990, Fes and Cairo 1994-95) of feeling ill at ease with the environment during their teenage-years, which made them search for answers to fundamental questions of human life in political and religious literature, while at the same time attaching importance to and gaining a growing consciousness about what was going on in society. Taken together, according to the women, these reflections culminated in the decision to take on the *hijab* bearing witness to their faith in Islam as holding the solution to both social and more existential questions. These women reported on reactions from family, friends and school, ranging from scepticism to strong objection, indicating that attaching oneself to Islamist ways has not necessarily been the most wise decision.

Though not necessarily approving of their political goals (including those concerning gender politics), we want to emphasize that these women are ascribing their identity to a project of changing their society, and that one outcome of this, in itself, is *empowerment*. Empowerment is usually considered an important consequence of women's participation in feminist activities. Until recently, women shaping their identity within a religious framework has been approached with more ambiguity — or not approached at all. Countering modernity, which is to some extent on the agenda of such women, has been taken as sufficient evidence of the purely regressive character of their activities. New conceptual frameworks today allow us to draw a more differentiated picture of women who choose a religious frame for their activities and voice ambiguous feelings towards modernity. An example is a recently published work on female Christian youth activities in Denmark at the beginning of this century.[8]

To give an indication of the extent and character of this empowerment when it comes to female Islamists it may be useful to give specific examples.

8. Christensen, 1995.

During a stay in Fés, Morocco in 1994 the activities of female Islamists were observed. These activities seemed to be directed at increasing the intellectual abilities of the adherents, increasing the practical knowledge of political organizing and raising an interest for national and world politics. One sort of activism where all these objects meet are the so-called Islamic celebrations. These celebrations take place in various surroundings, private and public and they may be gender-segregated events or gender-mixed events. A certain programme of features are largely followed on each occasion in short consisting of the following: The opening session is a reading of the *Quran*. Then a religious song follows, accompanied by drums played by a small group of people who are also the leading singers, and most of the audience joins in. The next feature is a few words of welcome from the toastmaster and the programme continues with humorous sketches on themes of political or religious awakening, alternated with singing. A lecture on some aspects of Islam may also be included in the programme at this kind of event as a more direct way of informing.

When asked directly, the women in charge of such events stated that the object is primarily one of socializing, and only when pushed a little would they concede to other aspects, such as conveying an impression of practicing and convinced Muslims as happy and cheerful people, or the transmitting of religious and political messages. Yet there may be other and more subtle implications of actively joining and subscribing to the view of the world as presented to the individual at these kinds of events. The celebrations taking place in private homes are open to everyone and invitations are spread by word of mouth; for example through a visit to the mosque, or between students at university, although nobody in the audience is addressed directly. These occasions are clearly suitable for gathering new adherents. The celebration and the coming together of many people (perhaps 40-50 women even in a private setting) provides a perfect opportunity for the distribution of books and pamphlets by Islamic ideologists popular in the Islamic movement, and of cassettes and samples of the Quran, in simple as well as luxury editions. The participants as well as the organizers are predominantly younger people up to 35 years of age. Many, but not all female participants, wear a headscarf or another form of clothing signalling a Muslim commitment. Islamic celebrations are moreover one of the activities in which many young people take part without any formal relation to Islamic movements. The claim here is not that one visit to an Islamic celebration makes any difference to any one individual, but rather that joining a chain of events and becoming involved, not only socially, but perhaps also emotionally, certainly makes a difference.

This is not a final analysis of Islamic celebrations as they take place in Fes, Morocco, or anywhere else, it is merely a suggestion of their inherent educational qualities. The essential result of this educating effect may be an ability to find one's bearings — the establishing of a basis from which to act and relate to the modern world.

There is a certain kind of empowerment related to personal conviction which is again related to access to discourse. Here we wish to point to the fact that the activity of Islamic celebration is one way of obtaining access to, in certain circumstances, an empowering discourse. When conviction is combined with the acquisition of skills and access to discourse the result may be an almost outright directory of action. This directory of action specifies, for example, how to behave individually and as a group; which intellectual activities to perform; how to interpret situations of a political nature, and it is the reason why Islamic activism as a whole, should be regarded as an empowering act. It could also serve as an example of the mechanisms of discourse on a local level.

Public Discourses

Though it is evident that female Islamists do have access to discourses, often taking the shape of strategic arguments, the female Islamists are certainly not free to create just 'any' discourse on the Muslim woman. On the contrary, *the Muslim woman* as a public discourse is contested, usually not out of concern for Muslim women and their room for manoeuvre, (as examples below will demonstrate), with the result that the space for creativity left for women who want to fulfil the ideal of a Muslim woman is significantly narrowed. The context, or the battlefield, of this dispute is not one but rather several public spheres.

While the public is usually understood as being the space of the mass media in a nation state, John Keane[9] suggests a more comprehensive concept of the modern public, differentiated at three levels, each constituting a stage for non-violent controversy over relations of power: A macro level, where the global public — mostly consisting of all types of communication media world-wide — encompass hundreds of millions of people affected by transnational and global power relations. Then the public which includes the stages of negotiation within the borders of the nation state, where millions of people share national mass media. And finally the public on a micro level of local spaces for dispute, ranging from social movements to informal forums such as a coffeehouse.

9. Keane, 1994.

   It is striking that the Muslim woman is disputed at all levels and moreover that these disputes are reflected in the arguments of female Islamists themselves. Below we will tentatively, and in the brief manner that this presentation allows for, apply these levels to the discourse on the Muslim woman.

Global Aspects in National Debates

It has been argued that the history of colonial domination created some areas of cultural resistance in the Middle East, one of these being 'women'.[10] While this has had an impact on the mutual cultural categorization between the West and the Middle East, it has also made a firm imprint on regional and national public discourses. Throughout this century 'the woman question' in the Middle East has as a result been informed with nationalism or cultural nationalism, as it is usually labelled in this connection.[11] A glance at the Middle Eastern media shows quite clearly that this is still the case today; cultural nationalism has taken the form of Islamism and 'the Muslim woman' has therefore become a subject of dispute. Two front page stories in the Egyptian media will serve as examples:

1) In August 1994, preceding the Egyptian school year which begins in October, the Egyptian Minister of Education announced new regulations regarding the school uniform in public schools. Along with other new regulations, the length of skirts of female pupils and their headscarves were mentioned in his decree; a maximum length of the skirt was defined and the headscarf was forbidden at all levels including secondary schools. At first these measures provoked a debate in the written media, and not surprisingly was met with fierce attack from the Islamist opposition, who, for instance, voiced their critique in the pages of *Esh-Sha'b*.[12] The minister soon withdrew from his first intention, limiting the decree to primary schools and declaring that a female pupil should be allowed to wear a headscarf if her father signs a paper of approval, because, as the minister explained in an interview in *al-Ahram* (the largest Egyptian paper, usually depicted as a government organ); 'the Ministry would not oppose the authority of the father'.[13] Allegedly the objective of the decree was to protect the pupils and their parents against oppressive measures from school

---

10. Kandiyoti, 1991.
11. Haddad, 1985; Hatem, 1987; Ahmed, 1992.
12. A twice-weekly organ of the Labour party and today considered an Islamist organ since the Islamization of the party during the eighties. See, for example, issues of August 26th and 30th, 1994.
13. *Al-Ahram*, September 18th, 1994.

leaders. As a sequel to this affair, the minister changed the curriculum for home economics, not in words but in pictures; a new edition of schoolbooks was published in which all the women portrayed were 'stripped' of their hijabs.

The case had legal consequences, as the minister was taken to court by two fathers of female pupils in primary school and accordingly a group of Islamist lawyers scrutinized the legal grounds for such a decree which was published in full length in *Esh-Sha'b*. The decree was attacked for violating the rights of the individual. It was claimed that rights such as to choose how to dress, what to eat, how to live was stipulated both in the Egyptian constitution and in Islam. The minister was therefore violating Islam in prohibiting the free choice of dress.

However, as the dispute intensified throughout the autumn, another argument took over in the columns of *Esh-Sha'b*. The focus was no longer the right to choose, but the duty of young girls to wear a headscarf. Juridical analysis was replaced by personal reports of fathers complaining that they were not allowed to undertake the correct Islamic education of their daughters, and of schoolgirls who were banned from school because they insisted on fulfilling 'the Islamic duty of covering the hair'.[14]

It seems probable that the 'covered schoolgirl' during this contest between the minister of education and the Islamist opposition became a symbol of the virtue of Islam in opposition to encroachments committed by the secular state. Probably the dispute as a whole revitalized the veil as a symbol of opposition to the government — a symbol which in the Egyptian public was otherwise rather diluted by the middle of the nineties.

The struggle was fought in the national public sphere, i.e. in the parliament, the courtroom, and in the written media. It is striking, however, that none of the female Islamists (though small in number and very assertive), who have access to part of the Egyptian media and usually comment on issues relating to women, had contributed to the dispute on the use of the headscarf in schools. Interviews conducted in the autumn of 1994 and one year later indicate that female Islamists nevertheless feel affected by the dispute. One prominent female Islamist reported (interview November 1994), that she felt trapped in a corner by this case. She did not consider it a duty for schoolgirls in primary school to cover their hair, on the contrary, she was of the opinion that it would be 'psychologically unhealthy'. Yet, she did not feel comfortable about voicing this point of view in public, because it would be taken as an approval of the task of the minister. In her view, any decree from him on this matter was illegitimate.

14. *Esh-Sha'b*, October 21st, 1994.

However, other female Islamists were involved in the case at the local level, both as teachers and mothers sending their daughters to school. Interviewed in November 1995, two female teachers at a private Islamic school reported with pride a 'new wave' of veiling among their pupils after the decree. They interpreted this trend as the will of the pupils to show their opposition to the ministerial decree and a good 'lecture' in solidarity with the Muslim cause. The effect, according to one of them, was disappointingly no longer visible after a year. A mother to a teenage girl reported that she was earlier of the opinion that her daughter should not wear the veil before the girl felt ready for it, but changed her mind when she found that there were too many obstacles to hinder her daughter from making 'the right' decision.

Clearly, this political power game fought at the national level over the Muslim woman, has had an impact on more local stages in terms of discursive innovations, such as in the school and the family.

Another example, originating from a global level, deserves brief mention:

2) A much larger front page issue in the Egyptian media in the autumn of 1994 was the UN conference on population and development which took place in Cairo in September of that year. The conference spurred a heated debate in all the Cairo papers from early summer and on throughout the autumn, mainly fought over views on women. This event brought more actors onto the stage, from feminist groups to the state sponsored religious establishment. Discontentment with the draft programme for the conference was voiced in the Islamist media and in columns written by Islamists in most of the other papers as well. The overall objection was that the mere acceptance of the placing of the conference in Egypt was to give in to Western concepts of family and gender relations.

A handful of female Islamists took part in the NGO forum of the conference, promoting major Islamist issues: the protection of the family in opposition to the emancipation of women as an isolated goal. Others voiced the same critique in the media. Meetings were held by female Islamist students on the issue of the conference and there are reports of debates at the university between feminists and Islamists as a follow-up on the conference.

This event no doubt provided a unique opportunity for some female Islamists to articulate their standpoints within their own ranks as well as in public dispute with representatives of other parties concerned. At the same time their opportunity to mould the discourse on the Muslim woman was probably restricted: This international event, where global issues were raised and disputed, once again fuelled a narrative which wove together woman, culture and colonial domination in the Egyptian context; a discourse of colonial origin.[15] The Muslim woman as a symbol of resistance to foreign domination was reinvoked.

Today, female Islamists have some access to the Egyptian public media. In Egypt the middle class was partly Islamized during the eighties and nineties, and most female Islamists who contribute to the public debate in the media are solidly grounded in the middle class. But female adherents of political Islam are certainly found in other social layers, and other settings in the Middle East as well.

Defining the Muslim Woman

The discourse on the Muslim woman is reflected in the activities of less visible female Islamists such as university students who do not belong to elite segments of society, nor do they contribute to the media in any form. However, they *receive* fragments of the discourse on the Muslim woman from, primarily, the media and relate actively to it regarding their commitment to Islam. They articulate the choice they have made to become convinced and practicing Muslims in terms of this discourse. In the words of 24 year-old Iman, a student of Islam at the University of Fes: 'I have become a committed Muslim, because Islam is the liberation of women'. In this way of presenting her religious conviction there is a resonance of a Western, even global public condemnation of Islam as being suppressive to women.

In fact the choice is often presented as a *gendered* choice by the women themselves. The argumentation of those women in general is based on the advantages of a Muslim way of life particularly for women. In contemporary Morocco, for instance, the female Islamist is less actively present in the media whereas she is certainly visible on the streets of the larger cities. As some of these young female students have noted, they have no Moroccan role model to follow. However, this does not prevent them from giving prompt answers when asked about what a real Muslim woman is. Soumia, who is 31 years old, and an engineer and teacher at a technical college in Fes says: 'A Muslim woman is primarily a Muslim being. With regard to faith, there is no difference between women and men in Islam'. Another young woman in Fes, Samira, a 21 year-old student at a teachers college, has a more elaborate answer: 'A Muslim woman is a woman who is not pursuing her desires, who has returned to God, who follows the Quran and hadith, who wears the hijab. On the street she has her eyes lowered towards the ground. She has a great education, she is cultivated, she can communicate, she speaks, she goes right to peoples'

15. Ahmed, 1992.

hearts, she has to know everything about the religion so that she can answer questions'.

The answer to this question is burdened with preconceptions about Muslim women. The point being: It is not what you expect it to be! This surprise-effect is not only used in an interview-session with a social researcher from Northern Europe, but it is also a central ingredient in the activities of female Islamist students to the extent that they ostentatiously add literary references and Quranic citations as they speak, and to the extent that they hastily voice their approval of a professional career for women. Further, this effect may be a device for gathering new adherents, but also for enlarging the room for manoeuvre for a committed Muslim woman.

For young women who are committed to the Islamic cause there is much at stake when it comes to a definition of the Muslim woman and her tasks and options, since this definition has a direct influence on their own way of life. In the justification of a position as a young Muslim woman as well as in the social practice of young female Islamists there is evidence that the elaboration of a definition of the Muslim woman, at the same time, is an ongoing construction of identity. The young female Islamist finds herself squeezed in her efforts to construct an identity as a young Muslim woman as the definition of the Muslim woman is a veritable battlefield between different parties on a local, national and global level. Female Islamists are not, however, leaving the discussion of the Muslim woman to their male counterparts. As one Moroccan female university professor, herself of an Islamist standpoint, put it when interviewed in 1994: 'The Muslim woman has no one to defend her' — except herself, one might add.

Concluding Remarks

Having presented some of the schisms related to existence as a young, committed Muslim woman, we shall now return to the political climate of polarization mentioned at the beginning of this brief outline. We would like to suggest that the recognition of some approximation and overlap between religious and secularist discourse and between Islamism and feminism would provide an opportunity for pointing out some unnoticed barriers for women in the Middle East. In fact, on closer inspection all the parties concerned find the fundamentalist position difficult to maintain.

Hatem (1994) has pointed to the convergence between secularist (liberalist) and Islamist discourses regarding women in the case of Egypt. This convergence is particularly relevant considering that conditions for women are always expected to undergo radical changes for the worse whenever the frame for that change is Islamism, or for that matter Islam. Another scholar, Abdullahi An-Na'im (1995), draws attention to the degree of interaction and overlap in practice between secularist and religious discourse on the rights of women. In short, a secularist position should not be regarded as a promise of any pro-women measures in comparison with an Islamic position.

Next, feminism and Islamism are not opposites in every sense. There is some ongoing mutual approximation, with Middle Eastern feminists tending to Islamize so as not to distance itself from the mass population and Islamists appropriating feminist ideas in order to attract women.[16] The paths of a post-colonial feminist and a veiled Islamist may, therefore, cross. This is partly due to the fact that they respond to the same problems of women — and none of these positions can claim coherence in a Middle Eastern context.[17]

If women's emancipation is in fact viewed as never in the absolute, but as a constant striving towards an improved social situation and increased influence, the judgement of female adherents of Islamism, would also, we believe, be more balanced. The dead-end of the present state of debate is aptly identified by Helen Watson in her observation on evaluations of the veil. She claims that 'Images and ideologies of the veil remain contested and polarized as long as analysis attempts to evaluate the degree of constraint represented by the practice of veiling'.[18] Thereby she is indicating that women engaged in Islamism should not perhaps be placed in the schism of liberation versus coercion at all. Thus, as Dialmy (ibid.) puts it, feminism is not exclusively liberation, and Islamism is not exclusively repression. When emphasis is on the actual activities and social practice of women, rather than on the ideology which has been chosen to explain and legitimate those activities, the women taking part in Islamic movements are as much engaged in 'self-realization' and the successful shaping of their lives as are adherents of a Western concept of women's emancipation. To grasp the proportions of the choices made, a knowledge of the context in which the women have to manoeuvre is required. As far as female Islamists are concerned, we have tentatively called this context the discourse on the Muslim woman.

16. Dialmy, 1996.
17. Abu Odeh, 1993.
18. Watson, 1994: 154.

Bibliography

Abu Odeh Lama, 1993. Postcolonial feminism and the veil: Thinking the difference. *Feminist Review*, (43).

Ahmed, Leila 1992. *Women and Gender in Islam. Historical Roots of a Modern Debate*. New Haven: Yale University Press.

An-Na'im, Abdullahi 1995. The dichotomy between Religious and Secular discourses in Islamic societies. In Afkhami, Mahmaz (ed.), *Faith & Freedom. Women's Human Rights in the Muslim World*. London: I.B. Taurus.

Bucaille, Laetitia 1994. 'L´engagement islamiste des femmes en Algérie'. *Monde Arabe Maghreb-Machrek*, (114).

Christensen, Hilda Rømer 1995. *Mellem backfisch og pæne piger, Køn og kultur i KFUK 1983-1940*. København: Museum Tusculanums Forlag.

Christiansen, Connie Carøe & Lene Kofoed Rasmusssen, 1994: *At Vælge Sløret. Unge Kvinder i Politisk Islam*. København: Forlaget Sociologi.

Dialmy, Abdessamad 1996. 'Féminisme et Islamisme dans le monde Arabe. Essai de Synthèse'. *Social Compass*, Vol. 43, (4).

Foucault, Michel 1978. *The History of Sexuality*. Introduction. New York: Pantheon Books.

Göçek, Fatma M. & Shiva Balaghi (eds.), 1994. *Reconstructing gender in the Middle East. Tradition, Identity and Power*. New York: Columbia University Press.

Haddad, Yvonne Y. 1985.' Islam, Women and Revolution in Twentieth-century Arab Thought' *Women, Religion and Social Change*. Eds., Haddad & Finlay. Albany: State University of New York Press.

Hakiki-Talahite, Fatiha 1991. 'Sous le voile ... les femmes', *Les Cahiers de L´Orient*, (23).

Hatem, Mervat 1986. 'The Enduring Alliance of Nationalism and Patriarchy in Muslim Personal Status Laws: The case of Modern Egypt', *Feminist Issues* 6, (1).

Hatem, Mervat 1988. 'Egypt's Middle Class in Crisis: the sexual division of labour', *Middle East Journal* 42, (3).

Hatem, Mervat 1994. 'Egyptian Discourses on gender and political liberalization: Do secularist and Islamist views really differ?' *Middle East Journal*, Vol. 48. (4).

Hessini, Leila 1994. Wearing the hijab in contemporary Morocco: Choice and identity. In Göçek, F.M. & S. Balaghi (eds.), *Reconstructing gender in the Middle East*. New York: Columbia University Press.

Kandiyoti, Deniz (ed.) 1991. *Women, Islam and the State*, London: Macmillan.

Keane, John, 1994 . Den offentlige sfæres pluralisering. *Tendens*, Vol. 6, (2).

Mernissi, Fatima 1993. *Islam and Democracy. Fear of the Modern World.* London: Virago Press.

Mir-Hosseini, Ziba 1996. Stretching the limits. A Feminist Reading of the Sharia in post-Khomeini Iran. In Yamani, Mai, (ed.), *Feminism and Islam. Legal and Literary Perspectives.* London: Ithara Press.

Moghadam, Valentine (ed.) 1994. *Gender and National Identity. Women and Politics in Muslim Societies.* Helsinki: The United Nations University.

Watson, Helen 1994. Women and the Veil. Personal responses to global process. In Ahmed, A. & Hastings Donnan (eds.), *Islam, globalization and modernity,* London: Routledge.

The Middle East

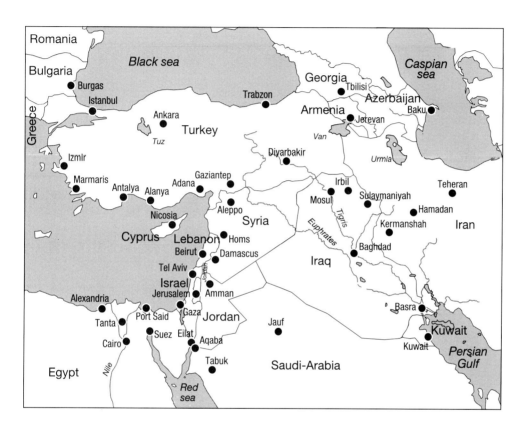

The Significance of Oil in the Middle East and North Africa

Meliha Benli Altunisik

Introduction

Oil was discovered in the Middle East at the beginning of the twentieth century. The first major discovery was in Iran. However, it was not until the end of World War II that the Middle East had become the centre of international oil. The institutional framework of a concessionary system and the absolute dominance of major international oil companies remained almost intact until the late 1960s. From that period onwards, the oil producing states in the Middle East and North Africa sought to redefine the basis of their relationships with the companies in question. These efforts culminated in the early 1970s in the oil-producing states themselves gaining full control. This new power and the subsequent four-fold price rise in 1973-74 resulted in an enormous influx of revenue into the coffers of these states.

Nevertheless, the impact of the increased revenue on the political economy of the Middle Eastern oil exporting states has not always been positive. On the contrary, the oil wealth created as many economic, social and political problems as it solved. In this article I will discuss the domestic and regional political implications of oil in the area. I will argue that oil revenues decisively influenced the state structures and the regimes' relations with different groups within their societies. The sudden influx of revenues at the beginning of the state formation process resulted in fairly less developed institutional capabilities. Furthermore, by using the newly found wealth, the political elite in these countries reinforced their authoritarian rules and reconstructed the traditional structures in their respective societies. However, starting in the 1980s, the oil revenues began to drop, in line with changes in the international oil market. These developments highlighted the vulnerability of these regimes. In addition to its domestic implications, the revenue from oil has had certain implications for regional politics in the Middle East and North Africa. While during the 1970s it was the positive, integrative aspects of oil which were stressed, by the 1980s in particular, oil began to have a negative influence on regional politics.

Oil and State Formation

In most of these countries the discovery of oil coincided with the state formation process. The oil revenue helped the regimes to extend their authority over their territory and to consolidate their power.[1] Later, increasing oil exports accelerated this process. For example, through its policies the Saudi monarchy created a new business elite, which shared the same tribal affiliation with the bureaucratic elite to replace the Hijazi merchants.[2] The latter, with their independent financial base, were seen as a possible threat to the regime. Similarly, in Libya the Qadhafi regime sought to consolidate its power in the mid-1970s with a new political structure; the *Jamahiriya* system, which aimed at a total restructuring of political, social and economic relations in Libya.[3] In Iran with the allocation of an increase in the oil revenue, the Shah tried to undermine the power of the bazaar, the landlords and the Ulema; which constituted the traditional basis of the regime.[4] On the other hand, the amirs in Qatar and Kuwait were successful in maintaining the continuity of their rule; this was due, in no small part, to the oil revenue. In both of these countries the merchants, who constitute the most influential social group, gave up their historical claim to political participation in exchange for a large share of the oil revenue.[5] In some cases the ruling elite preferred to use violence to undermine the power of different social groups in the society which were seen as a possible threat to their survival. The Sunni Baath regime, for instance, felt so threatened by 'the Shi'a commercial classes and their co-sectarians, who formed the majority of the Iraqi population, that it took every opportunity to eliminate the Shi'a leadership in both economic and socio-religious realms through mass deportations, imprisonment and violence'.[6]

1. Of course, parallel to the production of oil, or in some cases before that, the colonial regimes were very influential in the process of state formation and consolidation in the region.
2. Kiren Chaudhry: 'The Price of Wealth: business and state in labour remittance and oil economies' *International Organization*. Winter, 1989: 103-45.
3. Meliha Benli Altunisik: 'External Vs. Internal Revisited: The Political Economy of Economic Reform Policies in Libya (1987-1993)', Ph.D. Dissertation, Boston University, Boston, 1994.
4. Some scholars have argued that the fact that the regime could not create an alternative basis of support was one of the reasons for the revolution. See, for instance, Afsaneh Najmabadi:'Depoliticization of a Rentier State: The Case of Pahlavi Iran'. In H. Beblawi and G. Luciani, (eds.): *The Rentier State*, London: Croom Helm, 1987.
5. Jill Crystal: 'Coalitions in Oil Monarchies: Kuwait and Qatar' *Comparative Politics*, July, 1989: 427-43.
6. Kiren Chaudhry: 'Economic Liberalization and the Lineages of the Rentier State', *Comparative Politics*, October 1994: 16.

Once these regimes were able to undermine the power of their rival groups, with the aid of the oil revenue, they tried to buy the society off, hoping to prevent any kind of social opposition. Regardless of the type of regime, in all of these countries the state played a crucial role in the economy. This was quite natural since most of the GNP came from oil revenues that accrued directly to the state. However, the state's role was largely limited to the distribution of this revenue to the population. The rentier state not only provided goods and services but it was also generally the major employer in the economy. Yet these states lacked well-developed administrative machinery. This was due to the fact that, unlike most others, the oil-exporting states were lacking in those institutions designed for tax collection and information gathering. Although distributive tasks also require some degree of bureaucratic development, the political elite generally preferred patronage relationships as the basis of their distribution.

Through their distributive policies, the regimes also helped to reinforce traditional structures. For instance, even regimes like Iraq and Libya, which have been rhetorically hostile to traditional structures, reconstructed tribal, regional, family affiliations through their allocative policies. This was seen by these authoritarian regimes as being necessary to their survival. In the absence of any meaningful political expression and opposition, these structures constitute the most important institutional tie between the state and the society.

Oil has also been very important for the Middle East as a region - not just for the oil-producing states. The sudden influx of oil wealth into the region had two immediate practical results. First, the amount of capital flowing from the oil-rich states to the oil-poor increased considerably. Second, and what is more important, the migration of both skilled and unskilled workers from the oil-poor to the oil-rich states reached a record level during this period. These two developments increased hopes in some circles in the possibility of oil playing a crucial role in the economic integration of the region. And, although it soon became clear that these hopes were largely unfounded, the increased oil wealth of the exporting states had clear political consequences. Contrary to the 'radicalism' of the 1950s and 1960s, the 1970s witnessed the ascendancy of two conservative states in the region, namely Saudi Arabia and Iran. Saudi aid in particular was effectively used to induce former radical states such as Egypt and Syria. However, oil revenues also created regional tension because of the enormous polarization of wealth that resulted. The gap between the oil-rich states and oil-poor states became more paramount with the influx of large amounts of windfall revenues into the region in the 1970s. This created what

Barry Buzan calls a 'structural political threat'. [7] In fact, this resentment only became apparent during the Gulf War.

The Period of the Oil Bust

The period of oil boom, however, ended at the beginning of the 1980s. The oil prices started to drop in 1982 and they collapsed in 1986: The price of oil declined from about 28 dollars to about seven dollars per barrel.[8] The downward trend continued for the most part thereafter. Implications of these developments for the oil-exporting states have been tremendous. Throughout the 1980s and 1990s there was an enormous decline in oil revenues. This happened despite the fact that two major oil producers, namely Iran and Iraq, were at war during most of the 1980s. Later, the Iraqi invasion of Kuwait in August 1990 and the Gulf War which followed created a small boom. Then the embargo effectively removed all Iraqi and Kuwaiti oil from the market. The prices almost doubled. This was not surprising: The combined production of the two countries in July 1990 was 4.7 million b/d(barrels per day); 20 percent of OPEC oil production in that month, and almost 9 percent of the global supply in the third quarter of that year. What was surprising was that the boom did not last very long. Soon the prices started to drop again. In the summer of 1993 there was even a small crash.

Why has there been a downward trend in oil prices for most of the 1980s and 1990s? Why did the two most important crises, namely the Iran-Iraq War and the Gulf War, not significantly alter this trend? Part of the reason for this was that Saudi Arabia and a few other producers increased their production to offset the loss in supply. But the most important reason behind these developments was a far-reaching transformation of the world oil market. In the 1980s and 1990s there was a decline in the demand for oil. This sharp drop in demand was in response to the rapid increases in oil prices that took place in the 1970s. Economic slowdown in the industrialized countries, the substitution of other fuels for oil, conservation and other investments in new energy-saving technologies all pulled the demand for oil down over the years. Moreover, there was especially a drop in demand for OPEC oil. Since the 1970s the non-OPEC oil has become more competitive.[9] The organization's market power has been in long-term and irreversible decline. In 1982, for the first time,

---

7. Barry Buzan: *People, States, and Fear: An Agenda for International Security Studies in the Post-Cold War Era*, London: Harvester Wheatsheaf, 1991.
8. For more on 1986 oil crisis see Robert Mabro, (ed.): *The 1986 Oil Price Crisis: Economic Effects and Policy Responses*. Oxford: Oxford University Press, 1988.
9. The main increases have come from Angola, China, Egypt, Malaysia, Mexico, Norway, Oman and the United Kingdom.

non-OPEC oil surpassed OPEC production. By 1985, OPEC's world market share of global production was 30 percent, down from 54 percent in 1973. OPEC's problems were increased as a result of the organization's failure to produce a sustainable production quota. Hence OPEC's control of prices started to diminish. In its place a new model of the energy market has emerged. In this new model it is largely the market, not the OPEC resolutions, which began to determine the prices. As a Wall Street article put it, oil was becoming 'just another commodity'; traded in the spot and/or futures markets. By early 1984, spot marketing has been accounting for over half of world trade.[10]

Despite policies aimed at diversifying their economies, Middle Eastern oil exporters remained very largely dependent on the oil revenue. The fall of prices highlighted their immense vulnerability. As a result, these countries increasingly faced economic problems. They had serious balance of payment problems and their foreign exchange reserves were depleted. Some Middle Eastern oil producers, like Iraq, Algeria, and even Saudi Arabia, resorted to foreign borrowing. The economic crisis in Saudi Arabia prompted an IMF warning that 'a broad based review of policies' was needed — something unthinkable a few years earlier. By the end of 1994, Saudi Arabia's internal and external debt came to a total of 80 billion dollars; their foreign assets had fallen to under 20 billion dollars — from a high of 120 billion dollars in 1982.[11] In Algeria and Iraq the 1980s marked the start of a period of foreign debt. On the other hand, Libya, while not resorting to foreign borrowing, has nevertheless been facing a serious financial crisis since the oil revenues fell from 22 billion dollars in 1980 to some 5 billion dollars in 1986.[12]

In response to the financial crisis the oil-rich countries adopted austerity measures that aimed at decreasing state expenditure. They put development projects on hold and reduced the size of their foreign labour force. Most of them also adopted liberalization policies intended to increase the role of the private sector in the economy.[13] These policies posed a serious challenge to the legitimacy of the existing regimes. They built up popular frustration and

---

10. Daniel Yergin: *The Prize: The Epic Quest for Oil, Money and Power*. New York: Simon and Schuster, 1992.
11. Fareed Mohamedi: 'The Economy', in H.C. Metz (ed.). *Saudi Arabia: a country study*. Federal Research Division, Library of Congress, Washington, D.C., 1993.
12. See Altunisik, op. cit., 87.
13. See M. Altunisik, 'A Rentier State's Response to Oil Crisis: Economic Reform Policies in Libia', *Arab Studies Quarterly*, Autumn 1996: 49-63; and Kiren Chaudhry, 'Economic Liberalization in Oil-Exporting Countries: Iraq and Saudi Arabia'. In I. Harik and D. Sullivan, *Privatization and Liberalization in the Middle East*. Bloomington: Indiana University Press, 1992.

anger and generated new political pressures. Therefore, from the perspective of these regimes, the fiscal crisis created a security problem. Domestic political stability was undermined by a drop in economic performance resulting from external factors.

Oil has been central to the long-term viability of these regimes. Most of these states are all the more fragile because of the uneven process of development they experienced in their formation. As mentioned above, the influx of oil revenues allowed these regimes to buy domestic security with oil. An important part of their legitimacy has been based on their distributive functions. The financial crisis meant that they could no longer distribute as they used to and this gave rise to popular protests. The regimes adopted a carrot and stick approach to contain the pressures coming from their societies. They tried to contain the discontent by more repression and/or by co-opting.

The problem now is that there are few possibilities for increasing government revenues. Oil prices are likely to remain at current levels. While demand is falling, non-OPEC oil is becoming increasingly competitive. Iraq's eventual return to the world oil market is looming. All of this is bad news for Middle Eastern oil-producers. What is most important is the difficulty these regimes face in trying to increase their non-oil revenues. For instance, methods generally used by states faced with a fiscal crisis, such as imposing income taxes, are out of question because of the fear that they would increase public demand for political participation. The populace in these countries is also adamantly opposed to such measures. In Kuwait and Saudi Arabia, for instance, government attempts to impose new taxes were undermined by fierce opposition. Similarly, any further cuts in state expenditure would invite social protest. In fact, it is very hard to decrease state expenditure in these distributive states where an important part of their legitimacy rests on their allocative capacities. Military spending constitutes another big piece of the budgets of the countries in the region, including the rentier states. In fact, the region as a whole has the highest per capita military spending in the world. For years this has been juistified primarily by the existence of regional conflicts, chief among them the Arab-Israeli one. However, these regimes also wanted to achieve domestic security through military power. Because of this multi-faceted role of military might, these regimes, including the rentier ones, are reluctant to decrease their military spending. On the contrary, despite the fiscal crisis, the states continue their huge spending on armaments, increasingly so after the Gulf War. Therefore, there is no easy way out for the oil-exporting states of the Middle East. It is very likely that they will be confronted increasingly by such challenges in the near future.

New developments in the world oil market have also had regional implications. Declining revenues of the oil-rich states did not completely erase the resentment of the oil-poor states. On the contrary it added new tensions due to the knock-on effect of the decrease in oil rents in recent years. Aid from oil-rich countries to the oil-poor ones has declined considerably. Between 1980-1988 the two major Arab donors, Saudi Arabia and Kuwait cut their foreign aid funding by 63 and 91 percent respectively. Moreover, as part of their austerity measures, oil-exporting states reduced the number of foreign workers in their countries.[14] This policy not only put more pressure on the already strained economies of the donor countries, but also sparked tensions between the oil-rich and oil-poor states.[15] And finally, the decline of oil prices added a new tension; which is the competition between the oil-exporting states for their share of the market. Kuwaiti over-production to offset falling prices was taken by Saddam Hussein as an economic war and subsequently influenced the Iraqi decision to invade Kuwait.

14. Nader Fergany: 'Arab Labour Migration and the Gulf Crisis'. In Dan Tschirgi (ed.), *The Arab World Today*. Boulder, Colorado: Lynne Rienner Publishers, 1994: 91-99.
15. For instance, in 1985 the Libyan government expelled 30,000 Tunisians who were working in Libya as part of the austerity programme that was adopted as a response to the revenue crisis. This event resulted in a souring of relations between Tunisia and Libya and led to the eventual breakdown of diplomatic relations in September 1985.

To Get More Out of Less:
Managing the Water Resources for
Sustained Agricultural Production

Martin Hvidt

Water has been an avidly debated issue in the Middle East over the last decade or two — and for good reason. Water is a vital resource in all economies, but especially important in the Middle Eastern societies which have to be sustained and developed in arid environments.

Today, only Turkey and Lebanon among the Middle Eastern countries have the water resources they need to satisfy their demands presently and in the foreseeable future. All other Middle Eastern countries operate with a water deficit. At present, if they were to fully satisfy all their water needs, each country would need twice the amount of water they have today.[1]

There are a number of issues which make the water resources of the Middle East particularly problematic.

Firstly, the demand for water is increasing drastically in the region due to rapid population growth as well as an increase in demand from industry and the agricultural sector. It is estimated that the annual renewable water supplies will drop by 80 percent; from 3,430 cubic meters per person in 1960 to 667 cubic meters in the year 2025. The present water availability is estimated at 1,436 cubic meters per person.[2]

Secondly, the renewable water resources are finite and close to being fully exploited. The surface water is, at present, fully utilized while ground water resources are increasingly being brought under intensified use. There is very little scope for new sources of water. The implication of this is that all attempts to secure new sources of water are either, extremely expensive if based on technology (i.e. through the desalination of seawater), or politically dangerous,

---

1. Allan and Mallat 1995: 1. A substantial part of this water deficit is covered through the import of foodstuffs.
2. The figures are from the Water Resources Institute and the World Bank and summarized in Meed, 1994: 1-7. 1,000 m³/per person/year is the level commonly taken to indicate a severe scarcity of water (World Bank, 1993b: 26).

if threatening the size or quality of the water resources of a neighbouring country.[3]

Thirdly, most major water resources in the region are shared. The main river basins of the Jordan/Yarmuk, Nile, Tigris and Euphrates are the subjects of riparian disputes.[4] Only on the Nile is there a formal agreement on how to share the water resources. This, however, only involves Sudan and Egypt.[5] As of now, there is no internationally agreed legislation or any rules that can be used for the division of rivers.[6]

Fourthly, water quality is rapidly deteriorating as a result of the intensified use of each unit of water and the lack of effective measures to prevent further reduction in water quality.[7] Issues like agricultural run-off, untreated industrial and municipal waste water etc. in combination with low river flows, all contribute to this. In the cases where rivers are shared, the issue of water quality is always more prominent for downstream users than for upstream users.

For these reasons, journalists in particular have emphasized the notion of 'hydroconflict' as the likely outcome of the tightened resource. This point of view was fuelled strongly by the past general secretary of the United Nations, Boutros Boutros-Ghali, who in the mid-1980s, said that 'war in the Middle East could be started by disagreements over water'.[8] History, fortunately, has proven this viewpoint wrong and the evidence today points in the direction of an emerging level of 'hydrocooperation'.[9]

Among water specialists and decision makers in the Middle East, there appears to be a growing concern for more technical and quiet efforts to raise the efficiency of the present water supply systems in order to 'get more out of less'. One prerequisite of this effort is cooperation between both the different users and between the various states sharing the same resource.

One key measure, generally prescribed to make the optimum use of the available water, is to improve planning and management procedures to appropriate, allocate and utilize water. As Falkenmark points out, the main constraint for most countries, in the medium term, is the capability to develop a sophisticated and far-sighted water management strategy, along with the legislation and administration necessary to support these.[10]

---

3. Wolf 1995: 140.
4. Kliot 1993: Ch. 2-4.
5. Abu-Zeid and Rady 1992: 82.
6. See discussion of the existing framework in Kliot, 1993, Ch. 4; and Lowi, 1995.
7. Meed 1994: 7
8. Allan 1994: 13.
9. Wolf 1995: 140.
10. Falkenmark 1984: 158.

At present, the World Bank is forcefully introducing its 'comprehensive analytical framework for water resources management'. In short, this framework emphasizes an approach to the management of all water needs within a given country, the establishment of institutional and regulatory systems to provide efficient management, the creation of incentive structures, both for water users and bureaucrats, to include health and environmental resources in the planning, and finally the building of international relationships and agreements concerning international water resources.[11]

Agriculture plays a key role in these water management efforts. It alone accounts for approximately 80 percent of the total water consumption in the Middle East.[12] As a rule of thumb, in order to satisfy domestic and municipal demands, 100 m^3/year/person is required, while food production requires 1,000 m^3/year/person.[13] All of the Middle Eastern countries have well above 100 m^3/year/person.[14] This highlights the fact that, at present, there are no problems in covering the water needs for the domestic, municipal and industrial sectors in the Middle Eastern societies. There are, however, significant problems in supplying the huge amount of water required for agricultural purposes.

So far, Israel is the only country in the Middle East which, politically, has decided to cut back on the water supply for agriculture, in order to ensure the supply for others sectors of society.[15] Whatever foodstuffs cannot be produced within the country, must be imported.

Because agriculture is, by far, the largest consumer of water, it is within this sector that the greatest potential for water savings are to be found. Improving the efficiency of the irrigation system is seen as a prerequisite if agriculture is to retain its position as an important sector in Middle Eastern societies. The question is simple. How can larger amounts of agricultural products be produced with the same amount, or less water? The answer is far more complicated. It entails introducing a range of political, social, economic and technical measures.

In order to more fully understand the complexity of introducing such measures, this paper will review the current efforts introduced by the Egyptian

---

11. World Bank 1993b: 40ff.
12. World Bank 1993b: 26.
13. Allan and Mallat 1995: 19. 100 m^3/year/person is equivalent to a water consumption of 278 liters/day. In Odense, Denmark, as a comparison, the water consumption per person is approximately 200 liters/day or 73 m^3/year.
14. Meed 1994: 7.
15. Personal communication with Professor Aaron Soffer, Haifa University, April 8th, 1992. See also Lowi 1993, ch. 6.

water authorities to improve irrigation performance in the Egyptian irrigation system.

Improving Irrigation Performance in Egypt

Egypt has a history of nearly 7,000 years when it comes to practicing irrigation. Since the mid-18th century, new practices and technologies have gradually been implemented on a widening scale. In a final attempt to harness the Nile, the Aswan High Dam was inaugurated in 1971. This provided year-round water storage regardless of the season and flood control which has supplied agriculture with a steady, year-round and until recently, plentiful source of irrigation water. And thus, the Aswan High Dam provided the possiblity of raising the efficiency of irrigated agriculture.

Twenty-five years have elapsed since the High Dam was finished, and during this period the major improvements on the irrigation system have been in the main system and the installment of adequate drains. Until recently, *no* attempts have been made to change the way the farmers use water in their fields. Not until 1989, when serious attempts were made to initialize higher water use efficiencies in Egyptian agriculture.

Currently the Agricultural Sector faces three major problems:

1) The Problem of Lower than Potential Productivity
2) The Problem of Increasing Water Scarcity
3) The Problem of Changes in Economic Policy

The Problem of Lower than Potential Productivity

Egypt is blessed with good soil, good climatic conditions and a perennial source of irrigation water - the Nile. This provides excellent conditions for agricultural production and the application of intensive agriculture. This has resulted in generally high yields of most crops.[16] There is, however, considerable potential for increasing the agricultural productivity and quality of high-demand crops in the old lands through the wider adoption of improved technologies and cultural practices.[17]

It is estimated that the yields of some crops could be increased by at least one third on average, while the yields of selected crops like maize, sorghum

16. World Bank 1993a: 6-7.
17. World Bank 1993a: 13.

and groundnuts could be doubled.[18] Actual crop-yield evaluations from specific development projects confirm these estimates.[19]

Among the most fundamental reasons for public investments in irrigation systems is that good control over the water by the farmers is a prerequisite for the adoption of new agricultural technologies, such as fertilizer, pesticides, and high-yield grain varieties.[20] These improved technologies are primarily bio-chemical (in contrast to mechanical) and presuppose adequate and predictable water supplies.[21]

Even though the Nile is under full control today and the irrigation system in general performs satisfactorily — when water is plentiful[22] — research projects and studies provide ample evidence of the urgent need to improve farmer water control in Egypt.[23]

These studies document that control over irrigation water and its distribution along branch canals and watercourses (mesqas), is inadequate to provide the farmers with adequate, reliable and fair water distribution. This means that the farmers are not inclined to invest time and effort in improved farming practices and certainly not in the adoption of new agricultural technologies.

The Problem of Increasing Water Scarcity

The present water supply barely sustains the current demand in Egypt. And demand for water is increasing. Currently, the population is growing by 1 million a year. From the present population of approximately 55 million, Egypt is expected to face a population of about 63 million by the year 2000, and 86 million by the year 2025.[24]

Furthermore, hydropolitical issues threaten to limit the amount of water available to Egypt. For example, the two upstream states, Ethiopia and Sudan,

18. Stoner 1994: 199.
19. ILRI 1988: 62.
20. Barker 1978: 142; Haider 1987: 1; Levine 1986: 3; Richards and Waterbury 1991: 163.
21. Other major reasons for investment in irrigation systems are that irrigated land produces more food and reduces the risk of crop losses from drought.
22. Ispan 1992: 10-11.
23. See for example Abu-Zeid and Rady 1992: 96; EWUP 1984: 11-26; IIP 1990B: 9; Mehanna, Huntington and Antonius 1984: 139; World Bank 1993a: 26.
24. The figures used are from World Bank 1994: Table 1 and 25. For a further breakdown of these figures see Bos et al. 1992: 210 ff. The total size of the current population and its growth rate are subject to debate. United Nations figures for example maintain that the population in 1994 was approximately 62 millions, and project that the population by 2015 will reach 87 million, and by 2050 will reach 117 million. The current growth rate is estimated to be 2.2 percent (United Nations 1994).

have, at present, neither the political stability nor the money to engage in large irrigation development projects. If their condition is to change, however, Egypt would be left with a reduced portion of the Nile flow.

In 1979, the Minister of Irrigation wrote that 'Egyptian agriculture is considered to be one of the most consumptive of irrigation water in the world. This high consumption is not due to reasons related to soil, but is mainly related to the wasteful use of irrigation water'.[25]

Actual measurements point out that farmers generally apply 50 to 250 percent more water than is needed by the crops and for leaching requirements.[26] One reason for this vast over-irrigation is the lack of water control, because with lack of water control '... the general tendency of farmers is to irrigate too soon and apply too much water'.[27]

At present, Egyptian agriculture consumes about 84 percent of the water used in Egypt.[28] This means that it is in this sector that the greatest potential for applying water-conserving measures is found. Even relatively small changes in the on-farm water use on individual farms will result in sizeable savings on a national scale. Estimates of potential annual water savings of 15 percent are mentioned.[29]

The Problem of Changes in Economic Policy

In March 1990, the government of Egypt launched a comprehensive economic and social reform programme to facilitate the transition from a highly interventionist, centrally planned economy to one that is decentralized and market oriented. In the agricultural sector, this has meant the elimination of crop area controls, mandatory deliveries of produce to Government Cooperatives, and the elimination of administratively determined input and output prices.[30]

To achieve the full benefits of the free market, liberalizing cropping patterns require corresponding 'liberalization' of the water. Water deliveries are to be relieved of the rigid rotational system and changed into a demand system in order to accommodate the different needs of individual crops.

A second implication of this liberalization process is that the former procedure of the Government, to extract money from agriculture to improve and maintain the irrigation system, is being modified. The state alone simply

25. Samaha 1979: 253.
26. IIP 1993: 10.
27. Clemmens 1987: 60.
28. Abu-Zeid and Rady 1992: 94.
29. World Bank 1993a: 25.
30. World Bank 1993a: 9-10.

cannot pay for the improvements, operations and maintenance of the irrigation system. Mechanisms are to be set up to make it economically feasible for the farmers to invest their own money and effort in the improvment of the tertiary canals.

The IIP Improvement Effort

To rectify the above mentioned problems, the Egyptian Government and USAID has initiated the so-called Irrigation Improvement Project (IIP). This is a 90 million dollar pilot effort which is on its way to become a National Irrigation Improvement Project, and as such, is to be seen as a first step in the direction of bringing the Egyptian irrigation system in line with the demand it will be facing by the turn of the 21st century.

The project is designed to give guidance in the development of a process of water control and application to the Ministry of Public Works and Water Resources (MPWWR), including construction, training, capacity building, institutional and policy change. It field tests a shift from rotation to continuous flow at the branch canals, new application technologies at the mesqa level, and the formation of 1,200 Water Users Associations in a cross section of Egyptian environments.[31]

The IIP project is introducing a broad range of improvements at the ministerial level which aim to strengthen the institutional capacity of the Ministry in managerial and administrative skills, in operational policies and procedures and develop a rational interdisciplinary approach in planning, designing and implementing water resource projects.[32]

Furthermore, it introduces a range of changes at farm level. These encompass both technical and social features. The most fundamental change is to rearrange the institutional set up, by establishing WUAs. Worldwide IIP is a state-of-the-art project, in the way it involves the end users — the farmers — through the WUAs. Farmers are to participate in the design, implementation and maintenance of the physical structures and the allocation and distribution of water by WUAs themselves. More specifically, the WUAs are responsible for the operation and maintenance of the improved mesqas; the operation of the 'single point lift' pumping plant, scheduling irrigations among water users, collection of pumping charges, hiring pump operators, maintaining the mesqa and pumps and handling conflict among the users.[33] A WUA is defined as: a private organization owned, controlled and operated by member users for

31. Devres Inc. 1993: 14.
32. For a brief introduction to the aims of IIP see Devres Inc. 1993: 14.
33. See Hvidt, 1996, for an assesment of the implementation effort of WUAs.

their benefit in improving water delivery, water use and other organizational efforts related to water for increasing their production possibilities.[34]

Table 1: Characteristics of Irrigation Technology, Before and After IIP

Traditional Irrigation Technology		The IIP Technological Package	
Technique:	**Knowledge:**	**Technique:**	**Knowledge:**
Rotation system Private pumps Earthen low-level mesqas Multiple point lifting	Pump operation Traditional farming knowledge	Continuous flow in branch canals. Organizational pumps. Improved mesqas: - Raised lined - Pipeline Single point lifting	Pump O & M Mesqa O & M Accounting practices Irrigation scheduling Organization building Scientific know ledge of agricul- tural practices On-farm water management
Organization:	**Product:**	**Organization:**	**Product:**
Ad hoc cooperation. Shared ownership of e.g. pumps. Shared mesqa cleaning.	Low yielding crops.	Permanent organizations Delegation of responsibility Dissemination of knowledge.	- High yielding crop varieties. - Change in cropping pattern.

The Contents of the IIP Technological Package

The IIP effort can be conceived of as a technological package. Using the comprehensive and holistic definition of technology developed by researchers at The Aalborg School of International Technology Studies, Denmark, technology is defined as encompassing four interrelated elements, those of: technique, knowledge, organization and product definition of technology.

34. IIP 1990a: 3.

The table opposite provides a comparison between the traditional irrigation technology and the IIP technology.

As shown in the table, the IIP project seeks to implement changes in all four elements defining a technology. Significant changes are undertaken, both in the technical and management aspects of canal operation, in farmers' organizations and in the knowledge which is associated both with these organizations and the technical tasks they are to undertake; finally, potential changes in the outcome of the process, the product, and thus, in the productivity of agriculture.

A centerpiece of the IIP effort is the implementation of continuous flow in the branch and distributary canals. This means continuous availability of water in the canals, but not more water.[35] Previously only principal and main canals ran continuously, while branch and distributary canals operated on a rotational basis. The switch to continuous flow enables farmers to irrigate according to the water needs of the crops.[36]

Changing the Irrigation System

This section is reporting data on the impacts of the IIP effort to increase the performance of the Egyptian irrigation system.[37] Firstly, concerning changes in water control and following this, on changes in farm income. The purpose is not to make a detailed statement concerning the IIP effort, but to present some key findings resulting from the effort to improve the efficiency of the Egyptian irrigation system. It also proves how difficult and time-consuming redirecting agriculture can be.

Savings in water will not be dealt with, simply because the data is not available. The first stage of the effort to raise irrigation efficiency is to get the system operating technically and socially. Savings in water are expected to

35. For an in depth explanation of this concept see Hvidt 1997, ch. 1.
36. From a technical point of view, continuous flow is facilitated by the instalation of different types of flow control gates, and ultimately it necessitates a downsizing of all hydraulic structures to provide for good system operation.
37. The primary data for the subsequent analysis was collected during October and November 1992 in three Canal Commands in Middle Egypt; Herz-Numaniya and Beni Ibeid located close to the city of Minya, and Qiman Arus, adjacent to the city of Beni Suef. Data was collected through structured interviews undertaken by local interviewers. A total of 137 WUA council members were interviewed. The farmer interviews were supplemented by interviews with key informants in the areas, a review of the WUAs financial status and by physical measurements i.e. land savings. The data are reported in detail in Hvidt, 1997.

Table 2: Summary of IIP impact on Water Control

Indicators analyzed	Findings
Adequacy:	
Adequacy of water supply	74% of respondents rate the situation as improved
Number of days with critical water shortage	85% reduction
Night irrigation	87% reduction in reported number of night irrigations
Number of irrigations done at night	89% reduction
Source of irrigation water	Use of drainage water is eradicated
Reliability:	
Deviations from planned irrigations	86% of respondents rate the situation as improved
Fairness:	
Head-Tail differences along mesqa	Less Head-Tail differences.

Percentage figures are calculated for summer season

show up when farmers have gained confidence in the system. Experiences for surveys conducted in 1994 support this notion.[38]

Does the IIP Technological Package Impact Farmer Water Control?

Water control is defined as: the capacity to apply the proper quantity and quality of water at the optimum time to the crop root zone to meet crop consumptive needs and soil leaching requirements.[39]

In short, the term 'water control' can be thought of as the relative control over quantity and timing of water supplies. Water control is analysed as a multifaceted variable encompassing the three dimensions: adequacy, reliability and fairness. Each of these dimension have been operationalized using one or more indicators. The results of the survey are presented in Table 2 above.

The data in Table 2 provides evidence that the IIP effort has led to significant improvements in the water control situation.

38. Personal discussion Dr. Max Lowdermilk, Sept. 8th, 1995, Cairo.
39. Freeman et al., 1989: 10.

A bivariate analysis was conducted to examine the relationships between each indicator of water control and each of the four elements of technology. The following conclusion was reached:

1) The presence of a stable continuous flow regime in the branch canals was the single most important factor in securing water control at farm level.

2) Elapsed time between start of mesqas operation on improved mesqas showed a significant relationship with water control because continuous flow takes time to implement.

3) The strength of WUA organizations showed effect on water control at farm level.

4) The estimated increase in yields was found to be highly associated with the adequacy of water supply.

That the implementation of continuous flow is the single most important factor influencing the observed effects of IIP in regard to water control is understandable and in compliance with the investigator's expectations. Erratic and unfair water supplies in the main canals were the primary reasons for dissatisfaction with the traditional system.

Does the Shift to the IIP Package Lead to Higher Levels of Agricultural Productivity ?

Table 3 summarizes the survey findings relating the situation after the IIP implementation to the situation before.

The data in Table 3 shows that the IIP effort leads to sizeable decreases in the cost of irrigation. For example, in cost of pumping, labour time involved in pumping, and maintenance activities. Note especially the changes related to the capital cost of pumps.

Due to implementation of continuous flow and the specific design of the mesqa delivery system, the number of pumps decreases sharply.[40] This leads

40. Before the improvements 113 pumps were present along the surveyed canals, while there were only 24 after the change.

to a decrease of 73 percent in the capital investment in pumps. And the monetary amount is substantial. Per farmer, this saving is equivalent to a little less than half of an average net farm income in one year, which is found to be 1,296 Egyptian pounds (L.E.).[41]

The only factor that has increased after the shift to IIP is the capital cost of the mesqa systems. It is, however, a relatively small sum to be paid each year, because the Egyptian government has decided to subsidize the mesqa construction cost on concessional repayment terms.[42]

Table 3: Summary of Findings, Before to After, IIP

	Percentage Difference	In Monetary Units
Changes in Recurrent Cost:		
– Cost of pumping	36% decrease	9.4→6 L.E./one irr./feddan
– Labour time to irrigate	50% decrease*	
– Cost of labour time to irrigate	50% decrease*	6 h 30 min→3 h 10 min/one irrigation
– Cost of maintenance		59→29 L.E./feddan/ year
Pumps	29% decrease	
Mesqas	41% decrease	.77→.55 L.E./feddan/year
Changes in Capital Cost:		22→13 L.E./feddan/year
– Pumps (overall investment)	73% decrease	
– Mesqas	increased cost**	452,000→120,000 L.E.
Changes in Income:		65 L.E./year
– Income increased yields	increased**	
		440 L.E./feddan/year

* variations exist according to the specific cropping pattern
** not applicable to before — after scenario

41. Devres Inc. 1993: 37.
42. The farmers pay the full construction cost of the mesqa and the pump(s) through a 20-year loan, with one year grace period and no interest. (ARE Ministry of Irrigation 1994) and its by-laws. Thus the farmers will only pay approximately 15 percent of the total construction cost of the improved mesqa systems.

Table 4: Farmers' Perception of the Usefulness of the IIP effort, in Percentage of Reportings

	N=195*
Can irrigate when required	27.7
Increase in productivity	24.7
Time saving	17.0
Cost saving	10.0
Land saving	7.7
Road improvement	5.1
Less submersion of land	4.1
Less salinity	2.1
Irrigation scheduling leads to less conflict	1.0
Too early to know	0.6

* The 137 farmers were allowed to give more than one answer

Concerning the changes in farm income, only 3.6 percent of the farmers reported having introduced new crops after the shift to the IIP package (introduction of vegetables), whereas 35 percent of the farmers reported that they expected to introduce new crops within the next five years. A change in the farmers' earnings in the short and medium term is likely to come from changes in cropping patterns, from low value to high value crops, made possible by the improved water control. Using available data[43] it can be concluded, that estimated crop yield increases can generate an incremental income of L.E.440 per feddan for the project area.[44] They further point out that 'in addition, there will be some shift in cropping patterns to more profitable crops, but this has not been calculated at this time because it is unknown how this shift will occur given the recent freeing up of commodity markets in Egypt'. They estimate, however, that 'with proper crop husbandry and a shift to more profitable cropping patterns, a farmer's incremental income could increase two-fold to L.E. 880 per feddan'.[45]

43. Devres Inc. 1993: 35-36.
44. One feddan is 4,200 m².
45. Devres Inc. 1993: 37.

How do Farmers Perceive the Usefulness of the IIP Effort?

Table 4 presents the farmers views on the reasons why they found the IIP improvements useful for improving farm income. The data in the table shows that flexibility in irrigation, increase in productivity, time saving and cost saving, are the issues found most important by the farmers for increasing their farm income.

An additional indicator of the perception of the benefits of the IIP technology is that 44 percent of the farmers owning pumps prior to the shift to the new technology had sold their pumps within a two-year period after the implementation of the new mesqa systems. This indicates a high level of confidence among the farmers in the new technology.

It should be mentioned, that it has been of the utmost importance to the IIP effort, that it has succeeded in creating an extension service to support the WUA formation process, and the efforts to redirect farmers agricultural practices toward a more productive way.

Conclusion

Moving towards a water scarcity situation, Egypt has embarked on a program to improve the efficiency of the irrigation system.

This paper has dealt with the first experiences of this effort. There are a number of conclusions to be drawn.

Firstly, improving the efficiency of the irrigation system is a complex task, which includes changing not only the way the Ministry works but also the irrigation system and the way the farmers interact with it. To have water flowing on a continuous basis in the canals is as much a political as a technical task. Irrigation systems are man-made entities, and as such socio-technical by nature.

Secondly, although it is too early to make any final statements concerning the IIP effort, there is ample evidence that it drastically improves water control at farm level, and thereby the farmers possibility to plan and manage their crop production. This, is the fundamental stepping stone to higher productivity per unit of land and water.

Thirdly, the financial analysis showed that the improved layout of the mesqa systems, of which the WUAs are an essential part, make way for decreased irrigation costs and increased crop earnings. This provides a strong incentive for farmers to invest their time and effort in improving the performance of the Egyptian irrigation system.

Bibliography

ARE Ministry of Irrigation 1994. *Law No. 213 of year 1994. To modify some items of the Irrigation and Drainage Law.* Cairo, Egypt.

Abu-Zeid, M.A. and M.A. Rady 1992. 'Water Resources Management and Policies in Egypt'; Moigne, G.L., S. Barghouti, G. Geder, L. Garbus, M. Xie (eds.), *Country Experiences with Water Resources Management. Economic, Institutional, Technological and Environmental Issues.* World Bank Technical Paper Number 175. Washington: The World Bank: 93-101.

Allan, J. A., Chibli Mallat 1995. 'Introduction', Allan, J. A., C. Mallat (eds.), *Water in the Middle East: Legal, Political and Commercial Implications.* London: I.B.Tauris: 1-18.

Allan, Tony 1994. 'Management must supply and demand.' *Middle East Economic Digest*, (28), January: 12-14

Barker, Randolph 1978. 'Barriers to Efficient Capital Investment in Agriculture', T. W. Schultz (ed.), *Distortions of agricultural incentives.* Bloomington: Indiana University Press: 140-60.

Bos, Eduard, My T. Vu, Ann Levin, Rodolfo A. Bulatao, 1992. *World Population Projections 1992-93 Edition. Estimates and Projections with Related Demographic Statistics.* Baltimore: John Hopkins University Press, for the World Bank.

Clemmens, Albert J. 1987. *Arranged Delivery Schedules.* D. Zimbelman (ed.), Proceedings of the conference: Planning, Operation, Rehabilitation and Automation of Irrigation Water Delivery Systems, Irrig. and Drainage Div. (ASCE) Symposium held in Portland, Oregon, 1987: ASCE, New York: 57-67.

Devres Inc. 1993. *Evaluation of the Irrigation Improvement Project component of the Irrigation Management Systems Project.* C. Morgelard, D. Haslem, P. Hekmat, J. Layton, K. Swanberg, T. Weaver, F. Shahin, Washington.

EWUP 1984. *Improvning Egypt's irrigation system in the old lands. Findings of the Egypt Water Use and Management Project, Final Report.* Cairo, Egypt.

Falkenmark, Malin 1984. 'New Ecological Approach to the Water Cycle: Ticket to the Future.' *AMBIO*, Vol. 13, (3): 152-160.

Freeman, David M., with Vrinda Bhandarkar, Edwin Shinn, John Wilkins-Wells, Patricia Wilkins-Wells, 1989. *Local Organizations for Social Development. Concepts and Cases of Irrigation Organization.* Boulder: Colorado, Westview Press.

Haider, Mohammed 1987. *International Conference on Irrigation System Rehabilitation and Betterment.* Haider M. (ed.), Proceedings of conference: International Conference on Irrigation System Rehabilitation and Betterment, Volume 1: Proceedings, Leesburg, Virginia, October 27th-31st, 1986.

Water Management Synthesis II Project, Fort Collins, Colorado State University.

Hvidt, Martin 1996. 'Improving Irrigation System Performance in Egypt: First Experiences with the WUA Approach'. *International Journal of Water Resources Development*, Vol. 12 (3): 261-76.

Hvidt, Martin 1997. *Water, Technology and Development. Upgrading Egypt's Irrigation System.* London: I.B. Tauris. (Forthcoming, medio 1997).

IIP 1990a. *Irrigation Advisory Service Strategy for Building Strong and Sustainable Water User Associations* Discussion Paper (1). M. Lowdermilk, IAS Main office staff. Cairo, Egypt.

IIP 1990b. *Socio Economic study of Egypt's Irrigation management improvement challenge. Summary Report, Vol. 7. Final Report.* IIP Socio-Economic Team. Cairo, Egypt.

IIP 1993. *Water Management Monitoring and Evaluation Programme.* R.Oad, S. Mohamed, Cairo, Egypt.

ILRI 1988. *Annual report 1988.* International Institute for Land Reclamation and Improvement, Wageningen.

ISPAN 1992. *Irrigation Water Cost Recovery in Egypt. Determination of Irrigation Water Costs* (Vol. 1-2). Irrigation Support Project for Asia and the Near East. Report prepared for USAID/Arab Republic of Egypt and The Ministry of Public Works and Water Resources. Arab Republic of Egypt. Arlington, Virginia, USA.

Kliot, Nurit 1993. *Water Resources and Conflict in the Middle East.* London: Routledge.

Levine, Gilbert 1986. *The Challenge of Rehabilitation and Betterment.* D.A. Fowles (ed.) Proceedings of conference: International Conference on Irrigation System Rehabilitation and Betterment. Volume 2: Papers, Leesburg, Virginia, October 27th-31st, 1986. Water Management Synthesis II Project, Colorado State University: 1-13.

Lowi, Miriam R. 1995. *Water and Power: The politics of a scarce resource in the Jordan River Basin.* Cambridge: Cambridge University Press. (Cambridge Middle East Library, 31).

MEED 1994. 'A disaster that can be averted.' *Middle East Economic Digest*, (28), January: 7-8.

Mehanna, S., Richard Huntington, Rachad Antonius, 1984: *Irrigation and Society in Rural Egypt.* Cairo Papers in Social Science, Vol. 7, monograph 4. Cairo: The American University in Cairo.

Richards, Alan; John Waterbury 1991. *A Political Economy of the Middle East. State, Class, and Economic Development.* Cairo: The American University Press.

Samaha, M., Abdel Hady, 1979. 'The Egyptian Master Water Plan' *Water Supply & Management.* Vol. 3: 251-66.

Stoner, Roy 1994. 'Future Irrigation Planning in Egypt': P.P.Howell, J.A. Allan (eds.), *The Nile, sharing a scarce resource. A historical and technical review of water management and of economic and legal issues.* Cambridge: Cambridge University Press: 195-204.

United Nations 1994. *World Population 1994 (Wall Chart).* Department for Economic and Social Information and Policy Analysis, Population Division, United Nations, New York.

Wolf, Aaron T. 1995. 'International Water Dispute Resolution: The Middle East Multilateral Working Group on Water Resources.' *Water International*, Vol. 20, (3): 141-50.

World Bank 1993a. *Arab Republic of Egypt. An Agricultural Strategy for the 1990s.* A World Bank Country Study, Washington: The World Bank.

World Bank 1993b. *Water Resources Management.* A World Bank Bank Policy Paper, Washington: The World Bank.

World Bank 1994. *World Development Report 1994. Infrastructure for Development.* Washington: The World Bank.

The Challenge and Predicament of Human Rights Violations in the Mediterranean Context

Ihsan D. Dagi

Issues of human rights and democratization gained an immediate global interest, as well as hope at the end of the cold war. But initial hopes for a world respectful of human rights under democratic rules was hijacked by the eruption of nationalist fever, particularly in the former federal states of the communist world. But the revival of nationalism and micro-nationalism, far from removing the issues of human rights and democratization from the international agenda, has reinforced the need for international protection of human, and particularly, minority rights. The same need is also felt in the Mediterranean basin, where violations of human rights and the lack of democratic political process, particularly on the southern and eastern shores, breeds the sources of regional, as well as domestic instability and hence poses a security threat of a non-military kind to the North. Thus, this paper argues that the state of human rights in the Mediterranean countries concerns not only regional countries, but European security on a wider scale. It also argues that the southern Mediterranean countries should not be exempted from the global drive for the protection of human rights and provision of democratic models; such policies being justified due to the persistence of the radical Islamic challenge faced in this area.

Human Rights As an Issue of International Politics

Human rights have increasingly become a global concern, particularly since the late 1970s. It is just another scene in which we see the globalization of world politics as in issues of planetary policy on environmental protection and the quest for non-proliferation of nuclear weapons. Within the global politics of human rights there has emerged a multiplicity of linkages and interconnections that involve, but also transcend the nation-state. Thus the violation of human rights in one country may create unprecedented consequences among other countries, peoples and individuals. As territorial boundaries become increasingly insignificant, the transnational implications of human rights violations transpire as being unavoidable, which results in an increase in inter-state tension. The most striking case illustrating how human rights violations have a transnational impact and pose a security threat is the refugee crises. The cases of Bosnia, Rwanda and more recently Haiti, clearly illustrate that violations of human rights cannot be contained within national boundaries; that they have transnational implications which, in the end, invite regional or international interventions further complicating domestic problems.

The term human rights refers to basic physical integrity rights and civil and political rights as understood from a Western-liberal perspective. However, it must also be confessed that there is no universal consensus over what human rights consist of. There are arguments pointing to the distinct understanding of human rights in Africa, the Far East and Islamic world.[1] In fact these culture and tradition based conceptions are indigenous reactions to the universalization of human rights alongside a Western point of view and accompanying inclusion into Western foreign policy agenda. But points of disagreements are withering away with the end of ideological and superpower confrontations at the international level and the emergence of an international normative regime with the consensus among international political actors. Yet the seeds of confrontation derived from differing human rights conceptions should not be underestimated especially in the context of North-South relations since human rights have become another issue over which demands for international distributive justice clashes with a global liberal order, political and economic alike.

Human rights essentially deal with the way in which the political structure of a society is organized. Hence, at first sight it seems to belong to the realm of domestic politics. In the end, protection and promotion of human rights is a step towards the development of a human community that largely depends on the will and pursuit of the people who are affected by the provision of these rights. Therefore it seems that human rights fall within the domestic jurisdiction of the political community, that of the state. This is the realm of state sovereignty, which is traditionally regarded as the basis of society of states and where international politics ends.[2] However, normative and political transformation of international relations is forcing a convergence between the

1. J. A. Ferguson: 'The Third World', in J. R. Vincent (ed.), *Foreign Policy and Human Rights*. Cambridge: Cambridge University Press 1986: 215-22.
2. H. Bull: 'Human Rights and World Politics', in R. Pettman (ed.), *Moral Claims in World Affairs*. London: Croom Helm, 1979: 79-83.

domestic dimension of human rights and the international protection and promotion of them.

The concepts of national sovereignty and hence non-intervention which are often thought to limit the active promotion of human rights internationally are becoming more problematic in the face of changing structure of world economy and politics. The principle of non-intervention is based on the contested premises that we can know and distance state's internal and foreign affairs, that there is a domestic realm in which the state has the absolute sovereignty and in which foreign states have no legitimate claim whatsoever. [3] But in the contemporary world it is impossible to isolate a state's internal affairs from the effects of other states' or actors' policies and actions. If we cannot isolate a state's internal affairs from the outside involvement and influence, that is to say the impact of domestic and foreign policies of other states, it is very difficult to talk of the non-intervention principle as a guiding principle or common practice and value of world politics today. Thus, international protection and promotion of human rights as a fact has weakened this conventional view of world politics.

The changing and challenging international normative and political environment constitutes a significant constraint on national governments in their domestic human rights policy as well as foreign affairs. Democratic elements in the decision making process in the West, particularly in representational bodies such as the European Parliament, the Parliamentary Assembly of the Council of Europe, American Congress and national parliaments respond to the sensitivity of public opinion, which in turn make it very difficult to dismiss the growing demands for the inclusion of human rights issues in foreign policy making. As a result we have been witnessing an incorporation of the human rights concerns in foreign policy agendas of major powers.[4]

Additionally, activities of non-governmental human rights organizations are playing a crucial role in raising the global consciousness, and forcing the governments and inter-governmental organizations to take a stand. Furthermore international organizations like the United Nations and the Council of Europe have been trying to put human rights on the international agenda since their inception. The European Union too is emphasizing democracy and human rights in its policy of enlargement and bilateral

3. C. Beitz: 'Sovereignty and Morality in International Affairs', in D. Held (ed.), *Political Theory Today*. Cambridge: Polity Press, 1994: 37.
4. See for example, D.M. Hill (ed), *Human Rights and Foreign Policy*. London: Macmillan, 1989; A.G. Mower: *Human Rights and American Foreign Policy*. New York: Greenwood, 1987; P.R. Baehr: *The Role of Human Rights in Foreign Policy*, London: Macmillan, 1996.

relations. Recognizing human agony and security risks following human rights violations, the UN authorized intervention in Northern Iraq, Somalia and recently, Haiti. By the end of the Cold War and the disintegration of the Soviet Union, adherence to democracy and human rights has indeed become a common political identity on a global scale that sets the inspirational and political framework of the new international order. In fact, the CSCE process, from 1975 to the 1991 Paris Charter, represents the gradual legitimization of international human rights politics in world affairs.

To conclude, human rights as a subject of international politics poses two basic questions for individuals and policy makers. First of all it poses a moral question, a proper answer to which requires one to strip off all national allegiance. Does not an individual whose basic rights are violated by the state have a moral entitlement to turn to institutions and mechanisms going beyond national borders that may be able to bring justice to the individual concerned? The moral as well as legal answer is undoubtedly affirmative. There cannot be a moral defence of sovereign rights of the state so long as the state does not respect sovereignty and autonomy of the individual. On moral grounds the quest for justice and liberty transcends national boundaries and state sovereignty. The second question is a practical one; it takes us into the political realm which may create a forceful constraint over the policies of national governments and as such necessitates an evaluation of the international political milieu. Yet it may also prompt questioning of the 'secret agenda' of international human rights discourses. But one has to admit forthwith that human rights have acquired a moral, legal and political-practical place in the international arena, which in turn establishes the respect for human rights as a precondition for the international legitimacy of national government.[5] However the view that stresses instrumentalization of the human rights discourse is not groundless altogether. As now a legitimate subject of foreign policy making, human rights, beyond its universal principles and objectives can be utilized as a means to maximize national interest as a natural result of the very definition of 'foreign policy'. Yet politicization and instrumentalization of human rights in the international arena itself reveals the power, dynamics and support that human rights movements have acquired at the international level.

5. J. Vincent: *Human Rights and International Relations*. Cambridge: Cambridge University Press 1986: 130.

The Mediterranean as a Critical Region for Human Rights

Mediterranean countries, as a whole, are still some way from resolving overall questions of human rights. Despite differences in many areas, Mediterraneans share a heritage of authoritarianism, which remains as a historical residue in some societies while an actual practice in some others.

Looking at the Southern Mediterranean, human rights as understood within a liberal tradition do not constitute an element in the shaping of political regimes. The lack of democracy coupled with economic conditions creates obstacles for the provision and protection of civil and political rights. The Islamic fundamentalist challenge further complicates the domestic political process, and postpones the demolition of authoritarian regimes in the region. The countries that face powerful oppositions of radical Islamists, like Algeria, Tunisia, Morocco and Egypt, are tempted to clamp down on almost all opposition groups and this inevitably involves violations of basic human rights such as indefinite detention, disappearances, death in custody, press censorship, torture, etc.[6] Thus the Islamist challenge has dramatically led to an increased level of human rights violations. In those countries whose political leaders do not consider conciliatory measures but only military ones, the fear of fundamentalism is used as a pretext for the militarization of society. In turn this increases the influence and power of security forces in governmental process. Harsh measures taken against terrorists make the scope of human rights even narrower. In Egypt, for instance, security forces have extraordinary powers to keep suspects under detention without trial, and any association with a 'terrorist organization' can be enough for death penalty. In Algeria, Tunisia and Morocco, the participation of the Islamist opposition in the political process is banned, in Egypt seriously restricted. Civil liberties as a whole have been targeted as a means of curbing radical islamist movements. The way in which Islamist opposition is handled in Algeria weakens reformist, moderate and gradualist elements within the Islamist groups. It has led them to conclude that more revolutionary means are needed in order to get to power.

Political repression is nowadays fashionably justified in order to bar fundamentalists thought likely to capture power through electoral politics. But such a policy creates a vicious circle between the persistence of authoritarianism, thus evaporating popular support for existing regimes and hence further radicalization of politics. The fears of fundamentalism prevalent in the West are being skillfully manipulated by authoritarian leaders in the region. The impression that the West has exempted North Africa from the

---

6. See C. Humana, *World Human Rights Guide*. 3rd. Edition, Oxford: Oxford UP 1992; and *Freedom in the World: Political and Civil Liberties*. New York: Freedom House, 1992.

global drive for democratization and human rights provides the present governments with apparent international support for not democratizing the system, which in turn justifies the anti-Western stand of the fundamentalists. This is a process which fuels inter-state, inter-civilizational and intra-state frictions. If Huntington is right in his prediction of a clash of civilizations, the perceived open-ended support of the West for secular-authoritarian states of the Muslim world in the face of Islamic revival would certainly be the breaking point for an uncompromising confrontation between radical Islam and the West.[7] Such a break would also destroy any hope that remains for the integration of 'Islamic' movements and states into the international system, and force the former to resort to their 'revolutionary' deeds and discourse.

The threat of Islamic fundamentalism in the Muslim part of the Mediterranean is a transnational phenomenon that is considered likely to destabilize the whole region.[8] In fact there seems to exist a kind of common fate in resisting the spread of fundamentalism. Even the success of it in any regional country would make the spread easier. The Arab Maghreb Union, for instance, coordinate their security policies bearing such a prospect in mind. Current leaders of the Islamic Conference Organization seem to have adopted, as expressed in the last summit meeting, a similar strategy of containing radical Islamic movements and maintaining present political regimes by coordinating their policies against them. But if policies that are geared to prevent fundamentalist take-overs leave the people to choose between fundamentalists and dictators, nobody should expect any improvement in the condition of human rights.

Fundamentalism of any sort, religious or racist, stimulates and justifies the presence of the other. In North Africa, Islamic fundamentalists point to the revival of racist prejudices, attitudes and imposed limitations on Muslim migrants in Europe so as to vindicate their position and arguments; and conversely, the growing number of foreigners and their distinct life style increase the appeal of racists in the North. In contemporary international politics, the rights of minorities have gained a high profile interest, not only out of respect for ethnic nationalisms but out of fear that minority related issues cannot be confined within the country concerned, but are likely to pose regional, even international security risks. In a polity in which minority rights are not respected, a social and political tension and furthermore an armed conflict becomes inevitable. When conflict arises it quickly spills over neighbouring countries - at least in the form of population movements. The

---

7. S. Huntington, 'The Clash of Civilizations?', *Foreign Affairs* Vol. 72, (3), 1993.
8. H.B. Yahia, 'Security and Stability in the Mediterranean: Regional and International Challenges'. *Mediterranean Quarterly*, Winter, 1993: 6-14.

Mediterranean region is not free of ethnic tension, conflicts, and resulting ethnic migration; Mauritanians, Palestinians, Kurds, the Balkan Turks, Cypriots, Bosnians, Serbs, Albanians, etc. Disintegration of Yugoslavia and resulting ethnic clashes have revealed the need for a world in which the fears of ethnic groups being oppressed by majorities are eliminated through the establishment of pluralist policies that guarantee the rights of minorities.

Population flows do not always result from ethnic conflicts; revolutionary regime changes and economic hardship may also lead to mass population movement. Particularly in the South, both of these exist; a possible fundamentalist takeover in North Africa would create thousands, may be millions of migrants seeking refugee in the North.[9] The anxiety that French and Spanish governments have expressed regarding such a prospect on the other side of the Mediterranean is to a very large extent based on the concern that such a population movement would destabilize their own countries; a problem that France actually faces at present. North African migrants in France disturbs the demographic structure in some areas, serving as a support base for opposition groups (mainly Islamic) in North Africa and even threatening French democracy through providing an excuse for racist-ultra nationalist movements at home. Furthermore, the perceived threat of fundamentalism penetrating into the migrant communities in France leads the government to adopt strict measures to curb this process, but this, in the end, may create doubts about the plurality of French democracy and serves as a vindication for the National Front's enmity towards foreigners.

Being aware of the anxiety about population movements, some regional states exploit immigration release both as a foreign policy weapon and a solution for domestic economic hardship such as unemployment and lack of foreign currency; remember the Albanians fleeing to Italy. Unless a sustained economic development is achieved, it is hard to stop the economic refuge flows which are no longer acceptable to recipient countries of the North. The division of the Mediterranean between the wealthy North and poor South is a refugee generating fact. As the European Union members of Mediterranean countries adopt stricter immigration policies, the right for seeking refuge for political reasons is greatly threatened too. So there is a need to address the root cause, which are the prevailing political and economic conditions in the South. Without attempting to resolve the root cause, imposing stricter immigration policies is going to hamper the state of human rights for Southern people.

Human rights violations that generate a flow of refugees do not only create interstate tension and conflict, but an outside intervention might also be

9. J. Farley, 'The Mediterranean: Southern Threats to Northern Shares', *The World Today* February, 1994: 33-36.

provoked leading to further deterioration of regional stability. The war in Bosnia was poised to destabilize neighbouring countries as a result of the outpouring of refugees from there, and an outside NATO force under the UN umbrella has become heavily involved in the conflict. Earlier, following the Gulf War the exodus of thousands of Iraqi-Kurds into Turkey led to the intervention of multilateral forces setting up safe havens leading to the actual disintegration of Iraq. Recently, ethnic conflicts and resulting civil war with thousands of victims and refugees in Rwanda pulled France, the former colonial power, back into Rwandan domestic affairs. Most recently of all, waves of refugees resulting from the military takeover in Haiti constituted one of the reasons for American intervention within a UN mandate.

How To Meet the Human Rights Challenge

The presence of authoritarian regimes denying basic human rights, ethnic minorities from North to South demanding their minority rights, religious and racist fundamentalism complicating the prospect for democratization, and economic hardship, particularly in the South, all demanding immediate and radical solutions draw a picture of the Mediterranean that threatens the stability of the whole region, and is not very promising for the global prospects for democracy and human rights.

Mediterranean countries, first of all, should realize the fact that regional peace, security and stability is closely tied to the observation of human rights, the violation of which has implications which go beyond any particular country. When the issue is taken as a regional one, there is a need to establish an institutional framework with its principles and mechanisms to observe developments and deter human rights violations. Proposals for a Conference on Security and Cooperation in Mediterranean, the Mediterranean Forum or the Five + Five framework can provide such a platform. Especially a Helsinki type mechanism with its guiding principles, encompassing wider dimensions and follow-up meetings would constitute an encouraging and deterring regional mechanism for the future of human rights.[10] Such an attempt should naturally recognize the differences between Mediterranean countries but also get straight to reaching a consensus on the basic issues. The EU members among the Mediterranean countries should lead the process of institutionalizing the CSCM because they have the highest stake in regional stability. They are highly sensitive to developments in North Africa and the Balkans. In fact, a trade-off exists between the North — which is interested in containing

10. V. Ghebal, 'Toward a Mediterranean Helsinki-Type Process', *Mediterranean Quarterly*, Winter, 1993: 49-58.

immigration flows and establishing regional stability, and the South — which is in desperate need of economic development for which Northern help is necessary. The North can contribute to the economic and political development while the South provides the domestic conditions for regional stability.

In this context, economic development of the non-democratic countries in the region is crucial to prepare the conditions for the advancement of human rights. This would be encouraged by further integration of those countries economically into Europe and the world at large. Building economic inter-dependencies and institutional linkages would help the promotion of global values and prevent authoritarian tendencies to revive tribal nationalism or religious fundamentalism. Furthermore, the world at large should not exempt the development of pluralistic political regimes in the region. Particularly in the Muslim part of the Mediterranean, the democratization-fundamentalism dilemma should not be exaggerated. Any sign of double standards would weaken the moral as well as political standing of democracy, human rights and the West in the region. Authoritarian regimes would naturally exploit the fear of fundamentalism that prevails in the West to enhance and prolong their regimes. But, in the long term, the demands for representative politics cannot be barred by internal repression and international toleration of it. In the process of organizing a Mediterranean forum, the parties should be careful not to target any particular country or group. The impression that such attempts create a regional institutional body solely aimed at confining the spread of radical Islam will be damaging to the cause itself. Political Islam should not be portrayed as the common enemy since this would strengthen them not only in the Muslim countries of the South but in Northern Mediterranean countries where millions of Muslims live.

In short, the people of the Mediterranean should recognize the fact that in order not to be isolated from the international community in contemporary support for human rights, they should keep an eye not only on the provision of human rights in their own country, but also see the wisdom of setting up regional organizations to oversee developments in the whole area. The Mediterranean is too small a region to avoid the transnational repercussions of human rights violations.

Israel — Palestine

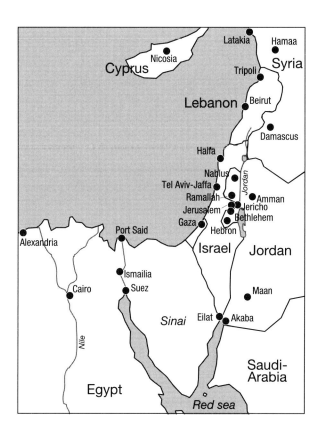

Human Rights and the Israeli-Palestinian Conflict

Torben Retbøll

The Israeli-Palestinian conflict is simple: two peoples, one land. The Jewish and the Palestinian people claim the same land. Both parties cannot achieve their goal at the same time. One excludes the other. That is why the conflict is so longstanding. That is why a solution is so complicated.

When discussing the question of human rights and the Israeli-Palestine conflict, it is useful to start with two official declarations:

1) Israel is a Jewish state, established on May 15, 1948, when the British gave up the old Palestine mandate.

2) Israel is a democratic state, whose declaration of independence promises equality under the law regardless of race, religion or gender.

Here already we meet the first problem, because the two principles are in conflict with each other. They cannot be combined. Israel cannot be both Jewish and democratic, as long as the state has got merely one non-Jewish citizen, and it does: about 20 percent of the country's inhabitants are non-Jews, most of them Palestinian Arabs.

Insofar as it is Jewish, it is not democratic. When the Jewish authorities have to choose between the Jewish and the democratic principle, they usually pick the former.

Another problem is the fact that the declaration referred to was never adopted as a part of Israeli law. Such a law would make it illegal to discriminate between Jews and non-Jews. That is not the case now.

No Constitution

A third problem is the fact that Israel does not have a constitution. In most states the rights and duties of citizens are written down in a constitution, which lays the foundation for the rest of the laws of the land.

Naturally, there is no guarantee that the state will respect its own constitution, but if you have a constitution, at least the citizens are able to see which rights they have in theory.

A committee was established to write a constitution in 1948. But the result is still not available. It has not been possible to agree on the words. How to formulate the rights and duties of the citizens in relation to the state? It is also difficult to define the concept 'a Jew.'

Israel is not the state of its citizens, as is the case with other states. Take Denmark for instance. The Danish state represents the Danish people, which consists of everybody with Danish citizenship, whether by birth or otherwise. Israel is different. There is no such thing as 'the Israeli people.'

Israel is a Jewish state, which claims to represent the Jewish people: the three million Jews in Israel as well as the twelwe million outside (in the *diaspora*). On the other hand, there is not much concern for the 20 percent of Israel's inhabitants who are non-Jews. They are Israeli citizens, true enough, but the state is not designed to defend their interests.

This is merely one example which demonstrates that Israel is different from all other states in the world.

European and Oriental Jews

To make the situation even more complex Israel contains European and Oriental Jews. The two groups are almost of the same size. The European (or Ashkenazim) come from Europe, the Oriental (or Sephardic) from the Orient, i.e. the Arab countries in North Africa and the Middle East.

During the first decades of Israeli history, the Labour Party and the European Jews dominated all leading posts in politics and the economy. In 1977, the Polish Jew Menachem Begin and his right-wing Likud-bloc won the election with votes from the Oriental Jews. Since then, right and left have had roughly equal representation in parliament (the *Knesset*).

Israel can be described as a society divided into three parts in which the European Jews are at the top, the Oriental Jews in the middle, while the Palestinians are at the bottom. This is merely a simple categorization based on ethnic criteria. Naturally, there are huge differences within each group if you look at income, private property and other assets.

These concepts and definitions are not just a dispute over words. They are essential, because the state is using them in theory as well as in practice: when parliament makes rules and regulations; when the authorities implement these rules and regulations.

Double Standards

Israel is a state which practices discrimination. The rights and duties of its citizens depend on who they are and where they come from. There are double standards. The state favours Jews. Palestinians are considered second or third-rate people. They are not required to do military service (as Jews are) and therefore they cannot receive the assistance and benefits to which former soldiers are entitled.

This discrimination is primarily found in the Occupied Territories (Gaza and the West Bank), but it also exists within the Green Line, i.e. Israel's internationally recognized borders until the Six Day War of June 1967. (Israel's annexation of East Jerusalem and the Golan Heights is not recognized by the international community). Discrimination is found in all essential areas:

1) education, work and housing
2) access to water and electricity
3) the right to organize and to express one self

Jews get better education, better jobs and better housing than non-Jews. Many Palestinian villages do not have access to water and electricity in the same quantities as Jewish settlements.

More than 92 percent of Israel's territory is reserved for Jews. It is owned by the state or the KLM, the Jewish National Fund, whose stated aim is to 'benefit people of Jewish religion, race or origin.' Non-Jews, about one fifth of the population, are not allowed to buy, rent, live on or work on this Jewish-owned area.[1]

Political Parties

For many years, the Palestinians were not allowed to form their own political parties, but only run on the Arab lists of Jewish parties. This changed with the election of 1988. Since then, they have been allowed to establish Arab parties, but only if they accept in advance the principle of Israel as a Jewish state which until recently did not recognize the PLO.[2]

The peace treaty of September 13th, 1993, meant that Israel recognized the PLO which was until then an illegal organization in Israel and the occupied territories. It also meant that the internal conflicts among Palestinians were

---

1. Uri Davis, *Israel: An Apartheid State*, London: Zed Books, 1987, Chp.1.
2. Nadim Rouhana, *Journal of Palestine Studies*, (71), spring, 1989.

sharpened. On the one hand the PLO endorsed the treaty, while on the other hand, Hamas and Islamic Jihad rejected it as too little and too late.

In spite of these problems, Israel and the PLO continued their negotiations concerning the practical implementation of the treaty. In April 1994, Israel began evacuating the Gaza Strip and the town of Jericho on the West Bank in order to prepare for the introduction of Palestinian autonomy in these areas. In September 1995, Israel and the PLO signed a new treaty extending Palestinian autonomy on the West Bank.[3]

There are Palestinian news agencies and publications, but they are subject to more censorship than the Hebrew media. What can be published within the Green Line cannot always be published in the occupied territories. Palestinian publications are closed down and Palestinian editors are deported without hesitation if they publish news and information unacceptable to Israel.

Many pro-Israeli observers outside Israel deny that any discrimination takes place. Discussions with them are not easy. In Israel, on the other hand, where this phenomenon is no secret, there is an extensive debate concerning the means and ends of the state.

The official argument for restricting or abolishing the rights of non-Jews is (as always) for reasons of national security. This argument is supported by the major political parties, the smaller religious parties and the militant settlers.

However, some Israelis claim that this discrimination is a disgrace on Israel's past and present, denying the official declarations about freedom and democracy, about peace and justice. This point of view is found in parts of the Israeli peace movement and parts of the Israeli press, which demonstrates courage and integrity by revealing and condemning the crimes for which their own state is responsible.

Hebron 1994

Baruch Goldstein is the name of an Israeli Jew. On February 25th, 1994, Goldstein, then 42 years old, killed at least 50 Palestinians who were kneeling in prayer in the Ibrahim Mosque in Hebron in the occupied West Bank.

Goldstein's massacre meant that the conflict between Israel and the Palestinians escalated once again. There was a curfew for the Palestinians of Hebron, but not for Jewish settlers. In the following days more people were killed or wounded. The massacre was condemned by all major parties. Not only the leader of the PLO, Yasir Arafat, but also the then leader of Israel, Yitzhak Rabin (who was killed by a Jewish settler in November 1995).

3. My articles in *Dagbladet Arbejderen*, October 12th and 13th, 1993; BBC World Service, *News Hour*, April 4th, 1994; *Information*, September 25th, 1995.

Later it emerged that the Israeli soldiers, assigned to guard the mosque, played a not too glorious role in the affair: they tried to prevent ambulances and doctors from reaching the wounded. One doctor and three nurses were wounded themselves while trying to assist the victims of the massacre. Several of those wounded died while waiting for medical assistance.

Later it also emerged that Rabin had been warned about Goldstein and his militant friends several months in advance: on October 14th, 1993, Goldstein had tried to burn down the mosque. Only quick action by the guards of the mosque prevented him from setting fire to the inflammable liquid he had poured over the carpet of the mosque. Two days later the Supreme Islamic Council in Jerusalem wrote a letter to Rabin, appealing for help:

Unfortunately we have never felt that the Israeli authorities have taken precautions against these hostile settlers.

Rabin did not respond.[4]

This was not the first time Israeli authorities were directly or indirectly responsible for the massacre of Palestinians. Other examples are Deir Yasin in April 1948, just before the establishment of Israel (254 dead); Doueimah in October 1948 (350-1,000 dead); Kibya in October 1953 (66-70 dead); Kafr Kassem in October 1956 (49 dead); Sabra and Chatila in Lebanon in September 1982 (1,800-3,500 dead); as well as the bombardment of the PLO headquarters in Tunisia in October 1985 (75 dead).

On May 20th, 1990, Ami Popper, a 21 year old Israeli, killed eight Palestinians in the village Rishon Lezion near Tel Aviv. This episode resembled Goldstein's attack in Hebron. However, while Popper appears to have been a mentally disturbed person, Goldstein was quite conscious about what he was doing.[5]

In comparison, PLO actions against Israel in the period 1967-82 cost 106 lives and 300 wounded (according to official Israeli figures).[6]

Kafr Kassem 1956

Israel uses tough methods. The rights of Palestinians are few or non-existant. The massacre of Kafr Kassem in October 1956 is a good example:

---

4. *Dagbladet Arbejderen*, March 9th and 11th, 1994.
5. My article in *Dagbladet Arbejderen*, June 20th, 1990.
6. *Le monde diplomatique*, July 1982.

On the same night as the Israeli army attacked Sinai, a curfew was issued in a number of Arab villages in Israel. This was done for reasons of national security.

In Kafr Kassem the curfew was announced one hour before it went into effect. A unit from the border patrol stopped some villagers on their way home. They had been working outside the village and could not possibly know anything about the curfew.

This situation had been predicted. But the commanding officer had responded: 'I do not want to see any sentimentality.' There was none: 49 persons were executed on the spot.

The aftermath of this episode is also worth noting: at first those responsible were given long prison terms, but these were quickly reduced.

The highest ranking officer was only condemned for having committed 'a technical error.' Another officer was later hired as an official with special responsibility for Arab affairs, a matter in which he knew a great deal.[7]

Levelled to the Ground

The tough methods are still being used. One method is to level a house to the ground should one of its inhabitants be suspected of terror, or should the house be in the way of a Jewish settlement.

On October 12th, 1993, the house of Mahmoud Mohammad Suleiman Khatib, home to ten people, was torn down.

Two police officers came looking for the family and told them the house would be destroyed. Since there was no telephone nearby, the family left the house to contact a lawyer. Shortly afterwards a force of 22 police cars entered the property followed by two tractors and a team of 80 workers. When the family returned, the house had been turned into rubble. Five hundred olive and peach trees on the property were also pulled up by the Israeli workers.

The next day the police came looking for the family again and showed them a document in Hebrew which the family could not read. The police said this was the order to destroy the home of the family. The document was dated October 13th 1993, the day after the destruction took place.

Khatib's property is on the outskirts of the village Hizmed and quite near Pizgat Za'ev, which is the largest settlement on the West Bank. It seems that the house was in the way of an extension of the Jewish settlement in the area.[8]

7. Sabri Jiryis, *The Arabs in Israel*, New York: Monthly Review Press, 1976.
8. *Dagbladet Arbejderen*, October 26th, 1993.

Torture

Another method is torture. For years, Amnesty International and the conservative British newspaper *The Sunday Times* have accused Israel of using torture, but this accusation has always been rejected by Israel.

In 1987, an Israeli government report concluded that agents from the Israeli secret service Shin Beth had been lying to the courts for 16 years and that they had been using 'psychological and physical pressure' against Palestinian suspects in order to get them to confess. But there was no demand to punish the agents.

In November of that year the then Israeli President Chaim Herzog made an official visit to Denmark. The Danish TV-News took the opportunity to ask him if the Shin Beth scandal undermined confidence in Israel's democracy. 'On the contrary. It increases confidence,' Herzog replied, and continued:

I know of very few countries where this would come out into the open, be officially investigated and where the authorities would ensure that it is never repeated and openly admit to the world that it happened and apologize. We are a model to the democratic world.

Torture is still being used, in spite of Herzog's assurance that it would never be repeated. But there is one change. The topic is no longer tabu. Brutality against Palestinians called in for questioning at Shin Beth is now openly being discussed in the Israeli media, says Joel Greenberg, Middle East correspondent for the *New York Times*, in an August 1993 article from Jerusalem. In June 1994, Israeli television showed a documentary film in which an Israeli soldier admits that torture of Palestinians is used by Shin Beth. Naturally, this development can be considered as progress. Or maybe it would be better if torture was not being used at all?[9]

Death Squads

A third method is death squads: Israeli soldiers who drive around disguised as Arabs and kill young Palestinians. Many groups, among them the Israeli human rights organization B'Tselem, have confirmed the existence of these patrols. Amnesty International and the Palestine Human Rights Information Centre in Jerusalem have also confirmed them directly or indirectly.

---

9. My book, *The Israeli-Palestinian Conflict on Danish TV* (in Danish), 1988; *Århus Stiftstidende*, August 18th, 1993; translated from the *New York Times; Jyllands-Posten*, June 16th, 1994.

However, Israel does not want information and debate about this matter. Reporters who tried to cover these activities have been physically abused and have had their press cards cancelled.

Jamal Ghanem, 19 years old, was one of the victims of the death squads. He was playing football when he was shot at close range by four Israelis who spoke Arabic and wore Arab clothes. Ghanem, who had seen the armed men coming towards him across the football field, raised his hands as a sign of surrender. Nevertheless he was shot and when he lay bleeding on the ground one soldier held him down with his foot while shooting again and again.[10]

Jewish Terrorists

The normal pattern is that Palestinians are arrested, charged and sentenced on a mere suspicion, while Jews (including the militant settlers) can get away with just about anything. But there are exceptions to the rule.

A small number of Jewish settlers have, in fact, been convicted of terror against Palestinians on the West Bank. However, they receive quite different treatment from that usually given to Palestinians:

Some of the guards sympathize openly with them, they get permission to leave the jail to visit their familiy and their sentences are often reduced.

On April 1st,1988, two settlers were released from jail. They were convicted of a series of attempts against Palestinians in the West Bank in 1983. One was released four months ahead of time and the other three months ahead of time, following a pardon from Israel's then president Chaim Herzog, who had already earlier reduced the second person's sentence of seven years for murder.

As Kurt Lyndorff, then Middle East correspondent for *Jyllands-Posten,* remarked, the timing of this was 'not exactly the most diplomatic,' because it was happening 'while young Palestinians are being given 14 months in jail for throwing stones during the popular uprising in the occupied territories.'

Kurt Lyndorff writes further that 'the pardon is being strongly attacked by Israeli human rights activists,' while on the other hand right-wing politicians demand that 'all members of the terror group be pardoned just as the majority of the 21 settlers have been since the trial in 1984.' Their crimes included attempts on three Palestinian mayors, attacks on schools and mosques as well as the Islamic University in Hebron, in which four were killed and 33 wounded.

On December 26th, 1990, three settlers who were sentenced to life long prison terms for murder were released having served less than seven years of the sentence. Amos Wollin, the Middle East correspondent for *Information,*

---

10. *Lies Of Our Times*, December 1992.

reported that outside the jail the three settlers were 'greeted by several hundred cheering relatives and supporters who carried them on their shoulders as heroes while people were dancing and singing nationalist songs.'

Representatives of the left wing movement protested this 'insult to law and justice' in Israel. The Peace Now movement called it 'a disgrace for democracy' and accused Chaim Herzog of supporting the right wing and abusing his right to pardon prisoners.

'This is a black day for human rights in Israel,' a spokesman for the Israeli League of Human Rights said. 'The release of these people after seven years is a strong message that when Jews are killing Arabs it is something to be forgiven, something not to be taken seriously.'[11]

Vanunu

The Jewish state is armed to the teeth with advanced military equipment. Some of it is produced in Israel, some of it comes from other Western countries (especially the USA). This equipment is being used for military actions against other nations, such as the bombing of an Iraqi nuclear reactor in 1981, and to maintain the so-called 'security zone' in the southern part of Lebanon.

It is a public secret that Israel also has nuclear weapons. About 200 nuclear warheads or 100 times the number which the USA suspects North Korea of having. But the USA is not demanding access to Israel's nuclear plants, nor is it threatening Israel with economic sanctions or war in order to get access.

Israel's 'secret' must not be revealed: at the moment the former Israeli nuclear technician Mordechai Vanunu is serving a sentence of 18 years for having talked about something which officially does not exist.

Vanunu was working in Dimona, the secret plant which produces plutonium for Israel's nuclear weapons. In 1986, he went to London where he told his story to the British paper The *Sunday Times*.

Just before his story appeared in the paper, he was lured to Rome where he was kidnapped by Israeli Mossad agents who brought him back to Israel.

In 1988, he was convicted for espionage and treason. The sentence was 18 years. Two years later, this verdict was confirmed by the supreme court.[12]

11. Kurt Lyndorff, *Jyllands-Posten*, April 2nd, 1988. Amos Wollin: *Information*, December 28th, 1990.
12. My articles in *Dagbladet Arbejderen*, September 30th, 1992 and March 11th, 1994; *Covert Action Quarterly*,(30), summer 1988; *Bulletin of the Atomic Scientists*, November 1992.

After the Hebron Massacre

On March 25th, 1994, five Palestinian human rights organizations issued a joint declaration[13], in which they evaluated the situation in the occupied territories one month after the massacre in Hebron. Tension was extremely high, they said, for the following reasons:

1) Hebron had been under 24-hour curfew for four weeks, causing total paralysis of the economic and social life of the community.

2) The one-year closure of the occupied territories had been strengthened and as a result, the social and economic life of the occupied territories had been critically affected.

3) Measures implemented by the Israeli authorities in response to the massacre had failed to address the root of the problem: armed settlers using violence against Palestinians.

4) The Israeli Defense Force had made the situation worse by their continued use of excessive and lethal force. At least 44 people had been killed by the military while hospitals reported having admitted more than 800 injured.

5) The Israeli authorities had detained at least 600 Palestinians, almost as many as were released in order to increase Palestinian confidence in the peace treaty of September 13th, 1993.

The five organizations called on the Israeli authorities to adopt the following measures: 1) The immediate removal of settlers and the withdrawal of military forces from Palestinian population centres in order to reduce provocations and confrontations. 2) A clear prohibition on the use of live ammunition in confronting demonstrators. 3) The immediate lifting of all curfews, and 4) The immediate lifting of the closure of the occupied territories.

The Security Council

On March 18th, 1994, the United Nations Security Council adopted a resolution condemning the Hebron massacre. This resolution was adopted after three weeks of deliberations in which the USA protested central passages about

---

13. Joint Alert by Five Palestinian Human Rights Organizations, *PeaceNet*, March 25th, 1994. Middle East Forum.

Jerusalem and the Israeli occupation. The USA abstained on two paragraphs in the text and thus marked a formal change in its foreign policy.

According to resolution No. 904 the Council was 'shocked' by the 'appalling massacre' and 'gravely concerned by the consequent Palestinian casualties ... as a result of the massacre.'

The resolution asked for 'measures to be taken to guarantee the safety and protection of the Palestinian civilians,' including 'a temporary international or foreign presence.'

The Council called upon Israel and the PLO to resume their negotiations for peace and called upon Israel to 'continue to take and implement measures ... with the aim of preventing illegal acts of violence by Israeli settlers.'

All 15 members of the Council voted for the resolution, paragraph by paragraph, except the USA, which abstained from voting on two clauses in the preamble. The first referred to 'occupied Palestinian territory.' The second referred to East Jerusalem as part of the occupied territory. By rejecting these passages, the Clinton government broke with the rest of the world and with its own political line since 1967.

But the President had much support from Congress in this matter. Both in the Senate and in the House of Representatives there were many members willing to sign a letter recommending Clinton to veto a resolution which referred to Jerusalem as an 'occupied' area.[14]

In October 1995, Congress went one step further when it adopted a resolution demanding that President Clinton transfer the Embassy of the USA from Tel Aviv to Jerusalem by no later than 1999. This is a *de facto* recognition of Jerusalem as Israel's capital. The resolution ignores the fact that the status of Jerusalem is an item for negotiations between Israel and the PLO which are not yet concluded.[15]

The USA not only supports Israel in the United Nations, but it also supplies a vital economic support of more than three billion dollars every year. This aid is given in spite of the fact that Israel is developing nuclear weapons and is violating human rights, on its own territory and outside.[16]

As long as the USA continues to finance the crimes of Israel, there is not much prospect for freedom and democracy or peace and justice in this part of the world.

14. Middle East Justice Network, US stands alone at UN Security Council, *PeaceNet*, March 26th, 1994. Mideast. News.
15. *Politiken* and *Jyllands-Posten*, both October 26th, 1995.
16. Jeffrey Blankfort, *Lies Of Our Times*, September 1992 and October 1993.

Created by the Enemy: Enemy Images as Nation Builders in Israel

Dag Jørund Lønning

Enmification is a process which goes beyond objective and historical conditions. It entails psychological processes that run very deep and which rapidly acquire their own momentum. Having an 'enemy' goes far deeper than merely having a competitor or an adversary. To have an 'enemy' is in a sense to be possessed. One no longer feels in command of one's own destiny; there is an enemy out there, and one's own fate is tied to his. And not only does one feel out of control, in an important psychological sense, one truly is out of control. Ultimately the enemy comes to dominate one's thoughts and feelings to the point where one is virtually bewitched by that combination of fear and hatred which Nietzsche defined as the 'absence of peace of mind'. In this sense the enemy comes to be defined as a malevolent kind of 'shadow' self.[1]

This essay addresses the effects of long-term conflict on individual life, worlds, and cultural interpretation frames in Israel/Palestine. The Israeli side is used as an example to demonstrate how the need of leaders for public legitimacy, as well as 'ordinary' people's urge to make cultural sense out of a very dangerous and complicated environment (interpretations which can backfire on politicians and other policy-makers) have worked together to produce a cultural meaning system, making *real* peace — meaning more than a cease-fire, between Israelis and Palestinians, extremely difficult and perhaps, in the foreseeable future, even impossible.

Conflict Dynamics and Cultural Manifestations

A nation involved in war consists, just like any other nation, of thinking and acting individuals. It consists of individuals doing war-like activities, but also of individuals living their lives and doing their ordinary tasks *in the shadow of the war*. This emphasis is put to show that wars and inter-group conflicts are nevertheless very special social contexts. Particularly so in protracted, long-term conflicts lasting for generations like the Israeli-Palestinian one.

1. Rieber and Kelly, 1991:

A conflict like the Israeli-Palestinian one has very different properties than a conflict which lasts only for a few years, even though the number of casualties may be much higher in the latter. The differences are in the interpretations made by the people who experience the conflict. In short-lived conflict, the war is conceptualized as an anomaly or a transient period. There was peace before the war and there will be peace afterwards. The war is a kind of liminal phase from one state of affairs to another. On the other hand, there has never been peace between Israelis and their Palestinian neighbours. There is no model, other than more or less Utopian history about Jews and Arabs living peacefully together in some ancient past, to build or conceptualize peace upon. Generation after generation has lived and died with the conflict. Conflict has become the normal order of things, or perhaps an anomalous normalcy. People are born, grow up, go to school, get married and have children — all *in the shadow of the conflict*. But, the emphasis, the hostilities are ever present. There is no way you can ignore them. Israel is far too small, and the conflict far too intense. Every individual has to relate to the hostile surroundings, not only socially — e.g. in terms of the avoidance of certain areas and certain people — but also culturally — in terms of making cultural sense out of the violent environment.

Here lies the greatest importance of the time-variable: Long-term intensive conflicts gradually become cultural or symbolic. A conflict which perhaps started with economic or territorial disputes, may gradually develop into a clash of totalized world-views or cultural meaning systems. Social groups are changed and formed through conflicts. There is no more effective 'cure' *against* cultural diversity and nothing more effective *for* inducing group cohesion than a long-term violent conflict. The possibility of obtaining direct and accurate information about 'the Other' shrinks drastically, and — theoretically through the processes of group-dynamics — and empirically — through the culture-building work of politicians, rhetoricians and lay-men alike, interpretations are inseminated and spread to ever widening audiences. One very effective strategy is the production of enemy images.

Through conflict dynamics, such frames gradually become more than just interpretations. They become conflict-maintaining mechanisms in their own right. In Israeli parliamentary elections — like in any other — politicians have to relate to the sentiments and interpretations held by people on the ground in order to gain new votes. Below we will see how even the current peace process has been interpreted, both by leading politicians as well as by laymen, according to a logic inherent in established enemy images.

In my previous work[2], I have tried to develop a particular methodology to be able to cope with such complicated issues. *First*, you need a theory of conflict dynamics, some aspects of which have been outlined above. *Second*, to validate this theory you need a special kind of data. Important concepts are rhetoric, macro-political events and individual interpretations. You need to scrutinize the public debate, as well as the rhetoric and the programmes of politicians and parties. Furthermore, you need to describe and analyse events which are considered important by the contending parties. And, most importantly, you need to gain access to individual interpretations of rhetoric, events and personal lives in the midst of conflict. To try to conceptualize the individual life-worlds, is the building block of a theory of conflict resolution which puts the individual at centre stage. *Third*, you need to gain access to a social field which may generate this kind of data. The particular field which has been the object of my studies — inter-ethnic dialogue and cooperation groups between Israelis and Palestinians — can be conceptualized as important barometers for studying the ethnic boundaries between Israelis and Palestinians. Challenging this boundary through attempts to create communication and friendship, they become the object of sanctions and contempt.

A Nation Built on Conflict

As a state, Israel is a unique phenomenon. The state was defined more or less before the nation itself existed as an *imagined community*.[3] The state was even defined before the nation was physically present. The 'usual' separatist process is the definition of a nation, followed by a claim for territory. The Israelis had to go the other way around. The growth and eventual victory of Zionism — the movement which has as its primary ideology the creation of a pure Jewish state to save the Jews from eternal persecution — has been described as one of the most astonishing and consequential historical developments of our century. Zionism started as a European elitist, non-religious phenomenon, but has grown into a world-wide movement supported by rich and poor, religious and non-religious, Western, African and Oriental Jews alike.

Likewise, the Israeli state: In the years following the state's formation, large numbers of Jews started to come to Israel from other parts of the world, particularly from Arab countries and the Balkans — Mizrahim and Sephardim. These people spoke Arabic, or other languages, brought with them totally different cultural traditions than the Europeans — the Ashkenazim — and even

2. Lønning, 1995.
3. Anderson, 1991.

adhered to different religious practices. The ideology of Zionism, on the other hand, was created in Europe. The symbols which the first immigrants used to communicate their new Israeli identity were also European, as is the image Israel has tried to establish about being 'the West in the Middle East'.
The Israeli leadership — also Ashkenazi — thus faced two serious problems or challenges. First, how to create a nation out of people with such different linguistic, cultural and partly religious traditions? Second, how to understand and interpret the presence and resistance of the local population in Palestine?

Some forty or fifty years later we can see a state, as well as a more or less (if not politically) united Israeli nation. It is still a 'European' state, though, with Ashkenazi Jews dominating both political and economic life. Cultural traditions of Sephardi and Mizrahi Jews exist predominantly within ethnic enclaves and on private backstages, but are not used as symbols to communicate the typical Israeli. But still we see unity. With such an extremely difficult point of departure, how has this been accomplished?

The impressive construction and insemination of a new language , modern Hebrew, has surely made an important contribution, but this in itself was not enough. A particular Israeli identity had to be constructed. A common denominator — bridging internal divides — had to be sought.

The Israeli answer to its two main challenges was to connect the two into one major frame of interpretation. The second challenge provided the answer to the first one. Zionism — the state's official ideology — had to be interpreted in its new local context. The Jews had achieved their state, but this state proved not to be safe. Thus, the prime ideal motivation of Zionism — to save the Jews from pogroms and persecutions — could be continued in the new setting. Despite all the differences, there is one common frame of historical experience which binds Jews, as being Jews, together, and that is suffering. Historically, Jews have been scapegoats over and over again when things have not been as they should be in their respective countries. Particularly so in Europe, but also — although less fervently — in Arab countries.

It is exactly this common historical tradition which became the backbone of the new Israeli national identity, and it also provided the interpretational logic for the conflict with Israel's Palestinian neighbours. Zionism says that Jews are persecuted *because they are Jews*. The hostility of the Palestinians was presented as yet another potential pogrom directed at Jews, being Jews. The nationalist aspects of the Palestinian struggle was under-emphasized, the Palestinians' moving rationale was — in Israeli national and international rhetoric — an urge to throw the *Jews*[4] into the sea.

In the first decades of Israel's existence, Palestinians were openly labelled anti-Semites by Israeli leaders. For example, the symbol of the Holocaust —

one of the greatest evils of humanity — has been taken out of its historical context and repeatedly been projected at the Palestinians who thus are presented as being capable of repeating what the Nazis did, if not harshly prevented by Israel from so doing. Symbols created during the Holocaust flourish in Israeli public discourse.

The most outspoken of the Israeli Prime Ministers was Menachem Begin. He repeatedly compared Arafat with Hitler, the PLO covenant with *Mein Kampf,* and even wrote in a letter to President Reagan after the invasion of Lebanon 'that the destruction of Arafat's headquarters in Beirut had given him the feeling that he had sent the Israeli army into Berlin to destroy Hitler in his bunker'.[5]

While perhaps not quite so extreme, such symbolic messages have been given at various occasions by every Israeli PM from 1948 until today.

Speech acts and speeches have consequences. Discussing the rhetorical devices leaders must develop to persuade followers, Bailey[6] writes: 'Because he must take action, the leader strives to simplify situations both for himself and for his followers... In fact, to work successfully on the mass he must... attempt to present them with a unitary set of values, freed as far as possible from qualification, ambiguity, and alternatives'. Messages such as the ones exemplified here, gain their own dynamics and repercussions when they are received and interpreted on the grassroots level. They provide an interpretative apparatus for the individual Israeli both to communicate his Israeli identity and explain the conflict with the Palestinians. A collective identity — 'us', the good, against 'them', the evil — has been developed through such processes.

Establishing connotations to such horrible manifestations of Jewish suffering, bridges internal differences by the use of one central logic: We are all Jews, and we must stand united in the face of our collective enemy. The most central symbol used to communicate Israeli identity is not 'what we are', but 'what we are not'.

4. During violent times, the term *Jew* consistently replaces *Israeli* in official and unofficial rhetoric in Israel. When the perpetrators are Palestinian, newspapers report about the *Jew* who was knifed, the *Jew* who was stoned, etc. Regarding internal crime, both perpetrator and victim are *Israeli*. Naturally, this is consistent with the logic of Zionism which states that Jews are persecuted beacuse they are Jews. See Lønning, 1995, for further exemplifications.
5. Segev, 1993: 399-400.
6. Bailey 1988: 54-55.

Emily Brontë uses the metaphor of the seed in her famous novel *Wuthering Heights*. When the seeds of hate are sown, they grow roots, ripen and bear fruits. I collected countless examples of rhetoric closely resembling Begin's during my fieldwork, from among politicians, academics and laymen. In the public debate, such symbolic production flourishes.[7]

Regarding the current peace process, many Israelis I have spoken to see the withdrawal to the borders of 1967 as equal to withdrawal to 'Auschwitz borders' — entrenched with a surrounding evil enemy. Furthermore, an uproar was created in Israel when it became known that Lech Walesa planned to invite Yasir Arafat for the 50th anniversary for the liberation of Auschwitz. Scores of Letters to the Editor appeared, and 'Oleg' — the Jerusalem Post cartoonist — pictured Arafat outside Auschwitz saying: 'It's never to late to learn a thing or two'. Foreign Minister Peres had to intervene personally, and could, after a couple of weeks, confirm that Walesa had changed his mind.

The result of such symbol production, along with actual violent events which have been interpreted according to the logic inherent in such frames, has been the production of an immense fear among Israelis.

Israelis involved in inter-ethnic dialogue with Palestinians have a large repertoire of stories to tell about fellow Israelis, who politically are ready to compromise with the Palestinians, but who nevertheless refuse to join a dialogue group out of fear. Dialogue members are told how lucky they are to be alive after having returned from a dialogue meeting in a Palestinian area. People are virtually terrified, and carry images about hordes of Palestinians with knifes waiting to attack the first *Jew* they meet. The theme of fear also surfaces at almost every Israeli-Palestinian dialogue meeting, where Israelis try to make Palestinians understand their fear, and the great personal sacrifice it is for them to be present.

Jerusalem is a very divided city, as is the rest of Israel/Palestine. The ethnic *boundary* almost paralleling a physical *border*. Israelis almost never go to the East if they are not forced to do so. During one of my fieldwork periods I lived on the so-called Green Line, the border separating pre-1967 Jerusalem. No violent incidents happened here during my stay, and the particular area where I lived is also known to be quiet. Nevertheless, almost all the Israelis I know refused to meet me there out of fear of what could happen to them. 'No, you have to come to the New City. I will be killed if I meet you there', people often told me.

If you compare this with the Palestinians, who have had probably four times as many casualties than the Israelis in the long war, this fear is more or less absent. Or, when it is there, it is directed at soldiers and other officials of

7. See Lønning, 1995 for examples.

the Zionist state, not at the individual Israeli. Thus, I believe the Israeli fears hardly originate from actual incidents alone. They are definitely fuelled by such incidents, but the roots can be ascribed to symbolic and ideological manipulation. These fears are an important and essential part of Israeli identity, and are frequently used by individuals to communicate this identity. 'Fear is internal to Israelism', one informant told me.

While Palestinian fears are directed at a particular collective political manifestation of their enemy, Israeli fears are directed at an almost meta-physical inherent property —some kind of a violent urge — of the individual Palestinian. The Israeli Anthropologist, Danny Rabinowitz, has studied these fears, and argues:

...in the eyes of Jewish Israelis, the stereotypical Arab is not so much one who is inherently stupid or incapable, as one whose first priority is to harm Jews at all times, regardless of costs and benefits.[8]

I have collected many examples of manifestations of such fears.[9] For example, the hysteria which was created in the Jewish part of Jerusalem when two young Palestinian girls were spotted in a hardware store with a special kitchen knife they wanted to buy for their mother. Or the story of an Israeli who wanted to commit suicide and figured that the best way was to wander unarmed into the West Bank. He ended up being delivered to Israeli soldiers by Palestinian Intifada activists.

That this feeling of fear and victimization crosscuts almost the entire Israeli political landscape was revealed to me during several inter-ethnic dialogue meetings. Most of the Israelis who attend such meetings are in favour of establishing some kind of a Palestinian state, either with or without East Jerusalem as its capital. These people are considered very radical inside Israel, and expect to have their radical ideas acknowledged by the Palestinians. This is not what happens, however. Because even though these Israelis are ready to compromise, they legitimate this readiness as an act of sacrifice and empathy on their part. Assuming that their Palestinian counterparts are ready to admit their historical guilt, the logic is often as follows: 'We are ready to forget what you have done in the past, and make a fresh start'. However, as Palestinians enter the dialogue with the exact opposite point of departure — that the Zionist occupiers are the ones to blame, and that the Palestinians are the ones who make sacrifices through their willingness to meet representatives of these occupiers in the midst of occupation — expectations and assumptions clash.

8. Danny Rabinowitz, 1992: 518.
9. See Lønning, 1995.

Israelis expect the Palestinians to recognize their radical ideas, Palestinians, on the other hand, often come out seeing these Israelis as extremists who are unwilling to admit their own past mistakes. For Israelis who advocate Palestinian rights in their own society, meeting Palestinians and experiencing not being accepted, can be emotionally very painful. As a result, many people— both Israelis and Palestinians — quit after *the first meeting*.[10]

Israeli sentiments of lurking danger and victimization has led to the development and articulation of another very important national symbol; *security*. That Israelis should be preoccupied with security would perhaps seem quite natural, taking terrorist activity into account. When you start digging a little deeper into the meaning of this concept, however, you nevertheless find that it means far more than securing politicians, airports and buses. It is not just a technical concept, it is a cultural construct in its own right which is closely connected to the rest of the symbolic universe used to communicate Israeli-ism. Security can be looked upon as a summation of the necessary strategies of how to deal with the Palestinians to prevent what happened yesterday — meaning pogroms and persecutions — from happening today. The symbol *'security'* carries positive connotations, and if an act can be legitimized according to the logic of the symbol, it will generally be accepted in the Israeli public. This legitimization occurred time and again in the media when Israeli soldiers shot Palestinian children — even when a 17 month-old baby was shot in the hands of his father! Regarding such incidents I was told many times — (even by left-wingers) something along the lines of 'it's sad that children must die, but it was probably necessary for security reasons'.

When a terrorist incident occurs in Israel, boundaries are placed on the Occupied Territories. Politicians employ the security concept as legitimization. Palestinians entering Israel are required to carry special permits, however, and there are, as far as I know, no incidents where captured terrorists have carried such permits. It is more or less impossible to control the whole border effectively, and persons wanting to detonate a bomb in Israel can easily manage to enter without permits. This is general knowledge among Israelis. Thus it is impossible to argue that closing the Territories leads to a halt in terrorism. On the contrary, it often leads to acts of revenge by Palestinian extremists. It has other effects, however. Firstly, it is collective punishment, as the flow of capital into Palestinian society is severely damaged. Thousands of Palestinians work in the Israeli construction industry. Secondly, and more importantly, it is a temporary measure against fear; simply reducing the

10. The difficulties of *the first meeting*, is well conceptualized using acting terminology. See Lønning, 1995.

Palestinian presence in Israeli streets. The mere event of facing and meeting Palestinians can produce fear.[11]

During the long-term closure in the Spring/Summer of 1993, Israeli state television had a long feature reportage called 'A smiling Jerusalem', where many Israelis were interviewed about how happy they were when they did not have to meet so many Palestinians any longer.

There is another very important symbol in Israeli discourse; *the soldier*. The Israeli soldier has won considerable fame on the battlefield, and he has also turned into something of a national sanctity. *'Our boys and girls'* is the common terminology for the Israeli Defence Forces. Men have to serve three years of army duty in Israel, women two. Furthermore, men have to do one month reserve duty a year until they become 50 years of age. This means that a considerable part of adult life is spent in the army, and Israeli society is constructed in such a way as to make this constant flow of personnel smooth and uncomplicated. As there is no possibility for legal conscientious objection,[12] nearly every Israeli, although not older immigrants, have experienced army life. It is thus a matter for constant discussion in the Israeli public debate. The average Israeli is immensely proud of the army, as it is the organization which — first and foremost — is responsible for providing the Zionist state with *security* against the external threat. Until now it has managed to do so with great efficiency.

The army pervades deeply into Israeli civilian life. First, without army experience, a lot of higher jobs are impossible to get. Secondly, as soldiers can be spotted on almost every street and street junction in Israel, there are several unwritten laws about how to relate to them. For example, car-owners are obliged to pick up soldiers before ordinary hitch-hikers.[13]

The soldier is a very potent symbol, but a symbol which regularly becomes the object of discussion in inter-ethnic dialogue meetings. Obviously, Palestinians have a totally different attitude to Israeli soldiers, and have a large repertoire of stories to tell about the atrocities of the Zionist army. Israeli dialogue members told me how painful these meetings could be. They had themselves witnessed such violence by the soldiers, but still had great emotional difficulties accepting it. At a dialogue for youth which I attended, the whole meeting ended in a catastrophe when the Palestinians staged a nationalist song about a young girl being mistreated by soldiers. Several of

---

11. See Lønning, 1995; Rabinowitz, 1993.
12. The number of young people going to jail for refusing to do army duty in The Occupied Territories increased after the outbreak of the *Intifada*. However, most of these people are members of the organization *Yesh Gvul* — 'There is a limit'.
13. A fact which hits Palestinian citizens of Israel hard.

the Israelis started crying, and they all left the scene claiming that the Palestinians had no interest in peace at all. After the incident, several Israelis told me that they know that such incidents have happened, and could not directly explain their reaction. One boy nevertheless told me that he felt as though he himself stood accused. The Israelis saw the song as an attack on them being Israeli Jews, not as — as was intended by the Palestinians — an attack on the occupation.[14]

I have now sketched what I believe to be a cultural meaning system with a great interpretative potential. Nearly every event and development concerning the Israeli-Palestinian conflict can be interpreted according to the inherent logic of this scheme. Israeli national identity is a very politicized identity, developed in opposition to an external enemy. And the development of the symbols and interpretations used to produce and communicate this identity can be conceptualized according to what Barth calls 'a logical train of thought':

linking an increasing number of facts or interpretations to one particular idea or schema... the idea or scheme gains in generality and validity, and progressively emerges as a more central theory in the cosmology.[15]

However, the problem begins when the macro-political environment which this meaning system was designed to explain changes. The current Israeli-Palestinian peace process has unleashed a great deal of ideological work in Israel; how is one to interpret a situation when your century-long arch-enemy suddenly becomes a political ally? The result of the ideological work which probably has taken place inside the Israeli government, has become what I do not hesitate to call a 'hybrid'. In their efforts to 'sell' the peace process to the Israeli public, politicians utilize the logic inherent in already established ways of seeing the Palestinians. The emphasis is put on *separation* — getting rid of the Palestinians, and thus partially at least, the realization of the Zionist ideology; the creation of a pure Jewish state. This is the bait which is to sell peace. The focus is on the enhancement of internal security; getting rid of the Palestinians means less fear. This was pondered over again and again by the late Rabin in his many speeches — called 'sensitizing campaigns' — after Oslo.

The rhetoric has been continued by the new Peres administration. In a statement supporting the peace process, the Israeli Foreign Minister Ehud Barak used a logic which clearly shows the connection between ethnically produced enemy images and politics in Israel: 'Those who have a Greater Land

14. See Lønning 1995: 108-18.
15. Barth 1987: 50.

of Israel vision say we should remain involved with the Palestinians who hate us'. (Pointing to Lebanon and Bosnia as examples of where mixed populations proved disastrous).[16]

Subjects which have been discussed at cabinet meetings include making closures of the Territories permanent, the building of a great fence between Israel and the Territories, etc. There have thus far been very few, if any, official statements saying that the occupation — producing human humiliation and suffering — was perhaps not such a good idea in the first place (cf. the statement by Barak).

It is easy to turn into a moralist, however, because a central question is: Could Israeli politicians actually have done otherwise? Probably not! Admitting ones own historical mistakes and utilizing altruistic concepts of peace would probably have failed, simply because long-term conflicts lead to the development of zero-sum world views. When it comes to the strategy which is currently being practised, it can be understood according to the cultural ideas people already hold.

The concept of peace which is being processualized does not challenge established images, but rather confirms these: There is an enemy out there, but if we can get rid of him, peace will be bestowed upon us.

Virtually every parliamentary election in Israel turns into a debate about which party can provide the most effective *security*. The Right has its answer with expulsion or continued occupation. The peace-process is being sold as the answer of the centre-left government coalition. There is no political party in Israel — apart from a few extreme leftist groups — which supports the idea of bi-nationality or integration.[17] It is also very telling that the dialogue groups — which actively work to bring Israelis and Palestinians together — has only experienced a very slight increase in members since the Oslo Accords.

In a long-term conflict like this, the 'grassroots'- level of the conflict are now virtually defining the political space for politicians involved in macro-political conflict resolution debates.

Group Dynamics and Cultural Cosmologies

Macro-political variables are definitely very important in a discussion of nationalist and ethnic conflicts, but — as Kapferer[18] so strongly emphasizes — there must be a deeper reason why nationalist symbols have such profound

---

16. *Jerusalem Post*, Nov. 24th, 1995: emphasis added.
17. See Barzilai and Peleg 1993.
18. Kapferer 1988.

effects on the individual. Such logic may create foes from friends virtually over night.

Kapferer argues that nationalists must make use of ontologies — or 'modes of being' — which are relevant to people's daily lives in order to be successful. Nationalism itself must take on a cultural shape — in the sense of actively exploiting experiences and ideas which people already hold. Another effective strategy is to work out answers to existing cultural dilemmas. In short, it must provide interpretative answers which make sense to the individual.

Barth argues that for new ideas and symbols to spread, they must add meaning *to* and not subtract *from* existing interpretations. A cultural identity system which has been developed through almost a century as an opposition to an enemy, cannot be changed overnight by the signing of a paper. The politicians who try to persuade Israelis about the advantages of 'Oslo', do exactly as Barth says. They try to add to established meanings, not challenge them. If I am correct in assessing that the presence of a Palestinian enemy has provided the cultural material upon which the *Israeli* — as opposed to *Jewish* — ethnic/national identity has been constructed, then novel ways of conflict resolution — directly challenging enemy images at the individual level — have to be developed.[19]

So far, so good, but where exactly did the individual go in all this? These interpretations have been made through a methodology which takes the individual's own interpretations as its point of departure, but the representations have ended up in something which looks like a very homogeneous and static picture of a collective. In a recent, inspiring work, Cohen (1994) —- after providing many examples of internal individual differences within groups — asks a very thought-provoking question: 'How is it that groups can cohere when their members perceive significant differences between them? How can the group 'speak' as a whole to the rest of the world when the internal discourse among its members is so diverse?'[20]

The strategy of producing external scapegoats to preserve internal unity is one strategy; one that is probably as old as the history of humans. I believe, however, there are other suggestions regarding Cohen's inspiring questions. My findings through fieldwork in Israel/Palestine revealed that Israel is as divided and individualistic as any modern society, perhaps even more so. Conflict-lines between, for example, modernists and traditionalists, rich and poor, black and white, orthodoxy and reformism, religious and secular, cross-cut the society. However, as in the top level of a segmentary lineage model, in dealings with Palestinians, the vast majority agrees on the basic principles

---

19. Newspapers are full of advertisements reminding people about this unwritten rule.
20. Cohen 1994: 23.

— albeit using different strategies — and that is the promotion of security and Zionism.

A film-maker opposing the occupation staged a film about Israeli soldiers serving on the West Bank in Jerusalem's 'Cinemateque' in 1993. This film created a lot of fuss in Israel, as it contained a lot of interviews with soldiers who had taken part in assaults on Palestinian children, etc. It was thus not difficult to read from the film that the film-maker was in favour of a total Israeli withdrawal. The means used and the main message was nevertheless more special. The film contained very little material on the Palestinians suffering under the occupation. The soldiers discussed how participating in the fight against children had affected *them and their families* — regarding psychosomatic problems and sleep-deprivation, etc. The main message of the film was that *the occupation is bad for Israel*, the Palestinians were absent. The film-maker on his part may very well be preoccupied with the Palestinians, but he has probably picked the only means which can communicate the problems of the occupation effectively to a wide Israeli audience. It is bad for *us*.

This is an indication of the problem of individuality in the midst of conflict — there may simply be no room for him as the conflict becomes totalized and collective. Prevalent interpretations and discourses may become hegemonic.

This is a 'brutal' statement indeed. If a society consists of thinking and living individuals with idiosyncratic ideas and experiences — Israel is actually a democracy — how can such individuals, to this degree, become captives of something as abstract as cultural meanings? Bourdieu utilizing the theory of hegemony — or *doxa* — argues convincingly that people are the makers of their own imprisonment through using and internalizing the discourses of the ruling class. Bourdieu's conceptualization of a doxic field — '(it) goes without saying because it comes without saying'[21] — definitely looks appropriate in the Israeli case. However, it is rather difficult to see the rulers and the ruled on the Israeli side regarding the Palestinians. Zionist pioneers probably used active manipulation to gain followers, but today the picture is far more shady. And with the peace-process the whole thing has turned upside-down, with people's ideas to a large extent defining the political space of leaders (see above).

Thus we have to look for more theory to be able to interpret this collectivization. Let us first approach our problem through the lens of theories of ethnicity. Barth's[22] seminal contact-paradigm stands firm. However, one must expect context to have a decisive influence on ethnic symbols and ethnic ideologies, and the Israeli-Palestinian conflict is obviously a very special kind

21. Bourdieu 1977: 167.
22. Barth 1969.

of social environment, very different from market-places in so-called multi-cultural societies, for example. How can we modify Barth's ideas to the study of ethnic conflict?

Some of the criticism which has been directed at Barth's work relates to his emphasis on the arbitrariness of ethnic symbols. I am not going to reiterate the positions within the so-called primordialist-formalist schism, but rather confirm that I share this scepticism. Particularly when it comes to the Israelis, my hypothesis is that the symbols which were used to produce this new identity were probably the only ones which could have produced the desired effect; simply because they — symbols of pogroms — were not arbitrary. These symbols probably have great personal significance to almost every Jew. Still, however, these symbols were utilized to interpret an adversary, and Israeli national identity has been produced in the face of this adversary. Thus, the contact paradigm stands, but we cannot totally reject primordial attachments.[23]

An interesting attempt to reconcile these different theoretical approaches to the study of ethnic conflict has been made by Scott Jr. Following Spicer, he argues that ethnic groups are formed in the face of opposition from an 'other'. Emphasizing the difference between Spicer and Barth, Scott argues:

Barth maintains that social interaction and acceptance are frequently the cornerstone on which ethnic distinctions are built and that cultural differences can persist *despite* inter-ethnic contact. Spicer, on the other hand, argues that these differences can persist *because* of the inter-ethnic contact, especially if the contact is one of opposition.[24]

I will quote Scott's further arguments at some length, because I believe they are particularly illuminating in the Israeli-Palestinian case:

We no longer need to dichotomize persistent and fluctuating ethnicity; rather, we can now place them along a continuum of *degree of ethnic solidarity*. This dimension constitutes the *dependent variable* in our model. And we need only one *independent variable* with which to explain it, namely, the *degree of opposition*. According to Spicer's theory, then, the degree of an ethnic group's identity will vary in direct proportion to the amount of opposition encountered by the group, the greater the opposition, the greater the degree of identity, and conversely, the lesser the amount of opposition, the lesser the degree of identity.[25]

Regarding primordial sentiments and symbols, Scott goes on to argue:

---

23. Naturally, this is exactly what inter-ethnic dialogue groups are all about.
24. Scott Jr. 1992: 158; emphases in original. Spicer 1971.
25. Ibid: 163; emphases in original.

But what role does primordialism play in this model? It seems best to place it as an *intervening variable* between the dependent and independent variables, such that the greater the degree of opposition, the greater the primordial sentiments engendered, and the greater the degree of ethnic solidarity expressed by the group. Opposition, then, does not lead directly to ethnic solidarity, but operates indirectly through the psychological mechanism of primordial sentiments. When opposed, members of an ethnic group will conjure up images of their 'glorious past', often intertwined with images of their ancestors' deprivation and suffering, which helps further to strengthen ethnic ties.[26]

Scott argues further that:

The direction of causation in this model is essentially circular, in that an increase in the belligerent expression of an ethnic group's solidarity or movement will lead to a greater opposition mounted against it, which in turn, will result in a further increase in the solidarity or movement, and so on. This circular causation is mainly what accounts for the escalating nature of ethnic conflict; once it begins, it seems to take on a life of its own, reaching ever higher degrees of irrationality and violence, and, at the same time, increasingly eluding attempts to resolve it.[27]

I believe this theory is valuable particularly in its emphasis on *context*. As an undergraduate I was very attracted to newer anthropological models emphasizing diversity on every aspect and sceptical to coherence. Looking around myself in Norway on the verge of the 21st century, I find no reason to reject such wisdom. Still, studying the Israeli-Palestinian conflict, I discovered that individual freedom has its limitations. However, just as there is a diversity of individuals and social situations, there is also a diversity of macro-political contexts. Some contexts are more demanding and extreme than others regarding the claims they put on the individual. And extreme contexts — we are talking about long-term conflict here — may also lead to the development of 'extreme' and rigid symbolic systems.

Scott's independent variable — the degree of opposition a particular group faces — goes a long way in explaining the relation between conflict escalation and symbolization, as well as differences and similarities between different conflicts. It also relates to the passion of ethnic conflict, and thus, indirectly, the restraints on individuality which is a concomitant aspect of conflict escalation.

However, to directly approach the (fate of the) individual in the midst of conflict, I have found it useful to cross the boundaries of anthropology and

26. Ibid: 163; emphasis in original.
27. Ibid: 164.

search within the discipline of social psychology; a discipline which has worked quite extensively on the problems of individuality, group dynamics and inter-group conflict.

Interesting social psychological theories have been developed, particularly regarding the concept of *enemy images,*. This is a concept which has become very popular in recent years, both in academic as well as in public discourse. However, we see few concomitant attempts to provide the concept with analytical properties. One such attempt has been made by Spillmann and Spillmann. The authors' main point is that enemy images have functions. They serve as devices to order and interpret a violent and conflictual reality, and may thus be conceptualised as some kind of *explanation-prediction-control-schemes*[28] — or, if we prefer, cultural interpretation frames.

Regarding ethnicity, what we have become accustomed to call *ethnic stereotypes* may have the same functions. Spillmann and Spillmann, however, make a qualitative distinction between stereotypes and enemy images: 'The function of enemy images corresponds to the function of stereotypes with the decisive difference that enemy images *dictate* orientation while stereotypes *help in orienting oneself*.'[29] I find this a very thought-provoking and useful distinction, which may provide another variable in our theoretical model of ethnic conflict.

However, context again becomes crucial. Spillmann and Spillmann make a close connection between the development of enemy images and the degree of conflict escalation. Enemy images resume the function of 'culture' only at the highest levels of conflict escalation, the level where totalized world-views crash. Furthermore, an important building block in this theory is that the individual gradually diminishes in importance, as well as from sight, as the conflict escalates. Their step-wise model of conflict escalation is closely connected to cognitive regression. It goes from misunderstandings and crushed expectations (level 1) to fluctuations between cooperation and competition (level 2). From the alternative of action to bring about a change in the other party without being willing to yield oneself (level 3) — to loss of empathy for the other, disappearing internal differentiation and development of fear (level 4). Level 5 is the ultimate. Here the conflict becomes totalized between entire world views and mythic representations. The concept of individuality looses its importance: 'What remains is one concept, one image, shared by all'.[30] This is the fully developed image of the enemy. Historically and contemporally, this looks like a very accurate description of the development of the Israeli-Palestinian conflict; a conflict which, cognitively, must definitely be placed at

28. Horton 1971.
29. Spillmann and Spillmann 1991: 71; emphases added.
30. Ibid: 70.

level 5. Enemy images, say Spillmann and Spillmann, have a range of different characteristics:

1) Distrust: (Everything originating from the enemy is either bad or — if it appears reasonable — created for dishonest reasons).

2) Placing the blame on the enemy: (The enemy is responsible for the tension which exists and is to blame for everything that is negative under the predominating circumstances).

3) Negative anticipation: (Whatever the enemy does is intended to harm us).

4) Identification with evil: (The enemy embodies the opposite of what we are and strive for, wants to destroy what we value most and must therefore be destroyed).

5) Zero-sum thinking: (Anything which benefits the enemy harms us and vice versa).

6) De-individualization: (Anyone who belongs to a given group is automatically our enemy).

7) Refusal of empathy: (We have nothing in common with our enemy; there is no information which could divert us from our enemy perception; human feelings and ethical criteria towards the enemy are dangerous and ill-advised).[31]

The concept of peace which is currently being processualized in Israel is not an altruistic concept built around ideas of empathy for the Other. The peace process has, according to my own data, as well as other independent sources, had no effects on established enemy images at all.[32] Most analysts — particularly media analysts—- have described this fact as 'surprising'. I would counter and say that it would be more surprising if the peace process *had* a marked effect. If we accept, at least as a hypothesis, that enemy images may gain the function of cultural frames, signing macro-political agreements do not change culture in the cognitive sense. Instead, as I have argued above, the political changes have been interpreted by the use of established images of the enemy.

We are dealing with a socially very flexible but cognitively very rigid construct. Enemy images as culture provide information about where to go,

---

31. Ibid.
32. For example Bredesen 1995; see also Barzilai and Peleg, 1993.

who to speak to, places and people to avoid, friends and foes. The fates of Israelis and Palestinians are tangled. They inhabit and lay claim to the same area — an extremely small but densely populated area — and are unable to avoid one another completely. Thus, a highly complicated scheme of how to survive in such an environment is very much in need.

It goes without saying that internal unity is extremely important. One needs clear guidelines about who is friend and who is foe, otherwise chaos would prevail. As the conflict becomes totalized, there is virtually no space for individualism. Furthermore, at level 4 of Spillmann and Spillmann's model, 'anyone maintaining contact with both groups becomes suspect'.[33] This is the clue to understanding the tragedy of the individual. A cultural meaning system as rigid as this carries inherent sanctions against offenders. Bruner argues that narratives are constructed when cultural norms are violated, or when unexpected things occur. Such narratives function to make cultural sense out of violations: '...the nature of narrative is built around established or canonical expectations and the mental management of deviations from such expectations'.[34] Israelis involved in dialogue with Palestinians are particularly exposed to such sanctions. I was told about or witnessed many instances of grave sanctioning against dialogue members. People were denied work promotion, had graffiti painted on their houses, telephones were tapped, etc. The sanctions experienced as most grave, however, are insults thrown in your face in public. The concept *of the self-hating Jew* is much in use. Historically, this term refers to individuals or Jewish communities in the Diaspora who in some way or another internalized the majority's negative attitudes to Jews and thus felt ashamed about and undercommunicated their identity. By the use of this historical symbol, Israelis involved in dialogue with Palestinians are told that by their acts they denigrate their own Israeli-Jewish identities.

An active female dialogue participant was called 'Korakh' in her synagogue. In Judaic cosmology, Korakh was a person who by his treacherous acts caused an earthquake which swallowed him. The same dialogue participant barely survived a vicious attack by an Israeli settler from the West Bank.

Furthermore, symbols originating from the Holocaust are also in use as sanctioning mechanisms. People are, for example, called neo-nazis. A very grave instance happened during a demonstration in Jerusalem, when a car stopped and several Jewish Israelis approached some young dialogue

33. Spillmann and Spillmann 1991: 69.
34. Bruner 1990: 35.

participants. 'I wish Hitler had killed all of you in the gas chambers in the Holocaust. You are not real Jews', one of the intruders shouted.[35]

Such sanctions, along with fear, effectively limit the number of people who are willing to join a dialogue group.

Sanctions occur when salient values of a collectivity are threatened or challenged. By the use of cultural schemata, humans put down a lot of work in 'reading' their social environment and adjusting their actions and attitudes accordingly. In a very interesting theory on the formation of public opinion, Noelle-Neumann discards the prevailing popular idea that public opinion formation is 'open' for everyone to see and based upon rationality and logic. On the contrary, says Noelle-Neumann, public opinion formation is based on the individual's more or less unconscious yearning to conform. Public opinion is social control. The fact that human beings are social beings and constantly strive to be accepted in their respective social groups have been left out of traditional theories on public opinion, Noelle-Neumann claims.

Human beings possess some kind of a quasi-statistical sense of reading the climate of opinion in their surroundings, Noelle-Neumann argues. This goes for all groups of society. Surveys have shown that this sense is often very accurate. This reading of the social environment is the most important link which connects the individual and the collective, according to Noelle-Neumann.

The most important innovation in Noelle-Neumann's theory, is the emphasis she puts on the individual's fear of isolation. Surveys have shown that individuals who perceive that they represent the minority within any kind of social assembly, will remain silent rather than speak up. This can be attributed to fear of losing out as a social being, as sanctions — the seriousness of which depends on the issue in question — may follow from the majority. Such fear of isolation may be biologically determined, following from the human social character. Individuals also seem to possess an internal mechanism which predicts which attitudes may lead to isolation in any given social setting. The work of the spiral of silence is particularly vital in issues of great moral concern to the community in question. Noelle-Neumann seems to be addressing the issue of challenging established ethnic boundaries in Israel-Palestine directly when she writes:

Where opinions and forms of behaviour have gained a firm hold, where they have become custom or tradition, we can no longer recognize an element of controversy in them. The controversial element, a prerequisite for the potential of isolation, enters only

---

35. An interesting question is also whether totally arbitrary symbols can produce the hostility and passion often present in inter-ethnic conflict?

after a violation, where firmly established public opinion, tradition, and morals have been injured.[36]

Sanctions that follow from transgressions, may be perceived 'as the conscious or unconscious *practical reaction of the community to injury* of its interests, a defence for the purposes of common security'.[37] Public opinion functions like a social tribunal. The collective sanctions, the individual fears isolation.

Public opinion as social control has integrative functions. The individual is linked to the collective, and the collective is manifested as a collection of individuals. The lower the level of culturally ethnic integration, the greater is the need for moral and valuational integration, Noelle-Neumann claims. And the more strict the social tribunal may become. Thus, one should expect strong sanctions against transgressors in plural communities which have built their internal unity on opposition towards an enemy 'other'. This, as I have demonstrated[38], is exactly what happens in Israel-Palestine. Noelle-Neumann even mentions collectively felt danger as a moving rationale — one of my own primary conclusions:

Perhaps the degree of danger to which a society is exposed, whether the danger comes from within or without, is the key: greater danger demands greater integration, and greater integration is enforced by heightened reactions of public opinion.[39]

The main points of this theory can be summarized by the following quotations:

Public opinions are attitudes or behaviors one *must* express in public if one is not to isolate oneself; in areas of controversy and change, public opinions are those attitudes one *can* express without running the danger of isolating oneself.[40]

Public opinion is an understanding on the part of people in an ongoing community concerning some affect- or value-laden question which individuals as well as governments have to respect at least by compromize in their overt behaviour under the threat of being excluded or losing one's standing in society.[41]

If we return to the question of context as some kind of an independent variable, the particularities of the Israeli-Palestinian conflict have produced several extremely 'value-laden question(s)'. Exclusion is costly, as we have seen

36. Noelle-Neumann, 1993: 63.
37. Ihering. Cited in Noelle-Neumann, 1993: 57.
38. Lønning 1995.
39. Ibid: 138.
40. Noelle-Neumann, 1993: 178.
41. Ibid: 179.

above. Regarding the Israeli dialogue members, most of them belong to the so called left Zionist parties. They thus adhere to vital aspects of Israelism, but reject Israel's treatment of and most Israelis' attitudes to Palestinians. For the large majority however — conceptualized through enemy images — these two are linked. For these Israeli dialogue members, there are thus few options available if they are to be accepted in Israeli society. One is to look upon dialogue as a part time activity, and take active part in the wider Israeli community. The entrance fee — to avoid sanctions — is the demand that attitudes and experiences from the dialogue are undercommunicated. The other option is an involvement in closed social circles where one's own attitudes are confirmed and appreciated by equals. The problem is only that the possibilities of these small groups — partly existing 'outside' society — to influence the wider community are limited indeed.[42] Both these options are practiced by Israeli dialogue members, individually closely connected to experiences and cognitive development as part of the dialogue.[43]

Although they have to *relate to* the value-laden questions, as they provide the backbone of Israeli identity, only one small group may afford to discard such meanings altogether. This is the small group of anti-Zionists, who denigrate the entire state of Israel as it is conceptualized today. To keep the overall picture of reality simple and manageable, however, the response to such groups by the majority is, exactly, conceptual exclusion. 'They are not real Jews', I was told repeatedly. It is also very interesting that mixed Palestinian and Israeli parties on the left, like for example, the Communists, in Israeli public discourse are referred to as *Arab* parties.

Conclusion

The fate of the individual caught within a cultural cosmology produced under a context of long-term passionate conflict is a tragedy. However, war starts through decisions made by individuals, and the real end of hate and hostilities in the former British mandate, Palestine, will only come through the creative thinking and behaviour of individuals. To release this activity, however, it is necessary to depict the processes involved in the imprisonment of the individual mind.[44] Thus I have tried to show how a particular system of symbols — established around enemy images — has become a self-fulfilling

---

42. See Lønning, 1995, for more examples.
43. See Lønning, 1995.
44. As are, unfortunately — because of a lack of legitimacy and, not least of all, money — the dialogue groups.

prophecy, capable of incorporating ever new phenomena, but equally, unable to change.

Mountains probably exist in the real world, but do they exist *as mountains* for *us*, as humans, without a preconception of what they are and what their properties are? The images we in Norway or the USA, or anywhere, have about the term 'peace process' may not coincide with the images which the actual contending parties have. The simple processual statement 'laying down weapons and making territorial compromises leading to peace and friendship' does not hold in Israel-Palestine simply because an important variable is lacking; culture. When the peace process is conceptualized through the cultural lens of enemy images, a totally different interpretation emerges: 'We are involved in the process because we want to get rid of our enemy'. The agreement may provide that opportunity. 'What is at stake here is not first and foremost technical issues like territory or water, what is at stake is a question of whole collective sets of identities communicated through symbols which have been developed and processualized through 100 years of continuous conflict'. To avoid losing out, this is the language politicians must use in their 'sensitizing campaigns'.

Like mountains in the *real* world, humans are presumably alike, distinguished only by, for example,phenotype and size. Ethnic groups and nations are cultural constructions, on the other hand — their identity symbols being arbitrary or not — and must also be studied as such. One purpose of this essay has been to show how culturally produced symbols — rather abstract stuff, after all, — may gain the ultimate power of legitimizing, on a large scale, the killing of fellow human beings, and secondly, preventing the instigation of peace. Humans who act according to the logic of enemy images may perceive themselves as perfectly rational. Killing a dehumanized being — meaning virtually one who has been deprived of his humanity — may mean little more than killing an animal.[45] This was clearly emphasized by the Auschwitz Commandant Rudolf Höss who was said to be a warm person and an excellent parent. His home, however, is said to have been lit by lamps made from the skin of Jews, a people who in the cultural meaning system of National Socialism were not conceived of as being human at all.

Conflicts, if they are allowed to develop, sooner or later become cultural, followed by a radically different dynamics. As a conflict becomes cultural, it — as Scott[46] argues — 'increasingly elude(s) attempts to resolve it'. Sensitivity

45. See Galtung, 1990; Spillmann and Spillmann, 1991.
46. Scott, 1992: 164.

to cultural dynamics should to a much larger extent become an integral part of international conflict research and conflict resolution.[47]

Bibliography

Anderson, Benedict 1991. *Imagined Communities. Reflections on the Origins and Spread of Nationalism.* London: Verso

Bailey, F. G. 1988. *Humbuggery and Manipulation. The Art of Leadership.* New York: Cornell University Press.

Barth, Fredrik 1969. 'Introduction'. In: Fredrik Barth (ed.): *Ethnic Groups and Boundaries. The Social Organization of Culture Difference,* Oslo: Universitetsforlaget.

Barth, Fredrik 1987. *Cosmologies in the Making. A generative approach to cultural variation in inner New Guinea.* Cambridge: Cambridge University Press.

Barzilai, Gad & Ilan Peleg 1994. 'Israel and Future Borders: Assessment of a Dynamic Process'. *Journal of Peace Research* Vol. 31, (1).

Bourdieu, Pierre 1977. *Outline of a theory of practice.* Cambridge: Cambridge University Press.

Bredesen, Inger Synnøve 1995. 'Fred uten forsoning'. *Mennesker og Rettigheter.* Vol. 13, (3).

Bruner, Jerome 1990. *Acts of Meaning.* Cambridge: Harvard University Press.

Cohen, Anthony P. 1994. *Self Consciousness. An Alternative Anthropology of Identity.* London and New York: Routledge.

Galtung, Johan 1989. *Nonviolence and Israel/Palestine.* Honolulu: University of Hawaii Press.

Horton, Robin 1971. 'African conversion'. *Africa* Vol. 41,(2): 85-108.

Kapferer, Bruce 1988. *Legends of People, Myths of State. Violence, Intolerance and Political Culture in Sri Lanka and Australia.* Washington: Smithsonian Institution Press.

Lønning, Dag Jørund 1995. *Bridge over troubled water. Inter-ethnic dialogue in Israel-Palestine.* (Bergen Studies in Social Anthropology, 49), Bergen: Norse Publications.

Noelle-Neumann, Elisabeth 1993. (2nd ed.): *The Spiral of Silence. Public Opinion — Our Social Skin.* Chicago and London: The University of Chicago Press.

Rabinowitz, Dan 1992. 'Trust and the Attribution of Rationality: Inverted Roles amongst Palestinian Arabs and Jews in Israel'. *Man.* No. 3, 1992.

---

47. Conflict resolution is not directly a subject of this essay. See, however, Lønning 1995 for an attempt to develop a model on how to challenge individually held enemy images and preconceptions.

Rieber, Robert W. and Robert J. Kelley 1991. 'Substance and Shadow: Images of the Enemy'. In Robert W. Rieber (ed.): *The Psychology of War and Peace. The Image of the Enemy.* New York and London: Plenum Press.

Scott. Jr, George M. 1992. 'A resynthesis of the primordial and circumstantial approaches to ethnic group solidarity; towards an explanatory model'. *Ethnic and Racial Studies* Vol. 13, (2).

Segev, Tom 1993. *The Seventh Million. The Israelis and the Holocaust.* New York: Hill and Wang.

Spicer, Edward 1971. 'Persistent Identity Systems'. *Science* 4011: 795-800.

Spillmann, Kurt R., and Kati Spillmann 1991. 'On enemy images and conflict escalation'. *International Social Science Journal* 43 (1).

Religion — Legitimizing the National Dream

Jørgen Bæk Simonsen

During the 19th century, religion was gradually regarded as something belonging to the past. In the West, scientific approach and scientific analysis was evolved as a new means of exploring and explaining the world in which mankind lived.

Religion, however, did not become a dead letter — neither in the West nor in the world at large. Religion was transformed, from being the sole explanation to becoming one of several ways to explain life in general and human behaviour in particular. When the UN, in November 1947, voted in favour of dividing the British mandate in Palestine into two states religion was once again used to legitimate practical political reasoning. This can be illustrated by the many references to religion in the various discussions between UNSCOP[1] and various individuals and groups during the summer of 1947 prior to the final UN-discussion on the future of the British mandate in Palestine.

The declaration of the independent state of Israel on the May 15th,1948 also uses religion as a means of justifying the new independant Jewish state of Israel:

The Land of Israel was the birthplace of the Jewish people. Here their spiritual, religious and national identity was formed. Here they achieved independance and created a culture of national and universal significance. Here they wrote and gave the Bible to the world.[2]

1. United Nation´s Special Commission on Palestine, established in May 1947 when the UN General Assembly for the first time discussed the future for the British mandate in Palestine consisted of eleven member-states who toured Palestine during the summer of 1947 conducting discussions with a great many persons. The report was presented to the UN on August 31 the same year. See *Records of the Second Session of the General Assembly, Supplements* Vol. 11. containing the statements of persons interviewed during the summer.
2. The content of this statement is dubious compared to historical scientific research — see inter alia Nathan Weinstock, *Zionism: False Messiah*, London 1979. Quotation from

Early on, the Bible became a much used reference cited in the arguments used by the Zionist movement when, after the formal establishment of the World Zionist Organization in Basel in 1897, it began to work towards realizing its future goal: a Jewish state in Palestine. In the declaration of independence, a shrewd link between the Bible and the goals of the Zionist movement is created by a most clever use of important historical landmarks: the Basel programme of 1897,[3] the Balfour-declaration of 1917,[4] the mandate from 1920,[5] and resolution 181 of the UN dated November 29th, 1947 leading the way to the UN partition-plan for the British mandate in Palestine. Listen to the following argument in the declaration of independence:

In the year 1897 the First Zionist Congress, inspired by Theodor Herzl's vision of the Jewish State, proclaimed the right of the Jewish people to national revival in their own country.

This right was acknowledged by the Balfour Declaration of 2 November 1917, and reaffirmed by the Mandate of the League of Nations, which gave explicit international recognition to the historic connection of the Jewish people with Palestine and their right to reconstitute their National Home.[6]

Although the declaration of independence uses arguments based on the specific status granted to the Jewish people in the Bible, the debate among Jews on religion and religion's ideological significance to the Jewish state has been very hard and one of the more important reasons for the lack of a constitution in Israel. Accordingly, we can find very different arguments even in the 1980s and early 1990s for the so-called right for Israel/the Jews to keep the occupied

Walter Laqueur, *The Israel-Arab Reader. A Documentary History of the Middle East Conflict*, Harmondsworth, 1970: 159.

3. In Basel the World Zionist Movement was created by Theodor Herzl and his friends. The Basel-programme formulated the following agenda for the new movement: 'The aim of Zionism is to create for the Jewish people a home in Palestine secured by public law', quoted from Laqueur, 1970: 28.
4. Cf. the promise made by the British foreign minister to The World Zionist Movement promising to help the movement to establish in Palestine 'a national home for the Jewish people'.
5. The San Remo Conference decided on April 24th, 1920 to assign the Mandate under the League of Nations to Britain. The legal text was confirmed by the Council of the League of Nations on July 24th, 1922. In the document the promise from Lord Balfour was incorporated in the legal text: 'Whereas the Principal Allied Powers have also agreed that the Mandatory should be responsible for putting into effect the declaration originally made on November 2nd, 1917 by the Government of His Britannic Majesty, and adopted by the said powers, in favour of the establishment in Palestine of anational home for the Jewish people...', quoted from Laqueur, 1970: 54.
6. Quoted from Laqueur, 1970: 159f.

territories in Gaza and the West Bank under continued Israeli occupation. From the Likud victory in the elections in 1977 until the early 1990s, political parties in Israel once again found and used arguments in the religious tradition for the Israeli right to Judea and Samaria — the name in the biblical tradition for the West Bank.[7]

It was not only the Jews who found political arguments in the religious tradition for their proclaimed right to Palestine. So did the Palestinians; when, after the establisment of the mandate in 1920, they had to face the systematic immigration of still larger numbers of Jews to Palestine.

The emergence of the Palestine National Movement after 1920 illustrates this fact. The genesis of Arab nationalism is still a matter of dispute among scholars,[8] and so is the genesis of Palestinian nationalism.[9] After the *intifada,* this debate has surfaced once again, forcing Palestinians in general to reconsider the relationship between nationalism and religion.

No formal poitical structure existed in Palestinian society when the League of Nations decided to hand over the mandate of Palestine to the British in 1920. Some Palestinians had joined forces with the Arab Movement headed by Husain ibn Ali (1853-1931) and his sons Faysal (1885-1933) and Abdallah (1882-1951) which led to the Arab Revolt in 1916. Based on promises formulated by Sir Henry McMahon (1862-1949) in the famous letter to Husain ibn Ali dated October 24th, 1915:

But having realized, however, from your last note that you considered the question important, vital and urgent, I hastened to communicate to the Government of Great Britain the purport of your note. It gives me the greatest pleasure to convey to you, on their behalf, the following declarations which, I have no doubt, you will receive with satisfaction and acceptance.

The districts of Mersin and Alexandretta and portions of Syria lying to the west of the districts of Damascus, Homs, Hama and Aleppo cannot be said to be purely Arab, and must on that account be excepted from the proposed delimitation.[10]

7. For an analysis of this see Ian Lustick: *For the Land and the Lord: Jewish Fundamentalism in Israel*, New York, 1988; and Laurence J. Silberstein, *Jewish Fundamentalism in Comparative Perspective. Religion, Ideology and the Crisis of Modernity*, London: 1996.
8. See inter alia Rashid Khalidi (ed.), *The Origins of Arab Nationalism*, New York, 1991.
9. See Muhammad Y. Muslih, *The Origins of Palestinian Nationalim*, The Institute for Palestine Studies Series, New York, 1988 and Ann Lesch, 'The Origins of Palestine Arab Nationalism', in William W. Haddad (ed.), *Nationalism in a Non-National State*, New York: Columbia, 1977.
10. McMahon´s letter October 24th, 1915 was a reply to demands made by Husain ibn Ali on the geographic extention of the future independent Arab State demanded by the Arab Movement. The extention was identical with the goals formulated in the so called

Subject to that modification and without prejudice to the treaties concluded between us and certain Arab Chiefs, we accept that delimitation.[11]

The promised independent Arab state never materialized and the former Ottoman provinces of the Middle East became mandates controlled by the French and the British. As a result, the Arab inhabitants in the mandates began the difficult struggle for full national independence. In the end, after World War II, national indepence was achieved for all, save the Palestinians.

This, however, is not our concern here. Instead we have to focus on the use of religion in the emerging Palestinian nationalism. As mentioned above, no formal Palestinian political structure existed when the British mandate was created. Accordingly the emerging Palestinian national movement developed, to a very large degree, to meet questions posed not by the Palestinians but by decisions taken by the British mandate on the one side and the Zionist movement on the other.

Ottoman Palestine was dominated, like the rest of the Ottoman Arab provinces, by large and rich families economically based on land and trade. Some of the families succeeded in obtaining important positions in the local Ottoman administration and thereby were able to support the local Palestinian population.[12] Politics, however, were in the hands of the economically important families — and some of them supported the Arab Revolt dream of establishing an independent Arab state in the former Ottoman Arab provinces following the revolt in 1916. There was some ideological reference to the Muslim tradition in the Husain-McMahon correspondance, but the Arab Revolt, as such, was not justified by religious arguments — nor was it founded on any clear definition of nationalism.[13]

After the establisment of the British Mandate, things developed differently. When Amin al-Husayni was elected *mufti* of Jerusalem in 1921, and at the same time installed as the prime important person in administrating the various *awqâf* in Palestine it became obvious that the British administration was interested in establishing a political framework for the Palestinians in which politics and religion were administered by the same person(s).[14]

Not surprisingly, Amin al-Husayni was conscious of using his new, formal

Damascus-Protocol, cf. George Antonius, *The Arab Awakening*, London 1938: 158f and 164f.

11. Antonius, London, 1938: 419.
12. Muslih, New York, 1988.
13. In the entire correpondance between Husain and McMahon no precise description of the political establishment in the future independent Arab state is stated.
14. Philip Mattar, *The Mufti of Jerusalem. Al-Hajj Amin al-Husayni and the Palestinian National Movement*, New York, 1988: 19ff.

political power to strenghen his and his family's position in the gradually
expanding Palestinian participation in the daily running of the British mandate
— thus repeating what other important families had done in Ottoman Palestine
for centuries. And when growing Jewish migration — with the third *aliya*
centering also on establishing the Jewish presence in the existing towns of the
British mandate — finally forced him to confront the British mandate, Amin
al-Husayni turned to religion to express himself.

In 1929, he and his colleagues arranged one of the early Islamic conferences
to attain, and possibly to sustain, international support for the Palestinians in
their effort to minimize the growing Jewish migration.[15] The effort was of no
immediate result — but it indicated the themes of an increasingly visible
Palestinian nationalism that saw light in the 1930s, i.e. the effort of combining
political nationalism with the classical Islamic political tradition — a
combination that in no way was particular to the Palestinians. The same trend
can be found in the writings and declarations of the Muslim Brothers in
Egypt.[16]

After the riots at the Wailing Wall - in August 1929, the Palestinians and
the British administration in Palestine again and again had to confront each
other. But it was not the *mufti* and his colleagues who introduced the *djihâd*
as a means of fighting both the British administration and the expanding
Jewish community in Palestine. This was done by Izz al-Din al-Qassâm, who
in 1935 began his political fight against the British[17] — with no great immediate
success, but which had important consequences later on. Accordingly, the first
sustained Palestinian effort to fight the British in 1936 was not specifically
legitimized by religious claims — but by a need to form an all-embracing
Palestinian alliance to fight the real threat to the Palestinians: Jewish migration,
and the support this was given by the British administration.[18]

The Palestinians lost the first round. When the British Mandate was
handed over to the UN, the Zionist Movement, compared to the Palestinians,

---

15. Cf. Martin Kramer, *Islam Assembled. The Advent of the Muslim Congresses*, New York,
    1986, 123ff and Jacob M. Landau, *The Politics of Pan-Islam. Ideology and Organization*,
    Oxford, 1994: 276ff.
16. See inter alia Richard P. Mitchell, *The Society of the Muslim Brothers*, London, 1969 and
    John Obert Voll, *Islam: Continuity and Change*, London, 1992 with examples of how
    these two trends was mixed also in other parts of the Islamic world. The same was by
    the way also visible with the Maronites in Lebanon cf. Albert Hourani, *Ideology of the
    Mountain and the City*, in Roger Owen (ed.), *Essays on the Crisis in Lebanon*, London,
    1976.
17. Cf. Nels Johnson, *Islam and the Politics of Meaning in Palestinian Nationalism*, London,
    1982 and Ziad Abu-Amr, *Islamic Fundamentalism in the West Bank and Gaza — Muslim
    Brotherhood and Islamic Jihad*, Indiana, 1994.
18. Mattar, 1988: 73ff.

was far better organized in terms of presenting its case. As mentioned above, the various discussions conducted by the UNSCOP during the summer of 1947 provide plenty of examples of claims supported by religion — both among Muslim Palestinians, Christian Palestinians, and Jews.

The establishment of the Jewish state materialised on the May 15th,1948 and the Jewish state has existed ever since. As the emerging Palestinian nationalism did not succeed in combining political nationalism with religious tradition (among other things due to the fact that Palestinians comprise both Muslims and Christians) the Palestinian nationalism that developed after the disaster of 1948-49 was secular.

This is clearly evident if one reads the 1968 Palestinian Charter which launched a nationalism based on clearly secular foundations. When in 1969, some of the Arab states decided to organize yet another *djihâd* in order to fight the Jewish state, it was not at all a means of argument proposed by the various Palestinian groups active in the fight for a future Palestinian state.

During the 1970s, the PLO managed to be recognized as the sole legitimate representative of the Palestinians — and managed finally, in September 1993, to also be recognized as such by the last two parties that hitherto had refused this: the US government and Israel. By signing the Declaration of Principles, the Jewish state recognized the PLO as the legitimate representative of the Palestinians, while the PLO for its part recognized the Jewish state's right to existence. At the same time, the two sides recognized their common right to the same land — the land that had been the focus of the fight since 1948.

The compromise contained in the Declaration of Principles was criticized by many Palestinians; not least of all, the large number living as refugees outside the occupied territories. The critique focused primarily on the giving up of a point of view which, up until September 1993, had been held as irrevocable: the right to return. But within Palestinian society in the occupied territories in Gaza and on the West Bank, new social forces had matured — and even long before the signing of the Declaration of Principles, the traditional right of the PLO to be regarded as the sole legitimate representative of the Palestinians was questioned by HAMAS.

In a historical perspective, the emergence of HAMAS had two very different preconditions. The one was the traditional role played by Muslim groups such as the Muslim Brotherhood in Palestinian society at large; the second had to do with the general ideological development in the Arab world at large, where political groups based on Islam from the early 1970s onwards became visible and active to an ever increasing extent.

This double background is discernible in the HAMAS-charter published in August 1988, which presents to the general public the ideas and goals of

the new Islamic group calling itself HAMAS. The goal is clearly stated in §
11 of the charter: the establishment of a Palestinian state based on Islam in the
entire geographic area founded as the British mandate back in 1920. HAMAS
here formulates a point of view held by the PLO until the mid 1970s, when
the more moderate part of the PLO headed by Fatah began talking about a
Palestine of a smaller geographic size.[19]

The legitimization in the HAMAS-charter, however, differs from the one
traditionally used by the PLO. In this charter, no reference is made to
nationalism in this context. The right of the Palestinians to a Palestinian state
is based on Islam. The Palestinians have a right to Palestine due to the fact
that Palestine was conquered by the Muslims in the 7th century — thereby
being a waqf (trust) for the Muslims until Doomsday. This is stressed without
reservation in §11:

The Islamic Resistance Movement (firmly) believes that the land of Palestine is an
Islamic *Waqf* (Trust) upon all Muslim generations till the day of Resurrection. It is not
right to give it up nor any part of it. Neither a single Arab state nor all the Arab states,
neither a king nor a leader, nor all the kings or leaders, nor any organization - Palestine
or Arab - have such authority because the land of Palestine is an Islamic Trust upon
all Muslim generations until the day of Resurrection.[20]

The historical and religious right of the Palestinians was neglected by a shrewd
alliance between the Zionists and the West. The charter offers this explanation:

The enemy planned and perfected their plan long ago so that they could achieve what
they want to achieve, taking into account effective steps in running matters. So they
worked on gathering huge and effective amounts of wealth to achieve their goal. With
wealth they controlled the international mass media - news services, newspapers,
printing presses, broadcast stations and more... They are behind the French Revolution,
the Communist Revolution, and most of the revolutions here and there which we have
heard of and are hearing of. With their wealth they formed secret organizations
throughout the world to destroy societies and promote the Zionist cause.[21]

If one compares this explanation to the one launched in the PLO-charter of
1968 there are some very interesting parallels. This seems to confirm the central
problem of Palestinian nationalism since its birth: the various demands and

---

19. Cf. Helena Cobban: *The Palestine Liberation Organization: People, Power and Politics,*
    Cambridge 1984: 20; and Omar Massalha, *Towards the Long-Promised Peace,* London
    1994: 161ff.
20. Charter of the Islamic Resistance Movement (HAMAS) of Palestine, *Journal of Palestine
    Studies* 22, 1993: 125.
21. Ibid. § 22: 129.

their verbal formulation have been forced by claims raised by others — the Zionist movement, the British mandate-administration and the pan-arab national movement created by president Nasser (who was actually the architect behind the PLO when it was formally created in 1964). The secular Palestinian leaders managed, after 1968, to obtain control of the PLO and they subsequently transformed it during the 1970s into a very strong national organization which slowly gained international recognition as the sole representative of the Palestinian population. But also a movement with a goal out of reach — the demolition of the Jewish state.

When the independent Palestinian state was declared by the PNC in November 1988, the Palestinians were forced to reinterpret history — and the legitimation of the Palestinian state to come was now based on the UN-declaration 181 of November 1947 — the one leading to the partition of Palestine into two states: one Jewish and one Arab.[22]

The PLO-charter of 1968 is silent on the principles according to which the future Palestinian state wil be run. It is first and foremost a legitimation of the rights withheld from the Palestinians after 1947 — when they alone had to pay the price for decisions taken by others when the UN decided to divide the British mandate, allowing the Jewish state to expand its territories and de facto accepted the neighbouring Arab countries of Jordan and Egypt to take hold of the rest of the Palestine that was established in 1920 by the League of Nations.

The same is through in the HAMAS-charter of 1988. This too is first and foremost a legitimation of rights to the land of Palestine comprising no concrete references to the principle of the future state — save a few references to *inter alia* the rights of non-Mulims — the Jews and the Christians who will be secured basic rights in accordance with principles established in Islamic *fiqh* — rights totally out of touch with basic values in modern political nationalism and for that matter in civil society.[23]

It can probably not be decided whether or not the secular nationalism developed by the PLO is a more effective ideology than the religious inspired ideology formulated by HAMAS and presented to the general public in the

22. Please note the wording of the UN declaration of November 1947. It does not refer to a Palestinian state, but to an Arab state in the part of Palestine that was not to be part of the Jewish state. Cf. also Edward Said, 'Intifada and Independence', in Zachary Lockman & Joes Beinin (eds.), *Intifada. The Palestine Uprising against Israeli Occupation*, London 1990: 5ff.
23. Cf. the Charter § 31. This remark is in no way intented to question the principle accept given in Islamic fiqh and Islamic theology to the other two monotheistic religions. In neither the Jewish tradition nor in the Christian tradition do we find anything similar. This however has nothing to do with modern political ideals and principles.

1988 charter. Both charters are historical documents formulated as a response to claims put forward by others. The secular nationalism followed by the PLO, however, did succeed in creating principles for a future Palestinian state, and nobody can seriously expect HAMAS to succeed in expanding this area into a state comprising the whole of the long gone British mandate of Palestine. HAMAS on the other hand can very well be depicted as a social force capable of mobilizing the rest of Palestinian society to once again attempt to seek the establishment of a nationalism in which parts of the Islamic tradition find a natural place in the formulation of a political entity able to sustain its followers in what it is all about: an all-embracing 'imagined community' in which the imagined ideas and goals will be able to meet the challenges of a changing world.

Bibliography

Abu-Amr, Ziad 1994. *Islamic Fundamentalism in the West Bank and Gaza — Muslim Brotherhood and Islamic Jihad*, Indiana.
Antonius, George 1938. *The Arab Awakening*, London.
Cobban, Helena 1984. *The Palestine Liberation Movement: People, Power and Politics*, Cambridge.
Hourani, Albert 1976. 'Ideology of the Mountain and the City', in Roger Owen (ed.), *Essays on the Crisis in Lebanon*, London.
Johnson, Nels 1982. *Islam and the Politics of Meaning in Palestinian Nationalism*, London.
Journal of Palestine Studies.
Khalidi, Rashid 1991, (ed.) *The Origins of Arab Nationalism*, New York.
Kramer, Martin 1986. *Islam Assembled. The Advent of the Muslim Congresses*, New York.
Landau, Jacob M. 1994. *The Politics of Pan-Islam. Ideology and Organization*, Oxford.
Laqueur, Walther 1970. *The Israel-Arab Reader*, Harmonsworth.
Lesch, Ann 1997. 'The Origins of Palestine Arab Nationalism', in William W. Haddad (ed.), *Nationalism in a Non-National State*, Columbia.
Lustick, Ian 1988. *For the Land and the Lord: Jewish Fundamentalism in Israel*, New York.
Massalha, Omar 1994. *Towards the Long-Promised Peace*, London.
Mattar, Philip 1988. *The Mufti of Jerusalem, Al-Hajj Amin al-Husseini and the Palestinian National Movement*, New York.
Mitchell, Richard P. 1969. *The Society of the Muslim Brothers*, London.
Muslih, Muhammad Y. 1988. *The Origins of Palestinian Nationalism*, New York.

Records of the Second Session of the General Assembly, Supplements, Vol. 11, New York, 1947.

Said, Edward 1990. 'Intifada and Independence', in Zachary Lockmann & Joel Beinin (eds.) *Intifada. The Palestine Uprising against Israeli Occupation*, London.

Silberstein, Laurence J. *Jewish Fundamentalism in Comparative Perspective. Religion, Ideology and the Crisis of Modernity*.

Voll, John Obert 1992. *Islam: Continuity and Change in the Modern World*, London.

Weinstock Nathan 1979. *Zionism: False Messiah*, London.

Two Movements of National Liberation — in Conflict or Peace Making?

Gert Petersen

Bearing in mind the extremely complicated historical background, it is greatly impressive and almost incredible what has been achieved in the last few years in the relationship between the Palestinians and Israelis.[1] The difficulty of the task was evident. Let me quote an excerpt from what I wrote in *FN-Orientering* No.5 in 1973:

Rarely has the background been so confusing as here.. Jews and Arabs can, with equal right, refer to territorial promises which England gave them during the First World War in order to win their military support. Morally, legal demands of equal value are counterposed: did not the Jewish Agency buy the land peacefully from Arab owners? Was not the State of Isreal established by the United Nations? But, are large parts of the present Israel not an old Arab national home; a home which many people had to flee as refugees? — To both questions my answer is — 'Yes.'

What we have seen in Palestine is the confrontation of two national movements, both of them carrying the banner of national liberation and self-determination.

The Jewish (Zionist) one emerged as an answer to the persecution of Jews in Tsarist Russia, France, Austria and other parts of Europe at the end of the former century, aiming at migration and the setting up of a Jewish state. Like many national movements, this one had a religious affinity, and therefore 'the promised land', Palestine (and not East Africa, as was discussed), was appointed the target land.

Unfortunately, the 'promised land' had, since Jahve's promises were supposed to have been made, almost been emptied of Jews and was mostly inhabited by another people, the Arabs. So, one must register, from the very

---

1. This manuscript was delivered before an extremely small majority in Israel changed Israeli policy. This does not, however, diminish the immensity of what had been achieved until then, nor the hope for this achievement to be reconstituted at a date not too far in the future.

beginning, a certain imperialist trend in the Jewish national movement. Among Zionists there was a divided reaction to this awkward fact. Some of them, ignoring the facts, simply claimed that at present Palestine was a 'land without people'. Others mirrored the general Western spirit of that period, i.e. the 'right' of Westerners to colonize the rest of the world (who asked the American Indians if they wanted the settlers?). Still others referred to the commands of God (Jahve). But quite a few of them did hope for a good co-existence with the Arab inhabitants and a sharing of the land with them.

All this does not change the fact that Zionism was a national movement aimed at setting a hitherto suppressed nation free. Nobody can claim truthfully that national liberation movements are above blame, very often the contrary is true. And the final, and decisive, impetus given the Zionist movement was the crescendo of persecution, in the shape of pure annihilation; the holocaust engineered by Hitler. This led to an overwhelming and desperate exodus of Jews from Europe, migrating — often in extremely difficult conditions and resisted by the Arabs — into Palestine. The outcome was the UN General Assembly decision in 1947 on the division of Palestine and the establishment of a specific Jewish state, — very much due to the bad conscience of the Western World after the holocaust which might have been prevented by military means.

The establishment of Israel was implemented in April 1948, and resulted in a war with the Arab inhabitants and the Arab neighbouring states, as well as instigating the fleeing of hundreds of thousands of local inhabitants; terrorized or fearing the terror of the Israelis.

Thus, the victory of the Jewish national movement is a grim story of much cruelty and injustice. But the State of Israel was set up on the bidding of the International Community (including the then Soviet bloc), and since then millions of Jews have been born in this State or have immigrated there - trusting in the validity of the decision made by the United Nations. Consequently, the undoing of this decision, i.e. the abolishment of Israel, would lead to even more human tragedies and an unlimited degree of destruction. Therefore, any sustainable solution of the Middle East conflict must respect the integrity of Israel, in spite of all the wrongdoings which came about during (and after) the emergence of the State.

This does not mean that wrong-doings should pass uncorrected. On the contrary, as much as possible must be corrected, and a solution must build on vital and important Israeli concessions to the other party in the national conflict.

This party is the Palestinians. Theirs is also a genuine national liberation movement. Its history is a bit complicated. In my view we have, since 1948, witnessed the emergence of a new nation, the Palestinian, which is a part of the general Arab culture and language community.

When the Jews began settling in Palestine, the Arabs in this country saw themselves as a part of an Arab nation: This included the people living in the Arab peninsula and the fertile crescent, all of them subordinated to the Ottoman Sultan. Their dream was to be liberated from Ottoman rule and to establish an Arab state in the said area. This was what they were promised by the British and French during the First World War. The promise was never honoured. This was partly due to the Balfour Declaration (the British promise to the Zionists), which led to the mandate of Palestine, and partly to the fact that the French imperialists wanted their slice of the cake (Syria, the Lebanon) and that the Saudi campaign (probably helped by British intrigues) upset the apple cart and 'forced' the British imperialists to carve up the Arab land, to the delight of the princes (Iraq, Transjordan).

Be that as it may be, the fact was that the Jews were a minority in Palestine. They bought Arab land from rich landowners who were willing to sell. This transaction created conflicts, but was fully legal. Much worse was their laying claim to the state, their wish to set up a new state. When they succeeded, they were only a small majority in the area allotted to them by the UN dividing plan. And after their conquests in the ensuing war, they have probably been a minority in their own state, at any rate for a short period. But immigration changed this picture quickly.

Thus, the Jewish national liberation movement achieved victory at the cost of another people which in turn, quite naturally started to develop its own movement of national liberation. But it was in a difficult position. The Arabs living in old Palestine and in the refugee camps were not only fighting the Israelis, they were also pawns in the power game of the Arab states. One factor was the Israeli Prime Minister Golda Meyer's refusal to accept the existence of a Palestinian people ('You can call them South Syrians,' she said), another was that a similar attitude was taken by Arab princes and presidents. Instead of establishing a core Palestinian state on the West Bank, King Hussein annexed this area as a part of his kingdom (changing its name from Trans-Jorden into Jordan). This annexation was only given up in 1988.

In the same way, a liberation movement was set up by Egypt's Nasser and — according to the memoirs of PLO leaders — treated as an instrument in Nasserite policies. It was the task of Yasir Arafat and El Fatah to 'liberate' this movement from its 'guardians'. This led to dramatic conflicts, in particular in Jordan and the Lebanon (with the Syrians).

In a way, the PLO became involved in a war on two fronts, which necessarily led to a stronger self-identification of the Palestinian people as

Palestinians, part of a broad Arab framework, but also a nation in its own right.

After the 1967 war, this sense of identity must have grown substantially. The core of Palestinians were now confronted directly by an enemy, an oppressive occupying power. The people in the refugee camps identified with the people in the West Bank and Gaza strip. In the following years they would become isolated from many of their Arab brethren (Black September in Jordan, Sadat's separate peace with Israel, the expulsion of the PLO from the Lebanon). Among the Palestinians there was growing awareness of their own situation.

But these years were also a time of confusion. The UN Security Council resolutions 242 (1967) and 338 (1973) were positive steps, in so far as they ruled against Israeli conquests and demanded the return of 'conquered areas' - but to whom? The 'Palestinian question' was treated solely as a question of refugees, and this was negative. In this desperate situation the PLO answered by radicalizing its Charter in demanding a total annihilation of Israel (1968). It may have sounded very heroical, but was far from realistic in this world. Even the Soviet Union, which played the role of a new 'guardian' of Arab interests, would not support this demand. Furthermore, this was the period of spectacular terrorist acts committed by the PLO. These acts focussed the world's attention on the 'forgotten' cause of the Palestinians, but to most people it did so in a negative way.

On the other hand, international recognition of the PLO and the Palestinian cause did make some progress from around the middle of the 70s. This was most spectacularly demonstrated by the UN invitation to Arafat to address the General Assembly.

Superficially, the return of the Sinai Peninsula to Egypt might look like the beginning of liberation, but the practical effects revealed a very different picture. Objectively, Sadat's separatism weakened the Palestinians, and right after this step the Israeli policy in the occupied areas became much harsher.

There were several motives behind the Israeli policy towards the occupied areas. The general one was security. Israel is a small country, certainly difficult to defend from behind the pre-1967 borders, and the feeling of being threatened is very real.

Two alternatives seemed possible. Either establish friendly relations with the neighbouring countries, cemented by diplomatic measures and international guarantees, supplemented of course, by a strong national defence and incorporating into this framework a *modus vivendi* with the Palestinians. Or else accept eternal enmity with the Arabs as being unavoidable and combine this with a very strong defence force with the establishment of a large 'glacis' area around the country (West Bank, Gaza strip, South Lebanon, Golan

Heights), permanently occupied by Israeli soldiers and heavily settled by armed Israeli civilians.

With regard to the first alternative, the areas conquered in 1967 could be used as diplomatic cards, to be played at the negotiating table within the framework of UNSC resolution 242. This is the 'land for peace' formula. Right after the 1967 war, many observers considered this to be the Israeli strategy. But already in 1970, when Ambassador Jarring investigated the matter on behalf of the UN, the Israeli government reacted very vaguely to his questions of withdrawal of troops and the drawing-up of borders.

According to the second alternative, the conquered areas would be annexed, or in some other way kept under the permanent control of the Israeli army along with an army of well-armed, civilian settlers. A formal peace arrangement would have a very low priority and would only be accepted if it confirmed the *fait d'accompli*.

By the end of the seventies, the latter alternative seemed to be the one chosen by the Israeli establishment. This was indicated by the settlers' policy and the increasingly brutal treatment of the Palestinian population. The background was now a coupling of the old security thinking (in its most radical version) with an even stronger fundamentalist thinking. The West Bank was a 'Biblical land', the right-wingers said; given to the Israelis by God (Jahve). Therefore, these lands should be taken over by Israelis and the Arabs should be 'transferred' (meaning: deported) to neighbouring Arab lands.

This way of thinking played a strong role in the first Likud era (Begin, Shamir), when the occupied areas in the East were constantly referred to as Judea and Samaria — their Biblical names. The idea was to colonize the West Bank, ideologically motivated by Biblical commands. In practical terms, the motive was much simpler.

In 1983 there were 20,000 settlers in the West Bank, and the then the War Minister, Mr. Sharon, predicted that in a few years there would be 100,000 or more. Why? 'Then we will not be able to give up the land,' Mr. Sharon said. It was the real motive behind the settlers' policy. (As a matter of fact there are now 150,000 settlers, and they really are a barrier to the peace process).

The real change in the situation was caused by the PLO, by — if I might put it thus, — a combination of the carrot and the stick method.

The carrot was the 1988 recognition of the Israeli State's right to exist and the acceptance of UNSC resolutions 242 og 338 as the basis of future negotiations. At the same time, the PLO National Council proclaimed the establishment of the State of Palestine. But what broke the deadlock was the radically new approach to the realities of the region, including the existence of Israel.

The stick was the rebellion, the *Intifada,* in the West Bank and the Gaza strip. The *Intifada* was of the utmost importance. Contrary to the early years of the PLO, when terrorist acts predominated, the *Intifada* was   and is internationally recognized as being — a genuine and very broad popular uprising, without firearms, explosives, etc. It was the struggle of David against Goliath, of people armed only with slings against submachine guns. Thus, the intifada created enormous international sympathy for the cause of the Palestinians.

More important still: it demonstrated to the Israeli authorities that the situation was completely uncontrollable and extremely unstable. It appeared also to be impossible to subdue the rebellion which went on and on, from one year to the next. When the PLO at the same time accepted the most important and dearest demand of the Israelis — to recognize Israel's right to exist — those Israeli forces who wanted a peaceful settlement with the Palestinians experienced an unprecedented strengthening. The soil was ripe for a security policy that broke with fundamentalism and the harsh alternative I mentioned earlier. So, in both the Israeli establishment and among the PLO leadership, ideas of a peace compromise began to develop. Secret talks led to the Oslo Agreement followed by open talks which led to the Washington Agreement.

Of course, many dangers still threaten this peace process. Both on the Palestinian and the Israeli side fundamentalism, based on religion, is deeply entrenched. And religious fundamentalism is an extremely dangerous barrier against peace, because it is purely emotional and reasoning is out of the question. It is the background of the Palestinian suicide terrorists, and the corresponding acts carried out by the Israelis, e.g. the massacre in Hebron and the murder of Yitzhak Rabin. One must hope that the present decision-makers on both sides will remain calm and that the general public will not fall prey to these provocations.[2]

Because there is no solution other than the peace process that we are going through at present.

The idea of old Palestine as a bi-national state is not feasible. It was advanced by Jewish Left circles (Hashomir Hatzair) in the 40s and looked wonderful, but neither the Jewish nor the Arab masses accepted it. For many years the PLO proposed a similar idea; Palestine as the land 'of the three creeds',with the religions representing nations. One has only to look at the Lebanon to see how unwieldy and perilous this model is. Then there has been talk of the 'extermination of Israel'. From one side this idea looked morally well-founded ('we had to flee before you'). But from the other side it was

---

2. Regrettably, it did, by a very small majority. But this does not change the essence of the following considerations.

completely immoral ('we ourselves had to flee from untold sufferings'). Two wrongs do not make a right. And moral considerations aside, this idea is totally unfeasible in the real world. Any attempt to put it into practice would lead to a terrible disaster.

In reverse, the idea of extermination of the idea of a Palestinian state is just as impossible. And this is what permanent Israeli *de facto* annexation and colonization of the West Bank and the Gaza strip amounts to. It would breed an interminable *Intifada* and one war after another and would in the end lead to a disaster of similar dimensions to the one referred to above.

Consequently, there is no solution other than that of the Jews and Palestinians sharing the territory of old Palestine (between the River and the Sea), as two independent and neighbouring states. This is an outcome based on the UNSC resolution 242 of 1967, but with the very important difference that the Palestinian question is now treated as a national question, among the states which (according to the Resolution) must live securely and in peace in the region, is also a Palestinian state.

If peace is reached on this basis, one may envisage a close economical and cultural cooperation between both states and other states in the region.

The matter of Palestinian statehood is not formally settled, and the Israelis are reticent, but a Palestinian State is the only logical outcome of the peace process, and surely the Israeli decision-makers know this. Until now, a home rule has been set up for 90 percent of the Palestinians in the Gaza strip and the West Bank; Israeli troops have been withdrawn, and the Palestinians are creating a democratic rule which is outstanding in the Arab world.

Admittedly, there are many extremely difficult problems still unresolved — such as the matter of paying compensation to refugees (or their return if possible), the final drawing-up of borders, the fate of the Israeli settlers, the distribution of land and water, and the status of Jerusalem. (And, of course, the question of the Golan Heights, but this is not a matter for the PLO). Still, with the withdrawal of Israeli troops and the establishment of democratic ruling mechanisms in what is to all intents and purposes a State of Palestine, the process is now on the point of becoming irreversible.

But in order to make it completely irreversible, much good will is still necessary — such as has been demonstrated since the great turn undertaken first by the PLO, led by Arafat and then by Israel, led by Rabin and Peres. This process has had its own dynamics: the idea of peace is becoming more and more rooted in the greater part of both peoples, in spite of much old suspicion, fear and hatred.

The necessity to 'overcome the yoke of history' and create peace and neighbourly relations is, in spite of disastrous set-backs, being increasingly accepted by a great strata of public opinion, although the solution cannot be a fully 'just solution', with two nations having equally valid claims (in a historical and legal sense) to the same territory. So, a great compromise leading to a good solution (instead of a 'just' one) is the only way out; a solution which entails greater advantages for both nations than continued struggle and mutual destruction.

The Middle East Between Agony and Progress:
Building a New Palestine

Johannes Dragsbaek Schmidt & Jacques Hersh

... the twentieth-century Arab is in revolt against foreign powers, against an alienated, hardened world, and against his own decadence.
Jacques Berque, *Arab Rebirth: Pain & Ecstasy*, Al Saqi - Zed, London, 1983, 50.

I am convinced that the path the government has taken is the path that will lead to the end of the control of another people. The Palestinians in the Territories are an entity different from us — religiously, politically, and nationally...
Yitzhak Rabin, January 1995.

The conflicting parties in the Middle East Peace Process have discovered that the aftermath of the Oslo accord did not bring about automatic and immediate peace; and while peace has become the buzzword, an end to the conflict has yet to be resolved. The wide differences in fundamental claims and expectations divide the two contracting parties; even if the schedule outlined in the 1993 Israel-PLO Declaration is met, a permanent agreement has yet to be reached. Israel aims at achieving security and stability and the Palestinian leadership needs support for a new state within a national entity.

Focusing on a comparative perspective of political cultures and changing national identities in Israel and the Occupied Territories in a rapidly changing international environment, this contribution suggests the need for an alternative understanding to comprehend the emerging new state structures in Palestine, where a new partnership between earlier opposed secular forces has been urged on by the challenge from Islamic and Jewish fundamentalism.

The Conflict Between Two Ideologies of Nationalism and Secularism

The end of the Cold War and the dissolution of Soviet-type socialism have profoundly affected the Middle East. On the geostrategic level the Palestinian-cum-Arab side has lost its former importance due to the disappearance of the Soviet presence and made the current peace negotiations possible. Israel, too, might experience in the long run, a loss of US interest for this nation as a strategic asset in the area. Furthermore, both Israeli and Palestinian national identities and secular political cultures seem to be moving in the direction of accommodating the perceived threat from fundamentalism. The outcome of this seemingly never-ending peace process can perhaps lead to a genuine 'banalization' of Israel's internal as well as international identity and the inevitable emergence of a Palestinian state. In short, a normalization of inter-state affairs accomplished through a final agreement between Israel and Palestine followed by a permanent peace accord between Israel and its neighbouring countries.

For the past fifty years Jewish and Palestinian nationalism has provided the two competing ideological discourses which fought political, military, cultural and economic battles over a tiny territorial entity located in the centre of the Arab world surrounded by Egypt, Lebanon, Jordan and Syria.

Although the two nationalisms originated under quite different circumstances, they both were nevertheless born as offsprings of the European experience. While Jewish political nationalism originated within Europe as a reaction to anti-Semitism, Palestinian nationalism had its roots in the anti-colonial struggle against British colonialism and European Jews' colonization.

Historically, Zionism was thus conceived on the basis of Eurocentric ideals and its heritage was colonialism, progression and an urbanized settler civilization based on Westernization, encompassing coherence in terms of societal force. The Jewish people, as it has evolved during the past 500 years, and the Zionist movement, as a political movement that gave birth to Israel as a nation, are deeply interwoven with the histories and cultures of Europe. Zionism has, in its political expression been successful in positioning itself as both victim and victor of the entire Jewish people. This is well encapsulated by Benedict Anderson: 'The ancestor of the Warsaw Uprising is the state of Israel.'[1]

The other nationalism, 'Palestinianism', could not — because of various internal as well as external reasons — materialize before it was too late; the rise of mass-nationalism was created and shaped as an encounter with Europe and invented as a response to the Zionist conquest of territory;[2] during the 1960s and 1970s Palestinian identity was revived in connection with the rise of two other competing nationalisms: On the one hand Nasserism with the idea of Pan-Arabism, and on the other hand a compartmentalized Arab nation

---

1. Benedict Anderson: *Imagined Communities. Reflections on the Origin and the Spread of Nationalism.* London: Verso, 1991: 205.
2. See among others Eric J. Hobsbawm; *Nations and Nationalism Since 1780. Programme, Myth, Reality.* New York: Cambridge University Press, 1992: 138 and 152.

consisting of many nationalisms without any single unifying element other than Islam and the Arab language. 'Palestinianism' became a janus-faced ideology trying to walk a line between Third World rhetorics about armed struggle, liberation and progress and a fundamental bias towards its heritage of traditionalism, a rural world-view of authoritarian family and political structures and always having to respond to actions and facts that seemed more or less irreversible.

Attempting to understand the origins and the evolutions of both nationalisms does not resolve the question of territoriality. Although victorious, the legitimacy of Zionism's claim to Palestine was not very strong. Scattered throughout the world for several millennia, Jews never ceased to identify themselves on the basis of their religion; that is as a special people distinct from the various brands of non-believers among whom they lived. But at no stage, at least since the return from Babylonian captivity, does this seem to have implied a serious claim for a Hebrew political entity. According to the Jewish religion, if such a state was to come about, this would be through an act of God with the arrival of a Messiah to deliver the Jews from their sufferings. Not until the very end of the nineteenth century did European Jewry — influenced by and rejected by newfangled Western nationalism — raise the banner of political nationalism and the demand for a national Jewish homeland.

Seen in this light it is an encroachment on international norms to identify the Jewish links with the ancestral land of Israel based on the merit deriving from pilgrimages there, or the hope of return with the arrival of the Messiah with the desire to gather all Jews into a modern territorial state situated in the ancient Holy Land — a territory with a non-Jewish majority. One might as well argue that good Muslims, whose greatest aspiration is to make the pilgrimage to Mecca, in doing so really intend to declare themselves citizens of what has now become Saudi Arabia.[3] Leading Zionists, aware of the weakness of their case, were willing to accept the offer of creating a Jewish homeland in Argentina or Uganda!

On the plane of political ideology the two nationalisms share a number of significant affinities. The most important is the nearly symbiotic nature of ethnic origin - Semitism - and the no less important religious monotheism of Judaism and Islam. Secularization has only had seminal success in the two experiences where a break with the importance played by religious practice and its influence in daily life as well as in political attitudes has not been consumed. Taking the symbiotic twin factor into consideration it is not surprising that secular forces in the Palestinian and Israeli secular political

3. Ibid: 47-48.

spheres share a common interest in containing the fundamentalist and anti-modernist forces in Israel/Palestine who are in opposition to the peace process.

The Quest for Peace by Unequal Partners

The battle between Zionism and Palestinianism was affected by the external support each could mobilize. The alignment of the United States with Israel while still nurturing a positive relationship to conservative Arab regimes has been to the detriment of the Palestinian cause. Israel has had almost unlimited access to economic and diplomatic, as well as military backing from the United States without losing the initiative. The Jewish lobby in Washington prevented the relationship from developing into a patron-client pattern. As far as the Palestinian nationalist movement is concerned it had to 'rely' on non-trustworthy friends, i.e. the former Soviet Union and its satellites, and competing Arab nationalist interests in the Middle East geopolitical sphere. The support of the world's most powerful nations for their regional allies made the so-called conflict between the Arab countries and Israel appear almost like an 'imaginary war'. Besides, taking Israel's possession of nuclear weapons into consideration overstates the term conflict.

As Duncan Clarke recently noted: 'Indeed, Israel's welfare, even survival, is dependent on its special relationship with Washington'.[4] Moreover, as a state whose economic and political well-being depends to an enormous degree on Western and especially American support— almost 25 percent of Israel's GNP today takes the form of American aid, which since 1967 has totalled the staggering figure of 77 billion dollars — we are entitled to draw the conclusion that Israel's occupation policies on the West Bank and Gaza are in fact subsidized by the West.[5]

This state of affairs along with the backing of the Jewish-American community has of course given Israeli politics its specificity both with regard to internal and external matters. Thus, as stated by an Israeli scholar, Israel is:

afflicted with an 'elite illegalism' that is central to the country's domestic political culture and international behaviour. Sustained partly by a pervasive security consciousness and born of genuine fears and the absence of a written constitution, elite illegalism

---

4. Duncan Clarke: 'Israel's Unauthorized Arms Transfers', *Foreign Policy* No. 99 Summer 1995: 89.
5. Edward W. Said: *The Politics of Dispossession. The Struggle for Palestinian Self-Determination*. 1969-94, New York: Vintage Books, 1995: 168.

deprecates the idea of the rule of law and assumes that 'democracy can work without a strict adherence to ... law.[6]

Israel represents a unique hybrid, combining democracy, with a system in which virtually everything is considered 'political', but also extremely centralized, with little diffusion of power and few checks and balances. Although belonging to the Western camp of liberal capitalism, 'Israeli commercial policy is the most protectionist in the democratic world. Israel has always had high tariff walls accompanied by even higher non-tariff barriers'.[7] The state owns dozens of industries including most of the energy companies, much manufacturing, all utilities, all public broadcasting, all the universities and academic research institutions, 93 percent of the country's land, and virtually all of the country's water supply. In 1992, the state also held most of the stocks in four out of the country's five major banks, including the two largest. Since 1948 the aim of Israeli economic policy has been to maximize political control, or at least political involvement, in every part of the economy.[8]

It is quite obvious that any economic relationship between Israel and the emerging Palestinian political entity, cannot be based on equality between Ismail and Isaac, but rather on unequal dependency in the mould of a David and Goliath relationship.[9] Approximately 90 percent of imports into the Palestinian territories come from Israel and between 70 and 80 percent of exports go to Israel. About a quarter of the population of the autonomous areas are supported by family members who work in Israel; however, these workers do not always have the necessary permits to enter Israel, since it is difficult to obtain them from the Israeli authorities. Airports, seaports, and other transit facilities are all under Israeli control.[10]

What Israel is doing to the Palestinians is set against a background of a long-standing Western tutelage over Palestine and the Arab world but also against a legacy of equally long-standing and equally unflattering anti-Semitism that, in this century, produced the Holocaust. The West cannot fail to connect the horrific history of anti-Semitic massacres to the establishment of Israel; nor can the West fail to understand the depths, the extent and the overpowering experience of suffering and despair that informed the post-World War II

---

6. Quoted in Clarke, 1995: 109.
7. Steven Plaut: 'Pork in Israel', *The National Interest,* Summer, 1992: 77.
8. Ibid, 78.
9. See the introduction in Johannes Dragsbaek Schmidt (ed.), *Ismael og Isak i det Forjættede Land (Ismail and Isaac in the Promised Land — in Danish).* Aalborg: Aalborg University Press, 1993: 9-23.
10. Muhammad Musli, 'Yassir Arafat's Dilemma', *Current History,* Vol. 94, (588), January 1995: 26.

Zionist movement. But it is no less appropriate for Europeans and Americans today, who support Israel because of the wrongs committed against the Jews, to realize that backing for Israel has included, and still includes, support for the exile and dispossession of the Palestinian people.[11]

According to Edward Said, Palestinians have, since 1948 been the victims of the victims, and are kept in this position to a great extent by Europe and the United States, both of whom look away and excuse Israeli behavior because the Hebrew state is still seen as a nation of survivors.

Islamists as Modernizers

Most Western scholars tend to regard Islam as a pre-modern force. However the most important pressures for political reform emanate from the myriad of Islamist movements that have emerged during the past two decades. As Augustus Richard Norton remarks:

It is a commonplace that the growth of Islamist movements is a reflection of Islam's inherent appeal over secular ideologies, which are often derided as alien and failed. There is some truth to this, but equally important, the Islamists have adopted a strategy of power seeking and have combined this strategy with a penetrating critique of government performance. The populist Islamist movements have tapped into a wellspring of discontent; they have not resumed the natural march of Muslim history. Of course, the failure of government to implement sharia (Islamic law) is often cited as part of the Islamists' critique, but central to that critique is the emphasis on corruption, malfeasance, and misbehaviour. The mistreatment of people at the hands of government is a constant refrain. The Islamist critique is persuasive because it rings so true'[12].

Misunderstanding of the resurgence of religious movements in the Muslim world is based on an over-emphasis of the violent anti-Westernism discourse and antagonism towards pro-Westerners in their own societies. In this connection it ought to be recalled that it was the American CIA which recruited and trained 'freedom' fighters from among the fundamentalist movements in Arab countries to fight in Afghanistan against the atheist Soviet troops! Nor should it be forgotten that Hamas was initially encouraged by the Israeli security apparatus in the occupied territories as a way of weakening the PLO. In addition, the popular support which fundamentalist organizations gets is often based on their philanthropical activities of organizing and helping the

---

11. Said, 1995: 167.
12. Augustus Richard Norton: 'The Challenge of Inclusion in the Middle East', *Current History*, Vol. 94, (588): 2.

poor who are faced with the inability of the modernizing state to fulfil their social duties. This has also been the case in the Palestinian territories after the PLO lost the funding of Saudi Arabia following Yasir Arafat's support for the Iraqi invasion of Kuwait.

Western scholars, often striking a tone that might be confused with apologia, have argued for the complementarity of Islamic concepts like consultation and consensus with democratic procedures. These analyses have missed the point; the crucial thinking among Islamists these days deals with questions of tolerance or civility, minority rights, and confidence and security.[13]

What is most important to understand is that political groupings like Hamas are much more than mere opposition groups: Hamas is a sentiment; it is an index of Palestinian frustration, just like the FIS in Algeria, and the Islamic movement in Iran led by Ayatollah Khomeini before them. In later years, the existence of Jewish fundamentalism in opposition to both the secularization of Israeli society and the peace process has also been revealed. Its clearest expression was of course the murder of Prime Minister Yitzhak Rabin.

The dilemma for secular forces in the area resides in co-opting religious activists in both camps who might otherwise transform traditional religious rites into militant political action. Nevertheless, if secular forces in the two camps fail to co-opt them, the new religious activists among Jews as well as Islamists, might transform traditional recourses such as praying and fasting into militant action. The idea of a return to Middle Age politics — a Clash of Civilizations — where politics is defined by the cultural struggle between those who want Israel to become like any other state and those who insist on a Jewish identity is a poor substitute to replace the old cliches about communism as the enemy, while the real question is a matter of solving the conflict by recognizing equal rights to each contracting party.

The Political Agenda of the Occupied Territories

Just like the confrontation between Zionism and Palestinianism has revolved around the question of land, the key to peace is likewise linked to how to defuse the problem. Israel has for some time been trying to establish a political culture unbound from the discourse about the territories. The centrality of territory seems somewhat to have abated also for the Palestinian side with only the demand for East Jerusalem as a minimal precondition. For the Israeli side the threat to this approach of delinking territory from the project of creating

13. Ibid: 3.

Eretz Israel evolves around fundamentalism, and there is no doubt that religious energy can be terribly dangerous. But 'Israel's dilemma is not whether deals with Syria or the Palestinians are worth the risk, but how to be Israel without the issue of the land'.[14]

Uri Avnery has remarked that 'the question is not whether the Oslo agreement is good or bad — but rather whether the implementation is progressing well and in good faith, and where it leads'.[15] There are a number of Palestinian agendas which must be solved before real peace can be accepted and final implementation achieved. One is that of the Palestinian diaspora who feels that the Israeli-PLO agreement ignores their concerns (primarily their right to return to their homeland within pre-1967 borders; also a not insignificant number claim a right to compensation for loss of their land in pre-1948 Israel); another is that of the Palestinians in the West Bank and Gaza, whose overriding priority is to rid themselves of all vestiges of Israeli occupation; a third is the status of Jerusalem; and a fourth is the obvious question of establishing the Palestinian state.

However, the most important obstacle to peace comes from rejectionists on both sides: among the Palestinians there are three groups which object to the peace agreement: radical rejectionists i.e. secular Left-wing organizations such as George Habbash's PFLP who doesn't want to give up the momentum of the uprising/Intifada; then there are the Yasir Arafat supporters who feel that their leader has gone too far in alienating many people, and finally the disenchanted members within Fatah who criticize their chief — sometimes in public: according to Muhammad Musli, these groups are, in contrast to Islamic fundamentalist forces, united in their calls for democratization. Six principal ideas govern their position:

1) The PLO executive committee, its chairman (Yasir Arafat), its central council, and its bureaucracy should not be arbitrarily superimposed on the Palestine Authority (PA), or on the limited local self-government the Palestinians have been allowed to establish as an interim measure under the Israeli-PLO agreement.

2) The pro-democracy political culture embraced by the Palestinians in the West Bank and Gaza must replace the autocracy and paternalism of Yassir Arafat and the Tunis-based Palestinian leadership.

---

14. Martin Woollacott: 'Israel must become a nation, not a land', *Guardian Weekly*, Nov. 19th, 1995.
15. 'Who is the Opponent?', *Tikkun*, May-June 1994: 38.

3) The institutions created, or about to be created, by Yasir Arafat should protect human rights and individual liberties, and should be staffed on the basis of merit and not patronage.

4) The political field should be open to every Palestinian. A constitution drafted by delegates elected specifically for the purpose should have primacy over the concerns and interests of entrenched elites.

5) All authority should flow from the people and should be exercised by elected bodies. This is the only way to assure the creation of government and leadership style suited to nation-building.

6) Yasir Arafat should take orders from one master — the Palestinian people — and not from the Israeli or any other party or quarter.[16]

But as long as these fundamental agendas and demands have not been met, the peace agreement cannot be implemented. Yasir Arafat's PA is caught as hostage to Israel in a number of ways. One is at the security level where the PA is expected to succeed where Israel's military and intelligence services failed in curtailing and quelling the Islamic groups and the secular opposition.

Every move, every remark Yasir Arafat makes is microscopically scrutinized by Israel. Worse, Yasir Arafat constantly has to prove to Israel that he is credible and trustworthy.[17]

The fundamental question for the PA as well as for Israel concerns the choice between inclusion or exclusion of oppositional forces in the peace process. If Fatah/PA excludes Hamas and other rejectionists the alternative might lead to a Palestinian civil war. If Israel cannot accommodate its rejectionists among the fundamentalists, Likud party supporters and essentially the Oriental Jews, no peace settlement will be implemented in the near future.[18]

---

16. Musli, 1995: 24-25.
17. Ibid: 26.
18. As Avi Shlaim points out, 'While there is broad consensus in Israel, encompassing both Likud and Labour, that places national security above peace, there is no similar consensus on whether Israel should be prepared to trade the territories captured in 1967 for peace with her neighbours.' The ideology of Greater Israel — Judea and Samaria — is the driving force behind Jewish fundamentalism. 'Israeli Politics and Middle East Peacemaking', *Journal of Palestine Studies*, Vol. 24, (4), Summer 1995: 20-31.

Conclusion: Changing Political Cultures and Nationalist Expectations

While the Jewish political movement in the form of Zionism succeeded in establishing the national entity of Israel, it has constantly striven to prevent Palestinian nationalism from achieving the goal of creating a Palestinian state. As such it would be ahistorical to ascribe the difficulties behind the peace process as entirely due to the fundamentalist fringes in either camps. Both secular nationalist movements presently have leaderships who, taking internal, regional and international constellations into consideration, reached the conclusion that the time was ripe for concessions and compromises. The Israeli government — supported by a significant segment of the population — has decided to share the same bed as the PLO-leadership — also supported by a war-weary Palestinian population. But the question remains whether the two nationalisms have abandoned the dreams for which they fought for.

The peace accords of Oslo I and Oslo II have set a process in motion whereby Israel is willing to see a Palestinian entity comprising, except for Jerusalem, the cities of the occupied territories while itself retaining control of the countryside where the implanted Jewish colonies will have access to the resources (land + water). As a matter of fact, since 1993 Israel has intensified infrastructural projects whereby a highway network would permit transportation to and from these Jewish settlements without coming in contact with Palestinian villages and towns. With all its limitations to the interests of Palestinian nationalism, Jewish fundamentalism in both Israel and the United States is nevertheless violently opposed to the process.

When Israel formally transferred to the PA responsibility for education and culture, health, social welfare, direct taxation, and tourism, some observers saw this as evidence of emerging, albeit hybrid, state structures. Furthermore, taking into consideration the combined fact that the PLO transferred its political state-type infrastructure from Tunis to Gaza and Jericho, and that the leadership of the Intifada (UNLU) had been building a sophisticated social infrastructure and a number of political institutions, an emerging new state seemed almost irreversible. Obviously, the state already exists, in part because its success in achieving international recognition will not depend on a commensurate ability to defend and control territory. External powers might come to the conclusion that there is little difference between autonomy and nominal sovereignty once the structure of the final peace settlement is put into place; 'As, importantly, the state will build on Palestinian nation-building since 1948 and on the consolidation of a new political system and social alliances in Gaza and the West Bank (including East Jerusalem) under the PA'.[19]

Or the Palestinian Utopia might become a reality through the emerging Israeli insistence on mutual 'separation' — a peaceful apartheid — consisting of sniffer dogs, border fences, guards and electronic surveillance, indeed a physical border between the Territories and Green line Israel.[20] Certainly Israel is still capable of 'cantonizing' the West Bank and the Gaza Strip, but as external powers have prolonged the conflict for nearly fifty years, it will also be up to these powers to 'encourage' Israel. Israel was after all created by the West, now it is time for the West to help in the creation of a new Palestine.

Yasir Arafat's leadership seems to have stabilized and the opposition (both secular and fundamentalist) has been weakened - as a result of the hardship the population was subjected to during the Intifada. Under these conditions the prospects are limited. Within the pro-peace forces among Palestinians, concern is mounting about the viability of an autonomous entity without access to the resources of land and water. The Palestinian media have put forward the example of Singapore as a city-state which has been able to survive on the basis of its human capital. With the same population but with less than half the territory which Oslo II grants the Palestinians, the city-state of Southeast Asia is seen as a success story with its remarkable performances within high-tech industries.[21] Can technology and capital fulfill the aspirations of Palestinian nationalism? This question depends not only on the ability of the PLO to establish a strong developmental state, but also on Israel as well as the Arab nations in the region, and transnational investment, technology transfers and not least market access.

While some forces within the Palestinian nationalist movement appear to put their hope in becoming a high-tech capitalist island in the Arab world, politicians within Israel's Labour Party — especially around former Prime Minister Shimon Peres — look to the creation of some form of Middle East Free Trade Area. Aware that globalization of the world economy is

19. Besides the legal basis of their statehood, to which both the US and Israel are parties by virtue of their acceptance of United Nations General Assembly Resolution 181 of November 1947, the Palestinians understand that their exercise of sovereignty over their land, resources, and people is the key determinant of their well-being and national survival. See the discussion about security and weak versus strong state in Yesid Sayigh, 'Redefining the Basics: Sovereignty and Security of the Palestinian State', *Journal of Palestine Studies*, Vol. 24, (4), Summer 1995: 7-8.

20. The Middle East, London, March 1995: 17-19. See also the argument by Sayigh, ibid: 18, that from now on the debate about Palestinian statehood must be given more concrete substance.

21. Jan de Jong, 'Israël, maître de la Cisjordanie', *Le Monde diplomatique*, December 1995: 19.

simultaneously stimulating economic and political regionalism, the future of Israel might be better served by surmounting the limitations of Jewish nationalism and becoming an integrated part of the Middle East. After all it is questionable how long the dependency on American economic and political support can go on.

If this argument is valid, then what we are observing is the trade-off of two nationalist political movements towards economic projects in order to become 'normal' societies. But it is still uncertain as to whether these scenarios are viable, since so many variables will have to be controlled.

The Transformation of Palestinian Civil Society and Its Role in Developing Democratic Trends in The West Bank and Gaza Strip

Manuel S. Hassassian

Introduction

Albeit there is no unanimity on the definition of democracy, many political theorists and thinkers have construed certain commonalities as to the parameters of democracy. Democracy for many, is a means of goverment which is close to human nature, and aspires to construct a civil society governed by equality and parity in the eyes of God and the law. It is a rational system stemming not from metaphysical foundations, but from the inspiration of experience, the human mind and the outcome of social experiences.

It is undeniable that the historical development of mankind, with its socio economic formation, enhanced the awareness of man and his development through social relations during the capalist technical age of human societies. It is also undeniable that this development has consolidated social classes based on pluralistic thought. However, in laying the foundations of social justice and equity, democracy has adamantly attempted to shape the nature of this concept.

Along this vein of analysis, the social scientist Sa'ad Al-Deen Ibrahim praises social justice as a concept and practice. He confirms:

.... that social justice is not based on the values of sympathy, pity and charity as sole moral values, but rather on practical considerations, most important of which is deeming social justice as a guarantee for stability and peace in society, and a necessity to enhance the participation of the society's members in public affairs and political rights...

Democracy is based on the institutionalization of society, through consolidating constitutional and legal foundations which restrict the power of the executive authority and identify the rights and duties of the people. Therefore, democracy thrives on the rules of rationality and certain trends and not on individual discretion. Actually, discussing the concept of democracy is in fact a discussion on the nature of state. The political society in essence is divided into the governors and the governed. What is needed is a balance between authority and freedom, rights and obligations, relations between the state and civil society, and the degree to which the state, as a legal and institutional entity, represents the structures and forces in the society. In other words, discussing the issue of democracy is in fact discussing the legitimacy of the state and the legitimacy of the political and social systems. Political democracy, therefore, is a national necessity because there are only two ways to achieve national unity; either by sheer force or through free administration, which is practised through institutions in a constitutional way. Democracies flourish when nurtured by citizens who are ready to practise their freedom by participating in public debate, by electing their representatives and by accepting the need for tolerance and harmony in a free life.

With the emergence of the New World Order, the values of Western Democracy are being accepted nearly everywhere, and the discussion of democracy is conducted within the framework of liberal democracy. Of course, there is an emerging divergence in support for the rhetoric and support for the reality of democracy.

The end of the Cold War culminated in the advent of a new era in world politics and international relations, that define its parameters in the context of globalizing democracy. World recognition of this globalization of democracy induced Third World Societies, albeit sluggishly, to achieve a relative state democracy. Hence, civil society as an operational concept had emerged as an overarching category; organically spanning democracy, development and peaceful management of conflict domestically, regionally and internationally. It is evident that the emergence of 'Civil Society' is mandatory, although not a sufficient condition for the development of democracy. It is no wonder that civil society poses great threats to autocracy and arbitrary rule, and is widely supported by many Arab intellectuals as well as at the grassroots, because it signifies change and prosperity to them.

However, an alert observer could detect the transformation of primordial social relations in the Arab world, into a fledgling civil society in concord with the New World Order. Several Arab states at least, have already embarked on democratizing their societies by introducing pluralism, tolerance and elections in to their culture of politics as ways and means of building civic institutions.

It should be noted that the procedural definition of democracy is still inadequately interpreted by Arabs; The Palestinians are no exception to this, because one cannot presume the existence of a culture of accommodation which would make democracy operational. Yet, the importance of a democratic Palestinian entity in the aftermath of the Israeli occupation cannot be overstated, for it is a pre-condition for peaceful coexistence with Israel.

The Palestinians spared no time in developing certain trends in democratic behaviour, entrenched in the culture of a nascent civil society, already initiated in the 1970s by the institution building and development of grassroot organizations.

This paper will emphasize the nature of civil society in the West Bank and Gaza Strip because it has been argued theoretically to be critical for the facilitation of democratic governance. However, 'Civil Society' is defined as sub-national participation in political and socio-economic organizations, independent of the State. There is no doubt that civil society has played a pivotal role in the sustenance of the Intifada, and functioned throughout the Occupation since 1967, to fill socio-economic as well as political gaps stemming from the lack of a national government. It provided 'inter alia' the individual and society with services that enabled them to survive the 'modus operandi' of occupation. More importantly, one essential question to be asked is: To what extent has Palestinian political culture adopted the ideals associated with democracy? To answer this question, it is imperative that we describe the Arab context of democracy; one that has been erratic in both substance and form.

The Absence of Democracy In the Arab World

Although pan-Arabism is proclaimed as a value among the ruling classes and widely shared as a sentiment by the masses, Arab society is highly heterogeneous in its structure and plagued by factionalism, parochialism, tribalism and regionalism. Futhermore, it suffers from foreign control, economic subservience, the power of traditional loyalties (religious, kinship and ethnic), and repressive socio-economic and political conditions. Above all, it is fragmented because it lacks genuine links between the political power base and civil society. The result is a crisis in the legitimacy and credibility of a leadership that only survives through practicing any authoritarianism. No wonder, then, that the central problem of Arab governements today is an absence of political accountability. This lack of legitimacy explains the unstable, autocratic and volatile behaviour of Arab regimes.

One of the explanations that has been advanced for the short-comings of Middle Eastern democracies is the suffering of the Arab World and the installment of ruling classes as regimes by proxy. It must be acknowledged, though, that not all of the impediments to Arab progress have been created by external forces. The prevalence of traditional loyalties and value orientations, as well as high illiteracy rates, has been a significant factor in slowing the pace of democratization in the Arab World. Moreover, the discord between Arab heritage and Western values has made it difficult for Arab Societies to absorb democratic ideas that were the culmination of a long process of development in the West. The lack of an Arab substructural system to respond to the Westernization and modernization process created a gap between reality and dream.

The absence of democracy in the Arab World is an outcome of successive failures by the nationalists and secularists to transform the fundamental social structures that perpetuate patriarchal societies. Unfortunately, the crisis of Arab intellectuals has also exacerbated the 'status quo' and hindered efforts to bridge the gaps in society. Most intellectuals are being co-opted by the political systems in the Arab World, and those 'refuseniks' suffer from alienation which prompts them to emigrate to the West. Above all, the region simply lacks the structural institutional framework for democratic participation.

Arab liberal thought failed to define democracy as a structure or a system of social transformation. It simply portrayed democracy as a panacea for Arab socio-political malaise. One of the major pitfalls of Arab liberal thought was its adoption of an idea from the West without understanding the need to build an economic infrastructure that could generate a social system responsive to democratic change. Value systems cannot be implemented without viable corresponding structural roots. The concepts of democracy were not emboldened by the ruling elites; despite the slogans of secularism, nationalism and freedom which they espoused in their defiance of colonialism.

The political systems in the Arab World use liberal and democratic terminology such as 'pluralism as instruments aimed at containing the street, rather than unleashing it'. Among the vibrant actors on the political scene today are the proponents of Political Islam, who categorically oppose the notion of freedom and democracy as *hulul mustaurada* (imported solutions). For the Muslim fundamentalists, Islam is the only viable option for the resolution of Arab problems on the socio-economic and political levels. In Islam there is *shura* (consulation) and *ijma'* (consensus) but no democracy. Democracy is viewed as an alien concept stigmatized by association with the Western hegemonies and imperialists motives in recolonizing the Arab Muslim World.

The ebb and flow of Islamic resurgence in the Middle East is correlated with the degree of success or failure on the part of secular Arab regimes in responding to the aspirations of the Arab masses. Arab nationalists and those in opposition attempt, to no avail, to put pressure on the Arab regimes to modernize, industrialize, build institutions, and above all protect basic human rights.

Democracy is not an absolute concept. In its ideal state it is intertwined organically with freedom. It strives to create parity between the individual and society through representative and participatory government. The process of institution-building does not come after the imposition of modernization, but before. A democratic government does not come immedialety after the holding of elections, but after all the institutions have been put in place. One is reminded of Samuel Huntington's famous quote that 'Democracy is not synonymous with progress'. Countries that lack the institutions (e.g. the Islamic countries) needed to cope with a politicized society cannot be expected to uphold such a system for long. Other writers have talked about Western Democracy 'starving on 1000 calories a day' — meaning that a hungry person has other concerns that relegate vague notions which they cannot visualize into the background. Thus, if Islam (e.g., purported Islamic socialization) is taking care of the well-being of people's everyday life, it will be immaterial to settle for a diffrent ideology or otherwise. Therfore, it would almost seem as if indigenous questions had indigenous answers. In any case, it is sobering to consider that although each of us and collectively as a society or nation hold certain beliefs, we live in a world of billions where others have options and prejudices that are no less firmly hold than our own. In these circumstances, 'Rationality' itself thus becomes a very subjective term.

It is evident however, that the imposition of Western style measures on Islamic countries will not spur economic prosperity or improve human rights conditions; and abrupt democratization may not serve as a panacea to socio-economic ills. In fact, socio-economic liberalization programmes, if applied in tandem could gradually lay the groundwork for a sustainable transition toward democracy. On the other hand, rapid democratization in Muslim societies would create imbalances in the social, cultural and religious value system, which would ultimately lead to its total rejection and failure. However, the question of Islam and democracy has been an ongoing heated debate among Arab intellectuals in the Middle East, and many apologists try to reconcile them. In reality, the gap is widening and the contradictions are even greater than ever.

The Evolution of 'Pluralism' in Palestinian Political Culture

Palestinian cultural expression has been organically interwoven with the political developments and realities, and along their political struggle, Palestinians succeeded in embodying within their national ethos a culture of resistance and a momentum of socio-political transformation. Palestinians have defined democracy in the context of human rights, civil rights and self-determination, and to a certain degree, they have emphasized changes in their educational system.

Undoubtly, the Intifada has been instrumental in encouraging the Palestinians towards institution-buliding, thus expanding the democratization process among the grassroots of the Palestinian Community through the growing number, and membership, of trade unions, professional associations, women, student and youth movements and the like. A great number of Palestinians regarded their participation in these organizations as a major mean by which to defy the Israeli occupation and establish democratic institutions.

Consequently, the notion of democracy became, alongside the ideas of national solidarity and struggle against occupation, a major ethos among Palestinians. And throughout the 1980s democracy was perceived as the basis of Palestinian solidarity, popular mobilization and steadfastness (*Sumud*). This democratic process gained momentum which culminated in sub-structural changes; the expansion of education and the growing political awareness among the lower strata of Palesinians, urban and rural alike.

The lessons of the past five decades or so — indeed, the lessons of this century, marked by conquest, occupation and colonization — have taught the Palestinians that unless democratic practices are implemented at every level of daily life — in the home, in schools, offices and factories, the new state of Palestine will emerge as a replica of the surrounding authoritarian Arab regimes. A large number of Palestinian intellectuals, including proponents of the fundamentalist wing of Palestinian politics, consider political pluralism and freedom to be basic ingredients of the future Palestinian polity. Hence, a multi-party system is upheld as the most desirable model.

To illustrate the process of democratization already in progress, it is important to shed some light on the labour unions, professional associations, and popular organizations. It is important to note here that Palestinian political factions were operating clandestinely because they were not allowed to practice politics under occupation. Yet, it could be asserted that all elections held in these organizations were based on partisanship.

Labour Unions

The Palestinian workers have undergone dramatic changes in the Occupied Territories, and reportedly, of about 160,000 workers in 1968, only 6 percent were organized in labour Unions. However, in the late 1970s, the number of the total Palestinian labour force increased to 230,000 in the Occupied Territories and Israel, with only 20 percent registered as members of trade unions.

Palestinians boast of having more than 100 labour unions, with a total of 40,000 members, organized since the early 1980s into three federations affiliated to the different PLO factions. Regardless of their objectives, they run their internal affairs in a bureaucratized manner based on democratic mechanisms such as elections and checks and balances.

The Student Movement

The student movement has, unlike the labour unions, been vociferous politically because of its politicized nature and assumption of a leading role in the struggle against occupation. Certainly, the student movement is considered to be avant-garde in its application of democratic practices because of its high level of education and exposure to Western liberal concepts.

The student movement is structurally and ideologically divided along the PLO's political spectrum in addition to the Islamists-Hamas. It is worth mentioning, that the six universities in the Occupied Territories accomodate 20,000 students, and that elections for the student senate have been conducted in a democratic fashion with a high percentage of students participation.

The Women's Movement

In the early 1980s, other new social organizations emerged which reflected a wider range of political participation, and the women's movement is a significant example. Comprised of some 15,000 members, they belong to the main factions of the PLO. These organizations have practiced democratic elections and have been highly active in socio-cultural, vocational and paramedical work as well as in national/political activities against occupation.

Professional Associations

Other organizations were established during the 1980s, these include associations of merchants, lawyers, physicians, engineers, writers and journalists. These associations have provided the intellectual and conceptual guidance for mass political participation in the national struggle against occupation. Democratic elections based on pluralism have predominated the activities of these associations and have reflected their structural hierarchy which is based on decentralized and delegated authority.

The Crafting of Democracy in a Future Palestinian State

The Palestinian Declaration of Independence, addressed the question of the type of regime in the future independent Palestinian State. In fact, the last paragraph in the Declaration emphasizes the full equality in rights among Palestinians, and that Palestinians will be able to enjoy their national and cultural identity. Further, the Palestinian State will safeguard:

Their political and religious convictions and their human dignity by means of a Parlamentary democratic system of governance, itself based on freedom of expression and the freedom to form parties.

Moreover, the Declaration has made it clear in the area of authority and representation that:

... the right of minorities will be duly respected by the majority, as minorities must abide by decisions of the majority. Governance will be based on principles of social justice, equality and non-discrimination in race, religion, colour, sex under the aegis of a constitution which ensures the rule of law and the independent judiciary...

In principle, the language of the Declaration reflects a philosophical commitment to the development of democratic institutions. By and large, the seeds of democratic growth already exist in Palestinian society.

1) Within the PLO and the National Authority emphasis has been placed on the importance of democratic procedures in relation to the decision-making process. A shift from consensus to majority politics is quite explicit in the decision-making process.

2) Palestinians in the Occupied Territories have established a tradition of elections, and the 1972 and 1976 municipal elections are good examples; not to mention the current on-going elections in the main professional associations, trade unions, labour unions, student movements, and women's organizations.

3) The high literacy rate among Palestinians has been instrumental in loosening the patriarchal, traditional social structure. It is known that the development of education is a prerequisite for a democratic civil society.

4) For many years, the Palestinians have been engaged in a heated debate among themselves concerning their future. Of course, the debate has led to a wider acceptance of the principles of negotiations and political compromise - two cornerstones of democratic development.

5) The concept of freedom is extremely important to the outlook of many Palestinian intellectuals and political elites in the Occupied Territories, and especially during this transitional period.

6) Emphasis has been made on democracy as a means to encompass cultural diversity and variegated points of view among the interior and exterior Palestinians living in the diaspora.

7) Repression of the Palestinian leaders of the Intifada has induced diffusion and a decentralization of power to the grassroots organizations.

8) Palestinians during the Intifada have established new patterns of collective behaviour and self-reliance — two charateristics of democratic behaviour.

9) The role of women organizations during the Intifada has undermined the traditional perception of women in the Arab world, and has brought the plight of women closer to social and economic equality.

10) The Palestinian leadership strata represents to a certain degree, a western-educated leadership that may play a pivotal role in the crafting of the new regime of the Palestinian state. Palestinians cannot afford to build a non-democratic state, because they will be heavily dependent, economically, on Western donor countries.

11) The impact of the Israeli occupation has prompted the Palestinians to become familiar with a political system that espouses the rule of law and democracy. Paradoxically, it has left a positive impact on the political culture of the Palestinians, who categorically reject a Palestinian authority that would become a replica of Arab authoritarian regimes.

12) The impact of the Intifada has been tremendous in institution-building, and in developing Palestinian socio-economic infrastructure in the Occupied Territories.

13) The emergence of a middle-class among Palestinians has been significant in the process of building a Palestinian civic society that would bolster a democratic Palestinian State or entity.

Based upon the above-mentioned observations, one might be tempted to assert that Palestinian society is evolving in a democratic manner which could enhance and bolster future relations with democratic neighbours like Israel and Jordan. It is worth mentioning, that democracy in Palestine has not taken root; it is still in process and could be considered a fledgling democracy. Giovanni Sartori, explained it best when he warned that:

... new states and developing nations cannot pretend to start from the level of achievement at which the Western democracies have arrived. In fact, no democracy would ever have materialized if it had set the advanced goals for itself that a number of modernizing states currently claim to be pursuing. In a world-wide perspective, the problem is to minimize arbitrary and tyrannical rule and to maximize a pattern of civility rooted in respect and justice for each man ... in short, to achieve a humane polity. Undue haste and overly ambitious goals are likely to lead to opposite results.

Definitly, this warning is applicable to the Palestinian political culture, because the Palestinians have never established their own State, and therefore it is premature to expect them to adopt Western democractic values to their society in no time at all.

Notwithstanding the many hurdles, there are good indications that Palestinian society will develop democratic principles and will establish a democratic political entity. According to Hisham Sharabi, a leading Palestinian scholar:

Only a free and democratic Palestinian entity alongside Israel will guarantee a genuine and lasting peace. An autocratic regime, such as exists today in many Arab Countries, would not last, and would inevitably lead to economic and political disintegration with unpredictable consequences.

Democracy cannot survive in Palestine if it only offers elections and multi-partisanship. Only real democracy can restore faith in the civic society and maintain self-fulfilment and aggrandizement. Futhermore, democracy cannot develop without a viable economic infrastructure, because the economy of the West Bank and Gaza is presently in a shambles. Therefore, an urgent need for stimulating economic development in the Occupied Territories is a pre-condition for political stability in the area.

There is no doubt that over recent years, serious structural problems in the economy of the Occupied Territories have come to light, and these require immediate attention:

1) Heavy dependence on outside sources of employment for the Occupied Territories' labour force.

2) Low degree of industrialization.

3) A trade structure heavily dominated by trade links with Israel and large trade deficits.

4) Inadequate public infrastructure and services.

5) Economic assistance to build Palestinian Institutional capacity (by the World Bank and the donor countries).

6) Promotion of a private-led sector of the economy with public sector involment.

7) Foreign aid is needed to support:
   a. Infrastructure projects
   b. Training and Education
   c. Technical Assistance
   d. Welfare programmes

To summarize a strategy of economic development for the Occupied Territories, a three-phased strategy has been espoused by the Palestinian National Authority.

Phase one: Moving from dependence to independence and its sub-strategies.

Phase two: Moving from independence to interdependence.

Phase three: The involvement of Israel and Palestine in other blocs (Interdependence with the Arab World-building bridges with the United States, Europe, Russia, and Japan).

Such a strategy would insure the building of an infrastructure that would synchronize best with the ideals of democracy. One could infer that only independent civil infrastructure can ensure a democratic society based on the freedom and rights of the individual. Democracy should evolve to be the supreme political value over ideological and factional adherence.

Palestinian Civil Society in the Making: Future Prospects

Ideally, civil society should both entangle itself in dealing with government intervention, and exhibit a dimension of tolerance within and among the institutions that it encompasses. The pertinence of civil society to the democratization process is solely based on the facts that 1) Popular institutions lay the groundwork for the grassroots training in the areas of plurality and democratic behaviour; and 2) Civil Society can counterpoise the autocracy of the State. The Palestinians experimentation with the development of Civil Society had developed certain exclusivity when compared with that of the Arab world.

There is no doubt that the Palestinians have contrived to build institutions and organizations that include an 'array of political parties, municipal service organizations, cooperatives, educational institutions, students senates, women's organizations, health care associations, charitable organization, trade unions, business associations, child care facilities, and religious groups (including welfare and social service organization run by these group), 'think-tanks', professional unions and syndicates (e.g. lawyers' guilds and medical associations) and chambers of commerce'.[1]

These variegated organizations and groups have developed over the last three decades in the Occupied Territories, and have been responsive in catering to the social needs of the Palestinians in the absence of any political national authority. Of course, the service rendered enabled the Palestinians to survive under Israeli military occupation. However, these diverse formations will culminate in the building of an infrastructure of civil and political institutions - a prelude to an independent Palestinian State. Futhermore, the structure of Palestinian civil society is emboldened by several significant attributes conducive to the process of democratization in the Palestinian autonomous areas.

One of the main attributes is the tolerance of divergent opinions, that has developed into a tradition among Palestinians especially within the political infrastructure of the PLO. The concept of pluralism within the factions of the PLO has been one of the banners which evolved to become an intrinsic value within the Palestinian social system. It is no wonder then, that today the opposition forces within the Palestinian political spectrum are respected and tolerated by the mainstream. This is an essential element indicating a level of 'civility' in civil society. Undoubtedly, the opposing groups would act as a check on the performance of the authority in a democratic enviroment.

---

1. Shukri Abed, unpublished article on Palestinian civil society.

Another major attribute is the development of a participatory culture in which elections and popular consent are the main sources of legitimacy. A good example to cite here is the active political participation of women. Today this stands as an essential part of Palestinian civil society, which in turn has crucial impact on the establishment and consolidation of pluralist thinking and democratic rule.

One could suggest that such attributes are already in operation in Palestinian society, and need only to be bolstered and legitimized by the Palestinian National Authority. It is fair to say, that Palestinian society has been severely distorted and affected by Israeli military occupation, and inspite of these distortions, the Palestinians had contrived to build a civil society which is still nascent in form and substance. The transition of Palestinian society from a traditional/rural to urban/neo-patriarchal is sincerely registered by social science observers. However, it is not yet adequate by Western standards. Therefore, Palestinians still have to struggle in the building process of their institutions and have to establish the pre-conditions for such an evolution. The economic factor is a vital one in fulfilling this objective, and Palestinians need to have the proper material and spiritual conditions to facilitate this process. Israel, Jordan and the donor countries are keys to the success of the process.

Conclusion

Although, the seeds of democratization exist in Palestinian society, one cannot assert that it has potentially developed. Despite the shortcomings, Palestinians have managed to transplant the seeds of a civil society, and these already have a distinctive impetus on the process of democratization. Definitely, the growth of a democratic civil society in the Occupied Territories will sustain itself in the post-occupation phase. Unfortunately, one can venture to assert that the subject of civil society in the Middle East in general and in Palestinian society in particular, is a relatively new focus of scholarly research and concern.

Most of the early research done in this area is considered as pioneering, but there is no doubt that the Palestinian democratic attitudes have become pervasive in the political culture at large.

The future of Palestinian civil society and its impact on the process of democratization, is organically intertwined with the political developments of the region.

The Peace Process in the Middle East — Explanations and Future Prospects

Ulf Bjereld

On September 13th, 1993, at an impressive ceremony held outside the White House in Washington, Israel and the PLO signed 'The Declaration of Principles on Interim Self-Government Arrangements'. In this Declaration, Israel and the PLO stated that it is time to put an end to the decades of confrontation and conflict and instead work for a just, lasting and comprehensive peace settlement. The ceremony was led by the US president Clinton and included the historic handshake between Israel Prime Minister Rabin and the PLO Chairman Arafat. Rabin and Arafat, together with Israeli Foreign Minister Shimon Peres, received the 1994 Nobel Peace Prize for their contribution to the peace process.

By signing the Declaration of Principles, Israel recognized the PLO as 'The Representative of the Palestinian people'. The PLO recognized Israel's right to exist in peace and security. Arafat also recommended that the Palestinians in the West Bank and Gaza Strip bring to an end the Intifada and reject the use of political violence and terrorism.

The Declaration of Principles contains a set of mutually agreed general principles regarding the five-year period of Palestinian self-rule. A Palestinian Interim Self-Government Authority shall be established and a Council shall be elected for the Palestinian people in the West Bank and Gaza Strip for a transitional period not exceeding five years, leading to a permanent settlement based on Security Council Resolutions 242 and 338. Israel shall withdraw from parts of the occupied West Bank and Gaza Strip. Authority shall be transferred from the Israeli military government to the authorized Palestinians, and a Palestinian police force shall be established. Negotiations between Israel and the elected representatives of the Palestinian people shall begin as soon as possible; these would include the questions of the status of Jerusalem, Palestinian refugees, security arrangements and the future of the Jewish settlements.

No matter how the peace process develops in future, the signing of the Declaration of Principles was a historical moment. For the first time in modern ages, Jews and Palestinians recognized one anothers legitimacy and agreed upon the rules for a continued peace process.

But why did Israelis and Palestinians succeed this time in reaching an agreement? History is full of attempts and ambitions to reach a solution, all of which have failed. And what are the prospects for the future development of the peace process? Are there any reasons for further optimism, or are the remaining questions about the status of Jerusalem, the rights of the Palestinian refugees and the future of the Jewish settlements so difficult that the possibilities of reaching a just and durable solution are in fact very small?

Ever since World War I, when Palestine was excluded from the Ottoman Empire to become a British Mandatory, there has been antagonism between the Palestinian and the Jewish groups of the population. The attempts to solve the conflict have been almost innummerable: The King-Crane Commission 1919, The Peel Commission 1936, United Nations Special Committee on Palestine (UNSCOP) 1947, the Bernadotte Plan 1948, the Jarring Mission 1967-73, the Rogers Plan 1969, Kissingers shuttle diplomacy 1974-77, the Camp David Treaties 1978, the EC Venice Declaration 1980, the Rogers Plan 1982, the Fez-plan 1982 and the Brezjnev-plan 1982. Even a brief enumeration tends to be of length.

Just a few years before the diplomatic break-through, the negotiation situation between Israelis and Palestinians was characterized as a stalemate. Sometimes, as a joke, it is said that the pessimists are always right when it comes to development in the Middle East. Hardly ever has the pessimism been so strong and unequivocal as it was at the end of the 1980s. It is true that the Palestinian revolt in the occupied territories — the Intifada — which started in December 1987 was a serious problem for Israel, but it did not significantly change the political and military power structure in the region. Israel stubbornly refused to recognize: the legitimate rights of the Palestinian people; the PLO as the representative of the Palestinian people, and refused to negotiate with the PLO.

The PLO and the Palestinians had, on their part, made some concessions. A few weeks after the Palestinian National Council in Algiers, November 15th, 1988, had proclaimed the State of Palestine, the PLO also, indirectly, recognized Israel's right to exist. The PLO also indirectly recognized Security Council Resolutions 242 and 338 and declared a renouncement of terrorism.

However, the Palestinian concessions were not unambiguous. Israel's right to exist was not explicitly recognized; the recognition of Security Council Resolutions 242 and 338 was accompanied by some reservations, and the renouncement of terrorism only referred to territories outside the State of Israel and the occupied territories of the West Bank and Gaza Strip. Military operations against Israel and use of force in connection with the Intifada could continue.

The Palestinian concessions were not followed by corresponding concessions from Israel. Apart from the strong support for the Palestinians in world opinion caused by the Intifada and Israel's harsh policies in the West Bank and Gaza Strip, the political gains for the PLO and the Palestinians were small. The Palestinians had used their last diplomatic card and could make no more compromises. Israel had no incentives to make any concessions at all. Any progress in the peace process therefore required a change in the power relations between the various parts in the conflict.

The end of the Cold War and the collapse of the Soviet Union caused great changes in the distribution of power between Israel, the PLO and the Arabic States. No matter how you see it, no matter what sympathies you might share, no matter how well-deserved Rabin's, Peres' and Arafat's peace prizes were, the most important single factor for the progress in the peace process in the Middle East was the end of the Cold War. The end of the Cold War and the collapse of the Soviet Union basically changed the strategic situation in the Middle East.

Israel

From an Israeli point of view, the new situation offered both advantages and disadvantages. The first sizeable advantage was that Israel's two counterparts in the conflict — the Palestinians/PLO and the Arab states — lost their most important ally when the Soviet Union ceased to exist. Israel no longer needed to fear Arab armies financed and equipped with high technology weapons by a superpower.

The disintegration of the Soviet Union also implied a solution of what is sometimes, a little cynically, called 'the demographic problem' of Israel. 'The demographic problem' is that population growth is twice as fast among the Palestinian minority in Israel than among the Jewish population. The difference in population growth rates means that the Jews run the risk of becoming a minority in Israel. If Israel, for example, annexes the West Bank and Gaza Strip, the Palestinians will be a majority in the population by sometime around the year 2030. If at that time Israel is still a democracy, the Palestinian population probably would make the most of that situation and elect a Palestinian Government in Israel. Israel would then no longer be a Jewish state.

But the disintegration of the Soviet Union solved Israel's demographic problem almost overnight. During the period of 1989-93 half a million Jews immigrated to Israel, most of them coming from the former Soviet Union. This immigration flow has to be compared with Israel's former Jewish population of about 3.5 million. After 1993, the immigration flow seems to have decreased considerably. Although the large immigration flow placed considerable economic strain on Israel, it also contained long-term gains because of the increased knowledge resources (many of the immigrants were well-educated). Israel also gains a stronger political position with a greater proportion of Jews in the population. Because of the immigration, the higher Palestinian population growth rate no longer poses the same threat towards the Israeli state.

The end of the Cold War also made it possible for the UN to reach agreement among the Great Powers in the Security Council over the decision to force Iraq out of Kuwait in the so-called Gulf War of 1991. The Iraqi invasion of Kuwait, and Saddam Hussein's bombastic rethoric and launching of SCUD-missiles towards Israel turned attention away from the Palestinian Intifada and world opinion subsequently showed a greater understanding of Israel's exposed position.

But the end of the Cold War brought not only advantages for Israel. The greatest disadvantage was certainly that Israel now is a less important ally of the United States. During the Cold War period, the USA needed Israel as a strategic counterpart to the Soviet Union's ambitions in the Middle East. But in the absence of the Soviet Union there are no corresponding Superpower threats to the USA's interests in the region. The need for Israel's services are therefore less than before and the possibility of the USA bringing economic and political pressure on Israel has increased. During the Cold War, the strong Jewish lobby in the USA could draw strength from Israel's strategic importance to the USA. Today this possibility is much smaller. This will probably decrease the Jewish lobby's credibility and influence. Israel is also just as dependent on economic support from the USA as it was before.

Palestine

The PLO and the Palestinians strengthened their postition in world opinion at the end of the 1980s with the Intifada. The Palestinian revolt received great attention in the news media. Photographs of heavily-armed Israeli military forces shooting at stone-throwing Palestinian youngsters and beating Palestinian prisoners were spread across the world. And Palestinian political concessions in the form of the indirect recognition of Israel and of Security Council Resolutions 242 and 338 was met with appreciation around the world. However, as we stated before, the gains made by the Palestinians and the PLO in world opinion was not followed by any corresponding political or military gains in the conflict.

The Intifada imposed a great strain on the Palestinian people. The economic and human suffering was great. Arafat's moderate leadership of the PLO was challenged; by Palestinian Islamists on the one hand, in the form of Hamas, which defined the Palestinian cause as a struggle of Muslims against Jews, and on the other by the Palestinian Left, which repudiated the peace process and instead stated that the whole of Palestine should be liberated by military means.

The PLO also lost much of its goodwill in world opinion during the Gulf War. The PLO was restrained in its criticism of Saddam Hussein and hesitated, like Jordan, in condemning the Iraqi invasion of Kuwait.

The end of the Cold War and the disintegration of the Soviet Union brought the PLO and the Palestinians face to face with the risk of national catastrophe. The disappearance of the Soviet Union meant that the PLO lost its most important ally. The Intifada was stuck and Arafat's leadership was challenged by Islamic fundamentalism and Left-wing Parties which rose in strength due to the disappointment over the absence of political gains. Ahead, the Palestinians could discern a scenario where Israel signed bilateral peace treatments with their Arab neighbour-states at the expense of the Palestinians. There was a risk of a situation where the world once again forgot the Palestinians and their terrorism would reappear as the only useful weapon. By the indirect recognition of Israel and Security Council Resolutions 242 and 338 in December 1988, the PLO had compromised as far as it was politically possible. The end of the Cold War made new Palestinian concessions both possible and necessary.

The Arab States

The Arab States also lost their most important ally with the disappearance of the Soviet Union. The political leadership in these Arab States realized that they therefore, in the foreseeable future, had no chance of challenging Israel in military terms. It is also possible that the disintegration of the Soviet Union gave the Arab Governments the legitimacy among their own populations to pursue a more moderate policy towards Israel.

The course of events during the Gulf War, and the 'infidel' US troups on Arabian soil was, in the beginning, a source of humiliation to the Arab States. The fact that the Arabs themselves were incapable of solving their 'internal' problems with Iraq and had to accept help from the USA placed a big strain on Arab self-esteem. On the other hand there was the loyal participation of the Arab governments during the war which was highly appreciated by the Western countries.

Jordan

Jordan was the Arab state which (apart from Iraq and Kuwait, of course) suffered the most during the Gulf War. At the time of the war, 23 percent of Jordan's imports came from Iraq. Jordan had no domestic oil resources, and 90 percent of Jordan's oil was imported from Iraq. The Iraqi invasion of Kuwait also meant that the 300,000 Jordanian guest-workers in Kuwait could no longer send money home. Jordan had to receive about 500,000 refugees during the war, a vast number considering that Jordan's entire population is only 3.5 million.

The domestic opinion in Jordan did not show a particularly negative attitude to Saddam Hussein's Iraq, and the political leadership in Jordan was under great pressure. On one hand, the Western states demanded that Jordan give loyal support to the sanctions against Iraq. On the other hand, there was no whole hearted popular support for such involvement among Jordan's own population and their participation caused severe damage to Jordan's economy.

Jordan's participation in the sanctions was half-hearted and Jordan found itself, along with the PLO, in the political wilderness. By some clever manoeuvering, however, King Hussein dealt with the situation and succeded in signing a peace treaty with Israel without severe domestic protest. (About half of Jordan's population are Palestinians). This treaty also opened the door allowing Jordan back into the diplomatic community.

Syria

Syria's restraint during the Gulf War made the country a more acceptable cooperation partner for the Western states. Syria is an old arch-enemy of Iraq and the Syrian leadership had no difficulty in accepting the sanctions. The Syrian policy also made it possible for the Western states to give Assad and Syria *carte blanche* in Lebanon. Today, Syria has adapted its policy to the new political circumstances and is striving to attain a peace agreement with Israel, where Syria hopes to get the Golan Heights back, a territory which was occupied by Israel during the 1967 war.

Conclusion

The end of the Cold War drastically changed the power-balance in the Middle East in such a way that compromises which had not been possible earlier, now became both possible and necessary. All parts in the conflict became more vulnerable to external pressures — to a far greater extent than during the Cold War.

The changed power-balance was mostly unfavourable to the PLO and the Palestinians. The concessions they now accepted (for example the direct recognition of Israel and the abandonment of demands for the whole of Palestine) came from a weakened negotiation position. The concessions Israel accepted (especially the recognition of the PLO and the withdrawal from the occupied territories) came from a position of strength.

The most important element in the peace process so far is that the various sides have recognized each other as legitimate negotiation partners with legitimate interests. This is important, since recognition is an irreversible process. One party cannot one day declare that they accept the existence of their counterpart and the following day say they do not.

It is now of considerable importance to, almost literally, consolidate the progress which has been made in the peace negotiations in the West Bank and Gaza Strip. With the shaping of a new infrastructure, the withdrawal of Israeli military forces and the training of a Palestinian police force, the two parties must make it credible, both to themselves and to the world that there is no turning back. The peace process must not be left vulnerable to possible shifts in government or leadership changes on either the Israeli or the Palestinian side. Today, it seems to be very difficult for any part to 'roll back' what has happened during the negotiations. On the other hand, there is still a risk that the process can be interrupted, which would be bad enough.

A key question remains about how Israeli public opinion will address the continuation of the peace process following the murder of Prime Minister Rabin. To many Israelis, Rabin was a personal guarantee that the Israeli concessions would never threaten the security of Israel. Rabin could, with his military past and his 'hawkish' political profile, fill this role.

Of course, it is also important that the world, and the USA and the EU in particular, actively contributes with economic support for development programmes in the region and that the peace process gets the politically support it urgently needs. The decision by the US Congress to move the US Embassy from Tel Aviv to Jerusalem is, in that respect, a disturbing turn of events. No state of any importance has situated its embassy in Jerusalem, because it would be to anticipate a negotiated solution to the Jerusalem question. If the USA implements the Congress decision, this will make it difficult for the PLO and the Palestinians to accept further compromises in the negotiations.

The negotiating parts have chosen to solve the small problems first and leave the big ones until later. It could be interpreted, it is true, that Israel and the PLO have chosen the easy option by simply postponing all the major problems. But it could also be seen as the only possible way. If the negotiations had started with, for example, the Jerusalem question, the refugee problems or the question about the future of the Jewish settlements, negotiations would probably strand before they got a chance to start. Instead, the negotiating parties are now hoping that the strategy of 'small-steps diplomacy' will shape new political conditions which can in turn bring those problems which today appear 'unsolvable' into a new, more 'solvable', light.

The end of the Cold War created a 'window of opportunity' for the peace process in the Middle East. The bipolar structure, with strong superpower interests in the region, was loosened and replaced with the change in power relations; new alliances, new political combinations and new compromises suddenly became possible.

In time, this flexible structure will probably be replaced by a new superpower constellation. This will increase the risk that the involved parts in the conflict form themselves along new superpower front lines, which will lead to new deadlocks in the conflict. The peace process is in a hurry — time is not on its side.

Israel and the Peace Process

Naomi Chazan

On the subject of ethnic, national and religious contradictions, we are all aware that ethnicity and religious identification inevitably enter into continuous contradiction with the state system, and that this is a 20th century phenomenon which will not disappear. One can muster history, one can distort history and one can invent history to serve political purposes. In other words, we must recognize that different people will present different histories according to their particular backgrounds and interests, as well as the moment in which they choose to reflect. This is the nature of history; contradictions are inevitable. We must find political solutions to these problems, and these political solutions will always require each side being satisfied with less than the minimum that they think they deserve. This is a point I wish to repeat because it is extremely important to me as an Israeli. We must get used to the fact that in order to resolve problems, we will have to make do with less than we think is conceivable to 'make do' with. This is a working premise in any concrete attempt to come to terms with deep seated religious, ethnic and national problems. The next point, and one which is most difficult to transfer and transmit, is that periods of reconciliation of the kind being described, are periods of uncertainty often accompanied by violence. The Oslo agreements address the following points:

1) Two peoples live in these lands.

2) This conclusion, though it seems obvious, is revolutionary in the context of the Arab-Israel conflict. Not only do two peoples live in the land, but two peoples must share the land.

3) In order to share the land we must recognize the mutual political rights of both peoples. I emphasize the political rights, of both peoples.

4) That the Palestinian-Israeli conflict is the key to resolving the Arab-Israel conflict — to achieving a comprehensive peace in the region.

5) Most importantly: in the Declaration of Principles, the purpose of the negotiations is laid down categorically: 'To achieve a historic reconciliation between our peoples'. Both Israel and the PLO have agreed to this. It is a statement of intent. What we began in Washington in September 1993, is not peace, but a negotiation process which will lead to peace. What is taking place now is not a result of the *Peace Accord*, but an integral part of the dynamic of a negotiation process which, upon its successful completion, will lead to peace.

The *Oslo Accords* are not just a series of words. They are an agenda with two stages as follows:

1) Interim accords.

2) A final settlement, which will be concluded within 5 years after signing the first phase of the *Gaza-Jericho Accords*, or the *Cairo Agreements*. In other words, we have entered into a process that we believe will lead to the results necessary for all peoples of the region to live in stability and justice. I am frequently asked, why has Israel done this? Why is this occurring now? Here are some of the various answers to this question:

There are few moments — they are very rare — in the history of the relations between peoples, when both sides understand that it is both possible and in their interests to accept less than they thought conceivably possible. We are in that phase now. There are three major Israeli interests, present and long-term future interests, that cannot be served without achieving peace between us and the Palestinians, and then with all our neighbours.

The first interest is *Security*. Having been born in Jerusalem in 1946, my first childhood memory is the siege of Jerusalem in 1948. My entire personal history consists of a series of wars; '48, '56, '67, '73, '82, the *Intifada*. Israel, during this period of time, developed a military capacity, an ability to defend itself. We have the strongest army in the Middle East. We have one of the best and most experienced armies in the world, and in my entire lifetime we have not been able to achieve the one thing that we strive for more than anything, security. However, there will not be security for Israel unless we can integrate into the Middle East. Security is therefore our first interest; we want, and we need, a peace agreement with the Palestinians and with all our Arab neighbours in order to ensure our security.

Interest number two is *Occupation*. The state of Israel was founded in 1948 as the political culmination of the national liberation struggle of the Jewish people. In creating a state to embody the principles and values of our Jewish heritage and Jewish culture, we came to occupy another people, the Palestinian people — in contradiction not only to our own needs and desires, but also the very Jewish values that initially inspired us. This occupation limits our freedom. I will be very clear; for our freedom to involve the domination of another people is anti-Jewish. Thus, our second and crucial interest in this peace is a Jewish one, and I will even venture to say, a Zionist one, because we can only be ourselves if we liberate ourselves from occupying the Palestinians.

The third interest is *Democracy*. Israel has succeeded in maintaining a democracy under the most adverse circumstances. We have lived in conflict since our inception. Many people have maintained that our democracy is a crazy democracy; we are rude to each other, we are uncivil, we are nasty, we scream, we yell — but we are very democratic. I have always believed that our democracy is the essential and fundamental source of our strength, because we would not have been able to survive without the democratic culture that we created during our first 47 years of existence. However, one cannot be fully democratic when there are 2.5 million people living in our midst who do not have fundamental human and civil rights. Occupation of the Palestinians is anti-democratic.

Does Israel have an interest in pursuing the peace process with the Palestinians, with Syria, and successfully concluded with Jordan? Of course we do: for security reasons, for Jewish reasons and for democratic reasons. And these interests are not passing interests. They are interests which will not be fulfilled unless we successfully complete the course we began with the *Oslo Accords*.

Since the *Oslo Accords*, Israel has discovered, as have the PLO and Palestinians, that when we undertake historic negotiations we will encounter two kinds of difficulties. The first relates to the engineering of the negotiation process. In other words there are only political solutions to ethnic and national conflict, but the political solutions must be the correct ones and they must be carried out well. The first set of difficulties that we have encountered — on all sides — relates to the parties' judgement and capacity to carry out the political objectives on which we all agree. I want to point out some of these obstacles in a language that illustrates that they are surmountable. The first set of difficulties is technical: Manuel Hassassian and I live ten minutes away from each other, but for Manuel Hassassian to reach my house, it can sometimes take him three hours! Israelis and Palestinians live in such a way that their lives are intertwined with thousands of details, and to agree upon those details — to separate them in order to interact in new ways — is a tremendously lengthy negotiating process. In stronger terms, I cannot think of an international negotiation process that is more complicated than the Palestinian-Israeli negotiations in terms of the sheer number of details. In the first rounds of the *Gaza-Jericho Accords*, we spent a tremendous amount of tiem trying to negotiate every single detail. For example, there are border crossings at Rafah and the Erez junction near Gaza, and there must be glass at the border crossings so that Israelis and Palestinians can jointly supervise who enters and who leaves. What colour should the glass be? Should it be dark, tinted, one-way glass? We negotiated three days over the colour of the glass. It was a mistake trying to negotiate every single detail because the basic principle of flexibility was lost in the shuffle. We have, I believe, learned our lesson.

The second problem is much more substantive. The greatest flaw in the Declaration of Principles, the *Oslo Agreements*, is that it did not pinpoint a concrete goal for the PLO-Israel negotiations. It was a mistake not to say from the start that the successful conclusion of the negotiations will ultimately lead to the creation of a Palestinian state alongside Israel. This lack of a concrete objective has created ambiguity during the negotiations. When these negotiations are concluded successfully — and they will be — there will be a Palestinian state alongside Israel, and we must get used to that fact.

Other objective problems relate not to the mode of the negotiations, but to real paradoxes that exist. I will raise two.

I used to study national liberation movements throughout the world. I never encountered, in all the cases that I studied, a situation where the struggle to reach independence continued while the transfer of power took place. In South Africa, for example, the struggle against Apartheid ended in 1991 and then the transfer of power began to be planned and carried out. But the Palestinian case is unique. While still struggling for recognition of the right to *self-determination*, they are also responsible for education, health and welfare, and a series of other items as well. Two processes: a struggle and the initial stages of state-building taking place simultaneously? I do not see a historical parallel that we can learn from; it is a real paradox. There is a second dilemma on this level. In the negotiating process, concrete results are expected. Political time is quick, it is dynamic. Every day which passes without a new agreement, or result, is a day where we move backwards, not forwards. However, institution-building takes a long time. It is a slow process and there is a contradiction between the political necessity of showing results and the institutional logic of building strong capable institutions. What a dilemma! Are there problems in the dynamics on an objective basis? Absolutely. And if we add to that the economic difficulties — some real, some manufactured — then this process is encountering the kind of problems anticipated when the political will to reach a solution exists, but the path is strewn with details, paradoxes, and economic difficulties. Therefore, part of the dynamic problems are objective, so I invite you to put yourselves in our position, remembering it is a joint Palestinian-Israeli position, and try to think together with us, and understand how we feel about these objectives. In the dynamic of the process, however, there are not only objective difficulties because, as I mentioned earlier — and I reiterate — when we are struggling for understanding, when we are searching for solutions to real problems, this is exactly the moment when ethnic, religious and racist antagonism arises. This is what has happened in the past year or so. There are opponents on both sides united, ironically, in that the basis of their opposition, among other things, is religious, sectarian, or ethnic. We have our opponents in Israel, and the PLO has its opponents within Palestine. These opponents to the process have another thing in common; they have nothing to lose by opposing the process. They want to stop it, and it is our common responsibility to make sure that they do not succeed.

The violence which we have experienced, especially over the past year, is most trying on the spirit and on the soul, and the uncertainty it has created impinges on our personal security. I can best convey this through a personal story. I have a marvellous seventeen year-old daughter who is an average Israeli teenager. In order to achieve 'financial independence' she sells jewellery in downtown Jerusalem three nights a week. At the end of December I was in Tel Aviv and I heard that there was an attack in downtown Jerusalem. An hour later I heard that the attack took place on the same street where my daughter worked. Another hour later, after trying desperately to call home and find out where she was, I received a phone call saying that she was working and that the attack had taken place right where she worked. I got into the car and drove from Tel Aviv to Jerusalem. Put yourself in the position of an Israeli 'dove', whose daughter was actually present in the place where an attack took place, and you were driving up from Tel Aviv to Jerusalem with me. It was the worst trip of my life. I reached Jerusalem, went straight there and found a very shaken seventeen year-old girl who had been missed — mercifully — by two shots. I took her home and said, 'well, what do we do now with the process?' and this delightful, intelligent seventeen year-old girl said to me, 'You know what we do? We continue and we fight for peace, and we don't let anything upset our routine'.

As you can imagine, I adore her, but sadly enough the inhabitants of Israel do not, and cannot, always react like my seventeen year-old daughter. We have been shaken up by a violence that we have not known before.

So, is the dynamic complicated? Yes, there is closure of the territories, and there is the expansion of settlements, which I have been fighting against for the past three years. And there is violence and there are objective difficulties. And we will surmount them; because the only way to prevent ethnic, nationalist and religious fundamentalisms from overcoming us is to apply the principle I presented earlier; there must be political solutions to political problems, and we must have the inner strength to deal with the objective difficulties as well as the current mood, which is not a good one at the moment. Despite the current climate of hesitancy and mistrust, I believe that with clear leadership and continued commitment to peace, we can resolve these issues. The dynamic of the current situation demands that we keep two things in mind. First, these negotiations and this peace are in our interest and, this being so, we will pursue peace and not allow the difficulties to divert us. Second, we cannot accept any alternative to the course upon which we have embarked. It is hard and it will be even harder, but if we do not succeed then we will have surrendered to one of the worst scourges in human history and that is to allow ethnicity and religious conflict a victory, when the use of the human mind and the human will can lead us elsewhere.

I suggest, therefore, that we do the following — and this I say not only in my private capacity — but also because I believe this should be the policy of the current government of the state of Israel. We must begin to tackle the serious issues which remain to be resolved by speeding up negotiations over the second phase of the interim agreements. The time has come to confront, among other matters, the issue of boundaries and the final status of Jerusalem.

Iran — Syria — Iraq

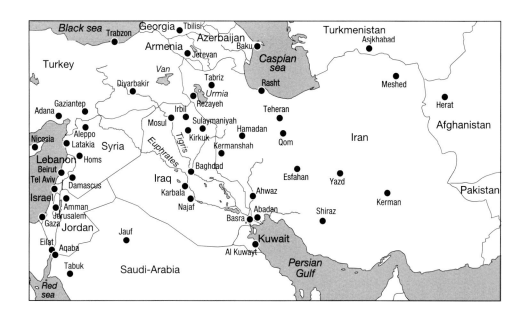

Black sea   Trabzon   Georgia   Tbilisi   Turkmenistan   Asjkhabad

Turkey   Armenia   Azerbaijan   Baku   Caspian
                     Jerevan   sea

Van   Tabriz   Rasht   Meshed
Diyarbakir   Urmia
            Rezayeh   Teheran   Herat
Gaziantep   Irbil   Afghanistan
Adana   Mosul   Sulaymaniyah   Hamadan   Iran
Nicosia   Aleppo   Kirkuk   Qom
         Latakia   Syria   Kermanshah
Lebanon   Homs   Euphrates   Tigris   Esfahan   Yazd   Pakistan
Beirut   Baghdad   Kerman
Tel Aviv   Damascus   Iraq   Ahwaz
Israel   Karbala   Shiraz
         Amman   Najaf   Abadan
Jerusalem   Basra
Gaza   Jordan   Jauf   Kuwait
Eilat
Aqaba   Al Kuwayt   Persian
Tabuk   Gulf
Red   Saudi-Arabia
sea

Iranian Fundamentalism — A Threat to the World

Maryam Rajavi

What is presently happening in my fettered country, Iran, namely the reign of the mullahs' medieval religious dictatorship, not only represents a national catastrophe for all Iranians, but is also the source of a global problem and danger which threatens stability and peace the world over.

Firstly, the mullahs have extended their state-sponsored terrorism across Asia, Africa, the United States, and Europe — including Germany, Switzerland, Italy, France and Norway.

Secondly, the clerics are exporting the cultural and political dimensions of fundamentalism, especially to Islamic countries and various Muslim societies. This is followed by an expansion of the fundamentalist extremist networks.

Thirdly, they oppose peace and advocate turmoil everywhere, as reflected in their regime's enmity to the Middle East peace process.

Today, virtually everyone is aware of the crimes perpetrated by Khomeini's inhumane regime within and without Iran. The clerics have executed over 100,000 of the youth of my country purely for political reasons, because they oppose the ruling dictatorship in Iran, and for defending freedom and democracy. The victims include intellectuals, university students and faculty members, high school students, teenage girls, pregnant women, elderly women, businessmen, merchants and even dissident clerics. In many cases, several members of a single family have been executed. Many more, some 150,000, have been subjected to the most barbaric, medieval tortures in the prisons of the Khomeini regime.

Nor is the appalling predicament of women under the mullahs' rule a secret. Inconceivable atrocities are committed against women on the pretext of combating improper veiling. Everyday, thousands of women are lashed, sent to prisons or viciously assaulted and insulted for very simple and trivial matters. These crimes are unprecedented in other areas of the globe. The rulers of Iran brazenly carry out hideous crimes under the banner of Islam. According to Khomeini's *fatwa*, virgin girls are raped by the Revolutionary Guards prior to execution to prevent them going to heaven. Those condemned to death have their blood drained before execution.

The export of terrorism, fundamentalism and belligerence of this regime, under the banner of Islam and revolution, is another well-established fact. It is evident in the regime's insistence on perpetuating the unpatriotic war with Iraq, which lasted some eight years and left millions dead or wounded and $1000 billion in economic damages on the Iranian side alone. It is also evident in the regime's formal enmity to the Middle East peace process, in its interference in the affairs of Islamic countries, in its decree to murder foreign nationals, and in its more than 100 terrorist operations throughout the world. Regrettably, the echo of these despicable crimes still lingers over this city. This is truly shameful.

A pivotal issue that needs to be addressed is how to confront this regime and the fundamentalism and terrorism it fosters. This is vital because all measures taken at the international level to curb the terrorist dictatorship of the mullahs have unfortunately proven futile.

For many years, particularly following Khomeini's death, Western countries indulged in a quest for a moderate current within the regime. They pinned their hopes on improving the regime's behaviour through expanding relations, particularly economic ties. Simultaneously, a number of big powers invested in a policy of appeasement in an attempt to ingratiate themselves with Tehran, and prevent the export of terrorism to their own countries. Consistent with this approach, the official European Union policy toward Iran today is one of critical dialogue. The experience of the past 16 years has confirmed, however, that none of these policies has borne fruit. They have failed to have any impact on the conduct of this international outlaw.

The inhuman and anti-Islamic *fatwa* against Salman Rushdie best illustrates the nature of this regime. The decree was issued seven years ago. All European efforts to change the regime's conduct through dialogue, discussion as well as economic and political incentives have failed to change the status quo. Khomeini's successors have time and again reiterated that the decree must be implemented. For seven years, the regime has used the Rushdie affair as a bargaining chip in seeking more concessions from the West. In other words, it has taken advantage of this issue and has gained greater concessions from the Western governments.

It is ironic that at a time when even the first prime minister of the Khomeini regime, Mehdi Bazargan, acknowledged in an interview with the German daily *Frankfurter Rundschau* in January that the mullahs have the support of less than five percent of the Muslim people of Iran, and lack both religious and social legitimacy, the international community nevertheless allows

Tehran to find a footing among Muslims elsewhere and advance their evil anti-Islamic, anti-human objectives. These policies allow the mullahs to turn Western countries into hunting grounds for their opponents. Indeed, the extensive economic and political ties with a number of countries, coupled with the kowtowing by some of its international interlocutors to terrorist and political blackmail, have been instrumental in prolonging this regime and delaying the establishment of democracy in Iran by the Iranian people and the Resistance.

Misperceptions about Mullahs, source of appeasement

Beyond economic interests or fear of this regime's terrorism — which in many cases justify and give impetus to them - these misguided policies and drastic miscalculations stem from the lack of a correct, objective understanding of the nature of the Khomeini regime, and of the roots and extent of its fundamentalist, backward outlook. For precisely this reason, these countries lose sight of the regional and international implications of their approach. This explains such misguided policies and the grave miscalculations about this regime so far. On the other hand, an objective appraisal or knowledge of the legitimate, democratic alternative to this regime, is lacking. This is an alternative which can bring democracy to Iran. This, exacerbates the misperception about the regime's durability, particularly among Western countries.

Let us look at a historical example. Although there are fundamental differences between the Khomeini regime and Hitler's fascism, in terms of their political, economic and military capabilities, a parallel may nonetheless be drawn with the conciliatory treatment of Germany by some European countries in the years preceeding the Second World War. This policy of acquiescence, embodied in the Munich Agreement of 1938, or the relations between the Soviet Union and Hitler's Germany until even the first or the second year of the war, stemmed from the notion that certain concessions at the expense of other countries, who were abandoned in their resistance against fascism, would force Germany to make peace. As if it were possible to stop Hitler's expansionism in this way. Hitler benefitted greatly from the policy, which enabled him to advance his goals. History is repeating itself.

The notion of the Velayat-e Faqih

In reality, the outlook and conduct of Khomeini and his regime neither belong to our age, nor compare to most dictatorships that have emerged in the twentieth century. This regime represents the most retrogressive form of medieval, sectarian dictatorship. Having failed to alleviate any of Iranian society's problems or needs, it is attempting to impose itself under the guise of Islam on the people of the world, especially Muslims.

The mullah's religious dictatorship is based on the philosophy of *Velayat-e Faqih*, presented in its present form for the first time by Khomeini. In his book, *'Islamic Rule'* or *'Velayat-e Faqih,'* written in the 1960s, Khomeini thoroughly explains his views. His theory is based, on the one hand upon imposing absolute authority over the populace, and on the other upon extending this authority to all Muslims, i.e. 'exporting revolution'. In his book Khomeini states:

The Velayat-e Faqih is like appointing a guardian for a minor. In terms of responsibility and status, the guardian of a nation is no different from the guardian of a minor.

These are Khomeini's exact words. During his reign, he repeated several times that if the entire population advocated something to which he was opposed, he would nevertheless do as he saw fit.

He even went so far as to write: 'If a competent person arises and forms a government, his authority to administer the affairs of society is the same as that of Prophet Muhammed. Everyone (meaning Muslims everywhere) must obey him. The idea that the Prophet had more authority as a ruler than His Holiness Imam Ali [the first Shi'ite Imam], or that the latter's authority exceeded that of the *Vali* is incorrect'.

With these words, Khomeini granted himself the same authority as the Prophet of God, but he did not stop there. Some twenty years later, in 1988, he wrote an open letter, published in the regime's dailies, lashing out at suggestions that 'government authority is contained within the bounds of divine edicts.' Khomeini wrote:

... The Velayat takes precedence over all secondary commandments, even prayer, fasting, and the hajj... The government is empowered to unilaterally abrogate the religious commitments it has undertaken with the people... The statements made, or being made, derive from a lack of knowledge of divinely ordained absolute rule...

In this way, Khomeini propagated the notion of the *Velayat-e Motlaqeh Faqih* (absolute rule of the jurist), something which his heirs and theoreticians within the regime went to extremes to stress and to perpetuate. Mullah Ahmad Azari-Qomi, one of the most authoritative theoreticians of the *Velayat-e Faqih* notion within the regime, wrote in this respect:

The Velayat-e Faqih means absolute religious and legal guardianship of the people by the Faqih. This guardianship applies to the entire world and all that exists in it, whether earthbound or flying creatures, inanimate objects, plants, animals, and anything in any way related to collective or individual human life, all human affairs, belongings, or assets...

This world view culminates in absolute ruthlessness and oppression when dealing with the issue of women. Azari-Qomi writes about the marriage of virgin girls thus:

Islam prohibits the marriage of a virgin girl without the permission of her father or her own consent. Both of them must agree. But the *Vali-e Faqih* is authorized to overrule the father or the girl.

In this way, this regime not only applies maximum political suppression on its citizens, but interferes in the most personal affairs of their lives, from compulsory veiling to varied forms of discrimination against women, to banning smiling in public and stoning women to death.

Misogyny is the most fundamental feature of the *Velayat-e Faqih*, and the structure of the clerical regime's system rests upon de-humanizing women. As far as women in the work force are concerned, they enjoy less than 10 percent of the opportunities afforded to their male counterparts. This ratio decreases as the quality of the job or its political importance increases. No women manage the affairs of society, particularly its political leadership. The regime's constitution absolutely and unequivocally bans women from positions as judges, the presidency and leadership.

All evaluations, laws and practices within this regime are based on the precept that women are weak and are the property and chattels of men, for which reason they have no place in leading or managing the society. A woman must stay at home, cook and bring-up children - the tasks for which she has been created.

The mullahs' misogyny has given rise to horrifying crimes and anti-human impositions; for example, the wholesale execution of thousands of women — even pregnant ones. The flogging and torture of women in public on bogus and superficial charges, execution methods such as firing bullets into their wombs, the 'residential quarters' in prisons designed to totally destroy these enchained and defenseless women, and the multitude of torture methods and atrocities invented by the mullahs, demonstrate the unparalleled savagery of their enmity toward women at every level and in every sphere of life. Why does the regime so barbarously and relentlessly suppress women? What explains the clerics' misogyny?

This enmity toward women is not merely a by-product of the mullahs' reactionary beliefs. If the clerics show the slightest laxity in their misogyny and gender-apartheid, allowing women to enter the social arena free of the reactionary restrictions unique to this regime, the mullahs' suppressive organs and institutions throughout society would lose their *raison d'être*. The clerical regime, a religious dictatorship, would subsequently lose its vitality, because the dynamism and conduct of the repressive forces in defending the theocracy is, first and foremost, rooted in safeguarding gender-distinction under the pretext of defending 'Islamic rule.'

The Mullahs' Foreign Policy

As far as the regime's foreign policy and the export of terrorism are concerned, both Khomeini and his successors pursue specific goals, unequivocally defined. Following Khomeini's death, Rafsanjani stressed: 'Islamic Iran is the base for all Muslims the world over,' adding that Khomeini 'truly and deeply hated the idea that we be limited by nationalism, by race, or by our own territory'. Elsewhere he says: 'Iran is the base of the new movements of the world of Islam... The eyes of Muslims worldwide are focused here...'

The book entitled *Principles of Foreign Policy of the Islamic Republic of Iran*, published by the Iranian regime's foreign ministry, formally states: 'Islam recognizes only one boundary, purely ideological in nature. Other boundaries, including geographic borders, are rejected and condemned.'

The mullahs ruling Iran dream of a global Islamic *caliphate*, much like the Ottoman Empire. They say the Islamic revolution will suffocate within Iran's borders and cannot be preserved without the export of the Revolution. Mohammad Khatami, Rafsanjani's former Minister of Islamic Culture and Guidance, who is also known as a moderate within the regime, writes: 'Where do we look when drawing up our strategy? Do we look to *bast* (expansion) or to *hefz* (preservation)?' In particularly, following the collapse of the Soviet Union, the mullahs refer to the split between Trotsky and Stalin in the 1930s, noting that developments in the Soviet Union proved the validity of Trotsky's theory of a 'permanent revolution,' and that the only way to preserve the Islamic regime is to foment Islamic revolutions in other countries. The slogan of 'liberating Qods (Jerusalem) via Karbala', with which Khomeini continued the Iran-Iraq war for eight years, reflected the strategy of '*bast*'.

Ali-Mohammed Besharati, the current Interior Minister and former Deputy Foreign Minister, stresses that 'the third millennium belongs to Islam and the rule of Muslims over the world'. By Muslims, of course, he means none other than the mullahs. Mohammad-Javad Larijani, a key foreign policy advisor to Rafsanjani, said: 'The true *Velayat-e Faqih* is in Iran. This Velayat is responsible for all of the Muslim world... One of its objectives is expansion...' Khamenei's latest emphasis that the Jews must be expelled from Israel and Israel annihilated are also an extension of this foreign policy.

The mullahs' outlook and theories about government and *Velayat-e Faqih* cannot in anyway be viewed as an interpretation of Islam. They are the first to offer such a criminal reading of Islam. This is unprecedented in Islamic history. Even many traditional clerics, more senior than or on par with Khomeini in Qom and Najaf seminaries, were strongly opposed to the *Velayat-e Faqih* perspective. In reality, the mullahs interpret Islam solely in terms of the needs and interests of their dictatorship.

The fact is that Khomeini and his clique lack any historical or political ability to govern a large nation with several thousand years of history and a rich culture. To stay in power, they see themselves as increasingly compelled to employ repression and religious tyranny inside the country, and export terrorism and fundamentalism, in an effort to expand the geographic sphere of their influence. For this reason, after Khomeini's death, contrary to all expectations that his heirs would pursue a 'moderate' path, they were forced to fill the void of Khomeini's charisma, the unifying element which gave the regime religious legitimacy, with greater suppression and export of fundamentalism. The Rafsanjani regime's record of terrorist activities abroad and interference in Islamic countries and the affairs of Muslims elsewhere is far worse than when Khomeini was alive.

How did Khomeini become a national and global threat?

For 14 centuries, since the Revolution, Iran and Iranians have always played a key role in shaping and advancing the policies and cultural identity of the Islamic world. Iranians wrote most books on Shi'ite and Sunni *Fiqh* and *Hadith*, on Arabic grammar and on interpreting the Quran. In philosophy, logic, mathematics, medicine, astronomy, chemistry and other sciences of the era, Iranian scientists led the Islamic world. The books of Avicenna, the renowned 11th century philosopher and physician, were translated into many languages and taught in Western universities until recently.

With an eye to Iran's vast land mass, geo-political position, population and many other factors, the country enjoys an exceptional position in the Islamic world. In the last 14 centuries, it has had a tremendous impact on Islamic countries. The mullahs have made maximum use of this potential to export their fundamentalism and advance their objectives. In other words, if a regime much like Khomeini's had assumed power in any other Islamic country, it would not have enjoyed such stature. It is not without reason that Larijani says that Iran is the only country capable of leading the Islamic world. This explains why the clerical regime in Tehran is the heart of fundamentalism throughout the world, just as Moscow was for communism.

Many fundamentalist currents existed in Iran or elsewhere before Khomeini's ascent to power, but they were nothing more than isolated religious sects. With the establishment of an Islamic reign in Tehran, they were transformed into political and social movements, and into serious threats to peace, democracy and tranquillity the world over.

In fact, the Khomeini regime uses propaganda, political, financial, military and ideological assistance, and beyond all these, its status as a role model and as a regional and international source of support, to direct Muslims' religious sentiments toward extremist, fundamentalist and undemocratic trends. The mullahs exploit Islam's spirit of liberation and its call to its followers to endeavour to establish justice and freedom, to further their medieval rule. Instead, consistent with the experience of the resistance (movement), the sentiments of Muslims and Islam's freedom-seeking spirit could have been and can be translated into a democratic and modern movement which, while respectful of Islam, aspires to a secularist, pluralist form of government.

What is to be done?

This paper has so far referred to the internal and international conduct of the Khomeini regime. But the fundamental question is: what is the solution?

On the basis of our 16-years of experience in the struggle for democracy, the only solution is to offer a political and cultural alternative to the Khomeini regime. I say political because this alternative must overthrow the regime and replace it with a democratic, secular government. The head of the viper is in Tehran and unless dealt with there, there is no hope of removing fundamentalism.

I say cultural because this alternative must present a democratic Islam, with a peaceful, tolerant culture compatible with science and civilization, to confront the mullahs' *Velayat-e Faqih* theory. Only thus can it prevent the mullahs from imposing themselves as the representatives of Islam in the minds of the people of Muslim countries.

Even before Khomeini's rule, we understood the danger of the *Velayat-e Faqih*, because we knew the mullahs and Khomeini intimately. While in prison in the final months before the Shah's fall, the Mojahedin leader, Mr. Massoud Rajavi, repeatedly pointed to backward religious currents as the main threat to the Iranian people's democratic movement and warned time and again against the dangers of religious fascism. In 1979, Khomeini succeeded in usurping the leadership of the Iranian people's anti-dictatorial revolution, relying on *marja'iat* (religious leadership) for religious legitimacy, deceit and the people's lack of experience and awareness. The Shah's widespread clampdown on organizations fighting for freedom, including the arrest and execution of their leaders, assisted Khomeini along the way. Relying on the overwhelming support of the people who longed for freedom and independence, he became a dangerous force, destroying everything in his path.

From the onset, as a democratic Muslim force, the Mojahedin saw it incumbent upon themselves to expose Khomeini's demagoguery and false portrayal of Islam. They thus represented a cultural, ideological and political challenge to the ruling mullahs, and embarked upon a relentless campaign to explain the facts to the people. For the first time, there was a cultural alternative to the Khomeini regime.

The teachings of the Quran and the life of Muhammed, the Prophet of Islam, are totally contrary to the behaviour of the new rulers. Like all great religions, Islam is a religion of compassion, tolerance, emancipation and equality. The Holy Quran often states that there is no compulsion in religion. As far as political and social life are concerned, it stresses consultation, democracy and respect for other people's views. Islam seeks social progress, and economic, social and political evolution.

Fourteen centuries ago, when people in the Arabian peninsula were burying their female children alive, Islam accorded women equal political, social and economic identities and independence. The Prophet of Islam profoundly respected women. The first Muslim was a woman, and four out of the ten original Muslims were women.

After two and half years, the resistance's endeavours paid off. Cracks appeared in Khomeini's religious legitimacy, and his use of the weapon of Islam began to lose its effect. The people no longer viewed Khomeini and the ruling mullahs as infallible. To prolong his rule inside the country, Khomeini had resorted to a blatant crackdown. Everyone knew that the Mojahedin, the largest opposition force seeking freedom, were Muslim themselves and that Khomeini's quarrel with them was not over Islam, but over preserving his dictatorial rule.

I lectured on Islamic teachings in one of Tehran's largest universities in 1980. Over 10,000 university students and intellectuals took part every week, and tapes and transcripts were distributed in their hundreds of thousands. The discourses exposed Khomeini's reactionary views promulgated under the banner of Islam, discrediting him among the religious youth. In a ruthless onslaught to curb the extensive influence of the Mojahedin in all universities, in spring 1980, Khomeini closed down all universities for the coming years on the pretext of a cultural revolution.

Another of the fundamental aspects of this cultural struggle has been to target the heart of the clerics' *Velayat-e Faqih* culture, namely the issue of women and the mullahs' ultra-reactionary, misogynous treatment of them. In this regard, we did not stop at simply exposing the clerics. In other words, our women, in diametric opposition to Khomeini's culture, advanced through unprecedented effort and assumed heavy responsibilities at the highest levels of the Resistance, to render as false Khomeini's utterly erroneous view. Owing to the misogynous nature of the mullahs' regime, the realization of freedom in Iran is, no doubt, contingent upon giving consideration to the freedom and equality of women in the course of the struggle to overthrow this regime.

The Iranian Resistance succeeded in incorporating women in the front lines of the movement and in the highest levels of military command, as acknowledged by most observers. In the political arena as well, we are witnessing the rise of women to important political positions. At the organizational and management levels, the highest positions are occupied by women. They have shown that when given the opportunity, they can excel in assuming responsibility. Today, 52 percent of members of the Resistance's parliament are women. Women fill the majority of positions within the National Liberation Army's high command. The leadership of the Mojahedin consists of a 24-member, all woman council.

A Democratic Alternative

Obviously, we did not stop at introducing a cultural alternative; we also gradually established a political alternative. In 1980, during the first presidential elections, Massoud Rajavi was a candidate for president. All religious and ethnic minorities, the youth, women, and opposition groups and parties supported Mr. Rajavi's candidacy. Sensing the danger, Khomeini issued a fatwa a few days before the election, banning him as a candidate because he had not voted for the *Velayat-e Faqih* constitution. Several months later, during the elections for parliament, the Mojahedin and other democratic forces announced a joint nomination. This time, despite the many votes cast for them, the regime prevented even one of the Mojahedin candidates from taking office through widespread rigging. In each of the election rallies of the Mojahedin in Tehran and other cities, hundreds of thousands took part.

In the first two and a half years of Khomeini's rule, the *Pasdaran* (Revolutionary Guards) killed 50 supporters and members of the Mojahedin in the streets. They arrested several thousand people, subjecting them to brutal torture. The regime also dispatched gangs of club-wielders into the streets to clamp down on dissidents. In contrast, the Mojahedin did not fire a single bullet, relinquishing their legitimate right to self-defence to prevent more violence and bloodshed. The Mojahedin's goal was to resolve the political problems through peaceful means.

On June 20th, 1981, in protest at the repression, the Mojahedin organized a peaceful demonstration. In a short span of time, some 500,000 Tehran residents joined the march. Khomeini issued a *fatwa* to suppress the demonstration. Guards opened fire indiscriminately, and hundreds were killed or wounded. Thousands were arrested and executed the same night in groups of several hundred.

Khomeini and other officials of his regime realized early on, even before the overthrow of the shah, that the Mojahedin could stand against both a religious and political dictatorship, due to their freedom-seeking and tolerant interpretation of Islam and their popularity and social base. In other words, the Mojahedin were the antithesis to the clerics. In summer 1980, several days after Mr. Rajavi addressed 200,000 Tehran residents in Amjadieh sports stadium, condemning the slaughter of the Mojahedin and dissidents in other cities, Khomeini immediately reacted by saying that the enemy was 'neither in the Soviet Union, nor in the United States, nor in Iranian Kurdistan, but in Tehran, right here in our midst'.

The Parliament-in-Exile

For our struggle against the mullah to achieve maturity, a political alternative —- a vast coalition of democratic opposition groups — was needed. Although the basis for such a coalition had taken shape in the first presidential elections and the parliamentary elections, after the start of the extensive, all-embracing suppression, this coalition had to be formalized and transformed into a political alternative. Thus, on July 21st, 1981, the National Council of Resistance was formed with the objective of establishing democracy in Iran.

After 14 years, the Council, the longest lasting democratic, political coalition in Iran's contemporary era, has 560 members. More than half of them are women. The council encompasses the democratic opposition, political parties, nationalist figures, Muslim, secular and socialist leaders, liberals and the representatives of ethnic and religious minorities. It acts as the resistance's Parliament-in-exile.

The Council's 25 committees will serve as the basis for the future coalition government and are carrying their tasks now. Following the mullahs' overthrow, the Provisional Government will be in office for no more than six months. Its primary task will be to hold free elections for a Legislative and Constituent Assembly. According to the Council's ratified decisions, in tomorrow's Iran, elections and the general vote will constitute the basis for the legitimacy of the country's future government. Freedom of belief, of the press, of parties and of political assemblies is guaranteed. Judicial security of all citizens and the rights stipulated in the Universal Declaration of Human Rights are also guaranteed.

All privileges based on gender, creed, and beliefs will be abolished and any discrimination against the followers of different religions and denominations will be banned. No one will be granted any privileges, or discriminated against, on the basis of belief or non-belief in a particular religion or denomination.

In tomorrow's Iran, the national bazaar and capitalism, personal and private ownership and investment toward the advancement of the national economy will be guaranteed. As for foreign policy, Iran will advocate peace, peaceful coexistence, and regional and international cooperation.

According to the Council's ratified plans, in tomorrow's Iran, women will enjoy equal social, political, cultural and economic rights with men. They will have the right to elect and be elected in all elections, and the right to freely choose their occupation, education, political activity, travel, and spouse. Equal rights to divorce and freedom of choice in apparel will be guaranteed for them.

The Current State of the Regime

In this way, after 16 years of the mullahs' rule, the overwhelming majority of people, from women to workers, to employees to university faculty, intellectuals and even the bazaar merchants and clergy who were hitherto considered the traditional basis of the regime, are deeply disaffected. Unemployment grips 50 percent of the labour force. With an inflation rate of over 100 percent, some 80 percent of the people live below the poverty line. Corruption and astronomical embezzlement by the regime's officials have eliminated any credibility the regime might have had.

Khomeini's death and the death of the last remaining grand ayatollahs; the lack of the minimum qualifications in Khamenei as the regime's religious leader; and the absence of an acceptable *Marja'-e Taqlid* (source of emulation) who would support the regime, have either eliminated or seriously undermined the last vestiges of the regime's religious legitimacy among the most retrogressive sectors of the society and the most traditional forces supporting it.

Today, religious fundamentalism does not exist as a social issue or problem in Iran. We are, rather, facing a form of fascism under the guise of religion which holds the reins of power. It is not without reason that, whereas at the end of the Iran-Iraq war in 1988 and Khomeini's death in 1989, more than 70 percent were volunteers ideologically loyal to the regime, today only 30 percent of the regime's Revolutionary Guards — its main suppressive arm — are volunteers. Even those remaining are receiving greater material incentives, and continue essentially because it is a well-paid job. In short, they have been transformed from a volunteer army to a suppressive mercenary force which fights against the people for its own survival.

On the international scene, however, the situation is very different. Although word of the regime's difficulties and internal crises and crimes against the people has inevitably reached the outside world, the policies of other countries toward the regime have not allowed the Iranian people's all-out resistance and more importantly, the resistance's cultural and ideological challenge to the mullahs, to extend beyond Iran's borders.

By the same token, the economic relationships between Western countries and Tehran's rulers, and the resultant petro-dollars are used only for domestic suppression — the suppression of vast numbers of people — the purchase of weapons and the quest to obtain nuclear arms and export terrorism and fundamentalism. A significant portion of the revenue has also been diverted into the mullahs' foreign bank accounts. For their part, the Iranian people have witnessed nothing but suppression and greater destitution.

The extensive economic ties with this regime have not only failed to contain fundamentalism, but have also emboldened the regime to persevere with these policies. Experience has also shown that the clerics use these connections as a cover to undertake more terrorist and fundamentalist activities abroad.

In short, the 16-year experience of the Iranian Resistance in dealing with the fundamentalist rulers of Iran and the experiences of international politics regarding Iran under the banner of the mullahs demonstrate that:

1) Any policy based on appeasing this regime is doomed to failure. Laws governing a religious dictatorship are different from the experiences and laws applying to the world community as we approach the end of the 20th century. This regime's laws emanate from the Middle Ages. Decisiveness is the only language with which one can and must communicate with this regime.

2) Any notion that would equate the conduct of the Khomeini regime with Islam is a strategic and dangerous mistake from which only the mullahs

benefit. The publicizing, support and recognition of the democratic alternative, which has the greatest respect for Islam as the religion of the majority of the Iranian people, and which at its core encompasses a Muslim democratic movement, is the only way to deny the mullahs the means of characterizing and exploiting opposition and decisiveness on the international level toward them as enmity to Islam.

In this way, the world community and Western countries will not be compelled to surrender to the blackmail of Khomeini's anti-human regime under the banner of Islam, to accept its double-talk on the cultural and religious distinctions of Iran and Islamic countries, or to tarnish the universal principles of human rights by giving concessions to this anti-human regime.

Furthermore, the people of different countries — especially Muslims — will to a great extent obtain the objective insight into the Khomeini regime that the people of Iran have arrived at, and few will be beguiled by the regime's Islamic posturing and demagogic slogans.

In other words, exercising decisiveness against the regime and support for the Iranian Resistance constitute two fronts against fundamentalism. On the one hand, by standing firm against the regime and supporting the resistance, the pace of change by the people inside Iran toward democracy and peace will be expedited. Thus, the material and spiritual source of support for fundamentalism will be eliminated and its heart will stop beating. On the other hand, by exposing the anti-Islamic nature of the mullahs in Western and Islamic countries and introducing the democratic alternative to this regime, the fertile grounds for the growth of fundamentalism will dry up. We have gained this experience with 100,000 martyrs.

The Iranian people are determined to bring democracy and peace to their homeland. Doubtless, a democratic Iran is indispensable to the return of tranquillity and lasting peace to the Middle East region and the eradication of terrorism throughout the globe.

The Significance of Religion — Islam and Modernity

Andreas Laursen

Introduction.

'Can an Islamic society be a modern society as well?' This is the question with which M.J. Larijani[1] begins his article about Islamic society and modernism. I shall return to his answer in the concluding section of this paper. In many ways, the question could have been the title of the present paper, the purpose of which is to examine whether modernity can be found in the discourse of the Iranian leadership today.

Iran is often perceived as a 'fundamentalist' state and, even if the word 'fundamentalist' is not used, as denouncing modernity: 'Islamic politics are centered on morality, not modernity'.[2] It is pointed out that Islam and modernity have existed in dialectical tension in Iran since the middle of the 19th century. During most of the 20th century, modernity was hegemonic but after 1979, Islamic discourse regained its long-standing hegemony.[3]

Modernity is a word which resists clear and easy definition. It is hard to find general definitions that are not directed at a marginal sub-issue. The dynamism of modernity is often pointed to as being its key characteristic: the constant change and the willingness to change so long as it is for the better; everything is amenable to improvement. Nothing can prevent human courage from taking on ever more ambitious tasks and finding ever more effective ways of achieving the desired results. Action is judged out of context, without reference to the traditions of the society in which these actions take place. Judgment is passed solely on the grounds of rationality and efficiency.

However, since this is an analytical paper, it is necessary to come up with a more workable definition. Some of the concepts which are mentioned in reference to modernity are rationality, secularism, unified order, law, individuality, national interests, scientific inquiry, economic growth, and

---

1. M.J. Larijani, 1995: 31.
2. Najmabadi, 1987: 204.
3. Haeri, 1992: 207.

popular sovereignty.[4] A key issue with regard to Iran is, of course, the idea of secularism; and the eventual question is whether a modern state with religious rule is an oxymoron. Similarly, there is the question of whether a religious society can accept the idea that things are amendable and that options are only valid so long as they are effective. Also, the lack of a moral imperative becomes an issue for any government which calls itself Islamic.

In order to analyse the problem of modernity and Iran in a manageable way, I have chosen an approach which examines Islamic attitudes within three particular areas. The three areas are chosen for several reasons: They were present in the sermons delivered in Tehran; they either reflect or have implications for modernity; they are all important areas in the debate between Islam and the West. The areas are the status of women, the nation state, and the economy. The second objective of this paper is to investigate the suitability of the Friday sermon as a medium of communication — in the present case, communication of modernity.

With regard to the Islamic discourse, this is, for the present purpose, found in the Friday prayers given in Tehran. In order to make the project manageable, I have qualified several of the factors which make up this study. I have taken Friday prayers, those conducted in Tehran during the period between the death of Ayatollah Khomeini in the summer of 1989 through to the first three months of 1995, as my primary source. The sermons were found in Foreign Broadcast Information Service (FBIS).

The Friday Prayer

The Friday Prayer in Early Islam

Friday worship in Islam is as old as the faith itself. Goitein traces the early origins back to the time of the Prophet Muhammed in Medina.[5] Friday was to become the holiday of Islam but not a day of rest as Saturday and Sunday are for the Jews and Christians respectively. Instead, Friday became the day of obligatory public worship. Goitein sees the choice of Friday as the designated day as being a very pragmatic one indeed. Friday was chosen because this was the market day for the Jews, the day before the Sabbath on which they purchased provisions for their day of rest. The Friday Prayer was held at noon when the market closed and before all the people started their journey home.

---

4. *The Oxford Companion to Politics of the World*, 1993: 592.
5. Goitein, 1966: 111.

The sermon delivered on Friday went beyond worship of God and beyond devotion.[6] From the very beginning, the gathering was a socio-political one. The prayer was a rally 'which manifested who adhered to the new religion and who failed to do so'. By taking part in the worship, the people could show their allegiance to Islam and to the ruler.[7] This, along with the religious worship, was a major function of the Friday Prayer.

The use of the Friday Prayer as a pulpit for political messages is well documented with regard to the time of the Prophet. By the time of the Umayyad Caliph Marwan, a highly official style was introduced[8] and the sermon became increasingly stereotyped and — according to Borthwick — irrelevant to the listener. This situation seems to have prevailed until the 19th century when a new vitality entered the sermon.[9]

The Friday Prayer in the 20th Century

When observing how several scholars emphasize the importance of the Friday Prayer in Islam, it is somewhat surprising that the literature dealing with this subject is rather sparse. A number of journal articles deal with the very general aspects of, or very specific issues regarding, the Friday prayer.[10] As for monographs, four are available in English; three deal with Arab countries and one with Iran. They each deal with specific countries — one or more — and are all textual analyses of actual Friday sermons.

Bruce Maynard Borthwick wrote his 1965 dissertation on the Islamic sermon as a channel of political communication and used sermons delivered over state radios in Jordan, Syria and Egypt.[11] The dissertation — which is guided by the then prevalent modernization theory as espoused by, among others, Karl Deutsch — examines the possibilities for the ruling elite to communicate its ideas to the 'traditional people'. Borthwick finds two modes of communication in the Middle East in the early 1960s, the first being the radio, representing the modern and largely urban form of communication, and the second, the traditional or face-to-face communication, which was prevalent in the rural areas. Between these two forms of communication there exists a 'communications gap'. The author finds that the ruling elite — with varying degree of success — used the medium of the Friday prayer to bridge the gap. With the revitalization of the form and language of the Friday sermon in the

---

6. Ibid: 122.
7. Borthwick, 1965: 28.
8. *Encyclopaedia of Islam*, 1927: 982.
9. Borthwick, 1965: 31.
10. See for example, Calder 1986; and Fathi 1979, 1984, 1987.
11. Borthwick, 1965.

late 19th century, the Muslim preacher reconnected, so to speak, with the rural population. Following the Second World War and the revolutions in several Arab countries, the new elites found the Islamic sermon a useful tool for communicating their policies and gaining legitimacy. The modernizing policies of the central governments were legitimized through reference to the Quran and the Hadith and propagated through the traditional medium of the Friday prayer.

The author goes on to examine whether this medium was useful for the communication of three core policies or ideas: Nation building, modernization and legitimacy. With regard to nation building, which is solely Pan-Arab nation building, the author finds the sermon an adequate medium since Arab 'nationalism' is rooted in Islam.[12] The goal of the modern government is in harmony with the myth of early Islam and without any commitment to a concrete programme. When, however, the issues relate to modernization and legitimacy, the subject becomes more concrete and harder to align with Islam. When the attempt is done, the result is strained and defensive.[13]

The book *Muslim Preacher in the Modern World*, by Richard T. Antoun[14] follows on chronologically from Borthwick's dissertation. The fieldwork for this book was conducted in a Jordanian village in the 1960s. However, although the author only uses sermons from this period for his textual analysis, he does include later developments in the village when relevant. The aim of the author is threefold:[15] To document normative Islam as it is propagated in the particular village by one particular preacher; secondly, to analyse the process by which the Islamic message is handed down and interpreted by the preacher, and; thirdly, to examine the experiential side of the worship, i.e. the affirmation by the preacher of an 'ultimate reality, a faith-driven society, and a personal commitment.'[16]

Whereas the sermons analysed by Borthwick were delivered over the state radio and appropriated by the ruling elite, the sermons in the Jordanian village were delivered by the local preacher. In time, the Jordanian government tried to guide the local preacher by sending him pre-prepared sermons, but the preacher denies ever having given a 'government' sermon. Perhaps it is due to this fact — the local and autonomous character of the village sermon — that Antoun finds the political content of the sermons to be minimal.[17] Another difference from Borthwick's analysis, and an issue which is relevant to this

12. Ibid: 193.
13. Ibid: 108 and 194.
14. Antoun, 1989.
15. Ibid: 1.
16. Ibid: 7.
17. Ibid: 128.

thesis, is the issue of modernity. As seen above, Borthwick found that the Islamic sermon was not very useful when it came to the promotion of modernity. Through his analysis of sermons, Antoun finds that: 'It is by no means clear that Islamization and/or religious resurgence works against such a transformation [modernization] or its cultural and psychological underpinnings'.[18]

The Prophet's Pulpit by Patrick D. Gaffney is an analysis of contemporary Islamic preaching in Egypt, as represented by the provincial town of Minya in Upper-Egypt. To make the analysis feasible, a threefold typology of preachers has been chosen to represent 'three approaches to transformation of charisma into everyday living'.[19] The three are the 'sufi priest-magician',[20] the 'traditional scholar and ethical teacher'[21] and the 'militant holy warrior'.[22]

Gaffney subscribes to the Borthwick's view that the Friday sermon has been reinvigorated. Old formalism has been shattered and the preacher has emerged as a 'pivotal figure in the redefining of symbols imparting the religious legitimation and moral affirmation of new social, political and economic options'.[23] Whereas direct and explicit involvement in political issues is rare in Upper Egypt, a moral perspective and assessment is common.[24]

If anything can clearly be deduced from a comparison of the above mentioned works on the Friday prayer it must be this: The diversity of the Friday sermon. As a number of authors have emphasized, Islam and aspects and practices within Islam are not monolithic.[25] Some sermons are sponsored by the government and have clear goals of mobilization of the population and legitimization of the governments policies.[26] Others are 'private', local sermons that transmit and interpret culture and give meaning; both intellectually and emotionally.[27] Even within a provincial town in Upper Egypt, several 'types' of preacher can be found.[28]

Finally, for the purposes of this paper, disagreements over the suitability of the sermon as a vehicle of communication should be noted, in the present case and particularly with regard to modernity.

18. Ibid: 142.
19. Gaffney, 1994: 181.
20. Ibid: 36.
21. Ibid: 38.
22. Ibid: 40.
23. Ibid: 118.
24. Ibid: 191.
25. Cole, 1992: 1; and Gaffney, 1994: 183.
26. Borthwick, 1965.
27. Antoun, 1989.
28. Gaffney, 1994.

The Friday Prayer in Iran

Following the Islamic Revolution of 1979, Ayatollah Khomeini soon reinstated the Friday sermon which had been abandoned during the reign of Muhammed Reza Shah; the first being held on July 27th, 1979. Khomeini appointed Friday prayer leaders in every major city who in turn appointed preachers for the smaller towns.[29] The institution became increasingly coordinated and centralized with the World Congress of Friday Prayer Leaders in December of 1982. The Friday sermon became a core institution and pillar in the Islamic theocracy.[30] It was clear from the start that the sermons were to be used as a political platform and in particular for the propagation of the Rule of the Jurist. The mosques were to be turned into 'prayer, political, cultural, and military bases'.[31] The politicization of the institution is also evident from the fact that a number of anti-governmental attacks in the early- and mid-1980's were directed at Friday prayer leaders.[32]

Haggay Ram has shown how the Friday prayer has been used for indoctrination and mobilization purposes during the first ten years after the revolution.[33] The author finds that the Shi'a cosmogonic myths were well suited to keeping up the revolutionary zeal and legitimizing the Islamic government. The stories of the Prophet, his family, and the Imams are, according to Ram, used extensively and interpreted according to need. One example is the story of Hassan, the son of Ali and brother of Husayn. Hassan is normally perceived as a rather weak man and not a martyr.[34] Khomeini is alleged to have said: 'I am a Husayn, not a Hassan'; meaning that he was a fighting man. In the Friday prayer, however, Hassan becomes a warrior and staunch opponent of the Umayyads.

Looking at the Friday prayer sermons delivered since the death of Khomeini, one can observe a continuity in the use of sermons as a political podium. It is clear from radio announcements that this use is openly admitted; when announced, the sermons are referred to as 'political religious rites of the Friday prayer' or the like.[35] As Khamenei observed, the Friday prayer is to diagnose and cure the ideological, cultural, and spiritual ailment of the society;

29. Arjomand, 1988: 136.
30. Ibid: 160.
31. Bakhash, 1984: 235.
32. Ibid: 219.
33. Ram, 1994.
34. Ibid: 49.
35. 89-245, December 22, 1989.

it is where hearts are made more robust and faith is fortified and God's soldiers are given bravery and courage to act.[36]

The Friday Prayer as Formal or Informal Speech

Initial impressions of the institution of the Friday prayer are of a somewhat formal sermon. With the long tradition and the religious implications, it seems natural to expect a formal speech. According to M. Bloch[37] this may have implications for the speakers in terms of their ability to address specific issues. In his essay, Bloch proposes a theory of 'Everyday Speech Acts' versus 'Formalized Speech Acts'. The model, which is based on seven criteria, is directed at 'traditional societies' but is still useful in regard to the Friday sermon because of its religious nature, even though the examples given by Bloch are taken from Madagascar, Bali, and New Zealand.

Initial help can be found in Antoun's examination of the Jordanian village sermon. In Chapter four, Antoun applies the analytic model espoused by Bloch to the sermons delivered by the local preacher. Investigating each of the seven criteria, Antoun finds that the local sermon probably has to be categorized as formalized speech.[38] Yet, the author found that, with regard to a particular incident in the village, the preacher was able to communicate on a specific issue; something that, according to Bloch's model, should not be possible with formalized speech.

What then are the implications of the above for the Iranian Friday prayer? Using Block's criteria, is the Friday prayer a suitable vehicle for the communication of individual issues within the overall framework of modernity? No one would be likely to characterize the Friday sermons as delivered by the Iranian leadership as 'everyday speech'. However, the Friday sermon does not fit the traditional image of formal speech. In any case, it appears less formal than the local sermon which Antoun dealt with. In the Jordanian case, Antoun found communication possible. This should indicate, that the communication of ideas is possible through the Friday sermon in Tehran.

Conclusion

The questions asked at the beginning of this paper were as follows: Can modernity be found in Islamic discourse? Is the Friday prayer sermon a

---

36. 91-180, September 17, 1991.
37. Bloch, 1975: 1.
38. Antoun, 1989: 116.

suitable vehicle for communication in general and for communication of modernity in particular?

Due to constraints on the length of the present paper, I have been unable to provide examples from the Friday prayers. I will, however, at this point, briefly summarize my findings:

With regard to the status of women, it was found that women are considered different from men and that equal treatment is, therefore, not logical. The Iranian leadership does promote and encourage education for women, but women's entry into the workforce is only welcomed in a few specific areas. Although women are not accorded equality, heavy responsibility for the welfare of the revolution is placed on women. With regard to female sexuality, recognition has now come from the chief executive. The statements made about temporary marriage did, however, receive an ambivalent reception. This is due to the fact that the institution of temporary marriage is seen as a male prerogative.

Examining attitudes toward the nation state and international relations, it seems clear that the traditional notion of Islam's inability to operate in a world of nation states has been refuted. In the sermons delivered and analysed here, an attitude of 'Iran first' is evident and any export of the revolution is to be done by example. The speeches about the united Muslim umma can be identified as feel-good rhetoric, since Rafsanjani points out how unlikely the scenario is before he elaborates on the issue. The promotion of the idea is good for the regime's Islamic credentials.

In the section on economy, it was found that the ideas promoted are 'strikingly similar to the Chicago school of 'trickle-down' economics'.[39] Emphasis is on private and foreign investment, although the regime continues to hope that heavy industry will pull the country forward. There is a strong motivation for hard work, even for one's own benefit, and also for education and science.

Before I draw any conclusions regarding these views and their relationship to modernity, I want to address the question of communication in the Friday sermon. As was found in the section entitled 'The Friday Prayer in the 20th Century', the Friday prayer in Tehran is not as formal as one might initially expect. In many ways it seems less formal than the village prayer which Antoun examined in Jordan. According to Bloch's model, the ability to communicate specific ideas depends on the degree of formality in the speech. However, Antoun found that even if the Jordanian sermons were categorized as formal speech, specific issues were effectively addressed through the sermons. This might call for a qualification of Bloch's model. For the present

39. Abrahamian, 1993: 138.

purposes, however, it would indicate that the Friday sermon can function as a vehicle for the communication of specific ideas.

Whether modernity can be communicated through the sermons is a separate question. It will be recalled that Borthwick found that Friday prayer sermons were not able to convey modernity. He found the reason being that the issues became too concrete and that the preachers were unable to fit the issue into the frame of the Islamic sermon.[40] Antoun, on the other hand, found that issues of modernity were effectively communicated.[41] With regard to the Iranian Friday sermon, it should be clear that the factors which worked to limit the communication in the case of Borthwick are no longer present. From the readings, the issues which represent modernity are not particularly concrete and, more importantly, the Iranian leadership has obviously found a way of incorporating modernist issues into an Islamic discourse. As shown by Ram and also found here with regard to hard work, the Iranian preachers make extensive use of Shi'a myths and do not hesitate to modify or re-interpret the myths to suit their purpose. The only factor which would be able to limit the suitability of the sermons as a means of communicating modernity, would be the leadership itself. Due to the total governmental control over the sermons, loss of popularity on the part of the government will automatically limit the effectiveness and usefulness of the sermons. Signs of this can be seen in reports indicating falling attendance at the sermons and in Rafsanjani's emphasis on the duty to attend.

I now turn to the main question of this paper; the relationship between modernity and the Islamic Republic. In the introduction, I asked whether Islamic discourse refuted, sought accommodation with, or attempted appropriation of modernity. As for the latter solution, an example of this can be found in the article by M.J. Larijani.[42] The author finds that modernism is a behavioural characteristic. The chief characteristic of modern man is rationalism. Other adjectives describing modern man are the following: realistic, calculating, and scientific. Something is missing, however; and this is responsibility and concern with one's origins. If man is irresponsible and rootless, he is no better than an animal. If, on the other hand, man is concerned with his origins, he is awakened and becomes intelligent and sensible. Larijani's argument is that the Islamic man has all the qualities of modern man AND an additional one: a moral outlook. In a well written and well argued but somewhat polemic article, Larijani attempts to appropriate modernity.

40. Borthwich, 1965: 193.
41. Antoun, 1989, Ch. 5.
42. Larijani, 1995.

In 1987, Najmabadi wrote an article about Iran's turn from modernism to moral order.[43] She found that modernity now took a back seat to moral order. She quotes from the then Speaker of the Majlis, who talks about how the values of Iran have been changed by the revolution, before which a big bank account and a big house were marks of value. This has, according to Rafsanjani in 1986, changed. This article interprets the revolution as a rejection of modernity.

The attempt to accommodate modernity can be found in an essay by F. Rajaee.[44] In this essay, Rajaee examines the works of Abdolkarim Soroush. The latter rejects the conclusion of Al-e Ahmad, i.e. that everything coming out of the West is bad and poisonous. Western thought consists of many different parts, and acceptance of one part does not indicate a complete surrender to the West. Soroush warns against the danger of fanatical religious zeal: 'We do not want the fate of Galileo to be repeated in this land under the rule of the Islamic Republic. We do not want religion to become an impediment of science.[45] Rajaee finds, when looking at Iran, a remarkable degree of adaptability.[46] However, the trend is not uniform. In certain areas there is no compromise. Behind the seemingly unpredictable policy of the Islamic leadership, Rajaee finds pragmatism. In all areas where compromise is necessary, things from the West, be they thought or material, are incorporated. On issues where compromise is not necessary, no compromise is found. A good example of this policy is family planning.

It should be clear which of the three attitudes to modernity the present analysis of Islamic discourse has uncovered. Within international relations and economy, compromise is sought and found. On the issue of the status of women, no compromise is sought. This is the general rule on issues of culture.

This paper has found, through a textual analysis of Friday sermons, that Iran attempts to accommodate modernity in areas where it is necessary. In addition, it was found that the Friday prayer can be a channel of communication. This includes the communication of modernity. The main impediment to this is the regime itself and its waning popularity.

Bibliography

Abrahamian, Ervand 1993. Khomeinism: *Essays on the Islamic Republic.* Berkeley: University of California Press.

43. Najmabadi, 1987.
44. Rajaee, 1993.
45. Ibid: 113.
46. Ibid: 116.

Antoun, R.T. 1989. *Muslim Preacher in the Modern World: A Jordanian Case Study in Comparative Perspective.* Princeton, NJ: Princeton University Press.

Arjomand, Said Amir 1988. *The Turban for the Crown.* Oxford: Oxford University Press.

Bakhash, S. 1984. *The Reign of the Ayatollah.* New York: Basic Books Inc.

Bloch, M. 1975. *Political Language and Oratory in Traditional Society.* New York: Academic Press.

Borthwick, B.M. 1965. *The Islamic Sermon as a Channel of Political Communication in Syria, Jordan and Egypt.* Dissertation 7282, Ann Arbor: University of Michigan.

Calder, Norman 1986. 'Friday Prayer and the Juristic Theory of Government'. *Bulletin of the School of Oriental and African Studies.* Vol. 69: 35-47.

Cole, Juan (ed.) 1992. *Comparing Muslim Societies.* Ann Arbor: University of Michigan Press.

Encyclopaedia of Islam. Leiden: E.J. Brill, 1927.

Farhi, Farideh 1990. 'Ideology and Revolution in Iran.' *Journal of Developing Societies.* Vol. 6: 98-112.

Fathi, A. 1979. 'Communication and Tradition in Revolution: The Role of the Islamic Pulpit'. *Journal of Communication.* Vol. 29: 102-6.

Fathi, A. 1984. 'The Social and Political Function of the Mosque in the Muslim Community.' *Islamic Culture.* Vol. 58: 189-99

Fathi, A. 1987. 'The Culture and Social Structure of the Islamic Pulpit as a Medium of Communication in the Iranian Constitutional Revolution.' *Islamic Culture.* Vol. 61: 28-45.

Gaffney, Patrick 1994. *The Prophet's Pulpit - Islamic Preaching in Contemporary Egypt.* Berkeley: University of California Press.

Goitein, S.D. 1966. *Studies in Islamic History and Institutions.* E. J. Brill.

Haeri, Shahla 1989. *Law and Desire - Temporary Marriage in Shii Iran,* Syracuse, NY: Syracuse University Press.

Haeri, Shahla 1992. *Temporary Marriage and the State in Iran: An Islamic Discourse on Feminine Sexuality. Social Research.* Vol. 59: (1): 201-23.

Larijani, M.J.: 'Islamic Society and Modernism.' *The Iranian Journal of International Affairs.* Vol. 7, (1): 31-58.

Najmabadi, A. 1987. 'Iran's Turn to Islam: from Modernism to a Moral Order'. *Middle East Journal.* Vol. 41, 1987: 202-217.

Najmabadi, A. 1993. 'Veiled Discourse - Unveiled Bodies.' *Feminist Studies* Vol. 19, 1993: 487-518.

Najmabadi, A. 1993. 'Hazards of Modernity and morality: Woman, State, and Ideology in Contemporary Iran.' in Hourani, A. (ed.): *The Middle East.* Berkeley: University of California Press.

Rajaee, F. 1993. 'Islam and Modernity - The Reconstruction of an Alternative Shiite Islamic World view in Iran'. *Fundamentalism and Society, Reclaiming the Science, the Family and Education.* Chicago: University of Chicago Press.

Ram, Haggay 1992. 'Crushing the Opposition: Adversaries of the Islamic Republic of Iran.' *Middle East Journal* Vol. 46: 426-39.

Ram, Haggay 1993. 'Islamic 'Newspeak': Language and Change in Revolutionary Iran.' *Middle Eastern Studies* Vol. 29, 1993: 198-219.

Ram, Haggay 1994. *Myth and Mobilization in Revolutionary Iran: The Use of the Friday Congregational Sermon.* American University Press.

The Alawites' Rise to Power in Syria

Mette Fenger

Syria's population reflects an extraordinary diversity of religious and ethnic communities. The Arab Sunni Muslims constitute the majority. The largest (Muslim) minority group are the Alawites, who make up twelve percent of the population. (The other major religious minorities in Syria are; the Druze, the Isma'ilis and the Greek Orthodox Christians. The principal ethnic minorities are the Kurds, the Armenians, the Turcomans and the Circassians).

In February 1971, Hafiz al-Assad became the first Alawite president of Syria, thus ending the leadership of the Sunni majority. The Alawites rise to power has not only changed the composition of the Syrian political elite, but has also moved the Alawites from a discriminated, socially and economically backward religious minority, to a group of significant power.

In the following, a short presentation will be given of this religious minority; what makes them a religious minority, and how does their religion differ from orthodox Islam?

Their rise to power has passed through different 'stages' and 'organizations' and these will be examined in order to describe how a minority group has succeeded in gaining power.

Problems caused by the fact that power is in the hands of a minority group will be discussed in the following section.

In the final section, some of the problems this minority group has had while being in power will be discussed.

The Alawites' History and Religion

The Alawites today number approximately 1.3 million, of whom about a million live in Syria. Three-quarters of the Syrian Alawites live in Latakia, a province in the northwest of Syria, where they make up almost two-thirds of the population.[1] Smaller numbers are found in other adjacent areas of the

---

1. Daniel Pipes, *Greater Syria*. Oxford: Oxford University Press, 1990: 159.

Middle East, mainly the Alexandretta and Cilicia Regions in Turkey and in the Akkar district of Lebanon.[2]

The bulk of the Alawites have for centuries lived in the Jabal Ansâriyya mountain range, (known today as Jabal al-Alawiyyîn) which runs parallel to the coast behind the port and coastal plain of Latakia. Most Alawites worked land owned by absentee Sunni landlords, under extremely onerous crop-sharing arrangements; traditionally, the towns were principally Sunni or Christian.

Their concentration around Jabal Ansâriyya, however, illustrates the principle that minorities survive best when protected by terrain from the attentions of the majority.[3] Central to the cultural identity of Alawites is their unique religion, but mystery shrouds this people's formative history, and an absolutely authoritative explanation does not exist.[4]

The generally accepted source of the Alawite religion, however, points to Muhammad ibn Nusayr (d.883)[5] as the man who founded the sect in Iraq in the mid-9th century. It was ibn Nusayr (Muhammad b. Nusayr al-Namîrî) that gave name to the sect, which was not officially known as 'Alawîtes' until September 1920, when the French occupational forces instituted the policy of referring to them by that name.[6]

The change in name has significance. Whereas Nusayri emphasizes the group's difference from Islam, Alawite suggests an adherent of Ali (the son-in-law of the Prophet Muhammad) and accentuates the religion's similarities to Shi'i Islam.[7]

Born in Iraq, the Alawite doctrine quickly spread into Northern Syria which, under the domination of the Hamdânids of Aleppo, offered a favourable terrain for the Shi'i propaganda.[8]

In the Mamluk period, Baybars made numerous attempts to convert the Nusayris to Sunnism; he forbade initiations into the sect and ordered the construction of mosques throughout the country. After an uprising by the Nusayris, Sultan Kalâwûn re-imposed the ban on all proselytism and repeated the order to construct a mosque in every township, for the maintenance of

2. Peter Gubser, *Minorities in Power: The Alawites of Syria*: 18; in R. D. McLaurin (ed.), *The Political Role of Groups in the Middle East*. New York: Praeger, 1979.
3. John F. Devlin, *Modern State in a Ancient Land*. Boulder, Col: Westview Press, 1983: 27.
4. Mordechai Nisan, *Minorities in the Middle East. A History of Struggle and Self-Expression*. London: McFarland & Company 1991: 98.
5. Ibid: 99.
6. Umar F. Abd-Allah, *The Islamic Struggle in Syria. Mizan Press*, Berkeley, 1983: 44.
7. Pipes: 159.
8. L. & A. Chabry, *Politique et minorités au Proche Orient*. Maisonneuve & Larose, 1987: 99.

which the local population was to be responsible. But Ibn Battûta, touring the region in the mid-14th century, relates that these mosques had been abandoned or even transformed into cattle-sheds or stables.[9]

The Alawite religious faith, or the Nusairi sect, is rooted in a doctrine whose ideas reflect multiple theological and philosophical influences.[10]

The popular religion of Alawism, especially that of women, who cannot be initiated and therefore have little knowledge of the doctrine and theology, retains traces of paganism — the worship of high places, springs, trees and beliefs in talismans, magic and *ziyaras* (burial places of holy people which are subject to pilgrimage).[11]

The worship of stars and other celestial bodies is a central part of Alawite ritual. One of the fundamentals of this belief connected to these practices is the reincarnation and transmigration of souls. According to Alawite belief, all human beings originated as celestial bodies but assumed their present form as a consequence of the Fall. The successive reincarnations and transmigrations of souls will end in their restoration as celestial bodies.

In the beginning of time, the souls of the Nusayris were lights, surrounding and praising God; then they rebelled against Him, disputing His divinity. From then onwards, they have been hurled down from the celestial heights and exiled on earth, where they are enclosed in material bodies and condemned to metempsychosis (temporal *nâsûkhiyya* for the elected, eternal *nâsûkhiyya* for the damned). During their fall, the supreme God appears to them seven times, calling for their obedience, but they refuse...(Encyc.).

To the Alawites 'Ali is the incarnation of divinity. The most significant belief distinguishing the Alawites from other Muslims is their strong focus on 'Ali, the paternal cousin and son-in-law of Muhammad, and his deification in their eyes. The Alawites believe in one God who manifested himself to the world seven different times. Each time God showed himself, he made use of two other persons who, along with God, make up an inseparable Trinity and which are called *al-ma'nâ,al-ism* and *al-bâb*. The *Ma'ana* (the meaning) indicates that God is the meaning, sense, and reality of all things. The *'Ism* (the name) is also called the veil, because behind it the *Ma'ana* hides its glory, but through it, the *'Ism*, the *Ma'ana* reveals itself to the people. The *Bâb* (door) is the entrance to knowledge about the *Ma'ana* and the *'Ism*.[12]

The seventh and last time God manifested himself, 'Ali was the *Ma'ana*, the most important part of this trinity. Muhammad was the *'Ism* and said to have

9. Ibn Battuta, *Ar-Rihla. Beirut: Dar as-Sadr and Dar Bayrut*, 1384/1964: 79-80.
10. Nisan: 99.
11. Gubser, and E.J. Brill, *Encyclopaedia of Islam*, Leiden: 22.
12. Ibid: 20.

been created from 'Ali's light. Salmân al-Fârisî, the Persian companion of Muhammad, was the *Bâb*, and the sole means of access to the meaning represented by 'Ali and consequently is superior in that sense to Muhammad.[13] Salmân al-Fârisî, the *Bâb* and their initials forms a secret formula consisting of the Arabic letters *'Ain-Mîm-Sîn*, whose meaning is only revealed to the initiated.[14]

The Alawites have some secret books, the most important being *kitab al-Majmu'a*, which is more sacred than the Quran, these are not shown to the uninitiated and they are not published. An 'Alawit, Sulaimân al-Adnî, who converted to Christianity, dared to put some of these texts in circulation in Beirut and was assassinated (1866) for divulging the sect's mysteries. (It was from Sulaimân's texts that Orientalists (Massignon, Strothman, Catafago) and missionaries of the 19th and 20th centuries gained access to a number of the Nusairi manucripts).[15]

They do not have any religious buildings, even though pilgrimages go to saints' burial sites (*awliyâ*). Their calender consists of Sunni-muslim, Shi'a-muslim (*'âchûrâ'*) and Christian (Christmas, Epiphany, Easter, Pentecost) religious festivals.

They honour many Christian saints and the Arabic equivalents of Christian personal names such as Gabriel, John, Matthew, Catherine and Helen are in common use.[16] They use lights, incense and wine in their liturgy as in Chistianity.[17]

From an (orthodox) Islamic standpoint, the religious beliefs and practices of the Nusairis set them off as a distinct religion, neither Islamic, nor Christian, nor Jewish, and they have been regarded as *kuffâr* (disbelievers, rejectors of faith) and idolaters (*mushrikûn*).[18]

Whatever the truth about the genesis of 'Alawism, the reaction of orthodox Islam was undeviating in its absolute rejection of it. Ibn Tamiyya (1268-1328), the still highly influential Sunni writer of Syrian origin, considered Alawites more infidel than idolators and called for *jihad* against them. In reaction, the Alawites adopted the ways of silence and *taqiyya*, (dissimulation to preserve the faith) hidden away in their refuge in the mountains.[19]

With respect to religion, the Alawites are split into different sects, the most important being the Shamsîs, who see the sun as the symbol of divinity and

---

13. Umar Abd-Allah: 46.
14. A. Nimier, *Les Alawites*. Edition, Paris: Asfar 1987: 17.
15. Pipes: 160.
16. Nimier: 18.
17. Abd-Allah: 48.
18. Mordechai Nisan: 99.
19. Nimier: 19.

the Qamarîs who 'prefer' the moon.[20] But not only are they split into different sects, the Alawites can also be subdivided tribally into four main confederations: the Khayyâtîn, Haddâdîn, Matâwirah and Kalbiyyah, who are scattered throughout the entire Latakia region and its surrounding areas. Many villages and their lands are divided among families belonging to different tribes.[21]

It should be noted that the leaders of the Alawites deny any connection or affinity with astral gnosticism or other deviations from conventional Shi'ism. In a formal proclamation issued in 1973, 80 religious personages, representing the various parts of the Alawite country, affirmed that their book is the Quran, that they are Muslim and Shi'i, and, like the majority of Shi'is, the Twelvers, that is, partisans of the twelve imams, and that whatever else is attributed to them has no basis in truth and is a mere invention by their enemies and the enemies of Islam.[22] And at a time of sectarian tension in the mid-1960s, the suggestion that the Alawite officers running the country published the secret books of their religion caused Salah Jadid to respond with horror, saying that, were this done, the religious leaders would 'crush us'.[23]

Frequently persecuted — some twenty thousand were massacred in 1317 and half that number in 1516 — the Alawites insulated themselves geographically from the outside world by staying within their own rural regions. Also, even though some Alawites may have wanted to live in the cities, they were always made to feel unwelcome by the traditional urban population which was either of another Islamic sect or Christian. These groups prevented the Alawites from obtaining gainful employment except of the most

---

20. Van Dam, *The Struggle for Power in Syria*. London: Croom Helm 1981: 22.
21. The 'Ulamâ' of the Islamic 'Alawî Sect in the Syrian Arab Republic and in Lebanon, Al-'Alawiyyûn. Man hum wa Mâ 'Aqidatuhum (The 'Alawîs. Who are they and What are their Beliefs?) undated and unplaced: 6-7, 16-20 and 27. Quoted in Hanna Batatu, *Some Observations*: 135 and *Pipes*: 160. Taymiyya ... wrote in a fatwa (religious decision) that 'the Nusayris are more infidel than Jews or Christians, even more infidel than many polytheists. They have done greater harm to the community of Muhammad than have the warring infidels such as the Franks, the Turks, and others. To ignorant Muslims they pretend to be Shi'is, though in reality they do not believe in God or His prophet or His book.' Ibn Taymiyya warned of the mischief their enmity could do: 'Whenever possible, they spill the blood of Muslims...They are always the worst enemies of Muslims.' In conclusion, he argued that 'war and punishments in accordance with Islamic law against them are among the greatest of pious deeds and the most important obligations' for a Muslim.
22. Pipes: 160, and Batatu, 'Some Observations on the Social roots of Syria's ruling Military Group and the Causes for its Dominance', *The Middle East Journal*, Vol. 35 Summer, 1981, (3): 335.
23. Gubser: 19-20.

menial kind and prevented them, at times physically, from taking part in the activities of the city.[24]

Jacques Weulersse explained their predicament:

Defeated and persecuted, the heterodox sects disappeared or, to survive, renounced proselytism…The Alawites silently entrenched themselves in their mountains…Isolated in rough country, surrounded by a hostile population, henceforth without communication with the outside world, the Alawites began to live out their solitary existence in secrecy and repression. Their doctrine, entirely formed, evolved no futher.[25]

And E. Janot describes the problem like this:

Bullied by the Turks, victims of a determined ostracism, fleeced by their Muslim landlord, the Alawite hardly dared leave his mountain region, where isolation and poverty itself protected them.[26]

After having read these two descriptions it is understandable why the Alawites were known for their practice of *taqiya* (religious dissimulation). They acquired a reputation as fierce and unruly mountain people who resisted paying taxes they owed the authorites and frequently plundered Sunni villagers on the plains.[27]

A permanent condition of poverty had compelled Alawite families to sell their daughters into servitude to rich Sunni households in the city. This disgrace remained a vivid experience into the twentieth century. Perhaps the only true redeeming feature of Alawite life, aside from a unique religious heritage, was a martial tradition as mountain fighters.[28]

Finally, in the 1970s, this pattern began to change. As with rest of the world, Syria is becoming more urbanized, and the Alawites are no exeption to the rule. Many are now migrating to major urban centres in search of employment and education.

The ascent of the Alawites took place over the course of half a century. In 1920, they were still the lowly minority just described; by 1970, they firmly ruled Syria. The stunning transformation took place in three stages: the French

24. Pipes: 164.
25. Jacques Weulersse, *Le pays des Alaouites*, Tours, 1940, Vol. 1: 54 quoted in Daniel Pipes: 164.
26. E. Janot, *Des Croisades au Mandat: Notes sur le peuple Alouïte*, Lyon, 1934: 37.
27. Nisan: 100.
28. Gubser: 19-20.

mandate (1920-46), the period of Sunni dominance (1946-63), and the era of Alawite consolidation (1963-70).[29]

The two major national organizations that were instrumental in the Alawites rise to power and eventual control of political life in Syria were the Baath party and the military.[30]

The French Mandate (1920-46)

In 1918, British and French troops occupied the Arabic-speaking regions of the Ottoman Empire and by 1920 had expelled the Arab nationalist regime in Damascus and divided the area between themselves (as they had agreed to do in the Sykes-Picot treaty signed two years earlier). Out of their share the French created in 1920 the two Mandates of Syria and Lebanon with their own locally recruited military organization, first called the Syrian Legion and later the Troupes Spéciales du Levant.[31] This was an army dominated by minority groups, not least the Alawites, who in the army saw a stepping-stone to social advancement and a means of breaking out of their poverty.

Building upon sectarian and regional consciousness, the French set about formalizing Alawite particularism in political and military forms.[32]

On August 31st, 1920, the French established the 'Autonomous Territory of the Alawites', and in July 1922 the Territory was proclaimed a State which, along with the states of Damascus and Aleppo formed the 'Federation of States of Syria'. A few years later the federation was dissolved and the state of the Alawites became the 'Independent State of the Alawites' headed by a French governor and a local council composed of nine representatives of the various minorities (nine Alawites, three Sunnis, three orthodox Christians, one Isma'ili and one representative of the other Christian minorities).[33]

Sunni tribunals were precluded from judging Alawite cases in their own state entity. In 1930 the state was renamed the Government of Latakia.

The Alawite state enjoyed low taxation and a sizable French subsidy. It also had it's own flag (a sun on a white background) and postage stamps.[34]

Meanwhile, Syrian Arab nationalism gained momentum in Damascus and other key urban centres and its leadership aspired to reintegrate the outlying

29. M.A. Faksh, 'The Alawi Community of Syria: A new Dominant Political Force'. *Middle Eastern Studies* Vol 20, (2), April 1984: 140.
30. N.E. Bou-Nacklie, 'Les Troupes Spéciales: religious and ethnic recruitment' *Int. Journal of Middle East Studies* 25 (1983): 645.
31. Nisan: 102.
32. Nisan: 102 and *Encyclopaedia of Islam*, New Edition, Leiden: E.J. Brill.
33. Pipes: 166; and Nimier: 35.
34. Nisan: 102.

provinces.[35] In 1936, this was achieved with the annexation by Syria of the Latakia entity which transformed it into a province of the new Syrian state. The flag of the Alawites was replaced by the Syrian Tricolour.

Given the Alawites' background of poverty and suppression it is not surprising that they were slow to develop an identity with Arab nationalism or the emerging Syrian nation. During the French Mandate the Alawites had little consciousness of being Arab. The French encouraged this by setting up a separate government of Latakia and fostering the development of an independent Alawite identity and 'a more conscious particularist spirit then they had previously possessed'.[36]

In the past, the Arab nationalist movement had always been closely associated with and controlled by Sunni Islamism: heterodox Muslims and other religious groups were assigned a secondary place.[37] Some Sunni Arab nationalists even tended to regard members of Arabic-speaking religious minorities as 'imperfect Arabs', which was deeply resented by these minorities, who perceived Arab nationalism as a continued Sunni supremacy in disguise - the only difference was that Arab Sunni were replacing Ottoman Sunnis.[38] There was then little sense of loyalty or commitment among the Alawites when their area was incorporated within the newly established Syrian republic of 1936, which remained under French control. They reacted as they had against the Mamluks, the Ottomans and the French in the early days of the Mandate: led by Sulayman al-Murshid, who claimed a prophetic vision and founded a new Alawite religious sect, the Alawites revolted against the central government before and after World War II.

From 1921 to 1945, three of eight infantry battalions in the Troupes Spéciales were Alawite units. Various minority peoples, like Druze, Circassians, Kurds, Isma'ilis, and Assyrians served in the army of France. The majority Sunni Arabs were conspicuous by their absence. But in Latakia and Antioch, in particular, some 90 percent of the soldiers were Alawites.[39]

Despite the fact that the French over-recruited from the Alawites and the Druze, they did so with great finesse. For example, after 1920, the French rarely recruited from the Alawite al-Bashaghira tribe, which had spearheaded a rebellion in that year. In the same way, the French were reluctant to recruit from the Druze Turshan clan who had rebelled against them in 1925. The over-representation of the Alawites and the Druze came instead from those groups

35. Albert Hourani, *Syria and Lebanon, A Political Essay*. London, 1946: 185, quoted in Gubser: 39.

36. Hourani: 185. Quoted in Faksh.

37. *Weulersse*, Vol. 1: 326, quoted in Nisan: 103; Batatu: 341.

38. N.E. Bou-Nacklie: 656.

39. Ibid: 647.

and factions, tribes and clans that had either remained neutral or were loyal to the French.[40]

The French aim was to divide the mandatory populations by pitting religious and ethnic groups, as well as factions within each group, against each other. They allowed one ethnic or religious group to be strongly represented in one institution, for example, the military's officiers corps, while weakening its representation in others, such as the parliament.[41]

One of the main reasons that the French recruited Alawites and Druze was that their high representation ensured that Arab Sunni rebellions did not succeed. Alawites and Druze could be counted on to counter the Arab Sunnis and their nationalist demands for unification and centralization ('Alawi over-representation in both the Syrian Legion and the Troupes Spéciales remained constant from 1921 to 1944).[42]

Post-Independence — The Period of Sunni Dominance (1946-63)

According to Daniel Pipes it was the Sunnis, and especially the urban elite, who inherited the government when the French mandate ended in 1946. Even after independence, the Alawites continued to resist submission to the central government. Sulayman al-Murshid led a second revolt in 1946, which ended in his execution. A third unsuccessful uprising, led by Murshid's son, took place in 1952. The failure of these efforts led the Alawite to look into the possibility of attaching Latakia to Lebanon or Transjordan — anything to avoid absorption into Syria. These acts of resistance further tarnished the Alawites already poor reputation among Sunnis.

When they came to power, the Sunni rulers in Damascus spared no effort to integrate Latakia into Syria (in part because this region offered the only access to the sea). Overcoming armed resistance, they abolished the Alawite state, Alawite military units, Alawite seats in parliament, and courts applying Alawite laws of personal status. These measures had some success; Alawites became reconciled to Syrian citizenship after the crushing of a Druze revolt in 1954 and henceforth gave up the dream of a separate state. This change of outlook, which seemed to be a matter of relatively minor importance at the time, in fact ushered in a new era of Syrian political life: the political ascent of the Alawites.[43]

The process of integration was enhanced by ongoing socio-economic changes and modernization. 'The growth in mass communications and

40. Ibid: 652.
41. Bou-Nacklie: 647.
42. Ibid: 652.
43. Pipes: 168.

transport was breaking the older pattern of community isolation; Syrians of all kinds were brought into closer touch with one another. Most notable was the vast expansion of the educational system and its increasing Arabization by government during the 1950s and 1960s'. Educational opportunities became more and more available to a greater number of poor Alawites, former peasants who sought social advancement for themselves and their people. In this way, a new and growing segment of the Alawite community became mobilized and began to play a major role in national political life — eventually controlling it.[44]

The Military and The Baath

Once they recognized that their future lay within Lesser Syria, the Alawites began a rapid rise to power. Two key institutions, the armed forces and the Baath Party, had special importance in their transformation.

Even though the special circumstances which had brought them into the military lapsed with the French departure, Alawites and other minorities continued after independence to be over-represented in the army.[45] The situation within the army was well described in a 1949 report: 'All units of any importance were under the command of persons originating in [religious] minorities'.[46]

One of the reasons for this was that the military retained its reputation as a place for the minorities. Patrick Seale observed that Sunni landed families: being predominantly of nationalist sentiment, despised the army as a profession: to join it between the wars was to serve the French. Homs (Military Academy) to them was a place for the lazy, the rebellious, the academically backward, or the socially undistinguished.[47]

The dire economic predicament of the Alawites and other rural peoples meant that they could not pay the fee to exempt their children from military service. More positively, those children saw military service as a means of making a decent living.[48]

The new secondary schools were significant because a secondary school diploma was required for entrance to the Military Academy. Whereas Academy applicants had previously been few in number and almost exclusively middle

---

44. Faksh: 140.
45. Pipes: 169.
46. Fadl Allah Abu Mansur, *A'asir dimashq* (Beirut 1959): 51. Quoted in Van Dam: 41; Faksh: 143; Pipes: 169.
47. Patrick Seale *Struggle for Syria*: London, 1965: 37.
48. Pipes: 169.

and upper-class, in the 1950s and 1960s they could be numbered in the hundreds, mainly from the lower-middle class and the rural areas.[49]

Once having moved into command positions, these officers brought in relatives and others from their sectarian, regional and tribal communities, helping them to advance and tending to favour their applications to the army, navy and air academies.[50]

Successive military coups d'état since the first coup of Colonel Husni al-Za'im in 1949, and the subsequent increasing politicization of the officer class in the 1950s and the early 1960s, brought about an ever-shifting composition of the senior ranks. Indeed, the history of the Syrian army in politics is a long saga of the struggles, as Faksh puts it, sometimes violent, among power factions or blocs (*kutal*) linked with different political ideological parties or interests.[51]

Thus it was as much factionalized as Syrian political life itself. During this period and until the Baath officers' coup d'état on March 8th, 1963, the most prominent factions in the army were headed primarily by Sunni leaders who apparently believed that reserving the top positions for themselves would suffice to control the military forces. Accordingly, minorities filled the lower ranks and for some years found it difficult to rise above the company level. However, as senior officers engaged in the power struggles, leading to resignations and the depletion of Sunni ranks, the non-Sunnis and Alawites especially, who were stood apart from these conflicts, benefited from the repeated purges.[52]

In addition to the military, Alawites also acquired power through the Baath (Resurrection) Party. From its earliest years, the Baath held special attraction for Syrians from rural and minority backgrounds, including the Alawites, who joined in disproportionately large numbers (especially at the Baath Party's Latakia branch).[53] The Baath Party, was the first political party in the Arab world created with the specific goal of achieving Pan-Arab unity.[54] It had two separate origins, one in Zakî al-Arsûzî, an Alawite who fled the district of Alexandretta when it was taken over by the Turks in 1939, the other in the Christian, Michel 'Aflaq and the Sunni Muslim, Salâh al-Dim al-Bitâr. All three of them were educated in Paris and later became teachers in Damascus. The

---

49. Van Dusen, Political Integration and Regionalism in Syria, *Middle East Journal*, Spring, 1972, Vol. 26 (2): 132.
50. Van Dam: 41.
51. Faksh: 143.
52. Faksh: 144, Pipes: 169.
53. Pipes: 169.
54. Ibid: 169

party began its work during World War II, was formally founded in 1947, and played a growing part in Syrian politics from that time on.[55]

It was especially rural migrants who went to Damascus for educational purposes who found the Baath appealing. They tended to be students of lower-middle-class origins, the sons of ex-peasants newly arrived in the towns. In Aleppo, for example, the Baath claimed as members as many as three-quarters of the high school students in some schools. Zaki al-Arsuzi who, as mentioned, was Alawite brought along many of his (rural) coreligionists to the Baath.[56]

As a reaction to the 'monopoly' the Sunnis had on the traditional nationalist movement, the Baath opened up for the Arabic-speaking religious minorities who were tolerated rather than accepted[57] and as mentioned above seen by some of the Sunni Arab nationalist as 'imperfect Arab's' because they were heterodox Muslims or not Muslims at all.[58]

In particular, two doctrines appealed to the Alawites and members of other religious minorities, such as the Druze and Isma'ilis, and these were secularism — the withdrawal of religion from public life — and socialism. It was, indeed, these aspects that drew them to the Baath Party more than it's Pan-Arab nationalism.[59] Such a secular, socialist polical system would in Faksh' words 'certainly weaken the traditional Sunni-urban establishment's hegemony in Syrian political life and, consequently, would eliminate the prevailing political and socia-economic discrimination against heterodox Muslim minorities'. Other secular parties which attracted many minority members was the SSNP, the Syrian Social Nationalist Party and the Syrian Communist Party.[60]

The party's disproportional expansion in the Latakia region gave the Alawites a strong base from which to gain power in the region in the 1950s and in the nation later.

The Baath Party and the other Syrian polical parties were dissolved with the unification of Syria with Egypt in the United Arab Republic, UAR, (1958 - 61) under the leadership of the Egyptian president Gamal Abdel Nasser.

But some Alawite groups chose to remain organized clandestinely and so maintained a certain measure of power and control in the Latakia region. Following the secession of Syria from the union in 1961, the earlier dissolution of the Baath proved to be a major political gain to the Alawites, for they now

55. Olivier Carré, 'Le mouvement idéologique ba'thiste', p. 186, in Raymond (ed.) *La Syrie d'aujourd'hui*, Paris 1980.
56. C. Kaminsky and S. Kruk, La Syrie: Politique et stratégie de 1966 à nos jours, Paris: PUF 1987: 11.
57. Ibid.
58. Van Dam: 32.
59. Pipes: 170.
60. Faksh: 141.

were the strongest and most organized force in the much-weakened national organization.[61]

The Era of Alawite Consolidation (1963-70)

After Syria's secession, considerable resentment was directed at 'Aflaq and Bitâr. Many educated Baaths criticized the opaqueness of Baath socialism and began to call for a more Marxist approach. The failure of the UAR brought the doctrine of Arab unity itself into question. Many Baaths came to believe that socialist revolutions within each Arab state would have to precede the implementation of Arab unity[62] these became known as regionalist because of their focus on the Syrian 'region', the Baath party's term for an Arab country. So it was a weak and divided Baath party that came to power in a coup d'état on March 9th, 1963 and therefore the Alawites were able, from their firm organizational regional base in Latakia, to increase their strength in the party and to position themselves in less than three years in high party and government positions.

Immediately after the coup, as the need to fill the many available government vacancies by party supporters became more urgent, the Alawites took advantage of the relaxed requirements for party membership to admit family members and friends, thus strengthening their position in the party.[63]

From the spring of 1963 until 1966, a confusing power struggle went on, with alliances shifting among the contenders. In February 1966, the regionalists seized power in a violent coup that drove 'Aflaq and Bitâr into exile.

The Coup's leaders were: (Alawites) Salah Jadid, Izzat Jadid, Hafiz al-Assad, and Ibrahim Makhous; and (Druze) Salim Hatum and Izzat Ubaid.[64]

The event marked an important change in Syrian post-independent history: Control of the Syrian army and Syrian political life had passed to the heterodox Muslim minorities, led by the Alawites; the Sunni majority was in a subordinate, inactive position. In 1966 and 1968, the Alawite faction terminated the other two minoritarian-sectarian factions (the Druze and the Isma'ilis), and became masters of Syria.[65]

The Alawite officers, themselves of peasant background, claimed to represent the interests of the peasants and workers, and actively pursued

---

61. Avraham Ben-Tzur, The neo-Ba'th party in Syria. *New Outlook*, 12 (January 1969): 27. Faksh: 141; Gubser: 42.
62. Marc J. Sievers, 'The Ideologi of the Baath Party and Syrian Politics', *Journal of International affairs*, Vol. 34, (2), 1980-81: 189.
63. Faksh: 141, 152..
64. Sievers: 190.
65. Faksh: 144.

policies which benefitted the rural areas at the expense of the cities. Although Sunnis held important positions in the Jadid or 'neo-Baath' regime, Alawites received preferential treatment in the army and held key positions in the army and government. The neo-Baath regime was basically indifferent to pan-Arab issues except for Palestine; it took a more Marxist and explicitly secularist line than the 'Aflaq-Bitâr leadership. Internationally, the regime aligned itself with the Soviet Union and received considerable Soviet technical and military assistance.[66]

On November 13th, 1970, Hafiz al-Assad, former head of the Syrian Air Force and Minister of Defence since 1966, effectively led a successful coup d'état in Damascus. His loyalist troops took over the radio and the press, arrested opponents, occupied offices of the Baath party, and put Salah Jadid and President Atasi in custody. Syria's tenth military coup d'état in seventeen years, was to be the last for a long time to come.

In February 1971, Asad became the first Alawite president of Syria following the consolidation of his coup and its culmination in a new regime.[67]

The Alawites accession to power through the military and the Baath Party provoked considerable conflict with the balance of the Syrian population, and particularly with the balance of the urban Sunni Muslims.[68] There have been two main reasons for this conflict — one based on sectarian grounds/reasons and one based on class differences. (Symbolized by the urban middle and upper-middle classes versus the rural peasant lower and lower-middle classes).

Nationalization of industrial and commercial establishments destroyed the economic bases of bourgeois power. (It should be noted that pressure on the commercial sector became less intense during the mid-1970s).

Land reform has been very extensive, with about 28 percent of the land being expropriated and redistributed. This has had the effect of considerably raising the living standards of the peasants[69] and eliminating the landlord's role as guardians between state and village.[70] Investment in the educational system benefited all classes but mostly the lower ones and increasing state employment has broadened the state-employed middle class.[71]

66. Sievers: 190.
67. Nisan: 105.
68. Gubser: 43.
69. Ibid.
70. R.A. Hinnebusch, 'State and Civil society in Syria'. *Middle East Journal* Vol. 47 (2), Spring 1993: 246.
71. Ibid.

Even though it is quite evident that each of these measures definitely benefitted the lower and lower middle classes, it can also be argued that they have hurt urban Sunni Muslims and Christians the most.[72]

There has been, in addition, considerable conflict between the Alawites and Sunni Muslims on the religious plane. The Alawite-dominated government has often attempted to diminish the role of Islam and the position of the Sunni Muslim religious leaders (*ulama*) in the state and society, usually in the name of the advancement of secularism and the elimination of the role of religion in the state and curtailing it in the society.[73]

By the mid-1970s the Alawites took another step in their relations with Sunni Muslims. To gain more credibility, President al-Assad sought and received affirmation that he is a true Muslim from Syrian Sunni *ulama,* and the Lebanese Shia *ulema* — specifically Musa al-Sadr — declared Alawites to be Shiite Muslims. Asad went on the *hajj* to Mecca and occasionally attended prayer services in Damascene mosques. He appointed Sunnis to senior governmental positions and sought to deflect ever-present suspicions that 'Alawite were inveterately hostile to Muslims, and that they were themselves non-Muslims'.[74] But these moves did not bring an end to the Sunni reaction and opposition, spearheaded by the urban-centered movement of *al-Ikhwan al Muslimun* (the Muslim Brotherhood).

The Muslim Brotherhood has been effective because it served as the main vehicle for rallying anti-regime sentiment — and not because of its fundamentalist cast. Sunnis joined the Brotherhood because of its proven record as the most durable and effective organization combatting Alawite rule.[75] There have been several clashes between the regime and the opposition especially from September 1976, when the Brotherhood began a major campaign of terror that just three years later seemed on the verge of overthrowing the regime. The Sunni revolt climaxed with two events: in June 1979, the Brethren massacred more than sixty cadets — almost all Alawites — at a military school in Aleppo; and in July 1980, they nearly assassinated Asad himself. Just when it appeared that the regime might fall, Asad responded with a horrible efficiency. He made membership in the Muslim Brotherhood a capital crime and 'hunted down its members without remorse'. Efforts to destroy the organization peaked in early 1982, when Asad assaulted the city of Hama. Muslim Brethren forces held the city from February 2nd for about ten days, killing the governor and several hundred other officials. In response, some

72. Gübser: 43.
73. Ibid: 43, 44.
74. Nisan: 110.
75. Pipes: 182

twelve thousand troops attacked Brethren strongholds with field artillery, tanks, and air force helicopters. In the end, thousands lost their lives.[76] The Brethren's challenge ended for some years.

Writing in 1983, Gérard Michaud observed: 'today it appears that the repressive machinery has succeeded in dismantling the fundamentalist movement in Syria. But for how long? And at what price!'[77] It should be noted that the rigid controls of the 1980s are being relaxed as the Islamic threat recedes, and the security forces are being 'reined in'. The religious schools and mosques are recovering their autonomy on condition that oppositional activity is eschewed.[78]

While the Baath's 'nation-building credentials' remained plausible and it seemed as if the regime were addressing the country's developmental problems, discontent over the Alawite role was muted and criticism could be deflected.[79] Anyone who dared to broach the subject of the regime's communal composition was immediately accused of encouraging sectarianism and acting as an agent for Syria's enemies.[80]

Since the mid-1970s, criticism of the Alawite role has widened and intensified for many reasons. As the regime got older, it lost much of its dynamism and direction and evolved into something that vaguely resembles the original, reasonably progressive Baath vision. Whereas during the 1960s the Baath tried to subordinate the military as its instrument, now it is the other way around. The regime has become a 'conventional-authoritarian military' one.

The regime has also lost support because of the dramatic spread of corruption. This accompanied the party's degeneration and the growth of a huge, inefficient public sector which increased government spending and the easing of restrictions on local capitalists after Hafiz al-Assad's 1970 coup.

Even though the Alawites hold a disproportionate share of key posts in the officer corps, internal security forces and the Baath Party, it should be stressed that there are a number of Sunni-Muslims in some of the most important government positions, which doesn't reflect a purely sectarian-based regime. The fact that Hafiz al-Assad surrounds himself with family (Alawite)

---

76. Pipes: 185.
77. Olivier Carré and Gérard Michaud (Michel Seurat), *Les Frères musulmans: Égypte et Syrie* (1928-1982), Paris 1983: 160.
78. Hinnebusch: 81.
79. The regime of Hafiz al-Assad was generally regarded as less doctrinaire than its predecessor on domestic socialism, popular armed struggle, and relations with the capitalist power of the west. Hudson, *Arab Politics*. Yale University Press, 1977: 252; A. Drysdale,'The Assad regime and its Troubles', *MERIP*, November/December 1982.
80. Drysdale.

and friends (many of whom are Sunni-Muslims) rather indicates a regime based on nepotism.

Who will succeed Assad? This is quite an interesting question...

Nationalism and Geo-Political Circumstances — The Kurdish Problem As An Example

Sami Abdul Rahman

Kurdish Nationalism and Geo-Political Circumstances

Since the end of the First World War, the history of the Kurdish people can in a sense be considered a struggle which has more often than not taken the form of direct clashes between the forces of the Kurdish National Movement (KNM) and the geo-political circumstances of the Middle East. This was particularly so in the case of Kurdistan which saw itself divided between four states; Turkey, Iran, Iraq and Syria, despite the promise stipulated in Article 64 of the Severes Treaty to create a Kurdish state on at least some part of Kurdistan within the former Ottoman Empire. The first curse of division had befallen Kurdistan in 1514 as a result of the Chalderan battle between the Persian and Ottoman Empires in which the latter annexed more than two-thirds of Kurdistan.

The history of the Kurds has been characterized by open revolts since the First World War in Turkey, Iraq and Iran. Sheik Sa'id, Sayed Reza in Dersem, (Turkey) Sheik Mahmoud Hafeed and Barzani (in Iraq) and the Mahabad Autonomous Republic led by Qazi Mohammed (in Iran). The ongoing movement which started in 1961 under the leadership of General Barzani led to the 1979 uprising in Iranian Kurdistan and the movement which began in Turkey in the latter part of the seventies. These are the most well known cases in question.

The (KNM) in its uprisings as well as in its peaceful endeavours has been striving to attain cultural, administrative and economic rights for the Kurdish people. Sometimes this takes the simple form of trying to end open discirimination and recognition of identity. In other cases it has aimed at autonomy, federalism or independence. The geo-political elements have been the real and permanent forces which have persistently obstructed any progress by the Kurdish National Movement.

Any achievement in any part of Kurdistan regarding Kurdish rights and aspirations not only raises the objections of the state directly concerned; but also provokes apprehension and fear of the other three states dividing Kurdistan among themselves, albeit to differing degrees.

The fact that Kurdistan is land-locked shows how effective the collaboration is between these four states in suppressing the KNM in any part of Kurdistan. This makes it extremely difficult and sometimes impossible for any material (even humanitarian aid) to reach the Kurdish people. Indeed any government who would consider extending help to the Kurdish people in its endeavour to promote its cause will have to take into account the reaction of the four states concerned; be that aid material, political or even purely humanitarian. It should be added that each of these four states has given limited support to Kurdish movements in one or more of the neighbouring states at different times according to rivalries, or in retaliation; never, however, for the purpose of promoting or assisting the Kurdish cause or rights, per se. On the contrary, this limited support has been withdrawn at times when the tactical reasons for it waned, creating a great deal of dismay, harm and suffering. Iraqi Kurdistan possibly represents the most striking case of contradictions between nationalism and geo-political environment; both for reasons of its history and its present unique situation, as well as for the important reason pertaining to what the future holds for it. Is Iraqi Kurdistan going to be back at square one again? (although realistically speaking, nothing ever goes back to square one exactly). Or is it going to be crowned as a sort of a Kurdish entity? It is noteworthy that modern technology, despite having put all sorts of armaments, including those of mass destruction at the disposal of the Iraqi regime and other regional powers, has at the same time reduced the effects of being landlocked, thanks to the new means of communications and information, such as satellite, telephone, fax and TV.

Iraqi Kurdistan has always been a Special Case

Iraqi Kurdistan was clearly covered by Article 64 of the Severes Treaty although it was never realized. A tripartite struggle over the present Valayet of Mosul was waged between the Kurdish leader Sheik Mahmoud who declared the independence of Kurdistan with himself as king in 1919, and the British colonial authorities who put him down quickly and planned annexation of the Vilayet of Mosul to Iraq under their mandate because of the oil in Kirkuk. Turkey, based its claim to the Vilayet on the assumption that it was not conquered militarily.

After sending a mission to Kurdistan to verify the will of the local population, the League of Nations decided that Kurdistan be annexed to Iraq under British mandate on conditions that the will of the Kurdish people be respected in making Kurdish the language of teaching and in courts, and that the local administration be run by Kurdish officials. This was respected to a certain extent by the mandatory power and ever since no Iraqi cabinet has been formed without including Kurdish ministers. As a precondition for Iraq to join the League of Nations, it passed the law of local languages in 1931, which laid the legal foundation for primary schooling in the Kurdish language.

In 1937 the Saad Abad Treaty was signed by Iraq, Iran and Turkey with the support of Great Britain. While this treaty stipulated cooperation in the face of the Soviet Union and the rise of Nazi Germany, it also called for coordination against Kurdish aspirations and revolts. It is not a coincidence that the Dersim uprising in Turkish Kurdistan took place that same year and was crushed with devastating cruelty.

Despite this treaty, the great events of the Second World War stirred the Kurds into struggling for their rights. The 1943 Barzani revolt was appeased by the central government through the granting of certain cultural and administrative rights. This was done on the advice of the British government which was in the midst of a bloody war. But in 1943, when the end of the Second World War was in sight, the British Royal Air Force played a decisive role in crushing the Barzani revolt. Barzani had led his tribe and many other Kurdish patriots into Iranian Kurdistan to form the best fighting force of the Autonomous Mahabad Republic. While the Kurds of Iraq and Iran formed an alliance to reap some benefit from their struggle during the turbulent years of the Second World War, Baghdad and Teheran were able to collaborate directly and through the good offices of colonial Britain - which was still the main international power in both states. It should be added that the political organization Khoiboon (independence) was working under the direction of the Kurdish princes of Badir Khans (Jaladat and Kameran) in Beirut, especially in the field of Kurdish political thought and culture.

Only one year after the Kurdish Revolution of 1961 the whole of the countryside of Iraqi Kurdistan was liberated from the forces of the central Iraqi government by the Peshmerga (Kurdish freedom fighters) under the leadership of KDP headed by Mostafa Barzani. I am of the belief that if Iraqi Kurdistan had an outlet to the sea, either directly or through a sympathetic neighbouring country it would not have taken long for Iraqi Kurdistan to become independent.

The signing of the March 1970 Agreement with the Iraqi government was the best document pertaining to Kurdish rights since Severes gained from any government. It promised a wide range of cultural, economic and administrative rights culminating in autonomy for the Kurdish areas (Kurdistan). The other three governments did not hide their displeasure and concern regarding this development. Every one of them fearing repercussions among their own Kurds; None of them, however, was prepared to grant any similar concessions.

In 1974 the Iraqi government regressed on its pledges towards the Kurdish people, the KDP and its president General Mostafa Barzani. Fighting broke out between the two sides amid unprecedented popular support and substantial financial aid from Iran and the United States for the KDP. That aid was tactical since as soon as Saddam Hussein promised to leave the Soviet sphere of influence and approach the American sphere of influence, the Algiers Agreement was signed on March 6th, 1975 by which all foreign aid to the Kurds was abruptly cut. It is significant here to note that the Shah, in a press interview commenting on the sad fate of the Kurdish uprising in Iraq, gleefully said, 'I am fully aware that there are more Kurds in Iran than there are in Iraq.' It is worth noting that Turkey, in the name of the highest echelons of government, heaped praise on the Algiers Agreement and expressed great pleasure for the 'end' of the Kurdish revolution which they considered a potential threat to all.

Syria was an exception this time, There, the Baath regime feared the rival Baath regime in Iraq, whose oil revenues had quadrupled in a couple of years and could become a serious threat if able to put aside the Kurdish problem, even temporarily. However, Syrian reaction was slow and discreet. So while the Kurdish leadership was able to out-manoeuvre the geo-political forces in 1970 thanks to the foresight of Barzani who exploited the acrimony between the Shah and the Baath, in 1975 that leadership was out manoevred not because of faith in the Shah, but because there was trust in the promises made by the American government. In August 1988, following the chemical warfare attacks by the Iraqi regime on Halabcha and Anfal which were linked to the presence of Iranian forces in Iraqi Kurdistan, Iraq and Iran agreed to the UN Security Council resolution 598 to stop their war. Iran did this without consulting the Kurdish leadership and despite many promises that such a decision would not be taken unilaterally and without prior consultations and coordination. This was one of the greatest tragedies to befall the Kurdish people. We had to face one of the biggest and most experienced war machines in modern times, (the Iraqi military) alone, and in a land completely depopulated through the forcible deportation of its people. Tens of thousands of fleeing Kurdish refugees entered Iran and several thousand found their way into Turkey and were given refuge for the first time in modern history; this was in some way due to the attitude taken by Prime Minister Özal.

At the end of the Iran/Iraq war, there was a concerted effort by the rulers of Iraq to turn their attention to Iran's allies; Syria and the Kurds. Syria welcomed the Iraqi opposition as well as the Kurdish opposition and tried to foster unity among their ranks. The Iraqi regime, however, continued to threaten and harass Syria.

Although the Kurdish movement was not destroyed by the events of 1988, it would nevertheless, in my view, have taken many years before the Kurdish National Movement regained its prominence had Saddam Hussein not invaded Kuwait. The country was depleted of its population (4500 villages out of 5000) and devastated.

The Second Gulf War and its Aftermath

Following the invasion of Kuwait, the preparations for the war to eject Saddam Hussein's forces from Kuwait and the subsequent American-led war with about 30 other countries participating directly or indirectly, highlighted the cruelty and despotism of the Iraqi regime. No one was better placed to bear witness to this than the Kurds. The writer himself was interviewed about a hundred times by the international media on TV, radio and journals during that period. The Kurdish uprising at the end of the war and its brutal crushing by the regime led to one of the largest exoduses in modern times (about 2 million people). Travelling to Turkey and Iran under the eye of TV cameras brought tremendous international support for the Kurds. This resulted in the safe haven north of the 36th parallel which eventually led to the liberation of the governates of Duhuk, Arbil and Sulaimani as well as parts of Kirkuk province under the protection of the Western allies (USA, UK and France), as well as in Turkey where the allied air force of the Poised Hammer force is based.

The liberated area was administrated loosely by the Kurdistan Front (an umbrella organization of the Iraqi Kurdistan parties established in 1988) and supported by a great deal of humanitarian aid from UN agencies, governments and NGOs, besides a great amount of good will and sympathy for the Kurds from all over the world.

In May 1992 elections for a Kurdish Parliament took place which were considered free and fair. A cabinet was chosen by the elected parliament which alerted not only Baghdad but Tehran, Ankara and Damascus as well.

In June the first congress of the INC (Iraqi National Congress) which was supported by the governments of the USA and Britain was held in Vienna, with Kurdish parties playing a major role. The congress accepted the right of the Kurdish people to be recognized on the basis of self determination within Iraqi unity.

Later that summer a delegation of the INC sent to the USA was met by government leaders including the then Secretary of State, James Baker. The issue of Kurdish rights was raised with him and with others before him:

Mr. Baker: 'The Vienna formula is good and acceptable.'
Mr. Barzani: 'But it is vague.'
Mr. Baker: 'Anything within Iraqi unity is acceptable'.
Mr. Barzani: 'What about federation?'

After some discussion it was shown that there was no objection to federation especially considering that the USA itself is federal. Indeed the 'Voice of America' ran a commentary expressing the American Government's point of view praising federalism as a solution for Iraq.

In early October the Parliament of Kurdistan passed a resolution unanimously calling for a federal relationship between Kurdistan and the central government. This rang alarm bells in the three neighbouring capitals and of course in Baghdad.

The second congress of the INC, indeed the biggest gathering ever of Iraqi political organizations took place in Salahaddin on October 1992, where a federalist system was finally agreed upon despite opposition by some of the Islamic parties.

Before the end of that year the foreign ministers of Turkey, Iran and Syria met to discuss the issue of Iraqi Kurdistan. A Kurdish entity with an elected regional parliament and government and a declared intention of federation accepted by INC and sympathized with internationally.

At that meeting, the three foreign ministers could not declare their opposition to a demand for a federal democracy in these specific circumstances. But they expressed their definite opposition to the division of Iraq, something nobody had called for. It was clear that they were expressing their fear and opposition to developments in Iraqi Kurdistan. The foreign ministers also decided to create a mechanism for this purpose by meeting every three months.

It is worth noting that the former Turkish President Turgut Özal was tampering timidly and clandestinely with the idea of a federative relation between Turkey and Iraqi Kurdistan with a view to the Kirkuk oil.

The mechanism agreed by the foreign ministers continued and it is still very much alive: they could not meet every three months due to difficulties between Turkey and Syria; they disagree on almost every issue other than the developments in Iraqi Kurdistan. The differences and rivalry between Turkey and Iran are also on the increase.

However, every communiqué from these foregin minister meetings speaks of their opposition to the division of Iraq and interference in Iraqi internal affairs, whereas actually they interfere in these internal affairs on an almost daily basis.

Between the end of 1992 and the end of 1993 when there was internal unity or at least there was no open schism, the Kurds looked forward to new development and new horizons. Many people thought if we continue working democratically and peacefully, if we hold the next elections for parliament in time and democratically, if we continue consolidating the regional administration step by step, the internal situation would stabilize and international support would increase for a Kurdish democratic entity in the midst of this jungle of dictatorships. It is worth noting that Kurdish democracy scored very highly according to a British institute which classified democratic systems all over the world — higher even than Israel.

Torture suddenly disappeared, there were no political prisoners, no censorship; Baath daily papers and other publications were freely available in Kurdistan. Kurdish culture began to flourish with arts and literature becoming more colourful. Minorities and women were gaining more care and attention and the promotion of their rights. For the first time, people were enthusiastically making decisions about their own future.

If developments had proceeded along these lines, would world opinion and indeed Western democratic governments ever have allowed an Iraqi dictatorship or forces of any neighbouring state to intervene and crush this Kurdish democratic entity?

The end of 1993 witnessed sadly the beginning of internal conflicts within Iraqi Kurdistan. A bitter armed conflict began between the Patriotic Union of Kurdistan (PUK) and the Islamic Movement of Kurdistan (IMK). Although tension had been rising between the two sides for sometime, it was undoubtedly the PUK which started the open conflict with a major attack on November 22nd, 1993. The fighting did not last long; but it certainly left a scar on the image of Kurdistan and on the fledgling Kurdish democracy.

The most serious and devastating armed conflict began on May 1st, 1994 between the two major parties of Iraqi Kurdistan, i.e., the KDP and the PUK, who together control the parliament, government and public life of the country. Again it was the PUK who started the armed attacks with the clear intention of changing the political balance using sheer military force, whereas the KDP had called for new general elections to settle the outstanding differences. If the IMK was no match for the PUK here you had a conflict between two parties who were comparable in resources and forces. This makes it difficult to foresee either one of them crushing the other. However, external geo-political forces do not wish to see either of them gaining complete control over the country.

This armed conflict has been going on intermittently ever since; bouts of fighting followed by truces, the latest being arranged thanks to an American initiative.

This internal conflict has inflicted deep wounds on Kurdistan and has left ugly scars on our image. It has impoverished our people and devastated its morale, weakening the forces which are supposed to be the vanguard in the movement towards realizing Kurdish rights and security and has also disheartened our friends and sympathizers in the international arena.

While Kurdistan has been preoccupied with fighting, the geo-political forces have not been sitting by idly, nor are they just watching and rubbing their hands gleefully.

The Turkish army has made more than one incursion into Iraqi Kurdistan, the largest was in March 1995. The PKK gives them the necessary pretext since it attempts to make its presence in Iraqi Kurdistan as conspicuous as possible.

Iran shifts its alliance from one side to the other according to how best it serves its purpose of increasing its influence in Kurdistan. Syria, which has less direct leverage in Kurdistan, is interfering by proxy through the PKK. The PKK unleashed a major attack on KDP positions on August 25th, 1995 with the declared aim of destroying the Drogheda (Ireland) Agreement. This agreement in principle was arranged between the KDP and the PUK via American mediation on August 11th, 1995. These actions lured the Turkish army into Iraqi Kurdistan. It is noteworthy that both Syria and Iran had shown their opposition to the Drogheda Agreement.

Prior to the PKK attack, hundreds of its militants passed secretly from Syria into Iraqi Kurdistan. The Iraqi regime, which had declared an internal blockade against Kurdistan since October 1991, added to the misery caused to our people by the UN sanctions, by sending car bombs and other explosives to be detonated in the squares and main streets of Kurdish towns. Saddam Hussein was now gleefully inviting the warring sides to go back to him saying that he alone had the solution.

It is very obvious that the internal conflict has weakened the forces whose foremost duty is to lead the people and the country towards its noble goal of national and democratic rights and overcome the hurdles on the way. It should be taken into consideration that when UN sanctions are lifted or loosened against the Iraqi regime, its potential to destabilize Iraqi Kurdistan will be far greater than it is now.

I believe that the only way out of this ever deepening dark hole is to seriously accept the American peace initiative and make comprehensive peace in Kurdistan and resume the political process and cooperation in place of fighting.

I know for certain that the KDP leadership has embraced the American peace initiative sincerely. Had the other side done the same, then there would have been light at the end of the tunnel.

Then, depending on our hard working and freedom loving people as well as appealing to what remains of the goodwill and sympathy of the international community and public opinion towards Kurdistan, one of the most outstanding symbols of suffering, we may resume the march towards the attainment and consolidation of our people's rights.

If this were the case, the geo-political forces would have far less leverage. While writing this article one can see that various possibilities exist and the dangers are immense: A great deal, however, depends on internal peace and unity of the Kurdish forces.

The Politics of Genocide: From Iraqi Counter-Insurgency to Ethnic Cleansing of Kurdish Areas

Khaled Salih and Kirsten E. Schulze

In 1988, during the last year of the Iran-Iraq war, the Iraqi President Saddam Hussein diverted a large number of his troops to mount a military offensive against the population of Iraqi Kurdistan. This operation has been conventionally regarded as the culmination of the struggle between the security forces of the Iraqi state and the Kurdish *pesh merga* fighting for autonomy. It was part of Saddam Hussein's broader counter-insurgency strategy against elements siding with the enemy: Iran. And while the questionable loyalty of the Kurds and the implicit threat to the integrity of the Iraqi state will not be disputed, this article suggests that counter-insurgency was merely a cover for a meticulously planned and smoothly executed policy of genocide. Indeed, the campaign, code-named *Anfal*, bears many of the genocidal characteristics found in the Holocaust, Cambodia, Bosnia and Rwanda. It was aimed at systematically eradicating the distinct and separate national identity of the Kurds.

The claim of counter-insurgency put forward by the Iraqi government for obvious reasons was supported by some journalists and academics such as Milton Viorst and Edward Said. Viorst in his article 'Iraq and the Kurds: Where Is the Proof of Poison Gas?' suggests that it was unjust to punish the Iraqi government 'for a particular crime that, according to some authorities, may never have taken place.'[1] He claims that Iraq sent its army:

to crush a rebellion of the Kurds who fought at Iran's side ... to stamp out the insurgency... hundreds of Kurdish mountain villages that the Iraqi army destroyed (were) to deny the rebels sanctuary ... If lethal gas was used, it was not used genocidally — that is, for mass killing... If there had been large-scale killing, it is likely they would know and tell the world. But neither I nor any Westerner I encountered heard such allegations.

1. Milton Viorst, Iraq and the Kurds: 'Where is the Proof of Poison gas?' *International Herald Tribune*, October 7th, 1988.

The well-known advocate of Palestinian refugee rights, Edward Said, during the Gulf War of 1991 agrees:

The claim that Iraq gassed its own citizens has often been repeated. At best, this is uncertain. There is at least one War College report, done while Iraq was a US ally which claims that the gassing of the Kurds in Halabja was done by Iran. Few people mention such reports in the media today.[2]

Said's response is interesting, given his image of the critical intellectual who does not allow himself 'the luxury of playing the identity game,' but rather presses compassionately for 'the interests of the unheard, the unrepresented, the unconnected people of our world.'[3] But it is more politically motivated than based on facts which, as this article demonstrates, were that Saddam Hussein was not pursuing a policy of counter-insurgency but one of genocide.

Genocide as a Means of Dealing with Ethnic Conflict

The conflict between the Sunni Muslim Arab Iraqi central government in Baghdad and the Kurdish population in the northern provinces can be described as an ethnic conflict. The Kurds are a distinct ethnic group with their own language, traditions and customs tied to a specific geographical area. Conflict between two ethnic groups can be regulated in various ways, ranging from management to termination. In broad terms, conflict regulation can be divided into two categories: methods for eliminating differences and methods for managing differences.[4] Methods for eliminating differences include integration or assimilation, partition or secession, forced mass-population transfers, and genocide. Methods for managing differences include hegemonic control, arbitration, cantonization or federalization, and consociationalism and power-sharing.[5]

---

2. *London Review of Books*, March 7th, 1991: 7.
3. In 1988 Edward Said wrote the following lines: 'In education, politics, history and culture there is at the present time a role to be played by secular oppositional intellectuals, call them a class of informed and effective wet blankets, who do not allow themselves the luxury of playing the identity game... but who more compassionately press the interests of the unheard, the unrepresented, the unconnected people of our world, and who do so not in the 'jargon of the authenticity' but with the accents of personal restraint, historical scepticism and committed intellect.' 'Identity, negation and violence', in *New Left Review* 1988, (171): 60.
4. Brendan O'Leary and John McGarry: *The Politics of Ethnic Conflict Regulation*. London: Routledge, 1993: 4.
5. Ibid.

The Iraqi regime under Saddam Hussein opted for methods of eliminating differences in accordance with the Baath ideology which stresses Arab unity and an overall pan-Arab identity as opposed to separate nationalism. A careful analysis of Iraqi policy towards the Kurdish minority over the past 30 years shows that government policy moved from assimilation to forced mass-population transfers to genocide. Conflict regulation on the Iraqi side did shift but only within the framework of methods of eliminating differences.

Forced assimilation, mass-population transfers and genocide, as in the case of the Kurds, often go hand in hand. Genocide is defined as the systematic mass-killing of an ethnic collectivity or the destruction of an ethnic community. Genocides are one-sided and they are intended to terminate ethnic conflict.[6] The Kurdish genocide of 1987-89 followed the key concepts: Definition — Concentration (or seizure) — Annihilation.[7]

Background to Anfal: Kurdish-Ba'thi Relations

The Kurdish quest for autonomy or even independence has not been an issue solely under the Baath regime in Iraq. In 1920, the Treaty of Sèvres, redrawing boundaries after the First World War, specifically provided for the establishment of local autonomy for the Kurds. However, that clause of the treaty was never ratified and was dropped from the Treaty of Lausanne. Thus, the area of Iraqi Kurdistan was forcibly incorporated into Iraq.

The area for this autonomy has no defined borders. It generally referred to the Kurdish territories. Today, these are located in parts of Iraq, Iran, Syria and Turkey. Not having received any territory or autonomy, a Kurdish rebellion broke out against the British mandate government. Baghdad and Britain's interest was in retaining the oil fields. Thus, when the issue of Kurdish statehood arose as demanded by Kurdish rebels, Britain convinced the League Nations to vote against it.[8] The rebellion was put down and when Iraq later attained independence, it took over the area administered by the British, including the Kurdish north.

Whereas the Kurds never had full control over their territory, they still retained a separate national, cultural and ethnic identity despite the efforts of Iraqi rulers to suppress that identity or forcibly assimilate them. With the take-over of the Baath, though, the Kurds had to fight more than just cultural assimilation; They had to continuously struggle against pan-Arabism and

---

6. Ibid: 6-7.
7. Raul Hilberg, *The Destruction of the European Jews.* New York: Holmes and Meier, 1985: 267.
8. Kanan Makiya, 'The Anfal.' *Harper's Magazine* May 1992: 54.

'Arabization' as Ba'thism did not include provisions for non-Arab minorities. Rather, it considered ethnic minorities which did not assimilate to be separatist and enemies of the Ba'th's goal of pan-Arabism.[9]

The relationship between the Baath and Kurdish political parties centred around autonomy negotiations for a period of over 24 years. These negotiations, however, were not motivated by the belief in the principle of autonomy or self-determination, but by the pragmatic political necessity of the Baath trying to consolidate its power.[10] Thus the Baath pursued a policy which called for negotiations when the party was weak, only to proceed toward the final goal — the destruction of the Kurds — whenever the party had gained sufficient power to go on the offensive.

The defeat of the Barzani rebellion in 1975 was the beginning of an anti-Kurdish policy under the guise of 'security'. Kurdish insurgents, especially Barzanis, were forcibly relocated to southern Iraq. Following the 1975 Algiers Agreement between the Shah of Iran and Saddam Hussein, Iraqi authorities began a campaign of evacuating the Kurds from the Barzan and Mergasur districts in the governorate of Irbil.[11] Then, a security belt was created along the borders with Iran, Turkey and Syria. Villages designated as prohibited zones were relocated to other regions. These zones were widened over time by the relocation of more and more villages. At the same time, Arabs from the neighbouring province of Nineweh were moved into the Kurdish areas.

While negotiations continued, Kurds were arrested because they were affiliated with a Kurdish political party, because they had been overheard criticizing the government or, in subsequent years, because they were accused of aiding Iran during the Iran-Iraq war. Whereas the Kurdish guerrillas did receive military aid from various sources,[12] including Iran, many Kurds were arrested solely for being Kurds.[13] This seemingly arbitrary action, though, periodically turned into a well-planned offensive. Whenever the negotiations came to a standstill or broke down completely, government forces clashed with the Kurdish guerrillas.

Arabization of the Kurdish areas, a policy in many ways rooted in the 1960s, and the policy of establishing prohibited areas created prior to the major operations of 1987-89 were followed by the destruction of thousands of Kurdish villages, chemical attacks against civilians, and most importantly the creation

9. Sa'ad Jawad, *Iraq and the Kurdish Question 1958-1970*. London: Ithaca Press, 1981.
10. Edmund Ghareeb, *The Kurdish Question in Iraq*. Syracuse: Syracuse University Press, 1981.
11. 'Eight Thousand Civilian Kurds have Disappeared in Iraq — What has Happened to Them.' *Report by a Preparatory Committee*. 1987.
12. The Kurds received military aid from Iran, Israel, the United States and Syria.
13. Makiya: 54.

of a detailed administrative framework for the systematic campaign of *Anfal* from March 1987 to April 1989.[14]

Defining The Target

The process of defining those who would be targeted by *Anfal* began shortly after Ali Hassan al-Majid, one of Saddam Hussein's cousins, was granted 'special powers' as the secretary general of the Northern Bureau of Iraq's ruling Baath Arab Socialist Party, in March 1987. At the first stage, al-Majid decreed that 'saboteurs' would lose their property rights. He suspended the legal rights of all the residents of prohibited villages, followed by the execution of close relatives of 'saboteurs' and of wounded civilians whose hostility to the regime had been determined by the intelligence services.[15]

In June 1987, the process of drawing irreversible boundaries - the red line between 'us' and 'them' - was legalised by issuing two sets of standing orders, which were based on a simple axiom with a result which few, if any, of the Kurds were able to comprehend: in the 'prohibited' rural areas, all Kurdish residents were synonymous with the *pesh merga* insurgents, and would be dealt with accordingly.

Implementing a shoot-to-kill policy, the first of al-Majid's directives was to clear the 'prohibited areas.'[16] The second constituted an unmistakable inducement to mass murder. Army commanders were ordered:

to carry out random bombardments, using artillery, helicopters and aircraft, at all times of the day or night, in order to kill the largest number of persons present in these prohibited zones.[17]

In clause 5, al-Majid ordered that:

All persons captured in those villages shall be detained and interrogated by the security services and those between the ages of 15 to 70 shall be executed after any useful information has been obtained from them, of which we should be duly notified.[18]

While still engaged in this phase of definition, the Iraqi authorities did not hesitate to test their chemical capacity. At least forty documented chemical

---

14. Middle East Watch, *Genocide in Iraq: The Anfal Campaign against the Kurds.* New York: Human Rights Watch, 1993: 12-13.
15. *Genocide in Iraq*: 8.
16. Middle East Watch *Bureaucracy of Repression: The Iraqi Government in Its Own Words.* New York: Human Rights Watch, 1994: 72. Also: Genocide in Iraq: 8-9.
17. Clause 4 as cited in Genocide in Iraq: 9 and Bureaucracy of Repression: 72.
18. Clause 5 as cited in Genocide in Iraq: 9; and Bureaucracy of Repression: 72.

attacks on Kurdish targets over a period of eighteen months were recorded. Iraqi aircraft dropped their first poison gas on villagers in mid-April 1987, killing more than a hundred people, most of them women and children. These attacks were the first signs of the degree to which the regime was prepared to go in killing large numbers of Kurdish civilians indiscriminately.

In order to create a buffer zone between 'us' and 'them', between the government and the *pesh merga*-controlled areas, a three-stage programme of village clearances or 'collectivisation' was embarked upon in mid-April 1987. During this programme's first two phases, between April 21st - May 20th, and May 21st - June 20th, more than 700 villages were burned and bulldozed, most of them along the main highways in government-controlled areas. Due to the war effort on the Iranian frontiers, the third phase was postponed, but accomplished by *Anfal*.

In terms of defining the target group for annihilation, the national census of October 17th, 1987, was the most important single administrative step of the Iraqi regime. Having created a virtual buffer strip between the government and the *pesh merga*-controlled zones by the village clearances, the Baath Party offered the inhabitants of the prohibited areas an ultimatum: to either 'return to the national ranks' — that is, abandon home and livelihood and accept compulsory relocation in a camp under the eye of the security forces; or to lose Iraqi citizenship and be regarded as deserters. This second option was subject to an August 1987 decree of the ruling Revolutionary Command Council, imposing the death penalty on deserters. Not choosing the relocation was, in effect, tantamount to a death sentence.

In the period leading up to the census, al-Majid encircled the target group further. He ordered intelligence officials to prepare detailed, case-by-case dossiers of 'saboteurs' families who were still living in the government-controlled areas. Thus, countless women, children and elderly people were forcibly transferred to the rural areas to share the fate of their *pesh merga* relatives. This technique of sieving the population was also crucial to the question of who should live and who should die during *Anfal*.

Concomitant with this phase of definition were military operations to destroy the habitat of the rural population. These operations started, characteristically, with chemical attacks from the air on both civilian and *pesh merga* targets, accompanied by a military blitz against the Kurdish military bases. After this initial assault, ground troops and *jash*[19] enveloped the target areas from all sides, destroying all human habitation in their path, looting and setting fire to homes, before calling in demolition crews.

---

19. Pro-government Kurdish militias.

As the definition process proceeded, so did the phase of concentrating, or seizure, of the target group. By now, convoys of army trucks stood by to transport the villagers to holding centres and transit camps. To prevent anyone from escaping, the *jash* had to comb the hillsides in the first instance, while the secret police had to search the towns, cities and complexes to hunt fugitives at a later stage. In several cases those who still managed to hide had to be lured out with false offers of amnesty.

The processing of the detainees took place in a network of camps and prisons that followed a standard pattern. Men and women were segregated on the spot. The process was brutal and did not spare the elderly. A little later, the men were further divided by age — small children remained with their mothers, the elderly and weak separated, and men and teenage boys considered to be able to carry a weapon were herded together, without any thorough checking of identity documents.

The women and children suffered grievously in their own ways. After a short time the guards dragged the older women violently away from their daughters and grandchildren and bundled them away to yet another unknown destination. In at least two cases, soldiers and guards burst into the women's quarters during their first night at a camp and removed their small children, even infants. All night long the women could hear the cries and screams of their children in another room. But above all the women and children in one camp endured the torment of seeing their husbands, brothers and fathers suffer; they were beaten routinely in front of their female relatives and, in the end, disappeared.

The first temporary holding centres were in operation, under the control of military intelligence, as early as mid-March 1988, peaking in mid-April and early May. The mass disappearances began shortly thereafter. At this stage, most of the detainees were transferred to a place called Topzawa, a Popular Army camp on the outskirts of Kirkuk. Others were trucked to another Popular Army barracks in Tikrit. Women and children were taken from Topzawa to a separate camp in the town of Dibs. Between 6,000 and 8,000 elderly detainees were taken to an abandoned prison called Nugra Salman in the southern desert, where hundreds of them died as a result of neglect, starvation and disease. During the last stage of *Anfal*, villagers from Badinan were detained in a huge army fort at Dohuk. The women and children were transferred later from Dohuk to a prison camp in Salamiyeh, close to Mosul. Although the majority of the women, children and elderly were released after an official amnesty to mark the end of *Anfal* on September 6th, 1988, none of the *Anfal* men were ever released. Only six people were able to to escape to tell the true story of what happened to tens of thousands of Kurds who were driven away in convoys of sealed vehicles from the camps to southern Iraq.

The process of defining those who were actually to be killed, if they managed to survive indiscriminate chemical attacks, the harsh conditions of the transit camps and occasionally torture, was under way long before the actual killing by the firing squads. Two days before the national census, that is to say October 15th, 1987, army and intelligence agencies were ordered to compile lists of the Kurds from the 'prohibited areas' and 'saboteurs' families. During *Anfal*, the captives were registered by name, sex, age, place of birth and place of residence. Accoringly, men between the ages of 15 and 50 years old from the 'prohibited areas' and families of 'saboteurs,' were sent to death in the south. The execution methods of the Kurdish men by firing squads is 'uncannily reminiscent of another'; that of the *Einsatzkommandos* in Eastern Europe occupied by the Nazis.

Some groups of prisoners were lined up, shot from the front and dragged into pre-dug mass graves; others were shoved roughly into trenches and machine-gunned where they stood; others were made to lie down in pairs, sardine-style, next to mounds of fresh corpses, before being killed; others were tied together, made to stand on the lip of the pit, and shot in the back so that they would fall forward into it - a method that was presumably more efficient from the point of view of the killers. Bulldozers then pushed earth or sand loosely over the heaps of corpses. Some of the gravesites contained dozens of separate pits, and obviously contained the bodies of thousands of victims. Circumstantial evidence suggests that the executioners were uniformed members of the Ba'th Party, or perhaps of Iraq's General Security Directorate (*Amn*).[20]

Motives for *Anfal*

Government action during the 1980s, during the Iran-Iraq war, makes it clear that the *Anfal* operation of 1988 was not an isolated incident aimed at destroying Kurdish guerrilla bases. Instead, *Anfal* has to be seen as part of a process; a long-term policy aimed at destroying the Kurdish people as a political, cultural or ethnic unit. From the beginning of the Iran-Iraq war onwards, Kurdish villages were shelled regularly by the Iraqi army, male Kurds were detained, and poison gas was used against non-combatants, women and children. The motives often cited for this military action are oil and security. However, both fail to explain the extent of the operations.

It has been argued that moving the Kurds from oil rich regions in Kirkuk and moving in Arabs from Nineweh was motivated by Iraq's interest in the oil fields in Kirkuk. Since the beginning of the autonomy negotiations, the

20. Genocide in Iraq: 17.

percentage of the oil revenues payable to the Kurds had been on the agenda. Kurdistan, and more specifically Iraq's pipeline through the area to Turkey, had become more important with the Iran-Iraq war. The oil revenues were needed to finance the war and the only way to transport the oil out of the country was through the Kurdish north. Syria had closed Iraq's pipelines in 1982 and shipping through the Persian Gulf was too much of a risk. Consequently, the Iraqi government had to increase its control-measures against the Kurds in order to safeguard not only the oil fields in the Mosul area, but also the only working pipeline.

The continuing negotiations over the royalties from these fields between the Kurdish leadership and the government, in addition to Kurdish sabotage against the pipeline,[21] make this argument seem quite plausible. The safeguarding of the pipeline had taken on such importance that Turkey committed itself to securing the pipeline and vital oil areas from Kurdish sabotage. According to an agreement signed in 1978 and an additional accord signed in 1984 between Turkey and Iraq, Turkey had the right to pursue Kurdish rebels into Iraqi territory. Some 12,000 to 20,000 Turkish soldiers were assigned this task,[22] Turkey undertook several operations against the Kurds, the first of which was in 1983. There were major attacks on Kurdish guerrilla bases in 1984, followed by further incursions in 1986 and 1987.[23]

However, forcible relocation of the Kurds and the moving in of Arabs onto that very territory, point to an ethnic motive. If the reason had been to vacate the land for oil drilling, there would have been no reason for moving in another set of residents. Furthermore, pumping up oil does not require removing people from the surface above in the first place. Moreover, it was not only villages in the oil regions that were relocated. Villages throughout all of Kurdistan were destroyed, with residents detained or deported. In many cases shelling and bombing of the villages preceded the relocation. Such action close to oil fields would have endangered them. This is not to say that oil did not play any role at all. But within the wider framework of anti-Kurdish policies, the relocation and 'Arabization' served a larger goal — the elimination of the political threat of Kurdish nationalism by destroying the cultural centres, the rural economy, and eventually a large section of the Kurdish people themselves.

21. Shahram Chubin and Charles Tripp, *Iran and Iraq at War*. Boulder: Westview Press, 1988: 106.
22. Anthony Cordesman and Abraham Wagner, *The Lessons of Modern War: The Iran-Iraq War*, Boulder: Westview Press, 1990: 207-8.
23. Chubin and Tripp, *Iran and Iraq at War*: 142.

From a security point of view, Iraq's military operations against Kurdish guerrillas have often been classified as counter-insurgency operations. The continued actions against the Kurds, it has been argued, were the central government's response to the existence of Kurdish guerrillas which were a threat to Iraq. Indeed, much of the activity carried out by the security apparatus, especially military intelligence, supports that conclusion. Internal security set up an extensive system of 'collaborators'. Under threats and sometimes torture, Kurds were recruited to work for the central government. A pro-government Kurdish National Defence, the *jash*, was set up under the control of the Iraqi Ministry of Defence. It fought on the side of the Iraqi army during the Iran-Iraq war. During *Anfal*, however, the *jash* reported directly to Iraqi military intelligence. Its major duty was to locate villagers who had escaped the Iraqi army round-ups.

Furthermore, the relocation of villages and deportation of Kurds has been justified by the fact that some Kurds fought on the side of Iran during the war. Thus, Kurdish areas close to the border served as points of infiltration for the Iranian army. The Kurdish guerrillas were seen as undermining Iraq's position during the war. They were classified as traitors and consequently subject to the highest form of punishment.

However, there are many factors which question that the central government's military campaigns were purely a measure of counter-insurgency. For one, the actual military threat emanating from the guerrillas, even in cooperation with the Iranian forces, is debatable. It has been claimed that the Kurdish and Iranian attacks were only of limited strategic value.[24] Kurdish attacks were not well coordinated, had little practical effect and did not force Iraq to divert significant amounts of manpower to the region in 1986-87.[25] Yet, during the following year the most extensive anti-Kurdish operation, *Anfal*, was launched.

But even accepting the argument that there was a military threat, existing or perceived, it remains a fact that many military operations during *Anfal* were not directed against the Kurdish guerrillas. The guerrilla territory was traditionally mountainous terrain even though the *pesh merga* had also moved into the plains. The Iraqi army, though, attacked villages and, more importantly, arrested civilians.

Also, during *Anfal*, no distinction was made between villages generally in opposition to the government, neutral villages and villages which had

24. Cordesman and Wagner: The Lessons of Modern War: 224-25.
25. Ibid.

cooperated with the Iraqi army for the past ten years.[26] Neither was there any distinction made between combatants and non-combatants. Large parts of Iraqi Kurdistan were systematically attacked, villages were burned, dynamited or bulldozed; their inhabitants, without regard for age or gender, were deported and detained. The nature of the *Anfal* operation suggests that it had little to do with counter-insurgency.

Operation *Anfal*[27]

The Iraqi army launched a military operation named *Anfal* [28] against the population of Iraqi Kurdistan from April to September 1988. The official aim of the operation was the 'cleansing of northern Iraq from saboteurs.'[29] However, saboteurs, as defined by written orders to division level officers, were all males between 15 and 60 years of age.[30] Further, villages in the designated 'prohibited areas' were to be completely destroyed and anyone resisting deportation was to be killed.

It consisted of a series of military offensives, eight in all, conducted in six distinct Kurdish geographic areas between late February and early September 1988.[31] It is important to note that in reality *Anfal* corresponded to something more than military offensives against the Kurdish villages and Kurdish resistance. *Anfal* meant co-ordination of many measures starting with destruction of thousands of villages; gathering rural populations after multiple chemical attacks; transporting them to the camps; processing the captives through isolating them and determining who should be sent to death; transporting different groups to different destinies — women and children to particular camps, elderly people to southern Iraq and the men aged between 15 and 50 to gravesites — under extreme secrecy; using firing squads to kill large groups of men near pre-dug mass graves and then covering the mass

26. Some of the *Anfal* victims interviewed claimed that no exceptions were made. Others, however, testified that having influential *jash* in the village saved it from destruction. But even villages not destroyed by the Iraqi army were subjected to round-ups as a consequence of which many men disappeared.
27. This description of the Anfal campaign is based on 159 Middle East Watch interviews with Kurdish civilian victims, Kurdish guerrillas, Iraqi military intelligence officers and members of the *jash*.
28. *Anfal* means spoils, as in the spoils of battle. The eighth sura of the Quran is titled al-Anfal and describes the victory of the Muslims over the unbelievers, whose possessions naturally became theirs.
29. *Analysis of the Operation End of Anfal.* Command Fifth Corps of the Iraqi Army, a document classified strictly confidential.
30. MEW interview with Iraqi military intelligence officer.
31. Middle East Watch, Genocide in Iraq: 14.

graves as well as denying any knowledge of their fates.[32] Despite its secrecy, Iraqi authorities did nothing to hide the *Anfal* campaign from public view. 'On the contrary, as each phase of the operation triumphed, its successes were trumpeted with the same propaganda fanfare that attended the victorious battles in the Iran-Iraq War.'[33]

All phases had a similar order of operation. The ground operations were preceded by the shelling and bombing of the target villages by the Iraqi air force. Often the planes, especially the ones immediately preceding the ground forces, released poison gas over the villages. Then army units surrounded the village and troops moved in to round-up the villagers. Sometimes the villagers were promised resettlement in modern complexes if they did not resist. In general, resistance was low or non-existent.[34]

The importance of this operation can be seen from the amount of troops used for its execution. 'Operation End of *Anfal*' was launched after the ceasefire with Iran. Twenty-five infantry brigades, 4 tank battalions, 4 mechanized infantry units, 102 National Defence battalions, 6 artillery brigades, 14 armoured battalions and 7 armoured units in addition to headquarter forces, the engineers corps, chemical weapons units, special commando units, the air force, intelligence, radar and watercraft units were involved.[35]

Seven divisions were used simultaneously to 'cleanse' areas of 'saboteurs'. Each division was split into convoys consisting of a commander of a brigade, one infantry brigade, two to five National Defence battalions, one unit of armoured forces, and supporting units. The duty of such a convoy, as outlined in a strictly confidential document from the Command of the Fifth Corps, was to attack an average of three designated villages per mission and round up or destroy 'saboteurs.' Often special forces were sent in parallel to different areas to round up the saboteurs and 'cleanse' a whole district at once. The so-called saboteurs were mostly civilian residents of the targeted towns and villages as a list in the same document of 'evicted saboteurs' proves. The list counted 3,268 women and 6,964 children. The only mark to be found under the section of 'losses of saboteurs' read: 'too many blood stains were seen in all places cleaned by the forces.'[36]

After the deportation of the villagers, the engineering corps moved in for the 'destruction and removal of the remnants of the saboteurs and their premises in the area covered by the operation.' What the engineering corps

32. Ibid: 4-54.
33. Ibid: 11.
34. Ibid: 11.
35. *Analysis of the Operation End of Anfal.*
36. Ibid.

in fact was removing were the remnants of Kurdish cultural life and the basis of the rural economy and infrastructure. The selection process of the prisoners, followed by deportations and summary executions further guaranteed the destruction of the family units as the basis of Kurdish national identity.

The military operation of *Anfal* ended with the imprisonment of a large segment of the Kurdish population and the killing of an estimated 180,000 according to Kurdish leaders.[37] Many more died during their imprisonment or immediately after their release in September 1988 following an amnesty. The released Kurdish women, children and elderly were trucked away from the prison and dumped near Irbil and left to fend for themselves. They were forbidden to return to their villages in order to rebuild them. Some were housed in new complexes along the road, others tried to find relatives to live with. Most of the former Kurdish areas were declared closed military zones. The only unrestricted place was paved roads along which the Kurds could resettle.

According to the International Red Cross, an estimated 60,000 simple housing units were destroyed.[38] Lists of villages declared 'prohibited' and thus marked for destruction numbered 1,062 villages which were destroyed since 1986.[39] Others claim that as many as 3,000 villages were destroyed.[40] The exact number is not known at this point.

The official aim of Operation *Anfal* was the eradication of the Kurdish guerrillas, the *pesh merga*, who were considered a threat to the central government in Baghdad. However, most of the people killed were civilians, the areas destroyed were not para-military camps but villages and farms. Indeed, Operation *Anfal* shows careful planning and execution of all orders. It was not a campaign which exacted a high civilian toll during the process of neutralizing the resistance. Rather, it was aimed at the civilians because the threat perceived by Saddam Hussein was not a 'military threat' but a 'political threat' inherent in the distinct and separate Kurdish nationalism. Operation *Anfal* was aimed at cutting this threat off at the root by eliminating the Kurdish people.

Unlike the use of chemical weapons, the *Anfal* campaign was never denied by the Iraqi regime. In a reply to a petition by a former Kurdish POW, the Chief of the Bureau of the Presidency informed the man that his 'wife and

---

37. Makiya, *The Anfal*: 53.
38. The International Red Cross estimated that some 60,000 were rebuilt in Kurdistan after *Anfal*. This was established during an MEW interview with one of the former IRC directors in April 1992.
39. Makiya, *The Anfal*: 57.
40. David Hirst, 'The War that never ends.' *The Guardian*, September 14th, 1988.

children were lost during the *Anfal* Operations that took place in the Northern Region in 1988.'

Over 4,000 Kurdish villages were destroyed, more than 100,000 rural Kurds had died in *Anfal* alone, and half of Iraq's productive farmland is believed to have been laid waste. The destruction campaigns of April 1987 - April 1989 which amount to genocide, had the *Anfal* campaign as its centrepiece. Thus the *Anfal* campaign should by no means be regarded as a function or by-product of the Iraq-Iran war. Rather, it was a rational, pre-planned enterprise in which modern techniques of management and expertise were effectively co-ordinated. Indeed, the Iran-Iraq war only provided Baghdad with a cover for its long-standing efforts to bring the Kurds to heel.

The Timing of the Operation

The date of the operation further suggests that this was not a purely military campaign aimed at a legitimate military target, defined in its broader sense as any combatant. When Operation *Anfal* was launched in April 1988 Iran and Iraq had already indicated their willingness to submit to international pressure to negotiate a ceasefire. The operation was launched to destroy the resistance in the north - not because some *pesh merga* were fighting on the Iranian side - but because the Kurdish resistance movement had started to call for an independent Kurdish state. The Kurdish parties and their respective *pesh merga* had come to an agreement after years of internal disputes. The central government no longer had the power to control Kurdish nationalism through divide and rule strategies. This unification marked the end of the illusion that some Kurdish parties had entertained the notion that they could negotiate with the central government. Thus, Operation *Anfal*, was a military reaction to a political phenomenon.

With the negotiations being conducted with Iran and the superpowers and with Arab world support behind him, Saddam Hussein exploited the situation for his own political gains. By the time the ceasefire had been negotiated, three phases of the operation had already taken place. All he needed to do was to deploy troops freed in the border zone with Kurdistan to execute the last phases.

Genocidal Aspects of *Anfal*

The Kurdish genocide of 1987-89 can be described as a distinct modern phenomenon.[41] Although mass murder is not a recent invention, contemporary

---

41. Zygmunt Bauman, *Modernity and the Holocaust.* Cambridge: Polity Press, 1989: 88.

mass murder within the perimeters of the modern territorial state is. It is 'distinguished by a virtual absence of all spontaneity on the one hand, and the prominence of rational, carefully calculated design on the other. It is marked by an almost complete elimination of contingency and chance, and independence from group emotions and personal motives.'[42] Modern genocide is thus a genocide with a purpose. It has initiators and managers with a particular view of the society. The purpose of modern genocide is 'a grand vision of a better, and radically different, society.'[43] Here a 'gardener's vision', projected upon a society is involved. As in the case of the gardeners, the designers of the perfect society hate the weeds that spoil their design. The weeds surrounding the desired society must be exterminated, it is a problem that has to be solved; the 'weeds must die, not so much because of what they are, as for the sake of the idea of what the beautiful, orderly garden ought to be.'[44]

The Baath rulers in Iraq have always desired to create a harmonious, conflict-free society - orderly, controlled and docile in their hands. The Kurds have constituted the main challenge to this pan-Arab vision. They have been viewed as the weeds disturbing the Baath garden. But the Baathis have been patient in materializing their vision. They have advanced their position by consolidating their power step by step, over more than twenty years. They have never given up their dream. 'When the modernist dream is embraced by an absolute power able to monopolise the modern vehicle of rational action, and when that power attains freedom from effective social control, genocide follows.'[45] And that is exactly what happened in the case of Iraq under the Baath Party. Five factors are important in producing a modern genocide.[46] In the case of Kurdish genocide of 1987-89 these were: 1) A radical anti-Kurdish drive; 2) The transformation of that into the policy of a powerful, centralized state; 3) The state being in command of a huge, efficient bureaucratic apparatus; 4) A 'state of emergency'— an extraordinary, wartime condition, which allowed government and bureaucracy to get away with things which

42. Bauman, Modernity and Holocaust: 90.
43. Ibid: 91-92.
44. Ibid: 91-92.
45. Ibid: 93-94.
46. Bauman, *Modernity and Holocaust.* p. 94. See also Sarah Gordon, *Hitler, Germans, and the 'Jewish Question'.* Princeton: Princeton University Press, 1984: 48-49.

could, possibly, pose more serious obstacles in time of peace;[47] and 5) The non-interference, the passive acceptance of those things by the population and the international community at large.[48]

Under these circumstances, the mass killing of the Kurds was presented as a bureaucratic task to be implemented by different state organizations. The violence was turned into a technique of solving this bureaucratic mission. The officials within the Party, the army, numerous intelligence agencies, and civilian administration were presented with a meticulously functional division of labour without any moral responsibility. Having been presented with a definition of the task, the bureaucracy in Iraq carried out the task to its end with a remarkable degree of rationality and efficiency. In the end, only the bureaucracy's ability to refine its methods and efficiency could sufficiently explain why not even a single soul managed to escape from *Anfal*'s firing squads. Once set in motion, refined and honoured and glorified, the machinery of murder developed its own impetus: after accomplishing its task faithfully in Kurdistan, it sought new territories where it could exercise its newly acquired skills.[49] Is it not possible to view the invasion of Kuwait, and the killing of the civilians there as the externalization of the Iraqi bureaucracy's 'domestic style of rule to foreign policy', a modern skill, efficiency and capacity seeking by now territories outside Iraq? A close examination of the language, symbols and circumlocutions used in Iraq's propaganda war to justify the occupation of Kuwait might reveal that the Kuwaitis were presented as yet another kind of weed to be removed from the Baathi vision of a united Arab world under that particular leadership.

Conclusion

The execution of Operation *Anfal*, the military and political activities leading up to it, the definition of the target, the timing and the creation of a

---

47. Recall Edward Said's attempt to create uncertainty about the events and Viorst's justification of repression by describing the Kurds as those 'who fought at Iran's side.'
48. Defence Department cable of April 19, 1988 notes that 'an estimated 1.5 million Kurdish nationals have been resettled in camps' and that 'approximately 700-1000 villages and small residential areas were targeted for resettlement.' The long section that follows is heavily blacked out. Further, US President George Bush's foreign analysts concluded that 'in no way should we associate ourselves with the 60 year Kurdish rebellion in Iraq or oppose Iraq's legitimate attempts to suppress it.' Quoted in James A. Bill and Robert Springborg, *Politics in the Middle East*. New York: Harper Collins College Publishers, 4th Edition: 387-88.
49. See Bauman, *Modernity and Holocaust*.

'bureaucracy of repression' show that *Anfal* was not a counter-insurgency measure, but genocide. Genocide, as defined by the 'Convention on the Prevention and Punishment of the Crime of Genocide' includes the intentional killing of members of a national, ethnic, racial or religious group or deliberately inflicting on the group conditions of life calculated to bring about its physical destruction in whole or in part.[50] The systematic destruction of the majority of the villages and with it the rural economy and infrastructure of Iraqi Kurdistan, the Arabization of the area along with the forcible relocation of many Kurds, followed by mass executions, the disappearance of most males and the imprisonment of the rest of the population under conditions which cost many more lives, fall under this definition of genocide. *Anfal* was designed to systematically eliminate as many Kurds as possible, it was launched after careful, long-term planning and intelligence gathering, and it was conducted with extreme secrecy as to its real aims. The orders for the operation came from the very top to fulfil calculated political goals. And thus, even though the operation had all the characteristics typical of counter-insurgency, it was not aimed at destroying insurgents, but at destroying the Kurdish population of Iraq, civilians and *pesh merga*, which were considered a political threat to the central government in Baghdad.

50. 'Convention on the Prevention and Punishment of the Crime of Genocide', article 2(a) and (c), as published in *Twenty-Four Human Rights Documents*. New York: Center for the Study of Human Rights, Columbia University, 1992.

Turkey

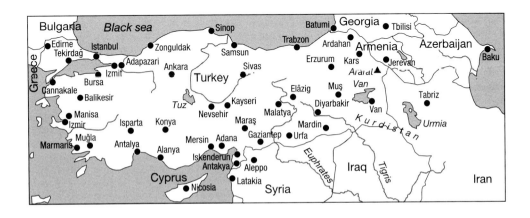

An Historical Account of Identity Formation in Turkey: The Impact of Nomadism

Selahattin Erhan

The Scope

This is a study of the processes of identity formation in Anatolia with particular reference to nomadism and the nomadic past of the main bulk of its population. While I include some discussion of earlier historical epochs so as to show the impact of political context on organization and identity formation among Anatolian people, my main concern is to demonstrate how particular contexts and relationships, socio-political alliances, kinship ideologies, etc. inform identity formation among the contemporary 'Turks'.

In the following pages I will emphasize the dialectical relationship between social composition and political organization. This will reveal the complex — and yet flexible — relationship between the socio-political formation and various identities of the people of modern Turkey, all of which are subject to change and frequently assume different forms under different circumstances.

At present, an indefinite variety of the world's population are often treated as fixed ethnic-units or as naturally evolving entities of this or another ethnic origin or ethnie. As against this 'primordialist' tendency, as it has been called,[1] some recent studies have adopted a more 'instrumental' approach to the analysis of ethnicity. Whereas the former approach held that 'subjective claims to ethnic identity derived from the affective potency of primordial attachments', the more recent view is that such claims result from 'instrumental manipulation of culture in service of collective political and economic interests'.[2] I suggest that in Turkey identity is formed around shifting alliances and situationally specific re-definitions of kinship groups, tribes, etc., not purportedly essentialist categories of ethnicity, which are themselves historical categories. I suggest that the Anatolian sense of identity is heavily shaped by its nomadic heritage, and hence is characterized by highly complex and flexible forms of socio-political organization, which normally supercede such narrow considerations. If one factor which seems to have determined the highly flexible sense of

---

1. See, e.g., Bentley 1987.
2. Ibid: 25.

identity in the Anatolian peninsula is its unique location in the midst of three continents, then the other major factor is physical mobility which allows greater flexibility to nomadic entities in terms of both identify and organization than a stationary life provides to sedentaries. As for the nomads in particular, the idea of genealogical descent is so frequently used by such groups to describe their social organization that many students have been led to accord an undue naturalism to their highly flexible, multi-faceted modes of organization. While denying such naturalism, I also argue that the long-held framework which suggests that Turks are of such and such origin indeed serves the people as a major basis of identity and a major means of maintaining their unity, in the face of the contrary tendency towards dissolution, which has resulted from economic pressures.

Previous Accounts of Nomadism in Turkey

The question of the historical formation of Turkish Anatolia has always been a major concern of serious scholarship in Turkey. Yet, very few of the authors who have devoted themselves to the study of Anatolian society have paid much heed to nomadism, despite the fact that it has substantially influenced the society since its first massive appearance there in the 10th and 11th centuries.

Turkish Intellectuals and Nomadism

Turkish scholarship has largely ignored the nomadic past of Anatolian society in terms of both intellectual interest and assessment of the historical roots and processes of the present social formation. Because of the casual references by Engels, for instance, who speaks of the Turks as having brought some kind of 'nomadic feudalism' to the region[3], some scholars have attempted to explain the Turkish social formation and its transformation in terms of feudalism.[4] A few others, such as Divitçioglu, have studied Ottoman society in terms of the Asiatic mode. However, not much has been done to foster investigation of the socio-economic bases of the Ottoman organization with respect to nomadism. More recent studies[5] do take note of nomads, but do not proceed to any elaborate analysis of nomadism in Turkish Anatolia.

To a large extent nomadism, or rather the nomadic origin of Turkish society, has been either a matter of mockery or of embarrassment for Turkish

---

3. Engels 1878.
4. For example Berktay 1983.
5. For example Keyder 1976; Kiliçbay 1982; Tezel 1977; Timur 1979.

scholars, depending on the ideological stand of the party involved. On the one hand, some have attempted to take very lightly the claim that the Ottomans established a world-empire out of a nomadic community. Hence, they have ruled out the possibility of seeking value in nomadic, as distinct from agricultural, origins. This is because nomadism was conceived of, in a misconceived rhetoric, as little more than heroism on horse-back, which led these authors to be apathetic towards nomadism and the scientific investigation of the nomadic impact on Turkish society, all the while holding fast to the Western notion of 'primitive nomadism'.[6] As a result, they saw no virtue in pursuing any serious work on the issue. Hence, nomadism is confined to the domain of historiography, whose predominant mode of investigation did not allow it to undertake detailed studies or descriptions of nomadic life and practices the way ethnography could.

Others, many of whom were historians, have been so conditioned by the ideology, uncritically adopted from western Europe and elsewhere, that civilization was essentially a sedentary quality[7] that, in the course of becoming 'modern' or 'civilized', they did not dare question the age-old stereotype by means of which the West has identified the Turks with 'barbarism' at least since the time of the first crusades. Nomadism and hence nomadic peoples, they were convinced, represented a primitive stage in the evolution of human society relative to agriculture. Paradoxically, these scholars were both proud of the heroic past represented predominantly by nomads, and ashamed of the possibility of their descent from nomadic peoples. What they did, instead of identifying the contribution of nomadic peoples to global civilization, and investigating how such 'primitive and uncivilized' people have established world-empires, was apologetically to try to show that Turks were not exclusively nomadic, as was imagined in Western discourse.[8] They took painstaking efforts to show scientifically that the massive waves of Turkic peoples into

---

6. To recall, evolutionary theory and certain disciplines which heavily relied on it, such as ethnology, maintained for a long time that pastoral nomadism preceded agriculture, and hence represented a more primitive stage in evolution than civilized cultivation, which was considered the 'great revolution' (For a critical exposition of this view, see Khazanov 1984). The myth of the epoch-breaking capacity of agricultural production has been criticized (e.g., see Johnston and Selby 1978) thereby opening the way to more fairly assess the historical significance of nomadism, long underestimated as a result of the highly romanticized and exaggerated evaluation of agriculture's role as *the* historical development towards civilization.

7. There are two words for 'civilization' in Turkish: 'medeniyet', and 'uygarlik'. Of these, the first is of much older usage. It is of Arabic origin, and is derived from 'medine', i.e., city. I am not sure at this point whether or not the prejudice against nomadism also entailed an Arabic or Islamic influence or component.

8. Sümer 1960.

Anatolia from the 10th century on comprised not only nomads but also settled, urban elements, and cultivators, who had actually formed the backbone of the subsequent Turkish dynasties.[9] Needless to add, they henceforth purported to announce to the world that the Turks were as civilized as any other people.

A Note on the Historical Literature

Partly for the reasons sketched above, and partly because the Ottoman archives are far from having been exhaustively investigated, there is as yet no coherent body of knowledge describing the activities and daily practices of nomads. Furthermore, much of what has been written about nomads since their arrival in Anatolia in the 10th century is from the viewpoint of the Imperial elites. For the Ottomans, who had the longest tenure of rule in the area, history-writing was largely conceived of either as keeping records of daily affairs (wills and wishes, orders and demands, etc.) and the 'great' exploits of the rulers or as an art akin to poetry relating the achievements of the previous rulers in a mythological tone.[10] The history of nomadism in Anatolia from the perspective of nomads themselves is effectively non-existent. Thus, information regarding a critical and vital component of 'Turkish' identity is largely lacking. The few sources that contain some information on nomads are the treatises written by some established urbanites for the originally nomadic dynasties, such as the *Siyasatnâma* of the vizier Nizam-ül Mülk of the Iranian *Seljuqlu* (1960 [orig. 1095]), and the *Secret History of Moghols* (1963). As yet, even such works are non-existent for the early Ottoman era, when the Ottomans themselves were still nomads.

Some historical studies do, however, provide information concerning nomad-state interaction. Of these, several archival studies focus on the Ottoman efforts to settle nomads: Refik's work (1930) on the 17th to 19th century Anatolian *asirets*,[11] Gökçen's work (1946) on the 16th and 17th century nomads in western Anatolia, Cengiz Orhonlu's study (1987) on the late 17th century settlements, and Yusuf Halaçoglu's volume (1988) on the 18th century settlements. Information on the earlier centuries, during which nomads were known to be most influential in the socio-political formation of the Ottoman,

---

9. See ibid.
10. Timur 1986: 72ff.
11. Gülöksüz identifies Refik's archival study *Anadolu'da Türk Asiretleri, 966-1200* (1930) as one on 'tenth to thirteenth century documents revealing the administrative measures taken to deal with nomadism and forced settlement of the Yörük and Türkmen' (1985: 43 note 4). The dates 966 - 1200 indicate the Islamic *hijra* calendar, and hence are to be read as 1650-1884, i.e., the 17th to 19th centuries.

and many other *Beyliks*[12], are still largely lacking. Apart from these, there also are several studies on specific regional developments which, however, do not provide much information on actual nomadic practices.[13] Thus, attempting to compile a comprehensive picture of the nomadic past in Anatolia is difficult. To overcome this difficulty, I have utilized as many sources as possible, including some that were remotely relevant. I am confident that this void will be filled by subsequent archival research.

A Brief Account of the Turkmen (i.e. Nomadic) Presence in Anatolia

The predominance of Turkmen existence in Anatolia began around the 10th century.[14] This nomadic presence was reinforced by a second major influx in the 13th century. Later, with the rise of the *Safevî* sect in Iran in the 14th century, migrations turned back towards the east[15] and remained so until the arrival of Tamerlane (Timur or Taimur the Lane) at the turn of the 15th century, which brought another major wave of nomads to Anatolia.

The founding of the Iranian *Safevî* state in the early 16th century, rooted in a 14th century *sufî* sect paralleled that of the Anatolian *Osmanli* in the west. The former remained much more loyal to the Turkmen who had founded it and who had borne the brunt of its establishment[16], while the latter rather swiftly changed its policy towards nomads once it was strong enough to do so.

Most of the incoming Turkic populations were nomadic although they contained full sedentaries as well.[17] Initially, therefore, the ruling group consisted mainly of Turkmen elements in administrative and military posts.[18] However, the dominant factions of the ruling elite changed through time at the expense of this nomadic majority. From the beginning of the 14th century, new *kuls* (subjects) were increasingly preferred over the Turkmen chiefs ('the equals') by the *Osmanli* leaders. By the second half of the 15th century, the military and administrative posts of the Empire were already occupied by a

---

12. Gibbons 1916; Cahen 1968; Uzunçarsili 1969.
13. For example Demirtas 1949; Sümer 1964, 1976b; Wittek 1944; cf. Sümer 1980.
14. According to Eberhard 'the main body of conquerors soon became settled in cities as a new aristocracy, or in villages as new landowners. Craftsmen, merchants, even clerks and scholars, emigrating later from Turkestan and Khorasan, naturally followed, and also lived in cities. But some tribal units of the time of conquest and some emigrating later from Khorasan remained nomads' (1967: 281).
15. Demirtas 1949: 38; Sümer 1980: 156.
16. Sümer 1976a.
17. See Inalcik 1951: 642; Gökbilgin 1957: 48.
18. Köprülü 1988.

class of *kuls* called the *kapikulu* (ibid.). Their advance gradually but systemati
cally removed nomadic chiefs from positions in the state hierarchy.

To exploit this political conflict between the subject *Yeniçeri* (janissary) and
the Turkmen (nomad), the princely contenders to the *Osmanli* throne regularly
sought assistance from the nomads. As a result, throughout the 15th century,
the struggles of the 'noble' Turkmen chiefs for power often manifested
themselves in the form of fights among the *seyhzades* (sons of the Sultan). A
succession of such fights began immediately after the collapse of central power
in 1402, leading to an era known in *Osmanli* history as the *Fetret Devri* (Inter-
regnum Period), and they occurred in every subsequent competition among
the *seyhzades* in the centuries that followed.

The persistent tendency was to assimilate nomads completely into the
subject category of *reaya*, commoners, along with the rest of the rural population, so as to divest them of their privileged *askerî* (i.e. military) position, and
hence power in general. Nomads did not accept this degrading attribution
easily.[19] 'We are *yürük*. We will not pay taxes like the *reaya*' was their recurrent
response to persistent *Osmanli* pressure. Active struggle against this policy
saved nomads at times, but worked against their interests at others. When
nomads proved successful, they were 'rewarded', and were either exempted
from certain taxes or allowed to pay no taxes at all, depending on the circumstances,[20] and hence were granted the *askerî* status.[21] Nomads enjoyed such
rights or privileges as long as they proved capable of retaining them by force
when they were at jeopardy. These 'privileges' were actually 'payments' for
certain services, duties, and obligations which were increasingly becoming non-
military and non-administrative.[22] Overall, nomads were an essential component of the *Osmanli* society, and they remained a significant force, thanks to
their organizational flexibility, and mobility as a mounted military force.

One of the major factors promoting nomadic survival in the Anatolian
peninsula was a new wave of westward migrations from Asia. The first
migration after the establishment of nomadism in Anatolia was the 13th
century Moghol influx. The second major influx of nomadic peoples came
about the time that the *Osmanli* were expanding at the expense of the Turkmen
Beyliks in Anatolia. The 15th century westward move was under Tamerlane,
and it successfully revived nomadism, despite the other factors working against
its preservation.

---

19. See Refik 1930; Gökçen 1946, *passim*.
20. Timur, 1979: 103.
21. For several instances in later centuries, see Gökbilgin 1957; Uluçay 1955, and Orhonlu
    1987 (1963).
22. Refik, 1930, *passim*.

In the long-run, the struggles of nomads demonstrated their power and the potential threat they presented. They also proved time and again the un-reliability of nomads as loyal, unconditional supporters of the throne. The *Kâ-nunnâmes* (Lawbooks) of the Empire, therefore, had to 'grant' certain rights to nomadic populations, as distinct from cultivators, though under very strict rules and regulations.[23]

At times, nomads were remembered by the *Osmanli* as old comrades. The long-settled *yürüks* in the Balkans were titled *Evlâd-i Fâtihân*, i.e., Sons of the Conquerors, when their military service was required in 1691. The *Osmanli* exempted them from all the taxes they had previously been forced to pay as *reaya*.[24] This policy encouraged not only the ex-nomads in the Balkans, but also many more in Anatolia, some of whom had no nomadic past, to join the privileged *askerî* class.

At other times, the *Osmanli* adopted a rather traditional means of securing peace and stability in the country. Along this line, a fresh attempt was made in Anatolia between 1691 and 1696 to settle the nomads as well as other communities on cultivable lands. In fact, the 1691-96 settlement project was a multi-dimensional one. To the *Osmanli*, rural settlement was the only way to counter the problems of decreasing rural population, crop damage caused by irregular nomadism, and external threat. Banditry and raids on dwelling areas were largely ascribed to the nomads — usually, quite rightly so.[25] In many cases, the disruptive groups were reported to have come from eastern Anatolia and Syria, where they had earlier been forced to settle.[26]

Large numbers of Crimean and Caucasian agricultural immigrants were settled next to the nomadic confederations, if not directly on the pastures used by nomads. Thus, in these border areas and trade-route passages vacated by the people during the upheavals leading to the *Great Escape*, not only was security expected to be maintained, but also a very critical balance was intended between the experienced cultivators and nomadic settlers. The incoming people had recently lost their ancestral lands, and were determined not to experience the same fate again. They represented a strong and intransigent foe for the nomads, who were not pleased at having been reduced to immobility. What is more, the two could successfully stand together against the advance of a common enemy, such as the *Shammar* and *Aneze* Bedouins of Arabia.[27] The presence of nomads as 'tribal' settlers was also seen as a factor

23. For example Çetintürk 1943.
24. Gökbilgin 1957: 255-56.
25. See Bayrak 1984.
26. For several examples of such cases of disturbances caused by nomads, see Uluçay 1955: 80ff, 105, 132, 142, 167, 183, 196, 215, etc.
27. Orhonlu 1987: 45-6.

that would control local 'feudalistic tendencies',[28] which had already emerged in the 17th century.[29]

The strict containment of nomads at one location year round, by preventing their seasonal migration, seriously damaged their reputation as unbendable people, and diminished their power over the territories through which they previously moved. However, it was not easy to prevent nomads from abandoning their assigned plots.[30] The land and its natural resources wereoften claimed by nomads to be insufficient. Furthermore, as settlers they were subject to recurrent attacks of stronger Bedouin (i.e., nomadic) groups from the south.[31] Finally, new taxes were imposed on them and were regularly extracted after they became 'sedentary', i.e., immobile. So, many of them left their settlement zones to avoid strict political control and taxation, and fled into areas where they could more readily cope with the pressures imposed by the governors.

Overall, nomads were a crucial component of the Anatolian social formation before and during the *Osmanli* rule.[32]

The *Osmanli* did not attempt to put an end to nomadism, instead they tried to keep nomadism at a level where it could not present a threat to centralism. The *Osmanli* continued to deploy nomads as warriors while trying to divide and settle them on distant lands when socio-economic conditions dictated it. Thus, they maintained a certain distance between the state apparatus and nomads, and withheld or at least tried to avoid giving any status, rights or privileges that they could not control later. It is this tension between the central authority and nomads which is conceptualized by some scholars as one of feudal forces and central despotic power.[33]

Both the last attempt to discharge nomads from the military duties and the final revival of nomadism came about under the *Ittihad ve Terakki* (The Union and Progress Party, the so called 'Young Turk') government. This

---

28. For example, in the 1840s, the Tanzimat government used some nomadic *aşirets* to complete the destruction of a *derebey* (local notable, 'feudal') family, which ran the *Muş Beylerbeyliği* (Muş Governorship) until it was annulled by the new government. The lack of governmental backing did not matter much since the official duty was assigned to the members of the same family for some time. Only after this family had been defeated, with the support of nomads, could government establish new administrative organs. Thereafter, the town of Varto became a *kaymakamlik* (district head-office) and Muş became a *mutasarriflik*, i.e., jurisdiction of 'provincial' (*sancak*) governor. (Firat 1983: 120).
29. Uluçay 1955: 71-74.
30. Orhonlu 1987: 81 ff, 88 ff.
31. Ibid., 90.
32. Köprülü 1988.
33. For example, Timur, 1979: 112; also 86, 107, 117, 127, and Yerasimos, 1974.

government was composed mainly of young officers of the army[34] which was being re-organized and modernized along western lines since the early 19th century.[35] The conflict between the Sultan Abdül-Hamid and the Government during the last two decades of the 19th and the first decade of the 20th century, however, led the former to seek support from nomads, who had proved themselves quite successful first in 1839 and then again in 1877 against one of the southward advances of the Russians.[36] The result was the formation of 36 new *asiret*, i.e., nomadic regiments, named after the Sultan Abdül-Hamid as the *Hamidiye* Cavalry Regiments.[37] The Sultan addressed the leaders of the resulting *Hamidiye* Cavalry Regiments[38] as 'my sons',[39] the implication being that he himself was a bigger 'chief' in alliance with them. The number of regiments tripled in less than two decades, and they soon became the main military power of the region, which was under continuous threat from both the Russians and the Iranians.[40] This revived the power and influence of nomads, especially in eastern Anatolia for another thirty years or so.

With the death of Sultan Hamid in 1909, the *alay* (regimental) chiefs found themselves in a dangerous vacuum. The new government did not seem to share the policy of the deceased Sultan regarding the regiments. Instead of the *sunnî*-oriented Islamicist policy of Abdül Hamid, the new government adopted an Ottomanist view, which it thought would (re-)unite the badly divided population of the Empire, Christians, Jews, and Muslims alike.[41] This policy found immediate support among the non-Hamidiye *alevî* communities in eastern Anatolia, who had suffered most severely from the divisive consequences of the earlier policy.[42] Partly because of being left powerless by the Sultan's death, and partly because of the threat posed by the alliance between the new government and the *alevî asirets*, some of these commander-chiefs rebelled shortly after the announcement of the era of the Second Constitution (*Mesrûtiyet*) in 1908, but were subsequently defeated by regular troops.[43] Only after these defeats and under strict governmental control did these irregular nomadic regiments give up fighting the new regime.

34. Çavdar, 1984.
35. Shaw and Shaw, II, 1974.
36. Firat 1983: 120-21.
37. Kodaman 1979.
38. Ibid.
39. Firat 1983: 125. During my personal encounter with the *Beritanli* I found out that some of the elder *Beritanlis* still referred to the Sultan Abdül Hamid, with much grief, as 'our father'.
40. Firat 1983; Kodaman 1987.
41. Çavdar 1984.
42. Firat 1983: 141 ff.
43. Ibid: 141.

The *Mesrutiyet* government did not dissolve the regiments but chose to control them more directly. Now, each regiment had a regular, professional Major as its second-in-command.[44] Again, according to the law, raiding and tax-gathering were no longer permitted.[45] In spite of these restrictions, the chiefs did not lose their power and authority either with respect to the troops or to the sedentaries of the region.[46] And they still proved helpful to the government in war. In 1912, they were put on alert because of the Balkan conflict in the west. The continuing threat of the Russian Empire forced the government to maintain and train *Hamidiye* regiments in the east. At the beginning of World War I in 1914, the *Hamidiyes* were sent to fight against the Russians. Though they fought to the best of their abilities, they were defeated. Most of them fled back into the mountains where they began to engage in banditry and raiding.

Those who stayed at the front were re-organized and gathered into two divisions,[47] which survived until about 1920. They adamantly resisted dissolution, and remnants of them (even after their official disbanding) caused the *Osmanli* government many headaches. Aside from trying to exact illegal taxes from villagers and non-*Hamidiye asirets*, they engaged in fierce fights with one another. Besides such inter-*asiret* warfare, the ex-commanders also turned into local 'despots' known as the *derebeys* of absolute power, with hundreds of armed men at their command. These and other events created widespread unrest in the region. The *Osmanli* found themselves on the losing side during the closing stages of World War I, and were in no position to put a stop to such illegal activities anywhere in the country. The capital Istanbul, on the western edge of Turkey, was under allied invasion. In the east, nomads and the *asiret* system were once again on the rise, and in the midst of the chaos created by the power gap at the centre from losing the war, raids and banditry became daily events.[48]

The *Hamidiye asiret* regiments were dismantled in 1918,[49] following the defeat of the *Osmanli* in World War I. After the 1919-22 War of Independence, the dismantling of all irregular troops, including the tribal fighters, and the establishment of a new central army, was put into effect. This completed the process of nomadic submission in Anatolia after five centuries of fierce struggle, though it was not without repercussions, which emerged in the form of a series of *asiret*-based upheavals between 1925-36.

---

44. Ibid: 141-42.
45. Ibid: 142.
46. Ibid: 141-42.
47. Ibid: 143-44.
48. Ibid: 155-56.
49. Ibid: 153.

One consequence of the establishment of the *Hamidiye* regiments was the division of the people into two antagonistic groups. Those who were serving in these regiments became 'the *Hamidiye*' vis-à-vis the others. For more than two decades, the previous names and titles of the people involved in the Hamidiye organization were subsumed under the more comprehensive and legally authoritative rubric of *Hamidiye*. Since religious affiliation (*sunnî* vs. *alevî*) was another concern of the *Osmanli* in appointing the increasingly willing candidate warriors as *Hamidiye*, sectarian antagonism[50] re-surfaced and rose to an unforeseen magnitude between the two groups, adding greatly to the strains felt between them later.[51]

The end of World War I was also the end of the *Osmanli* Empire. The victorious partners of western Europe had finally succeeded in dissecting *Osmanli* land into many parts, which added more fodder to the western colonial project. After the frustration of the Islamicist project of the Sultan Abdül Hamid, the Ottomanist policy of the *Ittihad ve Terakki* government also failed. Thus the end of the war also marked the end of an era and the beginning of a new one for the core of the Empire, Rumeli and Anatolia, for the people who would eventually define themselves as 'Turks'. The 'Turkish Nation', i.e., the 'imagined community', to use Anderson's phrase (1983), as long ago conceived by the West, and which the former *Osmanli* officials were in the process of creating, was now at last on its way to becoming a reality.

The Establishment of the Republic as the First 'Turkish' Nation State

From as early as the 11th century, Western Europeans referred to the incoming waves of people as 'the Turks' and the lands they came to as 'Turkey' and/or 'Turkomania'.[52] Thus, the Iranian *Seljuqlu*, the *Seljuqlu* of Rum and the *Osmanli*, to name only the better-known, were equally 'Turks' to even the most well informed west European. Thus, for four to six centuries, they called the Ottoman territory from Iran to Morocco in Africa and Austria in Europe 'Turkey' and referred to what is now northern Iraq and southeastern Turkey as 'Turkomania'. It was only after the foundation of a new, secular republican

---

50. This antagonism had its roots in the early 16th century conflict between *Osmanlis* and *Safevîs*, where the parties respectively held fast to the orthodox *sunnî* and *shi'î* sects of Islam. It is this historical conflict which in many ways has shaped the history of especially the eastern regions of Anatolia (e.g. see Firat 1983: 89ff.)
51. Although the *Hamidiye* regiments were disbanded in 1918, those who opposed the Seyh Said in 1925 used the devastating effects of the *Hamidiye* experience as an explanation of their mistrust of the rebelling forces, whom they identified with and hence referred to as 'the *Hamidiyes*' (Firat 1983: 158).
52. See Odo of Seuil 1148, and Marco Polo 1200s.

country over the remnants of the Empire in 1923, did the millenia-old 'Turks' begin to call themselves Turks.

The foundation of the new Republic in 1923 on the ashes of the *Osmanli* Empire as a central 'nation-state', identification of the people of the new country as 'Turks', and adoption of secularism in place of the abandoned *sharia* order were not welcomed by many including the ex-*Hamidiye* chiefs and commanders, who were gradually and effectively alienated in the process. The new government also began to implement new laws that would eventually shape the future of the new society being formed, and transform its identity from Ottoman to Turkish.

The new regime abrogated all the legal titles, official privileges, administrative and military rights and duties, such as collecting taxes, of the Hamidiye *asirets*.[53] Yet, according to Firat[54], even after the termination of these rights in 1918, many groups continued to carry out these activities by force until the 1920s, under the banner of the *Hamidiye*.

The introduction of the 1924 Village Act under the Republic was a major blow to nomadism, and hence to the former *Hamidiye asirets*. The Village Act converted the traditional grazing plots, highlands, and pastures that nomads had been using into the common property of (the nearest) villages.[55] Depending on their own productive orientation, the villagers chose either to exploit the pastures themselves, or to rent them to nomads (who were now stripped of this basic economic means) at high rates. As time went by, villagers began to voice their opposition to the increasingly powerless nomads at every opportunity. They used every incident 'as an excuse to exact high cash payments' from them.[56] These even included incidents like minor crop damage unintentionally caused during movements between *kislaks* and *yaylaks*, winter and summer quarters. Serious conflicts, even fights, broke out at times. At other times nomads resigned themselves, and over time appeared to become more and more submissive.[57]

The closure of the eastern and southeastern borders in the late 1920s and the 1930s curbed the migratory orbit of nomads drastically. It also reduced the area that nomads could exploit. More importantly, with the creation by the allied powers of World War I of a number of smaller countries in place of the *Osmanli* Empire, of which the closure of borders was the final affirmation, many nomads were left outside Turkey, in Iraq, Syria, and beyond in the

53. Firat 1983: 141 ff.
54. Ibid.
55. Tütengil 1969: 128.
56. Bates 1973b: 219.
57. Otyam 1978.

further south, i.e. on lands they used as winter quarters, and in Caucasia in the north.

The major forces that could still be taken as representative of nomads were the disbanded *Hamidiye asirets* left within Turkey. And the ex-*Hamidiye* chiefs were still very much attached to the late Sultan-Caliph who had been their only supporter. Their loyalty and allegiance lied with the abolished and deported (1924) *Osmanli* government.

As a combined effect of all these factors, a series of religious and *asiret* upheavals took place between 1925 and 1936, mainly in the eastern provinces against the new secular government and mostly in the name of re-establishing the caliphate. According to some, these 'revolts' were incited by the British, who at the time were trying to establish themselves in Iraq, and were not pleased with the continued claim by the new Turkish state to the Mosul, Kerkük and Erbil regions in British-occupied northern Iraq.[58] No matter what the purpose and extent of British involvement was, the crucial point in the present context is that the leading force in the most significant of all these upheavals, the 1925 Seyh Said rebellion, were the ex-*Hamidiye asirets*.

In order to gain support against the Republican government, the rebellion was presented to the world by some ex-*Hamidiye* leaders as a *Kurdish* movement. *Kurd* was a general term used to denote the people in the mountainous regions in eastern Anatolia.[59] Though known to outsiders as *Kurds*, this attribution was not acceptable to the non-*Hamidiye alevîs* in the region, who had already aligned themselves first with the anti-*Hamidiye* 'Young Turk' (i.e. the *Ittihad ve Terakki*) government, and then with the new secular-minded leaders of the Turkish Republic. Furthermore, they did not trust the former *Hamidiye* chiefs, and when invited to join the movement they refused to identify themselves as '*Kurds*', declaring themselves instead as '*Turks*'.[60] Nor was it attractive to the religious leaders involved, who also refused to identify themselves as Kurds.[61] In his testimony before the court, *Seyh Said*, the leader

---

58. See Mumcu 1991: 12 ff. For a defence of the British colonial position in these affairs, see Toynbee and Kirkwood 1926: 259-301, esp. 274 ff.

59. The people who have been commonly called *Kurd* at least since the 16th century, usually as distinct from others such as *Turks*, which meant 'plains villager', contain several groups of people who speak mutually unintelligible languages. The languages spoken today include *Zazaça, Kirmançe* or *Gurmançe, Terekemece, Hormekçe, Süryanice,* and *Türkçe*, among others. Until recently, the first two of these languages were considered to be two dialects of a single language. The current view is that they are two different languages (Izady 1988). This seems to recognize that '*Kurd*' is a socio-historical term and/or a social category rather than an ethnic one, as was long held in the western literature.

60. Firat 1983: 158.

61. See Mumcu 1991: 114ff.

of the rebellion, explained his intention as the restoration of the *Shari'a*. Another prominent leader, *Seyyîd Abdülkadir*, said that his intention was to frustrate plans for the establishment of Armenia in eastern Anatolia.[62] Many of the '*Kurds*' in towns and cities steadfastly refused to join them. As a result, the movement was practically confined to the mostly ex-*Hamidiye asirets* who adhered to the *Naqshibendî* doctrine.[63] It was announced as a *jihad*, i.e. holy war,[64] whose self-declared ultimate goal was to oust the 'infidel republican government', so as to re-establish the *sunnî* Caliphate, and bring the deported Caliph back as sovereign.[65]

In this regard, Toynbee and Kirkwood in spite of their tendency to present this politico-religious *asiret* upheaval as an ethnic uprising note that:

From a religious point of view, also, there seemed to be grounds for discord. The Kurds, like other primitive peoples, were capable of being roused to fanaticism on behalf of a religion to which they nominally adhered without either strict practice or deep understanding. So long as the Caliph remained, the Kurds kept more or less quiet; but, when the action of the Turkish Government in abolishing the Caliphate [in 1924] indicated that a non-religious and apparently atheistic régime had been instituted under the Republic, then the Kurds could be persuaded without difficulty by the religious leaders to take up arms against an infidel Government.[66]

As for the aim of the rebels, Toynbee and Kirkwood further state that:

The programme of the rebels was to re-establish the Sherî'ah or Quranic Law abolished by Mustafâ Kemâl's anti-clerical Government, and to proclaim Selîm Efendi, one of Sultan Abdül-Hamîd's sons, Sultan the Caliph.[67]

---

62. See ibid.; see also 120, 124, 127, 131ff.
63. Naqshibendî is an originally central Asian Muslim sect. According to Firat, it was brought to Turkey in the 16th century from Iraq, together with *Shafi'ism* (Firat 1983: 95.
64. Firat 1983: 171 fn.
65. Ibid: 165-66, and *passim*.
66. Toynbee and Kirkwood's work, 1926: 265, is quite typical in its attempt to present this apparently religious-oriented *asiret* uprising as an ethnic one. It contradicts itself when the facts manifest otherwise or indicate a much more complex picture. See also Robert Olson (1989), who, in his study of the Seyh Said Rebellion, suggests that the rebellion was essentially a nationalist movement by Kurds against the Turks. In light of the detailed evidence he provides regarding the gradual moulding and the ultimate purpose of this upheaval, this assertion is extraordinary. More precisely, the author makes this claim in spite of the fact that Seyh Said, the undisputed leader of the rebellion, was the hereditary 'Abbot' of the *naqshibendî târiqat* (sect), and that one of his first activities was to declare the restoration of the *sharî'a* order.
67. Ibid: 266.

The authors go on to describe the ensuing government response, which illustrates the dimensions of the 1925 incident and the way in which the Republican authorities regarded it:

A heavy hand was laid upon the Constantinople (Istanbul) press, which was held to be one of the contributing causes of disaffection and counter-revolutionary feeling, and more than a dozen Constantinople and provincial newspapers were suppressed. The teaching of religious doctrines which might subvert loyalty to the Republic was prohibited in the mosques. The Tribunals of Independence were re-established in various important centres ... and in June, some months after the rebellion had been extinguished, these Tribunals of independence ordered the closing of all Dervish monasteries in the Eastern Provinces on the ground that they were centres of intrigue and hot-beds of superstition. The discovery of a monarchical and religious secret society, called 'Order of Reform', organized in the same manner as many of the Dervish fraternities, encouraged the belief that every Dervish was an enemy of the new *régime*; and, on 3 September, the Government closed all the *tekkehs* and *türbehs*, abolished the titles and special costumes of sheikhs, dervishes and other *religieux* of the various orders, and thus ended this very ancient Islamic institution in Turkey, on the ground of its association with subversive movements in the country.[68]

Furthermore, the government took more direct measures to make sure that the insurgency did not erupt again. In addition to the severe punishment imposed by the Independence Tribunals on the leaders, some of the most significant of whom were put to death, in 1926 the government exiled the lesser leaders[69], transferred the people of some *asirets* involved to western Turkey, and dispersed them throughout the region.

To conclude, still in the words of Toynbee and Kirkwood, 'The rebellion was an unsuccessful protest against a policy of radical standardization and unification on Western lines, in which the variegated institutions of the *ancien régime* were being ruthlessly swept away'.[70] I would further add that its initial

68. Ibid: 269-70.
69. Firat 1983: 197-98.
70. Toynbee and Kirkwood, 1926: 274, manifest some contradictions in their account. For instance, they say just a few pages earlier that 'It must be remembered, of course, that the Kurds had never had any love for the ancien régime'. (1926: 271). If so, then why did they intend to enthrone a son of the Caliph, the sole representative of the supposedly hated régime, as the leader of the country?! Where did this affection of the 'skin-deep Muslim' Kurds for the Caliph (ibid: 265) and caliphate come from? What would 'the Kurds' gain by bringing a 'Turkish' monarch to power, and proclaiming him as 'Sultan the Caliph' in place of the secular Republican Government, if not the foregone religion? On the significance of a common religion for the new 'Turkish nation', compare these opinions on ethnicity with the authors' description of Muslim immigrants (from Greece) and their sentiments towards the 'Turk' (ibid: 210).

cause was also a limitation: the practical confinement of its religious component to the *Nakhshibendî* sect, and the idenitification of the rebel forces as 'the ex-*Hamidiyes*' by the non-aligned *asirets* of the region[71] were among the reasons for its failure. And this marked the end of the *Hamidiyes* who lost for good this time.

The Present Conditions of Nomadism in Turkey

In 1923, western Anatolia was relatively more developed than other regions in the country, with a fairly well-developed infrastructure, and a climate and soil composition amenable to agriculture. The massive population movements that started much earlier continued after the foundation of the Republic in 1923 as a result of bi-lateral agreements between Turkey and other countries such as Greece. Scholars generally agree that one of the consequences of the population exchanges initiated by these agreements, due to the loss of specialized labour, was a considerable decrease in the manufacturing and, in some specialized areas, agricultural capacity of Turkey.[72] Some argue, however, that while those who left took much with them in terms of experience and know-how in certain productive fields, the incoming Muslim populations possessed 'a business acumen and experience, a resourcefulness, and a spirit of enterprise', and also helped to foster modern commercial cultivation in the Turkish countryside.[73]

As for the conditions of nomadic survival in Turkey today, it is fair to say that contemporary nomadism is clearly dominated by the sedentary way of life into which it is becoming steadily incorporated. In contrast to the political

71. Firat 1983: 158.
72. For example, see Keyder 1981: 20 ff.
73. Toynbee and Kirkwood, 1926: 210, see also 207 ff. In their assessment of conditions in Turkey of 1926, present an example of scholarship that goes far beyond naive ethnocentrism. They describe Turkish people as 'the masses untouched by the enlightenment of Western ways and Western scientific progress' and define Turkish agriculture as 'the natural source of a primitive, land-loving peasantry'. (1926: 212) With this kind of an approach, the authors suggest that as a result of population exchanges between Greece and Turkey: 'The incoming Muslims ... were acclimatized to Greek life and thought; and, to some extent, at least, brought with them from Greece a business acumen and experience, a resourcefulness, and a spirit of enterprise, which will make itself felt as soon as they are sufficiently settled and established in their new country. They will help to fill the places of the evacuated Greeks and Armenians, and though their native language is not in all cases Turkish, they are co-religionists of the Turks and are at one with them in national feeling, and they may therefore contribute much to the development and prosperity of the country', (ibid: 210). I wonder why those in Anatolia did not learn anything from their Greek neighbours before the latter left for Greece.

power they held in 'living memory' i.e., the early 1900s, pastoral nomadic groups today are subordinate to the agricultural population. The regime today is explicitly on the side of cultivators as opposed to nomads. The official de-recognition of (nomadic) *asirets* as legal communities by the foundation of the Republic in 1923 undermined the leadership and made the allegiance of their members to certain *asiret* leaders contrary to the ideology of central government. Furthermore, the aforementioned Village Act of 1924 was designed to protect the interests of villagers against intruders such as nomads, who were *a priori* considered as 'the people of no land'. In most disputes between villagers and nomads, therefore, the law, and hence security forces, are on the side of the villagers.

Geographically, there is a 'clearcut contrast'[74] between western Anatolia and eastern Anatolia. In the west, nomadism is vestigial and is mainly practiced between the coastal plains and the plateaux near Kayseri (in central Anatolia) by a number of fragmented groupings 'belonging mainly to the Aydinli group'[75] and by the remnants of Bozolog[76] or *Boz-Ulus*. In eastern Anatolia, on the other hand, nomadism has experienced 'a much more vigorous survival'[77]. As a result of the developments and policies described above, eastern and southeastern Anatolia became a refuge for nomads. There are some pastoral nomadic *asirets* in eastern Anatolia such as the *Savakli* of the Elazig-Tunceli-Erzincan range which have as many as 15,000 members.[78]

74. Phanhol 1959: 529.
75. Eberhard 1967: 282; see also Bates (1971), who in his writings on the *yürüks* argues that their description by others as the 'Aydinlis' or 'Aydinli Asireti' is misleading. The *yürüks*, he claims, utilize this term mainly as a tool for proving their distinctiveness from the surrounding sedentaries of various 'ethnic' origin, though they do not belong to the *Aydinlis* as a whole (1971: 284, No.5). I do not think it is possible for any group to assume the name of another, unless it becomes a member of the latter through some kind of a 'contract', for example, by word, by joining forces for some time, by blood, or marriage relations. In Bates' case, it seems to be the marriages, if nothing else, that he has recorded in the Nogaylar köy of these *yürüks* (1973b) which enable all to claim attachment or belongingness to the *Aydinli Asireti*. Besikçi notes, on the other hand, that such attributions are of political and ideological significance. The ill will and even the hostility nomads and settlers feel towards the others is a consequence of sedentarization, as a result of which the two parties formed, as Besikçi labels it (1969a: 82), two 'castes', the members of each of which conceive of the other as subordinates (ibid: 90).
76. Yalman 1977, Vol. 2.
77. Phanhol 1959: 529.
78. See Aydin 1980: 143; Kutlu 1987: 53. The *Savak* (or *Savakli*) *asireti* is reported to be mainly *yaylaci* (transhumant) by Kutlu (1987; cf. Aydin 1980). In 1989, I conducted some research among them for comparative purposes. They identified themselves as herders predominantly. Therefore, I go along with Aydin, and consider them nomadic, who undoubtedly have sedentary elements as well.

Indeed, one of the most distinguishing social characteristics of the population in eastern Anatolia is its, as yet, undetached *asiret* affiliations which at times of inter-group conflict prove themselves to be a major basis for feelings of solidarity. In other words, the prevailing ideology which ultimately governs social relations in most parts of the region (including the sedentary population) is that of *asiret* organization, for example, genealogical kinship relations; social belongingness; and the notion of 'community', simply as 'a sense of belonging together'.[79] Largely as a result of this structure, eastern Anatolia did not seriously take part in the process of mechanization until the 1960s. Most people in eastern Anatolia were landless and organized in *asirets*, and the landlords would appear to have had very little to gain from using modern machinery. On the one hand, machines would replace large numbers of rural people, landless and landed alike, who for the most part belonged to the same *asiret* as their landlords. Thus, the calculation involved in adopting new machinery was not simply an economic one, in the crudest sense. The machines would perhaps bring about an increase in the yield, but on the other hand, once the machines were introduced, the *asiret* landlords would lose their 'dependants', i.e. the social base of their political power. In effect, then, *asiret* forces were threatened. The introduction of machinery to the area would have encouraged the break-up of fundamental social relations in favour of capitalist penetration.

In comparison with other regions, the level of mechanization in eastern Anatolia has remained low.[80] The region is highly mountainous in the east, and volcanic in some areas, like parts of the Urfa region in the southeast, where the fields are rocky and, as they stand, hardly suitable for cultivation. Moreover, as already indicated, *asiret* ties are still quite important and strong among the majority of the rural population, which precludes the landlords from investing heavily in tractors.

Over the last decade the effect has even begun to be felt in this region, which is now approaching a nomad-less state. Though the conditions of nomads in eastern and southeastern Anatolia are somewhat similar, and largely complementary in nomadic practices, the latter is now subject to drastic changes. The most comprehensive and most current of these changes is the GAP (*Güneydogu Anadolu Projesi*, the Southeast Anatolian Project). This devel-

---

79. Brow, 1990. Actually, this has been the case in most of Turkey. As Boran (1945: 67-68) notes for the villages of Manisa in western Anatolia, the quarters or districts of most of the towns and villages in Anatolia are still known by the name of the families or groups that initially settled there. Through the process of sedentarization the political term *mahalle* (which still signifies the group of closest families of agnates or even of affinals) has turned into a term indicating district of permanent residence (see Benedict 1974, and Ergenç 1984).
80. Erhan 1992: 95.

opment project, which involves a major part of southeast Anatolia, includes 13 sub-projects, the totality of which aims at a hydraulic complex able to irrigate 1,800,000 hectares, so as to increase agricultural production up to 50-60 times.[81] This figure is 300,000 hectares more than the total irrigated land in the whole of Turkey at present. The complex also includes 21 dams and 17 hydro-electrical power centres[82], which are expected to provide 22 billion kilo-watt hours of electric energy per year, a figure which is equal to the amount Turkey had in 1981.[83]

Preliminary planning began in 1936[84] with completion planned over a span of 30 years. At 1986 rates, it would have required a total of seven trillion Turkish Lira, a sum which is equal to the same year's national budget. The sub-systems of this vast integrated project completed so far provide only 2 percent of the projected irrigation needs, and 0.2 percent of the projected energy production. The final stages of the GAP were supposed to be finished by 1990. Several reasons, including the so-called 'Gulf Crisis' next-door, precluded the completion of the project on time. Partial opening of the Atatürk dam, the biggest dam of all within the GAP system, took place in September 1991.[85]

Despite the delay it seems certain that as far as the nomads of the region are concerned it allows them few alternatives — if they can be called 'alternatives' at all. The most obvious one is to settle down and cease to be nomadic. The other is to explore the possibility of either finding new *kislak* locations somewhere else or making the transition to settled or semi-settled animal breeding, assuming, of course, that the *yaylak* pastures will still be available for a while. And this is exactly what the *Beritanli* have been considering, ever since their official application for settlement in the early 1960s, preferably around their recently lost winter quarters (this coincided with the first steps for the GAP being taken by the government).

Many nomadic groups have actually been seeking government aid to settle since the 1930s and the 1940s. The underlying goal of state policy and settlement is to convert nomads into cultivating villagers, and to make them productive as soon as possible after they settle (APD 1971) so as to avoid them suffering the effects of a prolonged transition. Thus, the usual practice of governments before 1970, under Law No. 2510 which outlines the basic stipulations, has been to provide every possible assistance to those seeking

81. Balaban 1986: 5.
82. *Hürriyet* August 2nd, 1991: 2.
83. Ibid: 5.
84. According to Balaban, 1986: 3.
85. *Hürriyet*, July 31st, 1991.

rural settlement, including land, fields, housing, agricultural equipment, and the necessary infrastructure such as sheds, stables, and roads.[86] The principal conditions of eligibility were simple but very strictly followed. They were, as they still are, to own no landed property anywhere in Turkey, and to be married at the time of the official settlement survey.

Since the 1970s, however, these benefits are provided only as loans with easy credit terms (as low as 2.5 percent interest), payable in installments over 5 to 20 years. According to Law No. 1306, as amended in 1970, 'the property is not granted for free to the settlers, but rather they become indebted to the state for the disbursed expenses'. (ibid.) Perhaps because the settlement of nomads is not a primary concern of government in modern Turkey, in practice a group that requests settlement usually finds a place, and then notifies government agencies.[87] If the piece of land is public property, then its current value is calculated by experts, based on an assessment of the quality of its cultivable land, etc., and is transferred to the group after the roads and houses have been built by the state. If the land or village site belongs to private persons, as in the case of the *Beritanli*, then the government purchases it from its owner, to turn it over to the group when the necessary housing, roads, drinking water, stores, and the like have been provided. At the time of settlement, the state also provides some initial capital, based on agreement with the group. This may be either seed grain/wheat or animals.

Is 'Ethnicity' part of Nomad Identity or an Ethnographic Category?

In the literature, the issue of identity, as self-description and ascription by others, is usually subsumed by Western concerns of ethnicity. The identity of nomadic groups is either taken for granted as evident in their respective names or in historically significant socio-political appellations, or is submerged within the constraints of presumed ethnicities, and/or ethnonyms which are presumed to indicate mutually exclusive categories. Barth, for example, finds the *Baharlu* of the Khamseh of Iran to be referred to variably as 'Turk' or 'Arab' in the literature, thereby affirming that there is no necessary correspondence between language and the purported 'ethnic' identity of the *Khamseh* group. In this regard, Barth states that:

It is important first of all to be clear what the meaning of the ethnic appellations 'Arab', 'Turk', etc. are. A Western observer will tend to emphasize language as the crucial criterion, and in a very general way will find a correlation between the ethnic name

---

86. Gülöksüz 1985: 307.
87. An example of this is the *Beritanli*; for another example, see Bates 1973b.

applied to a group, and the language spoken by that group. Local people on the other hand use these names in referring to tribes as *political* units. I was frequently corrected, e.g. when saying that the Baharlu are Turkish. 'Turk' is used as a name for members of the Qashqai confederacy, whereas the Baharlu are members of the Khamseh and therefore 'Arab'. The frequent confusion in literature, assigning Arabic language or origin to the Basseri ... arises no doubt from this confusion of the political and linguistic reference of the 'ethnic' name.[88]

Barth notes along these same lines that the *Kashkuli*, 'one of the large tribes of the Turkish-speaking Qashqai confederacy', are therefore considered 'Turks', and 'do in fact speak Turkish. But they have traditions of being originally Lurs'.[89] In contrast with Barth, who cannot avoid referring to such terms as 'Arab', 'Turk', etc. as 'ethnic' names despite his awareness that they are not, the local people use these terms to signify a political aspect of their evidently multi-faceted identity. Apparently, the Turkish-speaking 'Arab' *Baharlu*, among many others[90], like the *Beritanli* of Turkey, have a very flexible sense of identity which does not allow any category to subsume another but permits multiple categories to prevail simultaneously. And unlike Barth, they are not concerned with any correlation between the language used and what Barth insists are ethnic appellations. That is, according to Barth's own presentation, it is not an issue for the local people whether a 'Turk' speaks 'Turkish' or an 'Arab' 'Arabic', or, *vice versa*, whether a Turkish-speaker is a 'Turk' or an Arabic-speaker an 'Arab'.

Bates[91] treats a *yörük* group of southeastern Anatolia as an 'ethnic' group as well. I would prefer to argue that the common name *yörük* acts as a socio-political and occupational term of address indicating the quality of being (originally) nomadic.[92] The *Beritanli* are called *köçer* (i.e. nomad) in the Elazig province (where they densely settled), and they are referred to as *yürük* (as are the *Savakli* of the same province) in the Erzurum province, to the north of the former, where some spend their summer. *Yürük* was the only word for nomad among those I interviewed in the Erzurum province, and it had no implication of ethnicity for the local people.

Besides the unwarranted presumption of approaching nomadic groups or organizations as being divided into mutually exclusive categories of ethnicity, another weakness in the literature is the overemphasis on the economic aspects of nomadic society, which leads to a neglect of cultural

88. Barth 1961: 131.
89. Ibid.
90. Ibid. 1961: 131-33.
91. Bates 1973b: 1, No. 2; see also Patai 1978.
92. Bajraktarevic 1934; Çetintürk 1943.

features, as well as the ideological and political dynamics of nomadic life. Comments such as that of Bacon[93], which suggest that nomads 'scorn agriculture', are either taken at face value as proof of the prevalence of a (frozen) universal dichotomy between pastoral nomads and sedentary cultivators, as mutually exclusive polar opposites[94], or as complementary economic practices[95], with little or no regard to the overlap between the two and the non-economic aspects of either party.

Bates notes that the rubrics 'nomadic pastoralist' and 'peasant' are utilized so as to imply 'an unwarranted dichotomy within what amounts to an ideal typology'.[96] In this context Spooner refers to the occasional shifts between nomadism and sedentarism in either direction as some sort of a continuous oscillation between two economic professions or productive activities: In reference to Bacon's aforementioned note, he asserts that 'Nomads and peasants hate and despise each other, and yet we know that nomads become peasants and peasants become nomads'[97], thereby implying that this attitude is a rather insignificant and misleading rhetoric which does not reflect actual occurrences and processes. Similarly, this is what leads Bates to entitle his article 'Shepherd Becomes Farmer', without much concern for the ideological aspects of either sedentary cultivation or nomadic pastoralism. The lack of interest in the implications of negative attitudes towards sedentaries and their life-style tends to reduce nomadism to a mere economic activity or a profession.

In my opinion, pastoral nomadism is not simply a profession. A shepherd may become a farmer through settlement, and a farmer may join a nomad group. But, as my study of the *Beritanli* reveals[98], considerations of identity do not always adhere to the type of economic activity in which people are engaged.[99] The settled *Beritanli* still consider themselves nomads, and they are so identified by their local neighbours.

Concluding Remarks

Where does this take us? What does this exposition of nomadism amount to? Throughout the text, I employed the terms Turkmen, Yürük, and *asiret* to indicate nomads, even though the general tendency in the literature is to use

---

93. Bacon 1954: 46.
94. cf. Nelson 1973.
95. Mohammad 1973.
96. Bates 1972: 48.
97. Spooner 1972: 126.
98. Erhan, 1992; see also 1989 and 1993.
99. See also Abu-Lughod 1986.

the first two terms to denote 'ethnic' groups whereas the third one is automatically translated as 'tribe' (or sub-tribe, in an Arabic context). In addition to being loyal to their historical and social implications, this is also because I consider the life-styles, productive relations, sense of identity and belongingness or organization, world views of these people crucial, and not any other features that may or may not coincide. And this is because these people themselves do the very same thing when they identify themselves, as Barth found out among the nomads of Iran.

Predominantly, people of Turkey are descendants of nomadic peoples. Given the social history of the region, even those elements within modern Turkish society with no direct link with any nomadic group seem likely to have adopted many traits of nomadic culture and logic. Many of their strengths and weaknesses, like tolerance and a sense of insecurity; the notions of family, relatives, friendship; the sense of belonging everywhere and nowhere in particular, or such attitudes as obedience to authority and running away from pressures or any oppression rather than resisting it, etc., seem to derive from this heritage. The collective subconscious of Turkish people reflects certain patterns of behaviour which tend to come out quite unexpectedly. For instance, one of the first questions a person utters when he/she sees an acquaintance is 'where is he/she from,' 'where does he/she belong originally',all of which are contained in the simple question, *Ne asilsin?*, (literally, how are you?) A single Turk can quite easily adopt to a new environment, granted that the host group does not deny him or her. But, when a group of people get together, even casually, especially in an alien environment, they will just as easily form a solidarity between themselves suggesting that they knew one another beforehand. Older people generally are addressed as 'aunt' or 'uncle'. The same age group address strangers as 'sisters' or 'brothers'. The younger generation are referred to as 'cousin', 'son', or 'daughter'. All of these are traits of tribally organized nomads, whose basic ideom in identifying *themselves* (as well as the 'others') is kinship. This I think is what we need to study, analyse; to dig out the implications of this nomadic heritage of Turks in their sense of identity, rather than settling for notions and/or categories that have developed within the particular contexts of certain societies, under definite historical conditions.

Bibliography

Abu-Lughod, Lila 1986. *Veiled Sentiments: Honor and Poetry in a Bedouin Society.* Berkeley: University of California Press.

A.P.D. (Arastirma ve Plânlama Dairesi) 1971. *Göçebe ve Gezginci Nüfusun Uzun Vadeli Iskân Plânlamas)*, T.C., Köy Isleri Bakanligi: Toprak ve Iskân Isleri Genel Müdürlügü.

Anderson, Benedict 1983. *Imagined Communities: Reflections on the Origin and Spread of Nationalism*, London: Verson Editions and NLB.

Aydin, Zülküf 1980. 'Aspects of Rural Development in Southeastern Turkey: The Household Economy in Gisgis and Kalhana'. Durham: University of Durham, Dept. of Sociology and Social Policy, (Unpublished Ph.D. Dissertation).

Bacon, Elizabeth E. 1954. 'Types of Pastoral Nomadism in Central and South West Asia,' *South-Western Journal of Anthropology* (SWJA), Vol. 10,(1): 44-68.

Bajraktarevic, Fehim 1934. 'Yürüks', *Encyclopaedia of Islam*, Vol. 4 (S-Z): 1176-77.

Balaban, Ali 1986. 'Güneydogu Anadolu Projesi (GAP) Entegre Sistemi, Planlama ve Uygulama Sorunlari' in *GAP: Güneydogu Anadolu Projesi Tarimsal Kalkinma Simpozyumu, 18-21 Kasim 1986*, Ankara: TÜBITAK, Ankara Üniversitesi Ziraat Fakültesi, T.C. Ziraat Bankasi, Ankara Üniversitesi Basimevi: 1-17.

Barth, Fredrik 1961. *Nomads of South Persia: The Basseri Tribe of the Khamseh Confederacy*, Boston: Little, Brown & Company.

Bates, Daniel G. 1971. *Güney-Dogu Anadolu'da Göçebe Yörük Yerlesmeleri Üzerine Bir Çalisma (A Study on the Nomadic Yörük Settlements in South-East Anatolia)*, in *Türkiye: Cografî ve Sosyal Arastirmalar*, E. Tümertekin, F. Mansur, P. Benedict (eds.), Istanbul: I.Ü., E.F., Cografya Enstitüsü: 245-92.

Bates, Daniel G. 1972. 'Differential Access to Pasture in a Nomadic Society: The Yörük of Southeastern Turkey'. *Perspectives on Nomadism*, W. Ironsand N. Dyson-Hudson (eds.), Leiden: E.J. Brill: 48-59.

Bates, Daniel G. 1973a. 'Shepherd Becomes Farmer: A Study of Sedentarization and Social Change in Southeastern Turkey', in *Turkey: Social and Geographic Perspectives*, E. Tümertekin, F. Mansur, P. Benedict (eds.), Leiden: E.J. Brill: 92-133.

Bates, Daniel G.1973b. *Nomads and Farmers: A Study of the Yörük of Southeastern Turkey*, Ann Arbor: The University of Michigan, Museum of Anthropology, Anthropological Papers No.52.

Bayrak, Mehmet 1984. *Anadolu'da Eşkiyalik ve Eşkiyalik Türküleri* (Banditry and Banditry Songs in Anatolia), Ankara: Yorum.

Benedict, Peter 1973. *Ula: an Anatolian Town*. Leiden: E.J. Brill.

Bentley, G. Carter 1987. 'Ethnicity and Practice'. *Comparative Studies in Society and History: an international quarterly*, Cambridge, London, New York, Melbourne, Sydney: Cambridge University Press, Vol. 29,(1) January: 24-55.

Berktay, Halil 1983. *Kabileden Feodalizme*, (From Qabilah/Tribe to Feudalism), Istanbul: Kaynak Yayinlari.

Besikçi, Ismail 1969a. *Doguda Degisim ve Yapisal Sorunlar: Göçebe Alikan Asireti*, Ankara: Dogan Yayinlari.

Besikçi, Ismail 1969b. *Dogu Anadolusnun Düzeni, Sosyo-Ekonomik ve Etnik Temeller*, Ankara: E Yayinlari.

Boran, Behice Sadik 1945. *Toplumsal Yapi Arastirmalari: 'Iki Köy Çesidinin Mukayeseli Tetkiki'*, Ankara: Ankara Üniversitesi, D.T.C.F., Felsefe Enstitüsü, Sosyoloji Serisi: 3, T.T.K. Basimevi.

Brow, James 1990. 'Notes on Community, Hegemony, and the Uses of the Past'. *Anthropological Quarterly*, Vol. 63,(1): 1-6.

Cahen, Claude 1968. *Pre-Ottoman Turkey (A general survey of the material and spiritual culture and history c. 1071-1330*, Translated from the French by J. Jones-Williams, New York: Taplinger Publishing Company.

Çavdar, Tevfik 1984. *Talat Pasa: Bir Örgüt Ustasinin Yasam Öyküsü*, Ankara: Dost, Kitabevi Yayinlari.

Çetintürk, Salahaddin 1943. 'Osmanli Imparatorlugunda Yürük Sinifi ve Hukuki Statüleri'. *A.Ü., D.T.C.F. Dergisi*, Cilt 2(1): 107-116.

de Planhol, Xavier 1959. 'Geography, Politics, and Nomadism in Anatolia', *International Social Science Journal*, (UNESCO), Vol 11,(4): 525-31.

Demirtas, Faruk 1949. 'Bozulus Hakkinda' (On Bozulus), *A.Ü., D.T.C.F. Dergisi*, Vol. 7 (1): 29-60.

Dyson-Hudson, Rada and Neville Dyson-Hudson, 1980. 'Nomadic Pastoralism' (Review Article), *Annual Review of Anthropology*, Vol. 9: 15-61.

Eberhard, Wolfram 1967. 'Nomads and Farmers in South-Eastern Turkey: Problems of Settlement'. *Settlement and Social Change in Asia*, Hong Kong: Hong Kong University Press: 279-96.

Eberhard, Wolfram 1967. 'Types of Settlement in South-Eastern Turkey'. *Settlement and Social Change in Asia*, Hong Kong: Hong Kong University Press: 297-311.

Eberhard, Wolfram 1967. 'Changes in Leading Families in Southern Turkey'in *Settlement and Social Change in Asia*, Hong Kong: Hong Kong University Press: 312-22.

Engels, Frederick 1978, (1878). *Anti-Duhring*, Moscow: Progress Publishers.

Ergenç, Özer 1984. 'Osmanli sehrindeki 'Mahallesinin islev ve Nitelikleri Üzerine'. *Osmanli Arastirmalari IV*, (The Journal of Ottoman Studies IV), Istanbul: Enderun Kitabevi, Edebiyat Fakültesi Matbaasi: 69-78.

Erhan, Selahattin 1982. 'A Conceptual Historical and Political Evaluation of Nomadism in Anatolia: the Beritanli Case', (Unpublished Master's Thesis), Ankara: The Middle East Technical University.

Erhan, Selahattin 1989. 'Hem Kalaba Hem Göçebe, ya da Beritanli Hâlâ Göçüyor.' *Tarim Orman Köy (TOK)*, Tarim Orman ve Köyisleri Bakanligi Dergisi, Sayi 40: 50-53.

Erhan, Selahattin 1992. 'Identity Formation and Political Organization Among Anatolian Nomads: The Beritanli Case', (Unpublished Ph.D. Dissertation), Austin: University of Texas.

Erhan, Selahattin 1993. 'The Beritanli and National Politics: Settlement and New Identities', *The Turkish Studies Association Bulletin*, 17 (2). Fall, 57-67.

Firat, M. Serif, 1983,(1948). *Dogu Illeri ve Varto Tarihi* (The History of Eastern Provinces and Varto), Ankara: Kardes Matbaasi.

Gibbons, Herbert Adams 1968,(1916). *The Foundation of the Ottoman Empire*, London: Frank Cass & Co. Ltd.

Gökbilgin, M. Tayyib 1957. *Rumeli'de Yürükler, Tatarlar ve Evlâd-i Fâtihân* (Yürüks, Tatars and the Evlad-i Fatihan in Rumelia), Istanbul: I.Ü., E.F. Yayinlari, No.748.

Gökçen, Ibrahim 1946. *16. ve 17. Asir Sicillerine Göre Saruhan'da Yürük ve Türk-menler* (Yürüks and Turkmens in Saruhan According to the Registers of the 16th and 17th centuries), Istanbul: Manisa Halkevi Yyl., Sayi 16.

Gülöksüz, Güven, Feb. 1985. 'The Beritan Nomads over Time and the Problems of their Settlement', (Unpublished Ph.D. Dissertation), Ankara: The Middle East Technical University City and Regional Planning.

Halaçoglu, Yusuf 1988. *XVIII. Yüzyilda Osmanli Imparatorlugu'nun Iskân Siyaseti ve Asiretlerin Yerlestirilmesi*, Ankara: Atatürk Kültür, Dil ve Tarih Yüksek Kurumu, T.T.K. Yayinlari, 7. Dizi-Sa. 92.

Izady, Mehrdad 1988. 'A Kurdish Lingua Franca?'. *Kurdish Times*, Vol. 2, (2) Summer: 13-24.

Inalcik, Halil 1951. 'Osmanli Imparatorlugu'nun Kurulus ve Inkisafi Devrinde Türkiyesnin Iktisadî Vaziyeti Üzerinde Bir Tetkik Münasebetiyle'. *Belleten*, 15 (60): 629-684.

Johnston, Francis E., and Henry Selby 1978. *Anthropology: the Biocultural View*, Dubuque, Iowa: Wm. C. Brown Company Publishers.

Keyder, Çaglar 1981. *The Definition of Peripheral Economy: Turkey 1923-1929*, Cambridge, London, New York, New Rochelle, Melbourne, Sydney: Cambridge University Press, and Paris: Editions de la Maison des Sciences de l'Homme.

Khazanov, Anatoli M. 1984. *Nomads and the Outside World*, Cambridge London, New York, New Rochelle, Melbourne, Sydney: Cambridge University Press.

Kiliçbay, M. Ali 1982. *Feodalite ve Klasik Dönem Osmanli Üretim Tarzi*, Ankara: Gazi Universitesi Yyl., No.8.

Kodaman, Bayram 1979. 'Hamidiye Hafif Süvari Alaylari; II. Abdül Hamit ve Dogu Anadolu Asiretleri'. (Hamidian Cavalry Regiments: Abdul Hamid the Second and Tribes in Eastern Anatolia), *Tarih Dergisi*, 32: 427-481.

Kodaman, Bayram 1987. *Sultan II. Abdulhamid Devri Dogu Anadolu Politikasi*, Ankara: Türk Kültürünü Arastirma Enstitüsü Yayinlari, Sayi 67.

Köprülü, M. Fuad 1981,(1926). *Türk Edebiyati Tarihi*, (3. Basim), Istanbul: Ötüken Nesriyat A.S., Yayin Nu: 157, Kültür Serisi.

Köprülü, M. Fuad 1988. *Osmanli Imparatorlugunun Kurulusu*, Ankara: T.T.K. Basimevi.

Köroglu, Meral Özbek 1980. 'Beritanli Asireti ve Yerlestirme Modeli: Toplumsal ve Mekansal Örgütlenme', (Unpublished Master's Thesis), Ankara: Middle East Technical University.

Kutlu, M. Muhtar 1987. *Savakli Türkmenlerde Göçer Hayvancilik* (Nomadic Animal Breeding among the Savakli Türkmens), Ankara: Sevinç Basimevi, Kültür ve Turizm Bakanligi, Millî Folklor Arastirma Dairesi Yayinl., 84, Gelenek - Görenek ve Inançlar Dizisi.

Lindner, Rudi 1983. *Nomads and Ottomans in Medieval Anatolia*, Bloomington: Univ. of Indiana Press, Ural Altaic Studies.

Marco Polo (nd-1200s). *The Travels of Marco Polo*, New York: Books, Inc. The World's Popular Classics, (Art Type Edition).

Mohammad, Abbas 1973. 'The Nomadic and the Sedentary: Polar Complementaries — Not Polar Opposites'. Cynthia Nelson (ed.): *The Desert and the Town: Nomads in the Wider Society*, Berkeley: University of California, Institute of International Studies, No. 21: 97-113.

Mumcu, Ugur July 1991. 'Devletçilik ve Kürtler'. (Etatism and the Kurds), *Cumhuriyet*, 31 Temmuz.

Nelson, Cynthia (ed) 1973. *The Desert and the Sown: Nomads in the Wider Society*, Berkeley: University of California, Institute of International Studies, No. 21.

Nelson, Cynthia 1973. 'Preface'. Cynthia Nelson (ed): *The Desert and the Sown: Nomads in the Wider Society*, Berkeley: University of California, Institute of International Studies, No. 21: 5-6.

Nizam Al-Mulk 1960 (1095): *Siyasat-nama or Siyar al-Muluk* (The Book of Government or Rules for Kings), Trans. from Persian by Hubert Darke, London: Routledge and Kegan Paul.

Odo of Deuil 1948 (1148): *De Profectione Ludovici VII in orientem (The Journey of Louis VII to the East)*, Edited, with an Eng. translation, by Virginia Gingerick Berry), New York: W.W.Norton & Company.

Olson, Robert W. 1989. *The Emergence of Kurdish Nationalism and the Sheik Said Rebellion, 1880-1925*, Austin: University of Texas Press (1st Ed.).

Orhonlu, Cengiz 1987 (1963): *Osmanli Imparatorlugunda Asiretlerin Iskâni* (Settlement of Nomads in the Ottoman Empire), Istanbul: Eren Yayincilik ve Kitapçilik Ltd. Sti.

Otyam, Fikret 1978. *Karasevdam Anadolum*, Ankara: Türkiye Yazilari: 7-68.

Patai, Raphael 1978. 'The Culture Areas of the Middle East'. *The Nomadic Alternative: Modes and Models of Interaction in the African-Asian Deserts and Steppes*, Wolfgang Weissleder (ed.), Cambridge: Cambridge University Press: 9-27.

Refik, Ahmet 1930. *Anadolu'da Türk Asiretleri (966-1200)* (Turkish Tribes in Anatolia: 1650-1884), Istanbul: Devlet Matbaas.

Shaw, Stanford J. 1978. *History of the Ottoman Empire and Modern Turkey I: Empire of the Gazis — The Rise and Decline of the Ottoman Empire, 1280-1808*, Cambridge, London, New York, Melbourne: Cambridge University Press.

Shaw, Stanford J., Shaw, Ezel Kural 1978. *History of the Ottoman Empire and Modern Turkey II: Reform, Revolution and Republic - The Rise of Modern Turkey, 1808-1975*, Cambridge, London, New York, Melbourne: C.U.P.

Sümer, Faruk 1960. 'Anadolu'ya Yalniz Göçebe Türkler mi Geldi?'. (Did Only *Nomadic* Turks Come to Anatolia? / Was it Only the *Nomadic* Turks Who Came to Anatolia?), *Belleten*, 24 (96): 567-94.

Sümer, Faruk 1976a. *Safevî Devletinin Kurulusu ve Gelismesinde Anadolu Türkmenlerinin Rolü*, Ankara.

Sümer, Faruk 1976b. *Karakoyunlular* (The Qaraqoyunlus), Ankara: Türk Tarih Kurumu Yayinlari, T.T.K. Basimevi.

Sümer, Faruk 1980. *Oguzlar (Türkmenler): Tarihleri — Boy Teskilati — Destanlari* [The Oguz (The Turkmens): Their History — Organization — Mythologies], Istanbul: Ana Yayinlari.

Tezel, Yahya 1977. 'Anadoluda Toplumsal Kuruluslarin Eklemlesmesi Açisindan Osmanli-Osmanli Öncesi Iliski', *Toplum ve Bilim*, 3: 3-30.

Timur, Taner 1979. *Kurulus ve Yükselis Döneminde Osmanli Toplumsal Düzeni* (Ottoman Social System/Organization During its Foundation and Rise), Ankara: Turhan Kitabevi Yayinlari.

Timur, Taner 1986. *Osmanli Kimligi* (Ottoman Identity), Istanbul: Hil Yyl., Hil Arastirma Dizisi, 3.

Toynbee, Arnold J., and Kenneth P. Kirkwood 1926. *Turkey*, London: Ernest Benn Limited, (Vol. 6 of 'The Modern World: A Survey of Historical Forces' series).

Tütengil, Cavit Orhan 1969. *Türkiye'de Köy Sorunu* (The Village Problematic in Turkey), Istanbul: Kitapçilik Ticaret Limited Sirketi, Kitap Bilim Dizisi No. 3.

Uluçay, M. Çagatay 1955. *18. ve 19. Yüzyillarda Saruhan'da Eskiyalik ve Halk Hareketleri* (Banditry and Popular Movements in Saruhan in the 18th and 19th Centuries), Istanbul: Berksoy Basimevi.

Uzunçarsili, lsmail Hakki 1969. *Anadolu Beylikleri ve Ak Koyunlu Kara Koyunlu Devletleri* (Anatolian Principalities and the Ak Koyunlu (and) Kara Koyunlu States), Ankara: Türk Tarih Kurumu Yayinlari.

Waley, A. (Trans.) 1963. *The Secret History of the Mongols and Other Pieces*, London.

Wittek, Paul 1944. *Mentese Beyligi* (Menteshe Emirate), Ankara: Türk Tarih Kurumu Yayinlari, T.T.K. Basimevi.

Yalgin (Yalkin/Yalman), Ali Riza 1977. *Cenupta Türkmen Oymaklari*, 2 Vols., Ankara, Istanbul: T.C. Kültür Bakanligi Yayinlari, Kültür Eserleri, No.14, M.E.B. Basimevi.

The Assyrian Community in Turkey

Joseph Yacoub

Introduction

Assyrians, Chaldeans, Syriacs, Aramaics, Suriyan: in short Mesopotamians. All of them are recognized groups, names which evoke a distant past; legendary names which we associate with the origins of civilization: Ninive, Babylon, Aram...

People forgotten by history, spread over a number of lands in the Middle East (Turkey, Iraq, Iran, Syria, Lebanon, Caucasus), the Assyrian-Chaldean-Syriacs have never been spared from persecution or attacks on their fundamental rights since the fall of Ninive, of Babylon and of the Aramean kingdoms of Mesopotamia. The catalogue of the martyrdom of these people is a matter of record, consigned to the numerous documents which now stand as a challenge to humanity.

In the large massacres of 1915-18, during the days of the Ottoman Empire, more than half of the population perished.[1] Indeed, in the 1935 documents of the League of Nations, one can read that:

The years of war changed the face of the ancient world. They witnessed the unravelling of dynasties and empires; the people, who up until that time had been oppressed, rediscovered their old freedom and there was a resurgence of revolutionary systems of government. It is probable, however, that relative to its significance, no other group of people has suffered trials and tribulations on a scale comparable to the denomination and Church known as the Assyrians.[2]

In a similar vein, the Orientalist Basile Nikitine wrote:

Of all the non-sovereign peoples who took part in the Great War, only the Assyro-Chaldeans remain in the shadows. Very little is known of them, they are not regarded as being of interest. Yet if we compare their losses to their numbers, the disproportion

---

1. Joseph Yacoub, 1985. *Les Syriaques massacrés par les Turcs, Le génocide Syriaque de 1915*, Paris: Gamk.
2. League of Nations, 1935. *The Settlement of the Assyrians, a work of Humanity and Appeasement*, (foreword) Geneva.

is striking, and the Assyro-Chaldeans have the right to hope that it is something which will draw attention and guarantee them a better existence in compensation for their sufferings.[3]

Throughout the entire period between the two Great Wars, this community was an international affair, regularly appearing on the day's agenda at the League of Nations. In this respect one could cite Lord Curzon, Minister of Foreign Affairs in Britain, and General Gouraud, the French HighCommissioner in the Levant. The former declared, on January 9th, 1923, that: 'The Assyro-Chaldean group is of little importance, but with its race, its history, its religion and its suffering, it excites more interest in the world than any other community of similiar importance'.[4] In turn, General Gouraud declared in 1920 that: 'This Assyro-Chaldean nation, which fought alongside the Allies during the war, has acquired numerous claims on our affections by the beautiful qualities of bravery she showed and also by the sacrifices which she made'.[5]

Assimilation and the Loss of Culture

Today, the Assyro-Chaldeo-Syriacs of Turkey view their existence as being threatened. Today, as in former times, the pressure brought to bear upon them to assimilate is both severe and unrelenting.

The policy of Turkish-ization affects all aspects of life from the ethnic identity to patronymic names. At the religious level, their liberties are continuously compromised, and Islamic religious schooling — through the complicity of the state — is obligatory for Oriental Christians, except in Istanbul where the dioceses still function. Activities in the monastries are reduced and subject to the approval of the authorites. However, no new churches are allowed to be built. On the linguistic level the situation is even worse. In this respect, the authorities show a complete rejection of all languages with the exclusion, of course, of Turkish.

On the level of education and social affairs, the Assyro-Chaldeo-Syriacs are completely lacking: no schools, not even at the elementary level, nor any social institutions. They are forbidden to open any educational establishments.

The process of Turkish-ization is aided by the matter of patrynomic and topynomic names. All of the Assyro-Chaldeo-Syriac places of domicile are affected by this policy. Cultural and architectural works only remain as ruins and scenes of devastation; ritual sites are abandonned and depopulated and

3. Nikitine's article, 1921. 'Une petite nation victime de la guerre, Les Assyro-Chaldéans'. *Revue des sciences politiques*, Paris, October-December: 602.
4. Blue *Book from the Conference of Lausanne.* Paris, 1923: 293.
5. *L'Action asyro-chaldéenne*, Beyrouth, May 1920: 22.

monuments are in danger. The alienation which leads to their dispossession touches on the forenames and surnames of people. The situation is aggravated by regular attacks by armed individuals and by gangs, who not only take people's possessions and abduct young girls, but also regularly carry out assassinations. All of this creates a climate of fear; the hope being that this will encourage people to abandon their villages. This objective is unfortunately succeeding: the Syriacs are leaving Turkey in large numbers. All the evidence suggests that in ten years from now the Syriacs will have abandoned thier land, their ancestral home, carrying with them only memories.

The Hakkari and the Tour Abdin — the National Homelands.

Since 1975, the emigration and immigration of the Assyro-Chaldeo-Syriacs towards Occidental Europe has considerably increased. More than 100,000 people from rural areas have found refuge in France, Belgium, Germany, Holland, Sweden, Austria, Norway, Denmark and Switzerland.

It is estimated that at present there are less than 5,000 in Turkey, compared to half a million at the turn of the century during the days of the Ottoman Empire; their numbers have never ceased to diminish with the passing of the years.

On the eve of the First World War, 10,000 Assyro-Chaldeo-Syriacs lived in the mountainous Turkish province of Hakkari.[6] Half of them were to be wiped out during the massacres of 1915 and the other half were forced into exile. Today, only a tiny number of families live there, divided between four villages to the south-west of these enclosed highlands.

Hakkari is situated in the extreme south-western part of Turkey in an area that covers a rough total of 25,000 km² divided as follows: arid mountains, 10,000 km²; wooded mountains — 5,000 km²; arable land — 10,000 km². It was a Vilayet (province) between 1856 and March 1st, 1888 when it was combined with the Vilayet of Van. Since that date it has had the status of a Sandjak

---

6. For the physical, human, administrative and ecclesiastical geography of this region in connection with the Assyro-Chaldeans, see: Etienne-Marc Quatremère, *Histoire des Mongols*. Paris, 1836; Grattan Geary, *Through Asiatic Turkey, from Bombay to the Bosphorus*. London, 1878, Sampson, Vol. 2: 1-257; Vital Cuinet, 'La Turquie d'Asie, Géographie administrative, statistique descriptive et raisonnée de chaque province de l'Asie mineure', Paris, 1891, op.cit: 716-60, T.2; Basile Nikitine, 'Les Kurds et le christianisme, Revue de l'histoire des religions', *Annales du musée Guimet*, Paris, 1922, Vol. 85, Ernest Leroux (Ed.): 147-56; Basile Nikitine, 'Le système routier du Kurdistan (le pays entre les deux Zab)', *Géographie*. Paris, May-June 1930, Vol. 58: 363-85; the excellent article by Jean-Maurice Fiey, 'Proto-Histoire chrétienne du Hakkari turc, L'Orient Syrien', Paris, 1964, T.O. IX: 443-72; D.C. Hills, *My Travels in Turkey*. London, 1964: 147-80; Réd., Hakkari: *Encyclopedie de l'islam*. nouv. Ed. Leiden: Brill 1971, T.3: 85.

(administrative department), divided into 11 Cazas (municipalities), 49 Nahies (districts) and 1555 Communes.[7] It is dominated by an immense mountainous massif through which the main Zab river flows. Access is very difficult and the mountains reach a high altitude, with a summit at 4,170 metres. Life is very harsh. Schulz, the first European traveller to have attempted to traverse the Hakkari region (1829) perished there along with his entire team. The only conquerer to successfully traverse the range was the Assyrian king, Sargon the First in 714 BC. The first proper road through this country was completed in 1932.[8]

The Hakkari became a stake in the struggle between the European powers, the Russians and the Ottoman Turks, because of its strategic value. It was also the scene of rivalry between the Catholic, Protestant, Anglican and Orthodox missionaries who sought to convert the Assyro-Chaldeans[9].

The entire population of the Hakkari sandjak, spread over this vast territory, was estimated at the end of the 19th century to be 300,000 inhabitants with more than 97,000 Assyro-Chaldeans, 160,000 Kurds, 20,000 Turks, 15,000 Armenians, 400 Yezidis and 4,000 Israelites. The Assyro-Chaldeans were divided between the following ten cazas: Djoulamerk (15,000), Albaq (10,000), Gawar (9,300), Shemsdinan (3,000), Mahmoudi (1,000), Nourdouz (3,000), Tchal (31,960), Beit-ul-Chebab (6700), Oramar (11,040) et Amadia (6,000). Mamouret-el-Hamid was the only caza which did not have any Assyro-Chaldeans among its inhabitants.

The Assyro-Chaldean Nestorians had a patriarch, the Mar Shimoun, whose seat was in the village of Kotchanes (Djoulamerk caza) from 1671.[10] There was also an archbishop of equal authority in the village of Mar-Khananisho (Shemsdinan caza) and a bishop in Achita (Tchal caza). As far as the Assyro-

7. The Sandjak of Van contained a total of 1,000 Assyro-Chaldeans in 1880, 3,850 in 1913 as well as a bishop's palace in the town of Van, the county town of the Vilayet and Merkez-Sandjak (county town of the Sandjak). 16 villages situated in the region of Van were occupied by Assyro-Chaldeans.

8. Today the Hakkari has become a province (Vilayet) with Colemirk as the county town, situated 200 km south of Van. This is the most dispossesed region in Turkey.

9. Pierre Deplaissan, 1899. 'La politique russe aux frontièrs de la Transcaucasie', *Echos d'Orient*. Vol. 3: 108-18; and 1904, 'L'Eglise nestorienne en Turquie et en Perse'. *Echos d'Orient*. Vol. 7: 285-92.

10. 'The patriarchal residence is in Kotchanes, a small village situated 13 km north of Djulamerg, at the bottom of a dramatic gorge. On the eastern side a rocky peak of more than 10,000 metres which rises as an impassable barrier and an examination of the other three sides also show very rapid and steeply climbing slopes. The desolation and the mood of the place evokes the idea of a tomb in which the spiritual leader of the ancient nation of Assyrians is buried'. (Vital Cuinet, 1891, 'La Turquie d'Asie', Vol. 2, op. cit: 652.

Chaldean Catholics were concerned, they had two primary schools, financed and run by their church which were in the Gawar caza and attended by 50 pupils. In addition, there was a bishop in the town of Amadia, in the caza of the same name.[11]

In looking at each caza in turn, how did the distribution of the Assyro-Chaldeans look? Approximately 15,000 lived in the caza of Djoulamerk, in the mid-west of the Hakkari sandjak, out of a total population of 33,900 inhabitants (14,100 Kurds, 2,800 Turks and 2,000 Armenians). Djoulamerk, Merkez-caza (county town of the district) was inhabited exclusively by Kurds (3,000) and Turks (1,600). The population of the patriarchal village of Kotchanès (800) was made up entirely of Assyro-Chaldeans. In Albaq, out of a total population of 42,870 there were 10,000; the other groups were: Kurds (22,580), Turks (5,690), Armenians (3,000) and Israelites (1,600).

Roughly 9,300 Assyro-Chaldeans were settled in the Gawar caza, out of a group of 26,200 inhabitants (12,800 Kurds, 1,900 Turks, 1,900 Armenians and 300 Israelites). An Assyro-Chaldean Catholic priest was resident in the small town of Diza, county-town of the caza from 1,885 onwards; sent from the monastry at Alqoch in northern Iraq by the Chaldean patriarch to serve the villages of the district. He was responsible for two schools with a total of 25 pupils. The commune of Mar Bishou housed a very old church in memory of the Abbot Bishou who lived in the 5th century and who is buried in the village which bore his name.

Turning to the Assyro-Chaldeans of *Shemsdinan* caza or Naoutchia (known in ancient times as Roustaqa) in the south east of the sandjak, they numbered 3,000 out of a group of 18,470 inhabitants (13,270 Kurds, 2,000 Turks and 200 Israelites). The small town of Nehri, county town of the caza was inhabited exclusively by Kurds (2,200), Turks (500) and a few Israelites (200).

Almost all the villages of this caza had churches dating back to the earliest days of Christianity. There is documented evidence of the presence of Assyro-Chaldean missionaries in the region as far back as the 4th century. On this subject, the geographer, Vital Cuinet wrote: 'Christianity appears to have once flourished in these lands'.[12] All of the villages belonging to the Nahié of Koumaro have been abandoned following the pillage and devastation caused

---

11. On the traditional costumes of the Assyro-Chaldean highlanders of Hakkari, see: George Percy Badger, 1852. The Nestorians and their rituals, London: Joseph Masters, 2 Vol.; Asahel Grant, 1845, *The Nestorians or the lost tribes*. New York: 385; W.W. Wigram, 1929, *The Assyrians and their neighbours*. London: G.Bell and Sons: 247; Surma D'Bait Mar Shimun, *Assyrian church customs and the murder of Mar Shimun*; Joseph John, 1961, *The Nestorians and their muslin neighbours*, a study of western influence in their relations, Princeton, N.J.: Princeton University Press.

12. Vital Cuinet, 1891. La Turquie d'Asie. Vol. 2: 745.

by the Kurds. The village of Déra Rech (Roustaka) was the residence of the Metropolitan Assyro-Chaldean Nestorian, Mar Khananichou. In the market town of Saté there is a very old church, famous for its door which is carved from a single bough of old vine. In the region of Ouchnou, to the east of Shemsdinan, on the Persian side of the frontier, the Christian remains testify to the existence of a very long history. In this respect the actual names of many of these villages carries a story: Bim Sourta (little altar), Nalos, Denkha, Ziaret (place of pilgrimage), called Cheikh Ibrahim by the Kurds, the name of the Assyro-Chaldean bishop Oraham; in the 13th century his episcopal chair was in Ouchnou and this tomb was also a popular pilgrimmage site. Likewise, it is worth noting that to the east of Ouchnou there lies an old Assyro-Chaldean cemetery known by the Kurdish name of Kabri Fala.

The Assyro-Chaldeans of the 'Mahmoudi' caza, situated in the north of the Sandjak, numbered 1,000 out of a total population of 31,680; (23,200 Kurds, 2,500 Armenians, 2,500 Yézidis and 2,480 Turks). The county town, Sérai, a market-town composed of around a hundred houses is to all practical intents and purposes occupied by Assyro-Chaldeans; the 2,000 Turks who are resident there are soldiers, customs officers, and sanitation workers — as well as functionaries living outside the town. In the town there is a Nestorian Assyro-Chaldean church.

In the north-west of the Sandjak, in the caza of 'Nordouz', there were 3,000 Assyro-Chaldeans, out of a total of 17,600 inhabitants; (11,000 Kurds, 2,600 Armenians, 1,000 Turks).

The county town of the caza 'Marané', is a small village of 400 inhabitants, all Assyro-Chaldean, apart from the odd Turkish government employee.

The caza of 'Tchal', situated in the east of the Sandjak, was secure in the sense that there were 31,960 Assyro-Chaldeans out of a population of 43,890 inhabitants; (11,090 Kurds and 840 Turks). The county town Tchal was a market town situated on a small tributary of the main river Zab. It contains a number of Assyro-Chaldean villages but is only inhabited by Kurds (800), Turks (200) and Israelites (200). As for the small, renowned village of Achita, all of its 6,000 inhabitants were Assyro-Chaldeans. The church of Mar Sawa is near Achita and was one of the episcopal residences and also one of the most famous Hakkari sanctuaries.

The eighth caza inhabited by Assyro-Chaldeans is that of 'Beit ul-Chébab' where there were around 6,700 out of a total of 18,700, (11,100 Kurds and 900 Turks). This caza is in the southwest of the sandjak. The Assyro-Chaldeans of this municipality were distributed between several nahiés (Pérouzan, Zirki, Mamoukran, Kewran...) all in the mountains. While in Elki, the county - town of the caza, the entire population (600 inhabitants) was composed of Assyro-

Chaldeans. The village of Proze was also made up of 500 homes, all Assyro-Chaldean.

At the centre of the Sandjak, the caza of 'Oramar' included 11,040 Assyro-Chaldeans out of a population of 15,040 inhabitants; (3,000 Kurds). A very old church in Oramar dates back to the end of the 4th century. Out of the 40 Assyro-Chaldean residences in the town of Oramar 11,000 Assyro-Chaldeans were distributed between the 32 villages of the Caza. The region of Oramar is dotted with very old churches such as Mari Mam, on the Roubary Chine, a tributary of the Zab. There is no more than a single family of Assyro-Chaldeans there, responsible for the upkeep of the church. There are two sanctuaries of recognized importance; Mar Zayia (because of the regular pilgrimmage to Mata) and Ma Bichou. In 1920, these churches were still intact, despite being repeatedly looted of manuscripts, cloth, bells, and other souvenirs removed during the war with the Kurds.

There were also items of Chinese porcelain brought back by from the Far East by Assyro-Chaldean missionaries. Basile Nikitine, Orientalist and former Russian consul in Ourmiah visited the region in September 1917. Nikitine tells of how, after the church of May Zayia was looted, a young Kurdish chief came to the door and surveyed his band carrying off the plunder. He writes: 'Soon all the Christian churches in the country will be lost in this way!'.

Aside from the sanctuaries of Mar Zayia and Mar Bichou, there were other churches which now exist only as memories: Mar Chimoun Bar Saba, in whose place the Kurdish Agha constructed his summer residence. Mar Guiwarguis in Beit Glal, known by the name of Khananiss, which when restored in the 6th century became even more famous as the domicile of Mar Guiwarguis the First (661-680), the Catholic patriarch; Mar Kourakios; Mar Odisho.[13] Mar Mariam; Mar Shalita; the church of the village Déra Banyié and Mar Talya in the valley of Tal (6th century).

Within the many layers of the Hakkari population, the Assyro-Chaldeans come second after the Kurds, who make up the majority of the inhabitants of the Sandjak. This land was furiously contested and finally confirmed as Turkish territory on December 16th, 1925, in a decision by the Council of the League of Nations — despite the fact that, at the time, the Turks made up no more than 6 percent of the population.

Several months before this decision was taken, a new massacre ensued following displacements to the Turkish interior, with the intention of encouraging dozens of Assyro-Chaldean families to abandon the territory.

This depopulation has continued since 1915. In 1985 there were no more than 450 Assyro-Chaldeans, out of a total of around 55,000 inhabitants, (the

---

13. The best known Hakkari sanctuary.

major part of whom were Kurds), still living in Hakkari in the caza of Beit-ul-Chébab, in the south-west of the country between the villages of Meer and Gasnakh. There is much to suggest that this haemorrage will persist and that in less than five years the anaemia will have finished off the febrile body. By June 1994, the village of Meer-Kovenkaya had already 'given up the ghost'.

Aside from this, in 1914 this country counted 223 Assyro-Chalden churches spread over 6 diocese and 10 districts, all of which fell directly under the jurisdiction of the Nestorian Patriarch Mar Shimoun.

If the Hakkari Assyro-Chaldean Christians have ceased to exist, it is due to Turkish, Kurdish, and Iranian intolerance, to the aridity of the land, to the harshness of the life, to the opprerssion of the Kurdish Agha's and the consequences of the Kurdish rebellion.

The Road to Exile

Over quite a number of years the news from Turkey has been alarming. This has in turn increased the massive exodus of Assyro-Chaldeans from the south and south-west of the country towards Europe,[14] fleeing from persecution by the Kurds and the Turks.

This mass departure began in 1975 and affects the provinces of Hakkari, Bohtan, Séert, Midyat, Dyiarbékir, Mardin, Tour Abdin, Ourfa and the Silop district.[15]

In 1995 the Assyro-Chaldeans were represented by no more than 5,000 people in the whole of Turkey. In time these people have fled their ancestral homelands, firstly towards Iran and Iraq and later to Lebanon, Occidental Europe and the United States. A large part of the population of Adana, Urfa, Diyarbékir, Mardin, Midyat now live in refuge in Syria, notably in the High Gezira (Hassaké, Kaméchlié, Amouda, Ras-el-Äin) and in Aleppo. The rest were massacred in 1915 and between 1923-27.

So, where are they today? The south-east region of Turkey shows progressive signs that a population of Assyro-Chaldéans is steadily establishing itself in Europe (France, Belgium, the Basque country, Germany, Austria,

---

14. Joseph Yacoub, 1987. 'Oubliés de l'histoire, les réfugiés Assyro-Chaldéens', *La Croix*, Jan. 14, Paris; J-P. Péroncel-Hugoz, 1990. 'Turquie: meurtres, discriminations, embrigadement religieux, la minorité chrétienne syriaque est victime de persécutions en Anatolie'. *Le Monde*, July 4; 'Menacés de disparition, l'appel à l'aide des chrétiens du sud-est de la Turquie', *La Croix*, Jan. 10, 1991.
15. The two following reports: *Les Araméens, chrétiens de Turquie, Comité de soutien aux réfugiés de Turquie en Belgique*, Bruxelles, January 1986; Antun Gôral, *Rapport sur les causes de l'émigration des chrétiens assyro-chaldéens du sud-est de la Turquie en Europe.* Södertälje (Suède), April 23, 1986, 23 p.

Sweden, Denmark) where, on the whole, people are managing to gain political refugee status.[16]

Certain details merit further attention.

The Population of Hakkari

The Assyro-Chaldeans of this region originally come from five villages: Baxyan, Ischy, Gasnakh, Meer and Oz.[17]

The 550 inhabitants of Bazyan abandonned their village. The massive exodus took place during a period of six months in 1984. Deserted of its population, the Baznay are now refugees in France. Some Baznay families have settled in Istanbul.

Ischy has suffered a similar fate. Settled today in the Val d'Oise and in Seine-Saint-Denis, there are no more than eight families left in the country, without passports and waiting to be allowed to settle in France. In June 1913 there were 200 Assyro-Chaldean families in the village, as well as a church and a priest. Today the church of Mar Yosep, is very old, and still standing, but in a general state of decay.

The same is true of Gasnakh, where two-thirds of the inhabitants are now

16. Luc Adrian, 1982. 'Venus d'Orient, les Chaldéens, Famille chrétienne', *Paris* No. 220, April 1: 26-30; Charles Sureau, 1984: 'Aller sans retour, Peuples du monde', *Paris* No. 178, December: 34-36; Sâdik Tanik, 1984. 'L'éxode des chrétiens Turcs', *La Croix* Dec. 11; Marlène Tuininga, 1984. 'Ces Turcs qui parlent la Langue du Christ', *L'Actualité religeuse*, November; Xavier Jacob, 1985. 'De la Mésopotamie à Paris: les Chaldéens, L'Assomption et ses oeuvres', *Paris*, No. 622, été: 20-22; 'Assyrians flee Turkey for safe havens', *The Assyrian Sentinel*, Hartford, No. 1, Feb. 1980: 1.

17. The names of Assyro-Chaldean villages have been changed into 'Turkish' ones. Here are a few examples of this:

Assyro Chaldean name	*Turkish name*
Harbol	Aksu
Betspen	Gurumlu
Bazyan	Dogan
Ischy	Ombudak
Gasnakh	Cevisagac
Meer	Kovankaya
Hoz	Ayirim

In May 1986, the Turkish Ministy of the Interior ordinated a new Turkish-ization of village names: 12,861 out of 34,957 communes were re-named. 80.65 percent of the villages in southwest Anatolia have been given Turkish names in this way. It has also been shown that the patronymic names of Assyro-Chaldeans underwent the same process of Turkish-ization in the 1930s. Are these not attempts at cultural annihilation?

living in France, Belgium, the USA and Germany. The other third (23 families) will shortly follow suit. The village of Meer has also not escaped this phenomenon of flight. The exodus which began in 1980 was accelerated in 1982; 700 people settled in Sarcelles, 500 in Clichy-sous-bois and 100 in Montlucon. Prior to the exodus, there were 90 families (1,000 people) living in the village. It had two Chaldean churches. 1980 saw the start of the steady progression into flight or exodus of 60 families (600 people) in the direction of Istanbul, France, Germany and Sweden. Of the Assyro-Chaldean families living in the village, thirty-five families were counted in 1986. In June 1994, however, there were none remaining; because of the circumstances, they had been forced to join their relatives in the diaspora.

In Oz only five people remain, all the others have fled and live either in France or Belgium.[18] In 1913 this village contained 500 Assyro-Chaldeans, a church, a priest and a school.

A Bohtan Without a Spirit

In the district of Silopi and Bohtan, there are ten Assyro-Chaldean villages: Harbol, Betspen, Hassana, Upper-Déran, Lower-Déran. Cenet, Azakh, Shakh, Mansouriah and Berhinci. In 1850, this region numbered 2,200 Assyro-Chaldeans, distributed between 22 villages. The village of Djeziret-Ibn-Omar counted 60 as well as a church and two priests; Faishkhabour also had 60 families, one church and two priests; Taikann had 15 families, one church, one priest; Guiguébadro had 12 families, one church; Tell-Kebbin had 10 families, one church, one priest; Beidar had 14 families and a church.

In 1918 Bohtan was home to some 2,760 Assyro-Chaldeans of which there were 420 in Hassana, 360 in Mansouriah, 60 in Mar Youkhanna, 180 in Shakh, 360 in Tilkuba, 960 in Djéziret-Ibn-Omar, 180 in Mar Akha, 140 in Azakh, 300 in Harbol and 160 in various other villages.

The most important site in the region is Harbol. Situated between two mountains and rich in coal deposits, it was entirely Assyro-Chaldean. It lies 8 km from the Iraqi border and is often caught up in Turkish military incursions into Iraqi territory in the pursuit of militant Kurds. Approximately 1,500 inhabitants out of a village of 1,800 people are now living in refuge in France,[19] Belgium and Germany, where they have been since 1980 because of Kurdish persecution. Today, the village is completely deserted.

The other villages of Bohtan have not been able to avoid the inescapable law of forced emigration. The history of the Assyro-Chaldeans in the village

18. In August 1986 there was not a single Assyro-Chaldean in the village.
19. There are 437 living in France.

of Betspen is peppered with violations, executions and suffering of every kind. Betspen is 10 km from Harbol and is a mixed Kurdo-Assyro-Chaldean village. Roughly 500 Assyro-Chaldeans (out of 544) were forced to abandon their land, their homes and their property. Starting in 1977 with Istanbul as their destination, the exodus escalated considerably in 1980, to the point where there are now no more that 30 Assyro-Chaldeans in the village. The others now live in Istanbul, France and Belgium.

As for the inhabitants of Hassana, they have found refuge in France, Belgium, the Basque country, Sweden and in Germany. The Assyro-Chaldeans of this village, like those of Azakh (300 inhabitants) and of Mansouriah (100 inhabitants), were the victims of a general massacre in 1915. They suffered tremendously from the pillage and maltreatment inflicted upon them by the Kurds and the Turks.

As for the region of Séert, there are none any longer living in that region when not long ago there was a flourishing Assyro Chaldean population. In 1913 they numbered 5,480. In 1928, prior to the Turco-Kurdish massacres, there were no more than 1,600 persons in all 36 villages and in the village of Séert itself. At present this region is deserted. Three villages (Dentas, Piroze and Hartvin) survived until 1968. But the inhabitants had to flee to Midayat (1968-72) and then later to Istanbul (1972-79). In 1980 they had come to settle in France. Other families stayed in Turkey, in Mersin, close to their own villages.

It is the same story in other parts of Turkey inhabited by Syrian Christians. As an indicative marker we can take the deserted country, the Tour Abdin (Mountain of the Believers). This has gradually emptied over a number of years and from 1970-76 all the inhabitants of the village of Kerbornan have found refuge in Sweden, in Germany and in Belgium.[20]

The Assyro-Chaldeans in France: The Hakkari in Sarcelles

The first people to come from these regions arrived in France on February 4th, 1974. They came as immigrant workers, under contracts of employment; all

---

20. For the cultural heritage of the Tour Abdin, see: Helga Anshüaetz: 1985. *Die syrischen Christen von Tur 'Abdin, Eine altchristliche Bevölkerungsgruppe zwischen Beharrung, Stagnation und Auflösung*, Würzburg: Augustinus-Verlag. Gabriel Aydin, 1984. *Deyr 'Ulzafaran, Antakya Süryani Ortodoks Kilesesi Eski Patriarhane Merkezi (in Turkey and occidental Syria)*, Holland: St. Ephrem Kloster, Glane/Losser, Bar-Hebraeus Verlag; Henno Suleyman, 1984, 1987. *Schicksalschläge der Syrischen Christen im Tur Abdin, 1915*, Holland: St. Ephrem Kloster, Glane/Losser, Bar-Hebraeus Verlag; Youssef Gibraiil al-Kass and Dr Elias Hadaya, Azakh, 1991, *Événements et hommes*, in Arabic, Alep, Ed. Ourhaï; *Ethnic cleansing in the Tour Abdin*, Jan. 1995, in Arabic, The Administrative Council of the Union of Syrian Association, Bahro Suryoyo, Södertälje. Sweden.

from the village of Bazyan (Hakkari). However, the first Assyro-Chaldeans to
obtain the right to asylum and refugee status dates only as far as 1978. At the
time, the concession of status was not eased by the fact that this community
has been entirely ignored.[21] With time, things have evolved in a, relatively
speaking, very positive sense.

At present, this community is better known and is generally well received
in France and by the French. Following the military coup d'etat on September
12th, 1980, the Assyro-Chaldeans had no choice but to flee *en masse* to the
Occident. Approximately 15,000 settled in France, the majority of whom
obtained the status of refugees. Some settled in L'Allier (Montlucon), L'Ain
(Miribel), Mont de Marsan (La Gironde), St-Pierre-Le Môutier (La Nièvre),
Liomoges (Haute Vienne), Laon (L'Aisne), Les Alpes de Haute Provence
(Limans), Le Rhône (Lyon, Villeurbanne, Bron, Vaux-En-Velin), Le Cantal (St-
Flour), Les Bouches du Rhône (Marseille), Les Alpes-Maritime (Nice), and La
Haute-Garonne (Toulouse, St-Jory); The greatest number are to be found
concentrated in the northern suburbs of Paris.[22]

Today, in the municipalities of the Paris region, the Assyro-Chaldean
community numbers around 8,000 individuals in possession of a political
refugee card. Numerous agricultural initiatives exist as projects to assist this
community, most notably in the Cantal area, but all have failed. Perhaps as
a result of their distribution and out of a fear of losing their identity and of
becoming cut off from their roots,these refugees prefer to stay together and
prefer to take work in the factories of Paris so as to be close to their fellow
countrymen.

In France, the Assyro-Chaldeans do not face great problems of introduction
or integration. At the same time, however, they wish to preserve their cultural
individuality and their ethnic, linguistic and religious[23] heritage. Now, the
maintenence of one's original culture in a country such as France, which is very
uniform, homogenized and assimilationist, is not without problems. The
Assyro-Chaldeans are very aware of this. Also, their community is searching

21. Joseph Yacoub, 1988. 'La communauté assyro-chaldéenne en France.' *Acceueilir* SSAE,
    Paris, No. 154, Dec: 10-13.
22. Hervé Viellard-Baron, 1991, 'Antillais, Magrébins, et Turcs chaldéens à l'epreuve de
    l'exil: l'exemple de Sarcelles'. Migrants Formation No. 86; and 'Sarcelles,
    L'enracinement des disaporas sépharde et chaldéenne'. *Disaporas*, GIP Reclus,
    Montpellier, 1995: 68-89.
23. Claudine Vermauwt, 1989, the integration of Assyro-Chaldeans in France, *L'insertion
    des réfugiés assyro-chaldéens de la région parisienne.* Université René Descartes Paris V,
    mémoire de DEASS; Frédéric Fourny, 1992, *Les Assyro-Chaldéens refugiés de Turquie,
    deux conceptions de leur insertion.* Mémoire de DEASS, Ecole de la Croix Rouge
    Francaise, Lyon; Morgan Le Coz, 1995, *La communauté assyro-chaldéenne de Toulouse.*
    Mémoire, Institut d'Etudes politiques de Toulouse, 120 p.

for itself and its religious and social responsibilities in such a way that it can insert itself and be integrated into French society without losing its character and without being completely dissolved in the dominant melting-pot. As well as the Association of Assyro-Chaldean Solidarity, a new organization exists today, based in Sarcelles; the Association of the Assyro-Chaldeans of France (AACF). This was initiated by Pétrus Karatay, of Turkish origin, known to his compatriots as 'Rayes' (president), because of his devotion. An ethnic trilingual (French-Aramaic-Turkish) biannual bulletin has been published since February 1994. It is entitled 'Hammurabai' (since January 1995), the name of the illustrious Babylonian king who reigned two thousand years before Christ. Its objective is 'To ensure the perenniality and development of Assyro-Chaldean culture for the sake of the Assyro-Chaldean community in France, and to encourage the maintenance of its cultural identity while at the same time seeking to introduce some of its members into French social life'.

The Assyro Chaldean Association has, since 1987, represented the community and contributed to maintaining a landmark of identity. Committed to the preservation of the community throught the generation of a broad fabric of initiatives and through the development of a network of solidarity and assistance. Their work has been eased and assisted by the geographic locations of the communities (village and regional) and through a system of merits and representation which is fairly analogous. With the risk of anonymity and isolation of its members in mind, it has formed firm bonds within the community; proposing socio-cultural, educational, sports, folklore and leisure activities. It helps the disadvantaged in legal and administrative matters and is an instrument of cohesion in the community, acting in tandem and partnership with the public authorities. It provides a number of courses; in religious education for a community strongly affected by religious belief;[24] as well as beginning and advanced courses in the Aramaic language which take place twice a week for adults and for children. The AACF periodically stages conferences on Assyro-Chaldean history and culture, as well as holding folklore evenings in which the most famous singers from the disapora community perform. On a recent occasion, trips to the United States or Australia were offered as a lively addition to the proceedings.[25] The AACF is an important part of the promotion of their identity. Their integration is most particularly wished for and is facilitated by their not being in contention with the rules of France, nor in any way in conflict, but is accentuated by their being in

24. On the pastoral question as faced by the Assyro-Chaldean community in France, see: Thérèse Turpin, 1988, 'Les Chaldéens: Questions pastorales'. in: *Venus de Turquie*. Cahiers de la Pastorale des migrants, Paris, special edition, 31,1: 94-7.
25. Hammurabi, September 1995, No. 8, Sarcelles: 10.

cultural and religious proximity with it, and by reasons of attraction which this country exerts on them. Without any doubt, these factors favour their integration. Religion, which could be a hinderance, as could the consolidation of their identity, are instead negligible factors and generate affinity with the host country.

It is likely that all such activities will grow over the next dozen years[26] and the same is expected to be the case in places other than Paris, such as Lyon, Marseille, Toulouse and Bordeaux.

The Assyro-Chaldean Community in Sweden: From Tour Abdin to Södertalje

There are around 35,000 Assyro-Chaldeans living in Sweden; 15,000 have acquired Swedish nationality. Nowadays, due to the flood of minority immigrants from the Middle East, Swedish researchers, sociologists and anthropologists have taken an interest in this community. The Swedish Research Commission on Immigration (EIFO), and the Institute of Social Anthropological Studies at the University of Stockholm have published a number of works, notably, *North to Another Country, the Formation of a Suryoyo Community in Sweden* by Ulf Björkland which appeared in 1981. This examines the Syrian Turkish immigrants from the sociological angle.[27] In this country, in Södertalje, there is also an important quadrilingual (Oriental and Occidental Aramaic, Arabic, Turkish and Swedish), monthly review 'Hujada' (Union) published by the Federation of Assyrian Association (Assyriska Riksförbundet i Sverige). The review has been in existence since 1978 and has without doubt had an immeasurable impact in terms of community bonds within the diaspora at the global level. The monthly publication *Bahro Suryoyo (The Light of Syria)* represents another trend, which is the Syrian association (Syrianska Riksförbundet i Sverige), and also deserves mentioning.

Recognized by the Swedish public authorities as mediators and partners, these associations continue to contribute to the improved integration of these immigrants into the Swedish melting-pot. At the same time they maintain the

26. On the Assyro-Chaldeans in France, see: Joseph Yacoub, 'Les assyro-Chaldéens: une minorité en voie d'émergence?' art. cit: 371-73; *Les réfugiés assyro-chaldéens de Turquie.* Forcalquier: CEDRI, 1986; *La Turquie et les Assyro-Chaldéens, nationalisme intégral et négation des minorités,* colloque Chrétiens du sud-est de la Turquie, Bruxelles, March 1991; *Ils seront des Chaldéens de France.* numéro spécial de la Pastorale des migrants, Paris, Service national de la pastorale des migrants, No. 43,2, 1991.

27. Ulf Björkland, 1981, *North to another country, the formation of a Suryoyo community in Sweden.* University of Stockholm, Department of Social Anthropology, and Swedish Commission on Immigration Research; Stefan Andersson, 1983, *Assyrerna. Wn bok om präster och lekmän, om politik och diplomati omkring den assyriska invandring til Sverige.* Stockholm: Tiden Förlag.

pure community characteristics which are necessary for the equilibrium and survival of its population. Without a doubt, the fact that these publications are issued in a country which, compared to the rest of the world, is very strong on communal social affairs, and actively promotes relations of such a nature is a great advantage; to the point where they benefit from a large distribution throughout the world, over and above their own community.

Germany

The same is the case in Germany, where the *Gesellschaft für bedrohte Völker* has, over the last twelve years or more, undertaken the task of alerting world opinion to the dangers which threaten ethnic communities in the Middle East. The periodical 'Pogrom' is filled with articles on the massacres of 1915-18, and the repression which has occurred since then. In 1978, Gabreiele Yonan, academic and militant involved in this association, published a book documenting the contemporary history of the Assyrians *Assyrer heute*, which is interesting in a number of regards.[28]

Belgium

Concerning the Assyro-Chaldeans of Belgium, the majority live in the Brussels region and have a number of dynamic associations of the kind which have on numerous occasions drawn the attention of the authorities, of social and humanitarian institutions as well as the Belgian press. In particular, mention is deserved of the important and prolific work carried out by the association: 'Droits de l'homme sans frontières', conducted by Willy Fautré.[29] This organization held a press conference in June 1994 at the Houses of Parliament in Brussels, under the presidency of Willy Kuijpers, to highlight the dramatic situation of the Assyrian minority in the Middle East.[30]

28. Gabriele Yonan, 1978, *Assyrer Heute, kultur, sprache, nationalbewegung der aramäisch sprechenden christen im nahen osten*, Hamburg and Vienna: Reihe Pogrom.

29. Natcha David, 1994, 'Turquie: l'exil des chrétiens d'orient', Ils rêvent d'avoir leur Elio di Rupo, venus du sud-est de la Turquie, les chrétiens sont près de 10,000 à Bruxelles, où ils forment une communauté quie veut s'intégrer. *Tendence, Entreprende*, October 3rd, Brussels: 61-63.

30. 'Turquie, les Assyriens, un peuple en voie d'extinction, dossier', *Droits de l'homme sans frontières* Nov.-Dec. 1992: 2-10; 'Les Assyriens, un peuple persécuté', *Droits de l'homme sans Frontiéres* leur consacre un numéro, *La Libre Belgique* Feb. 9th, 1993; 'Heurs et malheurs de la minorité assyrienne au Proche-Orient et en Belgique dossier', *Droits de l'homme sans frontières*, the Assyrian Democratic Organisation (ADO), Brussels.

Conclusion

What conclusions can we draw from all which has taken place in the south-eastern provinces of Turkey? If finally abandoned by Assyro-Chaldeans, whose present situation is so acute that there are no more than 500 poor souls haunted by the fear of persecution[31] awaiting permission to join their relatives in the countries of the diaspora.

Dispossessed of their ancestral lands and uprooted, without hope of return, those Assyro-Chaldeans still left in their country of origin will from now on be facing the inevitable prospect of migration to join the diaspora community which is desperately seeking to be integrated into the countries of Europe, while at the same time trying to maintain certain significant traits and marks of identity.

Poised as we are at the juncture of two eras, destabilized by having to deal with the radical changes of exile,becoming a compartmentalized society, changing from being a very traditional society to an urban one, being abruptly thrust into the modern world, and respecting the social rules of the host country, only time will tell whether the next generation will be able to retain its identity, to resist complete acculturation, the temptations of assimilation and the dangers of homogenization.

Bibliography

Blue Book 1916. *The treatment of Armenians in the Ottoman Empire*, Arnold Joseph Toynbee ed., London: Hooder and Soughton.

Chevallier, Michel 1985. *Les montagnards chétiens du Hakkari et du Kurdistan septentrional,* Paris: Publications du Départment de Géographie de L'université de Paris-Sorbonne, No. 13.

Cuinet, Vital 1891. *La Turquie d'Asie*, Paris: Ernest Leroux, 1890-1894, Vol. 4. II.

Fiey, Jean-Maurice 1964. 'Proto-histoire chrétienne du Hakkari turc, L'Orient Syrien', Paris: tome IX: 443-72.

Grant, Asahel 1841. *The Nestorians or the Lost Tribes*, London: John Murray.

Griselle, Eugène 1841. *Syriens et Chaldéens 1914-1917, leurs martyres*, London: John Murray.

Griselle, Eugène 1917. *Syriens et Chaldéens 1914-1917, Leurs martyres, leurs espérances*, Paris: Bloud et Gay.

---

31. 'Turquie, entre les islamistes et la guerre du Kurdistan', *L'Eglise en détresse dans le monde, faits et témoignage*, No. 84, Oct.-Nov.-Dec. 1994, Mareil-Marly: 90-94.

Heazel, F. N. 1934. *The woes of a distressed nation: being an account of the Assyrian people from 1914 to 1934,* London: Faith Press.

Joseph, John 1961. *The Nestorians and their Muslim Neighbours,* Princeton, NJ: Princeton University Press.

Magie, David 1918. *Report on the Assyrian christians,* Washington: National Archives of The United States.

Naayem, Joseph 1920. *Les Assyro-Chaldéens et les Arméniens massacrés parles Turcs,* Paris: Bloud et Gay; trad. English,' Shall this nation die'?, New York: Chaldéan Rescue.

Nikitine, Basile 1921. 'Une petite nation victime de la guerre: Les Chaldéens', *Revue des Sciences politiques,* Paris, Félix Alcan, tome XLIV: 602-25.

Nikitine, Basile 1933. 'Le problème assyrien', *Bulletin de L'Academie diplomatique internationale.* Paris, No. 4: 225-40.

Nikitine, Basile 1937. 'Assyriens (La question des)', *Séances et Travaux de L'Académie diplomatique internationale,* Paris, No. 11., vol. III: 33-44.

Rockwell, William Walker 1916. *The pitiful plight of the Assyrian Christians in Persia and Kurdistan,* New York: American Commitee for Armenian and Syrian relief.

Roux, George 1985. *La Mésopotamie,* Paris: L'univers historique.

Wigram, W.A. and Edgar T. A. *The Cradle of Mankind: Life in Eastern Kurdistan,* London: A. & C. Black.

Yacoub, Joseph 1986. *The Assyrian Question, Chicago: Alpha Graphic,* réédité en 1993, traduit en turc (suède).

Yacoub, Joseph 1988. *Un peuple oublié de L'histoire,* Paris: Groupement pour les droits des minorités, traduit en suédois.

Yacoub, Joseph 1986. *Les réfugiés assyro-chaldéens de Turquie,* CEDRI: Forgualquier.

Yacoub, Joseph 1988. 'Les Assyro-Chaldéens d'aujourd'hui', dans: *L'Afrique et L'Asie modernes,* No. 151, Paris: CHEAM, Winter.

Yacoub, Joseph 1988. 'La question assyro-chaldéenne', dans: *Guerres mondiales et conflicts contemporains,* Paris: FEDN, PUF, No. 151, July.

Yacoub, Joseph 1990. 'Les Assyro-Chaldéens, une minorité en voie d'émergence?', dans: *Etudes internationales,* Université Laval, Québec, Canada, June.

Yacoub, Joseph 1991. 'Les Assyro-Chaldéens, les derniers chrétiens syriaques de Turquie et d'Irak', dans: *Balkans,* Paris, No. 9, March.

Yacoub, Joseph 1994. 'Les Assyro-Chaldéens, une minorité dispersée', dans: *Hommes et Migrations,* Paris, January-February: 37-41.

Yacoub, Joseph 1995. 'La diaspora assyro-chaldéenne', dans: *Diasporas,* Michel Bruneau (ed.), Montpellier: Réclus: 55-67.

Yacoub, Joseph 1995. *Les minorités, quelle protection?*, Paris: Desclée de Brouwer, May.

Yacoub, Joseph 1996. *Babylone chrétienne. Géopolitique de l'Eglise de Mésopotamie*, Paris: Desclée de Brouwer, April.

Yohanann, Abraham 1916. *The death of a nation or the ever persecuted Nestorians or Assyrian Christians*, New York and London: Putnam.

The Construction of the Turkish Republic and Citizenship

Mümtaz Soysal

The Middle East is perhaps the most complex corner of the world. It is the cradle of the oldest civilizations, and of the main monotheistic religions. It is also an area where many ethnic groups exist, some arrived earlier than others. As Turks, we are latecomers; we came from Central Asia in the 11th century. This is why, normally, when one speaks of the Middle East, and this is also the case in Europe, one is tempted to speak of the earlier arrivals, whom people consider as autochthonous. But when you go down into the earlier episodes of history, it becomes clear that no one is in fact autochthonous and that, to varying degrees, they all have come from somewhere else. We are no exception and this we accept. Looking at it from a humanitarian point of view, this means that nobody has the right to ask us to go back to where we came from, because we have nowhere to go. This is our country; although others were there before us, we would like to make that country a country of human beings, regardless of their ethnic origins or date of arrival. That is one of the things which needs to be corrected from the outset.

Turks came to Anatolia by way of its eastern boundary. The exact date of the conquest of Kars, a town in what was then Armenia, was 1067, four years earlier than 1071, which is the date normally attributed to the conquest of Anatolia by the Turks.

Speaking of this particularity of the region, I can also assure you that even in our present century, Anatolia — which is commonly referred to as Turkey, including the Kurdish part — had a population estimated at ten million at the time of the Lausanne Treaty, this date normally being taken as the beginning of the history of the modern Republic of Turkey. Half of the population at that time, according to one American ethnographer (Justin McCarthy) was of non-Anatolian origin, namely Turks from different parts of the Empire, who had to leave their homelands, the places where they were born, and take refuge in Anatolia. Out of these ten million, five million were originally Anatolian and the other five million came from elsewhere. That is the second correction I wish to make.

Turkey accepted the fact from the beginning that half of its population was made up of refugees — who were not necessarily of the same ethnic origin. This has continued to be the case up until the present day: Today in Turkey there are more Turks of Bosnian origin than there are Bosnians in the present Bosnia. They are Slavs, their ethnic origin is not Turkish, but they are Muslims. When, in the 19th century, that part of the Empire fell into other hands, they chose to come to what is today called Turkey. We accepted this, because ethnicity does not interest us. This is the third point I wish to make.

In the first place our religion and religious culture, i.e. Islamic culture, refuses to enquire about the ethnic origin of people. People are equal as Muslims according to the concept of *Umma*. The concept of Umma comes before the concept of nation. In our Islamic culture the only distinction is between Muslims and non-Muslims. All Muslim subjects of the Ottoman state were referred to as the Islamic Umma, and in Islam, every single individual, because he or she is Muslim, is considered as the 'slave of God', and that slavery, the divine slavery, makes every Muslim individual equal with other Muslims. This means that he or she cannot be the slave of any human being. So in Islamic culture ethnic origin does not count. Ethnicity is not of interest to us. Secondly, in this century we imported the concept of 'nation' from France as a product of the French revolution. And there too, the concept of nation, theroretically, does not enquire about the ethnic origins of its citizens. In the nation-state, which is again a product of the French revolution which we adopted, theoretically speaking, peoples' ethnic origin does not count.

Since I am talking as a jurist to a group of ethnographers and social anthropologists, I must speak of the juridical situation to explain the difficulties, the problems that we are facing. We are aware of these problems, more than anybody else and this is the fourth correction I would like to make. Many people give the impression that they are the only ones who realize the problems, and that they know the solutions without thinking that we are the first to realize the problems and the contradictions between theory and practice. I will come to that, but first I will try to mix juridical history and ethnology in an illustrative way, by referring back to a discussion which took place in 1923 during the conclusion of the Lausanne Treaty which more or less established the present borders of the Turkish Republic.

To do that I will have to remind you of the importance of oil at the beginning of this century, and of the importance which the British attached to those areas of the world where they presumed there was oil. During the First World War, Britain had to import almost eighty to eighty-five percent of the oil which it used in its navy and because of this fact there was a tremendous interest in areas where oil existed. During the war Britain aimed, through a number of military operations in the Middle East, at the conquest of Mesopotamia, because it was known that the area contained very rich oil fields. I shall not explain at length the military operations, but one should bear in mind that on the day of the ceasefire at the end of the First World War — which in the case of the Ottoman State was October 30th, 1918, Armistice day, British troops had already occupied the whole of the Arabian Peninsula, a large part of today's Syria and a large part of today's Iraq, and the armistice line stopped just short of Mosul.

This is the picture and this is my introduction to the Kurdish problem, which started in 1919 when General Mustafa Kemal landed in Anatolia to start the revolutionary nationalist movement. This movement was ready to create a new state within the borders of the armistice line; the line that was traced by those who had concluded the agreement between Britain and France and the Ottoman government. The discussion about Iraq started on that day. The British did not stop at that line. After October 30th they continued to pursue their aims, using an Article in the Armistice agreement which gave them the authority to occupy other pieces of land for security purposes. So Mosul was occupied by the British after the date of the Armistice, as was northern Iraq too, and in fact parts of present day Turkey. General Ismet, the head of the Turkish delegation at Lausanne and number two in the revolution, tried to claim back the territories occupied after the Armistice, and he did so first on a legalistic basis, claiming a violation of the Armistice, but he did not succeed.

Now I find this introduction very necessary, because it brings me to a very important discussion that would also be of interest to the ethnologists and anthropologists.

Ismet's claims for the return of the occupied areas were turned down by the British delegation. Lord Curzon, the head of the British delegation, even made fun of these Turkish claims and said:

General, you are forgetting that you lost this World War, and we have occupied these parts because we won that war and we had the right of sword to go beyond the Armistice line'.

After this refusal, General Ismet changed his argument. He argued that these parts of Mesopotamia were inhabited by Kurds and two, three, or even four other ethnic groups. There are Turks, Turcomans, there are Arabs, some Jews; all the ethnic groups that you find in the Middle East. And he gave figures. These showed that there was a large Kurdish majority, and that together Kurds and Turks formed an absolute majority over the others. Those people of Turkish ethnic origin were not a majority. Arabs are a minority, according to the Turkish figures, not only vis-à-vis the Kurds, but also vis-à-vis the Turks.

So his argument, which I find interesting in this context, is that you should not separate people who, sociologically speaking, have lived together for centuries and who, except for the 20th century, have had cultural affinities: their languages may be different, but their way of living, the way they look at world affairs, the way they consider human relations are similar; in short their group behaviour is more or less the same, therefore they should not be separated. General Ismet pointed out that the borderline which the British wished to trace would force the Kurds to live together with the Arabs. There were other corners of the world where this was so and these included large parts of Anatolia where Kurds and Turks had lived together for centuries and, except for the 20th century, there had been no major conflicts between them. Therefore, General Ismet argued, they should not be separated.

Now, I find this argument very modern, very humane and it should have applied also to Turks and Armenians who lived together for centuries without conflict; but 19th and 20th century conflicts have created the separation between these ethnic groups.

So General Ismet's argument was, or should have been, to a Western mind, to a humanitarian mind, very acceptable. It did not take the oil into account. But the British very badly wanted that land and occupied it regardless of whether human beings should or could live together. That is the tragedy of the Middle East: nationalism encouraged by foreign interests.

The Turks of the Ottoman Empire were the last nationalists. After every other ethnic group became nationalists, the Turks turned nationalist in 1920. They had to, because the Sèvres Treaty of 1920 divided Anatolia between ethnic groups, and also gave parts of Anatolia as areas of influence to the French, the Italians, the British and the Greeks. The Lausanne Treaty, after the War of Independence (1919-23) traced the borders and left the Turks with a homeland of their own which they then called Turkey. This is another correction that needs to be made: Turks, before the nationalist movement of 1920, very seldom referred to their homeland as Turkey. In the Ottoman texts you see it referred to as Anatolia, as opposed to the 'Roman' lands of the Balkans. Before the Ottomans, the Seljuks referred to Anatolia as the Roman lands, because it was part of the Eastern Roman Empire, the Byzance.

The name 'Turkey' was not used first by Turks. It was used for the first time by the Crusaders on their way to the Holy Lands. Here they encountered people who had come from Central Asia, whom they had not expected to meet on their way. The first encounter between the West and the Turks occurred in a context of hostility and it was the Crusaders who referred to that land as Turkey because it was the land where they first saw the Turks. Later, the Western world referred to all the Ottoman territories occupied by the Turks as the Turkish Empire, whereas the Turks themselves called it the 'Ottoman State'. In a similar way this is what happened when the Spanish conquered North America and encountered a bird which they already knew from North Africa, which was then Turkish territory and they called that bird 'the Turkey bird', turkey. So the name of the bird comes from the land, and not vice-versa.

It was only in Lausanne that the West and the Turks together referred to that land as Turkey for the first time. The only part of the border which was not definitely traced at Lausanne was that border between the then British mandate-territory of Iraq, and Turkey. The Iraqi border was not agreed upon and remained in dispute and was referred to at another conference in Istanbul in 1924. Again it was not resolved but was passed instead to the League of Nations, and in the end the whole matter was referred to the International Court of Justice and an Estonian general finally traced the border.

The border goes right across an area where Kurds live and so the Kurds themselves were separated and politics traced that border. Now, within these borders, and this is the main point, Turks were to create a nation. It was the first time in Turkish history that one had to create a nation-state.

The concept was imported from the French Revolution and I should like to emphasize what it means to us to be a nation-state or what it meant to the French revolutionaries. A nation-state is a state in which the ethnic origins of the citizens should not be of interest to the government, because the state is made of citizens, and citizens, regardless of their ethnic origin, their religion, or their ethnicity are just human beings and as such they are equal. That is the theory. But Turkey, in its urge to create a nation state, has neglected the other requirement of creating a nation-state. The French revolutionaries created the concept of citizenship and they declared, in the first Universal Declaration of Human Rights, that citizens are equal as human beings and therefore should enjoy all the rights and liberties that man possesses as a human being. This is the task facing the nation-state. So on the one hand you have nationalism creating the nation within given borders, but at the same time, since Turkey declared itself a republic shortly after Lausanne, it also had the task of making each one of its citizens live as a human being, possessing inalienable rights which should not be violated. That is the requirement of the nation-state which Turkey has not been successful in accomplishing.

Why? Because of the outcome of the Lausanne negotiations and, especially, because of the subsequent Kurdish uprisings (while the Kurdish border remained in suspense), instigated by British interests in the region. From the documents which are now available we know that the Turkish rulers at the time assumed that Britain wanted to keep those areas, because they wanted to create a safety zone to protect their oil fields. So violence was used. Violence against violence, and there has been a spiralling rise of this violence ever since. This worried the rulers of the Republic whose main aim was the creation of a nation-state within given borders, but because they had to use violence against violence, because they were suspicious of any ethnically motivated activity, they neglected the other part of the requirements; the republican part, the part which called for the respect of the human rights of its citizens, to be themselves, to allow them first and foremost to speak their language, to develop their own culture and to enjoy all the rights that all peoples around the world should enjoy according to the Universal Declaration of Human Rights. But should we, because it was neglected until now, give up the concept of the nation-state, or the concept of a nation within which people, whatever their ethnic origin, should be equal as citizens? Our thesis is that the principle of the nation-state is right, that there have been mistakes in the past and that these should be corrected. They can be corrected within the larger context of democratization by creating a democratic republican state where, as was the case during the War of Independence — and as is the case now, except for one party — all ethnic groups could be reconciled, not as ethnic groups, but as citizens; through different political parties with complete representation and complete respect for human rights. These remain our objectives. They have not been reached yet and human rights have been violated by every ruling party in the past. There have been mistakes perpetrated recently, and these too should be corrected. But the basic principle of the nation-state which refuses to consider the ethnic origins of people and treats them as equals must remain. I would like to stress this point, because it is the right principle for our age. I believe that not recognizing the principle of 'non-ethnic citizenship' would be to turn the clock back to the Middle Ages.

Turkey and the Middle East

Osman Faruk Logoglu

Turkey is situated at the epicentre of the volatile, conflict-ridden Balkans, the Caucasus and the Middle East. Its political geography confers a unique role on Turkey with regard to the stability and prosperity of all these areas. As these regions are of critical significance for the security and well-being of Europe, the Turkish factor accordingly assumes a strategic bearing in European equations as well.

In the Middle East, even as a hesitant peace begins to dawn on this fatigued and stability-hungry region, old conflicts are refusing to go away and giving every sign that they will persist, though probably in different permutations. At the same time, new fault lines are already emerging as forebodings of hitherto unfamiliar types of tension and conflict in these ancient lands. In this environment, in addition to the familiar oil and religion, the key variables defining the politics of the area will now include water, ethnicity, fundamentalism, democracy and human rights.

As one of its integral components, Turkey is going to have a continual and central part to play in this complex Middle Eastern matrix. And to understand that role, we must look at its historical, political, social, economic as well as its military dimensions.

History

First, there is the fact of Turkish rule of the region for nearly four centuries. The Ottoman Turks conquered these lands, but respected the character and culture of the various peoples whom they came to rule. It was an empire that did not exploit or destroy the conquered domains. The Ottoman Sultan in Istanbul was an imperial, not an imperialistic suzerain. So long as outlying provinces paid their well-defined and strictly regulated taxes to the Ottoman treasury, they were left intact and to themselves.

The Ottoman system combined the seemingly contradictory elements of centralism on the one hand and of local power and authority on the other. The Sultan at the centre granted a large degree of autonomy to the individual far-flung domains of the Empire. But the Sultan also kept peace among them and exercised a unifying control over them.

Thus, the Middle East under the Turks was relatively peaceful and certainly not the scene of constant tensions or wars. Blood and tears are the legacy of colonialism, and chiefly the result of the policies pursued by Western powers after the departure of the Ottoman Turks. But while one may choose not to remember history, one cannot erase it. The Turkish imprint is an indelible facet of Middle Eastern cultures.

The Ottoman Empire gave birth to more than 20 independent states, most of them in the Middle East, and left behind a respectable legacy of administration and organization. History alone should accord Turkey a natural and knowledgeable say in the affairs of the region today.

One other point about history, i.e. contrary to what is sometimes alleged, is that Turkey is not faced with an identity crisis. It is true that Turkish identity is in a state of flux, but it is also a fact that it has been evolving around a relatively stable core for a very long time. Turks are proud of being citizens of Turkey and happy about living as Muslims in a secular, democratic society. Most would not hesitate to call themselves Western. In other words, for the average Turk, there is no inferiority complex in his relationship with the West. He is comfortable and unburdened and views his relationship with the European as one between equals. This is in part because he has been an integral part of the European political landscape starting early in the 14th century, fighting, trading, forming alliances, getting married with European enemies, friends and partners as the case might be. It has even been suggested that the concept of 'Europe' as such emerged as a result of the need to 'defend the faith against the infidel Turk'.

Yet there is also the fact that the Turks have never been colonized and have never lost their independence. The Republic of Turkey is the 16th State established by the Turks in the course of their existence. This provides the Turkish person with an ingrained sense of self-confidence and self-respect. This is why the process of Westernization that has been going on in Turkey for more than a century cannot be considered as something that was forced upon Turkey. Rather, it was a choice deliberately and knowingly made. It has not been a case of mere imitation, but an effort to learn and to improve. Turkish experience, therefore, contrasts with that of other Middle Eastern States and increases the importance and value of its role-model function today.

Politics

Turkey has, in the Middle Eastern context, a number of attributes which no other Muslim country in the region shares.

Turkey is the only country in the area governed by parliamentary democracy. It is the oldest and the only working, viable example of its kind in that part of the world. Aside from Israel, the next closest democracy to the east is India.

It is the only secular society in the Middle East with a predominantly Muslim population (about 99 percent).

The Turkish legal system and legislation are not based on religious precepts or principles such as the Islamic *shariat*. The laws, whether in civil or penal matters, are derived from the same sources as in most Western societies. All fundamental freedoms and individual human rights are under the guarantee of a civic constitution.

Turkey is again unique in combining the model of a unitary nation-state with a centralist political tradition on the one hand and a growing awareness of the importance of local government and its extension in practice on the other hand. This goes in tandem with the emphasis on individual human rights and the equality of citizens before the law. At a time when ethnic conflicts are ravaging our values and principles, the Turkish model offers a sound alternative.

Finally, Turkey has the singular distinction of being an integral and accepted part of both the West and the Middle East. It is a member of all the major Western organizations such as NATO, the Council of Europe, OECD and OSCE and is an associate member of the EU and the Western European Union (WEU). It is at the same time a leading member of the Islamic Conference and of the Economic Cooperation Organization.

Society

The great majority of the Turkish population is Muslim. But there are also small non-Muslim communities (Greeks, Armenians and Jews) with established minority status according to the 1923 Lausanne Treaty. There is, moreover, the fact that today's Turkey is the land for many different ethnic groups and emigres from former parts of the Ottoman Empire. These include, for example, Bosnians, Georgians, Abhazians and the Chechens. Still another fact of importance is the Turkish tradition of providing refuge to those fleeing persecution in their homelands over the centuries, whether to Sephardic Jews, the Bulgarian Turks, Afghans or the Iraqi Kurds.

Turkish society is a product of many civilizations and cultures, a synthesis that is not the lowest common denominator of its constituent parts, but their highest combination.

This intricate social texture is bound together cohesively by the common thread of citizenship in a secular regime. Social mobility is based on merit and not on subjective criteria. It is a society where there is no religious, racial or ethnic discrimination and a well-developed tradition of tolerance and acceptance of diversity. These are ingrained in the people's character so that behaviour consistent with these attitudes comes naturally and spontaneously.

Hence, the organization of Turkish society, too, offers a societal model combining successfully elements and structures that are diverse and different. It is a highly dynamic and creative society, always on the move, striving to get better and richer.

Economy

Turkey is a large, emerging market of 60 million people. Its foreign trade is constantly growing. But its economic importance goes beyond its borders and beyond its commercial value. It is ideally situated as a bridge between Europe and the Middle East. With its infrastructure and communications network as well as its financial services and free trade zones, Turkey will increasingly be the centre for international economic activities aimed at the Middle Eastern countries. The young and relatively inexpensive labour force and accumulated industrial experience and skills are additional Turkish attractions.

Not only Arab tourists, but also Arab investments and capital will continue to find a hospitable environment in Turkey. It will serve as a meeting point for Europe and the Middle East.

Europe needs secure and safe energy sources. Whether this is Middle Eastern oil or Central Asian gas and oil, Turkey is going to serve as a safe, stable, reliable, economic and environmentally preferred station for the transfer of these energy fuels from the east to the west. Its Western orientation in general and its NATO membership and EU association in particular make Turkey the most dependable storage and distribution terminal for vital energy resources. This is the reason why the Iraqi pipeline was built through Turkey. The same applies to the early Azeri oil. And it will be the case for the oil and gas from Turkmenistan and Kazakhistan. Moreover, the Turkish connection will bring substantial economic activity and lucrative profits to those European countries involved in this energy highway network of the 21st century.

Another key commodity in the Middle East is water. In the years ahead, the water issue will figure ever more prominently in the relations of the states in the region. Turkey has considerable water resources and has undertaken extensive and expansive programmes to preserve them and to enhance their utility and value. Most of the states in the region do not have enough water. Existing sources are meagre and face the risk of depletion or loss of quality.

Turkey, while not a water-rich country according to accepted definitions of the term, is in a position to supply water to parts of the Middle East. Several projects have already been put forward by Turkey to this end. The Turks are keen to use water as an instrument of peace and cooperation with its neighbours and beyond. There is no Turkish intention to deprive anyone of water, nor any unwillingness to address any questions through dialogue. Turks are prepared to accommodate the needs of its neighbours through optimal use of water resources. But this will and can only be done within the framework of Turkish national interests. Trying to challenge Turkey's sovereign rights over its water resources will not get anyone anywhere. Without Turkey, the water shortage in the Middle East cannot be tackled economically. With Turkish participation, collaboration over water would have a realistic chance of success.

Military

The strength of a country depends on the composition and quality of its various systems such as its politics, culture and economy. But one obvious index of strength is the military might of a country. Turkey is a democracy, with a long history of achievements and cultural accomplishments and a growing economy governed by free market principles. These are the ascending values of our times. But in the military sphere, too, Turkey has enormous resources at its disposal. In military terms, Turkey has to be considered a regional power because it has a large standing force of substantial means in terms of weaponry, training, professionalism and morale. Turkish national defence strategy places a justified emphasis on military preparedness in order to avert any designs from its surroundings against its territorial integrity and sovereignty.

In this connection, one must also keep in mind that Turkey is a member of the Western alliance and defence arrangements. As a member of NATO and associate member in the WEU, Turkey is poised, in defense terms, on the eastern front of Europe. Given the fact that the Middle East peace still lies in the future, it is important that Turkey continue to play a stabilizing and constructive role in this area.

The Middle East Peace Process

The foreign policy of the Republic of Turkey was based on one main principle enunciated by its founder Mustafa Kemal Atatürk as 'peace at home, peace abroad'. This axiom served as a guideline for Turkey's ties with its neighbours and its international relations. Hence, Turkish support for a just, comprehensive and lasting settlement of the Arab-Israeli conflict from its onset. Turkey was the first Muslim state to recognize and establish full diplomatic relations with the State of Israel when it came into existence in 1948. It has maintained its ties with Israel despite pressures over the many years from its Arab neighbours and friends to sever them. But the various Turkish governments stood their ground, arguing that Turkey's ties with Israel were not against Arab interests. On the contrary, Turkey could help the Arabs better through this dialogue with the Israelis. Having links with it did not prevent Turkey from criticizing and condemning Israel when appropriate.

The Turks supported the Palestinian cause from the start and established relations with the PLO early on and recognized the State of Palestine. Turkish support was not bound to any conditions. Throughout the years, the Palestinians and the Arab states had Turkish backing in all international forums even if they did not get reciprocal understanding on such issues as the Cyprus question which for Turkey has been a matter of national importance. Turkey has always called for the right of all states in the area to live peacefully with its neighbours in recognized and secure borders. It emphasizes today the preservation of the territorial integrity of states as a principal condition of avoiding the threat posed by ethnic nationalism.

The Turkish Government has taken a close interest in the Arab-Israeli conflict and been involved actively in the various efforts to find a solution. The parameters accepted by Turkey for a comprehensive, fair and durable settlement of the problem have been those defined by the various UN Security Council resolutions on the subject. Today, it is a vocal advocate of the Middle East process and a participant in all five working groups in the multilateral track of this process. The Turks believe that peace and prosperity are interdependent and therefore encourage economic cooperation in the area. The Islamic Conference provides one forum for such activity. When there is peace between Israel and the Arab states, Turkey's capacity, experience and means will help make it stick.

Turkey has also taken certain initiatives to carry over the experiences and results obtained in Europe through the CSCE (now OSCE) and the negotiations over conventional forces (CFE) to the Middle East. The Turkish point is that the region can benefit if some of the security and cooperation schemes that eventually worked in the East-West axis could be transferred to the Middle

East and adopted there. Formal proposals have been fielded in this respect. It is clear that it will take a long time before any such ideas can begin to take hold in this region. But Turkey is the one country that can advance such ideas in the Middle Eastern context in the hope of sowing the seeds for future breakthroughs. No other country in the area enjoys the first-hand experience in these matters that Turkey does.

Fundamentalism

Today Europe is very concerned with the problem of fundamentalism. This is conveniently, but wrongly, identified with and equated to Islam: despite the fact that the concept and the phenomenon of fundamentalism is historically of Western origin. It was the name of an aggressive religious movement that emerged in the United States after the First World War, antimodern in its instinct, action oriented and often associated with racist and sectionalist tendencies.

Be that as it may, one must still ask what Europe is doing about this menace? The answer unfortunately is 'not very much' and what little is being done is superficial and wrong. Measures such as pulling out one's diplomats and citizens, advising one's tourists, or hunting down individual terrorists, although appropriate, are not adequate. There must be a deeper soul searching in Europe about its relationship to Islam and the Islamic world. It must begin with more genuine and open-hearted debate. It must include a review of the policies pursued and attitudes exhibited toward Muslim immigrant communities that have been in Europe now for more than a generation.

The self-examination should extend to an evaluation of the tragedy in Bosnia whose victims, no matter how you define them, are primarily Muslims. Are the Bosnian Muslims victims of an unnamed fundamentalism in the Christian world?

Fundamentalism, when looked at in a broad view will be found to be a threat to both Christian and Muslim populated societies. The same applies to the state of Israel which is faced with its own version of the fundamentalist challenge. It is not something unique or limited to Islam. European countries are today experiencing a rise in racist, exonophobic tendencies. In a world which is getting smaller and more interdependent, European tolerance and openness to outsiders is diminishing. It is as if Europe feels sorry that it ever asked the immigrant workers to come to their countries and that most of their ills would be over when foreigners, but especially the Muslims, somehow all decide to leave and go back to where they came from. The treatment of immigrant communities is not consistent with the presumed values of the societies in which they live. This state of affairs marks nothing less than the onset of a fundamentalism in the West which is equally dangerous.

Nonetheless, Islamic fundamentalism is still a real and imminent danger, not so much for Europe, but for most of the Muslim countries themselves. Historically, the colonial powers fostered Islamic leanings as a means to stop communism. Today it is, among others, a response to chronic poverty, ethnic nationalism and way to overcome destitution, Islam is supposed to provide a consistent answer to earthly woes both here and in the next world. For the fundamentalists, there is only the nation of Islam. No other nationalities are recognized and unity is based not on ethnicity, but on Islamic precepts. Fundamentalism is also a reaction to fledgling aspirations of democracy, respect for human rights and the equality of women. Their interpretation of Islam identifies god as the exclusive and only source of sovereignty and authority and the principles laid by him as the eternal rules for societies to follow in every single aspect of their lives.

The direction which fundamentalism takes, in both Europe and the Middle East, will depend to a significant degree on the shape of the relationship still to be forged between Turkey and the EU. A most valuable gift which Europe provides to Islamic fundamentalists everywhere is that even a country like Turkey that has had intimate relations with Europe for hundreds of years and is a Western country in many respects, can nonetheless be shunned by the West. If that happens, the suspicion that the EU is a closed club of Christian nations will be justified. Hence, Turkey is the litmus test for both Europe and the Islamic world on the matter of whether Islam and Christianity can get together in a bond of mutual respect and understanding. This test will also reveal whether societies in both the East and the West will follow the path of secularization or unsecularization of their way of life.

Let it not be forgotten that Turkey is an important regional power, with a predominantly Muslim population, whose political regime is democracy, whose way of life is secular and whose economy is based on free market rules. It is a society where the rule of law prevails and where there is a constant drive to realize the highest level of respect for human rights by means of individual rights for all citizens who are equal before the law. The Turks are demonstrating that democracy, secularism and modernity are compatible with Islam. There is no other example. The democrats, the secularists in the Muslim countries look to Turkey because their own success is tied to the success of the Turkish model. Hence, important choices are awaiting both the Middle Eastern and the European countries, choices that will affect their common destinies.

The major weapon against fundamentalism is democracy, at both the individual and societal level. It is not enough that a country has a democratic regime. In addition, each person must have the habits of tolerance, understanding and respect for diversity and the rights of others as second nature, regardless of differences. If Europe wants to avoid the dangers posed by what it regards as Islamic fundamentalism, it must first try to understand the problem. But there is no doubt that the immediate order of business for Europe is to promote the democratic forces in the Middle Eastern countries. In this context, the closer integration of Turkey with the EU will be the defining index.[1]

1. The views in this contribution by Osman Faruk Logoglu, Ambassador of Turkey in Azerbaijan, (formerly Ambassador in Denmark), are those of the author and do not necessarily reflect the views of the Turkish Government.

Republican Citizenship Facing the Challenge of Identity

Nuri Bilgin

Certain fears have preoccupied Turkish society over recent years: Fear of the PKK, of terrorism, of slums, of migration to the cities, of fundamentalism, of military coups, of externally induced political currents, and of internal and external enmities are among the most common of these fears. These are, indeed, the fears that can be witnessed in all societies suffering from severe social problems. In addition, it is also possible to find some common points in the various reactions to these fears, exhibited by the societies in question. Rather than creating solidarity, these fears generally lead to individual insularity or collective withdrawal. Fear induces a lack of tolerance leading to a retreat to firmly protected towers, and a growing attachment to sources of security as power; military force, religion, or ethnic groups. As the tendency to follow the well known paths grows, the orthodox ideas grow more empowered. The ways of seeking solutions to the basic problems of the society tends to show a lack of consensus; deviations and differences tend to find a locus beyond the boundaries of legitimacy; the multiplicity of ideas appears to narrow as the increase in conformist pressures runs parallel with the retreat from beliefs.

In this context, the extent to which the Republic of Turkey has succeeded is open to question. Personally I believe that the Turkish Republic has been unable to realize the ambition of structuring herself as it had originally intended. Undoubtedly, there is no overwhelming difference between the present state of a society as compared to its initial projected ideal. It is known that a wide variety of ambitious social projects, ranging from religious to revolution, from innovations, to reformations, were actually never fully realized and that there was a continuous need to start again. Yet, these unceasing efforts to reconstruct society can only be effective if the social model in question remains valid. When we approach the problem from this perspective we are confronted with an important question: What is the model upon which the Turkish Republic rests and what are the current problems which the Republic needs to face?

The Trivet of the Turkish Republic

When the early constitutions of the Turkish Republic and the discourses of Kemal Atatürk are scrutinized as a whole, it becomes clear that the Republic, in terms of its basic principles, pursues an understanding which ranges from Kant to the French Revolution. This understanding stems from the principles embodied in the formation of nation-states and in the spirit of the *Universal Declaration of Human Rights*. Here, I think, the three determining factors are particularly worth emphasizing. These points, which complement one another are: the notion of a republic, the understanding of nationhood, and the perspective of modernization. Each of these three elements is of crucial importance in understanding the basic philosophy of the Turkish Republic more fully. First, let us focus on 'the notion of republic'. Republican thought, at its base, refers to the structuring of the public domain on the premise of law. That is, the concept of republic as a form of government in which legislative and executive powers are separated with legislative authority gaining the greater control, to a great extent conveys the meaning of the concept of Rule of Law *(Etat de droit)*.

The republic should be considered as an impediment to the divergence of the dynamics of civil society from human values - as it has been seen in the examples throughout history - and to the regression of civil movements into a state of nature (Today, countries all over the world are expected to incorporate their concepts of law with universal values, and with a different attitude to that of the past, international law approves of intervention in other countries in order to uphold these values). As far as the Turkish Republic is concerned, the second significant factor is her understanding of nationhood. As it has been known, during the period of emergence of nations, two different approaches appeared on the question of what constitutes a nation. These two approaches are: the concept of nation *based on social contract*, and the concept of *nation based on collective spirit*. The former, generally associated with the ideas of French Revolution, defines the nation as a community of citizens voluntarily united under the same principles. According to the understanding of the contract-based nation, initiation into a nationality is related to the individual's free choice and to his/her performance of voluntary participation. The acquired properties of *territory and voluntary participation* are much more important than such innate properties as *lineage* and *race*. Contrary to this, the concept of nation based on collective spirit considers history, tradition, and ethnic origin as determining factors in the formation of a nation, and identifies the individual with the community.

In this context, Atatürk's approach conceptualizes one's belongings to a nation as one's *citizenship*. This understanding of nationhood can be clearly seen in the 1924 Turkish Constitution. Article 88 of the constitution states that 'Turkish people, irrespective of their religious and ethnic background are called Turkish by citizenship', and those who come from different ethnic origins 'will become Turkish if they voluntarily choose 'Turkishness', and if they are accepted to 'Turkishness' by citizenship law'. On the other band, in *Medeni Bilgiler* (Civil Instructions) written in the early 1930s, Atatürk's definition of the nation as 'a political and social community established by the citizens united through the same language, culture, and ideal' reflects the same understanding of nationhood. This understanding, which links nationality with volition and elevates citizenship over ethnicity, is a natural outcome of the concept of a contract-bond nation in which belonging to a nation is based on acquired properties. At this point, qualities of the group are regarded not as being inherited by lineage but related to having lived in a particular territory along with commitment to the same beliefs and values.

Does the choice made by the Turkish Republic between these two concepts of nationhood still maintain its validity? Some observations on the subject may be helpful in answering this question.

There is sufficient empirical evidence indicating that the concept of nation based on citizenship is not solely a product of a fictive scenario or only of an ethnic choice of principle but is, in fact, able to meet the human needs of our age.

First of all, the predominance of citizenship over ethnicity is consonant with the previous experience of maintaining unity among the tribes of different ethnic origins in the history of mankind. As a matter of fact, throughout history great religions have demonstrated that the only way to keep cultures and people of entirely different origins together was to unite them in a transcendental identity by giving preference to citizenship over religious fraternity. Citizenship as a transcendental super-identity is the secular version of this.

Secondly, towards the modern ages in all parts of the world, rapidly increasing numbers of people leave their villages, their cities, or their countries for various reasons to live in other places. Among them, refugees and immigrant workers constitute an important majority for instance, let us consider the situation of 'Turkish' (including those of Kurdish origin) workers who live in Europe. As they live in a foreign country for a long time and as their children who were born there become grown-ups, their tendency to integrate with the host culture grows. As a consequence of this, either they want directly to assume the citizenship of the host country, i.e. they want to be French or German citizens, or they want the right to dual citizenship on the condition that they can keep their original identities, i.e. they want to be both Turkish and German or French.

Thirdly, overemphasizing the ethnic identities, giving priority to the modes of identification and conflicts based on ethnicity and sustaining such conflicts are distressing tendencies.

When the members of a community base their collective identities on certain properties that cannot be acquired and possessed by everybody, they will, by extension of this, lay claim to the world which would lead to prejudice and discrimination. Each collective identity is an inevitable consequence of discrimination and the demands of ethnic identity, in so far as they require the invention of 'the other' (Derrida's concept of constitutive 'outside').

Finally, as have been the case in most of the countries all over the world, when a society lacks cultural, historical, and linguistic homogeneity overemphasis of the dominant group's own collective identity and the consequent negation of the others weakens social integration. In such a society, dissolving the social bond leads up to an incurable anomaly and disintegration. Furthermore, it hinders the development of a culture of democracy in which the survival of differences is of vital importance. *Personal or collective identities may change with time, and different identities may serve the same functions.*[1] In this sense, it seems implausible and also unnecessary to be wrapped up in a definite collective identity and to perceive it as an immutable substance. This implies that overemphasizing the collective identity and assigning it a determining function seems to be harmful in many ways. Yet, exalting different identities and diversity in themselves may induce a failure to capture the truth in the sense that a lack of social integrity would also create problems.

Western intellectuals who make differentialist claims often transfer the models of individual differences developed in a society that has not experienced the problems of social integration to the level of communities. Apart from the methodological inadequacy of this approach, such efforts in fact encourage differentialist movements 'in someone else's home'. These countries' policies on immigrant workers, for instance involve integration at best and assimilation at worst and exclusion in the case of the failure of both of these.

Another factor: Since the day of her establishment, the Turkish Republic has adopted a modernist attitude in line with the tradition of *Enlightenment*. This attitude essentially considers economic growth as its main project and that principles of rational thought should be translated into general political and social objectives. Since its foundation the Turkish Republic has deployed policies whose aim is to mobilize the society in modernization, to annihilate

1. Bilgin, 1994.

all obstacles to modernization, to develop social patterns and personality traits amenable to modernization and to declare modernization as a national will. Yet, since all this effort was invested without the construction of an infra-structure, Turkey has failed to finance its political revolution. On the contrary, educational and cultural developments were given priority over economic growth. Modernization supported by developments of great diversity could, therefore, not have been realized.

The Rise of Identity

On the basis of a general evaluation, it would not be wrong to claim that the basic assumptions upon which the Turkish Republic was founded relied on a universalist orientation: The aim of the Turkish Republic was to establish a state of law, i.e. a secular system organizing the public life and adopting the priority of the laws over the people who make them, and also to realize a social scheme on the basis of contract-bound nation. However, the historical evidence obtained from the foundation of the Republic to the present day demonstrates that in the process of both searching for and constructing an identity, the Turkish Republic has had to experience the frustrations and conflicts stemming from the co-existence of the Enlightenment tradition, universalism, and modernization on the one hand, and of differentialism and nationalism on the other.

The situation has impeded the democratization process. Yet, the basic philosophy of the Turkish Republic holds the belief that democracy should be associated with the republic. In this belief, the fact that the Turkish Republic was a product of a revolution was the determining factor. Similar processes were experienced by the Western world in the 18th century. In Touraine's terms, in the Western world, historically, in the early stages:

...it was the general opinion that the society was traditional and unfair and that it consisted of customs and privileges; in this context, the political society or action was forced to break up the civil society; political society was developed in opposition to civil society; this Aristotelian view is an understanding of a revolutionary democracy which implies the idea of destroying everything, making a *tabula rasa*, and then re-creating everything.[2]

In this sense, republican thought considers the execution of sovereignty and of governmental power within the framework of the principles of the law. Despite the fact that this view maintains its validity even today, the principles

2. Touraine 1994.

of law in question have been adapted to the demands for universal equality and freedom. The main motivation behind this view is 'to impose restrictions on the governmental power through democracy, a more powerful principle or spiritual, ethical, and philosophical grounds'.[3]

The revolutionary character of the Turkish Republic from time to time, for practical reasons, tended to identify governmental power with the principles of law, and thus ignore the principle of priority of law. Furthermore, since these principles of law were formulated - though partly - in accordance with the pragmatic needs of the time without taking the dynamic of the society into consideration, they could hardly become effectively applicable. As a matter of fact, their applicability was rather forced from the outset.

Up until recent years, the concept of the citizenship-bound nation has maintained its validity in the discussions of political philosophy. However, today the validity of this understanding has started to be questioned particularly due to the failure of the modernization policies and the collapse of the strong universalist ideas. As a result, the concept of civil society gained importance, and differentialist, spiritualist, communalist and separatist movements and demands, in parallel with the increase in globalization all over the world, began to grow stronger.

The understanding of *Enlightenment* has been exposed to the challenges of tradition (Gadamer), of martyrdom (Bruckner), of magical thought (Moscovici), of empirical man (Kriegel) and of taking roots. Thus the 1990s seem to witness the emergence of differentialist movements in opposition to universalism in most parts of the world. Among these movements, nationalism, separatism, and fundamentalism along with the participation in small communities or groups are worth emphasizing. The common characteristic of all these movements can be defined as a kind of *search for identity*. In accordance with the social context to which they are bound, people try to meet their identity requirements through the membership of certain groups.

In this context, democracy has been threatened by various subversive ideas supported by non-political forces of the society, i.e. by the sense of ethnic and religious belonging. It seems necessary to seek solutions to these problems not only on political but also on sociological and psychological grounds. For it would be a mistake to consider the integrationist movements only as trivial outcomes of certain conditions. These movements have some psycho-social functions and are responses to certain questions. They can be interpreted, as the reactions of the ones who are excluded from the struggle between *in's* and *out's*. It is in this sense that these movements may be read by various countries as *the failure or damnation of modernization*. Search for collective identity appears

3. Ibid.

to be an exaggerated response of the poor, of the marginalists, of those who are marginalized and of those who are excluded; to their own state of poverty and exclusion. In spite of the fact that the search or need for identity is regarded as a fundamental necessity of individuals and groups, its prioritization due to certain conditions, (i.e. frustrations, the failure of modernization, the dissolving of social bonds, perception of the ethnic identity as a means for providing security, power, and prestige) supports the idea in question.

The Possibility of Multiple Identities: Citizen + the Single Entity

Today, general belief honours the idea that people cannot be regarded only as citizens, and the search for an ideal political system[4] which does not consider people's personal realizations as being related to their professional, national and sexual traditions, views, and interests no longer seems to be adequate. It has been thought that democracy should conceive of the individual with his/her specific characteristics, such as his/her cultural inheritance, imagination, sexuality, individuality, cultural identity and so forth. In addition, today countries all over the world are expected to incorporate their concepts of law with universal values (e.g. human rights). In a change to attitudes in the past, international law now approves of intervention in other countries for the sake of upholding these values.

Moreover, our world has not yet defused the tension between the universalist and differentialist movements. What is more important is that there have been strong psycho-social, cultural, and ethnic reasons indicating that humanity will be experiencing this tension for a longer period of time. Societies have been governed neither only by laws nor only by traditions and customs; the predominance of one of these over the other results in the return of the other in a more powerful way. From the ethnic point of view, on the other hand, societies can be consigned neither only to laws nor only to existential praxis, because both of them may become harmful when they become absolute and are against the nature of man. In short, neither universalism nor differentialism should be exalted in itself. A difference sanctified just for the sake of being a difference renders the idea of law, considered as having priority over human beings, impossible.

Therefore, the most plausible way appears to lie somewhere in between the two; attempting to associate universality with particularity and being able to live together with both universalism and differentialism. Democratic

---

4. Ibid.

pluralism requires mutual respect and allows the various sides to unite in a super-identity without losing one's own identity.

All these ideas circumscribe universalism on the one hand, and differentialism on the other, and suggest that people can be both the citizens of a country and/or a nation and *at the same time,* they can be a 'single' entity.

Following on from this it should then, in terms of the Turkish Republic, be possible to be both a citizen and Kurdish or an X. But is it possible? If so, how? In order to find a satisfying answer to this question first of all, one should explain what the concepts of citizenship and Kurdishness refer to in such declarations as 'I am Kurdish' and 'I am a citizen of the Turkish Republic'. The question of how it becomes possible and should be possible within the framework of a unitarian state requires careful thought. First of all, since all these people in question live together according to the principles of the same constitution, they are equal in terms of their rights and responsibilities. Thus, in terms of rights and responsibilities, to be Kurdish cannot be regarded as a source of, or a reason for, any kind of privilege.

How is it then possible to be Kurdish and a citizen or Turkish and a citizen? Here, two kinds of collective identities are in question. Let us think of them both as indispensable properties. Let us treat each of the two understandings in itself - the understanding that predominates citizenship and the understanding that the predominates ethnicity - as inadequate to meet human needs. The former appeals to a rational man, a voluntary creature; and conceptualization of this of man leads to abstraction. The latter, on the other hand, appeals to a type of person who has been enticed into the long term conditioning and emotional responses. Since this understanding also seems to be inadequate in meeting the requirements of the subjectivity to the universal values, and of co-existing in the same society, it leads to a complete deadlock.

There may be some factors (personal, conjectural, social, economic, political, etc.) which determine our preferences to one or the other of these two identities, and at the end everybody makes his/her own individual choice. But public life requires that individual choices should be combined into a certain framework. In this sense, the problem lies in declaring the identity in the public domain. In reality, these two identities should be able to co-exist. Besides, other kinds of identities, i.e. ideological, religious etc., are also possible. But let us take only one of them for the moment.

The answer to our question may lie in daily events that are completely free of our collective conditioning. For instance, personally I have different identities, i.e. political, professional, civil, geographical, etc. In practice, I use each of them simultaneously rather than in sequence. In other words, I do not wear them like an outfit; sometimes this one and sometimes that one. Instead, these identities can be regarded as circles expanded outward starting from 'me' and as strata intertwined with each other. Yet, this sort of topographical design has generally not been justified in practice. When one of these strata is removed the other one does not emerge. Therefore, it seems more plausible, for the present, to consider multiple-identities as a painting in cubic style which is composed of different parts, varying in size in accordance with the conditions, context, and relations, being seen simultaneously, and having connected with each other sometimes firmly and sometimes not, or intertwining with each other like ivy. This description seems to be the most appropriate to the purpose as long as a better one comes up.

In real life the tension experienced among multiple-identities has been defused in various ways. In most cases each of the different identities fits in well with one of the domains of life. According to the social context, a person may be a mother/father, a wife/husband, a leftist/rightist, a worker/officer, a driver/accountant/professor, a woman/man, a teenager/adult/elder, an employee/unemployed, etc. In a sense, identities and social context are integrated into *behaviour-settings.* Often, 'separation of domains' leads to the necessary solutions. And we turn back to the earlier question, to be simultaneously Kurdish/Turkish and a citizen can only become possible through a separation of domain. From the phenomenological point of view, this separation of domains can be determined by the process of deciding which one of those two identities under what circumstances is considered to have priority over the other.[5] It seems that ethnic identity gains control of daily life whereas citizenship predominates the public/political domain. In this case, what does it mean 'to be a citizen and Kurdish?' In order to answer this question, first of all, it is necessary to draw the line of demarcation around the frame in which we are seeking the answer. If Kurdishness has been demanded for a cultural identity, then its domain must be considered beyond the political domain (in fact, the Agreement of The Council of Europe on the Protection of National Minorities shares a similar understanding). Seeking the solutions to the problems of identity in the political domain inevitably leads to Kurdish Nationalism and to the understanding of nationhood based on Kurdish ethnicity. Therefore, Kurdishness should be conceived in terms of civil society rather than political society. At this point the following distinction may be helpful: In political terms everybody will adopt the idea of citizenship of the Turkish Republic and belongings to 'Turkish Nation' that does not have any ethnic reference. Kurdishness, on the other hand, will be restricted to the domain of civil society (in ethnic terms, Turkishness will also be considered

5. Graumann, 1983.

in the same way). More specifically, the concept of identity covers the activities concerning everyday life. What do the activities concerning everyday life refer to? Everything that forms the texture of daily life, such as consumption habits, clothing, practices, architectural activities, interior design, music, dancing, entertainment, family relations, human relations, except for the relations with official institutions communicating with others using any language one would wish, and so forth.

The realities that faced in social and psychological domains are not the facts discovered at the site of outsider's voluntary and arbitrary observations. While making the decision on what is possible and what is not, it seems more plausible to refer not only to the theoretical but also to the factual. When we closely examine the concrete examples of our daily life we realize that our problems are not as big as they were thought to be; at least, we are not faced with the problem of ethnic discrimination and racism on socio-psychological grounds. There are more similarities uniting Turks and Kurds than differences separating them. Views concerning the possibility of multiple-identities are not only the expressions of a strong desire or necessity, but also observations concerning daily life.

The Problems of Integration

A number of people have suggested that the basic problems of the Turkish Republic are not ideologically-based, but rather are directly related to national integration. Every society has to lay down the optimum conditions for unity and diversity. In our society today, the unification process undertaken by the government was partly completed. The Republic of the 1920s was different from the present one in terms of language, levels of income, ways of living and so forth. However, the Republic was unable to re-structure the new social divisions which emerged within years and to avoid the new inequalities. That is to say that the Republic was not able to organize the differences within the unity and the unity within the differences.

The main concern behind the Kurdish problem is the question of national integration. Yet, national integration should not be associated with only ethnic problems (as it is when dealt with in general terms). The problem of national integration should be approached from a wide variety of angles. This problem covers every situation in which there is the question of dominance of majority over minority and of the powerful over the weak. National integrity is based on social justice whereas citizenship is based on the dissolution of the ghettos. And only in this way does it become possible to establish the social bond and preserve its existence. The integration policy does not necessarily require giving up one's origins, rejecting national solidarities, or wiping out traditions, but in the end this policy should be based on *the logic of equality rather than of minority.*[6]

The choices made by the Turkish Republic for the universalist orientation, the understanding of nationhood, the system of law, and secularization maintain their validity even today. Yet, it seems necessary to modify and reshape this organization in such a way that it can allow the incorporation of the demand for differentialist movements. Insofar as the legitimacy of the preferences has been preserved on theoretical grounds, it would be for the benefit of the Turkish Republic to be confident, to give up being overly defensive, to enlarge the domain of legitimacy and to a certain extent to allow the anomalies. This seems the best way, for the present; one that leads towards the achievement of social peace and integration. The project of modernization still plays a meaningful role for Turkey and for similar countries. Yet, modernity should be regarded not as a process in which we have to participate at the expense of our own identities, but as a process that will be continually reconstructed in accordance with the challenges of the society and of the age.

Bibliography

Bilgin, N., 1994. *Sosyal Bilimlerin Kavsaginda Kimlik Sorunu*, Izmir: Ege Yayinevi.

Graumann, C. G. 1983. 'On multiple identities'. *International Social Science Journal*, Vol. 35,(2): 309-22.

Moscovici, P., 1994. *A la Recherche de la Gauche Perdue*, Paris: Calmann-Levy.

Touraine, A., 1994. *Critique de la Modernite.* (ed.) Paris: Fayard.

6. Moscovici, 1994.

An Imaginative Approach to the Problem of Turkey's Security in the 21st Century

Erhan Yarar

Preserving Turkish integrity in the 21st century remains a more difficult challenge than the development of the country itself. Turkey continues to retain its geostrategic significance in the face of a changing international order. In this study the importance of the geocultural position is also considered. It will be elaborated on the grounds that the concept of ethnicity threatening the security of the nation has been reconstructed from a neo-orientalist point of view. And a hypothetical approach as to the significance of this concept to Turkey in the future will be developed. The main theme of the study does not consist of what is understood by the elements of the concepts of ethnicity and regional security for the present.

It is plausible to expect that the people who live on the territory of the Turkish state pose a threat to the permanence of the state as a whole, or to alter it within the given framework of the state.

a) It is a fact that there is a desire to create an upper class. This upper class will wish to realize the necessary economic, social and political reforms all at once. It may take as given the period it takes for the state to implement the necessary reforms. The upper class will not be able to remain silent against the existing state rules. This class will no longer be a part of the society and so a narrow circle emerges in the definition of society. What keeps this narrow circle together can be understood in terms of the determining ethnic nature of this class. In this sense it is possible to expect that this class will attempt to have the competence for political administration in their *lebensraum* in order to protect and develop its own living standards. Finally, a conflict will emerge as a threat against the existing state order. In such a case the security of the state would be under threat in the classical sense.

b) In the case proposed above, there will of course be a lower class. This class will not be able to consider the existing administrative order as just. The pressures emanating from the upper class threaten the existence of the lower class. The existing central state would be far away from playing the role of a catalyst in this class conflict. The position of the state shall also be evaluated as another source of pressure. The lower class will attempt to resist these pressures and for this reason it will face internal leadership conflicts. History tells us that conflicts for leadership have a more serious nature within the lower classes but produce results over a shorter period of time. The elements that keep this class together are independent of this leadership conflict. Life in the lower class requires a clear-cut identity. This can be described by ones spoken language and appearance. It is necessary to evaluate them within the framework of alienation in ethnicity and is not changeable. The threat to the security is again present as this class aims to remove the state authority and the entire upper class.

c) In the face of these two cases, the state needs to fortify its identity so as to preserve its own order. Clearly both the upper and the lower classes will attempt to establish a legal framework for their *lebensraum*. This *lebensraum* clearly implies identity and therefore ethnicity. These activities will bring about the defence and security organizations of each class simultaneously. The state, on the other hand, in order to resist these new organizations will have to increase the capabilities of its classical defense and security structures, by fortifying its own organization with ethnicity experts. At this stage, a scientific dimension has been added to the field, which in turn will give rise to some conflict.

Some problems emanating on the grounds of existing boundaries, can also pose a threat to the permanence of the Turkish state.

a) Although a central government understanding still exists, the will for the expansion of local administration is there. It may be stipulated that trade benefits produced in the region are reflected only in the region in question. The unit which takes on the duty for the defence of the region will want to act independently from the central authority. It may also be demanded that living standards in the specific region be taken into account when the investment calculations are made on a national basis. A possible solution to this problem might be as follows; the taxes collected from the developed regions be invested in the same region again. In this case, a conscience for belonging to the region and a regionalist understanding will be fortified and a differentiated type of ethnicity will emerge. A region having a different character from the central authority will demand to have a role in the entire state structure. To achieve this, efforts must be made to keep to a minimum any risks in the

region regarding human loss, resource transaction, and environmental pollution. In order to terminate the violence in a less developed region the
developed region will not want to utilize its own resources. The state will
begin to lose its authority and as it will not be able to resist the threats on the
original borders a kind of boundary problem will emerge.

b) It will be hard to gain systematic and correct information nation-wide which
will pave the way for difficulties in decision making in the central authority,
moreover, as there will be leakings in the intelligence, the implementation of
decisions will go through a kind of lack of authority. The decision making
mechanisms utilized to solve problems emanating from the desire to provide
security on our boundaries, will not be freely applied in the face of the open
society conditions. It can be expected that the state forces seek to increase their
immunity against pressure and interest groups. In this case, a chaotic situation
within the authority can also be expected. This latter point will provide
extremely useful opportunities for terrorist activities that receive foreign aid.

The evidence for an increasingly globalized but indifferent world grow stronger
every day. Turkey as a state may suffer from these globalized relations.

a) The state will prefer to get smaller. In administrative issues the intervention
and competence of the state will be diminished. The territorial size of the state
will be questioned. The boundaries will be narrowed down on the basis of
natural resources and living standards. The bill for living within the new
boundaries can be viewed as the new identity that emerges within them.
Citizenship will be divorced from notions of birth place or settlement, but
rather indexed directly to capabilities, knowledge and implementation abilities.
This case represents a complete departure from today's understanding of
ethnicity. It is possible to accept this type of a state on the understanding that
it does not promise everything. While it is possible to expect the emergence
of an authoritarian regime, the base upon which the new ethnicity is founded
subjects its citizens to continual tests in order to perpetuate the new ethnicity,
but this has one fundamental ramification capable of destroying the state at
some time in the future: any citizen not able to keep up with the changing
standards of the ethnicity risks being discarded, i.e. excommunicated from
society. Being a member of the society therefore produces a combination of
abstract happiness and anxiety at the same time. It can be expected that a
person who is left outside the society may demonstrate aggressive behaviour.
Although it is inevitable for this state to be superior to other states in
technological terms, its continuity is in question.

b) Another point is the fact that the state, while keeping its own central authority constant, may be bound to develop drafts for the formulation of supra-national firms and branches or sub-states organized as the representative of the central state in the face of the reduction in land, resources and environment. It can be viewed as a union of states which works for the same common interests with a central decision making organization. What makes it different from today's situation is that it is not disturbed by ethnic considerations.

c) To be the forerunner in the region, or in a bloc, would be a possible way for the state to propose such an original perspective to influence the people living in those areas.

d) In the attempt to formulate a global system the state will have to strive towards becoming a centre for information. It will attempt to guarantee that local, regional, bloc and global alliances will not be formed so as to avoid being left outside the system.

It is reasonable to expect that new dimensions shall emerge in the concepts and ethnicities regarding the problems that are based on political, economic, religious and cultural motives.

Cultural gaps come into being when human beings and cultural values do not catch up with the technology that they have created together. By utilizing the speed that technology provides for communication, the ones who determine the agenda of the society form the first group. The ones who cannot keep up, either due to a lack of getting or reaching knowledge or lack of economic power, form the second group. The subsequent cultural gap is thus favourable to the first group and they therefore favour maintaining the advantage that they would gain. Thus a conflict will emerge between the first and the second groups. Therefore, what has to be done to overcome this situation is to provide the opportunity to take the affected group to a level above the mentioned cultural gap level. It is important to differentiate between the case when this opportunity is not provided and the case when it cannot be provided. The reasons for the latter shall be met by economic criterion, but to diminish the impact on the second group it is necessary to demonstrate that efforts are made to a certain degree. In the former case, the one and only reason has to be met by the fact that the investment which is to be made for the masses in the second group creates an unbearable burden for the first group. It can be further argued, and is a well-known anxiety for the first group,

that the output which the second group brings about might not match the investment made.

In short, the maximum interest gained during the period can be defined as the continuation of an exploitation in a modernized style and under bearable conditions. The extension of the conflict taking place now and in the medium-term emanates from the partisan groups that own the process instead of the classical method of pressuring the parties. The New Democratic Movement (YDH-Yeni Demokrasi Hareketi) is an illustration of a group of businessmen who want to get involved in politics in Turkey. It is a pioneer in this regard but at the same time a primitive example. However, it has been clear that the message which the YDH gives was not reflected in the results of the December 1995 elections; YDH only gained 1.3 percent of the votes. That some members of the TUSIAD, the largest body of employers, are now in the parliament, indicates the fact that they wish to have more active influence on events. Reports by TUSIAD on some serious social problems such as terror, also show a readiness on the part of businessmen to take the lead in Turkey's agenda, as never seen before.

Entities which defend the ones who are affected negatively by the situation seem to be insufficient. This creates an anxiety, hopelessness and distrust in society and even if the needs of the individuals are attempted to be met, a society composed of multi-individuals develops. What intensifies anxieties is the fact that the programmes of existing parties and other organizations are approaching one another and are now almost indistinguishable. Furthermore, increasing the number of parties prepared the way for new vote distribution. The leading characteristic of the election results is the fact that it does not give support to one or even two parties to govern the country. Clearly their myth can no longer sustain the original idea. In addition, they have adopted the values which they initially aimed to abolish and have also been unable to invent new values to sustain human life in the sense of substance and spirit. It is ironic that the parties in the second group are involved in a quarrel among themselves over leadership rather than presenting a united front against the ones who form the first group by passing through the stages of social violence and having an organization.

Although the suffering mentioned has been experienced at the lowest levels for the last 20 years in Turkey, it requires a more robust resistance than the one demanded 20 years ago in the face of the regional and global development for the forthcoming 20 years. It will be harder to furnish the security of the society under such conditions. In addition, those who experience a cultural gap will experience a kind of different war with the ones who are able to keep up with recent cultural developments.

For this reason the values that occupy the agenda in Turkey which are characteristic of the last century or the beginning of this century will be eliminated so as to be defined as a matter of contention. All of these values are proved to be the values that can be evaluated as concepts under bearable living conditions. Bloody wars have been fought simply to institutionalize these values. The defense of those who suffer from this cultural gap does not consist of this type of value but rather of those directly related to the survival of human beings. This last point demands some discussion as studies are still being done regarding what these concepts are supposed to be. In general the studies made by the ones who lead today's standards aim to manipulate masses in order to provide a rupture in the form of a clash deriving from the core of the conflict.

In recent history we see that either the paradigms of ethnicity, class, or nation, take the lead in turn. The thesis which says that the nation state would prevent conflicts between societies has proved to be invalid. It is historically proven that laicity has served for the necessities of the society when it moved towards industrialization at a time when it was understood to be a kind of alternative religion in the nationalist sense. However, this model lost its role between national cultural identity and the nation state in the context of belonging to the nation state. This last point has also been argued in Turkey.

A political party called the Democratic Peace Movement (Demokratik Baris Hareketi) was established to represent the case for the Alevis. Another political party which made Kurdish rights its central ideology has been in existence for five years.

Naksibendis and Nurcus, which are tarikats (religious orders), do follow a somewhat different route in contrast to the classical method of supporting political parties and they form new organizations. Furthermore they seek to promote their agenda through their own media. As recent events have shown it can be expected that they can form their own political parties.

It can be argued that there is no current advocate on the political stage representing the ideology which created the Turkish Republic. Those segments of society which support these values are left stranded, and therefore open to manipulation from any direction. Central parties reflect a sort of specific society representing a closer world outlook and this for sake of economic and political interests and legal privileges. At this point, ethnicity is either reborn or rebuilt anachronistically. Those who defend decentralization of the administration see ethnicity as a social necessity despite ethnic diversities. Those in this group who prefer regionalism develop while those who resist this do not give in to central authority.

Ethnicity lacks a common definition and semiotically it might be redeployed according to changing balances. Anderson's evaluation of the nation as an imagined entity may also be valid for ethnicity. The fact remains that during the import of nation building, religion was regarded negatively due to the developments in the West and has been regarded as part of the structure and traditions whose alteration was attempted. This contributes to the most crucial of political instabilities. Although religion constitutes an overwhelming identity in Afghanistan, ethnic identity prevents integration and thus tensions and conflicts have emerged. In the Bosnian conflict the frictions among the Muslims are strange to note. The assassination of Yitzhak Rabin should be questioned in the mentioned logical order as it has been the first case in the history of Israel and only the second in two thousand years of the history of Judaism. It has also been proved that Sunnism has not been a social adhesive in Turkey prior to 1980. This concept has been fixed for different meanings in time and space and it is not a dogma.

We are living in an environment where we are not citizens but rather members of the nation as defined by the state. 'The State' should only be understood as a political organization. However, it should also be emphasized that its position in the conflict stricken region delimits autonomy and will increase central authority. This point of view has been intensified by the developments in southeast Anatolia and northern Iraq. Turkey's relations with all its neighbours and the changes in its geo-political position make it difficult to realize the necessary reforms for an open society. However, this situation is supposed to pave the way for a civic society.

The essential problem on the eve of the 21st century is not that of the developed states' coexistence against conflict but one in which the masses have reached the first stage of their political conscience. The new geography of the ex-Eastern bloc which emerged following the changes in the post-1989 era show that micro-nationalism and ethnicity have proved to be overwhelming. These regions are awakening politically. The main characteristic of the first stage of political awakening can be denoted as their definition of the masses themselves in a narrow context as 'depending on ethnic privileges'; seeing how primitive it is to witness the expression of societal feelings. Unfortunately, the same thing also seems to be true of Turkey. There is an escape from political compromise on the grounds of not taking the complexity of social events into account but also from philosophical discussions — claiming the correctness of their own political and religious ideas affected by Manichean tendencies. In Turkey this case proves to be correct depending on religious or dogmatic mission. Identity depends on the view that the ones who belong to the ethnic group see all those who are not members of their group as being against them. In this type of collectivity the ones who wish to be the forerunners tend to create a society that conforms to their views. In Turkey, this is true for religious groups and for the extreme leftist or rightist organizations. In this case, attempts at political violence detaching economic policies from a rational structure and creating a milieu of ethnic intolerance depending on prejudices to ethnicity, formulate the basis for the implementation of the above mentioned policies. Leaders benefit from this in order to provide a specific position for their rule so that they may not be interrogated. Unfortunately, this happens to be true for the workers and trade union movements in Turkey.

It can be seen that most of the conflicts which have emerged in recent years in the world have been aimed at the establishment of a state. It is observed that those opposition groups which claim either autonomy or the separation from the existing state of a region inhabited by a particular ethnic population, leads to a conflict which is usually armed and most probably a war.

Essentially what differentiates the current situation from the classical trend is the fact that inter-state wars have been replaced by intra-state conflicts and wars. Situations along these lines are mostly observed within what is called the Third World. War between national armed forces has now been replaced by the devastation of unarmed masses in conflicts and clashes based on ethnic and political engagement. In some cases this leads to massacres condoned by the state.

Today, although interstate wars still continue, the use of classical methods along with the assistance of international law in ending wars is quite different from in the past. That in Turkey a similar event must occur is an aim of the terrorist organization, PKK. What needs to be questioned is the fact that the PKK does not carry the full representation of the native Kurdish people, and moreover that there are different groups depending on how they perceive ethnicity.

Another situation which should be mentioned here is the fact that organizations such as NATO, the UN and the OSCE which are utilized to put an end to such regional ethnic conflicts, were in fact formed with a different purpose in mind and in reference to other conflicts. In the present order of things they are redundant. The establishment of an organization capable of being able to cope with this new situation on a universal scale and the acceptance of its legal principles seems unlikely in the near future. In Turkey, it is often said that both political and administrative institutions remain quite incompetent most of the time. But there is very little effort being made regarding reorganization and this situation creates a threat to individual security. One argument against this point may consist of a reshaping of the concept of the nation state, however, this will not be discussed here. The question is one of naming the new problems of this era. The situation can be summarized as follows: The experience of mental and moral collapse, the systematic destruction of the elements which keep a society together, and thus having nothing in common, and finally, the belief that humanity is exhausted in its search for some form of awakening. In reference to this last point it can be said that human beings tend to come together either on the basis of ideological patterns, or ethnic, or religious elements, because they do not like to remain alone. Man, by nature, cannot cope with isolation from society. However, at this point it should be noted that since 1980 there has been a drive for consumption along with a lack of production in Turkey.

Attempting to force people to live together without a suitable set of moral values or the desire to share authority, where one group of people, persisting with consistent and indisputable messages, demands the control of the masses, resulting either in assimilation or disappearances. Most of the time the shortest method to actualize this policy has been made through the utilization of the concept of ethnicity which can easily be manipulated as there is no a clear-cut common idea about how to define it. This method has enabled people both to give a form to conflicts and to turn them into clashes. An estimated 87 million people have been killed in the wars fought during this century and a figure close to this have been disabled and wounded. This is greater than the entire number of casualties suffered since the beginning of history; most of these casualties are due to ethnic and religious wars. It is worth reflecting that a loss on such a scale also implies an enormous loss in genetical heritage. When an account of Turkey is made in the same vein, it is easy to see that, aside from those killed during the Turkish War of Independence and those killed in traffic accidents, the death toll due to terrorist activities before 1980, and in the events in the southeast after 1984, also constitute an enormous loss of genetical heritage in Turkey. When it is considered that the greatest investment for people regards the providing of security in a country, the mentioned matter implies a great risk.

It is plain that the new driving force for these extensive injustices is determined as ethnicity. However, peace and conflict research seem insufficient and the viability of the issue is almost completely disregarded. It is also clear that concepts such as self-determination have not been well evaluated by international authorities and institutions in a clear-cut and common manner. Neo-imperialism, which demands new fronts, can play with global concepts and provide the flexibility to re-fictionalize it in the longer term.

To abandon a concept to which the total security of a nation, and thus a state, is related, is not a matter which can be easily dismissed. It is not an unknown occurrence in today's world that wars are not only waged against the military power of a given nation, but also against nations themselves, in the same manner as the 'all-out-war' concept held by the Nazi regime during World War II.

In today's world a war fought on extended fronts threatens the welfare of the imperial powers. The shortest and cheapest way of settling and sharing new fronts is through the redeployment of the concept of ethnicity in the post-ideological wars' era. It has been supposed that ethnic conflicts are conflicts related to the internal affairs of a state, and considered that they have reflections of greater conflicts plus mostly dictatorial and/or repressive governments or simply by-products of larger conflicts. To the ones who approach change and development from a sociological point of view, the ethnic question has been evaluated as a suffering for the ones who are unable to pass to the modernity stage. Within the process of societal change leading from the traditional to the modern, from the simple to the complex, from particularism to universalism, ethnic problems have been perceived as obstacles to change. So, this can be regarded as a consequence of incomplete modernization. This view is praised by the upper class segment of society in Turkey. Moreover, it will not be wrong to explain the deterioration of moral values by this approach. The Weberian approach, which saw this as the problem of pre-modern societies at the present confronted with a deadlock regarding what it enumerated as the context of modernity. This can be exemplified with the Northern Ireland case. To the classical approaches of nation building, the ethnic question has been estimated only among sub-nation groups, so performing an obstacle for change. In the Marxist approach, the ethnic factor has clearly been given a secondary role. However, the point which cannot be ignored is the fact that the issue of an institutional framework that required the realization of a communist utopia was not handled by the founders of Marxism, but later first by Lenin and then with a severe hand by Stalin. This is a case of what practice has brought about.

The replacement of belief in the party and class with belief in the leader was seen in the Soviets and consisted of the 'ünschulung' of the masses. In close relation to this, a thesis which required the massacre of ethnic elements to fully control the masses, was developed to ensure the welfare of the leader, his group, and the party. In this sense ethno-cide was experienced just like genocide. It is clear, following the collapse of communism and the break-up of the dictatorships, why these nations are in the grip of ethnic conflicts.

In my opinion, the reason for this situation is not so different from Western style imperialism. There is no great difference between reducing ethnic elements and the characteristics which identify a nation, and preserving and propagating imperial interests, like creating nations according to geography.

For this reason, a new approach is necessary in order to understand ethnic conflicts and to define nations.

In providing Turkey's security we have to focus on the nation which makes up the state. Although there may be some deficiencies, the essence in the history of making Turkey a post-modern spirit is overwhelming, and for this reason they have exhibited some more developed attempts during that era. This issue naturally should be based on analytical studies to be conducted by political scientists and sociologists.

It can be assumed that an ethnic group can identify itself on the basis of either one or more of the following items: language, religion, tribe, nationality and race. Truly, such a definition raises more questions than answers in today's situation, but deriving from such a definition an ethnic group is considered to embrace people, nation, citizen, minority, tribe or community. Essentially, it can be thought that what comes up as an ethnic conflict is in fact that the arena in which a class or a group fighting for their interests are expanding their supporters by utilizing ethnic elements and thus are able to come together. By using ethnic elements a possibility emerges to hide the social, economic or political dimensions of the problem or issue in these conflicts. In this case the importance of ethnicity is diminished to the level of a 'leitmotif' to utilize them in moving masses.

In my opinion, ethnicity in Turkey, is intended to be used as an instrument both by internal and external powers. The clearest examples for this argument can be seen in the following polarization processes; Turk/Kurd, Alevi/Sunni, and even laic/anti-laic. Investigating HADEP from the point of view of Kurdish nationalism dimension is a topic in itself; and MHP for the Turkish nationalism dimension in spite of the fact that they gain considerable momentum.

In this sense, it is necessary to differentiate between conflicts of values or identity conflicts, and conflicts of interests. The necessity emerges from the fact that when a conflict persists for a very long period of time and at the same time involves violence, a conflict of interests may be resolved either by discussion or by bargaining. However, the problem is with the second type of conflict. The nation-building period, which began mostly in the 18th and 19th centuries, was proposed as a universal model and was even, sometimes, introduced with utopian ideas. For instance, for many centuries different societies continued to live on the same territory; however, during the mentioned period only one culture was chosen to be the dominant one. This caused the diminishing and even later on the disappearance of some cultures.

At the individual level, behavioural deteriorations begun to emerge and prejudices and enmities caused alienation. Until that time these groups existed as an ethnie-to-itself, but later they became an ethnie-for-itself. According to the supporters of an instrumentalist view, for effective action to take place it is necessary to have a rational choice, this ethnicity should be created as a political weapon, and it should be formulated, used, and be given a direction, or should be left outside the order. The problems we are confronted with are in fact the institutionalization of the changes in the individual by the politicians.

In Turkey, against all traditional values, children are massacred in separatist movements, terrorist activities and upheavals. Basically, all these problems can be evaluated as anachronous, so the question to be asked is this: Why they come to the fore in our country, which has been the cradle of so many civilizations? The answer may be as complex as the situation outlined above, and when foreign involvement is also included the degree of complexity increases.

When the United States is considering a foreign policy, reality can be observed. It follows the Middle East Peace Process with close interest due to the Jewish lobby in the States; it could not disregard the Afro-Americans when the South African problem emerged, although it has a structure based on White Anglo-Saxon Protestant values; and when one of its citizen's life is at stake, it can interfere with the problem of a Third World country. The content of the ethnic problems is justified by carrying them to the international arena. As to the Kurdish problem with the initiatives of the U.S., the Dublin Summit began to be organized as a series and thus this procedure represents a similar line with the above mentioned case. The Kurdish question is already on the international agenda. However, with the Dublin meetings, the PKK is articulated to the Kurdish elements and thus contributes to the process of the internationalization of the issue.

Events in the past indicate that we have also to analyse the core of an era in terror called 'substitutional terror'. As we witnessed, the Armenian terror organization ASALA handed the mission over to PKK, and PKK might do the same to a radical Islamic group utilizing terror as well.

In my opinion, the following points should be considered:

a) The process of the conflict is accelerated with foreign involvement.

b) The process is prolonged until the interests of the foreign entities are balanced.

c) When a balance is reached with the use of international pressure, a kind of yielding and compromise process begins, and for this reason the joining of official mediators either as individual persons or as institutions is provided. Recent events have also demonstrated that unofficial diplomacy has to be added to this point.

d) If a balance of interests cannot be reached, then either the ethnic factors or all other elements of the region are included in the process and thus the conflict turns out to be an all-out conflict.

It is understood from the current situation that an 'all-out-war' has not completed its cycle yet. Ethnicity is a tool to make this war perpetuate. Therefore, at this point it is time for a brainstorm to create the New Turkish Order.

The Reality of Turkey

Sefa Martin Yürükel

The Historical Perspective and the Process of National Construction

Anatolia and Thrace (Turkey), as they are today, were built in 1923 upon the ruins of the Ottoman Empire by the eternal leader and founder of the Turkish Republic, Mustafa Kemal Atatürk. In many parts of the former empire, there was a widespread displacement of inhabitants in the wake of its downfall; people belonging to ethnic cultural and religious minorites moved to Anatolia from the former regions of the empire: Albanians, Bosnians, Pomaks from Bulgaria, and from the Caucasus region there were the Chechens, Akbhazians, Georgians, Azeri, etc. This created a new situation in Anatolia. There was an increase in its already multi-ethnic diversity. Atatürk and his friends wanted to create a completely new structure to replace that of the Ottomans. Inspired by the rise in the 19th and 20th century of the nation-state in Western Europe, they set out to apply this centralised state model to Turkey in a radical break with the Ottoman system that was in place. Their aim was that Turkey should become a national state and its people should be one nation.

..The 'nation', and the ethnic group, appear as the ultimate guarantee 'when society fails'.[1]

Following the collapse, it was necessary for them to create a new model. This was based on the French model for a nation-state and republic. Right from the start of the national liberation struggle in 1919, it was Atatürk's plan to do this. In a similar fashion to that outlined by Hobsbawm above, Atatürk centred his struggle around two ethnic groups; first of all the Turks, and secondly, the Kurds. While these two groups were both Anatolian as well as being the largest ethnic groups in the country, and at the same time Muslim, Atatürk and his 'friends' realised that this was not sufficient for building the new republic: What they needed was a model into which all of these elements could be fitted. The potential of these two ethnic groups had to be mobilized in order to create the optimum conditions for the French model as well as gain political

---

1. Hobsbawm, E. 1992: 7.

authority. This was the only way in which he could create order in Anatolia. As Morgenthau puts it:

the nation needs a state, 'one nation-one state' is thus the political postulate of nationalism; the nation state is its ideal.[2]

To create this ideal nation state it was necessary therefore for Atatürk to use the idea of nationalism. It was clear to him that the nation state could not exist without nationalism. The establishment of the nation state was the only solution for Atatürk in order to break entirely with the former Ottoman system and at the same time to modernize or 'westernize' Turkey. In his opinion the Turkish people had never been a nation under Ottoman rule, or before.

The Turks are on their way to becoming a nation for the first time. There is now a national consciousness.[3]

Atatürk realised that this was a turning point, the Ottoman Empire could not be resurrected. At the same time, there was a political vaccum and a lack of authority. If Atatürk was unable to create this new republic then it would have fallen to the various imperialist powers and their interests in colonizing Turkey; France, England, Italy. Marx and Engels foresaw the collapse of the Ottoman Empire and analysed the consequences in the days when it was referred to as 'The sick man of Europe'. In their book, *The Eastern Question* (Dogu Sorunu) they wrote that 'Turkeys independence is necessary to avoid the Ottoman territories falling into the hands of the Russians in the likely event of the collapse of the Ottoman Empire'. This was the biggest problem as far as they could tell. In order to avoid the possibility of invasion and at the same time create a nation state, Atatürk set up a number of congresses during the liberation struggle.[4]

These congresses were vital in the creation of the national struggle, as well as the Republic and its authority. A number of resolutions were passed pertaining to the mobilization of the masses. An organized series of independent guerilla corps under the command of the *Kuvayi Milliye* (Political Authority) organization whose actions were ruled on at the various congresses. Their first task was to protect the *Misak-i-milli (National Pact)* — the borders of Turkey. A disciplined national organization was necessary in order to

---

2. Morgenthau, H., 1950: 155.
3. M.K. Atatürk 1920's: Teori 1994: 10.
4. The most important of these were: Erzurum, July 10th, 1919; Balikesir (1), July 31st, 1919; Nazilli, August 7th, 1919; Sivas, September 4th, 1919; Balikesir (2), September 22nd, 1919; Lüleburgaz, 1920; Edirne, May 9th, 1920. (Selek, S., 1987: 103).

mobilize society and create a large and strong field of authority in the country. In this way, during the liberation struggle itself, Atatürk had, with the establishment of the congresses, created a civilian authority for the nation-to-be, and a military organization in the form of the disciplined guerilla groups under the authority of the congress. This was, in effect, the foundation of a national state.

A 'nation', as I use the term here, only exists when a state has a unified administrative reach over the territory over which its sovereignty is claimed. The development of a plurality of nations is basic to the centralization and administrative expansion of state domination internally, since the fixing of borders depends upon the reflexive ordering of a state system.[5]

As Giddens makes clear, in order to succeed in the process of liberating Turkey and in the establishment of the Republic, as it occurred via the congresses and their resolutions, it became clear that Turkey could not be divided and that its unity was not open to debate. The soon to be established national state, was to be the republic of the Turks and the Kurds. This was made clear right from the very first declaration (the famous Amasya Declaration in 1919). Later on, in the process of sharing political authority, the non-Turkish groups had to accept that they existed as citizens and not as an ethnic group within the bounds of the new Turkish Republic. The French model was necesary to create a common cultural potential; one language, one flag, one parliament, one unified territory. All of these things were important if Atatürk was to establish a new republic in Turkey.

A nation is a historically constituted, stable community of people formed on the basis of a common language, territory, economic life, and psychological make-up, manifested in a common culture..it is only when all of these characteristics are present together that we have a nation.[6]

Stalin's formulation of the concept of the nation here is the same as that which Atatürk wished to implement in Turkey. The republic as founded by the Western bourgoisie, with Western understanding, and suited to the conditions in the West, involved great changes related to equality and democracy. As Lenin puts it;

---

5. Giddens, A., 1985: 119.
6. Stalin, J. cited in Hutchinson & Smith, 1994: 20.

We understand the republican concept, not in the structure of government, but upon what it is founded; that which all the democratic reforms are based on.[7]

In contrast to Lenin's understanding of the nation, Atatürk created an elite which gave rise to a system that built from the top downwards rather than the other way around. This is why the Kurds were to be seen as citizens rather than as an ethnic group.

The Amasya Declaration and the Historical Process

Mustafa Kemal Atatürk's speech as recorded in the Amasya declaration:

The accepted boundaries of the Ottoman rulers included the homelands of the Turks and the Kurds. It was impossible to remove the Kurdish people from Ottoman society. We are all in agreement on this.[8]

At the end of 1922, Atatürk and his commanders won a resounding military victory, at which point Atatürk announced that 'This new republic which we shall build will be the state of the 'Turkish people'. The Amasya declaration was signed by delegates from a number of ethnic groups. Later this declaration was ratified by the Erzurum congress:

All Muslim people make sacrifices on one anothers behalf and respect each other; They respect each others ethnic, social and local conditions and they are brothers.[9]

This was again underlined at the Sivas congress — here, the two ethnic groups saw themselves as being united as Anatolians. Officially, the Sivas congress sealed this brotherhood. It was therefore quite natural that the coming political authority should be divided between these two ethnic groups. A Kurdish delegate from Mus put it thus:

When we defeated the enemy it was a victory for fate. The blood which ran from our veins was Turkish and Kurdish blood.[10]

The Lausanne Treaty and Its Consequences

After the end of the liberation struggle in July 1923, the leader of the Turkish delegation, the second highest ranking in the republic, national leader General

7. Perincek, D., Lenin, Vol. 8; Kemalist devrim: 125.
8. Article 1A. declaration; Teori 1991: 18-19.
9. Article 1. ibid: 19.
10. Gologlu, M., Türkiye Cumhuriyeti: 76; Ibid: 19.

Ismet İnönü, represented both the Turkish and Kurdish inhabitants and he formulated their situation as follows;

The Turkish delegation is obliged to express its gratitude and great admiration to all the Turkish commanders who took part in the World War and in the War of Liberation as well as the sacrifices made by the Kurdish population in the liberation of the fatherland. In the fight against the Sultan and the Istanbul regime. In Anatolia, those who defended the front lines when the enemy invaded, particularly against the Greeks. The Kurds and the Turks worked hand in hand for the same ideal.[11]

The Lausanne Treaty covered the position of the Kurds in the formation of the new state; how to create unity and development and the division of authority. The Lausanne Treaty outlined how these matters were to be dealt with. The result was:

Article 39: There will be no official restriction on any Turkish citizen's right to use any language he wishes, whether in private, in commercial gatherings, in matters of religion, in print or at a public gathering regardless of the existence of an official language, appropriate facilities will be provided to allow citizens to use their own language before the courts.

Article 37: Turkey commits itself to recognising the stipulations contained in Articles 38-44 as fundamental laws and to ensure that no law, no regulation, and no official action stand in contradiction to these stipulations, and that no law, regulation or official action shall prevail against them'.[12]

These are important pieces of evidence in the understanding of how the Turkish Republic was founded. After the war of liberation and the establishment of the Turkish Republic, the new national bourgoisie in Turkey applied the French model. That is to say that the official language of the Turkish Republic is Turkish. Turkey is a unitary state. All people are equal citizens, etc. As a consequence of this, the existing ethnic groups in Anatolia, especially the Kurdish population, were degraded by the new Turkish national bourgoisie in the sharing of political authority. This was a denial of everything in the Amasya and Sivas resolutions.

11. Ibid: 20.
12. Kendal, 1982: 60.

Political Mistakes and the Construction of a Centralist Nationalist State and the Consequences of the Politics of Denial

According to the Turkish nationalists, the population groups living in Turkey had to have a common, single identity. The new national bourgoise and nationalist movements decided to rewrite the history of the people of Anatolia. All the above named resolutions were thereby censored; in books, archives etc. Their understanding of the Western norm and nation thus gave rise to a falsification of history. Turkey's multi-ethnic reality was thus altered. As Smith puts it;

A named human population sharing an historic territory, common myths and historical memories, a mass, public culture, a common economy and common legal rights and duties for all members.[13]

According to the Turkish nationalists'new historians, the Kurds — one of the oldest surviving populations of Mesopotamia and Anatolia — were described in the books and articles as 'Mountain Turks'. All the ethnic minorities, as well as the Kurdish population, were regarded by these ideologists of the Turkish state as being different kinds of 'Turks'. They might speak a little differently, but they were still Turkish. Morgenthau writes;

The dilution of the race through the admixture of alien elements corrupts the character of the nation and the purity of the race thus appears as the very essence of national power, and for the latter's sake national minorities must either be absorbed or ejected.[14]

This policy of denial and falsification carried on for years and finally met political opposition in the 1960s when accusations were levelled at the Turkish Workers Party by the state. The Turkish Workers Party accepted the real facts of the Kurdish people. The accusation was as follows:

The charge on page 54. Due to the harsh climate in Central Asia the Turkish tribes moved south and west. The Kurds are in fact a part of the Turani Kavim — the Turkish peoples.[15]

This shows how far the Turkish state was prepared to go in order to falsify the historical details. This understanding was a product of the adjustment of the Western model of the nation state. The Turkish nationalists' rewriting of history was actually done with the intention of creating the ideal nation. This

---

13. Smith, A., 1991: 14.
14. Morgenthau, ibid: 155.
15. Savunma: 346.

resulted in a strategy of assimilation regarding the various ethnic identities in Anatolia.

Nation and the Construction of National Identity

The Turkish nationalists applied themselves to the creation of these two things; in order to do this they had to create Turkish nationalism which they saw as being alpha and omega in this regard. Nationalism was one of the six founding principles of Atatürk's Cumhuriyet Halk Partisi (Republican Folk Party) aimed at mobilizing society. In practice, nationalism was seen an important method for the build up of the nation. As Ernest Gellner says:

Nationalism is not the awakening of nations to self-consciousness; it invents nations where they do not exist — but it does need some pre-existing differentiating marks to work on, even if, as indicated, these are purely negative...[16]

In this way, as Gellner makes clear, nationalism is used as a scheme in creating the sense of a nation. The Turkish nationalists in Turkey were using this method in 1919; even before the establishment of the Republic. This approach resulted in many upleasant events and caused much suffering, such as in putting down the Kurdish uprising. This has continued up until today.

The Multi-Ethnicity of Anatolia and Its Difficulties

Anatolia has been called the *Kavimler Kapisi* (The gate of the tribes). As mentioned above, Anatolia comprises many ethnic groups and this diversity is quite natural. The Turkish nationalists, however, never considered the problem of how to actually apply the model of the republic to an ethnically diverse place such as Turkey. No detailed policy was developed in this region. It was unthinkable to them that the model which they had imported from the West was not applicable. Their strategy was that all ethnic groups were to be assimliated into the nation. In the preface to his book; *The Ethnic Groups in Turkey (1992)*, Peter Alford Andrews wrote that 'the census figures for 1965 show that Alawi and Kurdish villages are noted as being either Sunni or Turkish.'

    This is also a product of the above-mentioned nationalist assimilation strategy. Since the foundation of the Turkish Republic and its replacement of the Ottoman Empire ideology with French Bourgoise state ideology, it has paid no heed to the reality of the ethnic communities and ultimately dictated from

---

16. Gellner in Smith, A., 1991: 71.

above in order to create Turkish identity and authority. The national leader General Ismet Inönü, stated the following at Lausanne:

The government of the Great National Assembly is the government of both Turks and Kurds; that the 'real representatives of the Kurds are equal partners in the Government of Turkey', and that although the Turks and the Kurds may speak different languages, these two peoples are not significantly different and form a single block from the point of view of race, faith and custom.[17]

These famous words were soon forgotten, as also was the Multi-Ethnic society, and the Kurds in particular were dismissed as an external factor by the Turkish nationalist elite when putting their ideology into practice. The Minister of Justice at the time, the famous Turkish nationalist intellectual Mahmut Esat Bozkurt, expressed his opinion as follows:

The Turk is the only *effendi* in this country and the only proprietor. Those who do not come from the pure Turkish race have only one, single right; to become servants and slaves. Let this be heard by all friends and foe alike and in all the mountains around us.[18]

The application of this layer of chauvinism on top of Anatolia's ethnic diversity affected the following groups: Yörükler, Türkmenler, Tahtacilar, Abdallar, Azeriler, Karapapaklar, Uygurlar, Kirgizlar, Kazaklar, Özbekler, Tatarlar, Balkarlar, Karacaylar, Kumuklar, Göcmenler, Dagistanlilar, Sudanlilar, Estonlar, yahudiler, Yezidiler, Zazalar, Ossetler, Ermeniler, Hemsinler, Arnavutlar, Molokanlar, Polonezler, Cingeneler, Rumlar, Almanlar, Araplar, Nusayriler, Süryaniler, Keldaniler, Cerkezler, Gürcüler, Lazlar, Kürtler etc...[19]

The existence of all of these groups was threatened by the elite of the national state. This chauvinistic attack levelled at non-Turkish ethnic groups prompted radical reactions among the Kurds. The Kurdish leadership, opposed to this policy, organized a series of uprisings between 1925 and 1938; Agri, Zilan, Kocgiri, Dersim, etc. These uprisings were a reaction to the broken promise of there being equality between Kurds and Turks in the newly founded state. These uprisings were generally considered to be led by reactionaries. The real intention was to force the state to stick by the promises it made at the congresses in Sivas, Erzurum and in the Amasya declaration. The two most important Kurdish leaders were the Sunni Sheikh Sa'id (1925) and the Alevi

17. Kendal, 1982: 59.
18. Bozkurt, M.E., 19th September 1930; Xemgin, E., 1989: 38.
19. Andrews, P.A., 1992.

Sayed Reza (1937-38). Their intention was to make their demands known through these uprisings. They used the same slogans which Atatürk used during the liberation struggle. They saw their battle as being the Kurdish war of liberation. Sayed Reza's last words before he was hanged in 1939 were; 'Yasasin Kürtlük' (long live the Kurds). The fight in other words would go on, as indeed it has — until today.

The propagators of the distorted history; the Turkish nationalists, put down these uprisings in a very harsh and bloody fashion. Around 15,000 people were massacred. Thousands of Kurds were forcibly displaced to Western Anatolia. The names of the Kurdish villages were systematically changed to Turkish ones, e.g; Dersim became Tunceli and so on. The Turkish national chauvinists did not stop there, but also started changing the names of people. This assimilation policy meant cultural and historical genocide for the Turkish state — as well as for the Kurds. From 1925 to 1938, the uprisings resulted in'206 villages completely destroyed, 8,758 houses demolished, 500,000 people moved from East to West, and tens of thousands were massacred'.[20]

These misguided policies are still being implemented today in areas such as; Hakkari, Sirnak, Sivas, Bismil, Cizre, Batman, Siirt etc. Former president Cemal Gürsel at the end 1960 in Diyarbakir declared, in an open speech to the people; 'There is no Kurdish population — you are all Turks. [21]

On the matter of cultural genocide, the well-known journalist Ekrem Usakligil wrote:

Ten years ago many foreign people referred to places called Kurdistan and Armenia. These remote places were far from the centre of Turkey, but the people were still Turks. The furthest outposts of the Ottoman Empire. The people mixed Arabic and Farsi with Turkish which is why they speak such a strange language. Today this negligence is being corrected by the school system. Hopefully, with the help of the schools, this Turkish dialect will be removed from our language.[22]

The oppressive measures taken in the systematic assimilation were successful in dissuading other ethnic groups from following the Kurdish example. Up until 1994, the suffering endured by the Kurds stopped any of the other groups from making any demands on the state. In 1994, the Laz ethnic group from Northern Turkey attempted to publish their own cultural magazine *Ogri* but were critized very strongly by the government, which then accused them of encouraging separatism. For several years this kind of political development created national paranoia in Turkey. This soon led to every single ethnic

20. Savunma, 1974: 364.
21. Hürriyet, October 25th, 1960.
22. Son Posta, April 11th, 1946.

demand being regarded by the state as a threat to the very existence of the nation. The majority of people in Turkey therefore followed the state-led suggestion and dropped all ethnic demands for the sake of the unity of the nation. It was as Balibar put it:

... a nationalism exacerbated by an 'exceptional' series of internal and external conflicts was able to idealize the goals of racism to the point of making the violence wrought by the great number of torturers possible and 'normalising' this in the eyes of the great mass of people.[23]

These policies also met opposition among democrats and socialists in Turkey. The opposition were accused of supporting separatism and undermining the existence of the Turkish state. To eliminate this opposition the government invoked paragraph 141 and 142 which entered the penal code in 1936, based on the laws of Mussolini in Italy. The use of these paragraphs implied that the republic's sense of itself as a democracy had in fact been discarded. On the basis of these laws, many intellectuals, socialists and democrats were sent to prison and lost their jobs. Many were sentenced to long terms in prison. The national state ideology forbid the formation of any new parties and all opposition organizations were banned. Lenin's view of the meaning of republic is mentioned above. The Turkish state adopted the term republic by name alone. Chronologically speaking, from 1922 onwards they have failed to, or else have only partially implemented the points outlined by Lenin. This applies not only to language, but also on the cultural and economic planes which a republic requires. The high ranking figures in the Turkish state have always regarded those people living in the Kurdish regions as a potential threat.

According to former Chief of Staff, the well known Turkish commander Marshal Fevzi Cakmak; 'In the eastern towns the opening of schools could encourage people and lead to the development of so-called "Kurdish" separatist movements'.[24]

Every single development in the Kurdish regions has been regarded with suspicion by the state. In the course of time this national state ideology has itself encouraged opposing ideology such as is the case with Kurdish nationalism which exploded again in a number of forms, including the ultra nationalist organization PKK's (Partîya Kârkeren Kurdistan —Kurdistan Workers Party) uprising in 1984. Those, who like the administrators of the

23. Balibar, E., 1991: 51-52.
24. Agaoglu, S., *DP'nin dogusu*: 159; Savunma: 343.

Turkish state, have not learned from political and national history, have contributed to the collapse of the possibility of assimilation. The Turkish state had in mind something like an 'imagined community' along the lines defined by Benedict Anderson (1991). The Turkish state's systematic nationalist policy and its dismissal of other ethnic groups has raised the awareness of these other groups who are now seeking, like the Kurds in 1984, to create their own 'imagined communities'. To do this the Kurds have built up their own nationalist organisations; the PKK, the KDP, Rizgari, AlaRizgari, Kawa, Denge-Kawa, Kurdistan Sosyalist Partisi, Bes Parcacilar, Kürt Hizbullahi, Tekoser etc. The Kurds are now speaking of their own nation in the same terms as used by M. Kemal Atatürk in the 1920s. The slogan used in 1984 by pan-Kurdist, Abdullah Öcalan, general secretary of the Kurdish ultra-nationalist organization, PKK, and leader of the guerilla forces ARGK, was; 'We will fight for a single handful of our soil'.

Abdullah Öcalan imagines himself as a kind of 'Ataküurd'. With this slogan he refers to war of national liberation in the same way that Kemal Atatürk did. The problem is that this kind of nationalist appeal to Kurdish society is not suited to the demographic structure of Turkey. There are no longer only Kurds in the Kurdish regions, just as the Turkish regions are not inhabited by Turks alone. As a consequence of the forced displacements in the past, the populations are now very thoroughly mixed together. Therefore, calls for Kurdish nationalism are in effect no different from the Turkish nationalists' in the past. In *Hujada*, the journal of The Federation of Assyrians in exile, Yashar Kaya, leader of the so-called 'Kurdish parliament in exile' (pro-PKK), referred to the Assyrian people as being 'Christian Kurds' in the same way that the Turkish elite called the Kurds 'Mountain Turks' as part of their assimilation policy. The result could be that the Kurds end up assimilating the other ethnic groups in the Kurdish regions. The Kurdish establishment of a parliament in exile and the guerilla organization ARGK, with one leader in a position of authority, are all very similar moves to what Atatürk did. The only difference between Atatürk and Öcalan is not that they belong to two different ages, but that Atatürk played a strongly anti-imperialist role, supported by Lenin and the revolutionary nationalist movements in the colonized world. Atatürk was also inspired by the national liberation movements in Egypt, Iraq, Tunis, Syria, Algeria, Bangaladesh, India, Pakistan, Afghanistan and the Philippines, etc. Atatürk influenced the identity of the revolutionary nationalist movements in all of these countries. Today, the ultra-nationalist organization PKK's leader, pan-Kurdist Abdullah Öcalan, plays a somewhat different role. Abdullah Öcalan is prepared to use the imperialist countries against Turkey in the struggle to create his own nation; 'the true

intention of the Turkish colonialists is....to assimilate the Kurdish population
— by political, cultural, economic and military means'.[25]

The violence of the Turkish state has given rise to opposing violence. The
Turkish state today uses the largest proportion of its GNP to carry out the
military operations necessary to fight the PKK in the Kurdish region. Economic
pressure in Turkey is forcing the state to consider alternative solutions. This
view is prevalent among members of parliament as well as military officers
and a portion of the bourgoisie. The Turkish population is concerned about
allowing their children to carry out their military conscription in Eastern
Turkey. More than 100,000 have deserted or refused to carry out their military
service. As Mikael Gravers puts it:

At a distance, their ethnic and cultural opposition to 'others' in the host country is often
sharpened. Appeals for assistance from home and a natural pre-occupation with self-
identification and images of a historical mission could enforce calls for the use of
violence to counter violence.[26] (Gravers, 1995 p. 142)

All of these developments have created a debate within the ranks of the
Turkish bourgoisie. On the strength of this, Professor Dogu Ergil was asked
to compile a report on the Kurdish problem in 1995. Within the ranks of the
military it is accepted that their is no military solution to the Kurdish question;
they too have begun to consider other solutions. At the same time, however,
the Kurdish question has entered the international arena. The European
Council and the EU Parliament have produced a number of reports on the
subject.

In Turkey itself, some politicians and socialists have begun to talk about
federation and autonomy. At the same time there has been an escalation of
state terror in the Kurdish regions as well as of the PKK's terrorization of
Turkish villages and citizens (for the simple reason that they are Turkish). This
has given rise to a general sense of fatigue among the population of Turkey.
The large cities such as Istanbul, Ankara, Mersin, Diyarbakir have seen an
influx of refugees from Eastern Turkey and this affects their populations
opinion of the problem. This creates a huge inversion of Turkish society at
large; in terms of economy, politics, demography, culture, and social matters.
Today people are divided over the solution to this question. Many think of
a political one and others of a nationalist solution; most are agreed that a
military solution is not possible.

25. Kürdistan Ulusal Kurtulus Problemi ve cözüm yolu, 1982: 184.
26. Gravers, 1995: 142.

Conclusion

The Western national state model and democracy has given rise to a strongly centralized system of national authority. But circumstances such as those present in multi-ethnic states like Turkey, or Bosnia, and the other countries of the Balkans, the Middle East and Caucasus, show that this model is not applicable universally. The models imported from the West to multi-ethnic Turkey were applied from above without creating or developing democracy, instead they used totalitarian power on the ethnic groups within the population. This created ethno-nationalism in Turkey — that is to say, to import a model or system from outside is not sufficient without the implementation of radical reforms — which is what Turkey is in need of. If Turkey is not democraticized, the development of ethnic nationalism will be a threat to the very existence of Turkey. In my opinion, Turkey should not import democracy from the West in a literal sense, but strive towards creating a form of democracy suitable to its multi-ethnic background. The other alternative is a scenario worse than that in Bosnia — the demography is far more complicated in Turkey than in Bosnia. Turkey has to accept the fact that it is a multi-ethnic country and has to build a balance in the division of political power and cultural autonomy between the various ethnic groups. That is to say that a democratic, economic, cultural, social, and political development, including the removal of power from large landowners and the redistribution of land to peasants in the east and southeast of Turkey, is the only feasible solution to running the country. What I have said here is nothing new; In the 1920s, Mustafa Kemal Atatürk, speaking in the towns of Eskisehir and Izmit, said that autonomy could be discussed. Finally, if Turkey wishes to maintain its political weight in the region then it must reinstate the declarations made at Amasya.

Bibliography

Andrews, Peter A., 1992. *Türkiyede Etnik Gruplar*. Istanbul: Ant Yayinlari.

Anderson, B., 1992. *Imagined Communities. Reflections on the origin and spread of Nationalism.* London.

Atatürk M. K., 1994. *Teori, cit. Perincek, D. Milliyetcilik Üzerine.* Sosyalist Parti Yayin Organi, Yön Matbacilik. Istanbul.

Balibar, E. & I. Wallerstein 1991. *Race, Nation, Class-Ambigious Identities.* London.

Cakmak, Fevzi cit. Agaoglu, Samet., 1977. *DP'nin Dogusu*: 159; Savunma: 343. Istanbul: Aydinlik.

Giddens, Antony, 1987. *The Nation, State and Violance.* Oxford: Polity Press.

Gürsel, Cemal, 1960. *Hürriyet Gazetesi.* Istanbul: 25. Ekim.

Gravers, Mikael, 1995. 'Nationalism and ethnicism in the present world order.' In: Yürükel Sefa M. (ed.): *The Balkan War/Krigen På Balkan.* Aarhus: Department of Ethnography and Social Anthropology, University of Aarhus: 139-46.

Hobsbawm, E., 1992. 'Ethnicity and Nationalism in Europe Today.' *Anthropology Today* Vol. 8, (1).

Inönü, Ismet, 1991. 'Kürt Sorunu ve Sosyalistler'. *Teori Sosyalist Parti Yayin Organi,* March. Istanbul: Yön Matbasi.

Kaya, Yasar 1996. 'Yalancinin Mumu Yatsiya Kadar Yanar', *Hujådå*; Assyriska Riksförbundet i Sverige, January, Vol. 19. (1). Series 211. Södertälje: 32.

Kendal, 1980. 'Kurdistan in Turkey, The Kurds and Kurdistan'. In Chaliand, Gerard. (ed.), *People Without A Country*, London: Zed. Press.

Marks & Engels, 1979. *Dogu Sorunu.* Sol yayinlari: 33-34; cit. Perincek, Dogu, *Kemalist Devrim.* Instanbul: Aydinlik Yayinlari.

Morgenthau, Hans J., 1984. *Politics among Nations; The Struggle for Power and Peace.* New York: Alfred A.Knoff.

Savunma, 1977. *TIIKP (Türkiye Ihtilalci Isci Köylü Partisi), Davasi.* Istanbul: Aydinlik Yayinlari, 2. Baski.

Selek, Sabahattin, 1987. *Anadolu Ihtilali* Istanbul: Kastas A.S. Yayinlari.

Smith, Antony, D., 1991. *National Identity.* London: Harmondworth.

Hutchinson & Smith (eds.), 1994. *Nationalism.* Oxford University Press.

Usakligil, Ekrem, 1946. *Son Posta Gazetesi.* Istanbul: Turkey, April 11th.

Teori, 1991. 'Kürt Sorunu ve Sosyalistler'. *Sosyalist Parti Yayin Organi,* March, Istanbul: Yön Matbasi.

Teori, 1994. Mustafa Kemal Atatürk, see Perincek, Dogu, Milliyetcilik Üzerine, Sosyalist Parti Yayin Organi, Aralik-Ocak, Vol. 60-61: 10. Istanbul: Yön Matbasi.

Wesanan, Serxwebun, 1982. 'ERNK- Program ve Taslagi'. *Kürdistan Ulusal Kurtulus Problemi ve Cözüm.* Köln: Serxwebun Verlag und Handels-GmbH.

Xemgin, E., 1989. *Kürdistan'da Insan Hakluri.* Köln: Agri Verlag.

Political Islam — An Anomaly of Liberal Democracy?

Elisabeth Özdalga

An important weakness of the modern Turkish political system is the widely felt apprehension of deep seated ideological divisions and openly declared divergent beliefs. The repeated military interventions speak their own language. They have been based on a mistrust in the institutions of democracy and a fear of total collapse should the ingrained ideological boundaries be too severely challenged. In other words, *pluralism,* one of the basic principles of liberal democracy, has been too narrowly defined.

Ideological conflicts and split interests have been conceived as a threat to the basic unity of the polity. A common conception is that anarchy is lurking behind openly expressed opposite views. This Hobbesian psychological syndrome is one important reason for the weakness of democracy in a country situated on the borderline between Europe and the Middle East.

Even if the expression 'diversity within unity' has become common-place, it points towards the question of what is an important missing link in the Turkish political system. In recent years the lack of tolerance has been particularly noticeable in the conflict between secularism and political Islam. The impatience with groups and people of different opinions is equally remarkable on both sides.

This intolerance is nothing new in the case of Turkey. If one leaves the non-democratic regimes of the Middle East aside, and limits the perspective to the European continent, one is struck by the difficulties met in establishing liberal democracy even in this part of the world. For the last century or so, authoritarian movements have repeatedly threatened and interrupted the democratic process. In this respect there are important lessons to learn from a closer examination of political developments in different parts of Europe as compared to Turkey. When doing so, one should not be limited to present conditions, but apply a wider historical perspective.

On the way to Vienna for the First European Conference of Sociology in August 1992, I had the American sociologist Carl E. Schorske's famous book *Fin-de-siécle Vienna* as a travel-guide. This singular work contains an informed account of the politics, culture, architecture, and science in Vienna at the turn of the century. Schorske is also well-known for his very readable work, *The Great Schism. German Social Democracy 1905-17*. On re-reading his book about Vienna I was struck by the similarities between political life in Vienna and Austria at the turn of the century and recent developments in Turkey.

Apart from an analysis of the scientist Sigmund Freud, the artist Gustav Klimt, and the architects Camillo Sitte and Otto Wagner, *Fin-de-siècle Vienna* contains a discussion of the emergence of three modern demagogues: Georg von Schönerer, Karl Lueger, and Theodor Herzl. Georg von Schönerer was a confirmed anti-Semitist, a forerunner of and source of inspiration to Hitler. Karl Lueger was also a leader who knew how to turn the anti-Semitic sentiments in Austria to his own political advantage. He became the founder of the Christian Socialist Party in Austria. Theodor Herzl was the founder of Zionism.

What was the secret behind the success of these leaders? At the turn of the century, Austrian society was characterized by a deep-seated crisis. The Liberal era, which had mainly been supported by a progressive bourgeois class, had come to an end. In the Reichstag elections of 1895, the Liberals lost control over Austrian politics once and for all. In their place the political initiative was passed over to political groups which, in different ways, were critical of Liberalism; socialists or social-democrats, extreme nationalists or supporters to the idea of pan-Germanism, Christian socialists, Czech nationalists and Zionists.

The Liberal era emerged after the 1848 revolution and was established during the reign of the Emperor Franz Josef (1848-1916), an era of glory and modernization for Austria in general and for Vienna in particular. This was the period of the great architectural reconstruction of the capital, when the famous Ring with all its grandiose and pompous buildings came into being: residential houses as well as public buildings like the Opera, the National Theater, the Art Museum, the Natural History Museum and the Reichstag. The motto of this era was Ritter von Schmerling's, 'Wir können warten. Wissen macht frei', which expressed a strong belief in future, progress, and reason. This was a time when bourgeois elite groups were feeling safe and confident concerning the liberal values of freedom and individualism. Based on these values there was no difficulty in deciding what was morally defensible or reprehensible, what represented progress or retrogression; and science certainly scored higher than religion.

Towards the end of this glorious century, however, groups other than the bourgeois class proper had begun to put their imprint on politics in Vienna. On the one hand non-Germanic groups such as Czechs, Croats, and Serbs had started to demand national independence. Many Hungarians were also dissatisfied with their involvement within the framework of the 'Double Monarchy.' On the other hand peasants, farmers, artisans, and workers had started to ask for democratic rights. Universal suffrage had still not been accepted and the right to vote was dependent on one's level of income.

To a large extent, the new political streams of thought also emerged as a reaction to liberal ideology. The new currents of thought were inconsistent and more like 'ideological mosaics'. This produced apparent confusion as to what was to be regarded as progressive and reactionary, and what could be accepted as a common ideological measuring rod. Georg von Schönerer for example, the Nationalist and pan-Germanist, represented an ideology, which combined attitudes and values from many different social strata. In Schorske's words it contained:

Aristocratic élitism and enlightened despotism, anti–Semitism and democracy, 1848 grossdeutsch democracy and Bismarckian nationalism, medieval chivalry and anti-Catholicism, guild restrictions and state ownership of public utilities. Every one of these pairs of values the nineteenth-century liberal would have seen as contradictory. But there was a common denominator in this set of ideational fractions: total negation of the liberal élite and its values.[1]

At the turn of the century the traditional political elite had been struck by confusion and paralysis. On the one hand there was a weak, impotent political leadership within the framework of the established parliamentarian institutions, whilst on the other, the broad masses of the people, impatiently waiting for social and political (democratic) reforms. So long as no solutions were taken by the Reichstag the masses were not afraid of taking to the streets. The combination of these two factors had momentous consequences. It was in this atmosphere that demagogues such as Schönerer and Lueger launched successful political careers.

Schönerer won the support of the masses through his anti–Semitism and extreme nationalism. Lueger on the other hand formulated an ideology based on Christian, Catholic values. In Schorske's own words:

Catholicism offered Lueger an ideology that could integrate the disparate anti-liberal elements which had been moving in contradictory directions as his career developed: democracy, social reform, anti-Semitism, and Habsburg loyalty. Conversely, Lueger could give Catholicism the political leadership to weld together its shattered social

---

1. Schorske: *Fin-de-Siècle Vienna. Politics and Culture.* Cambridge: Cambridge University Press 1981: 132.

components into an organization strong enough to make its way in the modern secular world.[2]

In this way Austrian political history offers an interesting illustration of how religion, here in the form of Catholicism, was used as a tool in the political struggle. Through the Christian Socialist movement religion was given a new status, which at the same time could be turned into a revival or upswing for the Church itself. It is interesting to note that this occurred during an epoch characterized by confusion and strong insecurity concerning already accepted values and ideologies, as well as a strong distrust and suspicion of the existing political system.

These factors suggest the existence of a highly relevant ground for comparative analyses between Turkey and other countries in Europe concerning the relationship between religion and politics. The explanation behind the success of the Islamic movement in Turkey since the end of the 1960s is closely related to factors which resemble the ones that led the Christian Socialists to power in Austria in the 1920s.

Turkey has never had any Liberal political party worthy of the name, but it has had advocates of a rational approach to political decision-making and social reform. During the inter-war era the Republican People's Party promoted many of the ideals of the French revolution in an élitist manner: equality, national self-determination, secularism, progress, along with certain reservations about freedom and individualism. For the modernists themselves these values were accepted as a matter of course, and as long as the Kemalist élite was the controlling power no great misunderstandings would arise concerning the content of the defended values. In other words, nobody would question the direction of what was to be regarded as progressive and what was to be repudiated as reactionary within this given ideological frame of reference.

After 1950 and the transition to a parliamentary multi-party system, this picture changed. The Democratic Party (1950-60) represented, in economic terms, a more liberal view than the RPP. In terms of religion too, the parties represented opposite views: DP regarded itself as more liberal (and therefore more progressive) on these questions, while the circles around the RPP would interpret DP's position as outright reactionary. The RPP representatives saw themselves as *the* guardians of the principles of laicism and progress. In 1950, after the interruption of the political monopoly of the RPP, different political values were mixed in and therefore the ideological commitments also became more confused than before.

2. Ibid: 140.

During the inter-war period politics had been in the hands of a well educated, and therefore also relatively homogenous and united, elite. After 1950, when the barrages were opened and the masses let into the stream of politics, the well-known ideological categories of the previous period also began to be questioned. The ideological mixture, which resulted from this process was particularly strong in connection to the emergence of the Islamist 'National Salvation Party' at the beginning of the 1970s. This political movement, represented by the National Salvation Party during the 1970s and the Welfare Party since the beginning of the 1980s, unequivocally illustrates the existence of an 'ideological mosaic' very similar to the one Schorske had observed in his analysis of the Austrian Christian Socialists.

Ever since they appeared on the political scene the Turkish Islamists within the NSP and the WP have been strongly opposed to all foreign interference — economic, political, and cultural. They are very suspicious of large capitalist interest and want to support the small local Turkish capital owners at the expense of the more powerful, metropolitan ones. They oppose the existing social and economical inequalities and aim at a fundamental reformation of society in the direction of a more equitable distribution of wealth. Their view concerning the role of women in society is traditional. Even if women should have a right to higher education, their main duty is within the family. Old religious traditions concerning family life and relationships between the sexes are upheld with great care.

The movement is democratic and non-democratic at one and the same time and represents a mixture of elements taken from socialist, as well as conservative ideologies. Thereby it seems that Islam has become for the NSP, and its successor the WP, what Catholicism was to the Christian Socialists in Austria, namely an ideology which grants cohesion to what otherwise stands out as a disparity between the various ideological elements and values.

With the help of religion, the Islamists have been able to bind together different ideological fragments into one coherent political programme. They have thereby also been able to summon the support of very different social groups; rich and poor, industrialists and workers, wealthy farmers and poor peasants, educated and uneducated, men and women, Turks and Kurds, young and old. People belonging to very different social groups and classes have found a common ground for political action within this movement.

Many social scientists have taken an interest in the authoritarian and/or totalitarian social and political movements of inter-war Europe. The explanation of different conservative mass-movements, like Christian Socialism, Fascism, and Nazism, has been especially difficult, since they are not easily explained in rational terms. The sociological literature therefore exceeds in explanations which have seen these movements as based mainly on instincts and emotions. They have also pointed to the emergence of what has been called 'mass society'.

One of the first representatives of the idea of mass society, used as a conceptual tool for the explanation of totalitarian political movements, was Ortega Gasset. His theory built on the assumption that individuals in modern society had become atomized. According to Gasset, men in mass society react like animals, which means they act on the basis of their emotions rather than reason. In this process human beings lose their integrity and sound moral judgement, and become an easy target for demagogues of different kinds.

Theories of mass society have been severely criticized by Marxist as well as Weberian sociologists.[3] Such contributions have been condemned, because they overemphasize the role of emotions and feelings in political action. Human beings in modern society cannot be looked upon as irrational creatures, who in the first instance can be pulled in one direction, and in the next instance in the other. The critics of the theories of mass society have instead stressed the existence of deadlock within the existing political institutions. They have pointed to the difficulties in making one's voice heard within the framework of the existing system and the limitations of available options for action. The real cause of the support of the masses for an undemocratic leader or an authoritarian political party has to be looked for in the institutional and political arrangements of the society at hand, not in the psychological deficiencies of its citizens.

This critique deserves to be taken seriously, especially in relation to recent developments in Turkey. To approach political Islam as if it expresses nothing but ignorance and religious fanaticism will only lead to further deadlock. Democracy will prosper through open dialogue and therefore it is important to avoid categorical condemnations and instead try to reach a deeper sociological understanding of the underlying structures.

One way of doing this is through the further development of comparative perspectives. This paper only contains a suggestion as to what may provide a fruitful approach in that direction. To relate recent developments in Turkey to what happened in Europe during a similar social conjuncture, is a way of broadening the horizon. Thereby one will be able to approach to daily events with greater distance and serenity. History constitutes an invaluable source of human experience. In the light of earlier European history one can learn that a political movement based on a religious ideology is not an anomaly in

---

3. See Sandor Halebsky, 1976. *Mass Society and Political Conflict. Towards a Reconstruction of Theory*. Cambridge: Cambridge University Press.

a modern democracy. In the light of a more comprehensive perspective, devils — as well as angels, mostly turn out to be normal human beings.

Bibliography

Gasset, Ortega, 1972. *The Revolt of the Masses.* London: Unwin.

Halebsky, Sandor, 1976. *Mass Society and Political Conflict. Towards a Reconstruction of Theory,* Cambridge: Cambridge University Press.

Schorske, Carl E., 1981. *Fin-de-Siècle Vienna. Politics and Culture,* Cambridge: Cambridge University Press.

Turkish Media after the 1980s

L. Dogan Tiliç

Introduction

The year 1980 is a crucial date for any socio-political or economic analysis of Turkey. Analyses often begin with 'Before 1980', or 'After 1980' as if '80 referred to the birth of the Messiah. In this article on the Turkish media, it can be seen that the year 1980 — which was the year of military intervention and the beginning of subsequent years of military rule, will continue to serve as an historical watershed. Many references to 'before '80' or 'after '80' are therefore used.

In the years following the coup d'état of 1980, Turkey began to experience a period of structural transformation. Both the European Union countries and the USA began to present Turkey as a model for the new independent states of the former Soviet Union and the Middle East. This role has been warmly welcomed by the Turkish state and governments from the early '80s until today. The role was indeed nothing more than how Turkey had presented itself to the West during its 150 year old Westernization process. The fall of the Soviet Union and the emergence of new independent states in Central Asia and the Caucasus was a new factor that made the West consider Turkey, much more seriously than before, as a *bridge* between East and West.

The Motherland Party (ANAP) of the late President Turgut Özal came to power in 1983 and ruled the country for the following 8 years. Turkey was more and more closely integrated with the world economic system in those years, mostly through IMF-directed policies. The results of this 'great transformation', as Özal liked to call it, were export-promotion development strategy (accompanied with many cases of corruption such as sending empty boxes abroad to get credits or tax returns from the state), temporary restoration of law and order on the basis of the depolitization of the society under the terror of a military regime, a worsening income distribution, emergence of a new type of individualism, further attachment to the values of the market economy, etc. All these developments, formulated within the ideological framework of the New Right, also continued under the rule of the centre-right and centre-left coalition governments until the mid '90s. Islamic groups and the Welfare Party (RP), being the best organized of them all, benefitted from the consequences of this transformation which harmed the middle and lower-middle class masses. The support given to the RP rapidly increased in the suburbs of the big cities, and the urban poor who backed the revolutionary leftist groups turned to the RP, which succeeded in presenting itself as a party that challenged the system.

The so called years of the 'great transformation' in the early '80s were really identical with an important transformation in certain aspects of the Turkish media. 'The market-based and outward oriented strategy for economic modernization adopted in the 1980s, has produced a short cut to a more information based economy'.[1] A World Bank report prepared in 1992, concluded that Turkey had used its resources for a transition to an information-based economy. 'As a matter of fact, the massive investments in communications in the 1980s were unprecedented in scale and this increase went hand-in-hand with an absolute, as well as, a relative decline in investments in virtually all other sectors of the Turkish economy. Investment in information technology picked up sharply in both the public and private sectors, especially in the second half of the decade, when the state-owned PTT (Post, Telephone and Telegraph Directorate) absorbed approximately 1 percent of the country's total GNP, every year. This was equivalent to approximately 4 percent of Turkey's total capital formation and higher than practically all other OECD countries, surpassed only by 1.07 percent in Brazil. This investment shift to a communication based infrastructure was accompanied by striking changes in Turkey's media environment'.[2]

Methodological and Theoretical Framework

Following the military coup in 1980, the changes in Turkey's media environment was really striking, as Prof. Kaya said. First of all, in the early '80s the socio-political structure of the country, which was characterised by having very little room for democracy, made it almost impossible to talk about a *free press*.

The functioning of the media in any country can be studied, firstly; by focusing on the socio-political structure of that country which in general provides an *atmosphere* of survival for the media. Secondly; the structure of the *media ownership* has to be analysed. *The media institution* can be a third level of abstraction to study the media. The *Journalist* is in the fourth place and the *Receiver* — readers, listeners or viewers, come last. To look at each of these five

1. Kaya, 1993: 87.
2. Kaya, 1993: 87.

aspects would be, methodologically, the most comprehensive and suitable way of dealing with the media of any country.

Theoretically, I assume a relationship of domination-determination from above among the five dimensions of the media mentioned. The political structure of any country imposes the limits of freedom on the media of that country. Media owners, either through laws or through his or her business relations, or through other indirect means, immediately feel the state and government imposed conditions of functioning. He or she determines the general frame and line for his/her media. Journalists and their work are very much influenced by the above mentioned interventions. They are often told from above what to do and what not to do. The way of telling them things varies from physical oppression to indirect pressures and bribing. The journalist, on the other hand, may have a limited influence from his position within the media institution. Receivers, at the bottom of this relationship, are almost in a hopeless situation. They are just under the bombardment of messages and have almost no way of responding. Not to buy the paper, not to listen to the radio, or not to watch TV; boycotting the media is the only chance receivers have to exert their influence on the media. However, to organize such a boycott among the atomized receivers is very difficult. The more democracy there is in a country, the better it is for a free media.

Looking one by one at each of the above mentioned dimensions of the media in Turkey would give a better understanding of the striking changes in the country's media environment after 1980, as well as a real picture of the existing situation.

Political Structure in the '80s as the Media Atmosphere

The military coup of the 1980 closed all political parties and the Parliament. Tens of thousands of people were imprisoned and tortured. A totalitarian constitution was imposed on the people with a referendum during which no anti-constitutional propaganda was allowed. The newspapers were strictly controlled. It was impossible to write on certain issues. Martial Law commanders dictated to the papers what to write and what not to write. Politically banned leaders of the centre-Right and centre-Left parties; namely Süleyman Demirel and Bülent Ecevit had almost no chance to have their voices heard in the media. The state radio and TV only served the generals. Martial Law commanders could close the newspapers anytime they liked. Media owners had to choose between closing down their newspapers or adopting a pro-junta or low profile line which would not disturb the coup leaders. They took the second option.

General Kenan Evren, the leader of the coup, became the President of the country during the referendum for the constitution. In 1983, elections could only be held with the participation of parties and candidates that had the permission of the generals. The Motherland Party (ANAP) founded by late President Turgut Özal won the election, getting more than 40 percent of the votes. The limited revival of political life in the country meant some increased freedom for the press. The then PM Turgut Özal developed personal relations with some newspapers and journalists. Those days marked the beginning of a new type of journalism which was mostly regarded as being inside the power circles and to make public what was dictated by those circles.

The Kurdish rebel campaign which began in August 1984 became another reason for the state to tighten freedom of the press. Certain newspapers were not allowed to be distributed in the eleven South-eastern and Eastern provinces which were ruled by emergency law. The Kurdish question was, at that time, a very risky topic to write about. Journalists were trying to find their own ways of describing the Kurds without using the word 'Kurd'. To use the word 'Kurdistan' is still punishable by law since it is considered as an act of separatism. Many journalists and writers were sentenced by the State Security Courts (DGM) for using these words. Article 8 of the Anti-Terror Law banned separatist propaganda. It was under this Article that many writers, artists and journalists were imprisoned and fined. It became the nightmare of intellectuals in the later years. The law was so vague that anything could easily be considered as separatist propaganda.

The journal *Bizim Gazete* (Our Newspaper) published by the Istanbul Journalists' Association reported in its October 1991 edition that 'during the 8 years under ANAP governments, a total of 1,392 legal cases were made against journalists. Also, 26 laws restricting and obstructing press freedom were introduced during the 8 years. A huge number of newspapers and journals were confiscated. In one year, 18 journalists were put on trial charged with 'having insulted the President, under Article 158 of the Turkish Penal Code'. In 1991, there were 29 books confiscated, 121 newspapers and journals were banned, or censored. Some were forced to stop publication and others were confiscated. During the 8 years of ANAP governments, five journalists were killed.[3]

In November 1991, a coalition government was formed by the centre-Right True Path Party (DYP) of the current President, Suleyman Demirel and the Social Democratic Populist Party (SHP) of Erdal Inönü. They promised democratization to the people. In his first trip to Diyarbakir; the regional capital of the Kurdish populated and troubled south-eastern provinces, Demirel said

---

3. THRFT, 1992: 119.

that the Turkish state recognized 'Kurdish reality'. Optimism for the improvement of Turkish democracy and the living conditions of Kurdish citizens was high. However, things got even worse for the press. Journalists were beginning to be killed. In June 1992, Oktay Eksi, president of the Turkish Press Council, wrote an open letter to PM Demirel and said 'If things continue like this, be aware that Turkey will be listed in front of Colombia, which is famous for the massacre of journalists... The attacks against the Turkish press have broken all records since you took office and five journalists have been killed by unknown gunmen during this time'.

In January 1994, the Turkish Press Council announced in its report that 1993 has been a bad year for the press. Indeed all the reports about the press in the first half of the 1990's began with a sentence saying that the previous year 'has been a bad year for the press'. In 1993, eight journalists were killed and 51 others were attacked. Sixteen attacks came from the security forces, four from other public officials, and seven from leading members of political parties. In the same year, newspapers and magazines were attacked seven times and police raided newspaper offices fifteen times. There were ninety-five journalists taken into custody and forty-nine of them were arrested. The International Federation of Journalists (FIJ) listed Turkey on the top of its list of dangerous countries in 1993, while placing it third as far as the murder of journalists was concerned. The Committee to Protect Journalists (CPJ) declared that Turkey was more dangerous in 1992 than Yugoslavia, where 9 journalists had been killed. In the same year the number of journalists killed in Turkey reached thirteen. In 1993 this number came down to eight and in 1994, four journalists were killed in bomb attacks not directly targeted at them.[4]

Turkey has a press history of 160 years. During this time, until the end of 1994, forty-four journalists were killed. Almost half of them were killed in the years 1992 and 1993. In those days, the then PM Demirel and Interior Minister, Ismet Sezgin, ruled-out the possibility of state involvement in any of the attacks and publicly labelled some of the victims as Kurdish militants who were engaged with the outlawed Kurdish rebel party PKK. In March 1993, following an investigation into the murder of journalists in Turkey, CPJ reporter Andrew Yurkovsky said 'The CPJ believes that the Turkish state is implicated in two killings and the PKK has taken responsibility for or has been blamed for another two'.

During the first half of the 1990s, PKK kidnapped many Turkish and foreign journalists. These kidnappings were another threat for free journalistic activity in the country's Kurdish populated and troubled south-eastern provinces. The kidnapped journalists were kept in the mountains for days.

4. TIHV, 1995: 247-318.

However, PKK always returned them unharmed. The Turkish state, on the other hand, claimed or suggested that in most of these cases the journalists went with the PKK guerrillas of their own free will.

Much fewer killings took place in 1994. But journalists and writers were sentenced to a total of 448 years, 6 months and 25 days of imprisonment and fined some 2,400,000 dollars in that year. Forty-one percent of the cases in the State Security Court in Istanbul were cases against the press. In thirty-four incidents, seventy-six journalists were beaten or insulted by the security forces and other public officials while they were on duty. International journalists' organizations reported in early 1997 that there were about 150 journalists in jail all around the world, and half of them were jailed in Turkey.

These are the conditions under which the Turkish press has been functioning since 1980. Of course, the pressure was felt most by those in the opposition media; pro-Kurdish, leftist and sometimes Islamist. The mainstream media very often remained silent and did not take a strong position against the oppression of the so-called marginal press. However, without being aware of such conditions, it would not be possible to give an overall picture of the Turkish media.

The Media Owner

The 'great transformation' of the 1980s has also meant a striking change in the structure of media ownership. The press employed the latest technology that could easily compete with American or European newspapers. This investment into communication technology was a consequence of the transition to an information based economy mentioned above. In March 1990, the state monopoly of TV and Radio Programming and Transmissions, which was protected by article 133 of the 1982 military constitution until July 1993, was de facto abolished. 'Taking advantage of the opportunity created by high-power satellites with transmission footprints that covered mainly Western Turkey, and development of cheaper antennas capable of receiving direct satellite broadcasts, a private sector station then owned in part by the son of the late President Turgut Özal began broadcasting into Turkey from Germany and effectively, and surprisingly, challenging the TRT (Turkish Radio and Television Corporation) monopoly'.[5] Turkey's first private television channel named Star 1 was later followed by others. The first private TV channel was owned by Rumeli Holding, a firm that has dealings in a wide sphere of business operations ranging from construction to banking. Later, other private

---

5. Kaya, 1993: 88.

TV stations; namely Show TV, Tele-On, HBB, and Kanal 6, followed the path of Star 1.

Private radio stations followed the example set by television. In 1992 and 1993 they spread all around the country. Many of them were small local radios, but some of them were national stations owned by important businessmen. The high technology in the press, the entrance of TVs and radio into the country's media life, turned the business into a very expensive and highly competitive one. Under the new conditions, ownership patterns were changed considerably. Apart from the traditional journalist families such as Simavis and Karacans, new entrepreneurs, who had made their capital accumulation in other fields, entered into the media business. Traditional owners began to escape from the sector to invest in other areas.

In the first years of the 1990s, the transformation from traditional media ownership was rapidly achieved. In mid-1995, the mainstream media was already under the control of the conservative corporate forces whose initial goal was to further increase their interests. The media, and the other businesses of these owners, were in permanent need of new credit and other subsidies for the press. Thus, they were stuck to the source of power. 'It is no secret that several influential figures of the Turkish press have established 'client' relations with government officials in order to seek business advantages'.[6]

In the last decade, it came as no surprise to intelligent readers to see how the banner headlines on front pages were changing from supporting, to severely criticizing, the government. This shift often meant the satisfaction or dissatisfaction of the media-owner over a business deal with the government. Government used the 'carrot and stick' method to control the media. The stick, besides the anti-democratic laws and pressures described above, was cutting state subsidies and sending inspectors to the media-owners other business concerns. The carrot was just the opposite: Giving credits to the businesses of the owner, awarding very lucrative public bank advertisements to his media, etc.

Holdings Controlling the Turkish Media

Today, the Turkish mainstream media are under the control of six holding companies. The *Dogan Group* of Aydin Dogan, functions in many areas including banking, textile, trade, insurance, tourism and automobiles. The group owns Alternatif Bank, Türk Dish Ticaret Bankasi, Ray Insurance Company, Pen Tourism, Hür Imports, AD Publishing, etc. Kanal D, one of the most popular of the private TVs, the mainstream dailies *Hürriyet* and *Milliyet*

---

6. Kaya, ibid: 89.

(number 2 and 3 in circulation; 722,000 and 667,000 in December 1995), the tabloid dailies *Meydan, Posta* and sports dailies, *Spor* and *Fanatik*, radio stations Radyo Klüp and Hür FM, and several magazines besides printing houses and a distribution network.

Dogush Group is active in the areas of construction, banking, engineering, insurance, trade, tourism, food, etc. The most important companies of the group are Dogush Construction and Trade, Garanti Bank, Türk Körfez Bank, Antur Tourism, Dogush Air Transportation, Filiz Food Industry, General Automobile Marketing and Trade, etc. The group has a 20 percent share in Kanal D TV and Radio Forex.

Dinç Bilgin Group is proud of functioning only in the media sector. However, it also has interests in Pamukbank, Interbank, Yapi Toko Bans-Russia, Bank Kreis AG-Germany, Inter Overseas-Iceland, Inter Capital-Iceland, Çukurova Steel and Halk Insurance Company. Bilgin owns the highest circulation daily *Sabah* (735 thousand in December 1995), other dailies such as *Yeni Yüzyil*, *Takvim, Bugün* and the sports dailies *Fotomaç*, and *Taraftar* as well as several magazines and a distribution network. ATV, one of the most popular private TV channels, belongs also to Bilgin, as does Medya TV.

Uzan Group owned the first private TV station. The son of the late President Turgut Özal, had a financial involvement in this group.The group owns Imar Bank, Adabank, Cukurova Electric, Kepez Electric, Rumeli Electric, Rumeli Cement, Trabzon Cement, Ladik Cement, Shanliurfa Cement, Gaziantep Cement, Rumeli Holding, Çestash Anonim, Eltem-Tek ASH, Standart Construction, Yapi Trade, Tunceli Cotton Thread. Star TV, Kral TV, and Kral FM radio station. According to rumours growing in journalistic circles, the group is also interested in owning a daily newspaper.

Erol Aksoy owns Avrupa and Amerika Holding, two banks in France and the USA, Iktisat Bank, Factofinans, Atlas Financial Renting, Emek Insurance, Uzman Hayat Insurance, Showpa Marketing with TV, Edatur Tourism and some publishing companies. Show TV, one of the leading private TVs, CINE 5 TV, and Show Radio, are Erol Aksoy's investments in media. In early 1997, Aksoy also bought the *Aksham* daily.

Two more businessmen entered into the media sector in 1997. Nergis Holding, owned by the textile tycoon Cavit Çaglar, opened NTV which broadcasts news only. In April 1997, one of the country's leading companies, Construction Ceylan Holding, started broadcasting with CTV.

Ihlas Group is the leading representative of Islamic capital in the country. It owns Yurtbank, an automobile marketing company, International Hospital, Ihlas Foreign Trade, Ihlas Marketing, Ihlas Food, Ihlas House Equipment, Ihlas Fair Organizing, etc. TGRT TV, TGRT FM radio, and the daily *Türkiye* belongs to the group, as well as the Ihlas News Agency.

Fethullahcilar, a growing Islamic sect of the late 1980s and 1990s, also invested a lot in the media sector. The highest selling Islamic daily *Zaman*, which has a circulation of over 350,000, and Samanyolu TV, as well as some radio stations and many magazines, belong to followers of this sect led by Fethullah Gülen. *Zaman* also started publishing in Azerbaijan, Uzbekistan and Bulgaria in 1993. It was later published in all Central Asian republics, and in 1997 in Russia. It was even distributed freely to the homes of citizens in crucial times of hot political debates. Even though a sect cannot be considered as a holding and it has ideological interests in investing in the media, the Islamic media as a whole became one of the biggest groups in Turkey.

Indeed, in parallel with the rise of political Islam in the country, Islamic media spread all around Turkey and became quite influential. As soon as the private radio and TV stations entered into the market in 1992, the Islamic media occupied a rapidly increasing place among them, both in the countryside and in the metropoles. The government was worried about their spread and began to impose a legal framework to control the media. In the early 1990s, there was no law permitting the operation of private TV and radio stations. Islamic media experienced a boom under such conditions and suddenly over 200 Islamic radios, and 40 TV channels, appeared throughout the country. There are now more than five Islamic daily newspapers; four of which have been in print for years, and over 40 weekly and monthly pro-Islamic periodicals are printed and sold in the major cities.

The media monopoly of a few holdings began to worry several business circles and political parties. The media was also engaged in the campaign war of the political parties along with the leaders they supported. A paper or TV supporting one leader was turned into a weapon against the other. A report published late in 1995 in the magazine of TOBB (Turkey Chambers and Stocks Union), said that the various holdings used the media as a *weapon* against their economic rivals and politicians. The report also said that governments used a 'carrot and stick policy' against the media; using subsidized paper, official announcements, cheap public bank credits and investment promotions. The

TOBB report said that holdings did not indeed enter into media business for profit after 1980s. Media was a power centre which they liked to control. 'It was seen that the main aspect of the media was not profit-making. Many capital groups wanted to have the media to exert their power of influence. The money they lost in the media was considered as a *defence expense* by the capital groups. There has not been any serious resistance to the tendency among some greedy businessmen and bankers towards buying the media in order to grow and strengthen their groups, and to use the media against their business and political adversaries' announced the report.[7]

Media Institution

The mainstream media institutions turned into commercial business companies under the above mentioned conditions. The necessary distinction between the news and commentary disappeared. Not only the news but even the headlines were full of comments which changed each day in accordance with the interests of the owners. A chief editor of a mainstream daily could publicly say that his main duty was to take care of the interests of his boss, rather than inform the public.

The Turkish media institutions of the late '80s also turned into show business and entertainment companies. Most of the radio and TV stations chose entertainment as their prime function, and informing the public was almost forgotten. Even the news programmes of the widely watched TV stations were giving some limited information, while mostly entertaining the viewers. Baudrillard says that there is no reason to presuppose that the masses want to live in the brightness of being informed, and that it might be more helpful to suppose that the people just want to be entertained before they die. However, Postman points out that this entertainment is indeed 'amusing ourselves to death'.

One of the biggest problems of the Turkish press was over-commercialization, and the introduction of the *lottery* gimmick, as a result of belonging to Holdings that have interests in many other businesses. The announcements of lottery campaigns, that would begin some days later, almost occupied the whole front page of the mainstream dailies for several days. Everything was given to the readers; from bread to TVs, houses, holidays, automobiles and kitchen equipment. Tradesmen and shop owners in Anatolia threatened the dailies by boycotting them, since their sales drastically fell as a result of the promotion campaigns. Things such as glasses, knives, plates, etc. which they sold in their shops were all given away by dailies. On July 1st,

7. Sönmez, 1995.

1993, an Istanbul based tabloid daily *Super Tan* carried the promotion war to an insane extreme by 'marketing women'. The paper announced its new promotion campaign on the front page with the following words: 'Unbelievable! *Super Tan* is doing what has never been done before. Dial the magical telephone numbers and catch the chance of spending a night with the stars of your dreams...' The paper also printed the naked photos of four belly dancers with whom the reader had the chance of spending a night. The reaction from women's organizations was very strong and many journalists were ashamed. However, the promotion wars continued. A year later, on July 3rd, 1995, the local daily *Olay* in the South-eastern Gaziantep province began to give graves to its readers, in protest against the promotions in the mainstream media, with the slogan 'Everything belonging to this world has already been given away in promotion. We think of your next world'!

The professional hierarchy within the institution of the media was also distorted by the 'great transformation' of the 1980s. While conducting research for my doctorate, I encountered many Turkish journalists who complained that the posts of editors, sub-editors and correspondents were not distributed on the basis of journalistic merit and skills but rather on the basis of being close to the owner or dealing successfully with the other businesses of the owner. Groups, teams or fractions of journalists taking care of each other began to emerge in each media organization. A correspondent could come to a position or secure his existing position when he accepted to become 'a man of the fraction leader' or member of a group. Together, the members of a group could change from one institution to another. 'I can come with my team' became a frequently heard sentence when 'important' journalists were bargaining with owners to transfer from one newspaper or TV to the other.

Journalists

The journalists of the country also experienced a transformation since the 1980s from what could be called a 'traditional' to a 'new' type of journalist. This 'transformation' was perfectly described as 'corrosion' by prominent Turkish journalist Erbil Tushalp. The wide income gaps did not exist between traditional journalists as they do nowadays. They could be considered mostly as middle and lower-middle class people who entered into the profession mostly with a missionary mentality. They believed that they had to do something against the ills of society and they considered journalism a way of correcting such ills. 'Break your pen but never sell it', was the most popular motto among traditional journalists. According to an 'old' generation journalist, now writing books, the journalists who refused to sell their pens are now considered naive and old-fashioned.

Since the 1980s, a new type of journalist, who considers the business as a profession by which simply to earn a living, has emerged. In this period, the media turned into a type of owner's *gun* to be used in his deals with business rivals and the state, and journalists became the *trigger men* of the boss. Many youngsters entered into the business, considering it as 'a short-cut to fame and fortune'. About a dozen media stars who earned thousands of dollars (US) attracted newcomers to the job. The income distribution among Turkish journalists is perhaps worse than that in all other sectors. A few stars receive monthly salaries of 30-40,000 dollars. The editors, who actually do the work, rank below the stars in the hierarchy and receive about 2-4,000 a month. The majority of correspondents, who are at the bottom of the scale, receive about 250 dollars per month,(1995 rates).[8]

The most important characteristic of the Turkish journalists today, in contrast to those from before the 1980s, is not being organized. Unions were pushed away from media institutions. The owner forced the journalists to choose between either being a member of the union or working. Hundreds of journalists were dismissed in one day from their newspapers in the early 1990s. They were not in a position to make any protest because they were not organized, and also due to the lack of solidarity. Ironically, journalists without any union themselves, defended the union rights of demonstrating public workers and civil servants.

Several of the older generation of journalists who remained in the media after the 1980s adapted themselves to the new commercialized journalism and began to do other things which were considered ignominious previously. Correspondents reporting about a political party often identified themselves with that party and several of them became parliamentary candidates of those parties afterwards. Journalists were often seen in the ministries 'helping' businessmen or citizens that had certain dealings with that ministry. Those who could not adapt themselves left the job or continued to function under editors less skilled than themselves. The job satisfaction which is believed to be high in journalism turned into dissatisfaction in many cases. During interviews in my PhD reseach, several Turkish journalists said 'I feel like a pro-stitute' in responding to the question 'Who is a journalist?'.

Since the papers were not indeed selling by dint of the news but for other reasons, good journalists were given secondary importance in the media. The media invested in technology, luxury buildings, etc. but not in human resources. Old generation Turkish journalists often complained that the

8. 3D, 1994: 4-9.

newcomers were not qualified and mostly ignorant of the main socio-political questions of the country and the world.

However, specialization was also a new aspect of journalism after 1980s. In many papers and audio-visual media, journalists began to feel the necessity to specialize in certain issues. The very simple specialization in sports, politics and economics of the old days was not enough to cover the developments post-1980s.

Journalism in its new form became a profession mostly occupied by the well-educated offspring of the upper-class. Being close to the political and economic power circles became extremely important, since everything happening within those circles was considered as news. 'The children of those circles have the highest chance to get into journalism, because they are already in the circles where news is considered to be', said a journalist.

Receiver as Reader, Listener and Viewer

The receivers have usually no chance of responding to the messages distributed by the newspapers, radios and TVs. Having an influence on the journalist, media institution, and the owner, is almost impossible for the receiver. After the 1980s, despite the increase in the number of different media available, the content did not diversify. The readers bought newspapers mostly because of the 'gifts' supplied with them. A reader in the late 1980s and early 1990s, who bought a newspaper from a kiosk and exchanged it again after cutting out the coupon, stands in strong contrast to the reader of before the 1980s who read the newspaper all the way through to the very last sentence, cut out articles which were of interest, and identified strongly with that newspaper.

A middle-aged Turkish journalist, who spent 20 years in the job, said that the number of readers has drastically decreased since the 1980s. 'Sales of the dailies today are below sales of the 1960s. In 1960, total daily circulation of newspapers was around 2 million. If you exclude the promotion readers, the total circulation of dailies is 2.7 million today. The population was 35 million and there were less than 50 thousand university graduates in 1960. Today the population of the country is 60 million and we have 1 million university graduates.'

Not to buy a particular paper is the only way the reader can register a protest against any disliked content. Promotions could break this resistance to a great extent, even today. However, in the last year a reaction to the promotions began to develop among readers. In various cities, readers began to collect signatures against promotions. They called for a boycott of the newspapers containing gift coupons.

Thousands of Alevites, a minority Islamic group in Turkey, demonstrated in front of the Star TV building in January 1995 in protest against a showman's joke which had insulted them and the demonstration almost turned into a small revolt. This was a spontaneous reaction by a group of people, naturally organized by being members of the same sect. However, to organize the slowly growing reactions of the atomized readers, for the sake of a more democratic, informative and objective media, is far from having been reached.

Concluding Remarks — Turkish Media and the Middle East

The general picture of the Turkish media, described above, demonstrates that both the reader and the journalist are not in a strong position to influence the media and its content. The Turkish media, as in many countries, is formed by its relationship to the capital and state. Media, capital, and state, are the three corners of the Turkish ruling elite's triangle.[9]

Turkish journalists are not organized among themselves. They have no contact with their colleagues in Middle Eastern countries. The lack of free journalism in many Middle Eastern countries is another main reason for this gap between the Turkish and Middle Eastern journalists. News about Middle Eastern affairs, and countries, often finds its way to the Turkish media through the big international news agencies such as Reuters, AFP and AP.

Employing foreign correspondents in other countries is a new development for Turkey. The foreign news performance of the Turkish media has increased considerably in the 1990s compared to the '80s. However, most of the foreign news, even about Turkey's neighbours enters the country through the Western capitals. Despite the fact that only 40 percent of the foreign news in Turkey's mainstream dailies is from Western Europe, 90 percent of the Turkish foreign correspondents are based in European countries.[10] The Turkish media has no correspondents in many Middle Eastern countries nor in several of Turkey's neighbouring countries. The semi-official Anatolia News Agency (AA) has the widest foreign correspondent network. In January 1996, AA had offices in Washington, New York, Athens, Komotini (Greece), Brussels, Strasbourg, London, Bonn and Rome. It employed correspondents in several Central Asian republics in the mid-90s; namely in Baku, Alma Ata and Tashkent. It had an office in Moscow since the late '80s. An office in Sarajevo was established in mid-1995 and another one in Sofia the same year. But the offices in Cairo and Baghdad were closed due to economic reasons. In January 1996, the only place

9. Otan, 1995.
10. Tan, 1989: 11.

in the Middle East where the AA had an office was Tehran. The Turkish press and TVs did not even have that.

According to a research conducted in 1981,[11] 49.3 percent of the foreign news that appeared in Turkish newspapers was from Western Europe, 17 percent from the USA and 16.4 percent from the Middle East. It can be said that news from Western Europe has occupied more place in the Turkish media in the last two years due to the customs union agreement between the European Union and Turkey. News from the Turkic republics of Central Asia might also have increased their share, while the percentage of Middle Eastern news may have decreased.

The anti-democratic media atmosphere in the Middle Eastern countries is another reason for the lack of any relationship between the Turkish and Middle Eastern journalists. The very close relationship between journalism and political power in Middle Eastern countries is also an indicator of the anti-democratic structure of those countries. The closer the media is connected to the source of power, the more democracy is threatened in a country. The media of such countries often reproduces the official policies of their respective states especially concerning inter-state conflicts. It can be said that none of the Middle Eastern countries present a better picture when compared to the five aspects applied to the Turkish media in this paper.

The water of the Euphrates, an important issue of conflict for example, is always reflected in the media in accordance with the official polices of the Syrian and Turkish states. It would be possible in Turkey to find ideas deviating from the official point of view, but not in Syria.

Forgetting that Middle Eastern countries were once part of the Ottoman Empire, and that they are today neighbours or much closer than many European countries geographically, the receiving of information about these countries via Western information centres is a definite handicap for the Turkish media. There seems to be no way, in the short run, to overcome this handicap unless the priorities of the country and the structure of the media change. Even though it is quite difficult, journalists are the only part of the media capable of developing links further. Exchanging information between them is a unique way of getting first-hand knowledge of the problems or realities of their respective countries.

11. Tan, 1989: 105-6.

Bibliography

Baudrillard, Jean 1983. *In the Shadow of the Silent Majorities ... Or the End of the Social.* Trans. P. Foss, P. Patton and J. Johnston, New York: Semiotext.

Bizim Gazete, 1991. Istanbul Gazeteciler Cemiyeti Yayini, Istanbul: Ekim.

3D Dergisi, 1994. *Bas Küfürü Kap Parayi.* Sayi 1: Ekim.

Kaya, Rasit, 1993. 'Media Politics in Turkey.' *International Politics: A Balkan Review of Current Affairs.* Athens: Summer-Winter.

Otan, Ümit, 1995. 'Babitelli'. Izmir Kitapligi, Izmir.

Postman, Neil, 1985: *Amusing Ourselves to Death: A Public Discourse in the Age of Show Business.* Vilny.

Sönmez, Mustafa, 1995: *Ekonomik Forum.* Aralik.

TURKEY: Human Rights Report 1991. Ankara: HRFT Publications, 1992.

TÜRKIYE: 1994 Insan Haklari Raporu. Ankara: TIHV Yayini, 1995.

Tusalp, Erbil, 1995. *Çürüme* Istanbul: Papirus.

Turkey in a State of Fear

Erik Siesby

Turkey and the European Union are gradually approaching one another. This process could be speeded up if the Turkish political leaders would understand the meaning of European integration: a process which will result in a multicultural, democratic European society.

Turkey has a good foundation for becoming part of a multicultural European society — because Turkey, like the old Ottoman Empire, is a multicultural society — even though official ideology does not recognize this fact. Instead of enjoying the rich cultural variety (Alawites, Sunnis, Kurds, Jews, Armenians) which exists in Turkey, the various groups fear each other. The various Turkish governments have, since the time of Kemal Atatürk, feared the Kurds in particular.

Fundamentalism

Turks oriented towards the West fear Islamic fundamentalism. The fundamentalists fear the influence of Western Europe.

Separatism

The government and the military suffer from fear of 'separatism', i.e. attempts to create a separate Kurdish state in the Southeast of the country. Many violations of human rights are due to this fear of separatism. Many completely non-violent newspapers and political parties have been banned because of articles and political speeches which mention the needs, wishes and demands of the impoverished population in the southeastern part of Turkey. Such statements have been interpreted by the authorities as expressions of 'separatism'. A long list of great Turkish authors, journalists and politicians have served long prison sentences for such statements. The Turkish Grand National Assembly has refused to follow the advice of the European Parliament to repeal Article 8 of the Anti-Terror Law in accordance with which many of these people have been convicted. Instead, Article 8 has been amended with the fortunate result that a considerable number of these prisoners of conscience have been released. However, Turkish law contains, many other restrictions on the freedom of expression, and the great defender of the cultural rights of the Kurdish population, the famous and courageous sociologist Ismail Besikci, is still in prison serving sentences that add up to over 200 years. Why? Because he has written what he sees as the truth about the fate of the Kurdish population in Turkey.

If anyone would like either to support or to criticize Besikci's views he would, of course, be free to do so in any democratic country which respects freedom of expression. It would then be up to each reader to decide whether Besikci or his critics were in the right. That is the way in which democracy works. As the Turkish public has been prevented from studying Besikci's writings, no such exchange of views can take place. Besikci will have to spend the rest of his life in a Turkish prison, and the Turkish reading public has been deprived of an opportunity to expand their mental horizon by studying Besikci's writings as well as those of his critics. A democratic dialogue between opposing views is a search for truth. The most disastrous fear in Turkey is the fear of truth.

Fear of truth

The Kurdish people have lived in the mountainous area in the south-eastern part of Turkey for more than six thousand years. Their language is Indo-european and thus related to Persian. From 1924 until a few years ago the Turkish government has persistently denied the existence of a Kurdish population in Turkey. The Kurds were called 'Mountain Turks' and their language 'a Turkish dialect'. Their songs were given Turkish texts and their traditional Kurdish names were not allowed. In the twenties, Turkish officials came to the Kurdish villages to rename both the villages and the inhabitants. A whole village population could be given the same surname 'Öztürk' which means a 'real Turk'.

The forced assimilation of the Kurds did not succeed completely. In the south-eastern part of Turkey where approximately 80 percent of the population are Kurds the Kurdish language and culture prevails. The oppression of the Kurds has resulted in several uprisings which have all been suppressed by the army.

In 1984 a Marxist Kurdish independence movement PKK (the Kurdish Workers' Party) led by Abdullah Öcalan, known as 'Apo', began to attack military and civilian targets in Turkey. The movement was of a modest size in the beginning, but grew, in spite of attempts by the military to suppress it. The fact that no Kurdish organizations were allowed contributed to the growth of this movement. Where else could the young Kurds turn to express their anger at the oppression?

Article 5 of the Turkish Statute no. 2908 prohibits '...associations which claim that there are on the territory of the Republic of Turkey minorities based on race, religion, sect, culture or language, with the intention of destroying the indivisible unity of the Turkish State's territory and nation...' This provision has been used to prevent the formation of organizations which might represent the Kurdish population and with which the Turkish government could have conducted a dialogue concerning the political and cultural demands of the Kurdish population.

Kurdish political parties such as HEP and its successor DEP have been banned. Kurdish members of parliament have been imprisoned or have left the country. The mainly Kurdish party HADEP has not yet been banned, but its activities have been hampered in many ways. The newspapers which have supported HADEP, for instance *Özgür Ülke* and *Yeni Politika*, have been banned. One of 'Yeni Politika's journalists, Tepe, died while in police custody. According to the police he committed suicide. Altogether 13 members of HADEP have been killed, among them some of the party's leading personalities. Eleven members of the party are now being prosecuted.

During the presidency of Özal (1991-93), mentioning the existence of a Kurdish population was allowed, and newpapers written in the Kurdish language were permitted. Özal understood that the Kurdish problem could not be solved solely by force of arms. He recognized that a large part of Turkey's population had a Kurdish identity, language and culture. Özal died too soon. Since then, any statements in favour of Kurdish rights risk being characterized as an expression of 'separatism', a criminal act.

In 1994, I wrote a report on the demands of the Kurdish population in the south-eastern part of Turkey on the basis of interviews with several leading personalities with knowledge of the attitudes and demands of the Kurdish population. I concluded that none of those interviewed considered an independent Kurdistan a Kurdish demand. The demands were:

1) Respect for human rights in South-east Turkey.
2) Respect for the Kurdish identity, language and culture.
3) Economic development.

Professor Dogu Ergil made a comprehensive study of the political attitudes of the Kurds at the request of the Turkish Chamber of Commerce (TOBB). Ergil reached similar conclusions. The vast majority of the Kurds are not separatists. However, according to Ergil approximately 42 percent want a federal system, which would give the population of those areas, where Kurds are the majority, more influence on the local administration — including the school system. First of all, however, they want respect for their human rights.

Fear of the villages

Several hundred thousands of soldiers, security forces, among them the dreaded 'Özel Tim', and village guards are hunting a few thousand PKK activists. Officially they are called 'Terrorists'. The Kurds call them 'guerillas'. Over and over again the government has declared that the PKK terrorists have been defeated. Over and over again the PKK activists have re-appeared.

For more than five years, towns and villages in the South-east have been 'evacuated': Sirnak, Lice, Cizre, Kulp and Digor are almost empty ruined towns. More than 2,600 villages have been evacuated and destroyed. Some 31 forests, fields and orchards have been burned. This destruction of a huge area is the result of an unsuccessful fight against PKK's fighters (terrorists or guerillas).

More than 3 million people have lost their homes, their property, their traditional social surroundings, and now live a miserable life on the outskirts of big cities threatened by epidemics.

Neither the Turkish Medical Association nor 'Medecins sans Frontiéres' have been allowed by the Turkish authorities to offer these poor people medical service. Not even the International Committee of the Red Cross has been given access in order to assess the need for assistance to the evacuated villagers. The Turkish authorities' attitude towards these humanitarian organizations violates Article 39 of the Moscow Document on the Human Dimension of the CSCE: 'The participating States will; —increase their preparedness and cooperate fully to enable humanitarian relief operations to be undertaken speedily and effectively; — take all necessary steps to facilitate speedy and unhindered access to the affected areas for such relief operations; —make the necessary arrangements for those relief operations to be carried out'.

The evacuated villagers find it difficult to get jobs in the cities. They have little education. The women in particular do not speak Turkish. Employers hesitate in taking on these people. Young people especially experience a cultural shock and are forced to take the dirtiest jobs or become involved with drugs and prostitution.

The first time I encountered the phenomenon of evacuation was in 1990 in the town Siirt. A group of evacuated villagers told me that they lived in tents outside the town. 'Tents' in this case meant four poles covered with plastic sheets. One of the villagers had lost two children. They had not survived the cold winter.

In the province of Diyarbakir, I visited five evacuated villages. The village guards had forced the villagers to leave one village. It happened several months before my visit. Now some villagers had returned to rebuild their houses and to harvest their crops. Three days before my visit the village guards had returned by night and burned all the grain fields.

The village guards were originally villagers who were ordered to fight the PKK and to prevent them from hiding in the villages. The village guards of course risked being killed by PKK. For that reason alone, many refused to become village guards. This often resulted in evacuation and destruction of the village. Now the village guards have developed into a paramilitary corps which is being used to attack other villages. Unofficially the corps of village guards numbers 60-100,000. They are well paid. In return they risk attacks by PKK and the contempt of their fellow Kurds.

Three villages which I visited recently were totally destroyed. A nearby mansion belonging to a rich landowner, an 'aga', was untouched.

An evacuated villager, whom I met outside Mersin, told me that a Kurdish village had refused to participate in the local election on March 27th, 1994. They protested against the election system which they found unfair. They protested against the presence of armed soldiers in the polling station. The village was punished by bombing from airplanes. Four villagers were wounded. The hospital refused to treat them, because they would not declare that the PKK had bombed the village.

A village ('köy') Halis Aksakal ('Seyhan' in Kurdish) consisting of 85 houses was evacuated in May, 1995. In a neighbouring military camp an explosion took place. A soldier was killed and two wounded. Next morning the soldiers came collected all villagers in the school house and separated men from women. The men were beaten up and all houses destroyed. The soldiers stole everything of value and destroyed the rest, They even stole carpets from the mosque. A villager: 'This is a mosque!' The soldier: 'This is not a mosque, but a church! — You are Armenians!' — This was intended and understood as being an insult. An old man of 63 was tortured until 9 p.m. The soldiers stole chickens and killed donkeys and other animals.

An old man with a long beard and turban, who came from the village 'Islam Köy' containing 15 houses, near the town of Kulp, told me that on May 18th, 1994 the soldiers came to the village. Without warning they burned the village and all 36 animals, as well as all property. The village was surrounded by tanks. Aeroplanes and helicopters (American 'Copras') flew over the village. It was a mountain village which could be used as a hiding place for the PKK. 'Tevfik Ates' consisted of 75 houses. The soldiers ordered the men to become village guards. When they refused, houses and animals were burned.

Fear of the Police

The police are omnipresent in the South-east, wearing uniforms or plain-clothes. The police have informers everywhere. It is thought-provoking that the police have not been able to detect the perpetrators of the many murders which are committed in the South-east. Kurds are being shot in the back by 'unknown perpetrators'. The local population know who the perpetrators are.

An everyday story which illustrates the police methods: Adnan Gül was a student at the Dicle University outside Diyarbakir on the right bank of the River Tigris ('Dicle'). On October 24th, at 07.45 he was stopped by the police outside his room. The police drove him out of the city towards Urfa. A cloth, a 'pushy', was put over his head to prevent him from seeing. At a crossing the car made several quick turns so that Adnan lost sense of direction. Later on another person entered the car, a person who apparently knew Adnan. He knew what Adnan had been doing last summer. The police now accused Adnan for working for Dev Sol ('Devrim Sol' a leftist revolutionary movement) and tried to persuade him to co-operate with the police by promising money and women. When he refused, he was asked whether he knew four persons, who in the spring of 1994 had been killed during an attack on a dwelling which housed an illegal movement. At first he denied any knowledge of these people, later he had to admit that he knew two of the four from his village.

There were two policemen in the car; a coarse one and a relatively mild one. The coarse policeman said, 'I shall kill you!' He then loaded his gun and held it to Adnan's head during the drive. 'Let us get rid of him!' he said. Adnan asked, 'What have I done?' to which the coarse policeman replied; 'What have you done for your country?' He was then once again ordered to become an informer for the police. The police wanted him to move in with some of Adnan's acquaintances and to take part in their activities — and then to keep them informed. The coarse policeman said, 'You have one minute. We have lifted the border between life and death'. The mild policeman said, 'No, don't let us kill him immediately — let us kill him slowly!'. At eleven o'clock Adnan was released and was told to report to the police the next day at 6.30 p.m. I met him the same day in the morning. I was told that five similar events had taken place during the previous ten days.

Various requests were made to the higher authorities to seek protection for Adnan, and according to the latest report Adnan has returned to Dicle University.

On the same day, October 25th, four corpses bearing signs of having been subjected to torture were found on a highway outside Diyarbakir. One was identified as a person who had been in police custody.

The president of Dicle University is a high- ranking general. The university has its own police whose task is to supervise the left-wing oriented students. These same police also recruit informers.

The fear of the police is not without ground. Most of the complaints of torture deal with persons in police custody. Torture is prohibited and the courts deal with torture cases. In 1994 more than 1,000 cases of torture were brought before the courts. A handful, less than 10, were found guilty of torture.

A glimmer of hope

The fact that the report by Professor Ergil is supported by the Turkish Chamber of Commerce (TOBB) indicates that a large part of the Turkish business world want peace in the South-east. The war is enormously costly. No one dares to invest in the South-east. The great GAP project which should utilize the water resources of the Euphrates and Tigris does not provide the profit expected.

Another glimmer of hope is the fact that a court recently approved of a foundation for Kurdish culture and research. It is the first time since 1924 that an organization has been approved under a Kurdish name.

A group of intellectuals headed by the author Ismail Nacar is trying to conduct a dialogue with the government about the Kurdish problem.

The Fearless

The country is tormented by fear, but there are those who remain fearless: journalists belonging to the newspapers which are under threat, liberal minded and humane authors, officials of the political parties which represent the suppressed populations, and the human rights activists. 'Fearless' may not be the proper word. Of course they are afraid, but they overcome their fear. Any hope for a better future in Turkey is tied to these courageous people.

Water Disputes and Ethnic Conflicts in the Middle East: The Case of the Kurds

Omar Sheikhmous

Introduction

Many countries in the greater geographical area of the Middle East are experiencing varying degrees of water scarcity which has since the 1960s tended to become more acute because of population increase, rapid urbanization, pollution, waste, reliance on water-intensive agricultural crops, along with inefficient irrigational systems and bad management of existing resources.[1] Except for Turkey, Lebanon and Iran, which have sufficient or abundant water resources, all the other countries of the area are facing a difficult future in terms of meeting their water needs in the coming decades unless better methods of utilization are found.[2]

The whole area is growing short of water, although existing resources if managed well and amicably can satisfy the human, industrial and agricultural needs of the region. This, however, has proved to be difficult because of the passions involved and the pre-conceived ideas connected with discussing water and its related issues. Water, the colourless gold or 'white oil', in comparison with other natural and energy resources like oil, is considered irreplaceable and essential for survival. It is worth sacrificing and fighting for. In the spring of 1979, President Sadat of Egypt, a few days after signing the Camp David Accord with Israel, declared: 'The only matter that could take Egypt to war again is water'. Israel, likewise, threatened Arab countries during the '60s that they would attack water installation and diversionary schemes which were contemplated by Jordan and Syria. In 1990, King Hussein of Jordan issued similar warring statements. Syria and Iraq made similar threats in December 1989.[3] Historical precedents of disputes and wars over single springs and wells between old civilizations, city states and local communities in traditional societies of today are abundant. Furthermore, Middle Eastern power elites, who for the most part are not concerned with the well-being of their citizens

1. Beschorner, 1992-93.
2. The Economist, December 23rd, 1995, January 5th, 1996.
3. Bulloch & Darwish, 1993; Starr, 1991; Lowi, 1993; Beschorner, 1992/93.

because of the non-democratic forms of government that they have, still think in terms of pure power politics and zero-sum games instead of thinking about cooperation, joint regional well-being, and the common good.[4]

Three main areas in the Middle East and North Africa have been affected by long lasting disputes between states over sharing water. These are:

1) The Tigris/Euphrates basin involving Turkey, Syria and Iraq.
2) The Nile basin involving Egypt, Sudan, Ethiopia, Uganda and other East African States.
3) The Jordan basin involving Israel, Jordan, Syria and Gaza and the West Bank.

All these disputes have vascillated in intensity since the formation or independence of the states involved in the earlier, or middle, decades of this century. The Euphrates and the Tigris rise in the mountains of Kurdistan in southeastern Turkey. They are cross-border river basins and flow (especially the Euphrates) through the territories of Turkey, Syria and Iraq. Their relations have become conflictive in recent decades over sharing arrangements. Turkey as the upstream state argues that it is entitled to make full use of all waters in her territory, while Syria and Iraq demand an international agreement on equitable sharing among all three states. The conflicts between Turkey and Syria on the one hand, and Syria and Iraq on the other, are very sharp at times, e.g. the near-war situation between Syria and Iraq in the summer of 1975. Relations between Turkey and Iraq have not been as conflictive because the waters of the Tigris, although originating in Turkey, are mainly filled with abundant water tributaries in Iraqi and Iranian Kurdistan. Furthermore, Iraqi and Turkish political and strategic interests concerning the Kurds and Iran (after 1979) have been similar and coordinated.

Iran, as a country with abundant water resources is not reliant on major rivers originating in the Kurdish areas of Iran or the neighbouring countries, and is not therefore seriously involved in water disputes with them. The historical conflict with Iraq over the Shatt Al-Arab waterway concerns navigational rights and access to the Gulf rather than water sharing and has an indirect impact on the Kurdish ethnic conflict in these countries.

The Rivers in Question

The headwaters of the Tigris and Euphrates rivers and the main tributaries of the Euphrates are in Turkey (Kurdistan). Over 98 percent of Euphrates' flow

4. Schulz, 1992 and 1995.

originates in Turkey. It is filled by the Sajur (originating in Turkey), Khabour and Balikh as tributaries (originating in Syria). While 45 percent of the Tigris originates in Turkey and is filled by tributaries such as Al-Udhaim, the Greater and Lesser Zab and the Diyala, that originate in Iraqi and Iranian Kurdistan. The Tigris and Euphrates converge at Qurna in Iraq and are joined by the Karun river which rises in Iran. The combined rivers then form the Shatt Al-Arab that drains into the Gulf. The Asi (Orontes) river rises in Lebanon and flows through Syria in the Hatay (Alexandretta) region of Turkey. Some 90 percent of the average annual discharge of the Asi is used by Syria and its irrigation schemes have virtually halted the flow of the river into Turkey.[5]

Iraq or Mesopotamia of earlier times had for centuries used the Tigris and the Euphrates rivers as a downstream region. This caused no harm to upstream states. Syria's and Turkey's interest in the Euphrates increased during the 1950s as a result of population growth and initiation of large schemes of agricultural irrigation. By the mid-1960s, Turkey and Syria were devising unilateral projects to harness the Euphrates for irrigation and hydroelectric power production. Most significant was the construction of a dam at Tabqa in Syria (1968-73) and a series of dams in southeastern Anatolia in Turkey: Keban (1965-73), Karakaya (1976-87) and Atatürk (1983-92).[6]

Historical Review of the Disputes

The building of the above mentioned dams led to many manifested forms of conflict and disputes over water resources between Syria and Turkey on the one hand, and Syria and Iraq on the other, concerning demands on scarce water resources (i.e. less supply and greater demand) and depletion of the quantity and quality of water downstream because of upstream usage. The need for cooperation, however, took over and a first round of tripartite talks took place in 1965. They did not lead to an accord because Turkey made agreement on the Euphrates waters conditional upon a comprehensive agreement on the distribution of waters from all the rivers (meaning the Orontes) common to it and Syria. This was rejected by Syria because it would have meant recognition of the contested territory of Alexandretta (Hatay) that was ceded in 1939 to Turkey by the French mandated power in Syria which is still claimed by Syria as part of its territory.[7]

In 1966, Syria and Iraq began a series of bilateral negotiations that concentrated mainly on technical matters. Iraq claimed acquired rights to large-

5. Beschorner, 1992/93.
6. Lowi, 1993.
7. Seale, 1987.

scale historical exploitation as a downstream state. Syria refused the Iraqi claim due to new potential needs. Representatives of both states continued to meet every year for three years, and they discussed an apportionment that would give Iraq 59 percent of the river flow at the Syro-Iraqi border. Nonetheless, no agreement was signed.[8]

Syrian and Turkish relations, however, had been tense over many political issues since the 1930s, but more so after Syrian independence in 1946: e.g. Arab-Turkish historical antagonisms about the revolt of the Arab territories against Turkish rule during the First World War, loss of Alexandretta, Turkey's suspected designs on the Ottoman Mosul region, Turkey's recognition of Israel, and Turkey's integration into western defence systems (NATO and CENTO — later the Baghdad Pact). Furthermore, when the Syrian national-front government established cordial relations with the Soviet Union after 1955, Turkey used military maneuvers and concentration of troops along the Syrian border as a method of putting pressure on Syria. The most serious being the one of autumn 1957 that contemplated a possible military intervention by Turkey, Iraq and Jordan into Syria.[9]

Since the 1940s, up to the present time, Syrian and Iraqi relations have also been characterized by competition and conflict over regional dominance, leadership in the Arab world, Baathist legitimacy since 1968 and moves by both sides to destabilize and eventually topple each other's regime, through support and mobilization of opponents.

In 1973, the Keban and Tabqa dams became operational. The filling of the dams seriously harmed Syria and especially Iraq. In mid-1974, Iraq asked Syria to release additional waters from Tabqa which Syria subsequently did. This consequently led to a bilateral agreement between both countries limiting the amount of water to be stored in the Tabqa reservoir and thereby guaranteeing Iraq's agricultural needs. In the beginning of 1975, however, Iraq charged Syria for violating the agreement by reducing the flow, thus placing a rural population of three million Iraqis at risk. Iraq protested and took the matter to the Arab League. The Syrians denied the charges and blamed Turkey for cutting the flow of the Euphrates by half that season.[10]

The Arab League, Saudi Arabia and Egypt mediated between Syria and Iraq. In June 1975, Syrian and Iraqi troops were amassed along joint borders and war was nearly imminent between both countries. A more forceful mediation effort, however, by Saudi Arabia in August averted the threat of war and an understanding was reached. Syria announced in mid-August that

8. Shulz, 1995.
9. Seale, 1987.
10. Lowi, 1993.

it had accepted a Saudi proposal whereby Euphrates' water would be shared between Syria and Iraq on a 'proportional basis' in accordance with the amount reaching Syria from Turkey. Nonetheless, no agreement was signed and the water dispute remained unresolved.[11]

In 1980, the three states (Iraq, Syria and Turkey) agreed to establish a technical commission that continues to meet today without any agreement having being reached. In 1984, Iraq agreed with Turkey to accept a minimum flow of 500 cubic metres per second, but Syria refused to negotiate at the time. A similar agreement, however, was also reached with Syria in 1986 and bilateral discussions still continue between them.

The Present Disputes

Because of Turkey's rising water needs as a result of development and energy requirements, as well as the rising population, it initiated in 1983 the South-East Anatolia Project (GAP - Güneydogu Anadolu Projesi) that is intended to be completed in the year 2006. But Turkish needs cannot be compared to those of Iraq and Syria. The declared main aims of the project are to generate hydroelectric power, decentralize development, slow-down rural-to-urban migration, and appease the Kurdish population in the region through improvement of their economic conditions.[12]

The whole GAP project includes thirteen smaller projects, seven on the Euphrates and six on the Tigris, which involve 74,000 square kilometres with 4.5 million inhabitants. The project will open 1.6 million hectares of land to irrigated cultivation and will supply approximately 24 billion kilowatt-hours of energy from 66 hydroelectric plants. The final project will also result in 80 dams and 68 irrigation systems. The Turkish government hopes to sell the additional food production to countries in Europe and the Middle East, which are expected to import $20 billion worth of foodstuffs by the end of the century. However, because of the World Bank's refusal to give financial backing to the project, based on its earlier practice and principle, that there is no agreement on water rights between the riparian states, the project will take more than 50 years to complete because the present levels of investment are solely provided by the Turkish Government.[13]

GAP has raised Syrian and Iraqi anxieties over the availability of water for their own agricultural and industrial projects in the future. The largest of the sub-projects, the Atatürk dam was completed in 1989. In November of the

11. Ibid.
12. Beschorner, 1992/93; Starr, 1991; Schulz, 1995.
13. Beschorner, 1992/93; Starr, 1991.

same year, Turkey announced that it would hold back the flow of the Euphrates for one month in order to fill the lake behind the dam, starting in January 1990. As a result of this, and a unique drought in the Middle East that year, Syrian and Iraqi hydroelectric stations and irrigation schemes were functioning at reduced capacities. Syria was further forced to cut back on drinking water and electricity to Damascus, Aleppo and other cities. Experts forecast that by the late 1990s, the GAP will have a serious impact on the water flow to Syria and Iraq. Water quality could worsen since water used for irrigation in Turkey may carry salts, fertilizers and pesticides back into the river. For Syria, the Euphrates is the main single source of water for drinking, irrigation and industry, and partly for electricity.[14]

Unlike Syria, Iraq has access to the less exploited Tigris and its tributaries and can replenish the depleted Euphrates with Tigris water. Before the Kuwaiti crisis, Iraq was planning massive investment in more than 20 flood control, hydroelectric, water storage, and irrigation projects on the Tigris, its tributaries, and Lake Tharthar. A major scheme involves the diversion of water from the Tigris into Lake Tharthar and then into the Euphrates if its water is insufficient to irrigate crops.[15]

Neither Syria nor Iraq can do much to halt Turkish plans. Turkey is in a strong geographical and military position and is not dependent on outside finance or expertise. She arranged ministerial talks with Syria and Iraq on water issues and succeeded in containing the dispute.

When Syria and Iraq first protested against the GAP project in the middle of the 1980s, Prime Minister (later President) Özal proposed a 'Peace Pipeline' to serve both the Gulf and the Near Eastern countries. This went on from 1987 to 1991. It was proposed to take water from two Turkish rivers, the Seyhan and Ceyhan, and transport it via two pipelines, one on a western route from Anatolia through Syria and Jordan to the Red Sea shore of Saudi Arabia; while the eastern route would carry water through Iraq to Kuwait, eastern Saudi Arabia and the United Arab Emirates. Although the plan was feasible, it was abandoned in 1991 for security reasons (the Arab countries were reluctant to be at the mercy of Turkey) and because it involved Israeli participation. The current peace process between Israel and her Arab neighbours might pave the way for a future implementation of the pipelines.[16]

At the height of the tension in 1989, President Özal stated: 'I appreciate their fears... but we will not harm them. On the contrary, Turkey will more than make up for the water shortage. I have tried to convince Iraq and Syria

14. Starr 1991, Foreign & Commonwealth Office, 1992.
15. Beschorner, 1992/93; Schulz, 1995.
16. Beschorner, 1992/93.

of our positive intentions'. and in reaction to this situation as well as part of the general peace process in the Middle East, President Özal suggested that the Middle East Water Summit be held in Istanbul in November 1991.[17] Unfortunately, a number of factors contributed to the cancellation of the water summit which had many promising solutions on its agenda. Among these factors, the death of President Özal and the Gulf War, together with the collapse of the Soviet Empire and the emergence of the Central Asian Turkic republics, can be mentioned. The latest attempt to discuss water issues in the Middle East was made in a multilateral meeting held in April, 1994 in Muscat-Oman. Although Syria and Lebanon boycotted the meeting because of Israeli participation, over forty states and organizations participated to discuss co-operation and joint solution of water issues in the Middle East.[18]

The Ethnic Conflict

There is a tendency in all the countries that include parts of Kurdistan, i.e. Turkey, Iran, Iraq and Syria to treat the dissatisfaction, protest and rebellion taking place in their respective Kurdish territories as being incited from abroad (meaning Kurds and non-Kurds from other countries) and therefore nothing to do with their own misdeeds, injustices and repressive policies towards their own Kurds. They repeatedly claim that their citizen-Kurds are quite happy with their lot and cannot imagine that there are indigenous causes for their dissatisfaction or that their governments have committed terrible mistakes for decades in dealing with Kurdish grievances. They, consequently, claim that if foreign incitement ceased, the Kurds would be very happy and loyal citizens again. This is a marvellous exercise in self-delusion and denial of responsibility by the successive governments of these states. It is also an easy way out, due to the lack of willingness to find serious solutions to the problem, to project it onto others.

Turkey, for example, up until 1989 accused the Eastern European and communist states and movements of being behind the unrest among the Kurds. During the 1980s, they shifted the blame to the dispute with Syria over water rights and the initiation of the GAP project, forgetting that Kurdish demands for cultural and democratic political rights go back to the beginning of the establishment of the modern Turkish Republic and long before any dispute over sharing of water resources had ever developed.

Iraq, too, used to blame either British colonial power, oil monopolies, zionism, US imperialism, the Shah and Khomeini's regimes in Iran, Arab

17. Starr, 1991.
18. Schulz, 1995.

reaction, Nasserist and Baathist rivals and the Communist states, for the Kurdish resistance movement that started in 1961 and has more or less gone on intermittently until now. Syria, too, was accused of hostile support to the Kurds after the intensification of the water dispute in 1973 and more so in 1975. It never acknowledged its genocidal practices of mass murder, mass deportation and use of chemical weapons against the Kurds as a cause for resistance and dissatisfaction.

Iran, during the Shah's period, used to accuse the Soviet Union and Tudeh Party of inciting the Kurds, or alternatively the Shah would blame Iraq and Nasser's Egypt for his troubles with the Kurds. The Islamic Republic has followed the same path but added US Imperialism and Zionism to their external enemies that incite and support the Kurds, instead of scrutinising their own behaviour in treating the Kurds which is extremely contradictory to their own declared Islamic ideals.

All earlier empirical research on water disputes in the Middle East have not found a causal relationship between water disputes and ethnic or political conflicts, especially in the dispute concerning Turkey, Syria and Iraq.[19] There have been instrumental uses of the Kurdish ethnic conflict by respective states when the level of conflict over other contested historical, political, strategic and ideological issues were already greatly heightened. All other evidence seems to indicate that conflicts are still determined by deep political differences and that although water is part of a complex system of political and economic leverages, it has not, so far, led to an actual conflict that is directly and exclusively related to the control and exploitation of water resources.

Some of the clearest examples of such a policy were: Syrian support for Iraqi-Kurdish political parties (KDP — Kurdistan Democratic Party, and PUK — Patriotic Union of Kurdistan) from 1973 until now. Iraqi support for Syrian-Kurdish opposition forces during the 70s and 80s. Syrian support for the Kurdistan Workers Party (PKK) and other kurdish opposition forces from Turkey since 1980. Iraqi support for Iranian kurdish opposition forces after 1970 until now. Iranian support for Iraqi kurdish forces during the Shah's regime until the Algiers agreement of 1975. Iranian support for Iraq and Turkish Kurdish forces after 1979, especially during the 1980s. Turkish support for Iraqi-Kurdish forces during and after the occupation of Kuwait and the Gulf War (1990-91). Turkish support for Kurdish and other Iranian opposition forces after 1979.

Most of the heightened tension concerning water issues between Syria, Iraq and Turkey during the 1980s has centred around the GAP project, which is essentially a domestic project that aims at developing agriculture and agro-

19. Libiszewski, 1995; Beschorner, 1992/93; Lowi, 1993; Schulz, 1995.

industrial production for export and to raise the standard of living of the Kurdish population in the south-eastern regions of Turkey. GAP is also conceived by the Turkish government as an economic answer to Kurdish demands for self-determination. The project area covers the provinces of Gaziantep, Diyarbakir, Sanliurfa, Mardin, Adiyaman and Siirt. GAP further aims at creating at least 90,000 public sector jobs in the region and establishing agricultural and industrial growth poles to attract Western investors. It hopes to turn the area into a regional bread-basket: 'to mobilize regional resources, to eradicate regional disparities, to enhance productivity, to create employment opportunities, to raise income levels, to develop urban centres and to ensure economic growth and social stability in the region'.

Instead of improving ethnic relations, the Kurds are already showing signs of dissatisfaction and discontent because the local impact of the GAP is, so far, very controversial. The Kurds refer to the examples of the Keban Dam in Turkey, and the Dokan and Derbendikhan Dams in Iraq. The first, although it brought some benefits to the Kurds, most of the generated hydro-electricity was fed to Western Anatolia and there was discrimination in land distribution and job possibilities. In Iraq both dams were utilized originally only for flood control in Baghdad without any hydro-electric or irrigation installations. GAP further raised expectations which have not been realized and displaced 70,000 people from 117 villages who have not invested their compensation money in agricultural land but in buying houses in Sanliurfa. Some of the criticism maintains that too much emphasis has been given to dam-building rather than to the development of roads, educational and training and agricultural extension facilities. Farmers do not have access to adequate credit facilities nor have they received sufficient training in irrigation techniques. Salinization and waterlogging of the soil — as a consequence of over-irrigation — are already in evidence in the GAP area. Problems of land ownership, where 8 percent of the farmers own 50 percent of the land, discrimination in job and land allotment is widespread.[20]

Turkey alleged in the later parts of 1980s to have uncovered a Syrian plot to blow the Atatürk Dam. In 1987, Ankara also threatened to cut the flow of the Euphrates to Syria because of Syrian support for the PKK. In October 1989, Syrian MIGS on a 'training mission' shot down a Turkish survey plane well within Turkey's borders. Five people were killed in the incident, which was reportedly linked to Syrian-Turkish tensions over water.[21]

One of the hypotheses that is put forward for denial of Kurdish rights in the countries of the Middle East, and reluctance by these states to grant

20. Beschorner, 1992/93, Schulz, 1995.
21. Starr, 1991.

Kurdish autonomy and self-determination, is the wealth of Kurdistan in oil, water, fertile lands and other natural resources. Although, the policies of these states towards the Kurds can be more soundly attributed to their modern nation-building process in recently-established states and immature unitarian ethnic assimilationist notions, the above hypothesis might have some credibility in the strategic planning and thinking of the relevant states, if they have any!

It is therefore, extremely important for the Kurds and their nationalist movements, if they are interested in a peaceful solution to their question, to engage these states and their peoples in a very serious dialogue and discussions for repeatedly giving them legal and political guarantees for future cooperation and access to Kurdistan's oil and water resources, even when it gains independence, in order to alleviate the fears of these neighbours.

Bibliography

Beschorner, N. 1992/93. *Water and Instability in the Middle East*, (273), London: Adelphi.

The Economist, 1995. *Water in the Middle East*, December 23rd, 1995; January 5th, 1996. London.

Bulloch, J. & Darwish, A., 1992. (eds.) *Water Wars. Coming Conflicts in the Middle East*, London: Victor Gollancz.

Foreign & Commonwealth Office, January 1992. *Problems Over Water In The Middle East*. London.

Libiszewski, S. 1995, *Water Disputes in the Jordan Basin Region and their Role in the Resolution of the Arab-Israeli Conflict*, Occasional Paper, (13), August, Zürich: ENCOP.

Lowi, Miriam R. 1993. *Water and Power: The Politics of a scarce Resource in the Jordan River Basin*, Cambridge: Cambridge University Press.

Ohlsson, L. 1992. *Regional Case Studies of Water Conflicts*, Göteborg: Padrigu Papers.

Schulz, M. 1995. 'Turkey, Syria and Iraq: A Hydropolitical Security Complex.' in: Ohlsson, L., *Hydropolitics: Conflicts over Water as a Development Constraint*, Zed Books, London: 91-122.

Seale, P. 1987. *The Struggle For Syria*, London: I.B. Tauris.

Starr, Joyce R. 1991. 'Water Wars'. *Foreign Policy* (82), Spring: 17-36.

Alevis in Turkey and Europe

Mehmet Ali Ölmez

Modesty is a friend and hatred an enemy; we love our enemies, for to us the world is one.

Yunus Emre, Islamic mystic poet and student of Haci Bektash —
approximately 12 - 13th century.

Approximately a quarter of the total population of Turkey (Turks and Kurds) are confessed Alevis, (Alawites). In Western Europe there are about 2 million Turkish migrants, 1.9 million of whom live in the Federal Republic of Germany. It can be assumed that approximately 35 percent of the Turkish and Kurdish migrants living in Germany are Alevis.

Before going into the particular aspects of Alevitism/Bektashism, I would like to give a geographic indication of the areas peopled by Alevis in Turkey and in other countries; the largest areas are in the eastern Turkish provinces of Erzincan, Tunceli, Malatya, Elazig, Kahramanmaras, Adana, Antakya (containing the biggest group of Arab Alevites), Sivas, Kayseri, Yozgat, Corum and Ankara. Alevis also live in some provinces of Western Anatolia, e.g. Balikesir, Canakkale, Izmir, Aydin, Antalya and Isparta. Outside of Turkey Alevis can be found in Syria (mainly north of Damascus), Egypt, Albania and Greece.

Anatolian Alevitism arose through the migration of Turkmenian tribes in Central Asia through Iran to Anatolia (approx. AD900-1300). Apart from the influence of Iranian Twelve Shiitism, Alevitism contains elements of Shamanist, Christian and Jewish culture and religion. Alevis differ from Iranian Shiites as well as from Sunnites (orthodox Muslims, majority in Turkey) because they do not accept the Sunnah and Sharia (Islamic law as practiced, e.g., in Iran).

This means that Alevis reject the prescribed five daily prayers according to strict regulations, the month-long fast for Ramadan, the ban on alcohol and pork, the separation of the sexes and exclusion of women from politics and community decision-making committees. Alevi women do not have to conform to any particular regulations regarding clothing or the wearing of veils, they do not usually wear headscarves, veils or any other 'Islamic' clothing.

Alevis are in favour of laicism — i.e. separation of state and religion — because during the Ottoman Empire they were oppressed due to their liberal interpretation of the Quran. When Kemal Atatürk introduced the policy of laicism in Turkey, this was supported by the Alevis even though their order of the Alevi philosopher Haci Bektashi Veli was banned under the new state model. The Alevis hoped that the majority religion of the Sunnites would free them from persistent oppression.

In more recent history, Alevis have always supported democratic and human rights orientated parties, and are now voicing stronger demands for official recognition by the Turkish Government and the right to participate in the compiling of school books and religious instruction (officially the only religious instruction is Sunnite and it is compulsory). Furthermore, Alevis demand the right to practice their religion freely and protection against attacks by Islamic fundamentalist groups. In Germany and its neighbouring Western European countries, there is now an Alevi community in every major town.

Who was Haci Bektashi Veli?

Haci Bektash developed the Alevi philosophy and founded the order of the Bektashites between AD1200 and 1300. However, due to the centuries of oppression and extermination there are hardly any existing scientific sources of information, but, according to Alevi history passed down over the generations, Betkas lived from approx. 1248-1337. He travelled from Horasan in Iran through Iraq, Medina, Mecca and Syria to Anatolia. There he settled in the village of Karahüyük. Through the people he had met on his many travels he had become a wise and educated man and he gathered a large number of pupils who spread his teachings throughout Anatolia. Haci Bektash abolished the Arabic language within his order so that the impoverished, often nomadic Anatolian peasants could understand him. He wrote lyrical religious texts in the Turkish language and these are still passed on by word-of-mouth today.

There would not be enough time at this point to explain Haci Bektash's teaching principle of 'The Four Doorways'. The focal points, however, are: the striving for spiritual education, caring for the poor and for justice, and the practicing of peace and modesty. In place of compulsory religious prayers, Alevis practice a kind of religious, lithurgic festival in autumn or winter, called *Cem*. A *Cem* involves the following:

1) ritual prayer
2) ritual dance between men and women

   3) ritual poetry expressed in song
   4) ritual group meal
   5) special ritual drink

This festival has a major social purpose within the Alevi community; if anyone is excluded from the *Cem* for reasons of unacceptable behaviour, it results in great isolation. Nobody speaks to such a person or helps him with the harvest, etc. The person in question can, however, redeem himself by confessing to the *Cem* cult community, which then decides on a form of punishment. Disputes and other problems are also resolved during *Cem* festivals. I have already pointed out the special status of women in the Alevi community; during a *Cem*, the male and female participants are not separated, but usally sit in a circle so that they can look each other in the face.

   Most Sunnites accuse Alevis of maintaining a cult focussed on *Imam Ali* and of worshipping him as a god. As Alevis reject Sunnah and Shariah, they are accused of being without moral restraint. The prejudice levelled against them which hurts Alevis most deeply, is the idea that they commit incest during *Cem* celebrations. Such ideas originated during the Ottoman period and were spread in order to suppress the Alevi belief.

   The existence of approximately 20 million Alevis in Turkey is officially denied. The state simply 'overlooks' them and tries to create the impression that the population of Turkey is completely Sunnite. The subject of Alevitism is not mentioned by the state-controlled TV and radio corporation and hardly ever mentioned in the state-controlled press. Although Christians and Jews are officially recognised as religious minorities and have their own places of prayer, Alevis are classed as a sect, thus coming under the official ban on sects in Turkey.

   Although the right to beliefs and opinions is a basic human right, Alevis are forced to practice their religion and culture in secret. Article 9 of the Declaration of Human Rights and Article 9 of the Constitution of the Republic of Turkey both state that every person has the right to 'freedom of conscience, belief and conviction'. Even after the founding of the Republic, social, psychological and political pressure continues to be exerted on Alevis. The terrible massacre at Sivas, Turkey, on July 2nd, 1993 in which 36 people, among them many prominent musicians, writers and teachers had gathered for a religious festival to commemorate the death of a martyr, is only one example. Thousands of raging fundamentalists set fire to the hotel where the participants were staying, despite the presence of security guards. Hundreds of Alevis were also massacred in Turkish towns in 1977, 1978 and 1979.

The pressure has increased particularly since the municipal elections in Turkey in 1994. In the areas where Islamic fundamentalist parties were elected, Alevi municipal employees were removed from office, an Alevi culture centre in Istanbul was burnt down and in a TV programme a pregnant woman was publically accused of 'having committed incest like the Alevites'. At the end of March 1995, Islamic fundamentalists attacked university students who were not fasting for Ramadan.

I have already referred to the formation of Alevi communities in Germany and Western Europe, however, it should be added that they are hardly noticed by the German public but that they make efforts to come into contact with other institutions such as churches and initiative groups working against the expulsion of foreigners. Unfortunately the official representatives of inter-religious dialogue generally address orthodox Sunnites, being the biggest majority of Turkish people living in Germany.

This is certainly important for ensuring a peaceful co-existence between Germans and Turks, but more space should be given to drawing attention to the plight of Alevis in Turkey — which constitutes a violation of human rights — and in particular, church representatives responsible for Islamic matters should view themselves as contact persons for the Alevi communities and should extend their activities accordingly. This would certainly be more in line with the aim of achieving a variegated picture of the total Turkish population.

Bibliography

Dierl, Anton Josef, 1985. *Geschichte und Lehre des anatolischen Alevismus-Bektaschismus.* Frankfurt: Dagyeli-Verlag.

Gülcicek, Ali Duran, 1994, *Der Weg der Aleviten (Bektaschiten).* Köln: Ethnographia Anatolica-Verlag.

The Reconstitution[1] of History and Continuous History

Ilhan Ataseven

I am concerned here on the one hand with the making of (legitimate) history, religious history, and on the other hand with the maintaining of history (not legitimising it). The latter, I will argue, is in a sense an apolitical effort whereas the former is a political effort.[2] Making history is about choosing (remembering) events from the past that are considered relevant from the point of view of the legitimation of certain values and ideas that are supposed to be the basis of social order.[3] In the creation of social order, history is remade with 'new' images from the past (and it is contrasted to the prevalent history against which the 'new' history is struggling). This is necessary because 'there is a measure of complete arbitrariness in the very nature of any such attempted beginning. The beginning has nothing whatsoever to hold onto; it is as if it came out of nowhere.'[4] The maintaining of history is explained under the heading 'The Apolitical Effort'. The representatives of the Alevis in Turkey constitute one such political group, mainly occupied with the making of socio-religious history. The Turkish state is a political body which, even though not mainly occupied with religious history, cannot afford to disregard religion altogether. The a-political group, in my study is the Bektashi sufi-order.

There is a conflict between Alevis and Bektashis. This conflict has to do with definition of the terms. The founding father of the Bektashi order was Haci Bektash Veli. He was a sufi with a message to the people, in the language of the people (i.e. Turkish, not Persian, or Arabic). This message was dressed in Islamic clothes but the tradition of the people was woven into its texture. A sufi order was created some time after his death. Initiation into this order required training. To be an Alevi is to revere Haci Bektash Veli, his message, and the tradition of sufi Islam that he represented. One is born an Alevi; one

1. Clifford, 1986: 24, 'Cultural *poesis* — and politics — is the constant reconstitution of selves and others through specific exclusions, conventions and discursive practices'.
2. The arguments concerning the political effort are mutually valid, I believe, for official history as well as unofficial (oppositional) history.
3. Connerton, 1989: 3.
4. Connerton, 1989: 6.

belongs to a group of people that throughout history has clung to this kind of Islam, mixed with pre-Islamic Turkish traditons. To be a Bektashi is to be initiated into the order. This has nothing to do with belonging to a group of people that by tradition believe in something. Theoretically, one can belong to any tradition whatsoever, and still become a Bektashi, after having received the proper initiatory education. This distinction between what it means to be Alevi and Bektashi is not recognised by the Alevis.

The Political Effort

The Alevi[5] group and the state are visible (or, in a sense, official) and therefore a target for attack. In a world of contending value systems, these groups have to make history according to the requirements of the society they wish to represent in order to be legitimate. The mere existence of a visible political body provokes attack. This of course is a nuisance since a political body needs continuity in order to be able to achieve any benefit for a society or for itself. Continuity by consensus is hard to achieve since there are so many different groups of people, each with specific needs and wants. To be all encompassing, to make all (groups) fit into one (system), can hardly be done without using force. The state is a square hole and if people do not become square they are made square by some kind of force.

This can be illuminated by one problem within the academic world[6]: Imagine a theory, a way of conducting research, that by its age and the weight of its users is accepted, and legitimate. You take this 'ready made' theory and try to apply it to the world you are studying, and you make the world fit into the theory by choosing suitable pieces (in politics: followers) and by leaving out pieces that are not suitable (in politics: opponents). This is all fine, so long as the unsuitable pieces are suppressed, kept out of focus. But the very minute some researcher steps out of the frame of the accepted theory, using pieces of the world that oppose it, this accepted theory comes under attack and a defence strategy must be implemented. Disregarding alternative theories is one such defence: The alternative theory is new, it has few followers, it lacks tradition and, most importantly, it threatens all those who extract a feeling of security by supporting the accepted theory. Each follower is, after all, sheltering

---

5. The word Alevi is here used to designate those who claim to be the representatives of the community of Alevis (which is very much defined by the representatives themselves).
6. Clifford, 1986: 7. This is about choosing information: 'Strategies of (..) concealment, and partial disclosure determine ethnographic relations as much as they do the transmission of stories between generations'. I take this to be valid for 'generations' of researchers, politicians and people in general.

under a big, strong, almost non-moving type of comforting body, (the comfort of familiarity).

This is, in short, the force of a majority opposed to the force of a minority. One wonders then what chances the minority has against this well supported majority? A state (a major and heavy theory), may gain its legitimacy by majority support or by the illusion of majority support. If no alternatives are available, if you can choose only one way, then there is an illusion of support. The question of how one would choose, if other options were available, is a forbidden question. Nevertheless, questions of this kind are asked quietly, and alternatives do appear. Alternatives gain momentum from highlighting the shortcomings of the state. They are saying that there can be another safety, there can be a secure life without the shortcomings that are present in the broad theory. There can be a new life, a better one. Alternatives bring hope, they are messianic. A short glimpse of the sources that put forth the history of the minority will illuminate the position of the Alevis during the period at the beginning of Ottoman hegemony.

The Alevi Uprisings

The situation being as it was, the question arises in Turkish literature on the subject as to whether a connection between the rebellions and the Ottoman enemy, Shah Ismail and Shiism, existed. The connection to Shiism would then also imply a Mahdi thought behind the uprisings. Were the uprisings a result of Shia propaganda? No, because Alevi uprisings took place also during Mamluk rule, Seldjuk rule and Byzantine rule. They were uprisings in the name of democracy and had nothing to do with Shiism. The Alevi uprisings during the Ottoman period in Anatolia were independent and restricted to the Anatolian sphere and its people. This is confusing, since the uprisings, in the 'name of democracy', that took place in Persia during Seldjuk rule and in other places are also called Alevi uprisings. A definition of Alevi would then be, in accordance with the above argument, 'those who fight for democracy'. Well, of course there was Shia propaganda in Anatolia during the Ottoman period, and there was sympathy for Shah Ismail among a large following of the Anatolian people. But the Anatolian people, (however much they sympathised with the Shia ideology), never supported Shah Ismail's political ambitions.[7] They had however the hope that this brother in faith (Shah Ismail) could put an end to an unjust society. The connection to Shia religious ideology makes the Mahdi thought appear as a plausible explanation to the popular support for the uprisings. There is nothing, however, to suggest that people in general

7. Öz 1992: 148.

were familiar with the theological aspect of Mahdism, but their longing for an 'ideal society', has the same implications.[8] Also in connection to the Mahdi ideology, the Celali uprisings, in which the Alevi were involved, must be mentioned. Celal was a rebel who, during the reign of the Yavuz Sultan Selim, claimed to be the Mahdi. Later Celali became a technical term for uncontrolled, violent uprisings.[9] The Celali uprisings were led by soldiers from different backgrounds with no clearly defined ideology. This was the reason why they did not succeed and this was also the reason why they were popular: They were expressions of discontent, simply, with no complicated message.[10] The Alevi uprisings on the other hand were led by people who had a clearly defined ideology and they were continuations of an old tradition ('Eski bir gelenegi vardir').[11]

The connection to Iran is accepted, but the reasons for this connection are seen as incidental since the uprisings in Anatolia did not have the intention of supporting the political ambitions of the Safavid empire. This is obviously so. The reason why a large following of people risked their lives in uprisings was of course their dissatisfaction with their living conditions. But the motivation and the inspiration seems to have been taken from Iran and Shah Ismail who was himself a Turk. A concentration of uprisings can be seen from the time of the Yavuz Sultan Selim until the beginning of the 17th century.[12] This period coincides with the Ottoman wars against the Safavid empire.[13]

A pattern can be seen in these uprisings. They were all born out of discontent. The leaders claimed, in most cases, to be the Mahdi and there was in most cases a connection to Iran and Shah Ismail. The Shahkulu uprising illustrates this quite clearly. It was an uprising whose aim was the overthrow of the Ottomans and in this the Ottomans partly had themselves to blame. The Ottoman sultan Bayezid II had been paying the sheiks so that they would 'pray for them'. This helped the sheiks to increase their local power, but at the same time they were potential support for Shah Ismail. They were his representatives in Anatolia.[14] As success was achieved, however, the possibility of gaining

---

8. Öz 1992: 145.
9. Sertoglu 1986: 62.
10. Öz 1992: 143.
11. Öz 1992: 146.
12. Öz 1992: 152-206.
13. Yavuz Sultan Selim set out against Shah Ismail in 1514, Süleyman Kanuni around 1550. Murat III fought Iran during 1577-1589, Mehmet III in 1603. Ahmet I made peace with Iran in 1612 but went to war again in 1615. Osman II made peace in Serav 1618, and Murad IV started war in 1635 and 1638 (and finally Abdül Hamid fought Iran in 1778).
14. Öz 1992: 166.

independence appeared.[15] Thus, when the uprising was subdued by the Ottomans and Shahkulu was killed, the rebels sought refuge in Iran. They were not, however, received openly by Shah Ismail. Some of the rebels were even killed by him. Shah Ismail deduced correctly that too many of these unsuccessful uprisings (in his name) would eventually turn the Ottomans against him. Yavuz Selim attacked him in 1514.[16] Shahkulu himself was depicted as a 'prophet' and a 'mahdi' and those who did not believe in him were infidels. This Shahkulu was the base (üssü) of the Safavids in Anatolia.[17]

The representatives of the 'major theory', the state, do not in themselves last— they come and they go. They do not in themselves represent continuity. If, however, they can give the illusion of being the representatives of a continuity their position becomes legitimate. If they are representatives of a force that is not subject to the cycle of life, a force that is not born, and therefore cannot die, their claim to be valid leaders is hardly questionable. The struggle is then to convince potential followers that they are, in fact, representatives of such a continuous force. In my sources, Atatürk is depicted as being a representative of such a continuity.

Mustafa Kemal made the spiritual leader of the Alevis (Cemalettin Chelebi) a representative in the national assembly.[18] He did so because he recognized the Alevis as republican, secular, modern and democratic.[19] Mustafa Kemal had realized that a large part of the population in certain regions (Tokat, Amasya) was Alevi and that these were tied to a spiritual leader in Kirshehir. In order to reach the people, Mustafa Kemal found it necessary to contact their spiritual leaders; Alevi persons with authority. That Mustafa Kemal contacted the Alevi population is seen as a sign of his understanding that Alevis were predisposed towards equality, liberty and independence[20] — precisely those qualities that had previously made Seldjuks and Ottomans turn against the Turcomen. The contacts with Alevi and Bektashi representatives continued after this correspondence and Mustafa Kemal went to visit them in Haci Bektash, where he met with Cemalettin Chelebi Efendi and Niyazi Baba.[21]

---

15. Even if the reason for the uprisings is said to be the quest for democracy and justice there are many cases where the rebels are said to indulge in pillaging and looting (Öz 1992: 182-3) which was another reason for the Ottomans to take action against them.
16. Öz 1992: 172-73.
17. Öz 1992: 169.
18. Sener 1991: 72.
19. Sener 1991: 79.
20. Sener 1991: 51-52.
21. Niyazi Baba was the head of the Bektashi order community, i.e. he was of the Baba branch as opposed to the Chelebi branch who is considered to be an Alevi by the Bektashis.

Mustafa Kemal takes on a legendary character and with the passage of time things are ascribed to him so as to create a history that suits the situation at hand. Cemalettin Chelebi and Niyazi Baba are said to have been astonished by the way in which Mustafa Kemal talked about saving the nation, safeguarding the Turks and so on, to the extent that they wondered whether he was Haci Bektash Veli himself in disguise. People started to consider him as the Mahdi since he clearly took their side against the Ottomans who had been an enemy of the Alevis for as long as they could remember.[22] The language which Mustafa Kemal used when addressing the people might have given them reason to believe so..

'With the permission of God'; 'In the holy war'; 'Our pure nation'[23] is what he wrote to Niyazi Baba in Haci Bektash.[24] The result of the contact with Mustafa Kemal resulted in announcements from Alevi leaders with the purpose of gathering the Alevi population into the movement of Mustafa Kemal:

His excellency Mustafa Kemal Pasa (...) who is a glory to Islam...; It is a duty of ours to assist Ghazi Pasa's every wish in the exaltation and progress of the nation; ... 'Those who do not accept this have no relation to us whatsoever; ... Those who do not follow this advice of mine are not one of us. God will not support them; ... Our holy nation...; Don't listen to anyone, do not disregard what I say; ...It is his excellency M. Kemal Pasa who is thinking of your happiness and who will save you from slavery.. .[25]

God Almighty, who was never born and will never die, exists eternally, and is the best of allies. His will is accepted by all. But what is His will? Who can know? Who speaks the language of God? Who can communicate with God? These are crucial questions for a political leader who wants to draw on the legitimacy of God. If the political leader himself does not possess the necessary knowledge, if he is not trained in the religious sciences, if he cannot convince his subjects that he is in a communicative mode with God, he has to ally himself with persons who do have religious knowledge. Holy men, religious scholars, representatives of God on earth, all constitute a group of individuals that have the power to attract followers — as long as their communicative qualities are believed in — and can be used, through alliance, by others who want to attract followers.

Religion thus becomes a weapon. Just like a nuclear bomb, it has an enormous destructive potential and it provides security for this very reason. For example, the stronger a police force, the safer the protected society feels.

22. Sener 1991: 66.
23. 'Tanri'nin izniyle', 'kutsal savasta', 'Temiz ulusumuzun..'
24. Sener 1991: 52.
25. Sener 1991: 82-83.

On the other hand, the degree of threat a police force may constitute (towards the society it is protecting) is in proportion to its strength. The force/power is legitimate since it gives security to those subject to it, much in the same way as gangster protection politics is conducted.[26] If this force/power is threatened by an outside force, the security of the society may be threatened as well (or so the holders of the initial force would claim).[27] The religious weapon is, then, double edged and it can easily be turned against its users. My supposition is that holy men, men of religion, can function as power boosters for men of politics. I will try to show wherein their power lies and how it is used by others. In order not to get lost in theories about the origins of religion I take for granted the existence of a need among human beings for a belief in things beyond, or above, the visual world. I also take for granted that this belief has various inherent functions which include that of explaining the unexplainable, giving comfort in life, meaning to life, and acting as a super-ego, a conscience or an 'evil eye'.

A holy man may prove his holiness by performing acts that are usually considered to be impossible to perform for human beings. He may see things human beings cannot see (the future, the past and so on). It is popularly believed that he can do all of this because he can communicate with the divine. He is a mediator between the divine and the human. This role is possible to have if one can communicate in the language of the divine as well as in the language of man.

Holy men, however, exist in various forms. Their difference, as I see it, lies in those to whom they primarily are communicating the divine will. Are they men of the people (in their profane identity) or are they men of the elite (the ruling class)? In other words; do they speak the language of the people or the language of the elite. For a political leader, to have a holy man by his very side, tied to him, has obvious advantages. But the nearness is in itself a disadvantage, because it comes close to a state of things where the leader claims holiness for himself. The nearer the holy man, the less credible are the political leader's claims of holy guidance.[28]

I am pushing the argument here. There are of course nuances in the relationship between the leading class and the led class. There are situations where subjects of an empire are happy and content with the way the empire is being run. So long as they feel justly treated there is no need to question the legitimacy of the ruling class. In many cases though, this is not the case.

---

26. Lewellen, 1992: 117.
27. Lewellen, 1992: 187.
28. Holiness requires, in a sense, unattachement, i.e. universality. An act performed for the benefit of the performer himself is likely to upset those not connected to the performer.

When people are not treated as they would like, they question the way things are being done, and the persons doing them. It is when individuals from the led class start to verbalise a discontent that alternatives seem to pop up, or at least they become the centre of focus. And it is when discontent becomes unbearable that visions of better alternatives gain momentum. So people turn to individuals who can provide visions of this kind. A man of the people who has been given an insight to the other world, the divine sphere, is well suited to provide such a vision. He speaks the language of the people, or rather, the divine is speaking (directly or indirectly) through him to the people. Once a belief in the holiness of a holy man is established his authority is confirmed and the loyalty of his followers guaranteed.

If the political leader was dependent only on those in his immediate surroundings, that is the elite class, the holy man (of the elite) by his side might have sufficed to give him legitimacy. This is not usually the case, however, since the territory of an empire is inhabited by human beings, a very small number of whom belong to the elite class. To have control of large territory thus requires the support of those inhabiting this territory. Control is of course possible without support, but it is a lot easier with it than without it.

The holy man sets an example for others to follow. Either people accept and respect his example or they do not. His example is clear though, so long as he is alive, walking in the mud just like everybody else. With his death, this clarity vanishes. The problem of representation arises. Not only is there the question 'by whom should the holy man be represented', but also there is the question of interpretation — what is going to be represented. The message, the example, of the holy man, has to be interpreted and this becomes a highly ambiguous task, especially if written texts are absent. There are many levels of interpretation and they increase as time goes by. If the message of the holy man, at the time of his walking and talking on this earth, was transmitted orally, then one might assume there to be quite a high level of distortion. In a way this is true. But consider the possibility of the message being intertwined in simple and concrete stories of a character so general[29] that the distortion of a few sentences, the changing of a few words, does not alter the message. Even different versions of a story may serve the purpose of orally transmitted knowledge, to provide a little information at a time and allow the listener himself to reach a more complete understanding of the message through his own reason.[30] This is possible if the stories are not too abstract. Consider the fact that the message could be delivered in the form of poems and songs, then

29. General, here, in a limited sense, within a community, a certain class of society.
30. Clifford, 1986: 7.

the risk of relevant distortion appears even less. If the message, however, is to serve a political purpose, and if this purpose is to gain a large following, it has to be generalized (so as to suite people of differing traditional settings). And in order to avoid distortion it needs to be written down, canonized, thereby becoming rigid and running the risk of cracking by its own size.[31] When we, today, try to interpret events that took place many hundred years ago, we are then confronted with the problem of judging which sources are closest to the original message; whether it is the poems and songs which are still recited and sung, or the texts and the books which are still read? Well, texts of this kind are written with a purpose to be spread and with a purpose to impose ideas on the readers. Poems and songs might be written with similar purposes, but the difference lies in the use of them. Political/ideological texts are not recited on quiet evenings in front of the fireplace, whereas poems and songs are very much suited for this kind of atmosphere.

The Apolitical Effort

Generalizations require a high level of abstraction which gives way to a variety of interpretations. Furthermore, abstract reasoning is vulnerable since it lacks a connection to a concrete situation; it can be dismissed by saying that 'this is not in accordance with my (concrete) experience of life'.[32] Assuming that a political ideology has to have a certain degree of abstraction[33] so that it may be generalized into suiting different groups of people with different traditions, one can conclude that a political ideology is highly vulnerable due to its ambition to be all encompassing. This in turn is due to the lack of realism: there is no all encompassing way of life. Rules of life have to be tied to concrete situations, and made into habitual behaviour, in order to be legitimate. They have to be applicable.[34] The bigger the empire, the harder to make such rules, and consequently the greater the need to use force (to fit people of different shapes into the square hole of the state). Rule-governed behaviour is different from habitual behaviour. Rule-governed behaviour implies the

31. Lewellen, 1992: 189.
32. The abstraction is necessary because it leaves out those voices that do not fit into the generalisation, voices that make the abstraction invalid. (Clifford, 1956: 6-7).
33. 'There were two spheres of politics, each with its own hierarchy: The first is a sphere of traditional face-to-face politics based in personal relations, and the second, a sphere of impersonal, legalistic politics based on abstract principles'. Lewellen, 1992: 176.
34. Political ideology is, according to Connerton, equal to knowledge in an abstract and generalised form, and they are 'abbreviations of some manner of concrete behaviour'. In contrast a 'tradition of behaviour is unavoidably knowledge of detail', because everyday behaviour is not abstract but concrete (Connerton, 1989: 11).

existence of a choice, thus rules, in this case, are consciously applied, further implying the lack of automation in an act.[35] A conscious choice of behaviour involves an amount of angst— 'what if I choose the wrong thing?'— and furthermore it introduces the possibility of being influenced by external forces that may be in contradiction to the moral values of the individual.

In the Bektashi case, maintaining history, then, means accepting it as it is transmitted in the apolitical sphere. It means staying away from ambitions that require the support of a large following of people. By doing this, there is no need to try to interpret history in a way that would be ideally suited to as many as possible; there is no need to make generalizations, and abstractions are therefore not relevant. On the contrary, 'concretizing' is the main tool in maintaining history; through ritual movements of the body. The historical message is in the movements of the body. These movements symbolize meanings which of course need to be interpreted. What Connerton calls social memory is maintained through commemorative ceremonies. These ceremonies are partly concerned with acting morally and this action is connected to habit. Moral should thus be habitual in order to have some pragmatic effect. These habits are acquired in the same way as a native language,[36] that is, by imitation. The words are then loaded with meaning. In the context of Bektashi ritual the movements are imitated and then they are given a meaning (or vice verse), a moral message. Theory and practice become intertwined and a meaningful behaviour becomes (ideally) automatized.

The Bektashi order is not concerned with legitimizing its history and therefore it does not get stuck in discussions of what is the correct interpretation, or the credibility of interpreters and so on. This is not to suggest that the Bektashi order has no implications whatsoever for the political life of the society it belongs to. On the contrary, it has great implications, since by having no political ambitions it stays clear of attack. The Bektashi order is not visible, it has no body and it can therefore not be killed, not even hurt. It has an inherent continuity, i.e. it does not have to create continuity (by force). The effect this has on the political life is hard to measure but still I would like to hint at one possible way of influencing political life: A group with the ambition of maintaining a history, in the above mentioned way; i.e. partly by ritual, and that carries a message of morals and ethics, ideally influences people in their immediate surroundings according to this message. It does so, ideally, to the extent that a moral and ethical way of life becomes automatically generated in the individual. This individual may in turn influence the political life (he might become a politician). After all, 'real decisions are made in private

35. Connerton, 1989: 30.
36. Connerton, 1989: 30.

offices, over lunch, and in the hallways; leaving the more public arenas as showplaces for the government — as it should be — that is, the government of the [...] myth'.[37] In other words, decisions are taken in settings of an informal character where people enjoy a certain amount of freedom to behave 'as they are', less formally. Thus ethics and morals could influence politics. Politics always have an influence on people; bad if it lacks a dimension of ethics and morals; good if it possesses this dimension.

Bibliography

Clifford, James, 1986. 'Introduction, Partial Truths', in: Clifford, J. & George E. Marcus (eds.): *Writing Culture.* Berkeley: University of California Press.

Connerton, Paul, 1989. *How Societies Remember,* Cambridge: Cambridge University Press.

Lewellen, Ted C., 1992. *Political Anthropology,* London.

Öz, Baki, 1992. *Osmanli'da Alevi ayaklanmalari,* Istanbul.

Sertoglu, Midhat, 1986. *Osmanli Tarih Lugati,* Istanbul.

Sener, Cemal, 1991. *Atatürk ve Aleviler,* Istanbul.

37. Lewellen 1992: 194.

The Alevis and Politics in Turkey

Helga Rittersberger-Tiliç

Introduction

Turkey has always held an important geo-strategic position in the world. During the cold war period, Turkey was an important NATO partner against communism. In recent years, however, Turkey is expected to function as a barrier to the growing Islamic fundamentalism. The secular Turkish version of Islam is pointed out as an alternative, mainly to the Saudi Arabian and the Iranian versions. Nevertheless, among the laicist Turks as well as in the West, doubts have arisen over its continued role as a mediator between the Christian and the Islamic world.

Since the 1980s, Turkey has experienced a growing 'Islamization'. This finds expression in the ever-growing alliance of Islamic brotherhoods and sects with leading political parties. Thus, the Welfare Party (RP — *Refah Partisi*), a party which clearly represents a Sunni Islamic line, has gained increasing importance since the middle of the '80s.[1] Parallel to these developments, radical Islamic fundamentalist organizations have been increasingly visible on the public scene; through killings and attacks on known laicist intellectuals.

Although, at first glance, Turkey seems to be moving into a less laicist historical period, it is necessary to point out, that the enormous fragmentation of Turkey along ethnic and religious lines, makes it very complicated to establish a homogenous, Islamic alliance, as was seen in Iran. Islam in Turkey

---

1. The increase in the number of religious high schools can also be seen as an index of the growing Islamic tendencies in Turkey. Thus, while those schools (Imam Hatip Schools) were originally considered as professional training schools for religious officials, their status has changed and nowadays they have a status equal to other secondary schools, leaving the way open to the Universities. Aksit (1991: 146-47) describes this development, using official statistics, as follows: '... In the 1977-78 academic year, when the Justice Party, National Salvation Party and National Action Party were in a coalition government, the number of middle-level Imam Hatip schools jumped to 334, and at the lycée-level to 103, with a total of 134,517 students. In 1987-88 there were 376 middle-level and 341 lycée-level Imam Hatip schools, with approximately 240,000 students. In the academic year 1985-86, there were 4,400 official, secular, general middle level school and 1,206 lycées, with approximately 2.4 million enrolled students.'

is much more heterogenous than in many other Islamic countries. The official 'state' version of Islam which is presented as liberal, puts its emphasis clearly on a Sunnite interpretation. Institutionally it is represented by the Directorate of Religious Affairs which is responsible for the appointment of religious officials and the running of mosques, etc.

While, throughout the 20th century, Islam constituted an integral part of Arab society and provided an instrument against Western powers, the situation in Turkey was quite different. Atatürk and his reforms brought an interruption to the public activities of religious brotherhoods and sects. Only after Atatürk's death, in 1938, did the religious life of the country experience a revival of its traditional religious organizations.

During the nineteenth century, dervishes wandering through Anatolia recruited large numbers of followers. Two of the more recent religious leaders are Said Nursi (1873-1960)[2], the founder of the *Nurcu* order and Süleyman Tunahan (1888-1959) the head of the *Süleymancis*, who had a great impact on the religious life of modern day Turkey. In addition, Mehmet Zahid Kotku (1897-1980) and Fethullah Gülen (born in 1927) have to be mentioned here, as influential Islamic leaders.

Kotku, the head of the twentieth century *Nakshibendi* order[3] is seen as the leader of political Islam in Turkey. Kotku initiated Necmettin Erbakan in 1969, thus founding the first Islamic Party in the country; the Party of National Order (MNP — *Milli Nizam Partisi*), which in 1983 became the RP.[4] Fethullah Gülen, on the other hand, comes from the Nurcu movement.

After Atatürk banned the religious orders, Islam survived mainly in the countryside, where it mobilized forces against the urban-based, western-oriented elites. It was only after World War II that Islam actively returned to the political arena of Turkey. Following Nursi's death in 1960, Gülen established his religious empire. In the beginning this was more or less on a private basis, but grew increasingly public in the middle of the 90s. In 1994, Gülen went into the media, due to his meeting Tansu Çiller, prime minister of Turkey at the time. His field of activity is wide, but concentrates mainly on the educational sector (in the form of private schools, religious newspapers, TV- channels, etc.) Gülen represents the image of a liberal Turkish version of Islam. Clearly, he can now be seen as a rival of Erbakan and the RP, which represents the established form of political Islam in Turkey.

---

2. About Said Nursi see Çakir, 1990.
3. For a more detailed description of the *Nakshibendi* order see Mardin, I., 1991. Here, it might be interesting to point out that, among others, the family of the former President of Turkey, Turgut Özal, also belongs to the *Nakshibendi*.
4. Yalçin, 1994: 53 f.

The Alevi Version of Islam in Turkey

After giving this short overview about the dominant Sunnite versions of political Islam, we can now look at the Alevi version, which represents a large part of the Turkish population. Although, there are no precise statistics about the number of Alevis, they clearly constitute the second largest religious group after the Sunnites. It is claimed that there are 10 to 15 million Alevis, about a fifth of the total population, living in Turkey.[5] In geographical terms, they were concentrated in Central, West, and Northern Anatolia in the provinces of Sivas, Tokat, Yozgat, Nevsehir, Çorum, Amasya, Kahramanmaras and Erzincan.[6] These areas can still be seen as main areas of concentration. However, the ongoing rural-urban migration processes have obviously brought changes to this distribution.

Generally speaking, it can be claimed that all those, who see Ali as the rightful successor of the Prophet Muhammed can be considered as Alevi. In this sense, they can also be considered as Anatolian Shiites, who do not strictly follow the *sheriat* (Islamic law) as the Iranians do. Alevism constitutes a complicated mixture of Turkish Shamanism, Iranian Shiism, as well as certain Christian elements and Batinism.[7] At the same time, it has always been strongly influenced by the Bektashi Order of Dervishes, which gained prominence in European history as the Janissary military corps[8] during the Ottoman period. There exist strong parallels between Alevism and Bektashism; both regard Haci Bektash as their saint. Melikoff points out that Alevism was predominant among the rural population, whereas Bektashism was more typical of urban areas.[9]

Without going into further detail, it seems to be necessary to mention at least some of the main differences between the Sunnite and Alevi Islamic interpretations. The Alevis do not have the 'five -times-a-day' praying rule; they have no mosques and officially appointed religious officials; they have different fasting periods; men and women gather together for their religious

---

5. Andrews, 1989: 57. It should be emphasized that the majority of the Alevis are of Turkish and not of Kurdish origin, see Kehl-Bodrogi, 1988: 92.
6. Kehl-Bodrogi, 1988: 73 f.
7. Çamuroglu, 1992.
8. For a detailed description of the relation of the Janissaries and the Bektashi order see Birge, 1965: 46 f. and 74-78.
9. Melikoff, 1994: 34

ceremonies, and their religious hierarchy is based on religious leaders stemming from holy families *(dedelik)*[10].

The Historical Emergence of Alevism

The emergence of Alevism as an endogamous, ethnic-religious group has to be seen as the result of major social transformations. The growing polarization between Persia and the Ottoman Empire formed the ground for these developments. While Persia declared *Twelfth Imam Shiism* as the state religion, the Ottoman Empire installed a Sunni version of Islam. The Anatolian followers of the Safavids adhered strongly to their heterodoxy. The Safavids therefore found support among the Anatolian rural population, as well as from Turcoman tribes.[11]

The military troops, which consisted mainly of Turcomans, were called *Kizilbas*[12], a term which in time became commonly used for Alevis in general; with an added euphemistic connotation. Thus, even from the thirteenth century onward, mainly through the support of Turcoman nomadic tribes, the Safavids prepared for the establishment of its dynasty.[13] However, the declaration of Shiism as the state religion in Persia brought on a break with the Anatolian followers, who did not want to put aside their pre-Islamic beliefs and practices.

From the middle of the fifteenth century onwards, the Ottoman state increasingly supported the orthodox Sunni orders, mainly to gain greater control over the social and political life of the population. The Bektashi order on the other hand was regarded by the central Ottoman power as a centre of revolt.

In the late sixteenth century, the Ottomans systematically tried to destroy these revolutionary centres. As a consequence, the *Kizilbas* escaped into geographically remote areas to escape the reach of the central powers. In this social and spatial segregation, political activities lost importance, instead an orientation towards religious values took place. In this process, endogamous marriage rules acquired increasing importance and a strict hierarchical order along *holy family* lines was established. The main functions of these religious

10. *Dede* literally means grandfather. The main duty of the *dede* was to function as a judge and to keep peace in the Alevi community. A good description of Alevism-Bektashism and its philosophical-theological roots as well as its organizational hierarchy is given by Birge, 1965 and Kehl-Bodrogi, 1988.
11. Inalcik describes the revolts of the Turcoman tribes in the period 13th to 16th century in his study 'The Ottoman Empire', 1973: 186-202.
12. *Kizilbas* means literally 'red head', and was prompted by the red headcovering of the followers of Haydar, the sheikh of the Safavid order, Gökalp, 1980.
13. Roemer, 1990: 27-39.

leaders were of a juridical nature and acted as a counterpart to the central authorities.

The Alevi Culture

The Alevis, as followers of Ali, are usually considered to belong to the Shiite branch of Islam. However, their practices and beliefs are rejected as heresy by Shiite as well as Sunni Muslims. Elements of a folk religion separate them distinctly from classical Shiism. Some scholars find their rituals and customs closer to ancient Turcoman traditions. For our purposes, their most important features are to be found in their less rigid practice of Islamic ritual. Alevis, when asked about their religious beliefs, usually emphasize the value of correct behaviour, even to the extent of subordinating questions of dogma. This Alevi ethic is generally summarized as 'be — the master of your hands and tongue and loins' — which means do not steal, lie or have forbidden sexual intercourse.

They also have a rich mystic and folklore tradition. Another important aspect is that their women are not necessarily veiled and interact more freely in public surroundings. Women also take an active role in religious ceremonies and the shrines of holy women play an important part in Alevi culture. The consumption of alcohol is also allowed, even during religious ceremonies.[14]

Following the Alevi faith, Ali is the *ilmin kapisi*; the gate to knowledge. Knowledge is divided into four kinds, which are arranged in hierarchical order, for which they use the symbol of the gate to be passed through. The first one is *Sheriat* which they have in common with the Sunnites and which includes the five fundamental duties of a Muslim (professing the faith, prayer, alms-giving, fasting and pilgrimage). The Alevis place the Sunnites at this level and see themselves at a higher level, even by birth. The second gate is *Tarikat*, which is usually the term for a religious order. This second gate refers, among other things, to the religious ceremonies held in the form of *cem ayini*. The third gate is *Marifet*, which is explained as dealing with knowledge. Finally, the fourth gate is *Hakikat*, or esoteric knowledge.

Birge[15] reports how a mystic explained these four doors to him: '... taking the idea of 'sugar' as an example. One can go to the dictionary to find out what sugar is and how it is used. That is the *Sheriat*, Gateway to knowledge. One feels the inadequacy of that when one is introduced directly to the practical seeing and handling of sugar. That represents the *Tarikat*, Gateway of

14. There are, however, exceptions to this in that some Alevis oppose the consumption of alcohol.
15. Birge, 1965: 102.

knowledge. Tasting the sugar and having it enter into oneself is to go one step deeper into an appreciation of its nature, and that is what is meant by *Marifet*. If one could go still further and become one with sugar so that he could say 'I am sugar', that and that alone would be to know what sugar is, and that is what is involved in the *hakikat* Gateway.'

The central religious ritual is the *cem ayini*: A gathering of the community in a special house (*cem evi*) which can also often be a private house. The *Dede*, as the descendant of Haci Bektash, leads the ritual. Religious knowledge is transferred by these representatives of holy families, and they refer to Imam Cafer's catechism (*Buyruk*) as their written text.

The rituals are conducted by married couples. In the first part of the ritual, sins committed and problems inside the community are brought to light. Afterwards, religious matters are discussed and religious songs sung and the dervish dance (*semah*) danced. Lyrics play an important role in the Alevi culture, which also finds its expression in common competitions of singers/poets. Putting out the candlelight (*mum söndürmek*) at a certain time during the ceremony, and the fact that men and women are together in the same room, has always given way to Sunni accusations of promiscuity.

Beside the main religious institution of the *cem ayini, musahiplik* (companionship)[16] has to be mentioned. This stands for the life-long duty of two couples, who choose each other and provide each other with all kind of mutual help during their lifetime.

Beliefs and rituals are not usually divulged to strangers referring to the principle of secrecy, *takiyye*, which allows the Alevi to hide his/her religious faith. This can also be interpreted as a protective mechanism against oppression from the dominant Sunnite faith.

Despite this, the practice of Alevi culture, specifically the continuation of the *Dedelik* institution and *cem ayini* began to wane in general. The period after 1990 saw a revival of Alevi culture, partially taking shape in the frame of cultural-folklore events, presenting Alevi culture to the non-Alevites. However, in recent times there has been an increasingly audible demand from the Alevis for 'real' — freedom of religious practice and equality. These demands are combined with a political demand for a more democratic society.

Atatürk and the Alevis

The foundation of the Turkish Republic in the year 1923, and the secularization introduced by Atatürk, as well as the call for a national identity, awoke strong

16. Kehl-Bodrogi, 1988: 182-204, who emphasizes the importance of this institution to the social arrangements in the Alevi community.

hopes among the Alevis for an improvement of their ethnic-religious and social situation. With the declaration of the Turkish Republic, large-scale social, political and economic reforms led the Alevis out of their marginality. The removal of the caliphate and Islam as state religion, as well as the lifting of restrictions on religious orders, the freedom given to different religions, and a growing Western orientation, gave the Alevis hope that they would become equal members of the society.

In the year 1924, the Directorate for Religious Affairs was established. This directorate came under the direct control of the prime minister. From the beginning onwards, it represented a clear Sunnite line leaving no room to the Alevi heterodoxy. As was mentioned earlier in the introduction, the 1950s in Turkey were characterized by a growing revitalization and politicization of Sunnite Islamic orders and sects.

The Alevis, however, increasingly lost their organizational principles along the lines of holy families, due to the increase in rural-urban migration. They clearly constituted one of the most well suited socio-economic strata for engaging in this kind of migration process; being mainly small-scale agricultural landholders or agricultural labourers located in the remote, less fertile, mountainous parts of Central Anatolia. The result was a growing flood of rural Alevis into the metropolitan centres of Turkey.[17] In the metropolitan environment, mechanisms like endogamy and holy leaders, which had formerly reinforced group homogeneity, lost their importance. In the search for a Turkish identity, the Alevis gained some social upgrading, because they were presented as the protectors of original Turkish culture.[18] Atatürk realized this potential, which planted a desire in the Alevis to fight against the existing status quo.

The Political Polarization of the Alevis

The great majority of the Alevis supported the War of Independence, and afterwards stood behind the Kemalist Republican People's Party (CHP — *Cumhuriyet Halk Partisi*). Following the death of Atatürk, in 1938, calls for a multi-party system increased and it was finally introduced in 1946. Thus the CHP was joined by the Democrat Party (DP—*Demokrat Parti*).

The 50s and 60s in Turkey were characterized by drastic capitalist transformations. Foreign capital streamed into the country, rural-urban migration took

17. Although there are no official statistics, it can be assumed that they also constituted a large portion of the migrants on the international level, Naess, 1990.
18. Such ideas were also supported by the fact that the poetry, which played an important role in Alevi culture, had always been in the Turkish language. See Kehl-Bodrogi, 1989: 508.

off on a tremendous scale, as did migration to Europe. In time, economic as well as social differences among the Alevi and Sunnite population became a growing source of conflict.

In the 70s, the majority of Alevi youth were organized around Marxist factions, while the older generations continued to support the CHP under Bülent Ecevit, who defined his party as being of the centre-Left. In 1966, in an atmosphere of growing anti-Alevitism in Turkey, an attempt by the Alevis was made to gain representation through their own party. This saw the birth of the Union Party (BP — *Birlik Partisi*), which changed its name into Turkish Union Party (TBP — *Türkiye Birlik Partisi*) in the year 1973.

Rightist parties, like the National Salvation Party (MSP — *Milli Selamet Partisi*) were strongly opposed by the Alevis, because of their clear Sunnite line. The MSP was the follower of the National Order Party (MNP — *Milli Nizam Partisi*) which was founded by Erbakan in the year 1970. After the military intervention in 1971, Erbakan once again gained political influence in 1972, when he founded the MSP. In the late '70s, the MSP lost its power, while the Left was getting stronger.

The Left of the '70s, gave a special importance to organizing the Alevi population that was seen in the public as a homogeneous block supporting leftist ideologies. Growing anti-communism and increasing reactions against a Kemalist Western orientation found, on the other hand, growing support among the conservative Sunnite population.[19] Specifically, the rightist National Action Party (MHP — *Milliyetçi Hareket Partisi*) used this growing polarization. The '70s were characterized by escalating attacks on the Alevi population.[20]

With the military coup in 1980 these clashes ended, while the MNP continued in the form of the RP, in the year 1983. In the local elections of 1984, the RP achieved 4.4 percent; in 1989 they arrived at 9.8 percent; in 1994 they had already 19 percent, and in the general elections, which were held on December 24th, 1995, they reached a nationwide figure of 21.3 percent. The growing political power of this party is expressed in these percentages. Certainly, the RP was capable of changing its image of a rural based conservative religious party and found a base also in the urban areas of Turkey. This success can be partly explained by the growing dissatisfaction in the 1990s with the metropolitan municipalities, which were unable to cope with the large numbers of incoming migrants from the East and South-east of Turkey. The Eastern parts of Turkey had always constituted areas of traditional Islamic orientation. However, the ever growing poverty in the

19. Laçiner, 1985: 241-51.
20. Events of open conflict in the cities of Malatya, Sivas, Çorum and Kahramanmara's are to be mentioned in this context. Laçiner, 1985: 251-54; Kehl-Bodrogi, 1989: 65-68.

squatter housing areas helped to widen the electoral base of the RP. It has to be stressed that the Alevi population in general considered the increasing power of this party as a threat to its way of life.

Before the military takeover in the '80s, the Alevis were clearly a part of the leftist political scene. The period after the 1980s was, however, characterized by the increasing diffusion of Alevi votes across the political spectrum. There were unproven claims that some Alevi votes went to the established Right conservative parties like the Motherland Party (ANAP — *Anavatan Partisi*) and the True Path Party (DYP — *Dogru Yol Partisi*). Even the RP enrolled some Alevi members in an effort to adopt a softer line towards these people.

Today, the RP is clearly one of the best organized parties in Turkey. Using high-tech, modern marketing, advertisement techniques and propagating a kind of pluralism. With this image, it was possible for them to attract, besides the traditional rural population (mainly of Eastern Turkey), also the urban poor (rural migrants in the squatter housing zones of the metropolitan areas in Turkey). Aiming to be a *mass* party, they also tried to attract Alevis, but it can be said that this attempt was far from successful.

The new appearance of the RP has to be seen as an outcome of major transformations, which were brought to the country during the period of Turgut Özal (1983-1989), who introduced liberal economics. He saw his governmental period as the start of a so-called 'Second Republic,' questioning the Kemalist doctrines and giving further freedom to religious groups.

During the discussions about the 'Second Republic', some liberal intellectuals and Islamic intellectuals moved closer to each other in the search for a pluralist civil society. Despite the fact that several Sunni Islamic intellectuals were excited by the 'Second Republic' project, the Alevi intellectuals mostly stayed away from this discussion. Alevis, in general, felt themselves much closer to the strictly laicist 'First Republic'. They were, indeed, disturbed by the ongoing weakening of the laicism principle of the republic since the '50s.

Conclusion: The Recent Rise of Alevi Consciousness

Since 1985, and more intensively in the '90s, a kind of Alevi revivalism is realizable[21], which is mainly directed at a return to religious traditions and practices, asking for equal rights of religious expression. However, there appear to be two main lines emerging among the Alevis. One group emphasizes the

---

21. This period witnessed a great increase in Alevi publications, as well as in publications on Alevism and public discussions in the media.

religious, traditional values, and principles, and tries to develop a purely 'religiously-defined' Alevi consciousness. On the other hand, the second group puts the emphasis on the political characteristics of Alevis; traditionally defined as 'leftist' and 'democrat' hereby opposing a religiously-defined Alevi identity.

Prof. Izzetin Dogan, the founder and chairman of the CEM Foundation, is the leading representative of the first group. He has close relations to the conservative parties; especially to former Prime Minister, Tansu Çiller's True Path Party (DYP). Just before the December 24, 1995 elections, he tried to organize a campaign implicitly intending to diversify the Alevi votes that used to go to the social democrat parties as a block. His argument can be summarized as follows: 'Nobody shall consider the Alevi votes as if they are already in their pockets. Alevis will from now on vote for the parties that respect their rights'. This campaign actually coincided with the then Prime Minister Çiller's promise of giving 3 trillion TL (about US$ 130 million) to the Alevis from the budget of the Directorate of Religious Affairs. Dogan was simply advising the Alevis to give priority to their concrete interests, rather than sticking to any particular ideology.

The second group that reacted to this approach is larger. They are organized in Pir Sultan Abdal and Haci Bektash associations all around Turkey and in Europe.[22] They said that the Alevi votes were not for sale and argued that developing a religiously defined identity around which organizations and political behaviors would be formed, would open the doors for Alevi fundamentalism.

These discussions and various spontaneous Alevi uprisings in the early '90s made the state officials fear a second spate of Alevite-Sunnite confrontations, besides an armed Kurdish rebellion that obviously weakened the country by sucking economic and human resources. The Alevi prayer houses, known as *cem evi*, suddenly found sympathy among officials. Several leading statesmen, including President Süleyman Demirel, former Prime Minister Çiller and other ministers, participated in ceremonies laying the foundations of new *cem evis*. They realized the growing Alevi consciousness.

In the absence of strong left-wing organizations in which Alevis located themselves before the '80s, the Alevis now feel the need for organizations in which they can express themselves. The massacre of 37 intellectuals, mostly Alevis, in a hotel that was burned down by Sunnite Islamic fundamentalists during an Alevi cultural festival in the central Anatolian town, Sivas, marked the breaking-off of relations between the social democrats and the Alevi community. Social Democrat Populist Party (*Sosyal Demokrat Halk Partisi* - SHP),

---

22. Thus, in Germany a 'Federation of German Alevites' was founded in 1991, which nowadays is called 'German Federation of Alevi Associations'.

which was the coalition partner during the Sivas massacre in 1993, was accused of 'only standing by, watching the fire'.

Later in January 1995, a TV showman unconsciously insulted the Alevis by telling a joke which identified Alevis with incest. Thousands of Alevis gathered in front of the Star TV building in Istanbul, broke the windows by throwing stones and demonstrated all night. This was a striking sign which demonstrated that the Alevis were not content with being silent anymore, but would react to any oppression against them.

In the middle of March 1995, the 3-day-long revolt that erupted in Istanbul's Gaizosmanpasha district was a real shock to Turkey. Thousands of Alevi youngsters took to the streets, immediately after an Alevi coffeehouse was sprayed with bullets by unidentified gunmen and 3 people were killed. Alevis from other districts of Istanbul joined the revolt in Gaziosmanpasha, where over 20 persons were killed in the clashes with the police.

Finally, in late December 1995, another sign of growing Alevi consciousness was the emergence of an initiative to form a political party which presented independent candidates under the banner of the Democratic Peace Movement. The movement withdrew its candidates just before the December 24 election, in order 'not to harm the leftist parties by pushing them below the 10 percent nationwide election threshold'. The attempt to form an Alevi party independent of other leftist forces was not given indeed much credit by the Alevis themselves. Participation in the election rallies of the Democratic Peace Movement was very low. This was in fact a clear message from the Alevi community to the leaders of the initiative to step back. However, Ali Haydar Veziroglu, the leader of the initiative seems to be resolute in continuing his efforts to form an Alevi party. The fact that he bought a 50 percent share of the National Press Agency (*UBA* — *Ulusal Basin Ajansi*) in early January 1996 is an indication of his political commitment.

To conclude, it must be said that the Alevis still consider themselves as part of a modern, secular and democratic Turkey, despite the events which have occurred since the 1980s.

Bibliography

Aksit, B. 1991. 'Islamic Education in Turkey; Medrese Reform in Late Ottoman Time and imam Hatip Schools in the Republic'. In: Tapper, R. (ed.): *Islam in Modern Turkey*. London: I.B. Tauris: 145-69.

Andrews, P.A. 1989. *Ethnic Groups in Turkey*, Wiesbaden: Ludwig Reichert Verlag.

Birge, J.K. 1965. *The Bektashi Order of Dervishes*, London: Luzac.

Çakir, R. 1990. *Ayet ve Slogan. Türkiye'de islami Olushumlar*, Istanbul: Metis Yayinlari.

Çamuroglu, R. 1992. *Tarih, Heterodoksi ve Babailer*, Istanbul: Metis Yayinlari.

Gökalp, A. 1980. *Têtes Rouges et Bouches Noires. Une Confrérie Tribale de L'Ouest Anatolien*, Paris.

Inalcik, H. 1973. *The Ottoman Empire*, Worcester: The Trinity Press.

Kehl-Bodrogi, K., 1988. *Die Kizilbash - Aleviten*, Untersuchung über eine esoterische Glaubensgemeinschaft. Berlin: Klaus Scharsz Verlag.

Kehl-Bodrogi, K. 1989. 'Das Alevitentum in der Türkei: Zur Genese und gegenwärtigen Lage einer Glaubensgemeinschaft'. In Andrews, P., (ed.) *Ethnic Groups in the Republic of Turkey*, Wiesbaden: Ludwig Reichert Verlag: 503-10.

Laçiner, Ö. 1985. 'Der Konflikt zwischen den Sunniten und Aleviten in der Türkei'. In: Blaschke, J.; Van Bruinessen, M., (eds.) *Thema: Islam und Politik in der Türkei. Jahrbuch zur Geschichte und Gesellschaft des Vorderen und Mittleren Orients 1984.* Berlin: Express Edition.

Mardin, Sh. 1991. 'The Nakshibendi Order in Turkish History'. In: Tapper, R., (ed.) *Islam in Modern Turkey*, London: I.B. Tauris: 121-41.

Melikoff, I. 1994. *Uyur Idik Uyardilar. Alevilik — Bektashilik Arashtirmalari*, Istanbul: Cem Yayinevi.

Naess, R. 1990. 'Being an Alevi Muslim in South-Western Anatolia and in Norway. The Impact of Migration on a Heterodox Turkish Community'. In: Gerholm, T.; Lithmans, Y.G., (eds.) *The New Islamic Presence in Western Europe*, London: Mansell Publ. Ltd: 174-95.

Pehlivan, B. 1993. *Aleviler ve Diyanet*, Istanbul: Pencere Yayinlari.

Roemer, H.R. 1990. 'The Qizilbash Turcomans: Founders and Victims of the Safavid Theocracy'. In: Mazzaoui, M.; V. Moreen, (eds.) *Intellectual Studies on Islam*, Salt Lake City: University of Utah Press: 27-39.

Yalçin, S. 1994. *Hangi Erbakan*. Ankara: Bashak Yayinlari.

The Kurdish Question

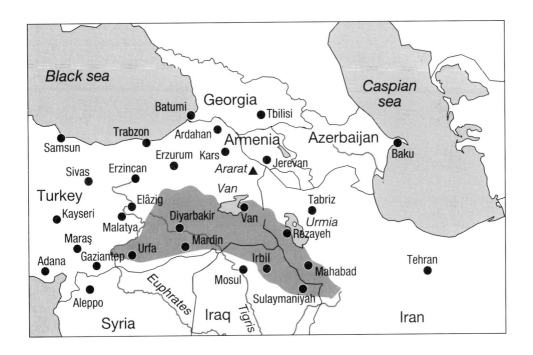

The Kurdish Question — Its History and Present Situation

Kemal Burkay

During recent years the Kurdish question has reappeared, more intensely than before, on the international agenda. For years, this question has been of fundamental concern to the countries of the region, and it has led to extensive internal controversies and economic and social crises. In order to further an understanding of the Kurdish question in its present dimensions, a summary of its historical and geographical background is necessary.

Language, Religion and History

The Kurds are, along with the Arabs, Persians and Armenians, one of the most ancient peoples of the Near East. The country they inhabit is called Kurdistan. The Kurds have their own language - Kurdish. Kurdish is a member of the Indo-European family of languages; like Persian, Afghan, and Beluchi, it is one of the Iranian languages. Kurdish is unrelated to the Arabic or Turkish languages.

Literary works have been written in the Kurdish language since the tenth century AD. Kurdish is a lively and rich language that has managed to survive despite all the oppression and bans to which it has been exposed. There are hundreds of poets, authors, and researchers writing in Kurdish. Many dictionaries and grammar books have been written for the Kurdish language. Kurdish folklore also has a very rich tradition.

Over time, various dialects have arisen within the Kurdish language. The most widely disseminated dialect is *Kurmanci*. It is spoken by about 90 percent of the Kurds in Turkey, in Iranian and Iraqi Kurdistan in the northern areas near the Turkish border, and by the Syrian Kurds — which is to say, by about 60 percent of all Kurds. The *Sorani* dialect is spoken by about 25 percent of the Kurds. This dialect is spoken in the middle and southern regions of Iranian and Iraqi Kurdistan. *Zazaki* is a third dialect which is spoken in certain regions of Turkish Kurdistan. In the southernmost parts of Kurdistan, *Gorani* and other dialects are spoken.

The great majority of Kurds, about 75 percent, are Sunni Moslems; about 15 percent are Alevi Moslems. The Alevis are in the majority in the northern and western areas of Turkish Kurdistan and in the Chorasan region of Iran. In Iran and Iraq there exist other religious groups such as Shiite Kurds *(Feyli)* and the *Ehlihak* ('the people of God'), who are closely related with the Alevis. In the various parts of Kurdistan, especially in the region where the borders of Turkey, Iran, and Iraq meet and in Armenia, there are Kurdish Yezidi communities. In earlier times, the *Yezidi* faith was a widely shared religious orientation. Its roots go back to Zoroastrianism. Finally in the middle regions of Kurdistan there are small groups of Christianity.

Kurds have played a significant role in the history of this region since its early epochs. A great deal of information on this can be found in numerous Greek, Roman, Arab, and Armenian sources. According to these, the Kurds founded several important states during the Islamic era, between the tenth and thirteenth centuries, including Shaddâdiden, Marvaniden, and Ayyûbiden — as well as others in the very distant past. Sultan Salahaddin (Salâh al-Dîn), the founder of the Ayyûbid state, which included Egypt, Syria, and Kurdistan, played a particularly significant role in history.

The Turks, whose roots are in Middle Asia, migrated to Anatolia via Iran after the eleventh century and founded the Seljuk and subsequently the Ottoman states. For a long time, Kurdistan was the theatre of military clashes between the Ottoman and the Persian empires. During this period, the Kurdish princes, sided first with one and then the other, thus maintaining their autonomy. But in the year 1638, Kurdistan was officially divided between these two states in the Treaty of Kasri Shirin. From that time until the mid-nineteenth century, both states made armed attacks on the Kurdish princedoms in order to destroy them.

The Kurds' struggle against these two great states took on a nationalist character at the beginning of the nineteenth century. Kurdish princes such as Bedirkhan and Yazdânsher, as well as religious leaders such as Sheik Ubeydullah, fought for the unity and independence of Kurdistan, but were defeated.

After World War I, the Ottoman Empire became a thing of the past: new states arose out of its former territory. According to the Treaty of Sèvres, which was signed on August 10th, 1920, the state of Kurdistan was also to be established in the region. But this intention was never subsequently implemented. In the Treaty of Lausanne, signed on the July 24th, 1923, that part of Kurdistan which had been part of the Ottoman Empire was carved up again. Part of it was included in the British and French Mandates, where Syria and Iraq later came into being. The largest part of Kurdistan remained within the state borders of the Republic of Turkey; which had been founded on the ruins of the Ottoman Empire.

The Ottoman and the Persian empires, which had divided up Kurdistan between themselves, did not question the existence of the Kurdish people at any time. The Republic of Turkey also initially defined its new borders as the 'borders of the *Misak-i-Milli* (National Pact), which included the areas occupied by the Turkish and Kurdish majority'. About 70 Kurdish Members of Parliament were present at the first session of the Great National Assembly in Ankara; they were officially designated as the 'MPs of Kurdistan'. The Turkish representative, Ismet Pasha, declared at Lausanne: 'The Kurds and the Turks are the essential components of the Republic of Turkey. The Kurds are not a minority but a nation; the government in Ankara is the government of the Turks as well as of the Kurds.'

However, after the signing of the Treaty of Lausanne, Ankara's policy rapidly changed. The structures of the new state were designed wholly in accordance with Turkish interests. The Kurdish language, the practice of Kurdish culture, even the concepts of 'Kurdish' and 'Kurdistan' were forbidden. The Kemalist leadership did not pay the slightest attention to the multi-cultural structure of Anatolia, which was in fact a mosaic of different ethnic groups. The cornerstone of their policy became the dissolution of other languages and cultures into the Turkish language and culture, to thus create 'a unified nation'. Article 39 of the Treaty of Lausanne, according to which the citizens of Turkey have the right to freely use their respective languages in all areas of life, was trampled upon, and the Kurdish language was totally forbidden in the educational system and the printed media. Speaking about the Kurds and criticizing the oppression of them was held to be a severe crime and was severely punished.

In 1925, the Kurds, led by Sheik Sa'id, rose up against this policy. However, this uprising was brutally suppressed; tens of thousands of Kurds were killed and driven into exile. There were more Kurdish uprisings in subsequent years; the major ones took place in Ararat in 1930 and in Dersim in 1938. The Turkish state waged war in Kurdistan on a permanent basis.

After 1938, there was a relatively peaceful pause that lasted about 20 years. However, it is not surprising that the Kurds — who had no national rights and were being subjected to massive oppression; being were forced into poverty and ignorance; seeing all peaceful and legal avenues of political struggle closed to them — began to arm themselves against the cruel oppression of the Turkish state. Since 1979, Turkey has ruled Kurdistan through military law, a State of Emergency, and a dirty war.

Similar developments unfolded in the other parts of Kurdistan. The Kurds living within the borders of Iraq, or southern Kurdistan, had also been resisting oppression since World War I. They staged uprisings that were led, first by Sheik Mahmud Barzenci (1919-32), then by Sheik Ahmed Barzani and his brother Mustafa Barzani (1932 and later). These uprisings also ended in defeat. But in Iraq, Kurdish identity was never denied. Moreover, because of these uprisings, the Kurds were granted certain cultural rights. They were given schools, universities, radio broadcasts etc. In this part of Kurdistan, Kurdish culture is relatively well developed.

The greatest Kurdish uprising in this part of Kurdistan began in 1961 under Mustafa Batzani and lasted until 1970. In 1970, the Kurds reached an agreement with the central government concerning an autonomous region. However, the government in Baghdad stalled the Kurds and ignored the conditions of the agreement. For this reason, the war broke out again in 1975. With several breaks, this struggle lasted until 1991.

The war against the Kurds has been expensive for Iraq. In order to halt Iran's support of the Kurds, Saddam Hussein's regime initially made territorial concessions to Iran. Then, to win back these areas, it started the destructive eight-year war against Iran which devastated Kurdistan. Iraq even used poison gas in its attacks on the Kurds. After this war ended, Iraq moved on to its invasion of Kuwait, the subsequent developments of which the reader is undoubtedly familiar with.

Saddam Hussein suffered a massive defeat in his war against the allies. The Kurds were initially subjected to mass expulsion, but later a United Nations declaration created a security zone for them. The refugees returned to their homeland. In what is now known as 'northern Iraq', i.e. southern Kurdistan, the Kurds created a parliament and a national government.

But the Iraqi problem has still not been solved today. The country is subject to a UN embargo, and the Iraqi Kurds are in an extremely difficult situation.

The State of Iran has conducted a policy of oppression against the Kurds similar to that of Turkey's Kemalist regime. After World War II, when Iran was occupied in the north by the Soviet Union and in the south by Great Britain, the Kurds were able to pause for breath and they quickly organized themselves. The Democratic Party of Kurdistan was founded and subsequently the Kurdish Republic of Mahabad was proclaimed. But soon thereafter, the government in Tehran, with the political support of Great Britain and America, annihilated the Republic of Mahabad.

But the Kurdish people's resistance has not ceased. When the Shah's regime ended in 1978, this part of Kurdistan could once again enjoy freedom.

Yet this phase did not last long either. It was soon followed by the attacks of the new regime of the mullahs. The armed resistance to this regime that began in 1979 is still continuing today.

To summarize; The Kurdish people have continually resisted the cruel oppression and colonialization levelled at them in these three, major parts of Kurdistan, both before and after World War I and up to the present day. They have struggled to keep their identity alive; to claim their national rights to have determination over their destiny. During this struggle, the Kurds have lost hundreds of thousands of their people and have been the victims of mass expulsions. Tremendous suffering has been inflicted on them. This is in fact a case of genocide. Unfortunately, however, neither the League of Nations nor the United Nations have lived up to their responsibilities in the face of our people's tragedy. They have remained merely witnesses to these events.

Geography and Population

The number of Kurds in the four parts of Kurdistan and within the borders of the four countries that have divided it up between themselves, totals about 35 million. This makes the Kurds, after the Arabs, Turks, and Persians, the fourth-largest nation in the Near East.

Kurdistan, which since time immemorial has been inhabited by the Kurds, has a territory of 500,000 km², which is as large as that of France. In other words, the Kurds are not a minority in their country — they are the majority. The Kurdish question is not the problem of a minority of the population of this or that country; it is the question of a divided country and a nation. Like all other nations, the Kurds too have the right to self-determination.

The borders that divide Kurdistan are neither natural, economic, nor cultural borders. They are artificial borders that have been drawn, against the will of the Kurdish people, and according to the interests of the forces that did the dividing and decided the balance of power. In many cases these borders have divided villages, towns, even families, and have had divisive and destructive effects on economic, social, and cultural life.

The largest part of Kurdistan, which in terms of both its population and its territory makes up about one-half of the total, lies in the north inside the state borders of Turkey. This part amounts to one-third of the total territory of Turkey, and includes more than twenty provinces in the 'eastern and northeastern regions'. Other parts, according to their size, are Eastern Kurdistan (within the borders of Iran), Southern Kurdistan (within the borders of Iraq), and Kurdish areas within the borders of Syria.

In all of these parts, a large number of the inhabitants — between 80 percent and 90 percent — are Kurdish. A certain proportion of the Kurds have lived there since earlier times or else, because of the migration and refugee movements in recent years, live in other regions and in the large cities of these countries. If we count these as well, then about 18 to 20 million Kurds live within the borders of Turkey, 8 to 10 million in Iran, 5 million in Iraq, and 1.5 million in Syria.

About one-third of the labour migrants who have left Turkey in the past 20 to 30 years to come to the countries of Europe are Kurds. If we add to this the number of Kurds from Turkey and the other parts of Kurdistan, who have fled to Europe in recent years for political and economic reasons, the number of Kurds living in European countries comes to about 1 million. Because of migration and refugee movements, Kurdish communities have also been formed in North America and Australia.

Natural Resources and Economic and Social Structures

With regard to its mineral resources, Kurdistan is one of the wealthiest countries in the world. Most of the zone extending from the Zagros mountain range to the Mediterranean, which has been known as the 'Fertile Crescent' since early times, falls within Kurdistan.

Kurdistan is rich in agriculture. The plains between the mountain ranges, especially in the warmer south, are well-suited to agriculture because of the composition of the soil and their favorable climatic conditions. The plateaus and mountain slopes have extremely fruitful meadowland. All types of grain, as well as high-quality fruit and vegetables, grow in the soil of Kurdistan. The Harran Plateau and the areas around Cezire and Mossul are grain reservoirs for the entire region.

Differences in temperature and elevation between the north and the south have resulted in the fact that Kurdistan has always been an important country for animal husbandry. Furthermore, Kurdistan is a reservoir of meat, butter, cheese, wool, and animal hides for the Middle East.

With regard to deposits of petroleum and other minerals, Kurdistan is a very wealthy country. A large part of Iraq's oil resources lies in Kurdistan, in the regions, around Kirkuk and Hanikin. Part of the valuable Iranian oil resources is also in Kurdistan, in the region around Kirmanshah. Turkey's oil resources are almost exclusively in Kurdistan (in the regions around Batman, Diyarbakir, and Adiyaman). Syria's oil resources too are mainly in Kurdistan, in the region around Cezire. Moreover, our land is rich in mineral resources such as iron, copper, chrome, coal, silver, gold, uranium, arid phosphates.

Furthermore, there are rivers in Kurdistan; these are at least as important, if not more so, than oil. The plateaus and mountains of Kurdistan, which are characterized by heavy rainfall and a heavy coat of snow in winter, are a water reservoir for the Near and Middle East. This is the source of the famous Tigris and Euphrates rivers as well as numerous other smaller rivers. With their water, the Tigris and the Euphrates give life not only to the Mesopotamian plains and the southern part of Kurdistan but also to Iraq and Syria. These rivers, which flow down from heights of three to four thousand meters above sea level, are also very valuable in the production of energy. Iraq and Syria have built numerous dams across these rivers and their tributaries. But the most important ones are a series of dams that were built by Turkey as part of the GAP project (Southeast Anatolia Project). The GAP project is still not complete, but it already supplies a significant proportion of Turkey's electrical energy needs. When the project is finished, both the generation of electricity and agricultural production, through the irrigation of this part of Kurdistan, will increase many times over.

Throughout Antiquity and the Middle Ages, Kurdistan lay on the trade route between the Far East and Europe (the Silk and Spice Road). More recently too, this significant position has continued. Interestingly enough, Kurdistan is today the most suitable region for the petroleum pipelines of Iraq and the Caucasus.

Kurdistan's extraordinary wealth and its strategic location are the most important reasons why our country is still divided and our people still subjected to so much suffering. For reasons mentioned above, Kurdistan drew the attention of the Western colonizing states in the eighteenth and nineteenth, centuries. The English, the French, and the Russians struggled for control over our country. Then, after World War I they divided it up once again, according to their own interests.

The Russians pulled out of the region after the October Revolution of 1917. The English and the French left the region as administrators after Syria and Iraq became independent. But their economic relations and their influence continue to exist in the region.

Not only the Republic of Turkey and Iran but also the newly formed national states of Syria and Iraq have done all that was necessary to keep control over those parts of Kurdistan that were granted to them, and to assimilate and exterminate the Kurds. They have brutally put down the Kurdish uprisings. In this regard they have in most cases cooperated and reached agreements between themselves. They have plundered the riches of Kurdistan and prevented it from developing economically, socially, and culturally.

For these reasons, our people are forced to live in poverty in this wealthy country. The colonial conditions, the constant insecurity, and the war, have prevented our country from developing its agriculture, trade, or industry. The capital that has been gained in Kurdistan has always flowed out of our country. The society has not been able to modernize, and the feudal social structures of the past have not been dissolved totally. The tribal social structure in the rural areas, the system of large-scale land ownership, the religious sects and associated sheikdom have remained. Even today, Kurdistan is ruled by a semi-feudal social system. There is no significant bourgeoisie or working class in the modern sense within its social system. The dirty wars that are being waged by the colonial states in order to put down the persistent Kurdish partisan wars as well as the popular rebellions — which have been going on since 1961 in southern Kurdistan (Iraq), since 1979 in eastern Kurdistan (Iran), and since 1984 in northern Kurdistan — have devastated our country. In view of this situation, in which everything is being brutally destroyed and people are fleeing en masse in fear for their lives, it would be senseless to expect any economic or social progress to take place.

Why Has the Kurdish Resistance Movement Been Unsuccessful to Date?

The twentieth century has witnessed the downfall of the worldwide system of colonialism, and the foundation of new states in former colonies and dependent countries. Why have the Kurds, with their long history and rich culture, not attained their freedom, even though they have continually waged resistance since the beginning of the nineteenth century and paid a high price for it?

There are both internal and external reasons for this. The feudal fragmentation within Kurdish society is one such internal reason. The tribal social structure, divisions between religious movements and confessions, and the institutions of large-scale land ownership and the sheikdom have always been obstacles to the unification of national forces. The medieval value structure of this system has resulted in the fact that a national consciousness has arisen only in part.

But these are not the essential reasons. We must not forget that many nations in Asia and Africa which have won their freedom have been backward with respect to their economic and social systems, in many cases even more backward than the Kurds. The true reasons that have prevented the Kurdish national movement from succeeding are external ones.

Initially the Kurds fought against two great empires, the Ottoman and the Persian. The balance of power was not in favour of the Kurds, and they had no external support whatsoever. But the Balkan countries, for example, attained their independence through the support of powerful Western states such as

Russia, Austria, England, and France. It was the English and the French that separated Arabia from the Ottoman Empire. These were the same powers that, in cooperation with the government in Ankara, carved up Kurdistan once again.

The Kurdish rebellions that followed World War I were opposed not only by Turkey and Iran but also by the French and the English, which had Syria and Iraq as part of their mandates. The English in particular used their own forces to put down the Kurdish national rebellion in Iraq.

After Syria and Iraq had gained their independence, the Kurdish national movement faced the alliance of these four states. One of the most detrimental effects of the division is that the territory of Kurdistan is surrounded by these four dividing states, i.e. by enemy forces. The Kurds have no connections with the outside world, either via land or sea. It is very difficult to set up contacts with the outside world. Even if friendly forces did exist which wanted to help the Kurds from the outside, there are no routes or points of access through which this support could reach Kurdistan directly. If the Kurdish national movement begins an armed rebellion in any of the parts of Kurdistan, it therefore requests a neighboring country to provide the necessary base areas or logistic support. But this neighbouring country is still one of the four states that hold another part of Kurdistan in its control. None of them are interested in a Kurdish victory. These states merely play the 'Kurdish card' against each other when they from time to time have problems with one another. This makes the Kurdish question, which is already difficult enough, even more complicated. Such relations are extremely problematic for the Kurdish national movement and occasionally bring Kurdish organizations into a situation where they are fighting against one another.

Aside from this, the Kurdish national movement has never received any substantial international support. The basic reason for this is that large and small states that are not directly involved in this issue put their own interests in the foreground and do not want to take a position that is opposed to the four states in the region (Turkey, Iraq, Iran, and Syria).

What is the Solution?

The Kurdish national movement has not been successful, for all of the reasons named above. On the other hand, the four states in question have not succeeded in their efforts to melt down the Kurds through assimilation or to eliminate them. On the contrary, Kurdish national consciousness has grown from year to year, having overcome certain feudal obstacles and acquired the character of a mass movement. The Kurdish national movement has organized itself and now includes all social classes and levels. Kurds in the various parts of Kurdistan have moved closer together. In all of these countries, Kurdish resistance has grown stronger; in the three largest parts of Kurdistan it has taken on the form of armed resistance which it has simply been impossible to eradicate.

It has also cost the oppressive countries dearly to deny Kurdish identity, deprive Kurds of their rights, and implement a policy of oppression against them. The governments of Turkey, Iraq, and Iran are compelled to wage continual war. This war consumes their financial resources and costs them human lives. In this respect Iraq, which has to deal with a *de facto* partition, is the most interesting example. But the situation in Turkey is no more rosy than it is in Iraq.

For Turkey, the policy of oppression against the Kurds is the greatest obstacle to democracy and domestic peace. One of the main causes of the frequent military coups in Turkey is the Kurdish question. The dirty war that has been waged for 13 years against the Kurdish people is consuming resources. Turkey's direct expenditures for the war amount to between 8 and 10 billion US dollars annually. The economy of Kurdistan has been totally crippled; agriculture, trade, and animal husbandry have collapsed.

A point has been reached at which the Kurdish question has precipitated a serious economic and political crisis in Turkey. Violence stretches over the entire social life of the country like a net. Chauvinistic nationalism and militarism are intensifying.

The government and official spokesmen continue to blame the PKK — the so-called 'handful of terrorists' — for the miserable situation. But the main responsibility for the present misery, and all the suffering that has been inflicted on both peoples must be borne by the Turkish state itself. The point that has been reached today is the result of a misguided policy that has been implemented for seventy years.

There is no doubt that this problem can not be solved by the army or the police. A peaceful solution is possible through dialogue and the recognition of Kurdish rights, and this is in the interests of both peoples. Thus peace and democracy could arrive in the country, and Turkey as a whole and Kurdistan in particular could enter into a phase of development.

During recent years, groups of reasonable people have been increasingly critical of the policy that has been implemented so intensely over the past seventy years and which has not achieved anything but has, on the contrary, led the country ever deeper into an *impasse*: They have committed themselves to a peaceful solution. Groups of businessmen and workers, intellectuals and the media are increasingly allying themselves to this point of view. The international situation is also forcing Turkey towards a change of course.

In recent years, the Kurdish question has developed from a regional problem into an international one. In this connection, the UN resolution to protect the Iraqi Kurds is extremely significant. Turkey, which wants to be accepted into the European Union, must adapt its political and cultural life to suit European standards, and put into practical effect the international treaties which it has signed.

The conclusion I have reached on the basis of all that I have presented so far is that the solution to the Kurdish question, despite the unfavourable present situation, is drawing nearer. In order to make a peaceful solution possible, as soon as possible, the peace initiatives at the national and international levels must be strengthened.

The Socialist Party of Kurdistan, of which I am a member, advocates a peaceful and just solution. Despite all the oppression and provocations to which the Kurdish people have been subjected, and are still being subjected, we have opted from the very beginning political and peaceful methods of struggle. In our opinion, the peaceful coexistence of peoples is possible, and therefore our party proposes a federation. We can find solutions that are similar to those developed in Spain, Belgium, or Switzerland. Turkey should grant the same demands— which it is making for the hundred thousand Turks on Cyprus, to the Kurdish nation of 20 million people within its own borders. For this to happen,however, there must first of all be a bilateral cease-fire and negotiations must be initiated.

In our view, a peaceful solution to the problem is also possible in the other parts of Kurdistan. In all parts of Kurdistan, the existence and rights of the Kurdish people most be respected. Federal solutions based on equal rights must be devised.

The question of the unity of the Kurdish nation is a question for the future. I believe that the Middle East region will see great changes in the future, as in other regions. The despotic, oppressive, and primitive regimes of today will go, relations between the peoples of the region will improve, and there will be a phase of rapprochement, as is happening now in Europe. The borders will lose their significance. Artificial borders, which today divide Kurdistan with barbed wire and land mines, will then also disappear.

The Kurdish Demographic Revolution and Its Socio-Political Implications[1]

Mehrdad R. Izady

Since the middle of the present century, all Middle Eastern population groups, with the exception of those in Afghanistan, have been experiencing rapid demographic growth. There has, however, been no uniformity in either the timing or growth rates of these groups. Thus, while the annual growth of Turks (the third most populous ethnic group in the Middle East) has been decreasing for the past 25 years, that of the ethnic Persians (the second largest) has been increasing. The growth rates of the largest ethnic group, the Arabs, and in particular those neighbouring on the Kurds, have, on average, reached a plateau. These are now, as in the case of the Syrians, showing signs of starting a decline. The Kurds, the fourth largest ethnic group in the entire Middle East-Caucasus-Central Asian region, have only recently, and belatedly, entered a period of extreme growth — a so-called 'population explosion' phase.

Living in an enforced state of fragmentation within the boundaries of over half-a-dozen sovereign states with various economic, social and health care regimes, each one of these segments of the Kurdish population displays the social and economic conditions of the given country where the group lives — rather than the trends of other Kurds across the borders. To complicate this further in most of the countries, within whose jurisdiction portions of Kurdistan lie, have refrained from carrying out an ethnic-based state census. In the case of Turkey, even the very existence of Kurds within the state was officially rejected, from 1965 to 1991. As a result of these impediments, no systematic study of Kurdish demography has ever been attempted. With the dramatic increase of interest in the Kurds, the question of their population dynamics has become the most important topic of interest after their political activities.

The Kurds are divided very unevenly among the local sovereign states. An inventory of the Kurdish population now places approximately 52 percent

---

1. The preliminary results of this study were first presented to the United States Congress, the House of Representatives, Sub-committee on Europe and the Middle East, November 15th, 1991.

of all Kurds in Turkey, 25 percent in Iran, and 16.5 percent in Iraq. There are also two smaller segments in Syria (5 percent) and in the southern republics of the former USSR: Azerbaijan, Armenia, Georgia, Turkmenistan, Uzbekistan and Kazakhstan (together they hold 1.5 percent of the total number of Kurds). Consequently, a minute change among the vast Kurdish population of Turkey is far more significant in terms of overall Kurdish demography than any major change within the tiny Kurdish community of Armenia.

Kurds constitute the second largest ethnic group in both Turkey and Iraq, where they represent between 20-25 percent of the total state population. Consequently, the impact of the Kurdish demographic revolution is felt most strongly in these two states. In Iran, Syria, Azerbaijan and Turkmenistan, Kurds are the third largest population group, constituting 11 percent, 9 percent, 2.1 percent and 3.8 percent respectively of the total population of those states. While the Kurds are also the second largest ethnic group in the Republic of Armenia, they account for only about 1.7 percent of the total for that state — representing negligible demographic weight.

Two important numerical factors set the Kurds of Turkey aside: 1) Turkey itself houses the majority of the Kurdish population (52 percent), and 2) Proportionally, the Kurds in Turkey constitute the largest proportion of a state's total population anywhere (24.4 percent). The first factor dictates that it is in the Republic of Turkey that any change in the economic or social conditions of the Kurds will have the most significant impact on Kurdish demography over all. The second factor suggests that due to their sheer size, Turkish planners should be the most interested 'outside' party in the ongoing Kurdish demographic revolution; and they are.

Since the first publication of the preliminary results of this demographic study, many newspapers and magazines in Turkey have republished its contents. They have also sounded warnings about a 'Kurdish demographic time bomb'. The most widely distributed Turkish daily newspaper, *Hürriyet*, published several articles during the month of February 1993 about a planned birth-control campaign for Turkish Kurdistan. The articles were accompanied by many cartoons. One depicted a pregnant Kurdish mother, looking at a pyramid of her babies and wearing a sinister grin (*Hürriyet*, March 23, 1993). The Turkish birth-control measures are blatantly brought to bear on the Kurds and Kurds alone. In fact, religious preachers have been instructed to remind the Kurds of their 'religious duty' to reduce their natural fertility.[2] Meanwhile, many of the figures in this study have been inflated, and my subsequent interviews distorted, not only by the Turkish press, but also by others as well,

---

2. *Hürriyet*, February 24th, 1993.

in order to paint a picture of the impending doom that will occur unless the Kurds are prevented from procreating.[3]

Clearly what is missing from all this media and official attention are the older, more optimistic studies and statements by Western and Turkish demographers which have recklessly misled the Turkish government for decades[4]. Ankara was assured that Kurdish demographics was not a factor worthy of her worry. The result? Instead of the Kurds disappearing, Turkish planners are now beginning to feel the weight of the 'Kurdish demographic time bomb', as the *Hürriyet* puts it, for which it is totally unprepared.

Trends: Past and Present

Like most places in the Middle East, poor health care and diet accounted for the slow Kurdish demographic growth during the nineteenth and early twentieth century. This was in contrast to the industrialized Western world, where a demographic boom was in full swing. Nevertheless, modest gains in absolute numbers were registered by the Kurds in the late nineteenth, and the first decade of the twentieth century. Kurds entered the twentieth century at only a marginal demographic disadvantage compared with most of their immediate neighbours. This, however, still meant a steady loss of relative demographic weight. This slow loss became acute between 1914 and 1950 and was brought about in the main by their less developed economy and health care system, but also due to extensive massacres, deportations, and famines which took place in the course of World War I and its aftermath. The turbulence dealt a serious blow to most inhabitants of the Middle East in general, but to the Kurds and the Armenians in particular. Population losses of up to 60 percent were registered in some Kurdish regions of the Ottoman Empire. Losses of the order of 5 percent to 10 percent in the Kurdish provinces of the Persian and Russian Empires were not uncommon. While the Kurds in Iran, Iraq and Syria found relative peace after 1930, and registered modest growth, in Turkey the continuing heavy military operations against the Kurdish insurgents,

---

3. In Iran, where up until recently the policy of the Islamic Republic has primarily been to encourage population growth, the state now decided there is some merit in reducing it; starting in Mahabad, the restive Kurdish city and capital of the 'Kurdish Republic' of 1945-46. The July 6th, 1994 edition of the daily *Ettela'at International* reports how 'Through the efficient distribution of contraceptives and adoption of other birth control measures, the annual population growth of Mahabad has fallen from 2.8 percent per annum to 2.3 percent'.
4. I have briefly discussed the inadequate scholarly treatment of Kurdish demographic trends in general, and that of Turkey in particular, in my book, *The Kurds: A Concise Handbook* (Washington and London: Taylor & Francis, 1992): 111-26.

followed by mass deportations and a high mortality rate in the countryside, meant a further loss of around 500,000 more Kurdish lives from 1918 to 1938.

From 1914 to the late 1950s, and with no exceptions, the neighbouring populations grew at a faster pace than the Kurds. To an outside observer, the Kurds seemed to be on their way out fast as major players in the area, if not, indeed, as a separate ethnic group. Their relative numbers were dwindling steadily. This demographic dip soon turned out to be temporary and self-correcting. The relative numeric loss of ground was to continue only until 1950, when it stopped and began reversing itself by 1955 – particularly in Turkey.

Even after this reversal, Kurdish growth rates remained dwarfed by those registered by the Arabs, and later the Persians. Since the middle of the 1960s the reversal of the previous half-century of decline has gained in momentum, and after 1970, Kurds' growth rates have outpaced those of most of their neighbouring ethnic groups, reaching levels usually qualifying as a 'population explosion'. (See Appendix 1, Table 1, p. 484).

At present the Kurds are steadily regaining the demographic position of importance that they traditionally held, representing 15 percent of the over-all population of the Middle East in Asia. Barring a catastrophe, the Kurds will displace the Turks to become the third most populous ethnic group in the Middle East only 10 years from now.

With a population of about 29 million in 1995, the Kurds are presently the fastest growing major ethnic group in the Middle East. They are now increasing by around 1 million persons per annum. This is expected to rise to 1.5 million per annum between the years 2005 and 2010, and be maintained until around the year 2020 when the total Kurdish population is expected to pass the 60 million mark. Afterwards, the annual growth rates should begin a gradual but steady decline, falling to just below 1 million per year after 2035, and then to half as much by the year 2045, when there will be about 85 million Kurds. Zero growth and demographic maturity should should be reached between 2055 and 2065.[5]

5. The projections given here were obtained by taking the median of the population growth rates projected for any given decade in Iran, Iraq and Syria, and applying the result to the total Kurdish population. The applicability of these demographic trends to the Kurds of Turkey is also obvious. Living deep in the Asiatic parts of that state, Kurdish socio-economic life and hence, demographic trends are far more reminiscent of those of their Kurdish brethren across the borders in Syria, Iraq and Iran than the quasi-European western Turkey. The projected median rate for the decade of the 1990s is the Syrian average, and for 2000 to 2020 it is the Iraqi average. After 2020, the projection becomes, predictably, less precise. Several trends can be considered; each depending on the degree of socio-economic integration of the Kurdish population within their respective states, but again, most significantly in Turkey. I have calculated a growth rate obtained by averaging the growth rates (rather than median rates above)

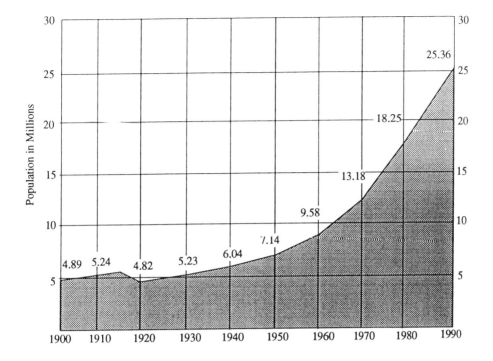

Fig. 1: Kurdish Demographic Trends in the 20th Century.

Socio-Political Ramifications

What effects will this Kurdish demographic revolution have on the states that now administer the various segments of Kurdistan? The answer lies partly in the nature of growth of their non-Kurdish population. Again, Turkey stands out: There, the Kurds are growing the fastest, while the majority ethnic group — the Turks, are growing the slowest of all major ethnic groups in the Middle East. (The proportion of Kurds in the Iranian and Iraqi populations will rise moderately only to fall after 2030. In the case of Syria, the rise will continue beyond 2050, but still in a very moderate fashion).[6]

for; Iran, Iraq and Syria and applied the result to the Kurdish population between 2020 and 2050.

6. The reason for this is the existence of large numbers of even lesser-developed ethnic groups within Iran and Iraq, whose own 'population explosion' phase will be last to arrive, resulting in an increase in their relative proportions. In Syria, however, the

With the current rate of 3.8 percent increase a year, the Kurds have sustained one of the highest growth rates in the Middle East for the past two decades. In this regard they were surpassed in their immediate neighbourhood only by the Iraqi and Syrian state averages in the 1980s, and now only by that of Syria alone. Kurds will replace the Syrians by the turn of the century as the fastest growing population group in the Middle East with a 3.9 percent rise per annum; i.e. the present average growth rate in Syria. The primary reason for the lack of abatement in the high annual Kurdish growth rates at present and in the near future, has been, and will continue to be, the particular socio-economic conditions pertaining to the Kurdish population in Turkey.

It should also briefly be noted that; The annual growth rate of the Syrian Arabs has very recently begun to drop; The Iraqi Arabs, after overcoming the shock of the Gulf War, are likely to reach a maximum of 3.7 percent annual increase from 1996 to 2005; The non-Kurdish Iranians are still increasing from their current 3.6 percent annual rate, and are expected to reach their maximum of 3.7 percent to 3.8 percent between 2000 and 2005.

Enjoying greater prosperity and better health care at the time when the Kurdish demography was stagnant, the Turks experienced a population boom. From the middle of the 1920s until the 1960s, the Turks grew at much faster rates than the Kurds (over thrice as fast at times). By 1955, the Kurdish ethnic component bottomed out at 18.6 percent of the total; or 3.9 million out of a population of 20.9 million. The harsh regulations regarding Kurdish ethnic-cultural expression were relaxed during the 1950s in Turkey, on the assumption that they were being assimilated successfully. Some publications even appeared in the Kurdish language.

The trend then reversed itself. The Turkish state censuses of 1955, 1960, and 1965 show this clearly. The Kurdish component had risen steadily to 18.6, 18.9, and 19.1 percent of the total, respectively. Dismayed by this unwelcome, and persistent demographic trend, the Turkish government ceased providing any breakdowns of ethnic and linguistic groups in the state census data from 1970 onwards. By 1980, Ankara had again embarked on a vigorous process of encouraging the assimilation of the Kurds and other ethnic groups into the majority Turkish community. Expressions of any form of Kurdish ethnic identity were banned, and the enforcement of the language ban was reintroduced by the military regime of General Kenan Evren in the 1980s.

While in Iran, Iraq, and Syria the non-Kurdish segment of the population is also growing rapidly, in Turkey this has not been the case for the past three decades. The demography of the ethnic Turks is now very European in

Kurds are the least developed ethnic group, and their faster growth rate, albeit slight, should naturally result in their steady proportional increase.

character, with growth rates of about 1.2 percent per year, resembling most other southeast European populations. On the other hand, Kurds coming from a more traditional Middle Eastern society in southeast Turkey, show all the characteristics of a Third World population experiencing runaway demographic growth. The demographic trends for the vast Kurdish immigrant population in the affluent Turkish cities on the west coast is not much different. There too, the Kurds form the lowest class in society, living in the most squalid conditions — conducive to maintaining large families and high birth rates. (See Appendix 1 — Table 2, p. 487).

While means are available to the Kurds everywhere in Turkey to reduce the high infant mortality from occurring, living as they do in the least economically and socially developed sections of Turkey, they have no incentive to curb their fertility. Kurdish literacy rates, for example, are less than half those of Turkish citizens. The per capita income in the Kurdish provinces lags behind at under 40 percent of the state average, and far below those of western Turkey. In one extreme case, the average per capita income of the remote Kurdish province of Hakkari in 1986 was a mere 6 percent of that for the province of Kocaeli on the Bosphorus.[7] Consequently, the persistence of a stagnant economy and low literacy, and a lingering of traditional patriarchal values have kept Kurdish mothers largely unemployed and very fertile. At the same time lack of a social welfare system to support the elderly encourages having many children as insurance for old age. Expansion of the state's labour market and its increasing appetite for a young work force has been an added incentive for having more children. As an example of this; between 1950 and 1980, the youthful population of the same Kurdish province of Hakkari grew from 44.4 percent of the total under the age of 15 to 50.4 percent. The corresponding figures for Turkey were 41.2 percent (for 1950), dropping to 38.5 percent (in 1980). This has occurred despite the fact that the infant mortality rate for that province is still at 21 per thousand live births per year.

Had the Kurdish population been assisted in integrating into the mainstream of economic and social life, their growth rate would have begun to slow down at around the present time. Instead it is picking up at an even faster, albeit uneven pace.

---

7. Lale Yalçin-Heckmann, 'Tribe and Kinship among the Kurds', Frankfurt: Peter Lang, 1991: 79-96; Philip Robins, 'Turkey and the Middle East', London: Pinter, 1991: 28-30.

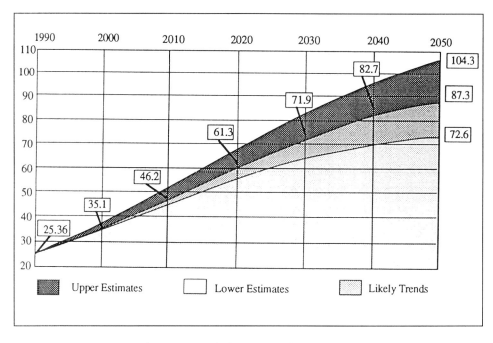

Fig. 2: Projected Future Kurdish Demographic Trends to the Year 2050

Remarks: The higher estimate employs the highest natural rate of increase among the paradigm populations (of Iran, Iraq and Syria) and applies it to the total Kurdish population. The lower estimates does the reverse. (See also footnote 3). Even if the Anatolian Kurds (i.e., the majority of all Kurds) were to be immediately integrated into all facets of Turkish national life and a democratic, fully-representative economic and political system were to be established, the lower estimates will not be achieved. Instead, a population figure of about 80 million might be expected for 2050.

It is not at all unreasonable to expect the phenomenon of rapid population increase among the economically and sociologically disenfranchised portion of Turkey's population to follow the same radical trends already in place in South Africa (white vs. black population), Israel (Jewish vs. Palestinian population), former Soviet Union (Slavs and Balts vs. the Asiatics), and the United States (white vs. non-white populations). It is useful to remember that in 1900, Europe contained a third of the world's total population. It now has less than a tenth. Similarly, South Africa's white population constituted about 38 percent of the total at the turn of the century. This dropped to 20 percent by 1970, and at present the figure stands at around 10 percent of the total.

Although they constitute only about a quarter of the total state population, the Kurds in Turkey now account for half the annual state population growth, registering an average of 3.8 percent per annum (for the decade of the 1990s) against 1.2 percent for the ethnic Turks. John Maynard Keynes once observed that 'the great events of history are often due to slow changes in demography, hardly noticed at the time'. Kurds may prove this thesis just one more time.

The implications are easy to understand. In the case of Turkey, for example, unless the Kurds are vigorously and quickly integrated into the main-stream of Turkish society, and their economic conditions improved to the level of the affluent (and far less prolific) citizens of western Turkey, first, the Turkish element of the Republic will be numerically overwhelmed in Asiatic Turkey (Anatolia) between AD 2020 and 2025. Then, in the space of another 15 to 25 years, Kurds will replace Turks as the largest ethnic group in all of Turkey: 'Turkey' will be predominantly Kurdish! This is interesting for a state which (officially) still does not admit there are any Kurds within its boundaries. Only since 1991 has there been reluctant muttering about the existence of people 'with Kurdish affiliation' or 'of Kurdish descent' in Turkey.

Geographically speaking, the general economic pull towards the west within Turkey has gradually shifted the Kurdish demographic centre of gravity towards the heartland of that state. In many cities that were only partly Kurdish in the past (e.g; Antep, Maras, Adana, Malatya, and Kirsehir) are now rapidly coming to have a Kurdish majority. There are already large Kurdish colonies only miles from the capital of Ankara; to the south, east and northeast. The Kurdish immigrant population of Istanbul has been estimated at over 1 million, which makes it the city with the largest Kurdish population, larger even than those in Kurdistan itself. As recently as in the 1970s, Kurds could have easily gone unnoticed by any casual traveller in the prosperous western cities of Turkey. This is no longer true; the Kurds have become a very visible, noisy, youthful, and impoverished multitude to be seen everywhere in Turkey — east or west. In fact, referring to southeast Turkey as being home to the Kurds is rapidly becoming an outdated statement. As early as 1991, the Turkish President Özal used to repeatedly tell foreign journalists that 'the main body of the Kurdish people is not in East Anatolia anymore. It is integrated into this society (i.e., western Turkey)'.[8] Özal later fine-tuned his broad estimate in 1992, announcing on Ankara television on the October 14th, that, 'Sixty percent of the Kurds live west of Ankara'.[9] This was not greatly exaggerated.

---

8. *Los Angeles Times*, May 1991.
9. Ankara TRT Television in Turkish, 1800 GMT, October 14th, 1992, as cited on FBIS-WEU, October 15th, 1992: 28.

The aging of the more developed and less prolific ruling ethnic element in Turkey should gradually tip the balance of the ethnic composition of the country. This is true of the workforce, and in particular, of the armed forces. As this happens, the Kurds will gain more than their general proportional weight in the total state population implies. In contrast, under normal circumstances, the electoral system favours the older groups of the population over the young; they have more eligible voters, and are more electorally oriented than a youthful population. The increasingly aged ethnic Turkish population will continue to outnumber Kurdish voters for at least the next half-century. But the relationship between Turkish and Kurdish citizens of the Republic is far from normal. Therefore, while the allegiance of the Turkish voters is quite naturally spread across a number of parties; in the main, the uneasy Kurdish minority are expected to continue voting as a bloc. It is only by voting as a bloc, the Kurds realize, that they can most effectively influence the elections in favour of Kurdish interests. This practice will, hence, more than compensate for their numerical disadvantage due to their youthful population.

Voting as an ethnic bloc, the Kurds already wield increasing power in the Turkish state elections (that is, when they are not flagrantly banned from participation, or when their parliamentary representatives are not arrested and imprisoned in Ankara). In this respect, Kurds are emulating the electoral power exercised by the ethnic Turkish minority in Bulgaria. There, with a mere 11 percent of the state population, the Turkish voting bloc has become the decisive one in that admirably democratic, multi-party state.

The situation will be, however, quite different with regards to the armed forces which are comprised of young men (and eventually women). Increasingly, there is a much greater proportion of 18-year-old Kurds than Turks. The former Soviet Union is a prime example of how unbalanced this situation can become, vis-à-vis the composition of the armed forces. Upwards of 40 percent of military conscripts were Asiatics at the time of the dissolution of that superstate in 1991. This despite the fact that their general demographic weight was just about 25 percent. What will the percentage be in the Turkish national army of the year 2020, when over 36 percent of the state population is expected to come from the much younger Kurdish ethnic element? How does the state plan to implement its internal policies if they remain unfavourable to the Kurds, and with an army that, only fifteen years from now, is bound to become largely Kurdish? To avoid this, the state could of course abstain from enlisting Kurds and as a result progressively reduce the overall size of the armed forces. This seems unlikely, as a restless Kurdish population will require an even larger army to keep them in line. Again, the South African example comes to mind. Barring some very urgent and drastic changes in their internal, economic and social policies towards the Kurds, Ankara can expect that, in little over a generation, they will have a fragmented and barricaded society of wealthy and aged Turks in a sea of impoverished, young Kurds.[10] In Turkey at least, in order to win their century-old struggle, Kurds need only to make love not war.

10. The prospect of this crucial demographic weapon; *La revanche des berceaux* ('The revenge of the cradles' — a term once employed by the French Canadians to atone for their loss of political power to the Anglo-Canadians), has not escaped the attention of local state governments or the Kurdish leaders *per se*. Nor has it escaped the attention of the Government of the United States. It is one of the linchpins of American foreign policy in the region. The unsettling demographic predictions for Turkey prompted an extension of this study following its first presentation to the U.S. Congress.

Appendix 1, Table 1: Kurdish Demographic Trends in the 20th Century

	TURKEY			IRAN			IRAQ			SYRIA			USSR	Total	Percent
Year	All	Kurds	%	All	Kurds	%	All	Kurds	%	All	Kurds	%	Kurds	Kurds	Change
1900	13.3	2.96	22.3	10.0	1.19	11.9	2.25	0.56	25	1.75	0.10	5.70	0.07	4.89	
1910	14.2	3.14	22.1	11.8	1.36	11.5	2.29	0.57	25	2.00	0.11	5.50	0.06	5.24	7.16
1920	13.1	2.95	21.7	10.0	1.19	11.2	2.50	0.62	§26	2.10	0.19	^9.0	0.05	4.82	¤8.02
1930	14.4	2.95	20.5	12.1	1.21	10.0	3.00	0.75	25	2.25	0.25	^12.9	0.07	5.23	8.51
1940	17.8	3.39	19.1	13.8	1.40	10.1	3.80	0.87	23	2.50	0.25	10.40	0.13	6.04	15.49
1950	20.9	3.97	19.0	17.5	1.80	10.3	4.77	0.96	20	3.25	0.28	9.80	0.12	7.14	18.21
1960	27.8	5.25	18.9	22.6	2.35	10.4	6.50	1.44	22.1	5.43	0.38	9.20	0.16	9.58	31.37
1970	36.0	6.98	19.4	28.7	3.19	11.1	9.80	2.25	23	6.60	0.53	9.00	0.23	13.18	37.58
1980	46.0	9.97	21.7	29.0	4.37	11.2	12.10	#2.81	#23.2	9.10	0.82	9.10	0.28	80.25	38.45
1990	56.7	13.80	24.4	*55.6	6.11	*11.0	¤18.8	3.90	#20.7	12.60	1.18	9.40	0.34	25.36	38.98

All populations in millions. Figures have been rounded to the nearest decimal point. (See Remarks next page).

Appendix 1   *Remarks* to Table 1:

For states like Iran that conduct their general census in mid-decade, the figures for the end of each decade are calculations based on their average annual growth rates.

§   The census taken by the British mandate authorities of Iraq in 1922, and submitted at Lausanne in 1923, supplies a figure of 520,264 Kurds (494,007 Muslim and 26,257 Yezidi), living in the contested Vilayet of Mosul. This figure excludes all Kurds south of the Diyala-Sirwan river (i.e. the southern borders of the Vilayet of Mosul),in the rest of Iraq.[11] It is reasonably conservative to add another 100,000 for these unaccounted Kurds to the Iraqi census figures. The total Kurds for Iraq in this period, would thus be 620,264.

^   Mainly due to influx of Kurdish refugees from Anatolia. About 50,000 of these had moved on to Lebanon, Jordan and Palestine by 1945.

¤   From 1975 to 1991, nearly 2m Arabs (mainly from Egypt, Palestine and Sudan) and Asians were invited in by Iraq for permanent settlement. This helped to boost that state's total to 18.8m in the decade of the 1980s (i.e., a 55.4% growth), and consequently to reduce the Kurdish share of the total. The Gulf War changed this picture once again. Nearly 2.6m Iraqi residents left the country. Among these were 1.5m Arab and non-Arab guest-workers who can be assumed to be gone forever. The Kurdish (arriving since 1975) and the Shi'ite refugees (arriving since 1991) in Iran number about 1.5m. The war-related casualties and its immediate aftermath of nearly 0.2m should also be further subtracted from the Iraqi total. The outcome must then be adjusted for the natural growth for the three year, 1991-93 period. Iraq had just over 18m people again by the end of 1993.

Since 1975, large numbers of Iraqi Kurds have been forced into neighbouring countries — Iran in particular. While most will eventually return, some are bound to stay, or move outside the Middle East altogether.The number of Kurds remaining in Iraq in 1992 could have been as low as 3.5m, constituting only about 19.4% of the total Iraqi population of about 18 million. Conversely, if the 1.2m refugee Kurds, many living in Iran since 1975, were all to return to Iraq, in view of the marked reduction in the state's total, their share of the Iraqi population would jump to over 25%. This would be about the same

11.   See, V. Minosky, 'The Mosul Question', *Bulletin of the American Library in Paris*, (9-10), 1926, Table 1. Reprinted in The Intetrnational Journal of Kurdish Studies, 7, (1-2) 1994: 28.

demographic weight the Kurds had in Iraq on the eve of its independence in 1932.

* In the past 15 years, Iran by far has been the country with the greatest number of refugees in the world. It now houses an estimated 4.5m of them. Even though the Kurds are still growing slightly faster than the state average, the influx and settlement of these masses would have resulted in a marked drop in the Kurdish demographic share of the state's total. But these refugees included large numbers of Iraqi Kurds, arriving there between 1975 and 1992. Nearly 0.5m Iraqi Kurdish refugees, particularly those living there prior to 1990, seem now to have permanently settled in Iran.

Table 2: Present and Near Future Kurdish Demographic Trends

A: Annual figures for the number of Kurds in the decade of 1990s (at 3.65% average annual growth rate)

Year	1990-91	1992	1993	1994	1995	1996	1997	1998	1999	2000
Turkey	13.8	14.3	14.8	15.4	15.9	16.5	17.1	17.7	18.4	19.0
Iran	6.1	6.3	6.6	6.8	7.0	7.3	7.6	7.8	8.1	8.4
Iraq*	3.9	4.0	4.2	4.3	4.5	4.7	4.8	5.0	5.2	5.6
Syria	1.2	1.2	1.3	1.3	1.4	1.4	1.5	1.5	1.6	1.6
CIS	0.34	0.35	0.36	0.38	0.39	0.41	0.42	0.44	0.45	0.47
Totals	25.4	26.2	26.6	28.2	29.2	30.3	31.0	32.4	33.7	35.1

B: Projected Trends to 2050

Year	1990			2000			2020			2050		
State	Total Pop.	Total Kurd	% Kurd	Total Pop.	Total Kurd	% Kurd	Total Pop.	Total Kurd	% Kurd	Total Pop.	Total Kurd	% Kurd
Turkey	56.7	13.8	24.4	65.9	19.0	28.8	87.5	32.8	36.8	105.8	47.8	45.2
Iran	55.6	6.1	11.0	73.9	8.3	11.2	130.6	15.0	11.5	192.5	21.5	11.1
Iraq*	18.8	3.9	20.7	22.6	5.7	25.2	38.2	9.6	25.1	53.0	13.0	24.5
Syria	12.6	1.2	9.4	17.2	1.6	9.3	28.0	2.9	10.4	33.7	3.9	11.6
CIS	0.3			0.5			0.9			1.1		
	25.4			35.1			61.3			87.3		

C: *Comparative Population Growth Rates, Recent Past and Near Future*

	Past State Population Growth: Annual Rates (%)			Projected State Population Growth: Overall Rates (%)		
State	1965-73	1973-84	1984-90	1990-2000	2000-20	2020-50
Turkey	2.5	2.2	2.1	16.2	32.7	20.9
Iran	3.0	3.1	3.6	32.9	76.7	47.4
Iraq	3.3	3.6	3.9	#20,0	71.8	38.8
Syria	3.4	3.4	3.8	36.5	62.8	20.4
KURDS	3.5	3.8	3.8	36.5	71.8	43.1

Remarks to Table 2:

— All populations are in millions.
— All figures rounded to the nearest decimal point.
— CIS, The Commonwealth of Independent States, refers to the territories of the former Soviet Union, dissolved in 1991.
* Beginning with the year 2000, figures for Iraq assume returning home of some 200,000 Iraqi Kurdish refugees from Iran.The large proportional increaseof Iraqi Kurds is due to emigration from Iraq of nearly 2 million (mostly Arab) workers by 1995.
# Pre-Gulf War estimates for Iraqi state growth for the decade ranged over 40%. War-related losses of all kinds and the demographic stress in its aftermath will result in Iraq achieving no more than half as much, or about a 20% increase for the decade.

Sources:
Current state population figures and their future projected growth trends, except for Iraq, are all based on *World Population Data Sheet* (Washington: Population Reference Bureau, annual report sheets for 1988, 1990, 1992).

Thoughts on the State and the Kurdish Identity in Turkey

Baskin Oran

The Adoption of Assimilation Policy by the Turkish State and its Reasons

To put it simply, and broadly speaking, State policy on group identity can be divided into two main categories: Assimilation and Integration.

Assimilation is an attempt by the State to homogenize society through the elimination of all forms of divergence; cultural, religious, ethnic, linguistic etc. If in any given society there is a high rate of diversification, and in particular if prosperity is low, then it is not unusual for this policy to be implemented by means of force. When this occurs, the unity of the State can be achieved for a limited time, but it is usually very difficult to create and keep the desired unity for long. This is because unity, as in a marriage, is something that can only be voluntary and cannot be imposed.

In integration, however, the purpose is to create a unity between diversities. In an analogy, where assimilation could be likened to a 'grinder', integration would be a 'salad bowl' in which all the ingredients of the salad (sub-cultures) retained their distinctive characteristics and the main taste stemmed from the dressing (the upper-culture).

Since its foundation in 1923, The Turkish Republic has opted for the first alternative. Hence, in what follows, I shall offer my thoughts on the underlying reasons for this choice, in relation to both the internal and the external contexts:

The Internal Context: The Legacy of the Ottoman Empire.

1) The impact of the '*Millet* System':

The Turkish Republic is an extention of the Ottoman Empire, at the core of which was the *Millet* System. At the very heart of this concept lay religion. Every religion (and, in the case of the Christians, every confession) was considered a different *millet*[1]. Accordingly, all Muslims, regardless of their other differences, belonged to the same 'Muslim Nation' (*umma*). Therefore, Kurds

---

1. 'Millet' which then meant 'religious community', is used for 'nation' now.

were never considered to be any different from Turks despite their diverse ethnic, linguistic features etc.

When the Republic was founded, the legacy of the *Millet* System was very well suited to the nationalist policy of a State that did not allow multiple identities.

2) The Young Turk tradition:

In the second decade of the 20th Century, the Young Turks (*Ittihat ve Terakki Firkasi*, The Party of Union and Progress) dominated the political scene in the Empire. Their 'Turkification' policies of course excluded any cultural identity other than Turkish. Mustafa Kemal and the other architects of the Republic all came from this school of thought and were to apply the principals of this powerful heritage.

3) The anticipation of the Ottoman disintegration:

The Ottoman Empire went through a rapid fragmentation during the 19th Century leading up to the point of its final collapse at the end of the First World War. Indeed, the Empire which once spanned three continents was reduced to a small nation-state squeezed into the Anatolian Peninsula. Since the Republic inherited almost the same mosaic of peoples, the concern about a similar occurrence happening terrified both the Turkish people and the elite. The fear of losing the precious peninsula also contributed a great deal to the intolerance with which cultural identities other than Turkish were regarded.

4) The Kurdish Uprisings:

The above-mentioned worry turned into sheer paranoia when there was a serious uprising in 1925 started by the Kurdish underground organization *Azadi* (formed in 1923); a mere sixteen months after the advent of the Republic. Only in 1938 was the State able to put out the fire created by these uprisings.

The External Context: The Fascist Atmosphere of the Inter-war Years

In the years between the two World Wars, the Turkish Republic was founded and Kemalism was developed as the nationalist ideology. This period, during which the Kemalists fought the Kurdish uprisings, was characterized above all by Italian, German, Eastern European and Balkan integral nationalisms; the slogans of which found resonance among the Kemalists: *Ein Folk* - The Turkish Nation; *Ein Reich* - The Turkish State; *Ein Partei* - The People's Republican Party founded by M. Kemal, the *'Ein Führer'*.

Much in the same way as the *Millet* System mentioned above, the international feeling was very well suited to Turkish nationalism as formulated by the Kemalist elites; who were themselves students of French Jacobinism to begin with.

In conclusion then, all of these internal and external issues contributed to the strong tendency towards assimilation in the Turkish Republic. I shall now turn the discussion towards the reasons for the failure of this assimilationist policy.

Reasons for the failure of the State's assimilation policies towards the Kurds

One must admit that the Turkish State has been quite successful in its nation building project. Bosnians, Pomaks, Albanians, Cretans, Circassians, Abhaz, Tatars, Georgians, Laz etc. were successfully united under the generic name and common cultural identity of the Turkish Nation ('*Türk Milleti*'). This is perhaps easily accounted for by at least two factors. Firstly, all these peoples were Muslims, and the non-Muslims in Turkey were less than three percent of the whole population. Secondly, all these peoples were Balkan or Transcaucasian immigrants. One must draw attention to the fact that immigrants, in contrast to autochtonous peoples, are rather more inclined to adapt to their new country rather than assert their own nationalism.

The one significant exception to the success of Kemalist nationalism was the Kurds; an autochtonous people. Today the failure of Kemalism's nation-building process with regard to the Kurds — at least a sizable proportion of them, seems obvious. I shall propose the following reasons for this failure:

Historical Reasons

1) The concept of 'nation-state' relies on the assumption that state and nation are identical. This understanding, however, falls short of capturing the reality in the Middle-East where practically all States are multi-national and all peoples are trans-frontier.

2) Assimilationist policy in Turkey did not only affect the Kurds, but also made the Turks blind to the issue. Up until the 1990s there was no public opinion favourable to the demands of the Kurds, because 'the Turk on the street' was not even aware that there were Kurds in Turkey, let alone a Kurdish problem. It was only after the PKK (Kurdistan Workers' Party) began its terrorist activities in 1984 that people in general first heard about it.

3) Kurdish nationality is too deeply rooted and powerful to be assimilated. The first Kurdish 'nationalist' newspaper *Kurdistan*[2] came out in 1898 — only three years after the publication of *Mesveret*, the Young Turks' newspaper. Furthermore, along with the *Mesrutiyet* (Second Constitution-1908) various Kurdish associations and publications which highlighted Kurdish cultural characteristics (language, epics, myths, etc.) flourished. After the *Mütareke* (Armistice of 1918) there were others claiming independence. As was stated earlier, the very secret revolutionary organization (*Azadi*) which started the 1925 uprising[3], was founded before the Republic was declared and the Kurdish rebellions were not to be put down until 1938. Consequently, the memory and bitterness of such a deep rooted and intensive nationalist conflict were passed on from generation to generation and the awareness of Kurdish conciousness was perpetuated.

Structural Reasons

1) The concept of a 'common fatherland' relies heavily on national economic activity. 'Common national sentiment' can only be developed in those areas included in the 'national economic market'. Because of the late arrival of the impact of Turkish industrialization — due to the mountainous nature of the terrain and the tough climate — the high concentration of Kurds in Eastern Anatolia were only recently included in the latter concept. On the other hand, Kurdish nationalism flourished there very early. Had it been the other way around, i.e., had the common economic market included this part of the peninsula before Kurdish nationalism was born, assimilation might have stood a chance.

2) Even in countries which seem to enjoy much more prosperity and a strong sense of national unity, we observe the appearance of nationalist movements in cases where economic disparities juxtapose confessional, religious, ethnic, etc. differences. Eastern Anatolia has been at a constant disadvantage ever since the world trade routes shifted away from there (16th Century).

---

2. For a complete collection (transcription) of this first Kurdish newspaper see Mehmet Emin Bozarslan (ed. and translator), *Kurdistan, Ilk Kürd Gazetesi* (1898-1902), 2 Cilt, Uppsala, Deng Yayinevi, 1 Kasim 1991, 580s. + Facsimile.
3. The Sheik Said Uprising of 1925 was so called because the secular and modern nationalist *Azadi* leaders who came from the ranks of the Ottoman Army and of the *Hamidiye* Regiments (irregular Kurdish troops organized by Abdülhamit II to combat Armenian nationalism) knew they could influence Kurdish people only through a religious leader, hence Sheik Said.

In the present atmosphere of globalization, communication and transportation links with Eastern Anatolia have improved. However, what travelled through these channels was not economic development, but information alone. So therefore the Kurds' relative depreciation has further increased through comparisons with the Turkish west. Hence, their 'awareness of being neglected' has also grown to an intolerable level.

3) Modernization without development creates social mobility, which in turn, creates new demands. Institutional inability to meet these demands forces the system to collapse. This is precisely the situation in Turkey today. The system denies or rejects new demands (such as broadcasting in Kurdish, for instance), and insists on assimilation as though it were still possible.

4) Deeply rooted Kurdish nationality, ill-defined industrialization, urbanization, and education, inevitably led to the rise of the Kurdish intellectuals. Needless to say, in underdeveloped countries, intellectuals lead—and even create— nationalism.

Ideological and Political Reasons

1) Secularism was a fundamental principle of the new 'nation-to-be'. Thus, the first act of the Republic was the abolishment of the Khalifate. The Khalifate, however, symbolized the only link between Turks and Kurds: Islam. Dismantling this tie gave rise, in an atmosphere of persistent emphasis on the Turkish element, a further strengthening of the sense of discrimination among the Kurds.

2) The leading policy of the Republic vis-a-vis the Kurds, such as the one represented by Field Marshal Fevzi Çakmak, was based on the strategy of preventing Kurdish nationalism through the isolation of the Kurds. This policy was rigidly enforced up until the 1950s. Therefore, assimilation was applied by only a handful of civil administrators, military personnel and teachers.

3) The upper-identity which the Republic sought to impose upon the Kurds could have reached the province by means of industrialization alone, but under these conditions it did not. On the contrary, the province came to the large cities of the west after the 1950s due to domestic migration for economic and educational purposes. Indeed, both in developed and underdeveloped countries alike, big cities have always been the cradle of nationalism. Turkey was no

exception to the rule, as the contemporary Kurdish nationalist elites flourished among the university youth in major cities like Istanbul and Ankara.

4) The Ottoman Empire, like all other large empires, was based on the respect shown to various identities (Turkish, Greek, Armenian, Jewish, Kurdish, Laz, etc). The Empire gathered all these diverse *lower-identities* under the *upper identity* of 'Ottomanism', which was identical to none of these. The Turkish Republic inevitably inherited this rich variety of lower-identities and yet the upper-identity it imposed eliminated all others but one: Turkish. The term 'Nation of Turkey' (*'Türkiye Milleti'*) used by Mustafa Kemal during the War of Independence was never to be heard again after the date of the declaration of the Republic (October 29th, 1923) as it was definitely replaced by that of 'Turkish Nation' (*'Türk Milleti'*)[4]. This led, at least one of the lower-identity groups, namely the Kurds, who fought alongside the Turks[5], to feel left out after the war.

5) The most important issue to be considered when discussing assimilation is the meaning implied by the word 'Turk'. The term had three different but interrelated meanings in Turkey: Firstly, it referred to citizenship. All the citizens of Turkey were called Turks. Secondly, within the international atmosphere of nazism and fascism, the term soon gained ethnic connotations closely related to racism. This second usage of the word was to prevent the integration of the Kurds into the third meaning of the term, the most important one — that of nation.

When Kurdish nationalism found a sympathetic international audience in the ethnic nationalist context of the 1990s, the chances of assimilation finally fell to nil.

Cultural Autonomy, the Turkish State, and the Kurds

Why is cultural autonomy— in different ways— so important to both the Kurds and to the State? In other words, why do the Kurds want to have a different cultural identity and why is the Turkish state so reluctant to concede this?

The answer to the first question is easy: Social identity, needless to mention, is of enormous importance to the individual. In particular, being

---

4. See my *Atatürk Milliyetçiligi — resmî ideoloji disi bir inceleme* (Kemalist Nationalism, a non-official interpretation), 3rd ed., Ankara, Bilgi Publ., April 1993: 208.

5. This was because of two common denominators: Anticipation of the Armenian vengeance, and the will 'to liberate the Khalifate'.

unable, under pressure from the State, to use the mother-tongue which one has spoken since birth can be seen as a hindrance par excellence, and one that alienates the individual from society. Even further, this socio-cultural alienation should be seen as one of the most important factors underlying the rebellion of this group[6].

The answer to the second question is also easy: As I have already noted above in 'The legacy of the Empire', in the atmosphere which made assimilation impossible (at least for the Kurds) the Turkish State is worried that; 'To recognize Kurdish identity by conceding cultural autonomy, would be to risk the disintegration of the country, as they would surely then demand their independence'.

To this, the best remark perhaps is made by the renowned novelist Yasar Kemal (who calls himself 'The most Kurdish of all the Turks and the most Turkish of all the Kurds'); 'If we refuse to give them cultural autonomy, will they not then ask for independence?'

In actual fact, the fear of the Turkish State is not that ridiculous. Until now, all nationalisms began as cultural nationalisms and only stopped at the final objective— independence.

But what about today? In the era of globalization where the nation-state begins to 'wither away' under the influence of 'bourgeois internationalism', will Kurdish nationalism in Turkey today go as far the 'final objective', or will it end at an earlier stage, such as cultural autonomy?

I will try to answer this, the *million dollar* question, by developing four criteria barely touched upon by a very distinguished student of nationalism, the late Ernest Gellner, at a lecture he gave in Ankara in December 1993.

During his lecture, Professor Gellner had modestly answered my question on the future of Kurdish nationalism in Turkey by saying that he did not 'know much about Kurdish nationalism', but would nevertheless, 'say a few things in general' on the conditions for the success of nationalist movements. He then cited the following four criteria: numerical strength, density, historical continuity, and motivation.

Numerical Strength of the Ethnic Group

The size of the ethnic group is important in the strive for independence. Today, there are many members of the UN with a population of a few hundred thousand only. Turkish citizens of Kurdish descent are estimated to number

6. See Professor Dogu Ergil's articles on pluralism and multi-culturalism in his *Bir Düz Bir Ters* (Backward-Forward), Istanbul, Milliyet Publ., 1995:146-65 and 215-20.

12 million. This would no doubt qualify the Kurds to set up an independent country of their own. Therefore, this criterion is fully met.

Concentration of the Ethnic Group in a Particular Region

If a nationalist movement of an ethnic group is concentrated in a particular region of a country, its chances of achieving independence are greater. Today, it is widely estimated that some sixty percent of the Kurds live in western Turkey; well away from their home region in the east and the southwest. Given the great disparity in the prosperity levels of the two parts, these people can hardly be expected to return within the next successive generation. In Istanbul alone there are two million Kurds. Therefore, I do not believe that this criterion is met. (*A minus*).

Historical Continuity of the Movement

There is perfect continuity in the Kurdish nationalist ideology and movement in Turkey. Themes like cultural autonomy and the like put forward by the Kurds today are to be found in *Jin*[7], published in 1918-19. Except for the relatively brief period of 1938-1959 there is practically no break in the nationalist movement. I think this criterion is fully met. (*A plus*).

Motivation towards Independence

Are the Kurds fully motivated to set up an independent Kurdish state of their own or do they find it somehow more suitable to their interests to stay in Turkey? Unlike the other three, this criterion is subjective and therefore much more important than the others, so I would like to study it in more detail:

1) Geopolitical Position of the Future 'Independent State':

If the piece of land to be independent is located adjacent to a border line rather than in the middle of the country, and if it enjoys objective conditions for survival, its chances of gaining independence are greater.

Presumably, the most suitable area for an 'Independent Kurdish State' would be southeastern Turkey, along the Syrian and Iraqi frontier. This case would be a positive advantage (*A plus*). On the other hand, the fact that it would be landlocked and surrounded by at least four (surely hostile) countries

---

7. For the transcription of this periodical, so important to Kurdish nationalism, see Mehmet Emin Bozarslan (Ed. and translator into Turkish), *Jîn* (Kovare Kurdî Tirkî), 1918-1919, Vol. 5, Uppsala, We anxana Deng, 1985, 1986, 1987, 1988.

(Iran, Iraq, Syria, and Turkey), having no natural resources to rely on, and most probably troubled by tribal and other rivalries, would not positively motivate the Kurds. I think it's realistic, therefore, to put a *minus* sign against this one; which means that this criterion is only partly met.

2) The Possibility of Adopting an Irredentist Policy:

If the prospective 'independent state' has a chance to implement an irredentist policy following independence, then nationalist Kurds will be more motivated to support independence. Irredentism refers to a policy adopted by a State to include the people of its own ethnicity who live close to its borders. In this particular case this is Pan-Kurdism.

On the one hand, the Kurds live in three neighbouring countries (Iran, Iraq, Syria) and it should also be noted that following the Gulf War an embryonic Kurdish State was established in Northern Iraq as a 'Safe Haven'. On the other hand, however, the Kurds of Turkey are far different than those in the other countries; in terms of development, democracy, social class, leadership, and language. Moreover, the sense of unity among the Kurds has historically always been weak. Hence, this criterion is only partly met.

3) International Conjuncture

The atmosphere of the international arena should be suitable for the birth of such a State in such a sensitive part of the world. In this regard, we can list at least three points:

Firstly; a number of independent states emerged from the disintegration of the Soviet Bloc. This climate would appear to be conjusive to the establishment of a Kurdistan. However, the opposite could also hold true because of the chaotic picture created by these new states.

Secondly; the Organization for Security and Cooperation in Europe is placing heavy emphasis on the issue of human rights, minority rights, and local cultures. Furthermore, this is the age of 'ethnic nationalism'. On the other hand, Western countries are not seeking to foster independence at the cost of breaking up existing states; they only push for the introduction of cultural rights.

Thirdly; globalization has brought the 'Age of Nationalism' to the beginning of the end. Just as nation-states replaced the feudal order when European bourgeoisies needed to erect national frontiers to protect their economic interests against other bourgeoisies, the very same classes of the very same Western countries are now tearing down the very same frontiers to enlarge the 'national market' to encompass the entire globe. In this holocaust, one single culture, the capitalist culture of the West is encouraging, with ever greater speed and vigour, the whole world in the direction of 'international (read: materialistic) values'. Material wealth, more than ever, is everything. In this 'Age of Globalization', concepts like 'national pride' are fast becoming less important than blue jean brands. In such a cultural atmosphere, the fate of a new land, complete with economic and other problems, is bound to appeal less and less to the dreams of men. Therefore, I do not believe that this criterion is met.

Now, let us come to the last point in the question of 'Motivation', namely, *Expectation*. And since the score of minuses and pluses above is about equal, this point is so important that I would prefer to classify it as a fifth criterion rather than a sub-division of Motivation.

Expectation

In a world of 'globalization', where the materialistic values of the West flood every corner of the globe, raising material expectations like a rocket, which alternative would provide the Kurds of Turkey a better life; an independent Kurdish state, or Turkey?

If the Kurds were no longer prevented from enjoying the material and cultural life which they aspire to in Turkey, then there are strong chances that they would not go as far as independence. There are several reasons why they might do so: They have been living and inter-marrying with the Turks for five centuries. They might have scruples about the new independent Kurdish state because there is a feudal tradition of Kurds fighting against one another. The PKK's (nationalist Kurdish organization) use of terror as the main means of achieving independence is just as ruthless towards fellow Kurds as it is towards anyone else. Also, the new state would be landlocked by hostile neighbours and would have very few natural resources to live on.

If, on the other hand, the Kurdish people give up all hope of attaining the material and cultural life they aspire to in Turkey, this 'new hope' may well be very attractive to them despite all possible future difficulties. If both the material and cultural expectancies are not met at the same time, then the 'new hope' will grow ever bigger in their hearts and minds.In other words, the Republic of Turkey would have to provide the Kurds with both 'bread' and 'freedom'.

valid for the PKK. After the USA defeated Iraq, there was a revolt in southern Kurdistan under American provocation. The Iraqi administration suppressed this revolt violently. The PKK, who did not support Iraq in her war against USA, indirectly supported the Iraqi regime as it was suppressing the Kurdish revolt. But anti-Imperialism necessitates the pursuit of completely opposite policies in both phases. Iraq must be supported against attack by the USA, and the Kurdish people have to be supported against Iraqi suppression.

As can be seen, the narrow minded nationalist policy that Turkey, Iraq, Syria and Iran display to one another and the national oppression they apply to Kurds, reflect upon various groups of the Kurdish people. Even these groups cannot achieve Kurdish nationalism. Their vision is so narrow as to rely on relatively small divisions; a persistence of narrow, fragmentary policies.

Turkey, Iraq, Syria, Iran and Kurdish organizations are trying to legitimatize their narrow-minded nationalist and particularist policies by blaming their actions on each-other saying that they have no alternative. The foremost power is either that of the country of the region, or imperialism, or — quite often, both of them. Those who reply with killing when the region turns into a war area, do not take this anti-imperialist attitude seriously.

There is no doubt that Turkey is in the first rank, 'legitimatizing' the policy of solving questions in collaboration with the USA. This policy produces its continuous reply in the mountains as if it were echoing a sound from a valley. Consequently, the states and organizations of the nations which are under the oppression and threat of imperialism, to a greater or lesser extent, are positioning against each other. As the national question breaks away from the axis against imperialism, it turns into the struggle of the Turks, Arabs, Persians and Kurds with each other and internal fights between Kurds and Arabs. There is no victory, for either side. Resorting to compromise in favour of imperialism and creating new dependencies will lead the way to complete the national balance-sheets in a negative manner, especially in the long-term.

This scene grows more and more complicated. The imperialism benefitting from the inner-South contradictions, just about turns the Middle East into an international bloodbath like the Balkans and Caucasus. The only way out for the Southern countries and peoples is to have a common front against imperialism. Undoubtedly, this is not easy, and we cannot expect that all sides will agree on this matter, because for a century they have all been caught in an imperialist web.

The greatest and determining fact of our area is the contradiction between imperialism and oppressed countries and peoples. This contradiction will rest on confronting imperialism in Middle Eastern countries in various measures, with regard to all the peoples of the Middle East and their class. The question is to produce the policies based on this fact now and to make them applicable. The most important thing is to understand that the struggle against imperialism forms an objective basis for all the nations of the Middle East. National demands unite on that basis and initiate dialogue.

'Imperialist Turkey' — Theses Originating from Imperialism

In such an environment, theses on an 'Imperialist Turkey' are being put forward. Let us look at it in a socio-economic scheme. Turkey, having an annual average income per person of about 2000 Dollars (US) as the measure of her capital accumulation, apart from being an imperialist could not even take a position among the economically advanced part of the Southern countries. The road to advanced capitalism was closed for Turkey from the beginning of the nineteenth century. One cannot show even a single country which has jumped from the ranks of oppressed to the ranks of imperialism in the twentieth century. It is no longer possible to catch up with the advanced capitalist countries through a capitalist path.

In the political scheme, imperialism is the system of rivalry of a small number of advanced capitalist states for the hegemony of the world. Turkey does not exist as far as the USA, Japan, Germany and Russia are concerned. Furthermore, she does not exist among the second-class imperialist capitalist countries such as England, France, Canada and Sweden. Turkey cannot either be considered in the same category as Spain, Portugal, and East European countries situated on the North-South border.

Turkey's place on the map also determines its position in the socio-economic splitting of the world. Turkey is Asian, she is a country of the Third World. She is a so-called Southern Country. She entered the exploitation phase in the nineteenth century, has opposed this process through an anti-imperialist independence War at the beginning of the twentieth century, has experienced the development of a national capitalism and, thereafter, has fallen to a dependency relationship with imperialism again. But Turkey, like China and Iran, possesses the great heritage of an empire in the oppressed world. Turkey has never been a colony, she has always possessed a state. On the other hand, she has a tradition of struggling for liberty and at the beginning of this century she had realized a democratic secular bourgeois step by demolishing the Ottoman State. Her political accumulation has especially provided an advanced position among the Southern countries. Her geography 'stretching like a mare-head' from Asia to Europe, symbolizes Turkey's revolutionary potential. But this revolution cannot be a capitalist one but an anti-imperialist democratic revolution which turns uninterruptedly into anti-capitalist. The experience of

Turkey is the most distinguished example as it proves the impossibility of the transfer of a country from the 'oppressed pole' to the 'oppressing pole' of the capitalist system. A revolution, which will transform Turkey into an imperialist country in the course of time, under the leadership of the bourgeoisie, is impossible.

With regard to Turkey's relationship with Middle East and Central Asian countries,Turkey has created a relatively advanced 'human capital' for industrialization thanks to the Kemalist Revolution. This human capital does business in oil-rich countries like Saudi Arabia, Libya and the Emirates, with its business organization, engineers, technicians and relatively skilled labour force. The situation is rather different in Central Asian countries. The human capital of these countries is advanced when compared to Turkey. Turkey plans to enter these countries mainly to constitute open market institutions and to manage these institutions. Turkey, because she has the largest population among the Turkish republics, and moreover an independent state tradition, inherited from a great empire, is in the position of 'big brother''. But, dependency relations of the imperialist oppressed type— imperialist domination and exploitation — do not rise from such a position. Turkey cannot behave as an 'imperialist' in Central Asia. The most she can do is function like a bridge between western imperialists and Central Asian countries; she can only have a 'subcontracting' role.

The theory that Turkey is 'imperialist' or 'sub-imperialist' is not valid from the Turkish-Kurdish point of view, either.

Not only Kurds but also various other peoples were living in the centralized-feudal Ottoman Empire. The relationship between these peoples and the Ottoman Empire cannot be explained in the context of either imperialism or colonialism. During that period there were no 'nations'. The Ottoman Empire did not have an advanced capitalism, but rather was ensnared by the capitalism contained in imperialism.

The relationship between Turks and other peoples in the Ottoman state was never a relationship between 'oppressor' and 'oppressed'. All peoples, even the Christians, consisted of peasants and artisans, as well as feudal landlords and tradesmen. Moreover, trade was only in the hands of Christians, thus providing a domination factor in the economy. Karl Marx in his articles on the 'Eastern Question', explains in detail that the Turkish people in the Ottoman Empire were in an economically weak position, especially compared to the people of the Balkans. The national oppression of Kurds was born and became graver in line with capitalism's development.

The relationship between the Kurds and the Turkish national state which was established by the young bourgeois after the Independence War, was one of national dependency and inequality, but was not one of an exploiting domination. There was no placing of Turkish capital in the Kurdish areas of Turkey, and agricultural lands were not seized by the 'exploiting' Turks either — they are still in the possession of the Kurdish landowners.

Lenin always considered Turkey as a 'semi-colony' at the beginning of twentieth century and during the War of Independence. He continuously stresses the threat to Turkey of being exploited. In the 1920 Revolution, he pointed out that Turkey had become a kind of 'slave'. Since the War of Independence, although Turkey has been considered part of the capitalist system, it has also been seen as part of the 'oppressed world'.

In our era, *colonialism* is in hands of the imperialist states, and is manifested by *imperialism*. This is why the theory that Kurdistan is a 'colony' does not have a scientific foundation. Therefore,the theory of an 'Imperialist' Turkey now closes this gap. Things have gone full circle, and these two theories are difficult to reconcile.

A number of articles recently published in the Western press describe the hegemony of Turkey and Iran as that of 'imperialists' in the Caucasus and Central Asia. It has been claimed that Turkey wishes to rule over an empire extending from the Balkans to the Sea of China by the 21st century. Scenarios have been suggested which characterize Turkey as the 'great hegemonist of the 21st century'. All of these are reminiscent of stories such as 'Iraq governed by Saddam is a regional hegemonic power', or 'the danger of Arabian imperialism'. The Gulf War too, has been analyzed by some witless personalities as 'a war of re-division between two imperialists' on the basis of this.

The assertion that it is not the oppressed countries, but the oppressors who are imperialist in the capitalist world system, is manufactured to mask the real imperialists and to aggravate the civil wars in the South. The ruling classes find channels and forms that will reproduce their ideologies, even in the classes which they have oppressed.

The 'Imperialist Turkey' theory also stands in the way of Kurdish National independence. Facts are revolutionary. Those who announce that Turkey is 'imperialist', not only damage the construction of a common front against imperialism by the southern peoples, but they also prevent the unity of the Kurdish people; they fragmentize them. The so-called, 'imperialist Turkey' is the 'saviour' and 'the most democratic country' for Talabani and Barzani. Others declare that Iraq or Iran are 'imperialist'. Consequently, no difference is evident between USA and Germany and the Third World countries. Thus, the axis of struggle against imperialism has been broken and the opportunity lost to confront the national oppression and terror of the Turkish state.

The content of internationalism cannot be reduced only to solidarity with the Kurdish people. The most important solidarity is to organize and to mobilize the struggle of the Turkish working class against the dominant classes.

Internationalism favours the future of the Arabian, Persian and Turkish peoples. Supporting the oppressed Kurdish people is an ethical principle of highest degree. But internationalism necessitates a common physical basis along ethnic principles. This is the common basis of gaining advantage against imperialism. The thesis of an 'imperialist' Turkey aims to destroy this common basis by declaring that the Turkish nation is an imperialist-like power vis a vis the American and German nations. Turkish people are continuously discredited to the Kurdish people, while the Turkish chauvinists are discrediting the Kurdish people to the Turkish people. Thus, the common class feelings and affiliations between two peoples are continuously under attack and the imperialist ideological hegemony is intensified along two paths. The history of mankind is the history of struggles between the classes. And the struggle against imperialism is the class struggle in the international arena. Theories of an 'Imperialist Turkey' are aimed at this.

Globalization of the Kurdish Question

One very worrying development which makes the solution of the problem more difficult is the globalization of the Kurdish question. The United States has its finger on this, and more particularly, so does Russia. Germany lies in wait, and other European countries are also waiting their turn. In other words it has become a field where developments in the world have intensified.

The ruling classes of Turkey sought to renew their power in 1991 via early elections. DYP-SHP coalition government was established with great support from the right and the left to implement the 'Oppress-Dissolve' policy. The pro-Kurdish party HEP was on one wing of the coalition, and even the PKK had supported the SHP in the elections. Thus the new government began working with the support of the forces that it was later to oppress in the 1992 Spring Operation which had been designed ten months earlier.

State terror at first focused on the restoration of the state's authority which had been lost in many towns and districts. People and their leaders were assassinated by contra-guerillas, or forced to leave the region. Some 2000 villages were freed through the use of violence. The state succeeded in regaining control in towns and districts by benefitting from the mistakes of the PKK.

The state carried out a violent policy in collaboration with Hizbullah. This collaboration had, as a matter of fact, been brought to light by our (Workers) party. The PKK's competition with the state for religionism in the region helped Hizbullah to gain power. As Hizbullah gained power by collaborating, first with the state, and then with the PKK, popular forces in the cities lost their power dramatically.

In effect, the state took control of cities and districts with the help of the religious forces, and emptied the villages which were initially the headquarters of the struggle and resettled those peasants in the cities which were under the state's control. In other cases, however, the state as a result of collaboration with the PKK, in fact extended protection to some villages.

As a result of the Turkish government's violent policy of collaboration they became dependent upon imperialist states and the USA in particular. The USA is trying to direct Turkey towards the south via policies that she has pursued since the Gulf War, and has gone a long way in this endeavour. Besides the conscious imposition of the burdens of Kurdish migration upon Turkey, the PKK is seen as a factor which is forcing the Turkish government towards intervention beyond the southern borders. Imperialism has helped mould Turkey's recognition of a small Kurdish state with the ultimate idea of getting rid of the PKK. Therefore, Turkey's policy of violence has a dimension to it which may lead it to becoming a gendarme of the USA in the Middle East, and to the wars with neighbours. By not solving the Kurdish question in a peaceful way through liberty and equality, political authority forces Turkey to accept the USA's Kurdish scenario. Thus, the Kurdish question becomes internationalized and more open to interventions from imperialism, via the policies of the state on the one hand, and of the PKK on the other.

The reform side of the state's 'Oppress-Dissolve' policy arises from two necessities. One is the need to re-integrate Kurdish people who have been living under the threat of terrorism for many years into the system, and the second is, pressure from the West.

The USA wants reforms to realize its plan of 'Kurdistan under the patronage of Turkey'. However, this solution will not bring about peace and a 'humane' life, as is claimed by certain 'human rights' organizations in the West. On the contrary, the countries and people of the Middle East will be pushed into endless hostilities and wars with each other. Civil wars in oppressed countries, as seen in Somalia, Yugoslavia, Caucasia and Rwanda, are reasons for interference by the imperialists — in the name of 'human rights and peace'.

Today, it can be observed, that the state has begun to supplement their military methods with reforms. Hence in the Kurdish provinces, the religious forces,as well as the reformist and pro-Western wings of Kurdish nationalism, are being supported.

Since the election in October 1991, subsequent developments reveal that the PKK after the Gulf War took up a new orientation. During this period, the project of building a 'Common House' by uniting with working people in Turkey was replaced by attempts to seek the support of the West via closer alliances with some other states in the region.

The Kurdish movement has two models for the future: The Northern Iraq model; to build a Kurdish state via collaboration with the imperialists. The second is the people's model: The unity of the labour classes against imperialism and the ruling classes.

Any real change in Turkey depends on a common front between the labour movement and the Kurdish equality movement. This is an arithmetical necessity. Isolation between these two movements would preclude the possibility of revolution. Therefore, labouring classes and people demanding equality are dependent on one another. Internationalism is a *must* for the revolution of Turkey.

The PKK, because of its ties with the states within region, has primarily lost its ability to pursue independent policies. Following this and in order to solve the troubles imposed by the war that it had intensified, it sought support from the West. Imperialist countries, while supporting Turkish state violence, carried out the Westernization operation of the PKK and gained remarkable success. Today, the PKK leadership is looking for a role in the 'New World Order' and develops its policies with this in mind. This policy of relying on the large states of the West goes alongside religionism.

Following this, the PKK launched operations to attack the innocent and ordinary Turkish people, such as bombing the supermarkets (in Bakirköy) and the massacre of Turkish peasants (Basbaglar village). This line of action shows that the perspective of a common revolution and of a struggle along with the working class has been abandoned. This has triggered a serious reaction from the people in Turkey and provoked the national hostility and violence.

It is clear that the PKK-leadership was aware of the possible consequences of this line of action. Because it sees the way forward as being national hostility and enlisting the help of the West. It is clear that the models applied to Bosnia-Herzegovina and Northern Iraq have been adopted.

This line of action is not only the result of a political mistake. In essence, it is based on the 'Theory of Colony'. Declaring the countries and the nations of the oppressed world such as Turkey, Iraq, Iran and Syria as 'colonialist', is a theory produced by imperialism itself. In the strategy arising from this theory, where the chief enemies are Turkey, Iraq, Iran and Syria, inevitably the imperialists become the allies. The strategy repeated in Northern Iraq for 30 years, has clearly demonstrated how 'Colony Theory' has been in the service of imperialism. Proponents of this theory, however, explicitly state that the genuine allies of the Kurds are USA and Israel.

A CIA official recently announced on CNN that 'all agents' were concentrating on the southeast of Turkey and this is because the Kurdish issue has become one of worldwide interest and competition. Their analysis also indicates that Turkey is moving towards chaos. This is correct.

We believe that Turkey is moving towards a state of chaos, meaning internal conflicts, a subsequent Turkish-Iranian war, and wars in the Middle East. Former Chief of Staff of the Turkish Army, General Güres, announced that Turkey would take up the mission of intervening in crisis areas. This means that Turkey will become a subcontractor of the United States and will intervene in major clashes.

Bringing the Experience of Turkey's War of Independence onto the Public Agenda

A solution has become a 'must' in this case. What we are doing is bringing the experience of the War of Independence onto the public agenda. The War of Independence was Turkey's resistance during such a globalization. Today Turkey has entered a process of colonialization as was the case in 1919. That is Turkey is becoming a colony. This process operates by way of ethnic divisions and sectarian clashes. In the War of Independence the solution came when Atatürk landed at the town of Samsun. Of course the determination existed to struggle against imperialism. He began his efforts with an arithmetical calculation. He could not wage his struggle without unifying the Turks and Kurds. In his telegrams to Tayyar Bey and Kazim Karabekir Pasha, he always focused on the issue of unifying Turks and Kurds. Subsequently there is the Amasya Protocol, which is considered as the first constitutional document where Turkey is noted as a country of Turks and Kurds — Turkey's first official description of itself was as a country of Turks and Kurds. This formulation was also agreed on at the Erzurum and Sivas Congresses.

Kurdish national and political rights were guaranteed in the declarations released at the end of the congresses. Racial, social and geographical rights regarding Kurdish environmental rights were also guaranteed. This is also very important. Later in Lausanne, in 1923, Ismet Pasha described the parliament as being 'a parliament of Turks and Kurds', and the government as being a 'government of Turks and Kurds'. The Sivas and Erzurum congresses and the Amasya Protocol are documents of constitutional value.

We (The Workers Party) have been trying to persuade society to accept it. This problem can no longer be solved from within the Kurdish provinces (in Sirnak or Van for example) but has to be solved from Istanbul, Zonguldak or Ankara. In other words, solving this matter is not possible before the Turkish people are in a democratic and free position. We should convince the Turkish people about the solution to the Kurdish matter. This is why we have brought to light various documents (by thoroughly scanning the archives) and have put them before the people.

The solution used during the War of Independence should be adapted again to unify Turks and Kurds. Of course this will require amendments to the Constitution, as well requiring some non-constitutional measures. That is to say, we have an 'historical experience'. If we're able to put up a resistance against imperialism by regarding Kurds as free and equal, there is the possibility of a solution. In this respect, our efforts are based on *convincing* the Turkish people, as well as all the powers who play a determining role in Turkey's future. Sooner or later this solution will come onto the agenda.

Foreign intervention, by Russia, the United States or Germany will definitely cause this problem to accelerate. The process of globalization is being introduced throughout the world with ethnic clashes and religious sectarian conflicts. As the American ideologist Samuel P. Huntington formulated it: 'The age of ideological border wars is over. The age of ethnic and national wars has begun'. This is not only a sociological assessment. They want this to happen like this. They are causing the oppressed world to crumble. In the end, the New World Order will come to exist with the crumbling of this oppressed world.

Turkey should try to solve the problem with the Kurdish organizations in Iran, Iraq, Syria and in the Middle East by excluding the big imperialist countries. Turkey, Syria, Iran and Iraq are oppressed countries. Kurds are an oppressed people. They should exclude Russia, the United States and Germany and give up their narrow concept of nationalism and seek a solution together. Within this context, we favour Turkey's cooperation with its neighbouring states and the Kurds, and powers such as the United States or Russia should stop intervening in this matter.

Today the key to solving the Kurdish question is within the labour movement. Most notably, developing the labour movement can create hope among the Kurdish masses and can turn their orientation once again towards the common struggle and to building a 'Common House'. The working-class of Turkey can pave the way by carrying the qualities of friendship, national equality and freedom which it contains, and making them effective in the policies of the country.

To summarize: The Kurdish question is not a 'colonial' one, but rather one of national equality and liberty with regard to the 'oppressed world'. At the centre of the question, lies imperialism and feudalism. The Kurdish question cannot be solved in collaboration with imperialism. Besides this, policies strengthening the medievalist relations and religionism will only reinforce the social structure which nourishes the problem.

Therefore, for the first, any solution to the Kurdish question necessitates a determined struggle against imperialism. The chief enemy is imperialism.

Secondly, every national question is in essence, a peasant question; and requires a struggle for freeing peasants from every form of medieval ties.

The Workers Party is convinced of the fact that the Kurdish question can be completely solved by establishing a Labour Republic consisting of our people of different nationalities,together with equality, friendship and voluntary union. On the political scene any increase in the weight brought to bear by the working class, together with the Kurdish people, will bring remarkable gains and will foster the revolutionary solution to the question.

The Separation of the Kurdish People and Their National Struggle

Mehmet Bedri Gültekin

It is important that we examine the shape of the Kurdish national struggle in relation to it being quite distinct from other regional struggles. The chances of its success must be seen in the light of what has happened before. A broad examination of the Kurdish national struggle highlights two mutually opposing elements.

The first element is the fact that the Kurds live in a period of 'late nation forming'. It was in the nineteenth century that the region first experienced the effects of capitalist development and it was also when the people of the region embarked on the process of national forming. It was a great misfortune for the Kurds, while not having an independent political existence, to enter into the nation forming process later than their neighbours. Thus, right from the start, Kurdish national demands have been faced with the difficult obstacle of having neighbours who were already established as independent countries. The regional regressive reactionary force that obstructs the national desires of Kurds entered into a pact with imperialism in order to maintain the status quo. In this way, the obstacles ahead of the Kurdish national struggle grew. As a result, as we approach the end of the 20th century, and the question of the national struggle is in most cases a problem consigned to past history, the Kurds have yet to attain their basic fundamental rights.

The immediate result of this situation is that national feelings among the Kurds are very strong. The feeling of having waited too long is one that could eventually be described as a national characteristic. In turn, however, it provides the basis of the strength upon which an independent national struggle will stand.

This fact is an objective one, the impact of which can also be seen in the way the Kurds have drawn the interest of international world opinion. As an unavoidable result of the intensive national oppression, Kurds have begun to grasp their national values more firmly. At the same time, this fact does enable the Kurdish national struggle to move in its own way, quite differently from the struggles of other peoples.

The second element is the result of the agonizing role of the 'being too late' effect. Whenever national problems appear in the world of today, it is a matter of concern. The most crucial factor to be drawn from this is a rapid 'internationalization'.

Today, only minor 'national' matters remain. There is a material base for handling and solving the common international problems, but the opportunities cannot be compared with those which existed in the past. It is 127 years since the event of the First Internationale. Today, the conditions required in order to achieve an organization of nations working together for a fraternal world cannot be compared with those in the world of the 1860s.

In most regions of the world, national problems are slowly becoming a thing of the past, and yet across most of the world, national problems have not been solved. It therefore becomes increasingly necessary to handle and solve in a perspective that exceeds national borders. As capitalism has made such problems international, it has also made their solutions international. The enormity of problems facing humanity, makes insufficient the idea of a solution which is limited to national boundaries. Today there exists a base for handling the Kurdish national problem with a perspective that exceeds the Kurdish national boundaries.

Kurds are now becoming much more a part of the Middle East at large. Both of these factors influence the Kurdish national struggle today. Both of them are a part of Kurdish reality. The factor of 'being too late' gives rise to the feeling that the Kurds are enclosed in their narrow national path. On the other hand, the 'to be international' factor directs this oppressed nation to the struggle of establishing a new world along with its neighbours.

Lesson from The Kurdish Democratic Party (PDK) Experience

How does being divided between four countries affect the national struggle today? For years, almost all the Kurdish organizations have proclaimed that it was simply a matter of the Kurds organizing themselves and their struggle in a different manner from other people in the region. Their argument was — 'If unity is to be established in any one of the countries as an outcome of the struggle by the people living in that country, this will naturally produce an alienation to the struggles of Kurds living in the other countries. In other words, this will mean accepting the division forced on the Kurds by imperialist and master countries in the region'.

Is the situation actually like this? Does division really mean that there are separate organizations within the struggle? Looking at the practices of the Kurdish Democratic Party, which is the main vehicle of Kurdish nationalism, and whose aim in the short term is for an independent and united Kurdish nation, may give us some idea about this. The Kurdistan Democratic Party is organized in all four parts of Kurdistan. It exists in Iran and in Iraq as a serious power, and exists as an organization in Turkey and Syria. Practicalities forced it to organize itself differently in each place, despite similarities in their programmes in the four countries. However, at times their interests clashed with one another; such as in Iran and Iraq.

Why does this happen? Because the struggle is aimed at the administrations of those countries rather than against an abstract target. In this situation, all other regional powers which exist outside the administration of that country become potential allies or else remain neutral. Therefore, for any Kurdish Party in any of the four countries, the enemies, allies, and neutral powers are constantly changing. A country which is an enemy to one of them can be an ally to another.

What has Iraqi PDK achieved so far? It has struggled against the government in Baghdad. At the same time it has maintained a traditional alliance with Iran. This alliance expanded somewhat during the 1970s. Iraq PDK has maintained cautious relations with Turkey, and has tried not to harm Turkey in its struggle against Iraq. Its relationship with Syria is similar.

Let's review the situation of Iranian PDK which is not greatly different from that in Iraq. In Iran, the PDK has been fighting against the government for several years. The Iraqi government has been the greatest ally of the PDK in Iran, which the Iraqi PDK has been fighting during this war. The attitude of the Iranian PDK towards Turkey is no different from the Iraqi PDK. It has tried to maintain the best relations possible.

Turkey PDK's situation was a little different. The Turkish PDK has submitted itself to the Iraqi PDK in the interests of the struggle being carried out in that part of Kurdistan. This is quite a comprehensible approach since its aim is to help the struggle in the region which has the best chance of succeeding. But the inevitable outcome of this policy has been to oversee the problems of the Kurds living on the borders of Turkey and as a result it remains passive towards them. Therefore the engagement of the Turkish PDK has not been so wide. In 1970, the organization risked struggling for Turkish Kurds as a means to gain power, and as a result of this the Turkish PDK lost the limited impact which it once had.

What can we learn from the experience of the PDK? Has the separation of the regional struggles attained the unity of Kurds divided between four countries? The answer is no. Even if it had been argued that each Kurdish organization in the four parts achieved what it wanted, the fact is that they might have attained more had they coordinated their efforts in respect to one another and the regional governments. Therefore, those who claim that this separation is the result of the different struggles, have not, in practice, progressed to being able to overcome the negative conditions in which Kurds exist.

Can we explain this situation on the basis of the PDK organization depending on Kurdish aristocratic or nationalist ideology? It is obvious that this explanation is not sufficient. On the contrary, here nationalism can only take the positive role of unifying the Kurds living differently in the four parts. But this positive role has remained limited due to the necessity of the struggle, and ultimately has not been successful.

Possible Allies

If we accept that the Kurdish traditional nationalist organizations are like this; does the practice of the PKK (The Kurdish Worker's Party) produce any different results? The PKK also defines its aim as being an independent and united Kurdistan. Let us look at the situation in practice. Taking the struggle in Turkey first: Being in alliance with Iran and Syria means that the struggle here will be based on the demands of the struggle taking place in Turkey. Because of the special status of Iraq there is no alliance, but the location is being used a base for the struggle taking place in Turkey.

In other words, in Turkey the struggle is being aimed at furthering the struggle taking place in Kurdistan. Why? Because this is a necessity. One cannot fight on four fronts simultaneously. There are no prior examples to support this anywhere in the world. Every struggle has to be carried out with a solid wall behind it.

Every struggle demands friends and allies. This is a general fact. This is valid from the stand point of administrations who are the target of the struggle, as well as the Kurdish national powers. The Kurds need friends and allies in their struggle for their national rights. These friends and allies may be sought at two different levels. Firstly, the people, workers and revolutionaries in the regions inhabited by the Kurds. Secondly, among the neighbouring states in the region. The traditional nationalist line represented by the PDK has sought alliances and friendships among the states of the region. As a result of this, over the past 50 years while the Kurds in Bahdinan and in Mahabat were coming under pressure, no support was forthcoming from the workers and people of Baghdad and Tehran. Naturally, we are looking at the matter from the standpoint of the Kurds. The responsibility of the Arabs, and the Persians in the application of national torture on the Kurds, regardless of the mistakes by the Kurdish organization, is a major responsibility which needs to be amplified. This is the main reason why the struggle for unity among the people of these countries has to be realized.

Despite all the shortcomings, the PKK has — until the Gulf War, displayed a different practice along non-traditional nationalistic lines. As a result the 'poor villages' movement in Botan has been echoed in Istanbul, Zonguldak and Ankara. The movement has been able to explain itself at Babiali (The Press centre in Istanbul). Such a situation shows us a way in which we can resolve the matter. Anyone wishing to suppress Botan, is forced to suppress both Istanbul and Zonguldak. The mutual support (solidarity) in the struggle has created a 'joint' destiny. This is of course an element which has a strong effect in the process of entering a new and different trend after the Gulf War. Up until this time, the PKK talked about establishing a 'Common Home' with the workers of Turkey and acting according to this idea. Now, however, they are trying to establish an 'alliance' with the workers in the region. To find a place for the Western Imperialists in the scenario, is now the main strategy for the PKK.

Today, the PKK has established itself in a position superior to the PDK model. The PDK with the support of the regional forces and Western forces has gained some 'success' in Iraqi Kurdistan. This has become a consideration for the PKK following the Gulf War.

In the struggle, one vital aspect of furthering Kurdish aims is finding allies among other nations. Naturally, throughout the struggle the contradictions between the regional reactionists can also be of some benefit. How to benefit from such conditions may be identified as much as the political conditions allow. But the important thing is to look in the right places when looking for allies; looking for allies among the regional governments is a dead-end task. Over the last eighty years the struggle as propagated by the PDK is a prime example of this. Those reactionary regional powers who confiscated the national rights of the Kurds in the region also gained some advantage from the fighting between the Kurdish factions. The pattern so far has thus been: whenever the Kurdish struggle reaches the point where there is light on the horizon, those powers who have done their best to undermine the Kurds in the region begin to relent in their suppression of the Kurdish movement. Over the past twenty years, there have been two important examples of the neutrality of Iran and Iraq during the 8 year war. In 1988, efforts were made to suppress Barzani's movement in Kurdistan in Northern Iraq following the 1975 Algerian Pact.

The only way to break down the efforts of the regional state creating a chaos among the Kurds, and overcoming the eventuality of Kurds being used against one another, is the realization of unity between the Kurdish struggle and the struggle of other people. Against all fronts of suppression, the best approach is the 'people's front'. The only context in which this would be possible is an anti-imperialist one: The divisions necessitate a *Joint Struggle* instead of a *Separate Struggle*.

What are the chances of the separate Kurdish regions achieving success alone?

When an agreement is reached among the Kurdish organizations, when the different powers are united, and when the struggle is directed into one single area, then the chances of success may be considered realistic. But this requires a joint Kurdish organization whose authority is accepted throughout the whole region. In addition, the organization in question should be able to sustain the Kurds who remain a little outside the region; this has been a long awaited and rather difficult matter. So far efforts in this area cannot be called successful.

Kurds live as separate entities under different socio-economic and political conditions. These conditions influence attitudes substantially. The development of capitalism, and differences arising as a result of this development, impose varying conditions on Kurds depending on where they live. Because the development of the four nations is at a different level, it is necessary for this matter to be addressed. It is also clear that differences brought on by variable degrees of political unity produce dissimilarities which in turn lead to different practices by the Kurds in each of these countries. This matter should be viewed as a independent objective, despite claims to the contrary. If the Kurds had lived within the boundaries of one single nation, the chances of success in organization and struggle would, without doubt, have been far greater. Why have the Kurds not achieved national unity up until now? Why have they not acquired their national rights - even on a small scale? All answers to such questions lie in the roots of the negative feelings that are created. Because throughout their history any struggle for national rights has faced more than one enemy, and because of the aristocratic-nationalistic leadership, the regional people were not united. Traditional nationalistic lines could not be applied. One could not expect the creation of a 'peoples front' against the 'conservative front' with this approach.

Kurdish national history clearly shows the necessity of a joint struggle by a divided nation. The concept of a divided nation brought about the separatist organization efforts, and the feeling of being a divided nation which necessitates struggle, knocks down their thesis.

The revolutionary perspective that the Kurds in their struggle unite with the people with whom they share a country, does not necessitate the alienation of the problems of Kurds living in other countries. On the contrary, the Kurds in their present situation may become a 'revolutionary cornerstone'. Kurds, with their revolutionary potential and physical location are capable of playing this historical role.

Today, the Kurdish problem is internationalized. Now each Western imperialist power has a Kurdish plan, and in their strategies towards the Middle East, the Kurds occupy an important place. It is necessary to indicate that this situation for both the region states and people is a major handicap. The New World Order proposes peace in the North and conflict and division in the South. The Kurds and the suppressed peoples of the region become the main subject of these conflicts and division.

This situation, instead of being resolved, is creating more chaos and adding to the problems. From the Kurdish standpoint, the toll is growing.

The only way to solve this problem is to disqualify the violent intervention of the imperialist powers. The governments of the region (Turkey, Iran, Iraq, Syria), cannot resolve it by suppressing the national movement. The reality is quite clear. The governments of the region and the Kurdish organizations should endeavour, through peace talks, to resolve the problem. This is the only way a solution can be brought about.

The Perspectives of the Kurdish Movement in Light of the Oil Strategies of the 21st Century

Orhan Kotan

Introduction

The messenger of doom began its journey when Germany turned its eye to the east. Kaiser Wilhelm set his eye on areas that were of interest to the Russians and British. He planned to connect his country to the rich fields of India and to enrich the British colonies with a railway project linking Berlin and Baghdad. The Ottoman Pashas dreamed of invading what they called 'Big Turan' country. This would extend German imperialism into the Caucasus, Central Asia and to the regions in the Russian sphere.

The hostilities in Serbia detonated the world. Bolsheviks from Germany gained control of the Kremlin. Tzarist Russia became a thing of the past.

The Ottoman pashas of the Committee of Union and Progress left the corpses of over 90,000 soldiers frozen under the gates to the Caucasus, the Alluhuekber mountains.

The Ottoman Empire was laid to rest. Germany was defeated. The Caucasus and Central Asia remained part of Russia while the rich oil fields of the Middle East remained in British hands. With the large oil reserves in the Hazar Sea out of the world's reach, the Middle East became the world's energy store in the 20th century.

The British Influence

The borders were drawn according to British interests, marked by the opening of an East India Company office in Baghdad (1806). All of the smaller countries, on what was the former Ottoman Empire, were reshaped according to British interests. The provinces of Basra and Baghdad were united under the British mandate to form Iraq. As a result of this the Republic of Turkey which emerged from the ruins of the Ottoman Empire was cut off from the oil reserves in the Middle East. This division was approved by world powers at Lausanne. At that time Kurdistan was divided into four parts in Turkey, Iran, Iraq and Syria respectively.

This structure defined the fate of the Kurds for the rest of the 20th century. The fate of Kurdish society was thus defined by oil. For the Kurds, this century has been a time of wars, massacres, migration and finally genocide by chemical weapons.

The Turkish Influence

This division is now — on the verge of the 21st century, once again receiving attention. The Berlin Wall and the Eastern blok countries collapsed one by one. The mighty Soviet Empire also collapsed. Thus in the Caucasus and the Middle East, independent states emerged with presidents who never seem to move from their chairs.

In the vacuum left by the collapse of the Soviet pole, Iraq invaded Kuwait, paving the way for the USA to enter the region with its own agenda. The Gulf War was a turning point which altered the sensitive equilibrium of the region. The Kurds were also affected and the political perspectives of the Kurdish movement gained a new shape and new content.

Into the vacuum caused by the Gulf War came the Kurdish uprising in Ranya, near the Iranian border (March 14th, 1991). *The Peshmerga* began to enter cities such as Süleymaniye, Erbil and Dohuk. Kerkuk fell after four days of fighting. On the 16th of March the world media entered Kurdistan. On March 18th, the Baghdad regime drove the Republican Guard into Kurdistan which was then saved only by intervention at the last minute by George Bush. On March 29th, the large cities ran out of oil. On April 30th, Iraqi helicopters were seen on the horizon. Thousands of people, fleeing from chemical weapons, began their journey to the Turkish and Iranian borders. The world observed these events via the media and the issue of the 36th parallel came on the agenda immediately afterwards.

The Kurdish Federal State thus emerged above the 36th parallel under the protection of the Rapid Reaction Force based in Diyarbakir. This resulted in the Kurdish problem becoming one of the most important topics on the world agenda. The geography of Kurdistan, which extends westwards into the Caucasus and Central Asia is a crucial element in the negotiations between Western Europe, the United States and Russia.

Turkey plays a very important strategic role in this. Turkey refused to address the matter of the Kurds, regarding it as an 'internal' affair.

With a Kurdish Federal State to the south and with the Caucasus and Central Asia in the North, the issue had begun to take on the proportions of a major regional, and also global, problem.

Turkey, took up a very narrow position — seeking to solve the Kurdish problem by military means alone. However, the Kurdish problem was in fact a sociological-historical problem and impossible to solve by oppression and assimilation.

The chronometer of history was ticking faster than it was thought possible. The Turkish Republic's official state ideology (which had begun to be written by the 'Takrir-i Sükun Law'), was based on the refusal to accept Kurdish existence. Official ideology in Turkey saw all its citizens as being Turkish; 'Everybody was happy because they were Turks'; 'The Kurds were Mountain Turks'; Kurdish, was a dialect of the Turkish language. Thousands of people, however, who fled the chemical attacks, both before and after the Gulf War, defied the official ideology of the Turkish state. There was an understanding between people on either side of Turkey's southern border as there was significant contact in terms of aquaintances and family relations. Turkish state officials on the other hand visiting the region recently had to use translators.

Kurdish leaders, considered as 'separatist rebels' by the Baghdad regime, held face-to-face discussions with the President at Cankaya. As a result of this the Kurdistan Democratic Party (KDP) and the Kurdistan Patriotic Union (KPU) were authorized to open bureaus in Ankara. There was now nothing to prevent Kurdish leaders travelling from Silopi to Diyarbakir (Iraq to Turkey) or even to Ankara. Kurds from other countries travelled easily into the Kurdish Federal State via Turkey. These things were a real shock to Turkish officials and prompted them to covertly change their ideology. The pronouncement that 'There are no Kurds. Everyone is Turkish and happy' changed into 'Kurds and Turks are brothers — to be Kurdish is no different, therefore Kurds are considered as first-class citizens of Turkey on equal footing with others.'

In the tumultuous period following the collapse of the Soviet Union, the concept of 'Big Turan Country' was an ideological shield for German imperialism. This gave rise to the slogan; 'A Turkish world from the Adriatic to the Great Wall of China'. This was quite worrying for Russia, Iran and, for other reasons, Western Europe and the United States.

The Trans-Caucasian Perspective

The war between Azerbaijan and Armenia began during this period. This was the first warning which Russia had of any ideas of enterprise in the Baku oil fields which had been inaccessible to world markets since 1917.

Georgia wanted an independent foreign policy but was warned off by the uprising in Abkhazia. Meanwhile, Ebulfeyz Elcibey, the president of Azerbaijan and an ally of Turkey was toppled by a small uprising, and Haydar Aliyev, an experienced politician (a politburo member in the former Soviet Union) became President.

Russia gave its first serious signal to Turkey; indicating the strategic importance of oil, Russia's ambassador declared that 'We will never hand over the oil fields to Turkey'.

The Grey Wolf

Turkey is well known for its political problems. Internal problems have always taken dominance over international matters. Following the collapse of the USSR, demands for a 'Turkish World' reached such proportions that an official assembly was convened in the tourist city of Antalya. Here a number of politicians and statesmen made fervent statements about 'hammering the anvil beneath the grey wolf's head, (a wolf that led the Turks across mountains to the open world)'. The head of the grey wolf was the symbol of the National Movement Party which made no attempt to disguise its racist and chauvinist intentions.

However, the world's attention was on quite a different matter!

The Oil Question

The world was busy trying to divide the Caucasus and Central Asia between them following the collapse of the USSR. This was a market of 170 million people with untapped underground and surface resources. Kazakhstan for example, whose borders extend from the Caspian Sea to the Chinese border with a surface area of 2 million square kilometers, has sufficient resources to supply all of Europe. Kazakhstan was formerly the centre of the Soviet nuclear programme. In 1991 it produced 140 million tons of coal, 110 billion kilowatts-hour of electricity, 8 million tons of iron and steel, 350 million tons of phosporous and 25 millon tons of grain. Kazakhstan's oil fields were as rich as those of Saudi Arabia.

The two World Wars marked the first divisions of these regions. Firstly the Ottoman Empire and Tsarist Russia were dissolved. The second division resulted in the Soviet Union being extended eastwards to include the area from the Baltic to the Black Sea.

A third 're-division' was on the agenda. This war was characterized by strategic equilibrium calculations and bloody internal struggles. The main focus of this division was once again oil. Oil being not only a resource but also a strategic factor capable of destroying all previous stability.

After the Gulf War, Iraq was isolated from the world oil market, particularly at the time when Kuwait and Saudi Arabia had to pay back their debts with their oil incomes. According to some predictions Kuwait and Saudi Arabia's foreign debts were around 50 billion US dollars. The sensitive nature of the international oil market was the main reason for the embargo being imposed on Iraq.

The market was threatened by the flow of oil which was to come from the Caspian and Tenghiz oil fields. While Turkey was concerned with its own agenda, the powerful industrial nations were busy discussing the implications of this new oil. The Kurdish problem was once again on the world agenda at this point. All the strategic lines drawn from east to west and north to south were centred on Kurdistan geography and stretched as far as the Mediterranean Sea. The oil pipeline which would connect Baku to Ceyhan, had to pass through the region of Kurdistan. In short, the most important connection linking Western Europe and the United States to the Middle East, the Near East and the Far East was Kurdistan. However, this region was overwhelmed by bloodshed and death. Armenia, the door to Central Asia, was to the north. Iran and Georgia had to be crossed to reach Azerbaijan. There was a deep seated conflict between Armenia and Turkey, dating from the beginning of the century. The Turkish-Armenian border was closed. The war between Armenia and Azerbaijan was central to the Kurdish problem.

To summarize, the sharing of Caucasus and Central Asian markets on the basis of oil was of urgent concern to the Gulf nations which depend on oil; to Iran which has access to the Indian Ocean and the Persian Gulf; to Russia which has claims on the former Soviet regions; to Armenia hoping to gain access to the world; to the Kurds who were fighting for their basic rights and freedom in a series of uprisings; and to Turkey — both geo-politically and historically.

After the first division of Azeri oil resources, the first emergency signs began to emerge. Azerbaijan became a 'country of coups'. Russia was not pleased with the 10 percent share it was given. Iran on the other hand received a 5 percent share and the United States was concerned about this. Turkey only received 1.75 percent.

Turkey, Iran and Russia each had a plan for how the oil would be transported to the Western markets. Thus, Caspian oil would:

a) be carried via Novo-russian harbours to the world market.

b) would flow via Iran and the Persian Gulf to the Indian Ocean.

c) would be transferred to the Mediterranean Sea via the Baku-Ceyhan pipe-line.

Iran opened an 800 kilometre railway connecting the Caspian Sea to the Persian Gulf. Russia, wanting full control of the planned route, invaded Cechnya to gain control of the oil refineries there. In contrast to Russian official statements, the Russian army came up against stiff resistance. This invasion brought things to the boiling point. Shortly afterwards, the United States brought the proposal for the Baku-Ceyhan Pipeline Project to Turkey. It happened so quickly that the U.S Ambassador in Ankara had announced it to the press on the basis of a simple fax message only.

The United States' Baku-Ceyhan project was welcomed in Turkey. This project, however, included 3 main requirements:

a) Turkey and Armenia had to be reconciled, the border reopened and the Azeri-Armenian war had to end.
b) Turkey had to solve the Kurdish problem since the proposed oil pipeline could not pass through a war zone.
c) An acceptable solution had to be reached over the Cyprus problem, which had persisted for 30 years.

Of course, the Cyprus problem was not directly related to the sharing of the Caucasus and Central Asia, but because this problem had remained in deadlock for 30 years, it was the main source of the Turkish-Greek conflict. In addition, while Turkey was taking steps to prevent the transport of oil via the Bosphorus (the Montreux Accord), Greece provided an alternative for the Russians. This would be a route which crossed Bulgaria to Greece, thus bypassing the Baku-Ceyhan project. The majority of Russia's oil tankers were Greek.

During the time in which the Baku-Ceyhan project was being debated, a delegation, which included the President of the Greek Parliament, visited the PKK President Abdullah Öcalan. During the meeting a photograph, later printed in the world media, was circulated. It showed a map without borders, with pipelines drawn on it. The names of cities and countries were in Greek. Russia also indicated its involvement in the Kurdish problem by helping the PKK to open a 'Kurdish House' in Moscow. The Baku-Ceyhan project proposed to Turkey was thus a composite of the region's strategic situation.

Kurds in a Global Perspective

Generally speaking, in light of the above, it is clear that good relations between states are a diplomatic gesture with no substance. It is the interests of the states which are the deciding factor. It is in Russia's interests to maintain the fighting in Kurdistan. Azerbaijan became the scene of coups, assassinations and sabotages, leading to the chaos in Georgia. Russia's interests come first. Russia is still capable of doing anything in the Caucasus and Central Asia; an area which it sees as part of its interior. The Russian soldier wants to wash his heavy army boots in the Indian Ocean. Moscow is determined to be the sole ruler of Caspian oil, which implies an interest in remaining a dominant power in the next century. Indeed, the oil route is so significant that Russia is quite open in its support of the PKK — the most senssitive aspect as far as Turkey is concerned. The opening of the 'Kurdish House' in Moscow occurred almost at the same time as the occupation of Chechnya. Turkey reacted immediately; the Minister of the Interior flew to Moscow and purchased 18 helicopters. This was characteristic of the Turkish administration: Instead of addressing the problem at hand they sought to bribe any state with an interest in the matter.

A White House spokesman gave a stern warning to Russia with regard to support for the PKK whom they described as a 'wild terrorist organization and drug dealer'.

Thus the PKK has become a tool in the hands of both Russia and the United States. The real problem is the political outcome of this struggle beetween the USA and Russia. Russia has no solution to the Kurdish problem. Russia is only trying to provoke matters. Chaos in the Kurdistan region ensures that Turkey is not included in the oil route. In one sense this means that the Kurdish problem will persist since oil is both the key and the fuse.

The United States uses the PKK to threaten Turkey, while retaining a package solution to the problem. The PKK is one of the most important 'trump cards' which the United States holds with regard to Turkey. The Dublin Meetings clearly showed this. The alliance between the PKK and Talabani is also a sign. This also explains why the PKK have marched on the KDP. It is also the reason why the United States gives clear support to the 'democratic solution' proposed by Western Europe and the Scandinavian countries. It is why the USA is lobbying for Turkey in Europe, and this in turn explains the popularity of Tansu Ciller in the United States, since she approves of these policies.

However, as pointed out above, countries like Russia, Greece and Iran are producing enough 'material' to sustain these authorities. This has provoked a wave of nationalist anti-Kurdish feeling in the country; the signs of which are visible on the street and in the media: top models sing the national anthem, TV announcers act as agitators of official ideology; people are urged to sing the national anthem at football matches. Slogans such as, 'Martyrs don't die', 'God damn PKK', 'Turkey is Turkish - and will stay Turkish' are now seen. The Turkish bourgeoise, concerned about the the 'whole' market, speak up in protest. The business community has proposed various solutions to the

Kurdish problem and (Türkiye Odalar ve Borsalar Birligi) is working out reports on the issue.

These facts indicate the contradicitions between the policies of the United States and Western Europe. These will last into the 21st century and affect the Kurdish policy of the Turkish state. For this reason, and on the basis of the Baku-Ceyhan Project, the Kurdish problem is included as part of a possible solution package for the region. In writing to President Clinton, the PKK president makes it clear that the PKK wants to be recognised as a 'party' and wants political representation. The United States is recommending an acceptable solution to Turkey through negotiations with the Kurdish legal representatives. And the PKK President needs help from the United States to reach a peaceful solution in Turkey. In describing the PKK as a 'terrorist organization and a drug dealer', the United States is making it plain that they do not see the PKK as any part of a politicial solution. The position of the Kurdish Parliament in Exile is dictated as a result of concern over this.

What of future prospects? It is difficult to predict what will happen, but the pattern which seems to be emerging indicates that there is no place for the PKK in the solution package put forward by the United States for the Kurdish problem. The Moscow meeting was only an opportunity for the White House to put forward its firm position. Involvement by the United States in developments in the Caucasus and Central Asia did not immediately follow the collapse of the USSR but only after the occupation of Cechnya.

After the Baku-Ceyhan project, the US embargo on Iran came onto the agenda. Iran has important claims on the oil route. The American embargo was intended to exclude Iran. The 5 percent share of Azeri oil given to Iran was taken back. From the American point of view, the Baku-Ceyhan route was not the only possible route. Oil resources with the potential to turn the world upside down could not be handed over to one state alone. It was also impossible to keep Russia out of this issue. If the Baku oil fields proved feasible, a single route from the Kazahkstan oil fields would be impossible. The geography of Kazahkstan and its relations with Russia dictated this. It is well known that Russia, not pleased with its 10 percent share (of Azeri oil), turned Kazakhstan into a country of coups and assassins. Some 32 percent of Kazakhstan's population was Russian. As insurance against Russia's planned oil route, the United States introduced the Baku-Ceyhan Project onto the agenda without Turkish assistance.

The collapse of the USSR provided Turkey with a perfect opportunity with respect to the geo-political position it had occupied over the last hundred years or so; the untouched markets of the Caucasus and Central Asia would thus open to the world. The world would have access to this huge market of 170 million people via Turkey.

But neither Turkey's technology, economic power nor its structural characteristics were able to use this dynamic. Turkish policy is in fact still frozen in dead slogans such as: 'A Turkish world from the Adriatic to the Great Wall of China!'

For Baku oil to reach the Mediterranean it must pass through Armenia. This would require an end to the Azeri-Armenian conflict and the Turkish-Armenian vendetta. While on a trip to the United States, Tansu Ciller opened an air corridor to Armenia. This prompted fears of genocide in Armenia.

Secondly, the oil route needs to pass through Kurdish territory. Here a war is raging, albeit unrecognised by the Turkish state. The de-facto Kurdish Federal State was a reality in northern Iraq. An oil pipeline connecting Kerkuk to Yumurtalik would pass though this region.

What was required was that Turkey recognize the political status of the Kurdish Federal State which would then be approved in turn by the United States and Western Europe. This would give Turkey a new form at the start of the 21st century. As neighbours, Turkey would have Armenia to the north, and the Kurdish Federal State to the south.

The Dublin conference focussed on the matter of examining possible solutions to the Kurdish problem in light of this situation.

Kurds in a Regional Perspective

Iran's exclusion from the proposed oil route with the Baku-Ceyhan project on the agenda made clear the need for a political framework for any acceptable solution to the Kurdish problem. Around the table were the United States, the Kurdish Federal State, and Turkey as an observer.

The conflict within the Federal state between the KDP and the KPU once again surfaced. Syria and Iran attacked the KDP and the KPU and gave their clear support to PKK. Immediately after the conference, the offical Turkish representative, Mumtaz Soysal, flew to Baghdad. Baghdad promised a collective military operation against the PKK. Baghdad asked Turkey to trust Saddam Hussein rather than Barzani. Saddam Hussein however blocked this operation and by improving relations with Baghdad, Turkey only polarised the situation further. The significance of relations between the separate parties should not be underestimated as it will have consequences far into the next century.

The United States and Europe have not fully embraced the concept of an independant Kurdistan. An acceptable and feasible solution must be found for Kurdistan whose geostrategic location puts it in danger. The Kurdish

Federal State therefore is still in need of protection. The Baku-Ceyhan project represents the protection required.

Turkey considers the city of Mosul to be within its borders (Misak-i-Milli). Turkey gave this region to Britain at Lausanne. Rightly or wrongly, Turkey does on occasions argue for its return. Opinion is divided in Turkey between those who consider it a necessary move and those who see it as dangerous. There is some concern that this would lead to a Turkish-Kurdish federation. The Kurdish problem is, however, an immediate and pressing problem for the Turkish government and one that cannot be ignored. The war shows no signs of ending as far as the military is concerned. The toll of casualties is high and affects Turkish society. The war has paralysed the economy. Every year around $8 billion is spent on this war. Militarist logic is dominant.

Parliament, universities and the press have been terrorized. The true nature of the war has been concealed from the rest of the world. Villages have been burned and destroyed; 3 million villagers live in the centre of big cities under very harsh conditions.

The United States and Europe are in consensus with regard to proposed solutions. The Turkish Administration must be supported against terrorism. Turkey, however, has to accept the political existence of Kurds within its borders as well as their basic rights and freedom. The United States and Western Europe are not proposing autonomy, federation or independence, but rather the recognition of Kurdish identity along with constitutional guarantees. The Kurdish political movements have debated the matter but do not take it seriously. The geometrical dimension of the problem is fairly broad. Recognition of Kurdish identity requires changes in the Turkish constitution. In connection with this it requires changes in the Penal Code and in the national education act. Establishing Kurdish identity requires major structural changes which in turn demand a change in attitudes. Ideological forms have to be exchanged for contemporary, democratic understandings. It is this point which is the main objection from the Turkish state.

Towards a Solution

The most important results in this context: For Kurdish society, acceptance of the Kurdish Federal State's political status on an international basis would be a great result. For Kurdish society, a sovereign Kurdish state on Kurdistan ground is no more than a pragmatic principle; however, a solution to the problem of Kurds in Turkey is critical. Without a solution to the Kurdish problem, the solution of other problems is impossible. Kurdish society has, oddly enough, reached the point where it will solve the Kurdish problem by its own intentions. Ideas such as autonomy and federation do not make much sense to ordinary people in Kurdistan. The demographic structure has been turned upside down, the degree of integration in society has reached such dimensions that any proposed solutions to the idea of a single common country are unrealistic. Today 60 percent of the Kurdish people live west of the Euphrates river rather than east of it. In the Adana-Tarsus-Mersin triangle this percentage is 35-40 percent. Kurds make up 50 percent of the population in the municipality of Adana. 22-25 percent in the Mediterranean and Aegean territory and 25-27 percent in Istanbul. Many of these people will not return to their original homes. Immigration, voluntarily or not has added a new dimension to the problem.

The nature of the Kurdish problem has therefore become a political-social problem rather than one of national liberation. Prolonged war does not change this fact.

There are also differences within the Kurdish movement. There are two sides to the policies of the PKK: 1) The acceptence of diversity and the idea that there are no class distinctions between the various groups; and 2) a more dictatorial approach. While there is no need to consider the prospect of national liberation in Northern Iraq there is a possibility of civil war. It remains to be seen how these two powers will resolve themselves in Northern Kurdistan (Eastern Anatolia).

The future of Kurdish society in Iraq is linked to international support for the Kurdish Federal State. In Turkey, the Kurdish society's future is tied to the fate of Turkish society. Turkish nationalism along with militarist policies will not work. Kurdish nationalism can likewise not be sustained through chaos and war.

In short, the key to the Kurdish problem is democracy in Turkey. The basic requirement is *complete* equal rights. In a democratic Turkey where Kurdish identity has been legalized, Kurdish people will respect their citizenship. There has to be common and free political practice. The solution *cannot be achieved* through the drawing of new borders, dividing thousands of people and creating geographical prisons. A solution requires finding a basic political status for people who share a common fate. This is not expressed in the general policies of the various Kurdish political movements.

Urgent practical-political steps are required, ratified by all the political powers. In Turkey the first step required is an end to the bloodshed via the recognition of the Kurdish national existence, the abolishment of the 'State of Emergency', the withdrawal of the Special Forces, abolishment of rural guards and the reconstruction of villages, towns etc. This resembles the solutions proposed by Western Europe and the United States. The need for a peaceful democratic solution is commonly accepted in Turkey, while the actual details of such a proposal are not yet agreed on. The DEP trial and debate on Article 8 of the Penal Code show that militarist logic and centralized national power is not sufficient for the socio-politic and socio-economic implications of such a strategic power equilibrium.

Political powers which are accountable to the world are dragging society into worse turmoil with their unreasonable, illogical policies and decisions. The latent threat posed by this turmoil is *fascism*. This is because the Kurdish policy of cowardly administrators whose actions lack foresight and thus rely on militarist logic are focussed on the power struggles of internal politics and thereby steadily feeding the rise of fascism. The most important indicator of this is the growing mass appeal of chauvinist nationalism which formerly occupied a marginal position.

Yugoslavia is a reality and Turkey is not on Uranus, it is on Earth!

Societal Security — A Solution to the Kurdish Problems?[1]

Grete Bille

Introduction

The multi-polar world which emerged from the end of the cold war has spawned an upsurge of ethno-national unrest, conflict and instability. New populist nationalisms, the rise of indigenous peoples etc. have placed the questions of ethnic secession, sovereignty, identity, and self-determination, at the top of the agenda of international relations.[2]

Although some scholarly discourse points to an emerging post-national era in which internationalization and globalization dominate, making ethnic conflicts and nationalism a secondary concern and increasingly irrelevant, it would probably be premature to proclaim the death of nationalism. There have been many such proclamations in the past. Other scholars, dealing with theories of globalization, have argued that the globalization and internationalization processes are of a more complex nature. They entail parallel processes of homogenization and heterogenization. This in turn makes it possible to understand, within the framework of globalization, the current proliferation and intensification of demands for cultural pluralism, growing ethnic conflict and nationalist ideals within unitary states. These demands are being applied by numerous, unrecognized and dissatisfied ethnic communities putting forward their own case for 'national self-determination'.[3]

Among those ethnic communities which pose a danger to regional and global peace and security in an international system of sovereign nation states are; the Kurdish communities in today's Turkey, Iran, Iraq and Syria[4]. They

---

1. A first draft of this article was presented as a paper entitled 'Stateless Nations and Societal Security: Kurdish Experiences' at the 13th Nordic and 1st Baltic Peace Research Conference June 29th—July 2nd, 1995, in which I was able to participate thanks to economic support from SNU.
2. Hutchinson & Smith 1994: 11; Ropers 1995.
3. Hutchinson & Smith 1994: 11-12; Sørensen 1995: 14.
4. In the following referred to as 'host states'.

regard certain areas within each of these states — the territory known as Kurdistan — as their homeland.

In the following, the concepts of societal security, ethnic identity and the stateless nation are applied to the Kurdish problems. This is an attempt to try and establish whether a solution can be found in terms of current security policies: These are in line with the concept of *societal security*, based on the European security situation in existence following the lifting of the overlay of the cold war superpower confrontation. In the section on *Kurds, Ethnic Identity and Conflict*, definitions are offered for some of the basic concepts of the discussion. In the section on *Kurds and Kurdistan* a brief presentation of Kurdish societies is given, while in the section *Kurds and Societal Security* the concept of societal security is dealt with and related to the Kurds. In the section *Kurds and Identity Budgets*, identity is explored in more depth and introduces the concept of identity budgets. In the section *Kurds, a Nation Denied*, the ambiguous position of the Kurdish society as a stateless nation is discussed, leading to the *Conclusion* in the final section on the problems at hand.

Kurds, Ethnic identity and Conflict

The Kurds and Kurdistan form a rich and uniquely interesting field of research in ethnicity, conflict and integration; as an example of identity formation in an *ethnic* group striving for modernity and development in a multi-cultural and hostile host environment; as well as for integration in the post-cold war global community of nations.

For seven decades, the mountainous area, known throughout history as Kurdistan, has been divided by the national borders of four states: Iran, Iraq, Syria and Turkey. Relations between these states are more commonly characterized by conflict than agreement. In addition to this, the Kurdish community, as a result of the forced migrations of the Ottoman Empire (and previous imperial dynasties), discovered themselves as being a diaspora; cut off from the ethnic homeland — their base and the fixed pole of their identity — by the boundaries of a hostile state. This has made any trans-boundary cooperation between fellow Kurds illegal, in the eyes of the majority populations and regimes of their host states, a treasonable act and a security threat at the very least. Moreover, the Kurdish homeland in the respective host states has come to function as an economic frontier[5], in many respects giving Kurdistan the status of a quasi-, or internal, colony.[6]

5. I draw here on a concept used by F.G. Bailey in *Caste and the Economic Frontier. A village in Highland Orissa* (Bailey 1957).
6. Aksoy 1992.

In this situation, the pre-modern Kurdish 'Ethnie', to use the terminology of Anthony Smith[7], latently prepared to develop a national identity in the modern period. Circumstances have forced it, as it were, to evolve into a multi-cultural and multinational environment of hostile majority populations of second generation nation states. Each of these is striving for their own national identity, acceptance and integration into the global community of modern nation states. As a consequence, the Kurds have had to form and develop their identity from a minority position vis-à-vis, and in opposition to, these very different majority cultures. This means that today they face a situation in which a 'primordial' Kurdish ethnic, based on family and localized clan loyalties — and to some extent influenced by identification with religious groupings — has in its search for a broader level of identity, evolved into a number of Kurdish ethno-national groupings or communities.[8] These are also in conflict with several state nationalisms which are in a formative stage. The Kurds have not been in a position to coin a pan-Kurdish common history, or develop an intellectual elite, or assert a literate linguistic community[9] — or indeed one political system and culture in agreement over what to disagree on.[10] As a result of this, several Kurdish ethno-nationalisms have emerged; each shaped by the conditions of identity formation in ethnic minorities; because ethno-nationalist movements, like ethnic minorities are both affected in their form and impact by the character of the societies within which they exist.[11] This influence works through the mechanism of opposition.[12]

Identity formation in ethnic minorities is predominantly characterized by opposition to the authority of the majority, as Maryon McDonald rightly points out in her outstanding work on Bretons in France, 'We are not French'. Surprisingly, McDonald discovered that Bretons come to identify modern Breton language schools with 'Frenchness'. This is because these schools are propagated, established and operated by the Breton movements. These are in turn rooted in the Breton intellectual elites at the universities and are perceived by rural Bretons as 'Parisian' or 'French'.[13]

---

7. Smith 1991.
8. The Kurdish society understood as a nation, or nations, with or without actual state project(s).
9. Smith 1991.
10. Bille 1994.
11. Wiberg 1995.
12. Barth 1969; de Vos 1982; McDonald 1989; Wæver 1995.
13. McDonald 1989. McDonalds's findings raise an interesting question, namely the question of 'who owns the identity', which is important in the context of the Kurdish problems, but falls outside the scope of this article.

It is in this context that today's Kurdish societies present an extraordinarily interesting and rich field for ethnic conflict research: Kurdistan has been caught in the crossfire of conflict between the different host states. It therefore offers innumerable possibilities for alignment and opposition between individual states and the different Kurdish societies (and groupings); between the different Kurdish societies (and cross-cutting groupings); between the states themselves in any possible combination; or all four states aligning themselves together on one dimension of the conflict: 'all for one, and one for all' against the Kurds. To be more precise, this effort is aimed against the formation of any Kurdish national identity which is seen as an indication of ambitions towards statehood, regardless of whether the Kurdish groups actually have a state project. All these conflicts are more often than not expressed in ethnic, ethno-nationalist and nationalist terms and translated into security concerns.

The complexity of the problems and conflict configuration may seem prohibitive to any comprehensive analysis, and this has undoubtedly had an effect. Most analyses of what might be termed the 'Kurdish problem' take an external perspective, and see the problems from the point of view of either: a host-state, the region (whether defined as the Arab World, the Gulf Region, the Middle East or others), or from a European (or Western) perspective. It is also commonly presented from the view of what is sometimes termed 'The International Community' which, more often than not, is undefined and can denote anything from the diffuse idea of a global moral community of various Human Rights Watch groups and other Non-Governmental Organizations, to the United Nations and its various institutions, to a euphemism for the USA. Any analysis which takes the Kurdish perspective usually turns out to be some form of Kurdish partisan statement.

To venture into a discussion of these complex questions by combining the concept of societal security with the concept of the stateless nation calls for a concise definition of both concepts, and indeed a number of precepts on which they rest; such as 'nation', 'nation state', 'ethnie', 'society' and 'security'. A discussion of 'integration', 'development' and 'modernization' is also needed, as these phenomena may or may not be instrumental in the dissolution, not of ethnic identities as such, but of ethnic identities as a driving force, or security risk.

At the Ethnic Studies Network conference in Elsinore, Denmark, on the 13th June 1995, in his paper on 'Political Science encounters with 'Ethnicity' and 'Race', Rupert Taylor did away with these concepts; He labelled them as social constructions, not of the societies studied, but of the political science academy. He acknowledged that there is 'something out there', which we are trying to grasp with these constructs, calls for more empiric (anthropological as it were) studies of what is really going on 'out there'.[14] Although any 'know-ledge' and its conceptualization *are*, as cognitive sociology has taught, undoubtedly a social construct[15], there is also no doubt that any expert community as well as the communities which they study, the local communities, may or may not have constructed an idea of a specific concept. A given combination of expert community and local community will thus exhibit one of four combinations of having/not having ideas of 'race' and 'ethnicity'. The problem may be to identify exactly what idea it is that passes for 'knowledge' in the respective communities. Simply doing away with the concepts of the given expert community amounts to 'throwing the baby out with the bath water'. This line of thought is a relapse into objectivist thinking, if not positivism; not distinguishing between an etic and an emic analysis: There is a set of facts, empirical truths defined objectively from the outside, which can be identified in the societies 'out there'. All we need are better microscopes! What is needed is not this kind of empirical study. What is needed are emic studies exposing whether local communities have concepts of race and ethnicity, and of religion for that matter, as an element of their understanding of self and other, as well as a solution to the problem. Hutchinson & Smith point out that this is perhaps the central difficulty in ethnic studies, partly caused by the interdisciplinarity of the subject; namely the problem of finding both adequate and *agreed* definitions of the key concepts[16] in order to incorporate these local understandings in an analysis of their importance to conflict relations and solutions.

This article attempts to identify useful techniques to determine whether an ethno-nationalist society or stateless nation, as it were, such as the Kurds, is capable — and permitted — in the existing, international system of nation states, to seek to alleviate their societal security concerns along the same lines as the civic societies of nation states do.

It is my hope that, by combining anthropological data and concepts with those used by the political science community, this analysis can contribute to both, and to the field of ethnic conflict studies as an interdisciplinary endeavour.

A comprehensive account of the Kurds and Kurdistan falls outside the scope of this paper, but before turning to the conceptual questions, a brief presentation of the Kurdish societies is necessary in order to facilitate the discussion.

14. Taylor, oral communication 1995.
15. Berger & Luckmann 1992.
16. Hutchinson & Smith 1994: 4.

Kurds and Kurdistan[17]

The Kurds can be defined as an Indo-European language group, belonging to a group of the sub-group of Iranian languages. Like modern Farsi, they descend from Old Persian, and the Kurds claim their ancestry stems from the ancient Persian groups of Medes. Some Kurds even claim that they are mentioned as early as in Hammurabi's law (c. 1750 BC)!

As an ethnic community with ambitions of nationhood, the Kurds and Kurdistan first surface in modern World History in 1920-23 (between the Sèvres and Lausanne Treaties). Kemalist Turkey was emerging as a nationalist successor state to, and in the wake of, the 'colossus on feet of clay'— 'Europe's sick man' — the Ottoman Empire, as it sank into the oblivion of its past glory.

In the decentralized administrative system of the Ottoman Empire, Kurdish identity, like other non-Turkish ethnic or cultural identities, posed no political problems, and numerous Kurdish principalities could function with relative autonomy within the empire. The internal social organization was expressed in kinship terms, and the conscious Kurdish perception of identity rested more upon affiliation to (endogamous) clans, chiefs and connected territory, villages with land, through family ties and religious bonds[18].

After World War I, the victors designed the new map of the former Ottoman territory according to a European logic of nation states. Much consideration was given to their own colonial and economic interests as formed by the rapidly accelerating industrial development in Europe and the ensuing economic dependence on crude oil. What the political elites of the successor states of the Ottoman Empire — first and foremost modern Turkey, but also the Arab political leadership — learnt from this painful process was the nationalist lesson; whatever you do, whatever you are, present and assert yourself as a nation, one nation, or you will be cut up into small unviable, unsustainable units, suffering from intolerable dominance by the great (and colonial) powers and unable to sustain sovereignty. In other words, what was taught and learnt, was nationalism[19]. While slowly discovering themselves a stateless nation, the same lesson gradually dawned on the Kurds: National self-determination is an attribute of nation states and nation states only.

The present Turkish-Kurdish problem, which may be seen as the key problem of the complex, was thus created by the conclusion of the peace pro-

---

17. In this section, no reference will be given to source material on Kurds and Kurdistan.
18. See M. van Bruinessen *Agha, Shaikh and State* for an outstanding analysis of Kurdish social organisation.
19. In the sense used by E. Gellner in *Nations and Nationalism*.

cess in 1920-23 and subsequently reinforced in the following years[20]. Since then, Kemalist modern Turkey has striven to build a national identity. Turkish nationality, as the basis for the Turkish state was modelled on the French example[21]. As any identity formation rests as much on the creation of an 'other' as of a 'self'[22], the result has been a reciprocal, self-sustaining process. The construction of Turkish nationalism and Kurdish ethno-nationalism with their respective matching enemy images and confrontations, have given rise to the seemingly insoluble conflict situation today.

Today, the ethnic conflict is perceived as one of terrorrism: State terrorism, or 'normal' terrorism, by the respective parties in an increasingly fierce and confrontational conflict. In this conflict there is absolutely no room for non-partisan contribution. One can either be terrorist, traitor or partisan; since prescribed identities have taken precedence over self-identification in the escalating conflict situation.

As far back as the 16th century, the division between the predominantly Sunni-Muslim, Arab and Turcophone Ottomans, and the predominantly Shi'a-Muslim, Farsi-speaking, Iranian Safavid empire divorced the smaller group of Iranian Kurds from the major part of the Kurdish groups (Ramezanzadeh 1995). Today, as mentioned above, the Kurds find themselves divided by the state boundaries of four host states. They are a minority in three different majority cultures. They have all experienced, and are experiencing, oppression. This oppression, however, takes different forms in the different states. They have all had the experience of witnessing oppressive majority regimes in their host states forming alliances with ethnic 'brothers' in neighbouring states. They in turn have done the same. The general excuse, for themselves *and* their 'brothers', is the law of necessity and (physical) survival.

In addition to these imposed dividing lines, there are also several internal divisions. Divisions between political groupings along the old clan boundaries. Competition for supremacy or even hegemony between clans/political groupings. Above all, there are divisions and competition for supremacy in defining the Kurdish nation (the question of who owns Kurdish identity). There is also rivalry over the monopoly on representing the nation; (stateless) nations, unlike states, do not have fixed rules and systems which regulate who can legitimately represent the group as a whole.[23] The Kurdish communities in Iran, Iraq and

---

20. The League of Nations' intervention in the question of the nationality of Mosul in 1929 is one example.
21. This statement is in fact grossly simplifying a very complex question, a fair discussion of which is completely beyond what is called for in this context. For a thorough analysis reference can be given to Isil Kazan, 1994.
22. Cf. e.g. Ropers 1995.
23. Wæver 1995: 7.

Turkey are divided into different ethno-nationalisms with their own political ambitions.

The social, regional, intra- and inter-state, as well as international conflicts affecting the Kurds are many and severe. A full inventory of these conflicts would be in place, but for this paper it must suffice to say that today the complexity and intensity of the conflicts make the outlook for Kurdish societies appear very bleak indeed. For a short period (1991-92), the UN intervention in the wake of the Gulf War created a safe haven in Northern Iraq. The ensuing, so-called 'democratic experiment' under this umbrella raised hopes in all Kurdish quarters. This hope has now — like other great Kurdish expectations in the past — along with the armed conflict between the Kurdish parties in Iraq, and the Turkish invasion — vanished into the thin air of the Kurdistan mountains. Once again, these mountains seem to the Kurds to be the only friends they have.

Kurds and Societal Security

What is societal security? Societal security is a concept denoting the concerns of a social collectivity which perceives threats, possible or actual, in identity terms, to the persistence of its essential character under changing conditions.[24] It is termed 'societal' to differentiate it from 'national security' which is in normal usage in security studies and denotes the security of nation *states*. 'Security' because it — like national security — deals with the survival of a social collectivity. It is a reconceptualization of the security field, stating a duality of *state* security and *societal* security; the former having *sovereignty* as its ultimate criterion, and the latter being held together by concerns about *identity*. Both terms actually mean *survival*: sovereignty is the name of survival for a state - survival for a society is a question of identity. Identity defence is triggered by forces both from below and above. That is to say, by forces that shake domestic society and by the emergence of an alternative identity, that appears as a potential substitute for the existing one.[25]

Societal security, then, deals with situations in which societies perceive a threat in terms of their identity[26] and although closely related to political security (dealing with the organizational stability of states, systems of government and the ideologies from which the legitimacy of these derive), it is distinct from this. Also, it is *not* about *the state*. A given society may often, at least partially, coincide with a state, but this is by no means always the case,

24. Wæver et al. 1993: 23.
25. Wæver 1995: 18.
26. Wæver et al 1993: 23.

e.g. as in the case of distinct minorities.[27] Further, the inventors of the societal security concept warn against confusion of their notion of 'society' with the use of the wider, more vague 'state population' which is both too narrow and too broad.[28]

This concept was developed by a research project group at the Centre for Peace and Conflict Research on the basis of more unspecified conceptualization in earlier works, notably Buzan. The object of the conceptualization of the phenomenon was to overcome the difficulty of International Relations theories to integrate categories like identity, nation and nationalism into the theoretical body of security studies.[29] In the societal framework the four main perceived threats to security are: 1) fundamental change of identities through changed composition of the population, 2) competition from other cultures through cultural imperialism (horizontal threats), 3) competition from other identities through integration (threat to minority identity) or fragmentation (threat to majority identity) and 4) majority monopoly on power structures used to disfavour the reproduction of minority cultural identity.[30] Central to the concept is also a differentiation between *referent object* (the entity in whose name security claims are pleaded) and *security actors* (the body or individuals who, in the name of the referent entity acts to secure it). It is the locus of reference (from the state to the society) which is moved by the concept. The same move is not necessarily made regarding the *security actor*, which may still be a variety of units; from state to various domestic groups, enterprises and/or individuals or combinations of these.

The approach has been criticized for moving towards emptying the concept of 'security' of all meaning by — like the idealist, activist, peace researcher — taking an 'everything is security' stand.[31] However, the widening of the traditional security concept and agenda was in fact carried out in two dimensions: One concerns security sectors or means (military, economic, environmental, political etc.) which by the development of 'societal security' are expanded by the societal aspect. The other dimension concerns the organizational level. Where traditional security studies deal with international, regional and state ('national') security, the societal security agenda also involves the level of domestic groups and individuals. Societal security then points to the fact that — in a paradoxical sense — the highest and the lowest level often meet, amounting to a statement that security is ultimately the

27. Wæver 1995: 2.
28. Wæver 1995: 10.
29. Wæver 1995: 1.
30. Wæver 1995: 10.
31. Ibid: 3.

security of individuals, of human beings, and in the last instance is the same as global security, making the security of *all* human beings equal.[32]

With societal security, the analysis moves towards a reformulation of the concept of *common security*. Originally coined in terms of military security, this denotes the interdependence of security on both sides of the arms race of the cold war.[33] This reformulation might eventually lead to a security consensus de-escalating ethnic conflict in multi-ethnic states. For Kurds, it might, in the long term perspective, mean that their fellow countrymen, the majority population in the host states, notably the ethnic-Turkish population in Turkey, will come to realize that 'without security for the Kurds (and other minorities), there is no security, and therefore also no (real) security for Turks', and — it goes without saying — vice versa. Since any assertion of Kurdish identity (stemming from Kurdish societal security needs) is perceived as separatism and, consequently, as terrorism, meaning a severe threat to Turkish security, any defence of Turkish national identity, unity and sovereignty can be expressed in military action (perceived by the Kurds *and* many Turks as State terrorism). This amounts to conditions of civil war, insecurity for everybody, and it thus contradicts security. Norbert Ropers points out that the failure of the quest of Yugoslavia and the Soviet Union for the establishment of multinational states demonstrates that even decades of forced political co-existence produce very limited common identity building; unless it is accompanied by positive social interweaving and *shared economic success*. And this is exactly what the present state of affairs in Turkey prevents.

The societal security approach is related to threats to identity. Since identities are relative and based on individual perspectives, it focuses on the question of how identities are politicized in order to avoid objectivist definitions of identity.[34] It is precisely for this reason that it becomes essential to approach an understanding of ethnic and national identity as the multifaceted, relative and operation/strategy oriented social phenomenon it is, even if it seems pretty one-dimensional in times of conflict. The idea that it is only possible to belong to one group, one place, was created by the political techniques of nation states for external delimitation and integration within,[35] not by individuals. As Håkan Wiberg puts it: 'Human beings normally have multidimensional identity budgets and in addition distribute their

32. Wæver 1995: 3.
33. Cf., e.g., 'the Palme Report'.
34. Wæver 1995: 18.
35. Sørensen 1995: 9.

identification between different levels on the same dimension... with shortage of time as being the only reason for making choices'.[36]

Kurds and Identity Budgets

To reiterate the centrality of identity to societal security concepts: Societal security suggests, as mentioned above, a reconceptualization of the security field in terms of a duality of *state* security and *societal* security, both effectively mean 'survival': Sovereignty is the name of survival for a state — survival for a society is a question of identity; The former has *sovereignty* as its ultimate criterion and the latter is held together by concerns about *identity*.[37]

George de Vos defines ethnicity as essentially a subjective sense of belonging[38] and goes on to stress exactly this problem of priority of multiple multidimensional identity and group loyalty of individuals in complex society, being dependent on orientation, perspective and the problems at hand.[39] De Vos shows that individuals in minority populations in multi-ethnic societies may choose between contrasting identities; such as ethnic identity and national identity — giving priority to either one as their loyalty focus changes according to orientation and problematics. This interpretation of identity priorities is clearly of a subjective, political character. In the same way that the societal security approach focuses on the question of when identities are politicized in order to avoid objectivist definitions of identity.[40] In the de Vos model of conflict and accommodation of different group loyalties, future orientation tends to motivate priority to ideologically defined loyalties; the subject having to choose between identification with a political (radical), religious or other morally founded social movements, while orientation towards the past tends to give priority to traditional family and cultural values, and obligations, as defined by the ethnic group. A presence orientation leaves the individual with a choice between general system loyalty as a holder of citizenship (civic loyalty), and specific loyalties to e.g. a professional or status group.

In addition, Håkan Wiberg stresses that multiple identity is not a question of either/or, but a question of both/and: When it comes to identities you can have your cake and eat it! Identity has several dimensions, Wiberg asserts, and introduces the concept of *identity budgets* for the individual's choice of priorities

---

36. Wiberg 1995: 37.
37. Wæver 1995: 13.
38. de Vos 1982: 16.
39. de Vos 1982: 18.
40. Wæver 1995: 18.

of identity.[41] This seems to be a very useful instrument for the analysis of intrastate ethnic conflict and, thus, of societal security of ethnic minority populations.

An analysis of Kurdish identity-budget configurations would be central to an analysis of the Kurds and societal security. It is essential to the understanding of the role of identity in repectively aggravating, and managing, the conflicts that face the Kurds today; in Iran, Iraq, Turkey and Syria - as well as in the CIS.

In this context, only a very limited presentation of some of the budget items and their politicized usage is relevant.

Representatives of the Turkish regime generally[42] refuse to see solutions to the problems in terms of national identities. No minority rights, no autonomy, no cultural rights can be granted: it is not necessary. In Turkey everyone is equal, regardless of cultural or ethnic 'background'. They are equal in citizenship. The human rights problems are general problems affecting everyone and are to be solved — by reinforcing democracy and the rule of law. Nationalism is old fashioned, and Turkish nationalism was not, and should not be, a point for the definition of identity. 'Turk' means bearer of Turkish citizenship, and all loyalties should be directed towards the general system.

The present problem is, however, simply that identity and loyalty cannot be imposed from above. Loyalties are subjective, individual and a matter of priority. The problem is not that the civic identity being prescribed in this scenario is absent; it is not. The problem is, that the system does not permit any national identity (other than Turkish) as *being valid* in the identity budget. If it did, this would facilitate integration of a multi-ethnic society into one multicultural, mono-civic-nation-state, sharing a multicultural civic society and common concern for its (joint) security. The challenge is to make good Turkish citizens, not Turks, out of good Kurds — by granting them cultural rights and equal status *with* their Kurdish identity; in the same way as the Finns succeeded in making good Finlanders out of their Swedish minority. The result of the ban on ethnic and national identities is exactly that the civic identity moves down the list, at least to second base — and probably even further down, behind religion, gender and profession — for Kurds and Turks alike.

41. Wiberg 1995: 33.
42. As did the former Turkish minister of foreign Affairs, M. Soysal, at the conference behind this publication, 'Contrasts in the Middle East: National or religious identification seen in a local-global perspective' April 29th, 1995, at the University of Aarhus, Denmark.

As this example shows, a discussion of modernity and traditionalism is also necessary. Ethnic identities (and what in sociology literature are often termed primordial loyalties) are given priority by orientation towards (an idea of) a special past heritage.[13] Special attention should be given to the role of gender identity formation within a minority identity. Women of many minorities struggling for some sort of recognition or independence[44] have stated that modernization of the female gender role *within* the limits of the minority culture have proved impossible; at least, so long as the struggle continues. The reason for this they state is that the female gender role is perceived as being an essential part of the past heritage — to be preserved in order to secure the society. It does not take much to imagine that modernization of the minority female gender identity of Kurdish women in Turkey would be seen as a serious threat to societal security. An important element of the ideology of Kemalism, on which the modern secular Turkish state is based, being to modernize the position and role of women in society. The dynamics of opposition involved, however, demand thorough study under the heading 'Modern states, 'traditional' minorities?', and taking Clastre's 'Society against the State' into consideration; current migration studies and theories of migration[45] as well as globalization theories.[46]

New nationalisms are often created from old ethnic identities as societies shake off their roots and become alienated by processes of modernization. The development of nationalism is also accelerated by the idea of the existence within the national soul of a deep meaning and a golden future — i.e. the ability to think along lines which make the *national* the supreme value and focus of unity.[47] When evaluating the Kurdish status as a stateless nation this should be taken into account.

Kurds all claim the same mythical ancestry and recall the same mythical heroes; all speak (or feel they should speak!) a Kurdish dialect[48]; share (to use

43. de Vos 1982: 19.
44. E.g. Same women, Inuit women from Greenland and Canadian Indian women have stated this at NGO workshops on minority women at the Nordic Forums on women as well as the UN world conferences on women. Also Kurdish women from North Iraq gave similar statements at a hearing under the NGO forum of the Social Summit in Copenhagen in March 1995 as well as at the UN World Conference on Women in Beijing, 1995.
45. For example, Sørensen 1995.
46. For example, Roland Robertson, 1992. *Globalization. Social Theory and Global Culture*, London: Sage; Jonathan Friedman's ideas of *Cultural Identity and Global Process*,1994.
47. Wæver 1995: 18.
48. It is beyond the scope of this paper to discuss how to determine what linguistic differences amount to distinguishing between different *languages*, and what only to different *dialects*. In any case, this differentiation is more a question of political power

an expression coined by Clifford Geertz and Ernest Gellner) 'a common enemy and the same misconception of a common history'. Irrespective of religious orientation they reconfirm their Kurdish identity through the same rituals — the most important being the celebration of *Newruz* as a 'national day' with bonfires, dancing and singing; and of course songs, music and dancing themselves on any occasion. The songs are often ballads commemorating past martyrdoms. All Kurds claim to originate from the homeland of Kurdistan (the diaspora groups, e.g. in Syria, very often taking the names of their village of (mythical) origin). Thus they may be seen as making up one ethnie, one ethnic community. The divisions, nevertheless, have such a scope and intensity that it is fair to say that there is no single pan-Kurdish nationalist movement today. Hence, no single Kurdish nation.

If there is a Kurdish ethnie, a Kurdish ethnic community, there is no evidence that this community can be asserted, sustained or reproduced under the current circumstances. If one can talk about several 'Kurdish societies', the question is, whether or not *these* can be asserted, sustained and reproduced as entities with separate identities — be it as 'ethnic, cultural, religious or linguistic minorities', 'local communities' or as 'autonomous regions' — under current circumstances in the host states and under the conditions and rules of the international society today. The question then is how can the Kurds secure their society — in the face of state monopolies on violence, cultural institution and legitimate representation, while facing a variety of legal systems of minority protection, declarations on the rights of indigenous people and other international legal instruments? To what means can the Kurds take recourse? To some extent this rests on recognition as some sort of stateless nation, i.e. on the good will of forces outside the Kurdish community itself.

Kurds, a Nation Denied?

Without the question mark, this is the title of a publication issued by the Minority Rights Group. This assumes an orientalist, exoticist[49] perspective, as it were, and takes for granted the fact that the Kurds form a stateless nation,

---

than it is a linguistic one — who was it who said: 'A language is a dialect with an army'?
49. I use the term 'exoticist' due to the lack of a better — and short — term to cover the attitude of many Western Europeans towards the Kurds, seeing them as the 'noble savage' of their 'near abroad', Europe's Indians, if you like. It is important to me to stress, that this image of Kurds (noble, savage, honourable, if martial), is not an attribute of Kurds. It is as much a product of our culture just as the Turkish image of Kurds as 'terrorists' is a Turkish product. And just like infatuation is not a quality of the object of the infatuation - it is a state of mind of the infatuated.

denied the right of self determination.[50] 'Stateless nation', however, like the
term 'Unrepresented peoples' (peoples, nations, not represented in United
Nations, as the UN is comprised of the international society of nation states)
is a concept that needs defining before an ethnic group can be classified as one.
Although 'Primitive societies are societies without a state'[51] — a state, that is,
in our Western sense of the concept, as has been pointed out by Evans-
Pritchard in his famous work on the Nuer — it does not follow, except in the
primitivist view, that stateless societies are also primitive. As Ernest Gellner
states[52], the nations of the world are too numerous, and often too small, for
them to actually have, or even aspire, towards a state of their own.

Both 'unrepresented peoples' and 'stateless nations' come in many and
varied forms and categories, the classification of which must include at least
three dimensions. It must also take into account the fact of the central concepts
used in the social sciences as well as in law. These have different, if partially
overlapping, meanings, just as the two professional communities hold different
concepts for central. It is therefore essential to distinguish between the legal
meaning and the social science interpretation of given concepts and terms, as
well as remaining aware of the centrality or marginality with respect to
concepts and terms in each context.

One dimension of defining or identifying a stateless nation is to determine
whether or not the people in question may be termed an 'Indigenous People'
(also sometimes termed aboriginals, autochthonous population). These can be
identified as those stateless nations, or rather non-nation peoples, which have
been included, and represented, in a working group under the UN. Since 1982,
this group worked in Geneva on the drafting of a declaration of the rights of
indigenous people. The work was finished in 1994 and the draft declaration
was registered with the UN Human Rights Commission.[53] By virtue of this
declaration, the definition of indigenous people under international law is
rather unambiguous. It is, however, by no means recognized by all UN
member states and thus, if the political will of host-states is absent, it is of little
use. The definition is that the society in question be the descendants of the
original populations having been conquered or colonized by European
immigrants, still living on the original territory, and now included as a
minority population in a nation state. It should be noted that the term of the
declaration is indigenous *peoples* and not nations. This denies indigenous

50. McDowall 1992.
51. Clastre 1977: 159.
52. Gellner 1992.
53. Hasager 1995.

peoples the right to national self determination that goes with the recognition of a *nation*.

In the legal and social science contexts, the questions to be asked are; which and how many of the criteria must be fulfilled by the people under investigation in order for that people to qualify as being indigenous? Included here are the American Indians (North and South); Inuit communities in America, Greenland, CIS; the aboriginals of Australia, the polynesians of Hawaii, and many, many others, but no one has ever dreamed of including the Kurds, except (of course) the Kurds (overlooking the definitional exclusion of the right to national self determination).

In a social science context, stateless nations are the traditional field of activity of anthropologists. They are — consciously or subconsciously — regarded as pre-modern societies, characterized by primordial loyalties; as being technologically inferior and organizationally and economically underdeveloped and not *yet* having reached the stage of statehood; which they are destined to reach, once they have undergone the development all societies must undergo, states Pierre Clastre.[54]

It is true that according to evolutionist theory, the history of civilization is about the evolution of stateless societies into (nation) states. Consequently, social and political collectivities without a state are relics of the past. Societies that have been passed over by the processes of modernization and global integration. In this framework, they are the wildlife form of human societies. In the world today there is, however, no more unexplored land. The development of a modern, all-encompassing global society of nation states is changing this, and stateless nations can no more live in a vacuum, as it were[55]. The reality of global integration is that, even if they are in the first phase of colonialism, all nations 'belong' to a state. It does not follow logically from this that all states 'belong' to one nation, some do, and some belong to more than one; not all nations, however, have their own state. This leaves a number of nations stateless. Among these are the Kurdish societies.

54. Clastre 1977: 160 ff.
55. In his *Cultural Identity and Global Process* Jonathan Friedman points to the fact that also premodern societies, stateless nations (including historic) — in short 'primitive' societies — the traditional field for anthropological research — should be seen in a global perspective, as it is precisely the processes of the global system and the position and status it prescribes for these societies that make them stateless, premodern, primitive. He calls for a global anthropology taking this into account in order to understand properly the dynamics of the relationship between the global system and cultural identities. For the problem of the Kurds and societal security, this may imply a conclusion pointing to the insight that the Kurds are denied self determination, because they, by global processes, are deprived of self determination.

A second dimension which may help us to distinguish stateless nations from national minorities, and to rank stateless nations according to the complexity of their problems, as well as contributing to the determination of the statelessness and nationhood of a given people, is to measure how many states are involved: In how many states do the people actually live, to what extent is this due to diaspora, and to what extent to the division of a homeland territory, and does the stateless people in one country have a national affinity to a nation state, neighbouring or other?.

The Kurdish homeland territory is divided between four nation states. In addition to this there is a widespread diaspora; partly due to forced displacements under past empires, such as the Ottoman Empire and the Soviet Union, and partly due to the movement of migrant work forces. This last fuses the Kurds with other Middle East/Muslim minorities in Europe. There is also — owing to the oppression and conflict — an exodus of political asylum seekers. The Kurds have no nation state to which they can claim affinity. Although Kurds everywhere do share an 'imagined community' (to use an Andersonian phrase), it is clearly not possible to treat them as one society, neither in a legal nor social-science — nor indeed in a political — context.

The third and last dimension is the question of 'entropy'; the relationship between nationality and regionality. In other words, the demographic question of relative regional distribution of the ethnic community as related to the mass of majority nationals in the state. Obviously, this is the decisive factor in whether or not a 'homeland' can actually be identified or defined as a regional territory in which the national minority is a majority. In the legal context, minority rights and other pertinent declarations (e.g. OSCE) combine the criteria of regionality with that of nationality differentiation in order to secure the group in question the minority rights prescribed by the declaration at hand, since status as a minority and status as indigenous entail different sets of rules.

In their host states, the Kurds (unlike e.g. the Saami of Sweden who have been outnumbered by immigration) are, or have been until recently, the majority population in the regions covering the pertinent part of the Kurdish homeland. Syria is the exception to this, as massive, forced migration has been undertaken in order to secure the state boundary. Besides this, the forced migrations of former times, the processes of modernization — and the armed conflict going on in the homeland — have dispersed the Kurds all over Iran, Iraq and Turkey. In Turkey this seems to be a deliberate process, aimed at changing 'the demographic composition of the region', as a recent official statement read.

In the context of social science, and indeed conflict research, the degree of territoriality has been related to an expected degree of conflict. Three ideal types (in the Weberian sense) can be identified: 1) clear territorial division of majority and minority population; 2) mixed majority/minority situation, equally distributed over the territory; and 3) a mixture. Although by no means without notable exception, it seems that a high degree of territoriality may cause greater aggravation in the majority population by increasing fears that the minority harbours secessionist tendencies. Consequently, although giving access to sets of rules of international declarations of minority rights, such as that of the OSCE, a high degree of territoriality may thus actually be a liability rather than an asset for a national minority when it comes to ensuring societal security. This has been proven by Kurdish experiences.

Conclusion

This overview shows clearly that societal security is pertinent to stateless nations such as the Kurds, in that it at least points out that asserting their identity constitutes a threat to the societal security of the host nation state.

Through an analysis of the many Kurdish dilemmas and paradoxes, it can be ascertained that stateless nations do have societal security concerns. This is probably what Kurdish, and indeed all, ethno-nationalisms in their struggle for recognition of some form or another are really about, whether or not these include state projects. Can a society be secured without the instruments and means of its own state?

One conclusion has already been suggested: societal security of stateless nations has to be defended by other strategies and other means than that of which nation state societies have at their disposal — as any attempt at using these (as e.g. armed struggle) would aggravate the majority population of the host states, causing further loss of security. Supra-national strategies should be studied for their applicability. This might involve legal instruments and bodies of the international society, primarily the UN, and OSCE; as well as sub-national strategies, such as cultural autonomy, inter-cultural exchanges, NGO networking.

As the legal system of the international society is predominantly built on nation states and state thinking, and to the degree that they build on ethnic definitions, they are also based on romanticist nationalist illusion.[56] It is my belief therefore that in the foreseeable future the Kurds too will have no recourse to any international legal instruments — be it rules for indigenous peoples or for national minorities — because there will always be a sufficient number of states who, fearing the consequences of their own minority

---

56. Wæver 1995: 22.

problems, will prevent any positive action. There is, in other words, a total lack of political will in all quarters.

This leaves the sub-national strategies, which for the most part are made impossible by their host states' perception of any assertion of minority identity as security threats to the state and its society.

It thus appears that for a national minority/stateless nation to be able to secure its society, it must; 1) be a minority to such a degree numerically that it poses no threat to the majority power holders of the societal security of the state; 2) have close affinity to the majority population in a neighbour state; or 3) have close allies (and common enemies) with one or more of the leading nations of the international society. It seems to me that the Kurdish societies do not fit any of these descriptions, their host states being those with powerful allies; their communities being too significant minorities to be taken lightly, and none of them having even a share in state ownership.

The prospects for solving the societal security problems of the Kurdish communities are thus indeed very bleak. As far as the Kurdish community in Turkey is concerned, recent developments point, however, to two factors which, if combined, may offer a way out of the deadlock of the spiralling conflict.

Firstly, it becomes increasingly obvious that the problems cannot be solved by military means. An armed conflict of this kind can have no victor. Both parties stand to lose considerably, and given the conflict-ridden situation in the region, it is becoming increasingly difficult to contain the conflict. It is already spreading into northern Iraq and is an element of Turkey's conflicts with its neighbour states, e.g., Syria. This disturbs the precarious power balance of the region and will increase international interest in — at least — bringing the conflict under control. This, in turn raises the probability that the pressure will increase, both on Turkey and on the Kurdish leadership, to bring them to the negotiation table.

Secondly, the economic factor is of great importance. The continued military campaign in itself places a great strain on the Turkish economy. Among the means implemented to bring East Anatolia under military and government control is a systematic destruction of the region's economy, including demolition of the infrastructure and means of production. This is particularly damaging to the economy of the entire country, as the loss of East Anatolian agricultural production has changed Turkey from net-exporter to net-importer of agricultural products. At the same time, circumstances prevent the Great Anatolian Project, designed to boost the economic growth of the region and the whole country with it, from getting off the ground. On the basis of this, the large Turkish enterprises, industries and trade have already begun to advocate a peaceful solution, and after the conclusion of the Customs Union agreement between Turkey and the EU, this internal pressure may be expected to increase at the same time as the Customs Union also makes the situation in East Anatolia a European (societal) security concern.

If the internal and external pressures are to succeed in bringing about a peaceful solution in Turkey, they must continuously and unambiguously call for cultural equal rights, democracy and power sharing amounting to a model for common societal security. In this way, the integration of the Kurdish community will be enhanced by the experience of common economic success as well as increase social interweaving, diminishing the aspirations for statehood within the Kurdish community in Turkey. Finally, a development along these lines in Turkey *may* have a positive effect on the socio-political development in the adjoining Kurdish areas.

Bibliography

Aksoy, Ibrahim, 1992. Conference paper. Copenhagen: *DKKM & Politiken*.

Bailey, F.G. 1957. *Caste and the Economic Frontier. A village in highland Orissa.* Manchester: Manchester University Press.

Barth, F. 1969. *Ethnic Groups and Boundaries. The Social Organization of Culture Difference.* Boston: Little, Brown & Co.

Bille, G. 1994. 'Fri byrd og lige værd. Det Radikale Venstre og højre-venstre dimensionen'. Unpublished MA thesis, Institute of Anthropology, University of Copenhagen.

Buzan, Barry, 1991. *Peoples, States and Fear: An Agenda for International Studies in the Post-Cold War Era.* Hemel Hampstead: Wheatsheaf.

Clastre, Pierre, 1977. 'Society Against the State'. In: *Society Against the State*: 159-186. Oxford: Blackwell.

de Vos, George 1982. 'Ethnic Pluralism: Conflict and Accommodation'. In: de Vos, George & Lola Romunucci-Ross (ed.), *Ethnic Identity. Cultural Continuities and Change*: 5-42. Chicago: University of Chicago Press.

Friedman, Jonathan, 1994. *Cultural Identity & Global Processes.* London: Sage Publications.

Gellner, Ernest, 1992. *Nations and Nationalism.* Oxford: Blackwell.

Hasager, Ulla, 1995. 'FN og indfødte folk', In: *Jordens Folk*, Vol. 43, (30).

Hutchinson, John, & Anthony D. Smith, 1994. (ed.), *Nationalism.* Oxford & New York: Oxford University press.

Kazan, Isil, 1994. 'Omvendt Osmannisme og Khanaternes Kemalisme'. Tyrkiets udenrigspolitik med særligt henblik på "det nye Europa", EU og de tyrkiske republikker efter opløsningen af Sovjetunionen. Unpublished MA thesis, Institute of Political Science, University of Copenhagen.

McDonald, Maryon, 1989. *We are not French. Language, culture and identity in Brittany.* London & New York: Routledge.

Ramezanzadeh, Abdollah, 1995. 'The Future of the Kurds'. Conference Paper, Second International Conference of Ethnic Studies Network, June 11-14th, Elsinore, Denmark.

Robertson, Roland, 1992. *Globalization. Social Theory and Global culture.* London: Sage.

Ropers, Norbert, 1995. 'Conflict Resolution in the International System', ms. for Wiberg, Håkan, (ed.), *Peace and War. Social and Cultural Aspects*: 86-117. Budapest: UNESCO.

Smith, Anthony D., 1991. *National Identity.* London: Penguin.

Sørensen, Ninna Nyberg, 1995. *Globale drømme. Migration og udvikling i et transnationalt perspektiv.* Copenhagen: CUF.

Wiberg, Håkan, 1995. 'Ethnicity, Identity, Conflict', in: *Proceedings of conference on 'From Nonviolent Liberation to Tolerance. The development of civil society in Eastern Central Europe*, Vilnius, 32-55.

Wæver, Ole, Barry Buzan, Morten Kelstrup & Pierre Lemaitre, 1993. *Identity, Migration and the New Security Agenda in Europe.* 1. 'Introduction': 1-14, and 2. 'Societal Security — the concept': 15-40. London: Pinter.

Wæver, Ole, 1995. 'Societal security — a concept and its consequences' Manuscript for publication in *Cooperation and Conflict*.

Appendix

International Conference on Contradictions in the Middle East —
A Token of National or Religious Identifications in a Local-Global Perspective
Held on April 29th, 1995 at the University of Aarhus, Denmark

Programme
Welcome speech by Senior Lecturer, Prof. (Dr.phil.) Richard Raskin, Pro-Dean
of The Faculty of Arts, The University of Aarhus.
Opening speech by Peder Mortensen, Middle East Archaeologist and Curator
of Moesgård Museum.

Speakers
The Turkish representative: Prof. (Dr.jur.) Mümtaz Soysal, former Turkish
Foreign Minister; member of the Turkish Parliament, TBMM, for the Democra-
tic Left Party.
The Kurdish representative: Prof. (Dr. jur.) Ismet Cheriff Vanlly, Chairman of
the Institute of Kurdish Scientific Research, Berlin.
The Israeli representative: Prof. Naomi Chazan, member of the Israeli
Parliament, the Knesset, the Meretz Party.
The Palestinian representative: Prof. Dr. Manuel Hassassian, PLO, the West
Bank, Bethlehem University.

Panel Debate
Chairman of the Panel: Carlo Hansen, journalist with the Danish newspaper
Aarhus Stiftstidende.
Participants in the Panel: The five above named representatives: Prof. (Dr. jur.)
Mümtaz Soysal, Prof. (Dr. jur.) Ismet Sheriff Vanlly, Prof. Naomi Chazan, Prof.
Dr. Manuel Hassassian.
Also: Helle Degn MP for the Social Democratic Party, former Minister of
Development and Cooperation, leader of the Danish OSCE delegation,
Chairman of the Danish Parliament's Commission of Foreign Affairs.
Prof. Dr. Mehdi Mozaffari, Institute of Political Science, University of Aarhus.
Jørgen Bæk Simonsen (Dr.phil), The Carsten Niebuhr Institute of Near Eastern
Studies, University of Copenhagen.
Prof. Per Bilde, Department of the Science of Religion, University of Aarhus.
Dr. Mohamed Bander, Iraqi Anthropologist.

Questions to the Panel were put by
Birgitte Rahbek, journalist with the Danish State Radio.
Prof. Jørgen Bang, Institute of Media Science, The University of Aarhus.
Sefa Martin Yürükel, reading for a masters degree at the Department of Ethnography and Social Anthropology, The University of Aarhus.

Contributors

Meliha Benli Altunisik — Department of International Relations, Middle East Technical University, Ankara, Turkey

Lars Erslev Andersen — Department for Contemporary Middle Eastern Studies, Odense University, Denmark

Ilhan Ataseven — Department of History of Religions, Lund University, Sweden

Nuri Bilgin — Social Psychology Branch, Faculty of Literature, Ege University, Izmir, Turkey

Grete Bille — Copenhagen Peace Research Institute, Copenhagen, Denmark

Ulf Bjereld — Department of Political Science, Göteborg University, Sweden

Faik Bulut — Writer, Istanbul, Turkey

Kemal Burkay — Kurdish Socialist Party, Stockholm, Sweden

Jorgen Bæk Simonsen — The Carsten Niebuhr Institute of Near Eastern Studies, Copenhagen University, Denmark.

Naomi Chazan — Knesset, Israeli Parliament, Meretz Party, Hebrew University, Jerusalem, Israel

Conni Carøe Christiansen — Department of Ethnology and Anthropology, Copenhagen University, Denmark

Ihsan D. Dagi — Department of International Relations, Middle East Technical University, Ankara, Turkey

Selahattin Erhan	Department of International Relations, Bilkent University, Ankara, Turkey
Mette Fenger	The Carsten Niebuhr Institute of Near Eastern Studies, Copenhagen University, Denmark
Mehmet Bedri Gültekin	*Teori,* Monthly Journal, Ankara, Turkey
Manuel S. Hassassian	Faculty of Arts, Bethlehem University, The West Bank, Palestine
Jacques Hersh	Research Centre on Development and International Relations, Department of Development and Planning, Aalborg University, Denmark
Jan Hjärpe	Department of History of Religions, Lund University, Sweden
Martin Hvidt	Department for Contemporary Middle Eastern Studies, Odense University, Denmark
Ole Høiris	Department of Ethnography and Social Anthropology, University of Aarhus, Denmark
Mehrdad R. Izady	Department of Near Eastern Languages and Civilizations, Harvard University, USA
Anders Jerichow	*Politiken*, Danish Daily, Denmark
Orhan Kotan	Writer, Stockholm, Sweden
Andreas Laursen	Department for Contemporary Middle Eastern Studies, Odense University, Denmark
Osman Faruk Logoglu	Embassy of Republic of Turkey, Baku, Azerbaijan

Dag Jørund Lønning	Chr. Michelsen Institute, Fantoft, Norway
Peder Mortensen	Moesgård Museum, Aarhus, Denmark
Baskin Oran	Faculty of Political Science, Ankara University, Turkey
Dogu Perinçek	The Workers Party, Ankara, Turkey
Gert Petersen	Folketinget, Danish Parliament, Socialist People's Party, Copenhagen, Denmark
Sami Abdul Rahman	Iraq-Kurdistan Democrat Party, Politburo, Iraq-Kurdistan
Maryam Rajawi	National Council of Resistance of Iran, Paris, France
Lene Kofoed Rasmussen	The Carsten Niebuhr Institute of Near Eastern Studies, Copenhagen University, Denmark
Torben Retbøll	Department of History, Cathedral School, Aarhus, Denmark
Helga Rittersberger-Tiliç	Department of Sociology, Middle East Technical Universty, Ankara, Turkey
Khaled Salih	Department of Political Science, Göteborg University, Sweden
Johannes Dragsbaek Schmidt	Research Centre on Development and International Relations, Department of Development and Planning, Aalborg University, Denmark
Kirsten E. Schulze	The Department of International History, London School of Economics, England

Omar Sheikhmous	Centre for Research in International Migration and Ethnic Relations, Stockholm University, Sweden
Erik Siesby	Danish Helsinki Committee, Copenhagen, Denmark
Mümtaz Soysal	Grand National Assembly of Turkey, Democratic Left Party, Ankara, Turkey
L. Dogan Tiliç	Agencia EFE (Spain's International News Agency), Ankara, Turkey
Joseph Yacoub	Université Catholique, Institut des Droits de L'Homme, Lyon, France
Erhan Yarar	The 21st Century Foundation of the Strategical Research Group, Ankara, Turkey
Sefa Martin Yürükel	Department of Ethnography and Social Anthropology, University of Aarhus, Denmark
Mehmet Ali Ölmez	Federation of The Alevi Communities in Europe, Bielefeld, Germany
Elisabeth Özdalga	Department of Sociology, Middle East Technical University, Ankara, Turkey

Index